D0706636

Modern Pricing of Interest-Rate Derivatives

Modern Pricing of Interest-Rate Derivatives

THE LIBOR MARKET MODEL AND BEYOND

Riccardo Rebonato

Princeton University Press

Princeton and Oxford

Copyright © 2002 by Princeton University Press

Published by Princeton University Press,
41 William Street, Princeton, New Jersey 08540

In the United Kingdom: Princeton University Press,
3 Market Place, Woodstock, Oxfordshire OX20 ISY

All Rights Reserved

Library of Congress Cataloging-in-Publication Data applied for.
Rebonato, Riccardo
Modern Pricing of Interest-Rate Derivatives: The LIBOR Market and Beyond /
Riccardo Rebonato
p.cm.
Includes bibliographical references and index.
ISBN 0-691-08973-6

British Library Cataloguing-in-Publication Data
A catalogue record for this book is available from the British Library.

This book has been composed in New Baskerville

Printed on acid-free paper ∞

Printed in the United States of America

10 9 8 7 6 5 4 3 2 1

To Rosamund
To my parents

Contents

Introduction

Rationale for the Book

The aim of this book is to present my views as to the most satisfactory approach to pricing a wide class of interest-rate derivatives. This approach falls squarely within the framework of the LIBOR market model. However, many competing versions, and even more modes of implementation, exist. I have not attempted to present a comprehensive, unbiassed review of all these possible approaches. Rather, I have chosen the particular version and the overall calibration philosophy that I have found most conceptually satisfying and practically useful. I have not been shy to express my opinions, but having strong views on a subject is, per se, no great virtue: I have therefore provided the reader with detailed reasons and explanations for my choices and preferences. Especially when it comes to its more recent treatments, I have consciously tried to cover an important version of the subject in depth, rather than its entirety in breadth.

Since 1973, the year of the Black and Scholes paper, both practice and theory have moved very rapidly in the derivatives area in general, and in interest-rate modelling in particular. Despite, or perhaps because of, this rapid development, the academic and practitioners' communities have not always communicated as productively as might have been desirable. Since my professional and academic experience straddles both fields, I have tried to bring theory and the practical trading experience together with as much 'constructive interference' as possible.

I imagine a rather diverse readership. All my readers should have in common a basic but solid knowledge of derivatives pricing, of the Black and Scholes model, of interest-rate products, of differential calculus and of elementary stochastic calculus. Some knowledge of stochastic calculus beyond Ito's lemma and some familiarity with modern probability theory would be helpful, but neither is a prerequisite. As long as they share this common ground, I hope that different types of reader will find the book useful. I have in mind, for instance: quantitative analysts, stronger in mathematical training than in trading experience, who want to deepen their understanding of how the modern interest-rate models work; practitioners interested in understanding the conceptual implications of the models they are using, up to what point these models can be pushed and trusted, and what aspects of financial reality they leave out; students who want to understand how asset pricing is currently applied to interest-rate derivatives; and researchers with an interest in improving upon and expanding the current approaches. The pace of the book might be a bit slow for some, but should not be too fast for any of these readers.

Plan and Structure of the Book

The book is organized in four parts, as shown in Figure 1. Part I opens with a historical introduction that traces the development of interest-rate derivatives modelling over the last 30 years or so. This introductory chapter aims to provide an indication as to why certain modelling choices have been adopted by the industry, to explain how the perspective of what constitutes an 'underlying' and a 'hedging' instrument has changed over time, and to illustrate how the required explanatory power of a model has evolved.

I then move on to laying out the mathematical and modelling framework of the standard LIBOR market model. The latter is shown to be characterized by imposing that the volatilities of forward rates should be deterministic functions of time. From this the observation follows that, given a pricing measure, forward rates cannot all be simultaneously log-normally distributed. This has deep consequences, because the lack of simultaneous log-normality for the forward rates would seem to indicate that their future conditional distributions are not known a priori, and therefore must be sampled via computationally intensive numerical methods (e.g., short-stepped Monte Carlo simulations). I show, however, that it is possible to introduce some very simple techniques that retain in an approximate but very accurate way the joint log-normality. Once these approximations have been enforced, I show (Chapter 5) that the drifts can be expressed purely as a function of the covariances. Therefore, within the validity of these approximations, the covariance elements are truly all that matters for pricing in a LIBOR market model context. This is the first important 'message' of Part I.

The attention is then shifted to the types of product that can be handled by the modern pricing approach. I show that their payoff functions must satisfy some, practically rather mild, conditions (related to the measurability and homogeneity of the payoffs). More importantly, I show that for all these products the Monte Carlo simulations that are typically used for valuation purposes can be carried out by evolving the yield curve either from one price-sensitive event to the next, or directly to the very final maturity. I have called these two modes of evolution of the yield curve the long- and the very-long-jump technique, to emphasize that, once the drift approximations referred to above are enforced, the computationally expensive short-stepped Monte Carlo evolution is never required (in the deterministic-volatility case). This is the second important result of Part I.

Part I is concluded by a chapter that shows how these numeraire- and measure-dependent drift terms can be expressed in terms of market-related

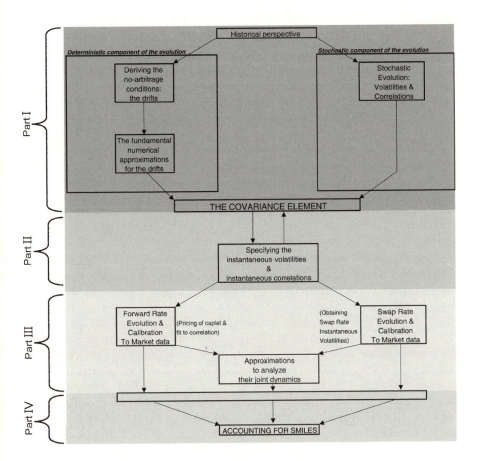

Figure 1   *Plan of the book.*

forward-rate volatilities and correlations. The focus is therefore naturally shifted to the analysis of these latter quantities, which constitutes the topic of Part II.

The logical development up to this point has highlighted the centrality of the marginal or of the total forward-rate covariance matrix to the whole modern pricing approach. The elements of this covariance matrix are, in turn, made up of instantaneous volatilities and correlations, and the LIBOR market model, which ultimately simply expresses no-arbitrage conditions for discrete-tenor forward rates, only and truly becomes a 'model' when these quantities are chosen. The quality of the whole pricing approach therefore hinges on the quality of these inputs, and Part II is devoted to exploring in considerable detail what the desiderata should be of plausible volatility and correlation functions. The task is made challenging (and interesting) because the market data available from the plain-vanilla instruments do not uniquely determine either the instantaneous correlation or volatility functions, and a strong element of financial judgement therefore necessarily enters the analysis. In this respect I explain why I place a great deal of emphasis on the condition of time homogeneity for the evolution of such quantities as the term structure of volatilities or the swaption matrix.

Part III assumes that, on the basis of the criteria presented in Part II, the user has chosen to her heart's content a satisfactory set of instantaneous correlation and volatility functions. In general, these chosen inputs will not automatically reproduce the market prices of the benchmark plain-vanilla instruments. The task undertaken in this part of the book is therefore to calibrate the model to the desired set of market data not only in an efficient way, but also, and more importantly, in a financially desirable way. In particular, tools are provided to explore the internal coherence and self-consistency of the caplet and swaption market, and to calibrate the model in a financially desirable way to a set of co-terminal swaptions.

Part IV moves beyond the standard LIBOR market model by presenting a combined framework to account for smiles. Again, the emphasis is placed on the financial mechanisms causing smiles, rather than on the mathematical models that can explain today's smile surface. In the course of this analysis I come to identify two different possible financial reasons for the types of smile surface encountered in the interest-rate arena. Correspondingly, I introduce two separate mechanisms to account for them. These are the displaced-diffusions/CEV approach coupled with the introduction of stochastic instantaneous volatilities. My main goal in so doing is not to obtain as close a fit as possible to the observed market smile, but to provide financially justifiable and convincing mechanisms capable of accounting in a sufficiently accurate way for the observed plain-vanilla prices. Almost as an added bonus, however, it so turns out that the quality of the obtained fit is very good indeed. Finally, I argue in the last three chapters that the standard LIBOR market model as it has evolved in the last few years is far more than a set of no-arbitrage conditions for forward rates. In its recent developments, it has become intimately enmeshed with the set of approximation and calibration techniques that have turned it into a practical and powerful pricing tool, and that I present and discuss in Parts I to III. I show in Part IV that the surprisingly simple, but very powerful, techniques that allow the efficient calibration of the model and evolution of the yield curve can be translated to the displaced-diffusion/stochastic-volatility setting in a natural and straightforward way. The last chapter presents and discusses empirical evidence concerning the swaption implied-volatility matrix, and its relevance for the stochastic volatility modelling. A general systematic procedure is introduced to assess the quality of a model when the term structure of volatilities it produces is stochastic.

As for the presentation style of the book, it has been strongly influenced by the use to which I have assumed it will be put by its presumably diverse readership. My ideal reader would begin on page 1, and would read the book sequentially (although, possibly, with a few breaks!) all the way to the end. To such a reader I must offer my thanks and some apologies. I have had in the back of my mind, in fact, the existence of a 'sub-optimal' reader who might prefer to read some sections out of their natural order, skip some chapters altogether, re-read others over and over, etc. A reader, in other words, rather like myself. For the benefit of this erratic reader, but possibly to the annoyance of the ideal one, I have therefore provided frequent indicators of the progress of the logical flow and of the direction ahead, and liberally posted reminders of the main results obtained on the way. I am aware that this does not make for elegant writing. I would at least like the ideal reader to know that I have not inflicted unnecessary repetitions out of sheer stylistic sloppiness or mental laziness, and that, in the end, it is all the fault of readers like me.

Acknowledgements

It is a pleasure to acknowledge the help, encouragement and support that I have received from colleagues and friends. In particular, I owe a debt of gratitude to Dr Mark Joshi and Dr Chris Hunter for stimulating discussions, useful suggestions and inspiring bantering. I would also like to thank Mark and Chris again, and Dr Peter Jaeckel, for invaluable computational help, and Dr Jochen Theis for careful reading of the manuscript and useful comments. Needless to say, I am solely responsible for all the errors in the text.

As I have acknowledged in my previous books, the seeds for many of the ideas that appear in my work were sown many years ago by Mike Sherring: my heartfelt thanks to him.

I am grateful to the staff at Princeton University Press, and to Richard Baggaley in particular, for the enthusiasm they have shown for the project and the help they have provided.

I have written this book in a private capacity, and the opinions expressed in it should not be attributed to my employer, the Royal Bank of Scotland, which, however, I wish to thank for providing a stimulating environment in which the ideas here presented have found intellectual challenge and practical application.

Finally, I hope I will be as supportive to my wife in her current and forthcoming book projects as she has been to me during the course of this work.

Part I

The Structure of the LIBOR Market Model

1

Putting the Modern Pricing
Approach in Perspective

1.1 Historical Developments

1.1.1 Introduction

The set of techniques to price interest-rate derivatives that stemmed from
the original work of Heath, Jarrow and Morton (HJM) in the late 1980s (HJM
1989) are referred to in this book as the 'modern' or the 'LIBOR-market-
model' approach. At a superficial glance, the differences between the various 'incarnations' of the approach might appear greater than what they have
in common. The state variables could be instantaneous or discretely compounded rates; they could be swap rates or forward rates; they might be normally or log-normally (or otherwise) distributed; the associated numeraire
could be a zero-coupon bond, a swap annuity or the money-market account;
and so on. Despite these non-trivial differences, these approaches share one
essential common feature: the recognition that the no-arbitrage evolution of
the state variables (however chosen) can be expressed purely as a function
of the volatilities of, and of the correlations among, the state variables themselves. Different choices of numeraires will give rise to different combinations
for these covariance elements, but this fundamental result, which goes back to
the original insight of HJM, is shared by all the approaches that will be dealt
with in this book. This result and its implications are sufficiently fundamental
and far-reaching to justify a self-contained and unified treatment.

Given the various 'versions', 'implementations' and choices of numeraires,
no general agreement exists in the financial community on how to call this set
of approaches: the terms 'BGM (Brace, Gatarek and Musiela) model' and
'Jamshidian approach' are often used, but 'pricing in the forward measure',
the 'LIBOR market model' and other terms are also frequently encountered.
Some purists insist on calling the approach simply the 'HJM model'. The
difficulty in establishing intellectual priority is compounded by the fact that

many of the key results were first obtained (and used) by practitioners but, for obvious reasons, not published in the academic press. I have therefore avoided any identification of the approach with names of academics or market professionals, and used the more neutral terms 'LIBOR market model' or 'modern pricing approach' – much as I am sure the latter may read rather quaint in a few years' time.

This introductory chapter is meant to provide a brief map of the development of interest-rate derivative pricing from its earliest (modern) days to the present. I have chosen to present such an introduction not only for its intrinsic historical interest, but also because it illustrates rather clearly that an uneven combination of market events, 'right choices made for the wrong reasons', computational expediency and sound judgement have conspired to produce the market standard that the later, more sophisticated, models have striven to recover. In other words, the modern approach is, justifiably, so loved by practitioners because of its ability to price exotic products while at the same time recovering exactly the prices of the relevant plain-vanilla options (caplets or European swaptions). I shall explain below how the market consensus has crystallized around the Black framework, partly for sound financial reasons, but partly also by historical accident. If this analysis is correct, there is nothing 'inevitable' about the current market standard, and it is quite possible that the target the modern approach has been trying to hit might in the near future turn out to be a rather rapidly moving one.

Indeed, this phenomenon is already becoming apparent: as discussed in Part IV of this book, in the last few years the prices of plain-vanilla options have been able to be strait-jacketed into their log-normal-rate Black framework only by increasingly complex ad hoc adjustments.[1] As a consequence, just when the pricing of exotic products had finally been successfully tuned onto the log-normal-rate wavelength, the prices of the underlying vanilla instruments have ceased to inhabit the same (Black) world. The brief account of the developments that brought about this state of affairs is presented below, and should give a clear indication of the fact that the 'modern' approach is virtually certain to be anything but the last step in interest-rate derivative pricing. The reader keen to delve into the quantitative aspects of the pricing can safely skip these pages. She would miss, however, not only a good story, but also some perspective useful in appreciating what aspects of today's market consensus are more likely to be challenged and superseded tomorrow.

---

[1] The malaise first became apparent with the appearance of implied volatilities monotonically decreasing as a function of strike. This phenomenon has acquired increasing importance since the mid-to-late 1990s. In addition, after the 1998 market turmoil, a distinct hockey-stick or U-shape for the implied volatility curve has appeared both for caplets and for swaptions. See the discussion in Section 11.1.

1.1.2 The Early Days

The relatively brief history of the evolution of the pricing of interest-rate derivatives can be subdivided into four distinct periods. The very first one corresponds to the use of the Black and Scholes (1973) (BS), Black (1976) and Merton (1973) approaches. In all these cases, the same distributional assumption (namely, the log-normal) was made for the underlying variable, and the resulting expiry-time distribution was integrated over the terminal payoff of a European option. For all of the three above-mentioned models, the solutions have a very (and deceptively) similar appearance, with the integration over the appropriate log-normal probability densities giving rise to the familiar cumulative-normal-distribution terms. The quantities that were typically assumed to be log-normal were bond prices (spot or forward), forward rates, forward swap rates, or bond yields. As for the products priced using these modelling approaches, they belonged to two rather distinct markets and yield curves: the Treasury/repo world, on the one hand, was the relevant environment for the pricing of plain-vanilla bond options, either directly, or embedded in once-callable or extendable-maturity structures; and the LIBOR environment, on the other, which provided caps and European swaptions.

The most straightforward approach (i.e., the use of the Black and Scholes formula with the spot bond price as the underlying) was popular, but it also came under early criticism because of the so-called pull-to-par phenomenon: in its original form the Black and Scholes formula requires a constant percentage volatility of the underlying. For a coupon or a discount bond, however, the volatility is certainly not constant (since the price has to converge to par at maturity). This fact was considered to be cause for little worry if the expiry of the bond option was much shorter than the maturity of the underlying bond (e.g., for a few weeks' or months' option on a, say, 10-year bond); but it would create discomfort when the times to expiry and maturity were comparable.

The 'easy-fix' solution was to consider a non-traded quantity (the bond yield) as the underlying log-normal variable. The main advantage of this approach was that a yield does not exhibit a deterministic pull to par. The most obvious drawback, on the other hand, was that the yield is not a traded asset, and, therefore, the Black and Scholes reasoning behind the self-financing dynamic trading strategy that reproduces the final payoff of the option could not be easily adapted. Despite being theoretically not justifiable, the approach was for a period widely used because it allowed the trader to think in terms of a volatility (the volatility of the yield) that was more independent of the maturity of the underlying instrument than the volatility of the spot price. With hindsight, and much to the relief of the academic community, this route was to prove a blind alley, and very little more will be said in this book about it.[2] Academics, of course and correctly, 'hated' the log-normal yield approach: not only did it make use as its driving variable of a quantity (the yield itself) of

---

[2]Yield-based approaches are still used to some extent in the bond option world. This asset class is not dealt with in this book, which mainly addresses the pricing of LIBOR derivatives.

poor theoretical standing (see, e.g., Schaefer 1977), but it was close to impossible to produce a satisfactory financial justification in terms of risk-neutral valuation for its use in a Black-like formula. In all likelihood, however, the trading community abandoned the log-normal yield model for reasons other than its lack of sound theoretical standing. As discussed below, in fact, the cap and swaption pricing formulas, which used log-normal forward and swap rates, were at the very same time gaining general market acceptance. Prima facie, these formulas appear deceptively similar to the log-normal yield approach. It so happens that, unlike the log-normal yield approach, these latter formulas can be justified theoretically. In the early days, however, this was rarely recognized, and papers showing the 'correctness' of the Black swaption formula were still appearing as late as the mid-1990s (see Neuberger 1990, Gustavsson 1997). Traders, although with a somewhat guilty conscience, were nonetheless still using the Black formula for caplets and European swaptions well before its theoretical justification had become common knowledge.

The reasons for the abandonment of the log-normal yield model must therefore have been rooted in causes other than its lack of theoretical justifiability. This constitutes more than a piece of historical curiosity: the fact that traders carried on using the Black formula for caplets and swaptions despite its then-perceived lack of theoretical standing turned the approach into a market standard. The subsequent realization that this market standard could be put on solid theoretical ground then provided the impetus behind the development of more general approaches (such as the LIBOR market model) capable of pricing complex interest-rate derivatives consistently with the (Black) caplet market. Therefore, without the somewhat fortuitous choices made during the establishment of a market standard, the current 'modern' pricing approach would probably not exist in its present form.

Going back to the pull-to-par problem, its 'correct' solution was, of course, to use the Black – rather than the Black and Scholes – formula, with the forward (as opposed to spot) price and the volatility of the forward as inputs. This route was often overlooked, and for different reasons, both by naive and by sophisticated market players. The naive traders simply did not appreciate the subtle, but fundamental, difference between the Black and the Black and Scholes formulas and the volatilities used as input for both, and believed the pull-to-par phenomenon to be relevant to the Black formula as well. The sophisticated traders understood that the Black formula, with the appropriate inputs, is perfectly correct and justifiable, and that no pull-to-par effect applies to a forward bond price (which remains of the same residual maturity throughout its life). They also realized, however, that something important was still missing. Much as the Black formula can give a perfectly correct answer for a series of options considered independently of each other, there is no way of telling whether these options inhabit a plausible, or even logically consistent, universe. In reality, despite the fact that different forward bond prices correspond to different assets, we also know that these prices are significantly correlated, but there is no mechanism within the Black formula to incorporate views about this joint dynamics. To make this important point clearer, let us assume that a trader were to give two different forward bond price volatilities as inputs for the Black formula for two options with different expiries on forward bonds with the same residual maturities. By so doing the trader is implicitly saying 'something' about the volatilities of the forward bonds spanning the period between the first and the second expiry, and the first and second maturity. Notice, however, the vagueness of the term 'something'. The relationship between the various volatilities is not strong enough to be of deterministic nature: given the volatilities for two same-residual-maturity, different-expiry forward bonds, the volatility of the forward bond spanning, say, the two expiries is by no means uniquely determined. At the same time, the relationship between the various volatilities is not weak enough for the various underlying 'assets' to be considered completely independent.

Sure enough, if an exogenous model existed, capable of providing self-consistent inputs (i.e., volatilities) to the Black formula, then all problems of consistency would be solved. Indeed, I have shown elsewhere (Rebonato 1998) that the Black formula can be rigorously extended to a surprising variety of path-dependent and compound-option cases (at least, as long as one is prepared to work with higher-and-higher-dimension cumulative normal distributions). However, paraphrasing what I wrote in a slightly different context (Rebonato 1998):

> ... what is needed is some strong structure to be imposed on the co-movements of the financial quantities of interest; ... this structure can be provided by specifying the dynamics of a small number of variables. ... Once the process for all these driving factors has been chosen, the variances of and correlations among all the financial observables can be obtained, analytically or numerically as the case might be, as a by-product of the model itself. The implied co-dynamics of these quantities might turn out to be simplified to the point of becoming simplistic, but, at least, the pricing of different options can be undertaken on a consistent basis. ...

These reasons for the early dissatisfaction with the Black approach are of more than historical interest because, paradoxically, the modern approach to pricing derivatives can suffer from the same over-abundance of degrees of freedom. I will argue that the need to impose the strong structure on the co-movements of the yield curve mentioned above is absolutely central to the modern implementation of the pricing approaches derived from the HJM family. But more about this later.

In parallel with the Treasury/repo market, the LIBOR-related market was also providing interesting pricing challenges. The demand for LIBOR-based derivative products was coming on the one hand from liability managers (borrowers) seeking interest-rate insurance via the purchase of caps, and on the other from issuers and investors seeking better returns or funding rates, respectively, via callable or puttable bonds. The coupons from the latter would then be swapped with an investment firm, who would also receive the optionality (typically a swaption) embedded in the structure. The mechanics of, and financial rationale for, these trades is an interesting topic in itself: the story of the search for funding 'advantage' that drove the evolution of financial instruments from the early once-callable coupon bonds to the 30-year multi-callable zero-coupon swaptions of late 1997/early 1998 deserves to be told, but elsewhere. For the present discussion it is sufficient to point out two salient features.

The first is that the consensus of the investment houses that were most active in the field was crystallizing around the use of the Black formula with log-normal forward and swap rates. This need not have been the case, since a caplet, for instance, can be equivalently regarded as a call on a (log-normal) rate or a put on a (log-normal) bond. Once again, despite the (rather unconvincing) rationalizations for the choice given at the time, the choice of the Black formula with the respective forward rates for caplets and swaptions turned out to be based on little more than historical accident. Without this choice, the development of the HJM approach would have taken a significantly different turn, and would have actually led to the market acceptance and popularity of formulations much easier to implement (such as the ones described in Section 17.3 of Rebonato (1998); see also Carverhill (1993) or Hull (1993)). Perhaps more importantly, had the choice of the put on a (log-normal) forward bond been made, today's term structure of volatilities for caplets would display a radically different smile structure (or, perhaps, no smile at all). And as for Chapter 11 of this book, which shows how to extend the modern pricing approach in the presence of monotonically decaying smiles, it might have been absent altogether, or relegated to a footnote.

The second important consequence of the market supply and demand for optionality was that investment houses found themselves as the natural buyers of swaptions and sellers of caps. Of course, it was readily recognized that these instruments were intimately linked: a swap rate, after all, is simply a linear combination (albeit with stochastic weights) of the underlying forward rates. However, the Black formulas by themselves once again failed to give any indication as to what this link should be: each individual caplet would be perfectly priced by the Black formula with the 'correct' input volatility, but it would inhabit its own universe (in later-to-be-introduced terminology, it would be priced in its own forward measure). Even more so, there would be no systematic way, within a Black framework, to make a judgement about the mutual consistency between the volatility of a swaption and the volatilities of the underlying caplets.

Much as in the Treasury/repo market, the need was felt for a comprehensive approach that would bring unity to the pricing of these different and loosely connected instruments. The search for a model with the ability to price convincingly and simultaneously the caplet and the swaption markets was actually to be frustrated until the late 1990s, and the progress made in this direction actually constitutes one of topics of Part III of this book. Once again, the story of the search for this particular 'Holy Grail' is in itself very interesting, and even has an almost dramatic twist, linked as it is to the ill-fated trades of a well-known investment house of the late summer of 1998. For the purpose of the present discussion, however, the salient feature of this early phase was the perceived need for a more comprehensive modelling approach that would bring unity and simplicity to what appeared to be hopelessly disjointed markets.

In moving from this earliest stage in interest-rate derivatives pricing to its adolescence, one last important factor should be mentioned: the caplet and swaption markets soon acquired such importance and liquidity that they became the new 'underlyings'. In other terms, the gamma and vega of the more complex products that were beginning to appear would be routinely hedged using caplets and European swaptions.[3] This placed another important constraint on the 'comprehensive' model that was being sought: since the price of an option is, after all, intimately linked to the cost of its hedges, the market prices of caplets or European swaptions (seen now not as options in their own right, but as the new hedging instruments) would have to be correctly recovered. From the point of view of the trader who had to make a price in an exotic product, it would simply not be good enough to have a model that implied that caplets prices 'should' be different from what the (Black-driven) market implied. This feature, in the early days, was to be found rather down the wish list of the desiderata for the model the trader would dream of receiving for Christmas. It was nonetheless to become one of the most compelling reasons for the development and the ready market acceptance of the modern pricing approach (namely, in the incarnation usually referred to as the 'market model').

1.1.3 The First Yield-Curve Models

The modelling lead was still taken at this stage by academics (namely, Vasicek (1977) and Cox, Ingersoll and Ross (CIR) (Cox et al. 1985)). Faced with the multitude of instruments (bond options, caplets, swaptions, not to mention the bonds themselves) in search for a coherent and self-consistent description, Vasicek and Cox et al.[4] made the sweeping assumption that the dynamics of the whole yield curve would be driven by the instantaneous short rate. The evolution of the latter was then assumed to be described by a stochastic differential equation made up of a deterministic mean-reverting compo-

---

[3]For a distinction between and discussion of 'in-model' (delta and gamma) hedging and 'outside-the-model' (vega) hedging, see Section 11.1.

[4]The brief account presented in this chapter barely does justice to the CIR approach, which is actually considerably farther-reaching, ensuring as it does that the resulting dynamics for the short rate is consistent with an equilibrium economy. Given the rather draconian nature of the assumptions the model has to enforce, this feature was perceived to be more of an intellectual bonus than of practical relevance. As a consequence, the trading community never placed much importance on this theoretically important feature, and regarded the CIR approach as a purely no-arbitrage model. The same applies to the Longstaff and Schwartz (1992) (LS) model.

nent and a stochastic part, with a diffusion coefficient either constant or proportional to the square root of the short rate itself. Given the existence of a
single source of uncertainty (as described by the evolution of the short rate)
the stochastic movements of any bond could be perfectly hedged by taking a
suitable position in a bond of different maturity. The appropriate hedge ratio was obtainable, via Ito's lemma, on the basis of the assumed evolution of
the single driver of the yield-curve dynamics (i.e., the short rate). Given the
existence of a single stochastic driver, the prescription was therefore given to
build a purely deterministic portfolio made up of just two bonds of different
maturities (in a suitable ratio). Once this step was accomplished, the solution
of the problem could therefore be conceptually reduced to the classic Black-
and-Scholes framework, where a stock and an option are combined in such an
amount as to give rise to a risk-less portfolio.

Despite the fact that the practical success of these first models was rather
limited, their influence was enormous, and, with exceedingly few exceptions
(such as Duffie and Kan's (1996) approach), all the models that were to be
developed up until the HJM approach was introduced were part of the same,
short-rate-based, research program. With hindsight, it might seem bizarre that
so much modelling effort should have been concentrated in the same direction. It might appear even more surprising, given the seemingly arbitrary and
unpromising choice for the driving factor, that the models spawned by this approach should turn out to be, after all, as useful as they have been. As usual, a
rather complex combination of factors conjured to produce this state of affairs
– some of computational, some of conceptual and some of purely accidental
nature. Cutting a long story to a reasonable length, a few salient features of
these early models are worth pointing out in order to appreciate how and why
the modern approach came to be. First of all, the Vasicek/CIR models had
both a prescriptive and a descriptive dimension. More precisely, if one took
as given a certain set of parameters, they showed what the shape of the yield
curve should be. If, on the other hand, one left these parameters as free-fitting
degrees of freedom, the model would then show what shapes the yield curve
could assume. In other words, if applied in a 'fundamental' way (e.g., by estimating econometrically the values of parameters – including the market price
of risk!), the model would indicate what the yield curve should look like today;
if used in an 'implied' manner, a cross-sectional analysis of prices would give
the best combination of parameters capable of producing the closest fit to the
observed yield curve. In either case, for a believer in the model, any discrepancy between a market and model bond price signals a cheap or expensive
bond, and, therefore, a trading opportunity. For the bond- or LIBOR-option
trader, on the other hand, the failure to reproduce the market price would
simply mean that the underlying was being mis-priced. In a Black-and-Scholes
framework, this was tantamount to being forced to price an option using the
wrong input, of all things, for the spot price of the underlying. The assessment of the usefulness of the model was therefore sharply different for the
relative-value cash trader and for the option trader: for the former the model,

however crude, had some explanatory power, and could, at least in theory, identify portions of the yield curve as cheap or dear; for the latter, the failure to recover the underlying correctly was too high a price to pay for the much sought-after self-consistency among prices of different options.

Relative-value traders, incidentally, tended to be somewhat intrigued by the fact that models with such a simple (or simplistic?) structure and sweeping assumptions did, after all, a very acceptable job at describing the yield curve. This partial, but encouraging, success was often taken as an indication that 'at the bottom there must be something right in choosing the short rate as the driving factor for the yield curve'. With the usual benefit of hindsight, one can venture a more prosaic explanation for this 'intriguing' degree of success: copious econometric research has shown that the stochastic evolution of the yield curve is explained to a very large extent by its first principal component. The loadings of the different forward rates onto this first principal component are also well known to be approximately constant. Therefore, virtually any rate, and, therefore, in particular, the short rate, could have been taken as a reasonable proxy for the first component, and hence for the yield curve as a whole. This way of explaining the partial success of the early short-rate-based models is not just another curious item in the history of derivatives pricing, but has a direct influence on many of the implementations of the modern approach.

1.1.4 The Second-Generation Yield-Curve Models

The third phase in this brief account of the path that led to the modern methods that are the topic of this book was ushered in by Black, Derman and Toy (BDT) (Black et al. 1990) and by Hull and White (1990) (HW) with their extended Vasicek and extended CIR models. The most salient feature of this class of models was the addition of a purely deterministic (time-dependent) term to the mean-reverting component in the drift of the short rate.[5] Minor as this feature might appear, it allowed the introduction of a simple but powerful deus ex machina capable of disposing of whatever discrepancy the stochastic and mean-reverting components of the short-rate dynamics would leave between market and model bond prices. Therefore, given an arbitrary market yield curve, however twisted and bizarre, the second-generation yield-curve models could always augment the mean-reverting drift with a deterministic 'correction' term capable of reproducing the market prices.

Needless to say, the relative-value bond traders and the option traders had at this point to part company, and all the model developments that were to

---

[5]The BDT model was originally introduced in algorithmic form, and its continuous-time equivalent presented only later (Jamshidian 1991, Hull and White 1990). Given the conceptual equivalence between the algorithmic, discrete-time version and its continuous-time counterpart, and for the sake of brevity, in the discussion of this section I have decided to treat all the yield-curve fitting approaches together, irrespective of whether the fitting itself must be obtained numerically or can be arrived at analytically. The Black and Karasinski (1991) (BK) model therefore also falls in this category.

follow have, if anything, widened their paths. Obviously, it could not be otherwise: a model that could account for any conceivable input shape of the yield curve automatically loses all explanatory power. This selfsame feature, however, makes it attractive for the option trader, who will be able to carry out her model-suggested delta hedging (by buying or selling bonds) at the prices actually encountered in the market.

At the same time, a new important type of relative-value trader became keenly interested in the models of the BDT/HW/BK family. These second-generation models might well have been able to reproduce any yield curve, but could not automatically account for the prices of all plain-vanilla options (caplets and European swaptions) – actually, if implemented as their inventors (correctly) recommended, that is, with constant volatility parameters, they failed to account exactly even for the prices of all the caplets. The explanatory mandate of these models was therefore transferred from accounting for the shape of the yield curve to assessing the reasonableness of the market term structure of volatilities. As a consequence, plain-vanilla LIBOR traders were put for the first time in a position to speculate that, *if* the yield-curve evolution was truly driven by the short rate, *if* its (risk-adjusted) drift was indeed of the prescribed mean-reverting form[6] and *if* its volatility had been chosen appropriately, then the model could give an indication that the relative prices of, say, two caplets could not be what was observable in the market. In other words, the second-generation models brought about for the first time the possibility of model-driven option-based 'arbitrage' trades. The story of these trades, and of the application of models to discover 'arbitrage' between plain-vanilla options, is still unfolding, and has been profoundly influenced on the one hand by the development of the modern pricing approach and on the other by the market events that followed the Russia crisis of 1998.

The class of market professionals who were still unhappy with second-generation models were, of course, the exotic traders. By the early 1990s – when the models of the BDT/HW family were mainstream in the financial community, and those houses boasting an 'HJM model' often actually had little more than a glorified version of the HW model in place – a variety of more and more complex trades were regularly appearing in the market. Beside the ubiquitous Bermudan swaptions, indexed-principal swaps, ratchet caps, callable inverse floaters, knock-out caps, index accruals, digitals and many other products were continuously being introduced. From personal experience, I feel confident to say that the years between 1990 and 1994 probably saw the highest pace in the introduction of new types of product. For those exotic traders who, like myself, had to carry out their hedges using caplets and European swaptions dealt with their colleagues from the plain-vanilla desks, the greatest desideratum that could at the time be requested of a model was

---

[6]In the case of the BDT model the mean reversion is rather sui generis, and is an artifact of its algorithmic description. See Rebonato (1998, 1999c) for a discussion. Since this distinction is not very relevant to the thrust of the discussion, and for the sake of simplicity, in this exposition I simply refer to 'mean reversion' *tout court*, without any further qualifications.

its ability to price at least the required option hedges for each individual trade in line with the plain-vanilla market. Much as plain-vanilla option traders wanted their hedges (bonds and swaps) correctly priced by the model, so exotic traders would have liked the prices of their hedges (caplets and/or swaptions) reproduced by the model in line with the market. And as for the latter, the caplet and European swaption markets back in the early to mid-1990s were still solidly anchored to the Black framework, with no smiles to speak of in all currencies apart from the Japanese Yen. The 'target to hit' for exotic traders was therefore both reasonably well defined and tantalizingly close to achieve.

1.1.5 The Modern Pricing Approach

It was approximately at this time that the first non-trivial applications of the HJM model began to be developed by front-office quants and to appear on their trading desks. This is the fourth and latest (but certainly not last) phase in the evolution of interest-rate derivatives pricing that I am describing. A puzzling fact is that the original HJM working paper began to be circulated as early as 1987, yet exceedingly few bona fide implementations were to appear before, approximately, 1993–94. There were several reasons for this delay. First of all the paper was cast in a relatively new language (or, more precisely, in a language that was new for the for the option community): set theory, measure theory and relatively advanced stochastic calculus. Techniques to solve analytically or numerically parabolic linear partial differential equations, which had been the staple diet of the pre-HJM quants, had little application for non-trivial implementations of the new approach. Similarly, recombining-tree techniques, so thoroughly and profitably explored in the wake of the Cox et al. (1979) paper, became of little use to cope with the non-Markovian nature of the log-normal forward-rate processes.

More generally, a whole new vocabulary was introduced to the trading community:[7] filtrations, martingales, sigma fields, etc., were terms more likely to be familiar to pure and applied statisticians than to the young physicists who had been recruited as rocket scientists at the main investment houses. So, not-so-old dogs suddenly had to learn not-so-new tricks.

Even as the intellectual barrier to entry was being surmounted, a technological impasse was becoming apparent: for meaningful and interesting implementations of the HJM model, closed-form solutions and recombining-tree-based techniques were of very little use. The obvious tool was Monte Carlo simulation. Despite the fact that the application to finance of this technique had been known since the late 1970s (Boyle 1977), the method enjoyed very little popularity, and tended to be regarded as a 'tool of last resort', to be used when everything else failed. The fact that the 'advanced' variance

---

[7]The introduction to the financial world of the concepts of martingales and stochastic integrals to characterize conditions of no-arbitrage pre-dates significantly the HJM paper (see Harrison and Kreps 1979, Harrison and Pliska 1981). Before HJM, however, this important work had remained mainly read and appreciated by the academic community.

reduction techniques of the day boiled down to little more than the draw-ing of antithetic variates and the use of a contravariate variable gives an idea of the rather primitive state of the financial applications of Monte Carlo tech-niques in the early 1990s. Coincidentally, and luckily for the acceptance of the HJM approach, a significant breakthrough for financial applications occurred in those very same years in the form of high-dimensional low-discrepancy se-quences of quasi-random numbers. By their ability to reduce, sometimes by orders of magnitude, the computational time required to perform a simu-lation, high-dimensional quasi-random numbers contributed to making the HJM approach a practical proposition.

The next big problem to be tackled was the so-called 'calibration issue', that is, how to make the HJM model reproduce the prices of the desired plain-vanilla options (i.e., caplets). In those early days the HJM model was perceived to be difficult to calibrate, and a small cottage industry quickly emerged, which began to spin rather cumbersome, and by and large ineffectual, numerical procedures to ensure that the market caplet prices could be recovered by the model.

This might appear extraordinary today, since, after all, one of the great-est advantages of the LIBOR-market-model approach is that it can be made to reproduce the market prices of plain-vanilla options virtually by inspection. If anything, it is the excessive ease with which this calibration can be accom-plished that raises problems today (see Parts II and III of this book). The HJM model, however, was originally cast in terms of instantaneous forward rates, which had no obvious equivalent in traded market instruments. Furthermore, the HJM paper mentioned the fact that, in the continuous-time limit and for truly instantaneous and log-normal forward rates, their process explodes with positive probability. Whilst perfectly true and correct, this statement, often re-peated and rarely understood, acted as a powerful deterrent against the devel-opment of an HJM-based log-normal market model. The fact that log-normal forward rates were considered to be a 'no-fly zone' obviously made recovery of the (Black) log-normal plain-vanilla option prices difficult, to say the least.

These fears were actually misplaced: as soon as the process is discretized and the forward rates become of finite tenor, the log-normal explosion disap-pears. Actually, however one numerically implemented a log-normal forward-rate HJM model (by Monte Carlo simulation, using a bushy tree, or in any other way), one could not have observed the dreaded explosion, hard as one might have tried. The discomfort in moving down the log-normal route was nonetheless both palpable and widespread, and encouraged a line of research devoted to the study of log-normal bond-price-based HJM approaches (which imply approximately normal forward rates). This was to prove a dead alley, but significantly slowed down the development of the standard version of the modern LIBOR-market-based approach.

As for the latter, it is fair to say that, before any of the now-canonical pa-pers appeared, it was simultaneously and independently 'discovered' by an-alysts and practitioners who, undaunted by the expected occurrence of the log-normal explosion, went ahead and discretized a log-normal forward-rate-based HJM implementation. These practitioners were more slaves of necessity than endowed with visionary foresight. The path they were forced to follow if they wanted to price a LIBOR-based derivative security using the HJM approach, can be approximately reconstructed as follows:

- Given a LIBOR-based path-dependent exotic product, they first of all had to specify the discrete points on the yield curve where the price-sensitive events occurred.

- This partition of the yield curve automatically defined a set of discrete-tenor forward rates. The next logical step was then to assume, plausibly if not rigorously, that these discrete forward rates could be regarded as the finite-time equivalent of the HJM instantaneous forward rates.

- At this point the no-arbitrage drifts for the latter (expressed in the original HJM paper in the form of integrals of volatility functions) had to be translated into their discrete-time equivalent. Not surprisingly, by so doing, integrals turned into summations, and continuous-time stochastic integrals had to be simulated using discrete-time-step stochastic quadrature.

- A numeraire also had to be chosen, and, by a natural extension of HJM's approach, the discretely compounded money-market account was 'invented'.

- Finally, a distributional assumption had to be made for the discrete forward rates. Given that so much in the approach lacked, in those first implementations, rigor and mathematical justifiability, why not try the forbidden explosive log-normal assumption? *If* it worked, after all, log-normality was still the standard for the plain-vanilla market, and the goal of pricing exotic and plain-vanilla options consistently would have been fulfilled.

This 'heuristic' approach did work. No explosion wrecked the computers of those who went ahead and tried the discrete-tenor log-normal implementation, and for the first time one could price *simultaneously* a series of caplets exactly in line with the market *using the same numeraire.*

Sure enough, pricing a series of caplets correctly had been a feat well within the reach of any trader capable of programming the Black formula on her pocket calculator for almost 15 years. But, as discussed above, these Black caplets inhabited separate universes (were priced in different measures), and therefore no other LIBOR security could be priced at the same time in an internally consistent manner. The exotic option trader could now for the first time use her Frankenstein model to price an exotic product (trigger swaps were the flavor of the time) and rest assured that, at the same time, the implied prices of all the 'underlying' caplets would be correct; and that they would be so, not approximately and by virtue of a possibly dubious choice of model parameters, but virtually by construction.

This account is somewhat stylized and simplified, but captures in a fundamentally correct manner both the genesis and the impetus behind the 'discovery' of the modern pricing approach. Needless to say, a lot of work still remained to be done to justify in a rigorous manner the procedure outlined above, and this is the area where the papers by Brace et al. (1995), Jamshidian (1997), Musiela and Rutkowski (1997a) and many others made a very important contribution. The importance of this body of work was much more fundamental than dotting the mathematical 'i's and crossing the financial 't's. These papers showed with clarity that any discrete-time implementation of the HJM model, and, therefore, in particular, also the log-normal one, was fully and uniquely specified by the instantaneous volatilities of, and the instantaneous correlations among, the discrete forward rates. More precisely, any discrete-tenor implementation was shown to be fully and uniquely specified by a series of integrals of time-dependent covariance terms. For each time step, that is, for each price-sensitive event, there would correspond one matrix with elements given by integrals of covariance terms; each matrix, in turn, would contain a number of entries proportional to the square of the forward rates still 'alive'. In its maximum generality, an implementation of the modern approach would therefore require the specification of a number of 'parameters' (i.e., the covariance integrals) proportional to the cube of the forward rates in the problem. It was no wonder that the market prices of benchmark plain-vanilla options could, if one wanted, be exactly reproduced!

Actually, this recovery of market prices, so cumbersome with the first- and second-generation models, could now be achieved with disturbing ease, and in an infinity of ways. Unfortunately, each of the possible choices for the instantaneous volatility functions (or for the above-mentioned integrals) would, in general, give rise to different prices for exotic products. Furthermore, if this fitting was injudiciously carried out, it could produce implausible, or even positively pathological, evolutions for such quantities as the term structure of volatilities or the swaption matrix. Much as discussed in the first part of this chapter, what was needed was once again some strong structure that would reduce the degrees of freedom in a systematic and financially transparent way, and yet still preserved the ability to achieve a market fit in a quick and efficient manner. Imposing what I have called above 'strong structural constraints' and enforcing internal consistency between different sets of state variables might not bear a great resemblance to choosing a traditional model, but in reality comes extremely close to fulfilling exactly the same function. This task is still an exciting ongoing research program, and constitutes one of the main topics of this book.

A second useful by-product of the formalizations provided in the papers referred to above was the realization that the modern approach, and, a fortiori, the HJM 'model', are not truly 'models' in the same sense as the HW, the CIR, the Vasicek or the BDT are. Rather, the approaches derived from the

HJM root simply provide conditions on the drifts of the forward rates if arbitrage is to be prevented, and, given a set of chosen instantaneous volatility and correlation functions, express these drifts purely in terms of these functions. It is actually the choice of the parametric form and functional dependence on the state variables of these volatility and correlation inputs that more closely resembles the choice of a 'model' in the traditional sense. After all, if any of the 'traditional' models were indeed arbitrage-free, they had to be a subset of the admissible HJM models. Therefore, there had to be a suitable specification of the volatility of the forward rates[8] that would reproduce exactly the traditional model.

This equivalence between the 'old' and the 'new' approach is actually extremely important. First of all, by embracing the new approach, one can rest assured that, at least in principle, no financially significant feature of a traditional model (such as, for instance, its mean reversion) will have to be abandoned. In other words, all the previously known models, as long as arbitrage-free, had to be just a subset of the HJM family. The modern approach simply provides a new, and often more flexible, vocabulary to describe the characteristics of a given 'model'.

The second, and arguably far more important, consequence of this equivalence is that the new volatility-based vocabulary forces the trader to express her trading views directly in terms of tradable, or at least market-related, quantities. With the modern approach, the option trader no longer has to 'guess' values for, say, the volatility of the consol yield, the mean-reversion level of the instantaneous short rate or the variance of the short-rate volatility, and hope that the opaque mechanism by means of which these inputs are turned into market observables will produce something reasonable. Admittedly, it is true that, with the modern methodology, the user still has to specify quantities not directly observable from the market, such as the instantaneous volatilities of forward rates. It is however possible to translate directly and transparently these choices into trading views about the future evolution of market observables, such as the term structure of volatilities or the swaption matrix. If sufficient liquid instruments were traded in the market[9] (i.e., if the market in forward-rate volatilities were complete), traders would not be forced to express such views, and could make use of any implementation of the LIBOR market model capable of correctly reproducing all the market prices[10]. The market prices of the plain-vanilla instruments (together with the associated serial options) would therefore give rise either to an effectively unique self-consistent parametrization of the LIBOR market model, or to no solution at

---

[8]Note carefully, however, that this volatility would not in general be deterministic. See the discussion in Section 2.3.

[9]Serial options complete the instantaneous-volatility market, but, depending on the currency, they are either illiquid or confined to the very short end of the yield curve. Serial options, and how they can be used to complete the market in instantaneous forward-rate volatilities, are discussed in Section 2.2 and in Rebonato (1999c).

[10]See the discussion in Section 11.1.

all. If any one market price could not be fitted (and assuming, of course, the distributional assumptions of the model to be correct), in this universe endowed with complete-instantaneous-volatility markets the trader could then put in place a replicating strategy capable of arbitraging away the offending plain-vanilla prices.[11]

Unfortunately, the instruments (serial options) that would be required to complete the market imperfectly spanned by caplets and European swaptions are far too illiquid and sparsely quoted to constitute a reliable market benchmark. Given this predicament, expressing a view about the plausibility of the model-implied behavior for such market observables as the term structure of volatilities becomes the main tool in the hands of the trader to establish whether the model parametrization being used is reasonable. This congruence between the trader's views and the model-implied evolution of the market is far more fundamental than a simple 'sanity check': any arbitrage-free model implicitly presupposes a self-financing dynamic trading strategy capable of reproducing the terminal payoff of the derivative product. This strategy, in turn, implies future transactions in the 'underlying instruments' (which, in the case of an exotic derivative product, are caplets and swaptions) with no net injection or withdrawal of cash. If a poorly calibrated model assumes an unrealistic future term structure of volatility or swaption matrix, it will produce the wrong set-up cost for the initial replicating portfolio. This, after all, is just a fancy way of saying that, by assuming the wrong future re-hedging costs, it will predict the 'wrong' price today for the exotic product.

Another important bonus of the modern pricing approach is that it can be equivalently cast in terms of (discrete) forward rates or of swap rates. This has two important positive consequences: first of all, given the ease with which the market-implied volatilities of the state variables can be recovered, the user can rest assured that at least one set of hedging instruments (caplets or swaptions) will be exactly priced by the model. It will then be up to user to decide whether recovery of the volatility of forward or swap rates is more relevant for the pricing of a given particular exotic product (see Jamshidian (1997) for a nice discussion of this point in the context of trigger swaps). At the same time, most complex exotic products require hedging positions both in caplets and in swaptions. It is therefore extremely useful to ascertain what swaption matrix is implied by a given forward-rate-based application, or what term structure of caplet volatilities is produced by the chosen swap-rate-based implementation.

More fundamentally, the modern approach provides the trader with the perfect tools to analyze the congruence between the two benchmark plain-vanilla option markets (caplets and swaptions). Needless to say, for a religious

---

[11] This statement requires careful qualification, since a finite number of instruments cannot complete the market in instantaneous volatilities, but can at most complete the market in instruments whose value depends on integrals over finite time intervals of the instantaneous volatility. In other words, if serial options, caplets and swaptions were simultaneously traded, one could conceptually create instruments that paid a unit certain payoff if one particular realization of each finite-time-interval integral of the instantaneous volatility occurred. This aspect is covered in Chapter 4.

believer in informationally perfectly efficient prices, markets are always congruent, and the inability to price simultaneously caplets and swaptions simply points to an inadequacy of the model used for the task. Alternatively, if the model is thought to be correct and it does manage to reproduce all the prices, the resulting volatility and correlations must reflect the market consensus about these quantities, no matter how implausible these might appear if compared, for instance, with historical and statistical evidence.

In reality, the picture is considerably more complex: on the one hand, there are the natural market flows and the actions of agents with preferred habitats who create an 'excess' demand or supply for certain products. The most obvious examples of this imbalance are, to name just a few: the 'natural' intrinsic mismatch between demand for caplet optionality (from liability managers) and the supply of swaption optionality (from issuers and investors in search of better-than-plain-vanilla funding rates or investment yields);[12] the recent and exceptional demand from British pension funds for long-dated GBP swaptions due to their need to provide fixed-rate annuities; the behavior of US investors who want to hedge prepayment risk inherent in their mortgage-backed securities; etc.

On the other side of the equation, such imbalances of supply and demand should in theory be ironed away by arbitrageurs, proprietary and relative-value traders who do not have a preferred habitat and can indifferently take either side of the market. However, I will argue in the next section that any inefficiency and market constraint reduces the ability of the arbitrageurs to exploit price discrepancies caused by an unbalanced supply or demand and to bring with their position-taking related markets in line with each other. In the caplet and swaption markets these imperfections and constraints are still abundant (and, if anything, they are likely to have increased in the past few years). For instance, a generalized reduction in the scale of the activities of proprietary relative-value arbitrage desks after the Russia events has had a detrimental effect on market liquidity. With poorer liquidity, it has become relatively easier to 'move the market' with a few well-placed large trades. This, in turn, has discouraged the activity of traders who, on the basis of a model, perceive a certain portion of, say, the swaption matrix cheap or dear relative to the underlying caplets. In this landscape of relatively poor liquidity, the rigorous discipline of marking positions to market has made the weathering of P&L storms in relative-value trades sometimes extremely painfully. The magnitude of 'temporary'[13] losses has often forced the closing out of positions, even when models, common-sense and trading experience would indicate that, given enough time, the mark-to-market losses would 'eventually' be reversed.

The bottom line of this digression is that a blind and unquestioning belief

---

[12]See, in this respect, the discussion in Section 9.1.

[13]If relative-value trades were put on in, say, long-dated swaptions, the 'temporary' period by the end of which the losses will, in all likelihood, be reversed (if the positions were held and model-hedged) could be as long as a decade or more. This, on the time-scale of a typical investment bank, can easily correspond to several generations of traders.

in the congruence of the caplet and swaption market requires a significant act of faith. This state of affairs creates for the trader a difficult situation, since the information from the two sister markets can neither be ignored nor fully accepted at face value. The issue of the joint analysis of these two markets, and of its impact on the calibration of the market model, is one of the main topics treated in this book, and is revisited in the final section of this chapter.

This somewhat stylized, but fundamentally accurate, account of the developments in interest-rate derivative pricing has brought us virtually to the current state of affairs. As in every good plot, there is a twist at the end: just when the market model has achieved the ability to value exotic products while, at the same time, correctly pricing the Black-model-driven plain-vanilla options, the market standard has begun to move resolutely away from the log-normal paradigm. This departure has been signalled by the appearance of smirks and smiles in the implied volatility curves. These plots, which, for a given maturity, should be exact straight lines as a function of strike if the log-normal assumption held true, first began to assume a monotonically decreasing shape as early as 1995–96 (see, e.g., Rebonato 1999c); after the market events that followed the summer/autumn of 1998, a hockey-stick smile shape then began to appear. This distinction is important, because I will make the point, in Part IV of this book, that different financial mechanisms are at play in producing these two features. I shall therefore argue that, if one wants to account for these distinct mechanisms in a financially convincing manner, different and simultaneous modelling routes are necessary. The first requires only relatively minor tinkering at the edges of the market model; the second calls for far more radical surgery.

In closing this introductory section, I would like to add two more remarks. First, it is essential to point out that the LIBOR market model as it is known today is much more than a set of equations for the no-arbitrage evolution of forward or swap rates: it includes a very rich body of calibration procedures and of approximate but very accurate numerical techniques for the evolution of the forward rates that have turned the approach into today's most popular pricing tool for complex interest-rate derivatives. Second, these calibration and approximation techniques have turned out to be, by and large, extremely simple.

Subtle as the reasons for its success might be, the fact therefore remains that, once the modern approach is properly implemented and calibrated, very complex computational tasks can be carried out with ease and in real trading time. (These are indeed the topics that I cover in Parts I–III of this book.) This state of affairs, however, makes extending the LIBOR market model in such a way that the observed smiles can be accounted for in a financially convincing way a very tall order. Not only must the resulting equations make 'financial sense', but the established calibration and evolution results must also be recovered, if not totally, at least to a significant extent. The treatment to be found in Part IV of the book has therefore been informed by these joint requirements of financial plausibility and ease of practical implementation for the calibration and evolution techniques that will be presented in the chapters to follow.

These topics arguably constitute the most exciting areas of current development in derivatives pricing. Rather than labelling this activity as the 'fourth phase' of model evolution, I prefer to post a brightly painted sign with the words 'Work in progress', and to wait and see which route the financial community will take in the years to come.

1.2 Some Important Remarks

The LIBOR market model allows the user to obtain *simultaneously* the correct prices of exogenous sets of (i) discount bonds, (ii) caplets and (iii) European swaptions. The recovery of the discount curve is virtually built into the construction of the model, and therefore comes, as it were, 'for free'. The ability to fit almost exactly to the two other asset classes, however, would appear to be a very important and desirable feature. I shall argue in the remainder of this book it will be argued that forcing the chosen model implementation to yield *simultaneously* the market prices of caplets and European swaptions is in most cases not desirable. I shall also repeatedly invite the reader to check the financial 'reasonableness' of the chosen parametrization.

Since caplet and swaptions are made up of the same building blocks (forward rates), both recommendations smack of heresy: Doesn't failure to recover market prices expose the trader to the possibility of being at the receiving end of arbitrage trades? Isn't the 'reasonableness' of a financial quantity irrelevant in derivatives pricing, given that the trader can 'lock in' via dynamic trading the implied values, however 'unreasonable'?

The answer to both questions does not so much lie in the 'in theory/in practice' dichotomy, as in modelling a given financial phenomenon within theoretical frameworks of different scope and generality. The bedrock of the whole analysis is to be found in the concept of no-arbitrage and in the efficient market hypothesis and its corollaries. Arbitrage, which can be defined in this context as the 'simultaneous purchase and sale of the same, *or essentially similar*, security ... for advantageously different prices' (Sharpe and Alexander 1990; my emphasis), ensures that prices remain anchored to fundamentals, and, ultimately, provides the strongest argument for market efficiency. Recall, in fact, that the validity of the efficient market hypothesis does not require investors' rationality (see, e.g., Shleifer 2000). It does not even require that the actions of the 'noise' traders should be uncorrelated. It does require, however, the existence of arbitrageurs capable of exploiting the moves away from fundamental value brought about by the (possibly correlated) noise traders. By virtue of the actions of the arbitrageurs, the values of financial instruments can never stray too far from fundamentals, and redundant instruments (as either caplets or swaptions appear to be in the LIBOR market model) must display congruous prices. When it comes to these LIBOR derivatives products, however, I shall argue that these quasi-arbitrage trades are in reality difficult and risky, *even if the trader could assume the underlying deterministic volatilities and correlations to be known with certainty.* In other words, even neglecting the market incompleteness that arises when these functions are imperfectly known, locking in the prices implied by the complementary sets of plain-vanilla options is far from easy. The 'accidental' factors that make this quasi-arbitrage difficult are several. Let me recall a few:

- *Agency problems* – The standard analyses in asset pricing assume that investors allocate their own wealth among the various available securities on the basis of their risk aversion. However, traders in general, and arbitrage traders in particular, typically do not act as principals, but as agents of investment houses (banks, hedge funds, etc.). As such, they are evaluated and compensated by managers or investors who do not share their market knowledge, and must base the appraisal of the traders' performance on their results over a relatively short period of time (see, e.g., Shleifer and Vishny 1997). A fundamental feature of this activity is therefore that 'brains and resources are separated by an agency relationship' (Shleifer 2000). If the strategy an arbitrageur has put in place is likely to show the market wrong only over a time-scale longer than the next bonus date, the trader might have to unwind the 'correct' positions before time.

- *Limit structures* – Arbitrage trades of this type typically reside on the trading book of a financial institution. Before the market can be shown the errors of its ways, large mark-to-market swings, possibly in the 'wrong' direction, can occur. Internal or regulatory limit losses may be hit, Value-at-Risk (VaR) limits breached and the positions might have to be prematurely unwound.

- *Market liquidity* – All of the above is more likely to happen in not very liquid and/or deep markets. The temptations for competing market participants to 'corner' the arbitrageur, once her positions are known or suspected, is increased by market illiquidity. This feature is compounded by the fact that these pseudo-arbitrage trades, to be 'worth the trouble', typically require very large notionals.

Indeed, the events alluded to in the previous section, connected with the caplet/swaption arbitrage trades of 1998, can be explained by a combination of all these three sources of market imperfections (or, one might say, of market reality). In my opinion, and to the extent that I have been able to ascertain the details of those trades, I can say that they were 'right'. In this context the word 'right' means that they would have probably brought the trader substantial gains if 'only' they could have been kept on for the best part of 10 years; if the market had not so violently swung against the holders of the positions causing very large mark-to-market losses; if the market had not been at the time so illiquid as to lend itself to manipulation; if the arbitrageurs had not been under the constraints of VaR and stop-loss limits; if the traders thought that their compensation, and the continuation of their gainful employment, would be decided on the basis of their (very-)long-term performance. As it happened, none of the above applied, the trades had to be unwound (at a substantial loss), and the caplet and swaption markets remained out of line.

So, is the efficient market hypothesis wrong? If the question is meant in the sense 'Are some of its assumptions incorrect or unrealistic?', the answer is obviously 'yes'. But, in this sense, *any* model is wrong – if it were not, it would not be a model in the first place. The more pertinent interpretation of the question above is instead: 'Are some of the assumptions so crude as to invalidate the results in some interesting cases?' If the question is understood in this sense, the answer is probably: 'It depends.' When speaking of a model I find it more profitable to think in terms of its appropriateness to a problem than of its correctness. The efficient-market framework has been proven to be extremely powerful and useful, and it provides a very robust tool of analysis in a wide range of applications. This does not imply, however, that the conceptualizations it affords, and the conclusions that can be derived from it, should be applied without question to every asset class and in every market condition. This is exactly what is done, however, when the model parametrization of the LIBOR market model is so chosen as to enforce perfect simultaneous pricing of caplets and swaptions. Given the difficulty of carrying out the 'arbitrage' trade that would bring their values in line with each other, I believe that assuming that the efficient market hypothesis should hold in the case of these instruments is unwarranted.

Does it matter? I believe it does, because the 'contortions' imposed onto the model by this over-perfect parametrization can produce very undesirable pricing and hedging effects. So, if a financially convincing parametrization of the LIBOR market model can be found that 'naturally' prices swaptions and caplets well, so much the better. If this is not possible, the trader will have to ask herself what future hedging instruments she is most likely to use during the course of the trade, and to ensure that their future prices (as predicted by the model) are not too much at variance with the real ones.

Isn't the whole approach, then, based as it is on dynamic replication of arbitrary payoffs, self-contradictory? It is only so for the believer in 'true' and 'false' models. Perfect payoff replication might be impossible, but a considerable degree of hedging can certainly be achieved. The trader who uses models as tools to aid the analysis will not be upset by this, and will know that using a model can be a useful crutch up to a point, but can become a hindrance if pushed too far.

In this book I shall analyze in detail additional and more technical causes of the near-impossibility to enforce via quasi-arbitrage trades the exact congruence between the two markets. These are linked to the fact that, even if the volatility and correlation functions that describe the model were deterministic, they are not perfectly known by the trader. Because of this lack of perfect information, the market is not complete. The difficulties are then compounded by the fact that, in reality, volatilities are unlikely to be deterministic, and, if stochastic, do not even appear to be describable in terms of simple diffusions (see Chapter 13). If this is true, supply and demand can, and in my opinion do, drive a wedge between the theoretical prices of caplets and swaptions. The main message that I tried to convey in this section will be expanded upon and will reappear as a recurrent theme throughout the book.

2

The Mathematical and Financial Set-up

2.1 The Modelling Framework

2.1.1 Relative versus Absolute Pricing

The branch of finance called 'asset pricing' deals, not surprisingly, with the problem of assigning prices to assets. There are two main strands, traditionally referred to as 'absolute' and 'relative' pricing. With the first line of inquiry one seeks to explain prices in terms of fundamental macroeconomic variables; investors' preferences and utility functions feature prominently in this type of approach. General-equilibrium models (such as the Cox, Ingersoll and Ross (Cox et al. 1985) or the Longstaff and Schwartz (1992) interest-rate models mentioned in Chapter 1) are typical examples of this approach. With relative pricing, on the other hand, one takes on a less fundamental task, and the attempt is made to explain the price of a certain set of assets, given the (exogenous) prices of another set of instruments.

In reality (see, e.g., Cochrane 2001), most problems in asset pricing are solved by a mixture of the two approaches, and even in the most dyed-in-the-wool relative-pricing applications there should be room for the judicious introduction of some absolute pricing considerations: this will be the case, in general, whenever the securities whose prices constitute the exogenous reference benchmarks fail fully to complete the market. This, in turn, will occur, for instance if jumps are present in the process for the underlying; if the diffusions are driven by stochastic volatilities; or, as we will see, whenever one deals with interest-rate instruments that depend on imperfectly known instantaneous (rather than root-mean-square) volatilities. In all these cases, more or less explicit assumptions about equilibrium market prices of risk (and therefore about risk aversion and utilities) appear alongside the relative-pricing approach. Some of these more complex aspects are dealt with in Part IV of this book, but in the present chapter I shall make use of sufficiently strong assumptions so as to be able to dispense with market prices of risk altogether. However, I shall frequently remind the reader, in Parts I–III that, even if the standard modelling framework assumes market completeness, reality is considerably more complex and interesting (and, for the trader, dangerous).

2.1.2 The Benchmark Securities and Model Calibration

The canonical modern pricing approach falls squarely in the relative pricing class. As mentioned above, the adjective 'relative' highlights that the price of the exotic instrument is obtained given the model prices of the relatively liquid plain-vanilla instruments that will be used in the dynamic hedging. These benchmark plain-vanilla instruments are swaps, FRAs, caplets[1] and (bullet) European swaptions.

Despite the fact that the ultimate goal is to price exotics, the most taxing part of the implementation of the LIBOR-market-model approach is arguably the consistent and financially realistic recovery of the prices of the plain-vanilla caplets and swaptions. This process is normally referred to as the 'calibration' of the model, and the choices of its parameters as its 'parametrization'.

The challenges that are encountered in the course of the calibration do not stem from the fact that recovering exactly the prices of at least one set (caplets or European swaptions) of benchmark instruments is difficult. On the contrary, and somewhat paradoxically, recovering exactly the prices of one set of variables is almost too easy. What I mean by this is that this perfect calibration can be achieved in an infinity of ways. For any of the resulting possible parametrizations, however, there may correspond substantially different possible prices for exotic LIBOR products. In a sense, the ability to distinguish good from poor (or, more realistically, better from worse) parametrizations is what a successful implementation of the modern pricing approach is all about.

In the next chapter I will show how an exact calibration to, say, caplet prices can be carried out, and will show why the resulting solutions are indeed infinite. In correspondence to each of these solutions, I will also obtain the no-arbitrage drifts for a variety of possible numeraires. The following chapters will then provide criteria to choose the financially most appropriate solutions from the set of the possible calibrations.

---

[1]Caplets are in reality instruments whose prices have to be imputed from the screen-visible brokers' quotes of caps for a set of maturities and strikes. The market adopts the following convention in quoting a cap implied volatility: given the strike, tenor and final maturity of the cap, the associated implied volatility is the single number that must be input in the Black formulas for all the component caplets in order to obtain the desired market price for the whole cap by adding up all the resulting caplet prices. Even in the absence of smiles, distilling from these the caplet prices is a far-from-trivial exercise. Just as in traditional yield-curve modelling, which requires a continuum of discount bond prices that are not directly traded, and whose prices are not screen-observable, I will always assume that prices for all the caplets are available to the trader.

2.1.3 The Relationship between the Present Treatment and Existing Literature – Overview of the Chapter

The standard modern approach to modelling the diffusive evolution of discrete (finite-tenor) forward rates in continuous time has been treated in detail in several articles and books (see, e.g., Jamshidian 1997, Musiela and Rutkowski 1997a, Brace et al. 1996, and the references in Section 2.3 of this book). It will be re-presented in the following in order both to allow the material presented in the book to be reasonably self-contained, and to emphasize the particular 'version' of the LIBOR market model that will be used in this book.

The treatment in Section 2.3 will be more formal, and requires greater mathematical knowledge than is assumed elsewhere in the book. My main goal in this section is to present the logical steps needed in order to build from scratch the particular version of the LIBOR market model that I intend to use. I will not prove theorems but simply show how they can be used as building blocks of the chosen modelling set-up. In so doing, my intention is to show which mathematical assumptions and definitions have a direct financial interpretation and motivation, and which are mainly technical in nature. Once this task has been accomplished, in the following chapters I will always assume (unless otherwise stated) that the 'technical conditions' are satisfied. In most situations this will hardly limit the scope of practical financial applications. It must be stated from the very beginning, however, that the mathematical treatment commonly found in the literature tends to convey an impression of greater generality for the approach than it actually enjoys: on the one hand, for instance, it allows the instantaneous volatility functions to be Lebesgue square-integrable, thereby giving room for much more 'pathological' volatility functions than any modeller might want to use. On the other hand, just a few lines into the classic treatment by Musiela and Rutkowski (1997a), the assumption is already made that the process driving the forward rates should be a Wiener diffusion (i.e., a process with continuous paths and infinite first and finite second variation), thereby substantially limiting the *financial* scope of the approach. In other terms, a great part of the mathematical complexity stems from the (esthetically understandable) desire to embed the treatment within a framework of great mathematical generality, without, however, by so doing, buying much financial flexibility: we might well allow the volatility function to reach infinity on an infinite number of zero-measure points, but there is no hiding the fact that the financially more relevant and 'mundane' cases of stochastic volatility or jump processes fall outside the standard treatment (see, however, Jamshidian (1999), Glasserman and Kou (2000) or Glasserman and Merener (2001) for extensions in one of these directions, and Joshi and Rebonato (2001), Rebonato and Joshi (2001a) and the treatment in Chapters 11–13 for a development of the other).

Different degrees of mathematical rigor have been used by various authors to present the mathematical foundations of the modern pricing approach. A compromise must always be struck between the scope and generality of a given approach, and the complexity of the mathematical formalism. Even in the relatively more formal Section 2.3, I have consciously tilted my treatment towards the simpler end of the 'complexity spectrum', but I have attempted both to provide pointers to more rigorous and general treatments, and to ensure that my approach should be as simple as possible while remaining mathematically correct.

Section 2.3, which contains the conceptual steps that are usually undertaken in describing the stochastic evolution of forward rates in the modern pricing approach, contains little original material. The order and choice of the topics of presentation, however, is not totally standard, focussed as it is towards providing in the most direct manner the theoretical framework suitable for dealing with the particular version of the LIBOR-market-model treatment I have chosen to present. I have typographically isolated Section 2.3 in order to indicate that it can be skipped by the mathematically well-versed reader who is already familiar with the standard set-up. It can also be skipped by the hasty reader who is not familiar with (or interested in) the conceptual lay-out and is more focussed on the results than on the detailed path that must be followed to reach them. For this type of reader, the definitions and concepts presented in Section 2.2 should be sufficient. While I have structured the book in such a way that this 'fast-track' approach should be possible, it should be pointed out that, by so doing, the reader will be ill-equipped not only to appreciate the scope and degree of generality of the standard approach, but also to understand some of the finer points that arise in more general and complex settings. This will be the case, for instance, when one wants to allow for stochastic volatilities (see Chapters 12 and 13).

Before embarking on this treatment, I present immediately below the definition and valuation of the building blocks of the LIBOR market model, that is, forward-rate agreements, swaps, caplets and European swaptions. Elsewhere, the book assumes knowledge of, or only briefly describes, considerably more complex products, such as trigger swaps or Bermudan swaptions. The reason for this asymmetry in my treatment is that the plain-vanilla instruments above enjoy a privileged status in the modern pricing approach, and a precise understanding of their characteristics and valuation is therefore indispensable for a proper understanding of the LIBOR market model.

2.2 Definition and Valuation of the Underlying Plain-Vanilla Instruments

2.2.1 *The Pricing of FRAs: Introducing Forward Rates*

From a purely theoretical point of view, the underlying plain-vanilla instruments at the trader's disposal are simply a set of pure discount bonds.[2]

---

[2] I will show later that, for the version of the LIBOR market model I have chosen to present, and for the products described in Chapter 4 (i.e., virtually all the commonly traded LIBOR products), the trader actually only requires a finite set of discount bonds.

The LIBOR market, however, typically operates off-balance-sheet, and transactions in physical assets (i.e., bonds) are in reality executed by traders in much smaller notional amounts than the principals of the associated off-balance-sheet products – see the discussion later in this section. Typically, the agents in single-currency plain-vanilla LIBOR transactions enter agreements whereby they promise to swap (fixed or floating) interest streams, without exchange of principals.[3] In addition, plain-vanilla traders also buy and sell options on these interest streams, as discussed later.

The simplest, most 'atomic', instrument is a forward-rate agreement (FRA). In working out the value of a FRA the crucial question is: 'Do two traders, with different subjective beliefs about the future, "have to" agree on the value of the FRA (and therefore of the forward rate)?' The answer depends crucially on the instruments they consider as primitive, and about which they most naturally express trading views. In the standard treatment, one assumes that the traders can observe the prices of the two discount bonds maturing at times T and $T + \tau$. I will argue later that this approach is unrealistic, not only because of the assumed absence of market frictions (a ubiquitous and relatively minor blemish), but in its specification of the fundamental instruments in which LIBOR dealers actually trade. Nonetheless, the logical flow of the argument that uses discount bonds as primitives is smoother, and the treatment more in line with the conceptual path usually found in the literature. I will therefore follow this approach. By entering a FRA, two parties agree at time t to exchange at time $T + \tau$ an amount of money proportional to the difference between a strike, K, also agreed at time t, and the LIBOR rate, $L(T, T + \tau)$, that resets at time T for payment at time $T + \tau$. The proportionality factor is given by the product of the notional principal, NP, times the accrual period τ (typically three or six months):

$$\text{Payoff(FRA)}_{T+\tau} = \text{NP}[L(T, T + \tau) - K]\tau$$
$$= \text{NP}[L(T, T + \tau)\tau - K\tau], \qquad (2.1)$$

$$\text{PV(FRA)}_T = \text{NP}\frac{[L(T, T + \tau) - K]\tau}{[1 + L(T, T + \tau)\tau]}. \qquad (2.2)$$

In Equation (2.2), the symbol 'PV_T' indicates the present value at reset time, T. Once the reset time is reached, the cash-flow occurring at time $T + \tau$ can be discounted to time T using the risk-less LIBOR rate because its magnitude is a known quantity determined by the reset of $L(T, T + \tau)$. The first term in the second line of Equation (2.1) is called the value at time $T + \tau$ of the floating leg of the FRA, and, similarly, the second term is called the value at time $T + \tau$ of the fixed leg.

---

[3] In the case of cross-currency swaps and swaptions, exchanges of principals at the beginning and/or the end of the transactions are common, but, typically, an exchange of interest streams is also present. The cash management associated with the exchange of principals gives rise to the so-called 'financing bias'. I shall not deal with cross-currency products in this book.

These two equations define the value of a FRA at expiry (time T) or payoff time (time $T + \tau$). They provide no indication, however, as to what the value of the FRA should be at any earlier time, that is, before the reset of the LIBOR rate. The value of the FRA at a time t prior to T is most easily expressed by introducing the concept of forward rate, $f(t, T, T + \tau)$. At reset the forward rate is set by definition to be equal to the corresponding LIBOR rate, L:

$$f(T, T, T + \tau) \equiv L(T, T + \tau).$$

Therefore Equations (2.1) and (2.2) can be rewritten as

$$\text{Payoff(FRA)}_{T+\tau} = \text{NP}[f(T, T, T + \tau) - K]\tau$$
$$= \text{NP}[f(T, T, T + \tau)\tau - K\tau], \qquad (2.1')$$
$$\text{PV(FRA)}_T = \text{NP}\frac{[f(T, T, T + \tau) - K]\tau}{[1 + f(T, T, T + \tau)\tau]}. \qquad (2.2')$$

As for earlier times, at any time t before T the forward rate is defined to be the strike that gives zero value to the corresponding FRA.[4] The ability to specify the forward rate at a time earlier than T is therefore predicated on being able to express the value of a FRA before its expiry, which is exactly the problem we set out to solve after Equation (2.2).

Equations (2.1), (2.1′), (2.2) and (2.2′) express the value of the FRA at time $T + \tau$ or T, respectively, while the definition of a forward rate mentions the equilibrium rate at time t. Since $f(t, T, T + \tau)$ is a stochastic quantity, at a generic time $t < T$ its realization at time T is not known. It would seem that two traders, even if they can observe the market equilibrium prices of the discount bonds that mature at times T and $T + \tau$, $P(t, T)$ and $P(t, T + \tau)$, might have different beliefs about the distribution of $f(T, T, T + \tau)$, and will therefore in general disagree on the value of the forward rate at a time before its reset.

There exists, however, a *static* replication strategy in the two underlying bonds, $P(t, T)$ and $P(t, T + \tau)$, that produces a payoff identical to the payoff of the floating leg of the FRA. The strategy is achieved by setting up, for each unit of the notional principal NP, a portfolio, Π, made up of a long position in the bond maturing at time T and a short position in the bond maturing at time $T + \tau$:

$$\Pi(t) = \text{NP}[P(t, T) - P(t, T + \tau)].$$

At time $T + \tau$ the value of this portfolio is equal to

$$\Pi(T + \tau) = \text{NP}\{[1 + L(T, T + \tau)\tau] - 1\} = \text{NP}\, f(T, T, T + \tau)\tau, \qquad (2.3)$$

where $1 + L(T, T + \tau)\tau = 1 + f(T, T, T + \tau)\tau$ is the value of \$1 from the discount bond that matured at time T, reinvested out to time $T + \tau$ at the

---

[4]Such a strike is also known as the equilibrium rate or equilibrium strike.

then-prevailing τ-period LIBOR rate. The last term on the RHS of Equation (2.3) is however equal to the first term on the RHS of Equation (2.1'), and therefore the floating leg of the FRA can be perfectly and statically replicated at time t by setting up the portfolio $\Pi(t)$. Under penalty of arbitrage, the values of the replicating portfolio and of the floating leg of the FRA must be identical, not only at time T, but at any time before that. It therefore follows that, if the two traders can observe the prices of the discount bonds $P(t, T)$ and $P(t, T + \tau)$ and can trade in them, the equilibrium strike of the FRA, and therefore the level, $f(t, T, T + \tau)$, of the forward rate at a time t before T can be unambiguously defined:

$$P(t, T) - P(t, T + \tau) = f(t, T, T + \tau)\tau P(t, T + \tau),$$

$$f(t, T, T + \tau) = \frac{P(t, T)/P(t, T + \tau) - 1}{\tau}. \qquad (2.4)$$

It is now a simple step to show that the present (time-t) value of the FRA is given by

$$\begin{aligned}
\text{PV(FRA)}_t &= \text{NP}[f(t, T, T + \tau)\tau - K]P(t, T + \tau) \\
&= \text{NP}[P(t, T) - P(t, T + \tau)] - \text{NP}\, KP(t, T + \tau)\tau. \quad (2.5)
\end{aligned}$$

Note that the replicating portfolio is static, that is, it does not require any readjustment throughout the life of the FRA. As a dynamic hedging strategy, which in general depends on the process of the underlying, is not required, any probability distribution such that the time-t expectation of $f(T, T, T + \tau)$ is equal to $f(t, T, T + \tau)$ will produce the correct price for the FRA. Therefore, any process – not necessarily a diffusion – such that this first-moment condition is satisfied will be compatible with a given market price for a FRA.

One important observation from this discussion is that forward rates do not contain direct information about real-world expectations of future rates, and are simply arrived at by a no-arbitrage argument. In general, not only expectations, but also a risk premium will affect the level of a forward rate, as discussed in Section 2.3.

2.2.2 Why the Bond-Based Description is an Idealization

The standard argument I have just presented puts, so to speak, the cart before the horse: in reality, a LIBOR trader *imputes* the prices of the discount bonds from the *observed* values of the FRAs (and of one spot rate). In trading practice the distinction is important: LIBOR traders mainly operate off-balance-sheet, and engage in transactions which are, by and large, unfunded (i.e., they have to borrow and lend amounts of cash – to purchase or sell bonds – which are a small fraction of the notional principals of their trades). Furthermore, the over-the-counter transactions entered into by a LIBOR trader are typically not collateralized, and traders tend to avoid as much as possible being owed large future cash-flows from risky counter-parties (even if, in present-value terms, these positive cash-flows are compensated for by shorter-term liabilities). The most common mode of operation is to engage in trans-actions where only net flows are exchanged, thereby significantly reducing the credit risk.[5]

Therefore, in order to express the risk of their positions, LIBOR traders often do work out the discount bond equivalent. However, their actual hedg-ing transaction will involve a relatively small outlay or receipt of cash, as the vast majority of the fixed and floating flows will cancel out. Indeed, it is very instructive, in this respect, to observe the behavior of a LIBOR trader who is asked to enter a zero-coupon swap (whereby a single large known payment – the fixed leg – is paid or received at the final maturity of the contract in exchange for periodic LIBOR payments – the floating leg). In this case the trader will face a different situation than if she were asked to price a stan-dard fixed/floating swap, since she will have to deal with a substantial cash management problem: if the single large coupon will have to be paid out at maturity, for instance, she will have to invest the proceeds from the floating leg throughout the life of the deal, and this will typically take place at LIBID, not at LIBOR (the London Inter-Bank *Offered* Rate).

The important point of this digression is that, contrary to the situation de-scribed above, where two traders *observe* the prices of the discount bonds and must therefore *agree* on the value of the forward rate, single-currency LIBOR traders will, in reality, have different subjective views about future realizations of the forward rate, find an equilibrium price by balancing supply and de-mand, and then agree on the discount bond prices that this price implies. In a way, the discount bond prices used by a trader are therefore 'virtual prices': she can use them to discount cash-flows when pricing a deal and to express the associated risk in terms of equivalent discount bond, as long as she does not have to trade them physically. Nonetheless, the conceptual set-up that un-derpins the LIBOR market model and the choice of numeraires is expressed more simply and elegantly if one assumes that discount bonds are the 'true' primitives. The two approaches are in the end equivalent, at least as long as the trader prices and analyzes largely unfunded transactions.

2.2.3 Plain-Vanilla Options on FRAs: the Standard Market Formula for Caplets

The plain-vanilla option instrument linked to a given FRA is the caplet, whose payoff at time $T + \tau$ is given by

$$\text{Payoff(Caplet)}_{T+\tau} = \text{NP}(f(T, T, T + \tau) - K]^+\tau. \qquad (2.6)$$

Due to the positive-part operator, $(\ )^+$, the present value of the caplet does depend on distributional features of $L(T, T + \tau) = f(T, T, T + \tau)$ other than

---

[5]This is the reason why the astronomical notional figures often quoted in popular accounts of the swap market do not really matter.

its first moment. The market standard is to assume that, when pricing a caplet with payoff at time $T + \tau$ as in Equation (2.6), the value of the forward rate resetting at time T is log-normally distributed,[6] with an unconditional variance linked to the implied volatility, σ_{Black}, by the relationship

$$\ln[f(T, T, T + \tau)] \sim G(\mu, \sigma_{Black}^2 T). \tag{2.7}$$

(In Equation (2.7), the expression $G(a, b)$ denotes a Gaussian distribution with first moment equal to a and second moment equal to b.) The no-arbitrage considerations mentioned in the previous subsection (see also Section 2.3) still hold, and therefore the time-t expectation of the forward rate resetting at time T must be equal to $f(t, T, T + \tau)$.[7] Equation (2.7) therefore becomes

$$\ln[f(T, T, T + \tau)] \sim G(\ln[f(t, T, T + \tau)] - \tfrac{1}{2}\sigma_{Black}^2 T, \; \sigma_{Black}^2 T). \tag{2.8}$$

Integration of the payoff function (2.6) over this log-normal distribution gives rise to the market-standard Black formula:

$$\mathrm{PV}(\mathrm{Caplet})_t = \mathrm{NP}[f(t, T, T + \tau)N(h_1) - KN(h_2)]P(t, T + \tau)\tau, \tag{2.9}$$

with

$$h_1 = \frac{\ln[f(t, T, T + \tau)/K] + \tfrac{1}{2}\sigma_{Black}^2(T - t)}{\sigma_{Black}\sqrt{(T - t)}},$$

$$h_2 = \frac{\ln[f(t, T, T + \tau)/K] - \tfrac{1}{2}\sigma_{Black}^2(T - t)}{\sigma_{Black}\sqrt{(T - t)}},$$

and where $N(\ )$ denotes the standard cumulative normal distribution. Note carefully that, at this stage, it is not a priori obvious that Equation (2.8) defines a well-posed option problem with a preference-free solution, that is, that no arbitrage will be incurred by pricing the caplet according to (2.9) and that there will exist, under the standard Black assumptions, a self-financing trading strategy capable of reproducing the caplet payoff. That this is indeed the case will be shown in a more formal way in the following section and more simply in Chapters 3 and 5. If the reader finds Condition (2.8), which fundamentally states that, in the absence of arbitrage, the diffusion that describes the forward rate should be drift-less, seems 'obvious', she should compare and contrast Formulas (2.8) and (2.9) with the deceptively similar, but fundamentally different, log-normal-yield bond model, referred to in Chapter 1, which cannot be financially justified.

---

[6] I neglect in this discussion the occurrence of volatility smiles, which are dealt with in Part IV.

[7] This statement implicitly assumes that the 'natural payoff' has been chosen for the discounting. See the discussion in Chapter 5.

2.2.4 The Pricing of Swaps

A similar treatment can be extended to the definition of swaps and European swaptions: a swap is a commitment to exchange the payments originating from a fixed and a floating leg. The fixed leg is made up an annuity, A, with fixed payments K occurring at pre-specified and (approximately) evenly spaced times T_i, $i = 1, 2, \ldots, N$. Since there is no uncertainty as to the magnitude and timing of these fixed cash-flows, the value of this annuity at time t is given by

$$A_t(\{T_i\}) = \text{NP}\, K \sum_{i=0}^{N-1} P(t, T_i + \tau)\tau, \qquad (2.10)$$

with $T_i + \tau = T_{i+1}$. As for the floating leg, FL, it is made up of a collection of payments, each of which will be determined by the reset of a LIBOR rate on a set of pre-specified dates, and paid on the payment date of the same LIBOR rate. Therefore the floating leg is simply equal to the collection of floating legs associated with a series of FRAs. Making use of the results obtained above, its value at time t is therefore given by

$$
\begin{aligned}
\text{FL}_t &= \sum_{i=1}^{n} \text{NP}\, f(t, T_i, T_i + \tau)\tau P(t, T_i + \tau) \\
&= \sum_{i=1}^{n} \text{NP}\, [P(t, T_i) - P(t, T_i + \tau)].
\end{aligned}
\qquad (2.11)
$$

(Notice that the number of payments on the floating leg, n, need, in general, not be the same as the number of payments on the fixed leg, N. If this were the case then the tenors,[8] τ, on the floating and fixed legs would also be different. To lighten notation, this possibility has not been considered, and the necessary extensions are totally straightforward.) If the notional principal is constant, it can be set to unity without loss of generality, and Equation (2.11) simplifies to

$$\text{FL}_t = P(t, T_0) - P(t, T_n), \qquad (2.12)$$

which, for a spot-starting swap, gives

$$\text{FL}_t = P(T_0, T_0) - P(t, T_n) = 1 - P(t, T_n). \qquad (2.13)$$

The equilibrium swap rate at time t, SR_t, is then defined to be the value of the fixed-annuity coupon that, at time t, gives zero value to a swap spanning the period $[T_{\exp}, T_{\text{mat}}]$. Therefore (see Equations (2.10) and (2.11)), it is given by the ratio of the floating to the fixed leg

$$\text{SR}(t, T_{\exp}, T_{\text{mat}}) = \text{FL}_t / A_t. \qquad (2.14)$$

---

[8]Tenors are precisely defined in Section 3.2 (see also Figure 3.1). For the moment it is sufficient to identify them with the accrual period associated with each payment.

A simple rearrangement of terms provides an alternative expression for the equilibrium swap rate, which highlights the fact that it can be regarded as a linear combination (with stochastic weights) of the underlying forward rates:[9]

$$\text{SR}(t, T_{\text{exp}}, T_{\text{mat}}) = \sum_{i=1}^{n} w_i f(t, T_i, T_i + \tau), \tag{2.15}$$

with

$$w_i = \frac{P(t, T_i + \tau)\tau}{\sum_{i=1}^{n} P(t, T_i + \tau)\tau} = \frac{P(t, T_i + \tau)\tau}{A_t}.$$

Expression (2.15) will be used frequently in later chapters.

EXERCISE 2.1 *Derive Equation (2.15) from Equation (2.14). Construct a static replicating portfolio made up of discount bonds that exactly replicates the payoff of a swap.*

2.2.5 Plain-Vanilla Options on Swaps: the Standard Market Formula for European Swaptions

A European swaption is defined as the option, purchased at time t, to enter at time T_{exp} a swap spanning the period $[T_{\text{exp}}, T_{\text{mat}}]$ with the fixed leg paying an annuity with a pre-specified coupon K. The standard market approach makes the assumption that the equilibrium swap rate is log-normally distributed with expectation equal to its value today, that is,

$$\ln[\text{SR}(T_{\text{exp}}, T_{\text{exp}}, T_{\text{mat}})]$$
$$\sim G(\ln[\text{SR}(t, T_{\text{exp}}, T_{\text{mat}})] - \tfrac{1}{2}\sigma_{\text{SR,Black}}^2 T_{\text{exp}}, \sigma_{\text{SR,Black}}^2 T_{\text{exp}}), \tag{2.16}$$

where now the quantity $\sigma_{\text{SR,Black}}$ is the swap-rate implied (Black) volatility. The payoff at time T_{exp} of the swaption is

$$\text{Payoff}(\text{Swaption})_{T_{\text{exp}}}$$
$$= [\text{SR}(T_{\text{exp}}, T_{\text{exp}}, T_{\text{mat}}) - K]^+ A(T_{\text{exp}}, T_{\text{exp}}, T_{\text{mat}}), \tag{2.17}$$

where $A(T_{\text{exp}}, T_{\text{exp}}, T_{\text{mat}})$ is the value at time T_{exp} of the annuity spanning the period $[T_{\text{exp}}, T_{\text{mat}}]$. Integration of this payoff over the log-normal distribution of the swap rate at expiry gives rise again to the Black formula

$$\text{PV}(\text{Swaption})_t = [\text{SR}(t, T_{\text{exp}}, T_{\text{mat}})N(h_1) - KN(h_2)]A(t, T_{\text{exp}}, T_{\text{mat}}), \tag{2.18}$$

---

[9]Needless to say, a linear combination with stochastic weights is, strictly speaking, not a *linear* combination at all if the weights depend on the independent variables (the forward rates). One of the recurring approximations used throughout the book, however, is that Expression (2.15) can very often be treated with little loss of accuracy *as if* it were a linear combination. The expression 'linear combination with stochastic weights' is therefore used throughout the book.

where now

$$h_1 = \frac{\ln[\mathrm{SR}(t, T_{\mathrm{exp}}, T_{\mathrm{mat}})/K] + \frac{1}{2}\sigma^2_{\mathrm{SR,Black}}(T_{\mathrm{exp}} - t)}{\sigma_{\mathrm{SR,Black}}\sqrt{(T_{\mathrm{exp}} - t)}},$$

$$h_2 = \frac{\ln[\mathrm{SR}(t, T_{\mathrm{exp}}, T_{\mathrm{mat}})/K] - \frac{1}{2}\sigma^2_{\mathrm{SR,Black}}(T_{\mathrm{exp}} - t)}{\sigma_{\mathrm{SR,Black}}\sqrt{(T_{\mathrm{exp}} - t)}}.$$

The important issue of the existence of a self-financing replicating strategy capable of reproducing the swaption payoff is not addressed at this stage. I will simply state without proof that, in a Black world, replication is indeed possible for the trader who knows the true (deterministic) volatility of the swap rate, who can trade without friction in the forward-starting annuity, $A(t, T_{\mathrm{exp}}, T_{\mathrm{mat}})$, and who can enter swap contracts without incurring bid/offer spreads.

It should also be noted that the simultaneous endorsement of the log-normal assumptions for all caplets and all swaptions creates problems of internal consistency, since, for instance, a swap rate, being a linear combination of forward rates, cannot be log-normal if the underlying forward rates are. The discussion of this issue is also postponed to later chapters (see also Rebonato 1999b).

2.2.6 Serial Options

Equations (2.1) to (2.18) provide the definitions of, and the pricing formulas for, the plain-vanilla instruments (FRAs, swaps, plus caplets or European swaptions) whose prices the LIBOR market model has the ability to reproduce exactly. While these results fulfill the main task of this section, it is useful for the purpose of future discussions to define the payoff of another type of product, the so-called 'serial option', which is not a plain-vanilla instrument, but which is deceptively similar to a caplet. The practical importance of serial options is rather limited, because they are neither very liquid, nor do they extend in expiry/maturity beyond a year or two. Conceptually they are, however, extremely important, because, if readily available for long expiries, they would allow the completion of the market in instantaneous volatilities and would fundamentally alter the treatment presented in Part III of this book (and, more importantly, trading practice).

To define their payoff, three different times must be specified, the option expiry time, T_{opt}, the payment time, T_{pay}, and the forward-rate reset time, T_{reset}, with $T_{\mathrm{opt}} \leq T_{\mathrm{pay}} \leq T_{\mathrm{reset}}$, but $T_{\mathrm{opt}} < T_{\mathrm{reset}}$ (see Figure 2.1). Given a strike K, the payoff at time T_{pay} is then given by

$$\mathrm{Payoff}_{T_{\mathrm{pay}}} = [f(T_{\mathrm{opt}}, T_{\mathrm{reset}}, T_{\mathrm{reset}} + \tau) - K]^+ \tau.$$

A serial option therefore pays at time T_{pay} the positive difference between a strike and the value of a forward rate at a time T_{opt} before its natural reset

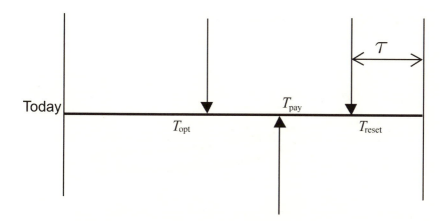

Figure 2.1 *The timings of the various events associated with a serial option. Note that T_{pay} may coincide with T_{opt}, but T_{reset} must always occur strictly after T_{opt}.*

time, T_{reset}. The crucial difference with respect to the case of a caplet is that one cannot assume that the instantaneous volatility of the forward rate will be constant throughout its life (see the detailed discussion in Chapter 6), and one cannot therefore simply 'pro rata' the root-mean-square Black volatility to take into account the fact that the option expiry occurs before the reset of the forward rate. This situation is depicted in Figure 2.2, which shows three different possible instantaneous volatility functions for a given forward rate that all give rise to the same root-mean-square (Black) volatility to be input in the market Black formula. They all therefore produce exactly the same caplet price. For a serial option, however, whose time T_{opt} is strictly smaller than T_{reset}, these three different instantaneous volatility functions would give rise to different root-mean-square volatilities out to time T_{opt}. Despite the fact that I do not provide a valuation formula for a serial option in this section, it is reasonable (and correct) to expect that it will depend on the root-mean-square volatility of the forward rate out to time T_{opt}, and, therefore, for the same market-observable caplet price, three different values for the serial option would be produced by the three instantaneous volatility curves (see again Figure 2.2).

EXERCISE 2.2 *Assume that you know not only today's price for the caplet expiring at time T_{reset}, but also today's market prices of other caplets. You might want to include in your information set the prices of the caplets expiring at time T_{opt} or T_{pay}. If you thought it could be useful, you can grant yourself knowledge of the prices of any other caplet of your choice. If you wanted, you could even assume that you knew the prices of a continuum of caplets. Would this additional information determine the price of the serial option uniquely? You can assume, for simplicity, that all the forward rates exactly and simultaneously follow a perfect log-normal diffusion. Explain.*

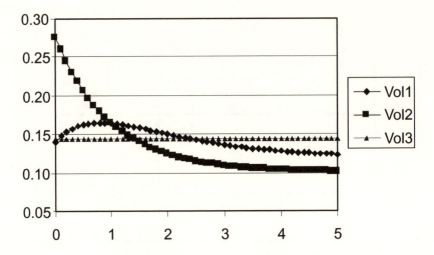

Figure 2.2   *Three possible instantaneous volatilities for a given forward rate that would give rise, over a five-year period, to the same root-mean-square volatility. All these instantaneous volatility functions would therefore give rise to the same price for a five-year caplet. Notice, however, that, if the expiry of a serial option on the same forward rate were to occur at, say, time t = 1.5, the root-mean-square instantaneous volatility over this shorter period would be very different in the three different cases, despite the fact that one would observe from the market the same caplet price.*

EXERCISE 2.3 *Suppose now that you also know the market prices of caplets of your choice that have occurred in the past. By analyzing the pattern over time of their associated implied volatilities, would you be in a better position to venture a choice among the three candidate instantaneous volatilities in Figure 2.2? Explain.*

There are several other subtle but important considerations that enter the valuation of a serial option, such as the fact that, at time T_{opt}, the value of the forward rate is not unambiguously defined by a screen-visible reset, but will depend on the details of the yield-curve construction carried out by the individual trader. At a more fundamental level, depending on the payment time, it will, in general, not be possible to assume that the underlying forward rate is an exponential martingale (i.e., drift-less). The derivation of the no-arbitrage drift for the forward rate in the case of a serial option can be profitably carried out as a simple application of the techniques explained in Chapter 5. At this stage, however, the important message from this discussion is that only if the prices of a double series[10] of serial options were observable from the market could a trader discriminate between different instantaneous volatility functions consistent with the same market prices of caplets.

---

[10]The series would have to be double because one would need the prices of serial options as a function both of T_{reset} and of T_{opt}.

2.2.7 First Discussion of Market Completeness

In general one calls a market 'complete' if it is possible to enter suitable trades in a series of 'fundamental' instruments such that one can produce with certainty a unit payoff for any possible future state of the world.[11] When this is the case, any additional security that pays an arbitrary (but known) amount in all or some of these future states of the world is redundant, since it can be replicated by trading in the fundamental assets. Let us now assume that, as is normally the case, a particular exotic interest-rate product has a payoff that depends on a particular portion of the instantaneous volatility function of a given forward rate (not just on the associated market-visible root-mean-square volatility to expiry).[12] The description of the state of the world of relevance for the exotic product would therefore have to include information also about the instantaneous volatility function of the forward rate. This being the case, if serial options were available, one could produce a payoff that depended exactly on the relevant portion of the instantaneous volatility, the market would be complete, the exotic product truly redundant and the only task left to the interest-rate option trader would be to find a parametrization of the chosen ('true') model that exactly reproduced the observed market prices of caplets, of serial options (and, possibly, of European swaptions, if the exotic product also depended, as in general will be case, on the correlation between the various forward rates). In the absence of serial options, on the other hand, the market in instantaneous volatilities is not complete, the trader cannot deduce uniquely from the traded price which instantaneous volatility is the 'true' one, the future payoff of the exotic product cannot be reproduced with certainty, and a parametrization of the true model such that all caplets and swaptions are exactly priced today would still not guarantee a unique price for the exotic instrument. These observations have profound implications insofar as the actual use and calibration of the LIBOR market model is concerned, and will be revisited at several points in the book.

The fundamental building blocks of the LIBOR market model have now been introduced. The following section presents a first derivation of the modern pricing approach that assumes greater familiarity with probabilistic and stochastic calculus concepts than elsewhere in the book. It can be skipped without loss of continuity, but some of the qualitative observations can be of interest also to the fast-track reader.

---

[11] There are many, more or less equivalent, definitions of market completeness. An alternative definition (Balland and Hughston 1999) is that a market is said to be complete if the given traded assets are insufficient to hedge a general contingent claim.

[12] More precisely, one should say that the payoff of the exotic product should depend on the integral of a function of the instantaneous volatility between two arbitrary times T_a and T_b. To keep the discussion simple, I will say that the value of the product depends on the instantaneous volatility *tout court*. The distinction is not pedantic, because the instantaneous volatility is defined by a continuum of values, while the value of a typical LIBOR product only depends on a finite number of these integrals. See the discussion in Chapter 4.

2.3 The Mathematical and Financial Description of the Securities Market[13]

Several treatments have appeared in the literature to describe the no-arbitrage dynamics of LIBOR forward rates: see, for instance, Brace et al. (1996), Jamshidian (1997), Musiela and Rutkowski (1997b), Rutkowski (1997, 1998) and Miltersen et al. (1997), to quote just a few. Whilst broadly equivalent, they display significant differences. Some authors (see, e.g., Rutkowski 1998) express the volatilities of the forward LIBOR rates in terms of volatilities of spot bond processes. Others (see, e.g., Jamshidian 1997, Musiela and Rutkowski 1997b, Rutkowski 1997) use the bond price processes only to define forward (price) processes, and avoid using spot bond price volatilities at all. More importantly, different treatments vary in the choice of the volatilities that are assumed to be a deterministic function of time. In this section I shall broadly follow the conceptual steps laid out, for example, in Musiela and Rutkowski (1997b) and Jamshidian (1997), and therefore my presentation will introduce bond price processes only as a means towards defining forward-price processes, will never require explicit mention of the volatility of spot bond processes, and will impose deterministic volatilities for the forward rates (to be defined) and for no other quantities.

2.3.1 Modelling Choices

What is the most convenient mathematical setting for the treatment ahead? Absence of arbitrage requires that, after appropriate discounting, the bond price processes become martingales. As for the forward-rate processes, depending on the choice of numeraire, they will be either martingales or semi-martingales. Both the forward rates and the forward prices will be required to be strictly positive. Therefore, strictly positive (semi-)martingales provide the natural mathematical description of these requirements. The standard LIBOR market model then deals with stochastic processes which follow continuous paths of finite quadratic variation. The innovations to prices and forward rates must therefore be compatible with this requirement. These desiderata suggest that the following setting can be appropriate.

Let us introduce a standard filtered probability space FPS $\equiv (\Omega, \mathcal{F}_t, P), t \in [0, T]$, which satisfies the 'usual conditions' (see, e.g., Dothan 1990, chapter 10, p. 232). Given this triplet $(\Omega, \mathcal{F}_t, P)$, one can then define on the probability space FPS:

- the set M of all real-valued (local) martingales;

- the set M_c of all real-valued (local) continuous martingales;

- the set M_c^+ of all real-valued (local) strictly positive continuous martingales;

---

[13]This section can be skipped on first reading without loss of continuity.

- the set A of all previsible (predictable) real-valued, finite-variation processes;

- the set SM of those semi-martingales made up of processes $X(t)$ such that $X_t = X_0 + m_X + a_X$, with $m_X \in M$ and $a_X \in A$;

- the set $SM^+ \subset SM$ of *strictly positive* semi-martingales.

The notion of arbitrage is closely linked with certain (too-good-to-be-true) strategies being impossible (i.e., having zero probability). Speaking of the probability of an event (zero or otherwise) only makes sense if the probability measure is specified. On the other hand, in the derivations below, we will move frequently between measures. It is therefore important that certain properties, such as strategies being an arbitrage, or processes being strictly positive semi-martingales, should be preserved as we move from one measure to another. We will therefore restrict the measure moves to take place between special sets of measures. This is made more precise as follows.

DEFINITION 2.1 *Two measures Q and P are said to be equivalent (denoted by $Q \sim P$) if they share the same null set (i.e., if events impossible in one measure are also impossible in the other).*

DEFINITION 2.2 *A measure Q, equivalent to P, is said to be an equivalent martingale measure if the process X is a martingale with respect both to Q and to P (and the Radon–Nikodym derivative dQ/dP has finite variation) (see, e.g., Duffie 1996, Chapter 6, Section F).*

Working with equivalent martingale measures is important because, if we preclude the possibility of an event (such as arbitrage) in one measure, we can rest assured that the same event will remain of probability zero in any of the equivalent measures we might want to work with. Another desirable property is that the sets SM and SM^+ remain invariant under a change of equivalent probability measures: if $Q \sim P \to SM(P) = SM(Q)$ and $SM^+(P) = SM^+(Q)$.

REMARK 2.1 *The concept of localization that appears in the definitions above becomes important if, for instance, the condition $E_P[|X|] < \infty$ fails to be satisfied (see, e.g., Dothan 1990, chapter 10, p. 240). It will not be of relevance in the treatment presented in the following chapters, but notice Jamshidian (1997).*

REMARK 2.2 *The standard definition of the elements of the set SM^+ requires that they should also have (almost certainly) sample paths that are right continuous and with finite left-hand limits (RCLL or cadlag). I shall make no explicit use of this property either, and will always assume this to be the case.*

There are deeper reasons for wanting to model prices and forward rates as strictly positive semi-martingales than their positivity. We would like to model price changes, for instance, as being made up of a previsible component (such as the pull to par of a discount bond), and a 'surprise' component, linked to the arrival of market information. The identification of price and forward rate processes with (strictly positive) semi-martingales is then particularly apposite because of the following:

PROPOSITION 2.1 *Each element in SM and SM⁺ can be uniquely (up to indistinguishability) decomposed into the sum of a pure martingale component, which is usually referred to as the 'innovation' part, and a previsible process, often called the 'predictable' part (Doob–Meyer decomposition theorem – see, e.g., Dothan 1990, Duffie 1996, Neftci 1996).*

To go any further with our modelling choices, we have to say something specific about the innovation part. The choice of the best description is not self-evident: it is not a priori obvious, for instance, whether the process path can be more profitably modelled as having a continuous or a discontinuous path (or a mixture of the two). Processes of finite first variation (such as Gamma Variance processes) are perfectly plausible, and in some respect very attractive (see, e.g., Madan et al. 1998 and references therein). Historically, however, processes with infinite first variation and finite second variation have probably been the first modelling tools for the description of financial processes (the literature goes all the way back to Einstein and Bachelier at the beginning of the last century). The evolution of this modelling program has led, via the Black-and-Scholes approach, all the way to the standard LIBOR market model. The following choice is therefore made about the innovation:

CONDITION 2.1 *As far as the martingale component of the Doob–Meyer decomposition is concerned, we will restrict our attention to innovations which are continuous martingales, m_X, with finite second variation and which are square-integrable.*

REMARK 2.3 *Because of the continuity condition above, jump processes fall beyond the scope of the standard treatment presented in the following (see, however, Jamshidian 1999, Glasserman and Kou 2000 and Glasserman and Merener 2001 for an extension of the LIBOR market modelling approach to the case of discontinuous processes). It is important to remember that continuous square-integrable martingales are characterized, inter alia, by having infinite first variation, and finite second variation. Infinite-activity processes – such as the Variance Gamma – are also outside the scope of the standard LIBOR market model.*

REMARK 2.4 *A few words on notation: The quadratic variation of $X_i \in \{X\}$, which we will use extensively in the following, will be denoted $\langle dX_i\, dX_i \rangle$ or, more simply, $dX_i\, dX_i$ or dX_i^2. Given two processes X_j and $X_k \in \{X\}$, their quadratic covariation will be denoted by $\langle dX_j\, dX_k \rangle$, $\mathrm{cov}[dX_j, dX_k]$ or, more simply, $dX_j\, dX_k$.*

These continuous, finite-second-variation martingales are important because one can show (Karatzas and Shreve 1988) that all such martingales can be represented in terms of Wiener processes, perhaps running at a modified-time clock. We can therefore restate Condition 2.1 with no loss of generality by saying that:

CONDITION 2.2 *As far as the martingale component of the Doob–Meyer decomposition is concerned, we will restrict our attention to innovations that are Wiener processes.*

Since (Levy theorem) any Wiener process relative to a filtration $\mathcal{F}_t$ is a Brownian motion, from now on we will equivalently speak of Wiener processes or of Brownian motions. We are therefore requiring that the innovation part in the Doob–Meyer decomposition of a (positive) semi-martingale should be of the form

$$\mathrm{d}m_{X_i}(t) = \sigma_i \, \mathrm{d}z_i(t), \qquad 1 \leq i \leq n, \tag{2.19}$$

with $\mathrm{d}z_i(t)$ the increment of a standard Brownian motion on P. Nothing has been said so far about the quantity σ_i (the volatility), which could, in particular, be deterministic or stochastic, as long as it is a Lebesgue square-integrable (L^2), adapted process (see, e.g., Duffie 1996, Chapter 8, Section H).

2.3.2 Two Useful Tools: Girsanov's Theorem and the Martingale Representation theorem

Most of the fundamental modelling choices have now been made. In order to obtain useful results we require two tools, which I state below without proof. The two theorems are usually referred to as the Girsanov or Cameron–Martin theorem and the martingale representation theorem, and they will constitute the cornerstones of the change-of-measure argument. The reader is referred to Karatzas and Shreve (1988) for a proof of the former.

Starting with the martingale representation theorem, let

- X be a strictly positive martingale with respect to the filtration generated by a P-Wiener process,

- $z(t)$ be a standard Wiener process under P, and

- $\gamma(t)$ be a real-valued (not necessarily deterministic!) previsible process, integrable with respect to $z(t)$.

Then, if some technical conditions are satisfied, the following theorem holds:

THEOREM 2.1 *Given X, γ and $z(t)$ as above, it is always possible to represent the martingale $X(t)$ in the form*

$$\mathrm{d}X_t = X_t \gamma(t) \, \mathrm{d}z(t) \tag{2.20}$$

Notice that the requirement that X should be a martingale with respect to the filtration generated by a P-Wiener process is essential to the proof, and reflects the fact that the Wiener process should be the only source of randomness in X.

As for Girsanov's theorem, let

- $z(t)$ be a standard Brownian motion under a measure P,

- $\mathcal{F}_t$ be the associated Brownian filtration, and

- $z_q(t)$ be defined by

$$z_q(t) = z(t) + qt$$

where q is an $\mathcal{F}_t$-adapted process which satisfies the Novikov regularity condition $E_P(\exp[\int_0^t q(u)^2 \, du]) < \infty$. Then (see, e.g., Mikosh 1998)

THEOREM 2.2 *The process* $M(t) = \exp[-qz(t) - \frac{1}{2}q^2t]$ *is a P-martingale (see, e.g., Neftci (1996, chapter 14, p. 291) for a nice sketch of the proof of this part of the theorem). The process* $M(t)$ *defines a new probability measure* Q, *equivalent to* P, *via the relationship* $Q(A) = \int_A M_t(\omega) \, dP(\omega)$. *Under* Q, *the process* $z_q(t)$ *is a standard Brownian motion.*

REMARK 2.5 *The new measure* Q *is often expressed in terms of the Radon–Nikodym derivative* $dQ(A)/dP(A)$. *The link between the latter and the market price of risk is interesting and profound (see, e.g., Duffie 1996, Baxter and Rennie 1996) but will not be pursued here for the sake of brevity and to keep the presentation as focussed as possible.*

   Why are these two tools important? As far as the martingale representation theorem is concerned, it allows the innovation part in the process X to be represented by an expression of the type $dX_t = X_t \gamma(t) \, dz(t)$. This provides more than a handy notational tool. We will see, in fact, that different versions of the LIBOR market model are characterized by

- identifying the process X either with forward rates or with forward bond prices, and

- requiring that, when one models the innovation part of X, the function γ should be purely a function of time.

In particular, if the identification is made between X and forward rates, one deals with the version of the modern pricing approach used in this book. So, a crucial part of the LIBOR market model deals with the identification of the measure under which the forward-rate processes can be modelled as strictly positive martingales expressible in the form $dX_t = X_t \gamma(t) \, dz(t)$ with *a deterministic volatility*.

   To see why we need Girsanov's theorem, recall that ultimately we are interested in setting up a price system that does not allow arbitrage. An informal definition of arbitrage is a *zero-cost* strategy whereby you never lose, and sometimes you win. So, for no arbitrage to exist, there must be, associated with the outcomes of this strategy, at least one negative outcome with non-zero probability. Consider then the set of all probability measures that agree as to which events are possible and which impossible (i.e., the set of equivalent probability measures). So, in moving between equivalent measures, we can 'reshuffle' in very complex ways the probability masses associated with the different events, as long as we do not turn impossible events into possible ones (with however small a probability) and vice versa. Assume that in a given probability measure in this set there is at least one negative outcome with non-zero probability. Then one can plausibly expect to find an *equivalent* probability measure that 'tilts' the probability of the various outcomes in such a way that the outcomes now constitute a fair game (i.e., with the likelihood of losses exactly counterbalancing the probability of losses). Under such a measure the reweighted outcomes therefore now satisfy the most important condition for being a martingale. Notice that this reshuffling of probabilities could not have produced this result if all the outcomes had been positive (i.e., in the presence of arbitrage). Therefore the ability to transform a probability measure into an equivalent one in such a way that a process becomes a martingale (Girsanov's theorem) is plausibly linked with absence of arbitrage. These comments could be profitably revisited after reading Sections 2.3.8 and 2.3.9.

2.3.3 Spot and Forward Bond Processes

We are now in a position to begin the financial treatment. Given a final horizon date $\widehat{T} > 0$, we can introduce a class of strictly positive, real-valued, adapted processes, $B(t, T_i)$, $t \leq T_i$, $0 \leq i \leq n$, $T_n \leq \widehat{T}$ (the bond prices), and we require that

- each such process should be a strictly positive semi-martingale, that is, an element of SM^+: $B(t, T_i) \in SM^+$,

- $B(T_i, T_i) = 1$ for any i, and

- $B(t, T_j) > B(t, T_k)$ for any $T_j < T_k$.

REMARK 2.6 *For notational simplicity, I shall often write $B(t, T_i) = B_i(t)$, or, more simply, just B_i if the time dependence is obvious.*

REMARK 2.7 *Since for the version of the LIBOR market model that I present below I shall simply need a finite number of forward rates, to be derived from the bond prices, I shall have to introduce only a finite number of bond processes, $B(t, T_i)$. Nonetheless, the evolution of each bond price process occurs in continuous time.*

REMARK 2.8 *It is easy to show that the condition $B(t, T_j) > B(t, T_k)$ for any $T_j < T_k$ is equivalent to requiring that there should be no arbitrage between the bonds and* *a continuously compounded money-market account (see, e.g., Musiela and Rutkowski 1997a). Since we will not make explicit use in the following of the money-market account (see Remark 2.9 below) this angle is not explored any further.*

REMARK 2.9 *Departing from the treatment of Musiela and Rutkowski (1997a), I shall not use, introduce or define the continuously compounded money-market account, nor, equivalently, the instantaneous short rate. As long as (i) the payoff of the derivative to be priced is measurable with respect to the filtration generated by the forward processes defined immediately below, and (ii) the payoff can be expressed as a function that is homogeneous of degree one in the bond prices, then neither the short rate nor the continuously compounded money-market account are needed for pricing and hedging purposes. Requiring the payoff to be homogeneous of degree one in the bond prices is not very restrictive, because requirement (ii) simply implies that it should be possible to express the payoff as the product of a function, however complicated, of the forward rates themselves times a bond (the numeraire). See Section 4.2 for a discussion of this point, and Jamshidian (1997) for a thorough discussion. This choice of avoiding the short rate and the money-market account also allows me to by-pass the discussion of issues of degeneracy of the bond price covariance matrix (see again Jamshidian 1997, p. 302). The notion of a discretely compounded money-market account can however be introduced, and is briefly discussed later on.*

For any $T_i \leq \widehat{T}$, and for any $t \leq T_i$, we also define the forward-price process (sometimes more concisely referred to as the forward process)

$$\mathrm{FB}(t, T_i, \widehat{T}) = \mathrm{FB}_i = \mathrm{FB}_i(t) = \frac{B(t, T_i)}{B(t, \widehat{T})}. \tag{2.21}$$

At this point we choose to work in the measure P under which, for any T_i, the forward process $\mathrm{FB}(t, T_i, \widehat{T})$ is a martingale. In other terms, the choice of $\widehat{T}$ (and of $B(t, \widehat{T})$) defines P as the measure under which the forward process $\mathrm{FB}(t, T_i, \widehat{T})$ is a martingale.

Given the assumptions about

- the bond price processes,
- the filtration, and
- the Wiener nature of the innovation processes,

we can conclude that, for any T_i, the forward process follows under P a strictly positive continuous martingale with respect to the filtration of a standard P-Wiener process. In other words $\mathrm{FB}_i \in M_{\mathrm{c}}^+$. Thanks to the representation theorem mentioned before, FB_i, being a strictly positive continuous martingale with respect to the filtration generated by a Wiener process, can always be represented as

$$\mathrm{dFB}(t, T_i, \widehat{T}) = \mathrm{FB}(t, T_i, \widehat{T}) \gamma(t, T_i, \widehat{T}) \, \mathrm{d}z(t), \tag{2.22}$$

with $\gamma(t, T_i, \widehat{T})$ a real-valued previsible process, integrable with respect to $z(t)$, and the latter is a standard Wiener process under P.

REMARK 2.10 *The condition that a martingale should be strictly positive is essential for the Representation (2.22) to hold.*

REMARK 2.11 *Despite the notation, which is commonly used in the literature and elsewhere in this book, the quantity $\gamma(t, T_i, \widehat{T})$ need not be a purely deterministic function of time (it might contain the forward price process itself, for instance). Therefore, one cannot in general say from Equation (2.22) that $\mathrm{FB}(t, T_i, \widehat{T})$ is log-normally distributed.*

REMARK 2.12 *We have required the measure P to be such that all the forward processes $\mathrm{FB}(t, T_i, \widehat{T})$ should be martingales. At this stage it is not obvious that one such simultaneous martingale measure should exist. See, however, the discussion in Section 2.3.9, where the result is stated that a necessary and sufficient condition for the existence of the martingale measure P is that no arbitrage should exist in the market.*[14]

Let us now consider two maturities $T_j \leq \widehat{T}$ and $T_k \leq \widehat{T}$, and define the new forward process $\mathrm{FB}(t, T_j, T_k)$ as

$$\mathrm{FB}(t, T_j, T_k) = \frac{\mathrm{FB}(t, T_j, \widehat{T})}{\mathrm{FB}(t, T_k, \widehat{T})} = \frac{B(t, T_j)}{B(t, T_k)} \qquad \text{for any } t \in [0, \min(T_j, T_k)].$$

Recall that we have chosen the measure P to be such that, for any T_i, $\mathrm{FB}(t, T_i, \widehat{T})$ should be a martingale, given that the 'forwarding' is carried out to $\widehat{T}$ (i.e., by dividing by $B(t, \widehat{T})$). The question then arises: 'When the forwarding is carried out to T_k (i.e., by dividing by $B(t, T_k)$), will $\mathrm{FB}(t, T_j, T_k)$ still be a P-martingale?' The answer to this question is given by a straightforward application of Ito's lemma, which provides for the dynamics of $\mathrm{FB}(t, T_j, T_k)$ under P (i.e., under the measure for which $\mathrm{FB}(t, T_j, \widehat{T})$ is a martingale for any T_j):

$$\begin{aligned} \mathrm{dFB}(t, T_j, T_k) = &- \mathrm{FB}(t, T_j, T_k)\gamma(t, T_j, T_k)\gamma(t, T_k, \widehat{T})\, \mathrm{dt} \\ &+ \mathrm{FB}(t, T_j, T_k)\gamma(t, T_j, T_k)\, \mathrm{dz}(t), \end{aligned}$$

with

$$\gamma(t, T_j, T_k) = \gamma(t, T_j, \widehat{T}) - \gamma(t, T_k, \widehat{T}) \qquad \text{for any } t \in [0, \min(T_j, T_k)].$$

REMARK 2.13 *In the expression above and in the following treatment, specifying clearly the measure under which a process is or is not a martingale is not a formal nicety, but is the crux of the argument.*

---

[14] A more careful treatment would require the introduction of the concept of 'No Free Lunch With Vanishing Risk' (NFLWVR). This angle is not pursued here, but see, for instance, Oksendal (1995) or Nielsen (1999) for a discussion of this point.

2.3.4 Changing the Measure

The equation above expresses the forward process for $\mathrm{FB}(t, T_j, T_k)$ in terms of a P-semi-martingale. We know, however, that this can be transformed into a martingale by using Girsanov's theorem, that is, it is possible to define

$$z_k(t) = z(t) - \int_0^t \gamma(u, T_k, \widehat{T}) \, \mathrm{d}u \qquad (2.23)$$

such that $z_k(t)$ is a standard (Ω, F_t, P_k)-Wiener process defined on an equivalent probability measure P_k, $P_k \sim P$, obtained on $(\Omega, \mathcal{F}_k)$ by means of a Radon–Nikodym derivative $\mathrm{d}P_k/\mathrm{d}P$. Under P_k

$$\mathrm{dFB}(t, T_j, T_k) = \mathrm{FB}(t, T_j, T_k)\gamma(t, T_j, T_k) \, \mathrm{d}z_k(t). \qquad (2.24)$$

REMARK 2.14 *When $T_k = \widehat{T}$, then*

$$\gamma(t, T_j, \widehat{T}) = \gamma(t, T_j, T_k) = \gamma(t, T_j, \widehat{T}) - \gamma(t, \widehat{T}, \widehat{T}) = \gamma(t, T_j, \widehat{T}),$$

$\mathrm{d}z_{\widehat{T}}(t) = \mathrm{d}z(t)$ *and $P = P_{\widehat{T}}$. This observation makes explicit the identification of the martingale measure P, previously simply defined as the measure under which $\mathrm{FB}(t, T_i, \widehat{T})$ are martingales, as the measure associated with the forwarding date $\widehat{T}$.*

REMARK 2.15 *Equation (2.24) shows that the change of measure effected by Girsanov's theorem is independent of T_j, that is, for any j it will turn a process $\mathrm{FB}(t, T_j, T_k)$ into a martingale.*

REMARK 2.16 *A remark on notation: The expression $\mathrm{d}z(t)$ can, in general, denote a vector of Brownian motions. When a Brownian motion is subscripted by an index, as in Equation (2.24) below, in this section the subscript always identifies a particular measure, and never the component of the vector $\mathrm{d}z(t)$. The meaning of the notation changes in later sections, but the different context should make the interpretation unambiguous.*

2.3.5 The Logical Steps up to This Point

Since quite a lot of ground has been covered so far, it might be useful to summarize the conceptual steps:

- First of all, we have introduced the bond price processes (positive, continuous semi-martingales). We have restricted our attention to the special but important case where the innovation part of the bond price process is driven by Wiener processes (with volatilities, at this stage, not necessarily deterministic).

- We have then introduced forward-bond processes, $\mathrm{FB}(t, T_i, \widehat{T})$, where the 'forwarding' was carried out to the last date in the trading horizon $(\widehat{T})$ – see Equation (2.22).

- Given this forwarding horizon, $\widehat{T}$, we have then chosen to work in the particular measure P under which the forward-bond processes are martingales.

- By construction, this measure P has been associated with the forwarding carried out to the final date $\widehat{T}$.

- We then observed, by applying Ito's lemma to a forward-bond process, $\mathrm{FB}(t, T_j, T_k)$, with the forwarding carried out to a *different* date, T_k, that this new forward-bond prices process was no longer a martingale under P.

- We therefore applied Girsanov's theorem to define a new standard Brownian process $z_k(t)$ and a new measure P_k, specific to each forwarding date T_k, under which the process $\mathrm{FB}(t, T_j, T_k)$ became a martingale.

Up to this point I have only given a rather hand-waving justification as to why we are so concerned with processes being, or not being, martingales. The importance of this requirement will become clear as we inject more financial content into the treatment.

2.3.6 The Forward-Rate Processes and Their Volatilities

We are now in a position to introduce the discrete-forward-rate processes. To this effect, let us define first a set of (finite-length) tenors τ_i such that $T_{i+1} - T_i = \tau_i$, and build today's forward rate resetting at time $\widehat{T} - \tau_N$ and maturing (paying) at time $\widehat{T}$ (the forward rate N) as

$$f(0, \widehat{T} - \tau_N, \widehat{T}) = \frac{\mathrm{FB}(0, \widehat{T} - \tau_N, \widehat{T}) - 1}{\tau_N}. \tag{2.25}$$

REMARK 2.17 *For the sake of simplicity and to keep the notation light, I have assumed that $\widehat{T} = T_{N+1}$.*

REMARK 2.18 *A more general treatment could have the tenor to be either discrete or continuous, giving rise to the discrete or instantaneous forward rates. Only the discrete case will be considered in this book. See, however, Musiela (1997a) for a discussion of the continuous-tenor case. For discrete tenors, the forward rate defined by Equation (2.25) is the strike that can be contracted at time 0 to give zero value to a forward-rate agreement (FRA) of expiry $\widehat{T} - \tau_N$ and paying at time $\widehat{T}$.*

As for the value today of the forward process $\mathrm{FB}(0, \widehat{T} - \tau_N, \widehat{T})$, it is fully determined by today's values of the bond processes $B(0, \widehat{T} - \tau_N)$ and $B(0, \widehat{T})$, and is given, by definition, by $B(0, \widehat{T} - \tau_N)/B(0, \widehat{T})$. The initial values of all the bond processes will in turn be made to coincide with an exogenously assigned term structure of bond prices, $P(0, T_i)$:

$$B(0, T_i) = P(0, T_i), \tag{2.26}$$

where the quantities $P(0, T_i)$ are required to be strictly positive, and strictly decreasing in T_i. By so doing one can rest assured that the forward-rate processes automatically recover the market yield curve (on the discrete points $\{T_i\}$). See Jamshidian (1997, Section 7, p. 318) about the non-uniqueness of the specification of $B(0, T)$ for a generic $T \notin \{T_i\}$.

The τ_N forward rate at a later time t is then given by:

$$f(t, \widehat{T} - \tau_N, \widehat{T}) = \frac{\mathrm{FB}(t, \widehat{T} - \tau_N, \widehat{T}) - 1}{\tau_N}. \tag{2.27}$$

Using Ito's lemma, and working under the measure $P_{\widehat{T}}$ (i.e., the measure under which $\mathrm{FB}(t, \widehat{T} - \tau_N, \widehat{T})$ is a martingale), one obtains for the stochastic differential equation of $f(t, \widehat{T} - \tau_N, \widehat{T})$:

$$\mathrm{d}f(t, \widehat{T} - \tau_N, \widehat{T}) = \frac{\mathrm{FB}(t, \widehat{T} - \tau_N, \widehat{T})\gamma(t, \widehat{T} - \tau_N, \widehat{T})}{\tau_N} \, \mathrm{d}z_{\widehat{T}}(t), \tag{2.28}$$

subject to the initial Conditions (2.25) and (2.26).

If we assume (impose) that the forward rates should be strictly positive, Equation (2.28) can be recognized to be a strictly positive martingale, and, by the martingale representation theorem, can be rewritten as

$$\mathrm{d}f(t, \widehat{T} - \tau_N, \widehat{T}) = f(t, \widehat{T} - \tau_N, \widehat{T})\sigma(t, \widehat{T} - \tau_N, \widehat{T}) \, \mathrm{d}z_{\widehat{T}}(t), \tag{2.28'}$$

with

$$\sigma(t, \widehat{T} - \tau_N, \widehat{T}) = \gamma(t, \widehat{T} - \tau_N, \widehat{T})\frac{1 + f(t, \widehat{T} - \tau_N, \widehat{T})\tau_N}{f(t, \widehat{T} - \tau_N, \widehat{T})\tau_N}. \tag{2.29}$$

CONDITION 2.3 *The standard LIBOR-market-model approach is characterized by imposing that the function $\sigma(t, \widehat{T} - \tau_N, \widehat{T})$ should be a purely deterministic function of time.*

REMARK 2.19 *As remarked before, in the general representation of a strictly positive, continuous process of finite second variation in terms of an exponential martingale, nothing constrains the 'percentage volatility' term to be a deterministic function of time. When one imposes that this should be the case for a certain set of quantities – say, for forward rates – then the deterministic or stochastic nature of the 'percentage volatilities' of other related quantities – say, $\gamma(\ \ )$ – is fully specified, and beyond the control of the modeller. Choice (2.29) is not the only possible one. One could have required, for instance, the volatilities of the bond processes to be deterministic functions of times – this is, indeed, the discrete-tenor forward-rate implementation of the HJM model as presented,* *for example, in Hull (1993), Carverhill (1993) or Rutkowski (1998). If this choice had been made, however, the distributional properties of forward rates would be different, their processes would no longer be positive, and the market-standard formulas for caplets would no longer be recovered. See Remark 2.20 below.*

REMARK 2.20 *By imposing a purely deterministic dependence on time for the quantity $\sigma(t, \widehat{T} - \tau_N, \widehat{T})$, one obtains that, under $P_{\widehat{T}}$, the forward rate $f(t, \widehat{T} - \tau_N, \widehat{T})$ is a lognormally distributed exponential martingale. When the payoff of the caplet expiring at $\widehat{T} - \tau_N$ and paying at time $\widehat{T}$ is integrated over the associated time-$(\widehat{T} - \tau_N)$ probability density, one recovers the market-standard Black formula. This justifies the name 'market model' for the approach.*

2.3.7 Associating Measures with Forward Rates

In constructing forward rates up to this point we have looked at one particular forwarding maturity in isolation $(\widehat{T})$. We now want to construct new measures P_{T_i}, each associated with different forward rates and forwarding maturities, such that the same properties enjoyed by $f(t, \widehat{T} - \tau_N, \widehat{T})$ under $P_{\widehat{T}}$ are obtained for $f(t, T_i - \tau_i, T_i)$ under P_{T_i}.

In order to do this, first of all we generalize and lighten the notation by setting

$$\widehat{T} = T_{N+1},$$
$$\widehat{T} - \tau = T_N,$$
$$\widehat{T} - 2\tau = T_{N-1},$$
$$\vdots$$
$$\widehat{T} - (i+1)\tau = T_i,$$

and

$$\sigma(t, T_i, T_{i+1}) = \sigma(t, T_i),$$
$$f(t, T_i, T_{i+1}) = f(t, T_i),$$
$$\tau_i = \tau \qquad \text{for any } i,$$
$$P_{\widehat{T}} = P_{N+1},$$
$$\mathrm{d}z(t) = \mathrm{d}z_{N+1}(t) = \mathrm{d}z_{\widehat{T}}(t).$$

With this new, simpler, notation, we then impose a condition exactly equivalent to Condition 2.3 above, namely:

CONDITION 2.3' *The standard LIBOR-market-model approach is characterized by imposing that, for any i, the function $\sigma(\ldots, T_i)$ should be a purely deterministic function of time.*

In the new notation, and making use of Equation (2.29), one can therefore write

$$\mathrm{d}f(t, T_N) = f(t, T_N)\sigma(t, T_N)\,\mathrm{d}z(t),$$
$$\mathrm{dFB}(t, T_N, T_{N+1}) = \mathrm{FB}(t, T_N, T_{N+1})\gamma(t, T_N, T_{N+1})\,\mathrm{d}z(t).$$

The procedure can be repeated: by making use of Equation (2.29) again, one can obtain for the volatility, $\gamma(t, T_{N-1}, T_N)$, of the forward process $\mathrm{FB}(t, T_{N-1}, T_N)$

$$\gamma(t, T_{N-1}, T_N) = \sigma(t, T_{N-1})\frac{f(t, T_{N-1})\tau}{1 + f(t, T_{N-1})\tau}.$$

Let us define now a new Wiener process $z_N(t)$ by

$$z_N(t) = z_{N+1}(t) - \int_0^t \gamma(u, T_N, T_{N+1})\,\mathrm{d}u = z(t) - \int_0^t \gamma(u, T_N, T_{N+1})\,\mathrm{d}u.$$

By Girsanov's theorem, as long as the function $\gamma(\ )$ satisfies the Novikov technical condition (and this requirement, in financial modelling, will hardly ever create a problem), this transformation defines an associated measure P_N, equivalent to P_{N+1}, under which $z_N(t)$ is a standard Brownian motion, and $\mathrm{FB}(t, T_{N-1}, T_N)$ is a (strictly positive) martingale (see Equations (2.23) and (2.24)). Given the definition of $f(t, T_{N-1}, T_N)$, and the assumption that all the forward-rate processes should be strictly positive, also $f(t, T_{N-1}, T_N)$ is a strictly positive martingale. As such, it can be represented as

$$\mathrm{d}f(t, T_{N-1}) = f(t, T_{N-1})\sigma(t, T_{N-1})\,\mathrm{d}z_N,$$

where, because of Condition 2.3′, $\sigma(t, T_{N-1})$ is a deterministic function of time.

One can proceed similarly for all the forward rates following the same steps (see, e.g., Musiela and Rutkowski 1997a): moving from one index $i + 1$ to the previous, from $\sigma(t, T_i)$ one can derive $\gamma(t, T_i, T_{i+1})$; from this quantity one can create a new Wiener process and an associated probability measure P_i. One then recognizes that, under the new measure, the forward process (and hence the forward-rate process) is a strictly positive martingale; one can therefore invoke the martingale representation theorem, impose the pure time dependence of the forward-rate volatility functions and proceed to the previous index i.

The final result of this procedure is the definition of a series of measures P_i, $1 \leq i \leq N$, under which each individual forward rate $f(t, T_i)$ is an exponential martingale with purely deterministic volatility, $\sigma(t, T_i)$. As such, it is log-normally distributed and the integration, under P_i, of the time-T_i caplet payoff,

$$\frac{[f(T_i, T_i) - K]^+\tau}{1 + f(T_i, T_i)\tau}$$

times the P_i probability density at time T_i provides the industry-standard Black formula.

Note that at no point in the derivation have the volatilities of the spot bond processes been used: only the volatility functions $\gamma(\ )$ associated with the forward price processes have been needed.

It is also important to point out that no two forward rates can be simultaneously log-normal under the same martingale measure.[15] The importance of this statement is not clear yet, because we have not explored the financial implications of certain quantities being or not being martingales (i.e., we have not yet made the link between martingales and absence of arbitrage). This task is undertaken immediately below.

2.3.8 Definition of Trading Strategies and Arbitrage

In oder to establish the link between trading strategies and arbitrage, recall, first of all, that the primitive assets in the economy are pure (discount) bonds. The bond processes have already been introduced, that is, they are the strictly positive, real-valued, adapted processes, $B(t, T_i), t \leq T_i, 1 \leq i \leq N+1$, $T_{N+1} \leq \hat{T}$, defined on the filtered probability space $\text{FPS}(\Omega, F_t, P)$, where the filtration F_t is always assumed, unless otherwise stated, to be generated by the N Brownian motions associated with the bond price processes. Following standard financial treatment we then define, also on the same probability space FPS:

- a trading strategy (see, e.g., Duffie 1996, chapter 5), that is, an adapted vector process $\boldsymbol{\theta}$, specifying at each point in time, and in each possible state of the world $\omega \in \Omega$, the units of each security i (i.e., of bond i) to hold – we will have all the generality we need, and more, by requiring that $\boldsymbol{\theta} \in L^2$, that is, that the trading strategy should belong to the space of the adapted processes satisfying the Lebesgue square-integrability condition

$$\int_0^T \boldsymbol{\theta}(u)^2 \, \mathrm{d}u < \infty, \qquad \text{almost surely for any } T;$$

- a gain process, $V(T)$, that is, the adapted process with continuous paths given by

$$V(T) = \boldsymbol{\theta}_0 \mathbf{B}_0 + \int_0^T \boldsymbol{\theta}(u) \, \mathrm{d}\mathbf{B}(u),$$

whose value at time T represents the gain from the trading strategy; and

---

[15]The statement obviously refers to spanning forward rates (defined in Section 3.2). Coterminal forward rates of different tenors can be simultaneously log-normal, but are virtually never used in the LIBOR derivatives problems the modern pricing approach deals with.

- the spaces H_1 and H_2, defined as

$$H_1 = \left\{ \boldsymbol{\theta} \in L^2 \; : \; E\left[\left(\int_0^T \boldsymbol{\theta}(u)^2 \, \mathrm{d}u \right)^{1/2} \right] < \infty, \, T > 0 \right\}$$

and

$$H_2 = \left\{ \boldsymbol{\theta} \in L^2 \; : \; E\left[\int_0^T \boldsymbol{\theta}(u)^2 \, \mathrm{d}u \right] < \infty, \, T > 0 \right\}.$$

One can show that if $\boldsymbol{\theta} \in H_1$ or H_2 the gain process is a martingale.

A self-financing trading strategy can then be defined as a strategy $\boldsymbol{\theta}$ that, in addition to satisfying the conditions above, requires no withdrawals or injection of cash throughout its life. If this is the case, a self-financing trading strategy must be such that its value at a future time t must be equal to the gain process:

$$\boldsymbol{\theta}_t \mathbf{B}_t = \boldsymbol{\theta}_0 \mathbf{B}_0 + \int_0^T \boldsymbol{\theta}(u) \, \mathrm{d}\mathbf{B}(u) = V(T).$$

(Note that this expression is clearly a vector equation, and an expression such as '$\boldsymbol{\theta}_t \mathbf{B}_t$' should be interpreted as a scalar product. The quantity $V(T)$ is therefore a scalar.)

In the financial context in which we are interested, an arbitrage is then defined as a self-financing trading strategy with respect to the bond price processes $\mathbf{B}$, with zero initial cost (i.e., such that $\boldsymbol{\theta}_0 \mathbf{B}_0 = 0$) and such that the gain $V(T)$ is never negative in any of the time-T states, and is positive in at least some of them (see Pliska (1997) for a more general definition of arbitrage and for a distinction between type-I and type-II arbitrages).

We have defined what an arbitrage is. We would like now to characterize price systems such that no arbitrage can be allowed. To do this it is useful to introduce the concept of a numeraire, $N(t)$. This is an arbitrary security (a bond, in our universe) with a strictly positive price in all states of the world. Such a security can be described as a strictly positive, adapted Ito process defined on the usual probability space FPS. If the price of any security in the universe of traded assets (again, bonds) is divided by this numeraire, one obtains a vector of relative price processes,[16] $\mathbf{Z}(t) \equiv \mathbf{B}(t)/N(t)$. We now have all the definitions in place to tell whether a system of prices (and associated forward rates) admits arbitrage.

2.3.9 Linking Absence of Arbitrage with the Martingale Condition

The build-up to the fundamental financial theorem that links absence of arbitrage with the martingale property of relative prices is almost complete. We simply have to introduce the numeraire invariance theorem:

---

[16]Some authors (e.g., Duffie 1996) define a deflator, by which they multiply, rather than divide, the asset price. The treatment carries through with little change.

THEOREM 2.3 *If a strategy is self-financing with respect to the vector of price processes* **B**, *and if* N *is a regular numeraire, then the same strategy is self-financing with respect to the vector of relative prices* **Z**.

REMARK 2.21 *The conditions that make a numeraire 'regular' are technical in nature, and will not be dealt with here. (The interested reader is referred to Duffie 1996, chapter 5.)*

Let B be a (bond) price process defined on the probability space $FPS(\Omega, \mathcal{F}_t, P)$. Recall that

- Q is an equivalent martingale measure if Q is equivalent to P, and the Radon–Nikodym derivative dP/dQ has finite variance, and

- we have required that $B \in SM^+$.

If these conditions hold, then

THEOREM 2.4 *If the price process B admits an equivalent martingale measure Q (i.e., if there exists an equivalent martingale measure Q under which B is a martingale), then there is no arbitrage.*

For the practical applications that we will present in the following, the above theorem is used in the equivalent formulation, which directly obtains from the numeraire invariance theorem:

THEOREM 2.5 *Given a numeraire N, if the process of relative prices* **Z** *admits an equivalent martingale measure Q_N (i.e., if there exists an equivalent martingale Q_N measure under which* **Z** *is a martingale), then there is no arbitrage.*

REMARK 2.22 *The requirement that* **B** $\in SM^+$ *is sufficient to guarantee that any $B_i \in$* **B** *can be chosen as a possible numeraire.*

The result in the theorem above was our final goal, and all we need for deriving the drifts of the forward rates (see Chapter 5). To enhance intuition, the reader might want to re-read the qualitative observations made at the end of Section 2.3.2.

Needless to say, many important and interesting aspects of arbitrage-free pricing in the LIBOR-market-model context have been neglected in order to make the treatment as simple and focussed as possible. The greatest omission in the development presented above is probably the precise specification of the class of payoffs that are replicable by a self-financing trading strategy based on the assets available in the economy, that is, such that $\text{Payoff}(T) = V(T)$. See Jamshidian (1997, Section 5, p. 311) about this point. It turns out that the requirements on the instruments that can be priced by replication within the framework presented above are essentially a measurability condition for the payoff function, and a (mild but important) restriction on the functional dependence of the payoff on the forward rates. More specifically, one can prove that an instrument will be replicable if its payoff is measurable with respect to the filtration generated by the realizations of the (vector) Brownian process $dz(t)$ at a finite number of times T_i. Furthermore, the payoff function will have to be homogeneous of degree one in the bond prices (or, equivalently, be decomposable in the product of a function homogeneous of degree zero in the forward rates times a discount bond). A precise treatment of this topic would require a rather lengthy and technically involved discussion. Given their importance, I shall however discuss both of these important concepts in an 'informal' way in Chapter 4 by introducing price-sensitive events.

3

Describing the Dynamics of Forward Rates

3.1 A Working Framework for the Modern Pricing Approach

The LIBOR market model allows the pricing of LIBOR products with discrete price-sensitive events by prescribing the continuous-time evolution of those forward rates that, together with one spot rate, define the relevant points of a discount curve. In this chapter I show that this is accomplished by requiring that the evolution of the forward rates should be a diffusion with deterministic volatility plus a drift term. I then show in Chapter 4 that the nature of the payoffs of the typical LIBOR products is such that they can be priced by moving the yield curve over 'long' time intervals. ('Long' in this context indicates a time interval from a few months to many years.) It will become clear that all the relevant LIBOR products can, and should, be handled by what I call the 'long-jump' technique, and that a wide and important class of products can be handled by the germane and more powerful 'very-long-jump' procedure. Both techniques are naturally derived by a series of manipulations of the diffusive coefficients (i.e., volatilities and correlations) of the forward-rate evolution.

Before embarking on this treatment, it is useful to provide a bird's eye view of the conceptual path that will be followed in the sections and chapters ahead (up to and including Chapter 5). This is accomplished in the rest of this section.

3.1.1 What We Need To Do

One of the fundamental results in derivatives pricing is that the present value of a financial instrument can be obtained as the discounted expectation (in the appropriate measure) of its terminal payoff. If the derivative to be priced is European, and depends on the realization of a single forward rate, the terminal distribution required to compute the expectation is simply

57

the *unconditional* distribution of the relevant rate. Exceedingly few products, however, are fully European, and can therefore be handled simply using our knowledge of the appropriate unconditional distributions: apart from plain-vanilla caplets, I can only think of European digitals, and knock-in or knock-out caplets, and then only when the index forward rate (which determines whether the caplet is dead or alive) is the same rate that determines the pay-off. For the more interesting products, the required expectation will be over a multi-dimensional density, and, for its evaluation, we will require information about the conditional probability of the joint occurrence of many forward rates at several different times. In other words, we will require the conditional probability of a given occurrence of the yield curve at time T_n, given a particular realization of the yield curve at earlier times $T_{n-1}, T_{n-2}, \ldots, T_1$. In Chapter 4 I show that a further distinction is important, that is, between products whose payoff is determined by the realization of several forward rates on their own reset dates, or by the realization of several forward rates at times other than their own reset dates. For the present purposes, it is enough to point out that the 'interesting' (i.e., non-European) cases will require knowledge of the joint conditional distributions.

3.1.2 *What We Would Like To Do*

Given this requirement, it would be very desirable if closed-form exact expressions were available for the unconditional and the conditional distributions of the forward rates. If this were the case, there would be no need to evolve numerically over short steps (typically, by Monte Carlo) an underlying process in order to sample the required conditional and unconditional distributions, because these would be known analytically a priori. Just as desirable would be to use distributions that are fully specified by a small number of descriptive statistics (say, expectations and covariances).

With these desiderata in mind, what would make our lives really easy would be the ability to impose that at least all the unconditional distributions should be Gaussian. Furthermore, since we would like forward rates to be strictly positive, modelling their logarithm as jointly Gaussian processes is a simple and appealing way to retain positivity in a Gaussian setting. There is no hiding that this modelling choice is mainly motivated by mathematical expediency, since no other distributions, and generating processes, lend themselves as easily to analytic treatment. However, simply knowing that the logarithms of the forward rates all have unconditional Gaussian distributions does not, by itself, solve the general pricing problem. This is because a process is not uniquely specified by its unconditional distributions – one also needs all the conditional ones (see, e.g., Baxter and Rennie 1996). Therefore, the next natural requirement that we would like to impose, if possible, is that also all the conditional densities should be jointly Gaussian. These desiderata can be made more precise by introducing the definitions and theorems presented below.

3.1.3 How We Would Like To Do It

The fundamental idea is the following: following Nielsen (1999), let us consider an N-dimensional stochastic process, $\mathbf{X}_t$,

$$\mathbf{X}_t = \mathbf{X}(t) = \{X_t^1, X_t^2, \ldots, X_t^N\},$$

and let us sample the vector process $\mathbf{X}_t$ on a finite number, n, of times $T_1, T_2, \ldots, T_n$, with $T_1 < T_2 < \ldots < T_n$. By so doing one can construct a random $(N \times n)$-dimensional matrix, called the sample matrix:

$$[\mathbf{X}(T_1) \quad \mathbf{X}(T_2) \quad \ldots \quad \mathbf{X}(T_n)].$$

The vector process $\mathbf{X}_t$ is said to be Gaussian if the distribution of every sample matrix is jointly normal, that is, if the joint unconditional distribution of the elements of the sample matrix defined above is jointly normal. Furthermore, if the process $\mathbf{X}_t$ is Gaussian, then the distribution of every sample matrix is fully characterized by the knowledge of nothing more than a finite number of unconditional mean and covariance functions, $E[X_i(t)]$ and $\mathrm{cov}[X_i(s), X_j(t)]$.

Given a filtration $\mathcal{F}$, one can then define a *conditionally* Gaussian process, by requiring that the conditional distributions of all the sample matrices should be jointly normal and independent of the realization of the stochastic process.[1] A result similar to the one stated above for the unconditional case then applies: namely, one can show that a conditionally Gaussian process is fully characterized by knowledge of the conditional mean and covariance functions, $E[X_i(t) \mid \mathcal{F}_s]$ and $\mathrm{cov}[X_i(t), X_j(u) \mid \mathcal{F}_s]$, $s \leq t, u$.

Clearly, any conditionally Gaussian process is Gaussian. In particular, a generalized Wiener (Brownian) process, $\mathbf{B}(t)$,

$$\mathbf{B}(t) = \mathbf{B}(0) + \boldsymbol{\mu}t + \boldsymbol{\sigma}\mathbf{Z}(t)$$

is both Gaussian and conditionally Gaussian. (In this expression, $\boldsymbol{\mu}$ is a constant, or, at most, a time-dependent, N-dimensional vector, $\boldsymbol{\sigma}$ is an $(N \times K)$-dimensional matrix, and $\mathbf{Z}(t)$ is the value at time t of a K-dimensional standard Wiener process.) Given the desiderata above, a generalized Wiener process would seem to be a perfect candidate for the modelling of the logarithms of the forward rates. More precisely, after identifying the vector $\mathbf{B}(t)$ in the expression above with the vector with elements given by the logarithms of the N forward rates, we would like to write for each individual forward rate, f_i,

$$\mathrm{d}\ln[f_i(t)] = \mu_i(t)\,\mathrm{d}t + \sum_k \sigma_{ik}(t)\,\mathrm{d}z_k(t),$$

---

[1]More technically, one must require that the process should be adapted to $\mathcal{F}$. The requirement that a process X_t should be adapted with respect to a filtration $\mathcal{F}_t$ means that the value of X at time t should only depend on information available at that time. In the context of the standard LIBOR market model, the information structure ($\mathcal{F}$) is generated by the evolution of the forward rates, and therefore the requirement of adaptness is certainly satisfied.

with known initial conditions, $f_i(0)$, and with $\mathrm{d}z_k(t)$ the increments at time t of standard orthogonal Wiener processes such that $E[\mathrm{d}z_i(t)\,\mathrm{d}z_j(t)] = \delta_{ij}(t)\,\mathrm{d}t$.[2]

What requirements should we impose on μ and σ in order to rest assured that the resulting process will be conditionally Gaussian? To answer this question, it is useful to analyze the properties of the time integral of the innovation part in the decomposition of $\mathrm{d}\ln[f_i(t)]$, that is, of the quantity $\int \sum_k \sigma_{ik}(t)\,\mathrm{d}z_k(t)$. The following theorem is useful (see again Nielsen (1999)):

THEOREM 3.1 *Let $\{\sigma_{jk}\}$ be a deterministic, square-integrable ($N \times K$)-dimensional matrix, $\{\mathbf{Z}_k\}$ a K-dimensional column vector of orthogonal standard Wiener processes, and s and t times such that $t \geq s$. Then the N-dimensional random variable, $\{y_i\}$, $y_i \equiv \int_s^t \sum_k \sigma_{ik}(u)\,\mathrm{d}z_k(u)$ is independent of the filtration up to time s (i.e., in our context, of the realization of the forward rates up to time s), and is normally distributed, with mean zero and an $N \times N$ covariance matrix whose (i,j)th element is given by $\int_s^t \sum_k \sigma_{ik}(u)\sigma_{jk}(u)\,\mathrm{d}u$. Furthermore, the stochastic integral process y_j is both Gaussian and conditionally Gaussian.*

From this theorem it follows immediately that, *as long as the drift term is constant*, a necessary and sufficient condition for the process $\mathbf{X}$ to be conditionally Gaussian is that the volatility matrix should be deterministic. As for the predictable part, can we relax the requirement that the vector μ should be constant? A simple theorem can be proven:

THEOREM 3.2 *Take a process $\mathbf{X}$ of the form $\mathbf{X}(t) = \mathbf{X}(0) + \mu t + \sigma \mathbf{Z}(t)$, with $\{\sigma_{jk}\}$ a deterministic, square-integrable ($N \times K$)-dimensional matrix, and $\{\mathbf{Z}\}$ a K-dimensional column vector of orthogonal standard Wiener processes. A sufficient condition for the process $\mathbf{X}$ to be both Gaussian and conditionally Gaussian is that the drift vector μ should be deterministic.*

It would be tempting to guess that the condition above should also be necessary. This, however, would not be correct, because even if the stochastic state variable $\mathbf{X}$ appeared in the drift term, the process could still be conditionally Gaussian. Nielsen (1999) provides the simple example of the one-dimensional Ornstein–Uhlenbeck process. Unfortunately, it is not easy to provide necessary and sufficient conditions for the process $\mathbf{X}$ to be conditionally Gaussian in terms of simple general properties of μ and σ.

If the conditions of Theorem 3.2 were satisfied, one could model the conditional joint distribution of the forward rates from time s to time t, $t > s$, as

$$\ln[\mathbf{f}(t)] \sim G(\mathbf{m}, \boldsymbol{\Sigma}),$$

with

$$m_i = \ln[f_i(s)] + \mu_i \tag{3.1}$$

---

[2]The requirement of orthogonality is not really restrictive, because, if the increments $\{\mathrm{d}z_i\}$ were not independent, they could always be made so by a suitable linear combination.

and

$$\Sigma_{ij} = [\hat{\boldsymbol{\sigma}}\hat{\boldsymbol{\sigma}}^{\mathrm{T}}]_{ij} = \int_s^t \sum_k \sigma_{ik}(u)\sigma_{jk}(u)\,\mathrm{d}u. \qquad (3.2)$$

In the expression above, $G(\mathbf{a}, \mathbf{b})$ denotes a multi-dimensional Gaussian distribution with vector of first moments $\mathbf{a}$ and covariance matrix $\mathbf{b}$.

If the conditions of Theorem 3.2 were satisfied, all the results and analytic solutions which are well known in the case of multivariate Gaussian distributions would be available. (See, e.g., Chatfield and Collins 1989 for a simple treatment.) In particular, the following would apply:

1. One could write immediately a closed-form solution for the value at time t of all the elements of the vector $\mathbf{f}(t)$, given their values at time s, $f_i(s)$, as

$$\ln f_i(t) = \ln f_i(s) + m_i + \sqrt{\Sigma_{ii}}\, Z,$$

with $\ln f_i(t)$ and m_i the ith elements of the N-dimensional column vectors $\ln \mathbf{f}(t)$ and $\mathbf{m}$, respectively, Z a standard Gaussian draw, and Σ_{ii} the ith diagonal element of the $\boldsymbol{\Sigma}$ ($N \times N$) covariance matrix. This property would therefore allow the evolution of the yield curve over as 'long' a step as desired. (See the more detailed discussion following Equations (3.15) and (3.16) in the example in Section 3.2.12.)

2. The multivariate density, Φ, would be given by

$$\Phi(f) = A\, \exp\{-\tfrac{1}{2}[(\mathbf{f} - \boldsymbol{\mu})^{\mathrm{T}}\boldsymbol{\Sigma}^{-1}(\mathbf{f} - \boldsymbol{\mu})]\},$$

with the normalization factor, A, given by

$$A = \frac{1}{(2\pi)^{N/2}\sqrt{|\boldsymbol{\Sigma}|}}.$$

(In the expression above the symbol $|\boldsymbol{\Sigma}|$ indicates the determinant of the matrix $\boldsymbol{\Sigma}$.) Knowledge of these multivariate densities would allow the association of an analytically computable probability to every possible state of the world.

3. The joint conditional densities of the forward rates would be simply expressible in terms of a finite number of expectations and conditional covariance matrices. Therefore, only a small number of moments would be sufficient to characterize *fully* these multivariate densities.

The theorems above also give the first indication that the covariance matrices play a central role in the modelling approach that we have been examining. Their importance will become even more apparent when we show (Chapter 5) that also the drift terms can be approximately expressed as a function of the same covariances.

If one were ready to strengthen the requirements on Σ, this modelling approach could be shown to enjoy another important advantage: if the vector process $\mathbf{X}$ were jointly conditionally Gaussian, the vector $\mathbf{m}$ deterministic and Σ constant, the state of the world (i.e., the realization of the yield curve) reached after a finite number, J, of steps would be fully described by the vector $\widehat{Z} = Z_1 + Z_2 + \ldots + Z_J$. In particular, the realization of the yield curve after any series of shocks, $Z'_1, Z'_2, \ldots, Z'_J$, adding up to the same vector, $\widehat{Z} = Z'_1 + Z'_2 + \ldots + Z'_J$, would be exactly the same: for instance, an up shock followed by a down shock of the same magnitude would produce the same yield curve that would obtain if the shocks took place in reverse order. In other words, for conditionally Gaussian processes with deterministic $\mathbf{m}$ and constant Σ, how one gets to $\widehat{Z}$ (the path) conveys no additional information, and the knowledge of $\widehat{Z}$ fully describes the state of the world at time J. When this condition is satisfied, the process is said to be Markovian (in Z), and can easily be discretized and mapped onto a recombining lattice. This mapping would, in turn, be very convenient for the evaluation of compound (e.g., Bermudan) options.

3.1.4 Why We Cannot (Quite) Do It

With the definition of conditionally Gaussian process and the tentative identification of the logarithms of the forward rates with these processes, we would seem to have put in place the setting that we require in order to price complex LIBOR products, that is, products whose payoff depends on joint discrete realizations of forward rates.

Readers who have followed the treatment presented in Section 2.3 already know, however, that forward rates can be assumed to be log-normally distributed *only in the appropriate measure*. The last qualifier is important. For an arbitrary numeraire[3] the drift terms in the diffusion for the forward rates are non-zero. It is true that there always exists one possible numeraire (see Section 2.3 and Chapter 5) chosen among the universe of tradable assets such that one forward rate (or one swap rate) is drift-less, and therefore, given the assumption of deterministic volatility, certainly log-normally distributed.[4] However, once this numeraire (a discounting bond) has been chosen, this feature can be true for at most one forward rate at a time, and all the other forward rates will have a non-zero drift.

---

[3]The numeraire can be arbitrary, but must be constructed from the universe of traded instruments. In the version of the LIBOR market model I have presented here, these assets are discount bonds. Since the latter are described by positive semi-martingales, a linear combination with positive weights of the fundamental assets always constitutes an admissible numeraire. Note carefully that, since the existence of an instantaneous savings account and of the instantaneous risk-less rate are neither used nor required in the present set-up, the continuously compounded money-market account is not one of the possible numeraires.

[4]For reasons that will become apparent, in the following, I shall call the numeraire that makes a given swap or forward rate a log-normal martingale the 'natural payoff' of the rate itself. I believe the term 'natural payoff' was first introduced by Doust (1995) in a narrower context.

Could one make a particularly inspired choice for the numeraire (perhaps by constructing some complex linear combination of discount bonds), so that several, or perhaps all, the forward rates will be simultaneously drift-less? It is easy to see that this is not possible either. The standard LIBOR market model is constructed to reproduce exactly the prices of caplets obtained by regarding each individual forward rate as log-normal. The drift-less log-normality assumption will produce the correct (Black) price if and only if the discounting of the payoff is carried out using the appropriate ('natural') numeraire – in this case the discount bond maturing at the final payoff time. The use of any other numeraire will introduce a covariance between the discounting and the payoff itself, which must be compensated for, if the same caplet price is to be recovered, by altering the drift of the forward rate. (See Rebonato (1998, chapter 3) for a detailed discussion and calculation.) With a complex pricing problem, which entails simultaneously several forward rates, once a particular numeraire has been chosen the presence of non-zero drifts is unfortunately unavoidable.

Therefore, in general one can rest assured that the proposed approach will be valid if the following two conditions are satisfied:

1. The payoffs to be evaluated must only depend on the joint realizations of the forward rates on a finite number of dates.[5] This is necessary if one wants to sample the stochastic processes at a finite number of points only.

2. The integrals of the innovation components from time s to time t, that is, $y_i \equiv \int_s^t \sum_k \sigma_{ik}(u) \, \mathrm{d}z_k(u)$, must be at most deterministic functions of time, and so must be the instantaneous drift, $\mu_i(u)$.

I shall show in detail in Chapter 4 that, for virtually all the payoffs encountered in practice, the first restriction is not at all onerous, and that such a discrete sampling is indeed all that is needed for the purposes of LIBOR derivatives pricing. The success of the pricing program highlighted above therefore hinges on the fulfillment of the requirements in Condition 2. I will show in Chapter 5 that, when the no-arbitrage conditions are imposed, the drift vector at time t will contain the time-t values of the state variables, $\{f_t\}$. The sufficient condition of Theorem 3.2 is therefore not satisfied. However, we also know from the Ornstein–Uhlenbeck example that, even if the sufficient condition fails, the process could still be conditionally Gaussian. Unfortunately, the type of dependence of the drift term on the forward rates is such (see Chapter 5) that this is not the case. As a consequence, the vector $\ln[\mathbf{f}(t)]$ is not jointly Gaussian (conditionally or unconditionally), no exact closed-form expression exists for the covariance matrices and, even if we had this informa-

---

[5]In addition, the payoff function must be homogeneous of degree one in the bond prices (or, equivalently, be decomposable in the product of a function homogeneous of degree zero in the forward rates times a discount bond). This condition is in practice very mild.

tion, knowledge of the conditional covariance matrices and of the expectation vectors would not be enough to obtain the joint conditional distributions.

Despite this, the presentation of the set-up up to this point has not been in vain. One of the main tasks of the present and of the next two chapters, in fact, is to show how this description of the vector of forward rates in terms of a conditionally Gaussian N-dimensional vector process sampled on a finite number of times can still be 'rescued', albeit in an approximate (but very accurate) way. The ability to do so will also be shown to be fundamental in order to carry out the so-called '(very-)long-jump' evolution of the forward rates described in Chapter 4.

It must be stated from the outset, however, that this 'rescue project' will only be partly successful: I will manage to show, in fact, that, given the knowledge of a random draw vector $\mathbf{Z}$ and of the yield curve at time s, the evolution out to time t can be carried out *as if*, over the time interval $[s, t]$, the drifts were deterministic. However, the value of this approximate deterministic drift will depend on the realization of the underlying Brownian drivers both at time s and at time t, and, for this reason, I shall call the approximate drift 'conditionally deterministic'. By constructing this approximate equivalent drift, however, the drift will depend on the filtration both at time s and at time t. The violation of this apparently 'technical' condition has deep consequences, and is connected with the non-Markovian nature of the forward-rate process, and with the lack of recombination of the bushy trees that evolve the yield curve from one price-sensitive event to the next. This latter feature, in turn, has dictated the choice of numerical techniques required to value compound-option products, such as, for instance, Bermudan swaptions (see Jaeckel 2000 and references therein). These topics will be discussed again in detail and in more concrete terms in Chapters 4 and 5.

3.1.5 The Link Between Conditionally Gaussian Processes and Smiles

As long as we impose that the volatilities of the various forward rates should be deterministic, and that the unconditional distribution of each forward rate, in the appropriate measure, should be log-normal, it is easy to see that the caplet prices will be given by the Black formula. The volatility input to this formula, in particular, will simply be equal to the root-mean-square volatility of the deterministic volatility. The resulting caplet prices that, by inversion of the Black formula, provide the 'implied' volatility will therefore by construction give rise to a flat smile (i.e., for each maturity, to the same implied volatility as a function of strike). Recently, volatility smiles of increasingly complex form have appeared in the smile surfaces obtained from the market prices of caplets and swaptions. When this is the case the identification of the Black (implied) volatility with the root-mean-square instantaneous volatility for each forward rate is no longer warranted. The problem of smiles is dealt with in later chapters (see Chapters 11, 12 and 13 in particular), but, without pre-empting future conclusions, I can already say that it is still possible to account in a financially convincing way for a large part of the smile surface by means of a relatively minor modification of the standard LIBOR-market-model framework (see also Andersen and Andreasen 1997, Zuehlsdorff 2001). In this generalized approach, not only is market completeness retained, but the implied (Black) volatility will be shown to be still the root-mean-square instantaneous volatility of a quantity simply linked to the forward rate itself. The analytical framework based on the approximate modelling of the forward rates as conditionally Gaussian processes will therefore still be directly applicable, after minor modifications, to the wider setting alluded to above.

Unfortunately, it turns out that this extension of the LIBOR market model is intrinsically incapable of accounting for certain more complex features of the smile surfaces that have recently appeared (post autumn 1998). A possible treatment to account for these additional effects is presented in Chapter 12 and requires a much more careful handling of the volatility component. In this more complex case the straightforward interpretation of the implied volatility in terms of the root-mean-square of some instantaneous volatility is no longer possible, and the definitions presented in this chapter will have to be revisited.

3.2 Equivalent Descriptions of the Dynamics of Forward Rates

The discrete forward rates that constitute the fundamental building blocks of the LIBOR market model are defined by taking suitable ratios of the bond processes, $\{B_i\}$. Therefore $n + 1$ bonds will allow the definition of n forward rates (plus one spot rate that will not be used directly, but which will affect the value of the chosen numeraire). Typically, the maturities of the bonds will be evenly spaced, but this need not be the case. Whether regularly spaced or not, forward rates such that the expiry time of one coincides with the payment time of the previous one will be called 'spanning rates'; furthermore, the time interval (in years) between reset and payment times of a given forward rate will be referred to as the tenor of the forward rate itself (see Figure 3.1).

Much as one can recast the same physics problem using a variety of co-ordinates, one can provide a description of the dynamics of these spanning forward rates in many equivalent ways. In this section I present a few of these equivalent formulations, which can be more transparent or computationally convenient in different contexts. Ultimately, my goal is to present a natural decomposition of the volatility terms into a 'historical' ('statistical') and a market-related component. The former can be extracted from econometric analysis, and will result in the apportioning of the overall responsiveness of a given forward rate among the different orthogonal driving factors. I shall show that, since the same factors are assumed to shock all the forward rates, this allocation of the responsiveness of the different forward rates to the various shocks is intimately linked to the correlation among all the forward rates. As for the market-related component, it can be obtained from the traded

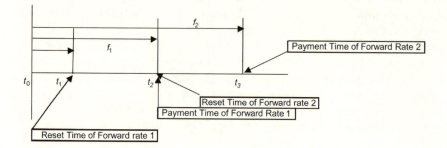

Figure 3.1   *The reset and payment times for two spanning forward rates. The time intervals between times t_1 and t_2 and between t_2 and t_3, respectively, are referred to as the first and the second tenor.*

prices of caplets and European swaptions, and is specific to one single forward rate at a time. This decomposition not only will provide a useful conceptual framework to analyze the dynamics of forward rates, but also will be directly mirrored in the treatment presented in Part III: Chapter 8 will deal with calibration to the instantaneous volatilities using market information; Chapter 9 will address the calibration problem (specifically, to the forward-rate correlation matrix) by bringing into play historical information; and Chapter 10 will show how a joint calibration that makes full use of market and statistical information is advisable when dealing with the evolution both of forward and of swap rates.

3.2.1 First Description: Each Forward Rate in Isolation

With these considerations in mind, the simplest starting point is perhaps to write:

$$\frac{\mathrm{d}\mathbf{f}(t)}{\mathbf{f}(t)} = \boldsymbol{\mu}(\mathbf{f}, t)\,\mathrm{d}t + \mathbf{S}(t)\,\mathrm{d}\mathbf{w}_Q(t), \qquad (3.3)$$

where

- $\mathrm{d}\mathbf{f}(t)/\mathbf{f}(t)$ is a time-dependent $n \times 1$ column vector of percentage increments of forward rates;

- $\boldsymbol{\mu}(\mathbf{f}, t)$ is an $n \times 1$ column vector of drifts, which can depend both on time and on the forward rates themselves;

- $\mathrm{d}\mathbf{w}_Q(t)$ is an $n \times 1$ column vector of correlated standard Brownian motions in the measure Q;

- Q is the pricing measure implied by the chosen numeraire; and

- $\mathbf{S}(t)$ is a real $n \times n$ diagonal matrix, whose ith element is equal to the instantaneous (percentage) volatility, σ_i, of the ith forward rate.[6]

In the following the notation $\mathrm{d}\mathbf{w}_Q(t)$ will be lightened to $\mathrm{d}\mathbf{w}(t)$ and, unless otherwise stated, it will always be understood that we are working in the measure under which all the Wiener processes are standard Brownian motions. It is also important to distinguish very clearly from the start between the time-dependent instantaneous volatility, σ_i, of the forward rate resetting at time T_i, and its implied (Black) volatility, $\sigma_{\mathrm{Black}}(T_i)$. The two quantities are related by the relationship

$$\sigma^2_{\mathrm{Black}}(T_i)T_i = \int_0^{T_i} \sigma_i^2(u)\,\mathrm{d}u. \tag{3.4}$$

The market-supplied Black (implied) volatility is therefore the root-mean-square instantaneous volatility. Description (3.3), with the accompanying linking Equation (3.4), provides the most straightforward and transparent representation of each forward rate in a Black-like world. In particular, as mentioned, one can always choose a suitable numeraire such that one of the forward rates has zero drift. When this choice is made, integration of the terminal caplet payoff over the probability density implied by Equations (3.3) and (3.4) directly leads to the Black formula.

The stochastic differential Equation (3.3) can be formally integrated to obtain the value of each forward rate f_i at time t:

$$f_i(t) = f_i(0) \exp\left[\int_0^t \mu_i(\{\mathbf{f}(u)\}, u) - \tfrac{1}{2}\sigma_i^2(u)\,\mathrm{d}u + \int_0^t \sigma_i(u)\,\mathrm{d}w_i(u)\right],$$

where $f_i(t)$ and $f_i(0)$ indicate the values of the forward rate at time t and today (time 0), respectively.

3.2.2 Introducing Correlation

What Equation (3.3) does not immediately provide is any information about the correlation structure among the different forward rates. This can be remedied by supplementing Equation (3.3) with the requirement that the different Brownian increments $\{\mathrm{d}w_i(t)\}$ should be linked through the $n \times n$ real symmetric instantaneous correlation matrix $\boldsymbol{\rho}$

$$\boldsymbol{\rho}\,\mathrm{d}t = \mathrm{d}\mathbf{w}\,\mathrm{d}\mathbf{w}^{\mathrm{T}}, \tag{3.5}$$

---

[6]A remark on notation and terminology: In this section I refer to a set of (possibly correlated) Brownian increments as 'standard' if they have zero mean and variance one. The term 'standard' does not imply that they should be uncorrelated. As for notation, the instantaneous volatility of the ith forward rate will be denoted either by σ_i (as above) or by σ^i_{inst}. The implied Black volatility of the same forward rate will never be denoted by the symbol σ_i, and will always be written as $\sigma^i_{\mathrm{Black}}$. No specific meaning should be attached to the positioning of the indices as super- or subscripts, as typographical convenience tends to determine their location.

where, as usual,

$$dw_i \, dw_j = \rho_{ij} \, dt.$$

(In what follows, I will always assume that the matrix ρ has full rank – more specifically, that no two forward rates are perfectly correlated.) Taken together, Equations (3.3)–(3.5) provide a perfectly viable formal description of the (discrete) yield-curve dynamics in terms of as many factors as forward rates (since it has been assumed that $\rho_{ij} \neq 1$ for any i, j: $i \neq j$). Such a description, however, can soon become not only computationally burdensome, but also unnecessarily detailed: for, say, a quarterly, 30-year swap, 120 forward rates would be driven by as many (correlated) factors, while at any one point in time one can optimistically obtain from the market at most 40/50 liquid prices (cash/deposit rates, futures prices and equilibrium swap rates). Reducing the dimensionality of the problem is therefore both desirable and necessary. From the description afforded by Equations (3.3)–(3.5) it is not obvious, however, how this dimensionality reduction can be accomplished in a systematic way.

3.2.3 A Second Formulation Using Orthogonal Brownian Increments

One alternative, and often more useful, description of the correlated dynamics of a set of forward rates can be achieved by defining

$$\frac{d\mathbf{f}(t)}{\mathbf{f}(t)} = \boldsymbol{\mu}(\mathbf{f}, t) \, dt + \boldsymbol{\sigma}(t) \, d\mathbf{z}(t), \tag{3.6}$$

where $d\mathbf{f}(t)/\mathbf{f}(t)$ and $\boldsymbol{\mu}(\mathbf{f}, t)$ have the same meaning as before, but now $d\mathbf{z}(t)$ is an $m \times 1$ vector of orthogonal Wiener processes. As for the matrix $\boldsymbol{\sigma}(t)$, it is a real $n \times m$ matrix whose (i, j)th element, $\sigma_{ij}(t)$, is equal to the loading onto the ith forward rate of the jth orthogonal Brownian driver. Notice that I have now explicitly allowed for the number of independent driving factors, m, to be smaller than the number of forward rates ($m \leq n$).

In financial terms, the element $\sigma_{ij}(t)$ of the matrix $\boldsymbol{\sigma}(t)$ gives the responsiveness of the ith forward rate to random shocks from the jth orthogonal Brownian motion. For a given i, the row vector $\sigma_{ij}(t)$, $1 \leq j \leq m$, can be interpreted as decomposing the volatility of the ith forward rates into components related to different, orthogonal sources of uncertainty. These independent factors are often interpreted as being linked to, say, shifts in level of the yield curve, changes in its slope or curvature, etc. (provided that these are indeed the modes of deformation associated with the orthogonal Brownian increments $dz_j(t)$). This type of description can therefore be naturally dovetailed onto the familiar decomposition of the dynamics of the yield curve by means of principal component analysis. Indeed, if the transformation from the processes $\mathbf{w}(t)$ to the processes $\mathbf{z}(t)$ has been carried out in such a way that the m factors happen to be the first $\mathbf{m}$ principal components, then the element $\sigma_{ij}(t)$ is proportional to the loading of the ith forward rate onto the jth principal component. More precisely, the $n \times 1$ vector of elements $\{\sigma_{ik},$

$1 \leq i \leq n$} is simply proportional, after scaling by the square root of the corresponding eigenvalue, λ_k, to the eigenvector of the instantaneous covariance matrix, as shown in detail below.

I have not assumed in this formulation that m (i.e., the number of driving Brownian processes) should equal n (the number of forward rates). In general, $1 \leq m \leq n$. For $m = 1$, Equation (3.6) corresponds to a one-factor description of the dynamics of forward rates, which are, in this case, all perfectly instantaneously correlated. More generally, for $m \neq n$, the correlation matrix implied by the $m < n$ factors will be different from the full-rank matrix ρ defined in Equation (3.5). The intrinsic limitations on the possible shapes of the correlation surface imposed by the dimensionality of the Brownian vector are discussed in Chapter 7.

3.2.4 Construction and Properties of the Covariance Matrix

Expression (3.6) above for the evolution of the forward rates is particularly convenient, because, given the orthogonality of the Brownian increments $d\mathbf{z}(t)$, one can immediately express the covariance matrix between the forward rates, Σ, as

$$\underbrace{\text{cov}\left[\frac{d\mathbf{f}}{\mathbf{f}}\right]}_{[n \times n]} = E\left[\frac{df_j}{f_j} \frac{df_k}{f_k}\right] = \Sigma = \underbrace{\sigma \sigma^{\mathrm{T}}}_{[n \times m][m \times n]} . \tag{3.7}$$

The result is obtained by taking the expectation of the product of terms of the form

$$\frac{df_i}{f_i} = \mu_i \, dt + \sum_{k=1}^{m} \sigma_{ik} \, dz_k \tag{3.8}$$

and by remembering the familiar Ito's rules, symbolically expressed as $dz_i \, dt = 0$ for any i, $dt \, dt = 0$ and $dz_i \, dz_j = \delta_{ij}$ (given orthogonality).

EXERCISE 3.1 *Derive Equation (3.7) starting from Equation (3.6). Alternatively, express in matrix form the covariance matrix starting from Equations (3.3) and (3.5).*

Note carefully that the measure under which the expectation is taken need not be specified, since all the equivalent measures linked by the Radon–Nikodym derivatives only differ by drift terms (Girsanov's theorem), which do not enter the calculation of the covariances.

By construction (see Equation (3.7)), the $n \times n$ covariance matrix Σ will certainly be real and symmetric, and, as such, can be orthogonalized. Notice, however, that the rank of Σ will be equal to m, the number of orthogonal driving factors. Therefore, when one orthogonalizes Σ, one obtains only m distinct non-zero eigenvalues, $\lambda_1, \lambda_2, \ldots, \lambda_m$. Only for $m = n$ will the matrix Σ have full rank, and will the description (3.6) be fully equivalent to Equations (3.3)–(3.5).

3.2.5 The Link Between the First and the Second Formulation

Comparing Equations (3.3) and (3.6), one can readily see that the former description places the emphasis on the total volatility of a forward rate, and prescribes a shock, $dw_i(t)$, that is forward-rate-specific, rather than risk-factor-specific. Equation (3.6), on the other hand, provides a complementary view, by focussing on the shocks, $dz_k(t)$, that affect the yield curve in its entirety, and specifying the impact of these shocks on the different forward rates. Clearly the two descriptions must be equivalent, and, by virtue of the orthogonality of the Brownian processes $dz(t)$, the elements of the matrices $\mathbf{S}$ and $\boldsymbol{\sigma}$ must be linked through the relationship

$$\sigma_i^2(t) \equiv \sigma_i^{\text{inst}}(t)^2 = \sum_{k=1}^{m} \sigma_{ik}^2(t). \qquad (3.9)$$

If, therefore, the instantaneous volatility $\sigma_i(t)$ is chosen in such a way that the caplet price is correctly recovered (i.e., if the root-mean-square instantaneous volatility is equal to the Black implied volatility), then a set of matrix elements $\sigma_{ik}(t)$ that satisfy Equation (3.9) for any t out to the expiry of the ith forward rate, T_i, are guaranteed to price the ith caplet correctly.

3.2.6 Variance and Volatility in the Two Formulations

Nothing has been said so far about the time- and state-dependent drifts, $\boldsymbol{\mu}(\mathbf{f(t)}, t)$, which embody the no-arbitrage conditions and which might, in general, depend on all the forward rates. We know, however, that, for a given forward rate, f_i, there exists one particular numeraire (the natural payoff of f_i) such that its drift term is exactly zero. In this case, in order to match the Black market price, and in the absence of smiles, the root-mean-square of the instantaneous volatility, σ_i, will simply have to be set equal to the Black implied volatility (see Equation (3.4)). We also know, from Girsanov's theorem again, that changing the numeraire, and therefore changing the pricing measure, will alter the drift but not the volatility of the Wiener process. If the drift is non-zero, and it does contain the stochastic variables $\{f\}$, the unconditional variance of the forward rate will depend on the drift itself, and, therefore, on the chosen numeraire. The price of a given security, however, does not depend on the numeraire. Therefore, irrespective of the numeraire and of the associated measure used, one can always use the instantaneous volatility that produces the Black implied volatility for the no-drift case, resting assured that the corresponding caplet will be correctly priced.[7] This observation is not trivial because it highlights that, in general, what determines the price of a caplet is the volatility (numeraire- and measure-independent) component, and not

---

[7]Indeed, if one so wanted, one could obtain the correct price for each caplet simply by using a constant instantaneous volatility equal to the Black implied volatility. I shall, however, strongly argue in following chapters that this is not advisable when pricing exotic products.

the (numeraire- and measure-dependent) unconditional variance of the forward rate. The two quantities would be simply related to each other only if the drift term were constant, or, at most, time-dependent. Since, however, the drift contains the stochastic state variables $\{\mathbf{f}\}$, variance and (squared) volatility are in general not interchangeable quantities, and it is only the latter that is directly related to the price of the plain-vanilla instruments.

3.2.7 A Third Possible Description

Another very useful description that achieves in a different way the decomposition among the forward rates of the loadings onto the various orthogonal shocks is the following. In the equation

$$\frac{\mathrm{d}f_i}{f_i} = \mu_i \, \mathrm{d}t + \sum_{k=1}^{m} \sigma_{ik} \, \mathrm{d}z_k,$$

divide and multiply each loading, σ_{ik}, by the volatility of the ith forward rate:

$$\frac{\mathrm{d}f_i}{f_i} = \mu_i \, \mathrm{d}t + \sum_{k=1}^{m} \sigma_{ik} \, \mathrm{d}z_k$$

$$= \mu_i \, \mathrm{d}t + \sigma_i \sum_{k=1}^{m} \frac{\sigma_{ik}}{\sigma_i} \, \mathrm{d}z_k$$

$$= \mu_i \, \mathrm{d}t + \sigma_i \sum_{k=1}^{m} \frac{\sigma_{ik}}{\sqrt{\sum_{k=1}^{m} \sigma_{ik}^2}} \, \mathrm{d}z_k$$

$$\equiv \mu_i \, \mathrm{d}t + \sigma_i \sum_{k=1}^{m} b_{ik} \, \mathrm{d}z_k$$

with

$$b_{ik} = \frac{\sigma_{ik}}{\sqrt{\sum_{k=1}^{m} \sigma_{ik}^2}}.$$

The caplet-pricing Condition (3.9) has been used in the equation above. This decomposition is very useful because one can easily prove that, if $\mathbf{b}$ denotes the $n \times k$ matrix of coefficients $\{b_{jk}\}$, and $\mathbf{b}^{\mathrm{T}}$ its transpose, there is a link between $\mathbf{b}$ and the correlation matrix ρ in Equation (3.5), given by

$$\mathbf{b}\mathbf{b}^{\mathrm{T}} = \rho.$$

EXERCISE 3.2 *Prove that, in non-degenerate cases, $\mathbf{b}\mathbf{b}^{\mathrm{T}}$ has all the properties of a correlation matrix, that is, it is a real symmetric positive matrix, with elements $\{b_{jk}\}$ such that, for any j, k, $|b_{jk}| \leq 1$. For $m = n$, show the conditions that must be satisfied by $\{b_{jk}\}$ to ensure that ρ should have full rank.*

The formulation

$$\frac{\mathrm{d}f_i}{f_i} = \mu_i \, \mathrm{dt} + \sigma_i \sum_{k=1}^{m} b_{ik} \, \mathrm{d}z_k \tag{3.9'}$$

is very useful because it decomposes the responsiveness of the forward rates to the orthogonal shocks into two conceptually distinct components. The first component (σ_i) only depends on the total volatility of a given forward rate, and is therefore linked to its market-given implied volatility: for the correct pricing of the associated caplet, the root-mean-square of σ_i will have to be equal to σ_i^{Black}. The second component ($\{b_{ik}\}$) is purely linked to the correlation structure, and can therefore be most directly related to the statistically obtainable correlation matrix.

The decomposition (3.9') is also useful because it achieves one of the tasks mentioned earlier, that is, the decomposition of the stochastic coefficient in the evolution of the forward rates into two conceptually distinct components: the instantaneous volatility, $\sigma_i(t)$, which contains no information about the correlation structure and which is directly related through its root-mean-square to the market information, as contained in the prices of caplets (see Equation (3.4)); and the terms $\sum_{k=1}^{m} b_{ik} \, \mathrm{d}z_k$, which have no bearing on the caplet prices (as long as Equation (3.12) below is satisfied), and contain all the model information about the statistically determinable correlation matrix.

3.2.8 Further Links with Principal Component Analysis

If one adopts the alternative (and, for $m = n$, exactly equivalent) description (3.6) rather than formulation (3.3), the integration of the corresponding stochastic differential equation gives

$$f_i(t) = f_i(0) \, \exp \left[\int_0^t \mu_i(\{\mathbf{f}(u)\}, u) - \tfrac{1}{2}\sigma_i^2(u) \, \mathrm{d}u + \int_0^t \sum_{k=1}^{m} \sigma_{ik}(u) \, \mathrm{d}z_k(u) \right]. \tag{3.10}$$

If one looks back at the definition of the real symmetric matrix $\boldsymbol{\Sigma}$, and one denotes by $\lambda_i(t)$ and $\mathbf{a}_i(t)$, $1 \leq i \leq m$, with $\mathbf{a}_i = \{a_{ki}, 1 \leq k \leq n\}$, its associated (time-dependent) eigenvalues and orthonormal eigenvectors, respectively, one can immediately rewrite Equation (3.10) as

$$f_i(t) = f_i(0) \, \exp \left[\int_0^t \mu_i(\{\mathbf{f}(u)\}, u) - \tfrac{1}{2}\sigma_i^2(u) \, \mathrm{d}u + \int_0^t \sum_{k=1}^{m} \sqrt{\lambda_k} \, a_{ik}(u) \, \mathrm{d}z_k(u) \right]. \tag{3.11}$$

On the other hand, as shown in Section 2.7, if one defines quantities b_{ik}, $1 \leq i \leq n$, $1 \leq k \leq m$, such that

$$\sum_{k=1}^{m} b_{ik}^2 = 1, \tag{3.12}$$

then the caplet-pricing condition can always be recovered for any number of factors simply by setting

$$f_i(t) = f_i(0) \exp \left[\int_0^t \mu_i(\{\mathbf{f}(u)\}, u) - \tfrac{1}{2}\sigma_i^2(u) \, du + \int_0^t \sigma_i(u) \sum_{k=1}^m b_{ik}(u) \, dz_k(u) \right].$$
(3.13)

Equations (3.11) and (3.13) show that the market caplets will be correctly priced if

$$\sum_{k=1}^m \lambda_k a_{ik}^2 = \sigma_i^2 \sum_{k=1}^m b_{ik}^2.$$
(3.14)

Looking at Expression (3.14), one can readily see that requiring that all the caplets should be correctly priced and that the Brownian increments should be orthogonal to each other is not enough to determine uniquely the loadings, $\{b_{ik}\}$, onto the forward rates. In particular, the principal component is but one of an infinity of possible solutions – at least for any number of factors greater than one (if $m = 1$, then, clearly, for any i, $b_{i1} = 1$). From the definition of the coefficients $\{b_{jk}\}$, it is clear that, if one simply requires that the increments $\{dz_k\}$ should be orthogonal to each other, the m vectors of elements b_{jk}, $j = 1, 2, \ldots, m$, will in general neither be of norm 1 ($\sum_{k=1}^m b_{ik}^2 \neq 1$) nor be orthogonal to each other ($\sum_{k=1}^m b_{ik} b_{jk} \neq 0$). It will always be possible, however, to rotate the $\{dz_k\}$ in such a way that these orthonormality relationships and the caplet Condition (3.12) are simultaneously satisfied. After this rotation, if $m = n$ (i.e., if the number of factors equals the number of forward rates), the description of forward-rate dynamics afforded by the $\{b_{jk}\}$ is exactly equivalent to a principal component decomposition.

EXERCISE 3.3 *Express the correlation matrix in terms of the coefficients $\{b_{jk}\}$. If as many factors as forward rates are retained, and an exogenous admissible correlation function assigned, indicate how the coefficients σ_{jk} in Equation (3.10) are related to the latter. If one imposes that the prices of the market caplets should be exactly recovered, are these coefficients unique?*

Clearly, if as many factors are retained as forward rates ($m = n$), any arbitrary correlation structure can always be recovered, and Expression (3.11) simply provides a transparent decomposition of the same information contained in Equations (3.3) and (3.5). In the more interesting case, however, when the user cannot 'afford' to retain as many factors as forward rates, an exogenous correlation matrix will, in general, not be recoverable, and Equation (3.13) will be shown in Chapters 8 and 9 to provide the most natural framework to ensure that the model prices the caplets correctly and recovers in an optimal way as much as possible of a desired correlation matrix. This decomposition will also be used extensively in Chapter 10.

3.2.9 *A Systematic Procedure to Reduce the Dimensionality of a Pricing Problem*

The description presented by Equations (3.11) expresses the evolution of the forward rates in terms of $m < n$ factors. Clearly, if one attempted to reduce the dimensionality of the problem simply by orthogonalizing the correlation matrix and truncating the summation over the resulting principal components to m terms, the total variance of the original problem would not be recovered, and, as a consequence, the caplet prices would no longer be correctly obtained. The question therefore remains of how this rescaling can be accomplished in an 'optimal' way. This will indeed be one of the main topics of Chapter 9. Already at this stage, however, the treatment presented so far provides a clear blueprint for the program ahead: whenever the number of factors is smaller than the number of forward rates, that is, for $m < n$, the user should attempt to determine the weights $\{\mathbf{b}\}$ such that $\sum_{k=1}^{m} b_{ik}^2 = 1$ (the caplets are correctly priced) and such that the correlation surface implied by this choice should be 'as good as possible'. For a given number of factors and a chosen criterion of 'goodness', this choice $\{\widehat{\mathbf{b}}\}$ not only provides the best LIBOR-market-model implementation that prices the caplets exactly, but is also the 'best' possible arbitrage-free m-factor model of the yield curve with deterministic volatility.

3.2.10 *Characterizing a Version of the LIBOR Market Model*

We are at this point in a position to characterize different versions of the LIBOR market model. Different implementations compatible with the same prices of plain-vanilla caplets are distinguished by three fundamental and conceptually distinct choices:

1. the choice for the shape of the instantaneous volatility function, subject to the root-mean-square constraint that

$$\sigma_{\text{Black}}^2(T_i)T_i = \int_0^{T_i} \sigma_i^2(u)\,\mathrm{d}u;$$

2. the choice of the number of factors, m; and

3. the allocation of the responsiveness of the different forward rates to the different orthogonal Brownian shocks, that is, the possible different choices for the coefficients b_{ik} such that

$$\sum_{k=1}^{m} b_{ik}^2 = 1$$

(i.e., the different possible choices for the correlation matrix).

Chapter 6 will deal with point 1. The issues raised in point 3 are dealt with in Chapters 9 and 10. The pricing impact of the number of factors (point 2) is dealt with in Chapters 7, 9 and 10.

For any number of factors, for any choice of the correlation matrix and for any instantaneous volatility function producing the correct root-mean-square (Black) volatility, the exact pricing of an exogenous set of market caplets can always be recovered. It is often said that the LIBOR market model is characterized by its ability to specify a forward-rate dynamics compatible with an exogenous set of caplet prices. For a given set of caplets, however, it does not make sense to speak of *the* associated LIBOR market model, since an infinity of possible combinations for choices 1, 2 and 3 above will give rise to the same caplet prices, but to substantially different dynamics for the forward rates. I will show in the following that, as we extend our horizon from caplets to more complex instruments (European swaptions or exotic products), progressively more information can be obtained about the shape of the instantaneous volatility functions, about the market-implied correlation matrix and about the number of factors needed to capture in an adequate way the important modes of deformation of the yield curve. Unfortunately, none of these more complex instruments provide independent information about one of these components at a time,[8] and it is up to the user to decide how much the observed price of a given exotic product (or of European swaptions) should be explained by the number of factors, by the shape of the instantaneous volatility function or by the correlation matrix. See, for example, Sidenius (1998, 2000) for a discussion of this topic. It is for this reason that the decomposition

$$\frac{\mathrm{d}f_i(t)}{f_i(t)} = \mu_i\,\mathrm{d}t + \sigma_{\mathrm{inst}}^i(t) \sum_{k=1}^{m} b_{ik}\,\mathrm{d}z_k(t)$$

can prove conceptually particularly useful, clearly splitting as it does the stochastic part of the evolution of a forward rate into a correlation component (the terms $\{b_{ik}\}$), an instantaneous volatility component ($\sigma_{\mathrm{inst}}^i(t)$) and a dependence, via the summation index m, on the number of factors. Another reason why this decomposition provides a useful working framework is that, as I shall show in Chapter 7, the shape of the model correlation surface is strongly and inextricably dependent on the number of chosen factors. This being the case, it could be very dangerous, for instance, for a trader who is using a small number of factors to attempt to force a near-exact fitting to a specific portion of the covariance matrix. By so doing, she would be likely to imply a financially implausible behavior for, say, the instantaneous volatility functions. More about this in Chapters 9 and 10.

3.2.11 The Link with Traditional Yield-Curve Models

In one guise or another, the choices 1 to 3 in Section 3.2.10 above are not specific to the LIBOR market model, and are common, implicitly or explic-

---

[8]The one exception could be serial options. They are unfortunately illiquid, and only cover a relatively short span of the maturity spectrum. See the discussion at the end of Section 2.2 and in Rebonato (1999c).

itly, to all arbitrage-free yield-curve modelling approaches. Since Equations (3.10)–(3.12), with the appropriate values for the no-arbitrage drifts, contain all the arbitrage-free approaches to evolving forward rates with deterministic volatilities, the possible choices 1 to 3 discussed in Section 3.2.10 provide a very general and transparent way to characterize different models. Despite the apparent bewildering variety of interest-rate models that have appeared in the literature, in fact, any two arbitrage-free, deterministic-volatility approaches cannot differ in any way other than by the number of factors they use, the shape of the instantaneous volatility they imply, and the allocation of the responsiveness of the various forward rates to the different drivers.

It is interesting to point out that the earlier short-rate-based modelling approaches (i.e., the approaches of the Hull-and-White (1993), Black-Derman-and-Toy (Black et al. 1990) and Black-and-Karasinski (1991) period) did not have the luxury of choice 3 (since, in a one-factor model, if one wants – and manages – to price the caplets correctly, there is no choice but implicitly to take the coefficients $b_{i1} = 1$, for any i).[9] Not only was this degree of freedom unavailable, but the shape of the resulting instantaneous volatility curves of the driving factor (the short rate) could not be independently assigned by the user either; rather, it was an opaque by-product of the chosen yield-curve dynamics. In this respect, the Black et al. (BDT) model is an interesting point in case. See Rebonato (1998, 1999c) for a discussion of the pathological nature of the short-rate mean reversion in the BDT model, caused by the need to price the caplet market and by the lack of the flexibility afforded by choices 1 and 3.

EXERCISE 3.4 *Starting from any of the standard descriptions of the BDT model, think how you would fit it to a set of caplet prices. Repeat the same exercise for a BDT-like model, that is, for a model where the short rate is still log-normally distributed, but the tree is now no longer forced to recombine. Comment on the resulting short-rate volatility in both cases, and compare it with the volatilities of the forward rates compatible with a given set of market prices in the LIBOR market model. In particular, how many solutions would you find in the BDT, the non-recombining-BDT and the LIBOR-market-model cases?*

More generally, as shown in the following (Chapter 7), both a set of non-flat instantaneous volatility functions and an imperfect instantaneous correlation can give rise to a significant terminal decorrelation among rates. However, the shape of the forward-rate instantaneous volatility was not an exogenous input for the short-rate-based models. Therefore, little could be done in the earlier approaches to produce a more desirable set of instantaneous

---

[9]Strictly speaking, the short-rate models specify a deterministic volatility for the short rate. The instantaneous volatility of the resulting forward rates is not deterministic, because it is a function of the short rate itself. This dependence is however very weak, and, for the purpose of the discussion, the instantaneous volatilities of the forward rates associated with the common deterministic-volatility short-rate models can be safely regarded to be deterministic themselves.

volatility curves if the model-produced ones were found wanting. In particular, if the calibration to market prices of a short-rate model produced, as it often did, virtually flat instantaneous volatility functions, for a small number of factors the terminal decorrelation produced by these early models would typically be very low. As a consequence, in order to achieve decorrelation among rates, researchers concentrated their efforts on increasing the number of factors. This was a route embarked upon more by necessity than by choice: it is not a priori obvious, in fact, whether the shape of the instantaneous volatility (choice 1) or the number of factors (choice 2 and the accompanying choice 3 that it permits) have a stronger pricing implication for a given product. I will show in the following (see Chapters 6 and 7 in particular) that the shape of the instantaneous volatility is at least as important as the number of factors in producing decorrelation. Furthermore, in certain situations the ability to impose a financially desirable shape for the instantaneous volatility function has greater pricing relevance than the dimensionality of the model. This is particularly true when the *instantaneous* correlation between the underlying variables is rather high, as is presumably the case for same-currency forward rates. More about this in Chapter 7.

3.2.12 A First Example

If one only wanted to price caplets, the formulations (3.11), (3.13) and (3.14) are unnecessarily complex. Indeed, if caplet pricing were all that the trader were interested in, and since one of the main virtues of the standard LIBOR-market-model approach is its ability to recover the Black market prices of the caplets, she would be better off simply using the Black formula. The richer treatments expressed in Equations (3.11), (3.13) and (3.14), however, become necessary as soon as more complex instruments have to be priced consistently with the caplet market (see the discussion in Chapter 1 and Section 3.1). To give a first concrete example of how the formalism just presented can be used for pricing purposes, let us consider a path-dependent instrument whose payoff condition is determined by the realizations of the forward rates at the times, $T_1, T_2, \ldots, T_k$, of k price-sensitive events (say, k barrier conditions). Let us also call the last price-sensitive event T, and $\mathcal{F}_{T_1}, \mathcal{F}_{T_2}, \ldots, \mathcal{F}_T$ the natural filtration generated by the resets of the discrete set of forward rates at the times of the price-sensitive events. In other terms, the information set, as described by the filtration $\mathcal{F}_t$, is updated simply by recording the realizations of the forward rates on the dates of their resets.[10] The implications of the requirement that the payoff should be measurable with respect to $\mathcal{F}_{T_1}$, $\mathcal{F}_{T_2}, \ldots, \mathcal{F}_T$ are discussed in detail in the next chapter. We can, however, already intuitively expect that, as far as the payoff is concerned, 'nothing relevant happens' between, say, today (T_0) and time T_1, the time when the first

---

[10]Loosely speaking, a function of random variables (say, a payoff) is said to be $\mathcal{F}_t$-measurable if it can be computed given the knowledge of $\mathcal{F}_t$ (i.e., given the resets of the discrete set of forward rates at the times of the price-sensitive events).

price-sensitive event occurs, or, more generally, between any times T_i and T_{i+1}. If the forward rates were conditionally log-normally distributed, and given the knowledge of their expectations and covariances, we could therefore directly evolve the whole yield curve out to time T_1, using, for instance, Equation (3.3), and attach a probability to each joint realization of the forward rates. Since this joint realization will, in turn, determine the price-sensitive condition, we can associate the same probability to the condition itself.

In the log-normal case, and for the simplest non-trivial choice of $k = 2$, if the drift were at most time-dependent, all that would be required (see, e.g., Rebonato 1999c, section 3.3.3) would be to evolve f_1 and f_2 according to

$$f_1(T_1) = f_1(0) \exp(m_1 \Delta t - \tfrac{1}{2} v_{1,1} + \sqrt{v_{1,1}} \, Z_1), \qquad (3.15)$$

$$f_2(T_1) = f_2(0) \exp(m_2 \Delta t - \tfrac{1}{2} v_{2,1} + \sqrt{v_{2,1}} \, Z_2), \qquad (3.16)$$

where

$$m_1 = \int_0^{T_1} \mu_1(u) \, du$$

$$m_2 = \int_0^{T_1} \mu_2(u) \, du$$

$$v_{1,1} = \int_0^{T_1} \sigma_1^2(u) \, du$$

$$v_{2,1} = \int_0^{T_1} \sigma_2^2(u) \, du$$

$$Z_2 = Z_1 \rho + \sqrt{(1 - \rho^2)} \, W$$

$$\rho = \frac{\int_0^{T_1} \sigma_1(u) \sigma_2(u) \rho_{1,2}(u) \, du}{\sqrt{v_{1,1} v_{2,1}}}$$

with μ_1 and μ_2 the (at most time-dependent) drifts of forward rates 1 and 2, respectively, and Z_1 and W two independent normal variates drawn from $N(0, T_1)$. To any couple $\{f_1(T_1), f_2(T_1)\}$ one can associate an outcome for the path-dependent condition (one could, for instance, calculate a two-period swap rate and check whether it is above or below a given barrier level) and a probability (which will be a function of Z_1, W and ρ). In other terms, given the nature of the payoffs, all that is needed is the evolution of the forward rates from one price-sensitive event to the next (perhaps separated by a time interval of several years), without making use of the realization of the processes at any intermediate time. In the next chapter I will refer to the procedure whereby the yield curve is evolved from one price-sensitive event to the next as the 'long-jump' technique (to distinguish it from the 'very-long-jump' technique, also described in detail in the next chapter).

As mentioned in Section 3.1, these discrete joint densities can be sampled using numerically different techniques, depending on the type of product.

In terms of a Monte Carlo simulation, for instance, this could mean that the evolution steps might have to be taken to coincide with the (possibly uneven) intervals between price-sensitive events; or, as shown in the next chapter, a single 'very long jump' (perhaps as long as 20 years!) could be sufficient for the evaluation of a product. In other terms, the simulation 'steps', Δt, would not have in any sense to be small.

It is important to stress again that, strictly speaking, these conclusions are only valid if the drift terms, which we have not evaluated yet, were at most a deterministic function of time. I shall show below (Section 5.2) that this is not the case. However, I will argue (Section 5.3) that the log-normal solutions can still be used with great accuracy even if the drift terms contain the state variables. The discussion presented above, and continued immediately below, of the truly log-normal case therefore retains its relevance.

3.3 Generalization of the Approach

3.3.1 Definition and Construction of the Matrices **TOTC** and **C**

One can generalize the reasoning presented above for the case of two forward rates observed at the first price-sensitive event, to the general case of a whole (discrete) yield curve described by n forward rates observed at the kth price-sensitive event. In order to determine their joint distribution, all that matters are the drifts and the (marginal) covariance elements, $C(i, j, k + 1)$, defined by

$$C(i, j, k + 1) \equiv \int_{T_k}^{T_{k+1}} \sigma_i(u)\sigma_j(u)\rho_{i,j}(u)\,\mathrm{d}u \tag{3.17}$$

$$\text{for } 0 \leq k \leq n - 1 \text{ and } k \leq i, j \leq n,$$

$$C(i, j, k) \equiv 0 \qquad \text{for } i < k \text{ and/or } j < k.$$

If the initial (time-T_0) yield curve was described by n forward rates, there will, in general, be n^2 non-zero elements in the set $C(i, j, 1)$, $(n - 1)^2$ non-zero elements in $C(i, j, 2)$, etc. (see Table 3.1). In particular, from Equations (3.4), (3.9) and (3.14), one can easily see that

$$\sigma_{\text{Black}}^2(T_i)T_i = \int_0^{T_i} \sigma_i^2(u)\,\mathrm{d}u = \sum_{r=1}^{i} C(i, i, r). \tag{3.18}$$

Furthermore, one can define the matrix **TOTC** with elements given by

$$\text{TOTC}(i, j) = \sum_{k=1}^{\min(i,j)} C(i, j, k). \tag{3.19}$$

Table 3.1   *The non-zero elements of matrix $C(i, j, 1)$, $1 \leq i, j \leq 3$, of matrix $C(i, j, 2)$, $1 \leq i, j \leq 2$, and of matrix $C(i, j, 3)$, $i = j = 3$, together with the sum matrix $TOTC(i, j)$, $1 \leq i, j \leq 3$. The first matrix links time T_0 to time T_1 and refers to the three forward rates (f_1, f_2 and f_3) that describe the yield curve at time T_0; only two forward rates have not yet reset at time T_1 (i.e., f_2 and f_3), and these enter the time-$[T_1, T_2]$ 2×2 covariance matrix. At time T_2, only one forward rate, f_3, has not yet reset, and the covariance matrix becomes a single number.*

$$
\begin{array}{|ccc|}
\hline
C(1,1,1) & C(1,2,1) & C(1,3,1) \\
C(2,1,1) & C(2,2,1) & C(2,3,1) \\
C(3,1,1) & C(3,2,1) & C(3,3,1) \\
\hline
\end{array}
$$

$$
\begin{array}{|cc|}
\hline
C(2,2,2) & C(2,3,2) \\
C(3,2,2) & C(3,3,2) \\
\hline
\end{array}
$$

$$
\begin{array}{|c|}
\hline
C(3,3,3) \\
\hline
\end{array}
$$

$$
\begin{array}{|lll|}
\hline
C(1,1,1) & C(1,2,1)   & C(1,3,1) \\
C(2,1,1) & C(2,2,1) + C(2,2,2) & C(2,3,1) + C(2,3,2) \\
C(3,1,1) & C(3,2,1) + C(3,2,2) & C(3,3,1) + C(3,3,2) + C(3,3,3) \\
\hline
\end{array}
$$

The matrix **TOTC**, which has been constructed by adding real symmetric matrices, is itself a real and symmetric $n \times n$ matrix and can therefore be orthogonalized. It is important to point out that, as long as no two forward rates are perfectly correlated ($\rho_{ij} \neq 1$, for any i, j: $i \neq j$), the procedure will in general produce n distinct eigenvalues and eigenvectors, λ_i and $\mathbf{a}_i$, $1 \leq i \leq n$, even if fewer factors than forward rates had been used in the construction of the matrix **TOTC**. By the properties of the orthogonalization of real symmetric matrices, the trace of the original total covariance matrix **TOTC** and of the new orthogonalized matrix are the same. The latter, therefore, is linked, via Equation (3.18), to the market prices of the caplets via the relationship:

$$
\sum_{i=1}^{n} \lambda_i = \sum_{i=1}^{n} \sigma_{\text{Black}}^2(T_i) T_i = \sum_{i=1}^{n} \int_0^{T_i} \sigma_i^2(u)\, \mathrm{d}u = \sum_{i=1}^{n} \sum_{r=1}^{i} C(i, i, r). \tag{3.20}
$$

3.3.2 Evolving All the Forward Rates to the Final Maturity

Some very useful intuitive insight can be reaped if all the forward rates are 'formally' evolved to the expiry of the last one according to

$$
f_i(T_n) = f_i(0) \exp\left[\int_0^{T_n} \mu_i(u) - \tfrac{1}{2}\sigma_i^2(u)\, \mathrm{d}u + \sum_{k=1}^{n} \sqrt{\lambda_k}\, a_{ik} Z_k \right]. \tag{3.21}
$$

The adverb 'formally' highlights the fact that some care must be taken in interpreting the procedure, since, by time T_n, all the forward rates but one will have already reset. As explained in greater detail in Section 4.2, one can think in terms of a set of equivalent stochastic variables, $\{\mathbf{f}'\}$, whose dynamics co-incides in a pathway fashion with that of the variables $\{\mathbf{f}\}$ up to the expiry of each forward rate, and whose volatility drops to a vanishingly small value after reset.[11]

Note carefully that a variety of matrices $\{C(i, j, k)\}$ can produce the same matrix $\{\text{TOTC}(i, j)\}$. The orthogonalization of the latter, therefore, cannot discriminate between different sets of matrices $\mathbf{C}$ that give rise to the same total matrix **TOTC**. Therefore, some of the information about the elements of the individual constituent matrices $\mathbf{C}$ will be lost if one simply works with the matrix **TOTC**, or with its eigenvectors and eigenvalues. Looking back at Table 3.1, for instance, one can immediately appreciate that all the covariance matrices $C(i, j, 1)$ and $C(i, j, 2)$ with elements $C(2, 3, 1)$ and $C(2, 3, 2)$ such that the sum $C(2, 3, 1) + C(2, 3, 2)$ is a constant give rise to the same element $\text{TOTC}(2, 3)$ (and, therefore, after orthogonalization, to the same eigenvectors and eigenvalues, and to the same forward rate dynamics). Each combination of elements $C(i, j, k)$ adding up to the same $\text{TOTC}(i, j)$ will, in general, give rise to different prices for a complex instrument. There is, however, one im-portant exception. From Table 3.1 and from Equation (3.19) one can see that all the matrices $\mathbf{C}$, such that the quantity $\sum_{r=1}^{i} C(i, i, r)$ adds up to the same value, will produce matrices **TOTC** with identical diagonal elements and with identical root-mean-square volatility for each forward rate out to its own ex-piry. This is important, because there exists a wide class of products such that their terminal payoff can be expressed purely as a function of the joint re-alization of the spanning forward rates on their own reset dates. For these products the orthogonalization of the matrix **TOTC**, coupled with Equation (3.21), does provide the correct answer for the joint probability of the differ-ent forward rates on their own reset dates, and, as a consequence, a correct pricing for the products in question. Chapter 4 will examine several instances of these products in detail.

3.3.3 First Introduction of the Long-Jump and Very-Long-Jump Procedures

Since the forward rates are evolved, via Equation (3.21), all the way to the last expiry date, the procedure will be referred to in the following as the 'very-long-jump' technique. The term 'long jump', on the other hand, will be reserved for the evolution of the forward rate from one price-sensitive event to the next. Note, however, that, even in this case, the jump can still be 'very long', because the price-sensitive events can sometimes be separated by as much as several years. I have chosen this somewhat inelegant terminology to contrast the two proposed approaches described above with a short-stepped Monte Carlo evolution, where the step size is not linked to the location in time

---

[11]Strictly speaking, one should independently require that also the drifts should approach zero. I shall show in Chapter 5, however, that these drift terms are a function of the volatilities, and therefore they automatically go to zero with the latter.

of the price-sensitive events, but is purely dictated by consideration of numerical accuracy of the approximation of the underlying stochastic process. I shall show in the following chapters (see Chapter 12 in particular) that a (mildly) short-stepped Monte Carlo evolution only becomes necessary in the context of the LIBOR market model when it is extended to the case of a stochastic instantaneous volatility. The important issue of long and very long jumps, and of their relevance in the context of the practical numerical implementation of the LIBOR market model, is examined in great detail in Chapters 4 and 5. At this stage, it is sufficient to notice that the volatility specification presented in this section ensures that the covariance matrix will be deterministic and that a finite number of these covariance matrices (plus a finite number of drift vectors) are all that is needed in order to carry out either the long- or the very-long-jump procedures.

3.3.4 Limitations of the Approach

Appealing as this program might be, its validity seems to be predicated upon the pure time dependence of the drifts. In reality I will show in Chapter 5 that the drifts are not a purely deterministic function of time, but also contain the forward rates themselves. Therefore the distribution of all but at most one of the forward rates will not be log-normal, and the appealing strategy of performing a joint evolution of all the forward rates from one price-sensitive event to the next would seem to become unfeasible. Using the concepts introduced in Section 3.1, the stochastic nature of the drifts is such that it violates the conditions for the forward-rate process to be conditionally Gaussian. In this case the user of the model would appear to be forced to progress the evolution of the yield curve using a Monte Carlo technique with sufficiently small steps that the stochastic variables can be considered approximately constant over each step. In brief, the approach presented above based on the orthogonalization of the covariance matrix and the (very-)long-jump evolution would appear to have been a case of wishful thinking. Fortunately, I shall also show in the following chapters that it is possible to approximate very accurately the joint evolution of the forward rates as if they were exactly log-normal, even in the presence of the state variables in their drifts. The accuracy of this approximation will be shown to be such that the yield curve can be accurately evolved in a single 'long' jump between price-sensitive events, separated perhaps by 10 years or more.[12] Even more remarkably, and, in a way, almost 'accidentally', once the above-mentioned approximation is enforced, also the drifts will be expressible in terms of the same covariance elements that drive the stochastic part of the evolution. Far from having to be abandoned,

---

[12]Time intervals between price-sensitive events as long as many years are not at all rare. They are common in products where certain features (such as exercise opportunities) only come into effect after an initial period, often referred to as a 'lock-out period'. For investor products such as structured notes, for instance, the existence of the lock-out period guarantees that an above-market coupon will be enjoyed by the purchaser of the note for a known number of years.

the orthogonalization approach presented above therefore has an even wider applicability once the drifts are included.

3.4 The Swap-Rate-Based LIBOR Market Model

Before moving on to the task outlined at the end of the previous section, it is important to mention a parallel possible treatment of the LIBOR-market-model approach that employs swap rates, rather than forward rates, as the primitive stochastic state variables. The derivation of the no-arbitrage dynamics of log-normal swap rates has been presented in detail in Jamshidian (1997). A less rigorous and general, but mathematically far simpler, treatment can be found in Rebonato (1998), where different, but ultimately equivalent, expressions for the no-arbitrage drifts of the swap rates can be found. In both treatments, the logical path proceeds by noticing that the value of the yield curve on a finite set of dates can be obtained not just in terms of spanning forward rates (see Section 3.2), but also, and equivalently, by means of co-terminal swap rates – see, in this respect, the discussion in Section 10.1. A numeraire can then be found for each swap rate individually, such that the swap rate itself, once assigned a purely deterministic volatility, is a log-normal martingale. In particular, the numeraire turns out to be the fixed-rate annuity associated with each swap rate. Under this assumption of deterministic volatility, and for this choice of numeraire, the market-standard Black formula for each associated European swaption is automatically recovered (see, e.g., Neuberger 1990, Gustavsson 1997, or Section 2.2).

Just as in the case of forward rates, not all swap rates can be simultaneously log-normal, nor can the joint log-normal assumption be valid for forward and swap rates at the same time. The pricing implications of this inconsistency in the market choice of using the Black formula for all European swaptions and caplets has however been shown to be small (see, e.g., Rebonato 1999b), at least for at-the-money strikes.

A possible reason for choosing swaps, rather than forward rates, as the fundamental building blocks is that certain important instruments (such as Bermudan swaptions, or constant-maturity-swap-based derivatives[13]) are most naturally hedged using plain-vanilla European swaptions. By using a swap-rate-based LIBOR-market-model approach, an exact recovery of the market prices of these benchmark products is very easy to achieve using an approach that exactly parallels the treatment presented in Equations (3.9)–(3.14) for forward rates. Therefore, the natural hedging instruments for the products mentioned above are automatically correctly priced. Furthermore, the hedging strategy is naturally obtainable in terms of plain-vanilla products the trader

---

[13]A constant-maturity swap (CMS) is a product whose payoffs are paid with the same frequency and on the same dates as those from a plain-vanilla swap, but with their magnitudes determined by the resets of different swap rates, each one of the same maturity – whence the name 'constant maturity'. CMS derivatives (such as CMS caplets) are options on these cash-flows.

will want to use, that is, swap rates and European swaptions.

Appealing as these important features may be, the swap-rate-based LIBOR market model suffers from two significant practical drawbacks. The first is that the no-arbitrage drifts turn out to be considerably more involved and computationally demanding and to require rather careful numerical handling. The second drawback is that the inputs of a swap-rate-based LIBOR market model are less directly related to market observables than the corresponding inputs for the forward-rates-based version. This is because the instantaneous volatilities of, and the correlation matrix among, the swap rates, instead of forward rates, are required to specify the model. Traders, however, tend to have less precise and well-formed ideas about swap-rate volatilities and correlations than about the same quantities for forward rates. Furthermore, small differences in the correlation between long-dated swap rates can imply very substantially different correlations between some of the associated forward rates.

In many situations, the advantage of an exact pricing of the most important hedging instruments outweighs the numerical burden, and this is indeed the view I have expressed elsewhere (Rebonato 1998) in the context of the pricing of Bermudan swaptions. However, in Chapter 10 I shall show how the market prices of a set of co-terminal European swaptions can be recovered almost exactly even using the much-simpler-to-implement forward-rate-based formalism. In addition, the trader can achieve this goal while, at the same time, retaining as much control as possible, after fitting the European swaptions, on the forward-rate dynamics.

Despite the fact that, in my proposed approach, forward rates are the state variables, the risk statistics of swap-rate-based products, such as Bermudan swaptions, can easily be expressed in terms of the 'Greeks' for the swap rates that the trader will most naturally use for hedging. So, for instance, the vector of vega sensitivities with respect to the co-terminal European swaptions can be easily obtained even when working with forward rates. Therefore, given the greater simplicity of the forward-rate-based LIBOR market model, the swap-rate-based approach will not be pursued any further.

4

Characterizing and Valuing Complex LIBOR Products[1]

4.1 The Types of Product That Can be Handled Using the LIBOR Market Model

From the discussion so far, the marginal and total covariance matrices, **C** and **TOTC**, can be expected to play a central role in the evolution of the forward rates that describe a yield curve. The next natural step is establishing the link between these matrices and the types of complex derivatives product the LIBOR market model has been specifically constructed to price. This analysis is important both from a conceptual and from a practical point of view, because it will inform the numerical techniques necessary to tackle the problem in practice. In fact, I will show that, for a very large class of products, the computational burden can be substantially alleviated if the simple-minded, 'brute-force' simulation approach is eschewed in favour of the more general procedures briefly introduced in Section 3.2, and more fully examined in the remainder of this chapter. This treatment will be shown to be closely linked to the material presented in the previous chapter, since these numerical procedures will make essential use of the construction of the marginal covariance matrices, **C**, and of the matrix **TOTC**.

Without pre-empting future results, I can already say that the maximum computational efficiency in the pricing of exotic products using the LIBOR market model is obtained when the size of the simulation jump is much larger than, say, the tenor (typically, three or six months) of the underlying product. I will show that, after choosing a common numeraire for all the forward rates, even in the case of a path-dependent instrument with, say, quarterly price-sensitive events, one can often carry out the evaluation by performing a single 'very-long-jump evolution' to the very last maturity date of all the forward rates. This very long jump can be safely carried out even if some of the

---

[1]I am indebted to Mike Sherring for many useful discussions about the ideas presented in this chapter, and the very-long-jump technique in particular.

forward rates will have expired 'on the way'. This technique is extremely powerful, and, in Section 4.2, will be applied, as a Case Study, to the pricing of a multi-look trigger swap.

4.1.1 Classification of the Products

With these considerations in mind, the products that fall within the natural sphere of tractability of the LIBOR-market-model pricing approach can be grouped into four different types:

1. path-dependent derivatives;

2. single-look options (simple or compound);

3. multi-look compound products;

4. path-dependent compound products.

The conditions at reset times $\{T_i\}$ which influence the payoffs of type 1–4 products will be referred to in the following as the price-sensitive events. Using the terminology introduced in Chapter 2, I intend to show that, if $\mathcal{F}_t$ is the natural filtration generated by the realization of the n forward rates observed at the times of the price-sensitive events, the payoffs of type 1–4 products can all be said to be $\mathcal{F}_t$-measurable. This measurability condition will then be shown to be one of the two requirements that must be satisfied for the applicability of the version of the LIBOR market model I have presented in Chapters 2 and 3. It will also be shown to be of assistance in suggesting the most suitable numerical technique for the evaluation of the various products.

4.1.2 Path-Dependent (Type-1) Derivatives

Starting with the first case, for type-1 products the payoff occurring at time T_n depends on the realization of a series of forward (or swap) rates on reset dates T_i $(1 \le i \le n)$. It is important for future discussions to make a further distinction between

- path-dependent securities whose payoffs depend on the joint realization of forward rates which, by the time of each price-sensitive event, have all already come to their own reset (type 1a);[2] and

- path-dependent securities whose payoffs depend on the realization on a series of dates of forward rates, some of which might not have reset yet (type 1b).[2]

---

[2]More technically, one can say that the payoff of type-1a products must be measurable with respect to the filtration generated by the realizations of the various forward rates at their own reset times, while the payoff of type-1b products is measurable with respect to the finer filtration $\mathcal{F}_t$ defined above.

The distinction is important because, as I shall show in the following, the latter securities can be handled by means of the 'long-jump' and the former by means of the 'very-long-jump' technique.

It is important to point out that sometimes a simple transformation of the variables in terms of which the payoff is expressed can turn a type-1b into a type-1a product. Consider, for instance, a four-period swap with strike K that can come to life on a single-look date, T, if the first forward rate in the swap (i.e., the forward rate resetting at time T) resets above a given barrier, H (up-and-in single-look swap). It can be easily shown that, after choosing the swap annuity A as the numeraire, the closed-form solution for present value of this security is given by

$$PV = [SR(0, T)N(h_1) - KN(h_2)]A, \qquad (4.1)$$

with

$$h_1 = \frac{\ln[\tilde{f}(0, T)/H] - \frac{1}{2}v_f + v_{f,SR}}{\sqrt{v_f}},$$

$$h_2 = \frac{\ln[\tilde{f}(0, T)/H] - \frac{1}{2}v_f}{\sqrt{v_f}},$$

$$v_f = \int_0^T \sigma_f(u)^2 \, du,$$

$$v_{f,SR} = \int_0^T \sigma_f(u)\sigma_{SR}(u)\rho_{f,SR}(u) \, du,$$

$$A = \frac{1}{\prod_{k=0}^3 [1 + \tilde{f}_k(0, T + k\tau, T + (k+1)\tau)\tau]}.$$

In these equations, $N(\ )$ denotes, as usual, the cumulative normal distribution, $SR(0, T)$ is the value at time 0 of the equilibrium swap rate for the swap that comes to life if the forward rate f resets above H at time T, $\tilde{f}_k(0, T, T+\tau)$ is the value at time 0 of the forward rate resetting at time T and paying at time $T + \tau$, after the numeraire-induced drift adjustment – described in Chapter 5 – has been applied, τ is the tenor of the swap – say, three months – σ_f and σ_{SR} are the instantaneous volatilities of the forward rate and of the swap rate, respectively, A is the fixed-leg annuity of the swap and $\rho_{f,SR}$ is the instantaneous correlation between the swap and the forward rate.

EXERCISE 4.1 *(Or, 'Where does the term $+\frac{1}{2}v_f$ in the Black formula come from?')*
One might wonder why in the Black formula the term $\frac{1}{2}v_f$ appears with positive sign, while, from Ito's lemma, one would have expected it to be negative. To see why this is the case, assume that the drift for the forward rate implied by the chosen numeraire has been

calculated, that is, assume that you know the value

$$\tilde{f}(T,T) = f(0,T) \exp \int_0^T \mu(u) \, du.$$

Derive Formula (4.1). Then obtain the Black formula for a caplet as a special case of Expression (4.1) when $H = K$ and the swap coincides with the forward rate used to monitor the knock-in condition. What happens to the fixed-leg annuity and to the drift adjustment to the forward rate in this limiting case? (You might want to answer this question after reading Chapter 5.)

If, instead of making use of the closed-form result, one wanted to perform a brute-force Monte Carlo evaluation of this product, one could be tempted to mirror the analytical treatment by choosing the annuity A as numeraire, evolving the four-period yield curve to time T after drift-adjusting the forward rates as appropriate, calculating the value of the swap, and enforcing the barrier condition by comparing the realized value of $\tilde{f}(T,T)$ with H.

If looked at in this manner, the product would seem to be a type-1b security, since, in order to evaluate the swap rate and the fixed-leg annuity, the value of the not-yet-reset forward rates that make up the swap rates is needed. An alternative decomposition of the payoff is however possible: one can first of all choose the zero-coupon bond maturing, say, on the maturity date of the swap as numeraire, and drift-adjust the forward rates as needed (see Chapter 5). One can then decompose the swap into four FRAs: the first FRA resets at time T, and comes to life if the associated forward rate resets above H; the second FRA resets at time $T + \tau$, and gives rise to a non-zero payoff if the first forward rate has already reset above H; similarly, the third and fourth FRAs reset at times $T + 2\tau$ and $T + 3\tau$, respectively, and whether they contribute a payoff still depends on the realization at time T of the first forward rate. If the barrier condition is triggered, the four FRAs will produce payoffs on different dates. How these payoffs occurring at different times can be combined together using a single numeraire for discounting will be explained later on, but one can already notice that, if looked at this way, the value of the knock-in swap only depends on the joint realizations of the forward rates on their own expiry dates, and the product can therefore be regarded as a type-1a security.

The manipulations needed to recast the problem in these terms might appear at the moment unnecessarily complicated, but I shall show in the following that the small amount of 'book-keeping' associated with this decomposition is a small price to pay in order to avail oneself of the very-long-jump procedure. Even in the more complex (but more common) case of a multi-look trigger swap,[3] in fact, the decomposition into FRAs shown above is still possible: in this case, each component FRA will pay the difference between

---

[3]The description and the pricing considerations that enter the evaluation of trigger swaps, captions, Bermudan swaptions and other securities are dealt with in detail in chapter 2 of Rebonato (1999c).

the forward rate resetting at time T_n and a strike, K, provided that none of a pre-chosen set of forward rates resets, at its own expiry, T_i, $i \leq n$, below a barrier level, H

$$\text{Payoff}_{(T_{n+1})} = [f_n(T_n, T_n) - K]\mathbf{1}_{\{f(T_i, T_i) > H, \ i=1,2,...,n\}}.$$

In this expression the symbol $\mathbf{1}_{\{\text{condition}\}}$ denotes the indicator function, which assumes a value of unity if the condition in the subscripted curly bracket is satisfied, and is equal to zero otherwise.

It is also important to stress the fact that type-1 (a or b) instruments are always obligation-type products, that is, their payoffs are contractually stipulated to depend on the realizations of screen-observable market quantities, and their exercise strategy does not depend on the future value of a discounted expectation. As a consequence, they lend themselves particularly well to evaluation via forward induction (i.e., in practice, a Monte Carlo simulation). The payoffs of path-dependent compound-option (type-4) instruments, on the other hand, can additionally depend on a complex exercise strategy, and their evaluation via Monte Carlo techniques, while still possible, is considerably more complex (see later). Multi-callable capped floating-rate notes are a typical example of this class of instruments.

In concluding the analysis of type-1 products, it is important to recall that their payoffs, whether decomposed or not, only depend on the realizations of the forward rates on a finite set of observation points. Therefore, one can say that their payoffs are measurable with respect to the natural filtration generated by the realizations of the forward rates at the times of the price-sensitive events – which coincide with the reset dates of the spanning forward rates. If one denoted this filtration by $\mathcal{F}$, one can therefore concisely say that the payoff of type-1 products is $\mathcal{F}$-measurable.

4.1.3 Single-Look (Type-2) Options (Simple or Compound)

Moving to type-2 products, that is, to simple or compound single-look options, only one price-sensitive event exists, and the payoff is determined by a condition that can be determined given the knowledge of the values of a set of spanning forward rates at a single future time T_{exp}. (The reset of the first forward rate in the set will often, but need not, coincide with the time T_{exp}. In either case, it is important to notice that at most one forward rate will have come to its own reset by time T_{exp}.) The simplest example is the evaluation of a European swaption in a forward-rate-based implementation of the LIBOR market model. In this case, the value of its payoff at time T_{exp} is given by

$$\text{NVP(Payoff)} = (\text{SR} - K)^+ A(T_{\text{exp}}, T_{\text{exp}+n}),$$

$$\text{SR} = \frac{B(T_{\text{exp}}, T_{\text{exp}}) - B(T_{\text{exp}}, T_{\text{exp}+n})}{\sum_{k=1}^{n} B(T_{\text{exp}}, T_{\text{exp}+k})\tau},$$

$$B(T_{\exp}, T_{\exp+j}) = \prod_{k=0}^{j-1} \frac{1}{[1 + f(T_{\exp}, T_{\exp+k}, T_{\exp+k+1})\tau]},$$

$$A(T_{\exp}, T_{\exp+n}) = \sum_{k=1}^{n} B(T_{\exp}, T_{\exp+k})\tau,$$

where SR indicates the swap rate resetting at time $T_{\exp}$, $A(T_{\exp}, T_{\exp+n})$ is the associated annuity, $B(T_{\exp}, T_{\exp+j})$ is the price at time $T_{\exp}$ of a zero-coupon bond expiring j periods thereafter, and $f(T_{\exp}, T_{\exp+k}, T_{\exp+k+1})$ is the value at time $T_{\exp}$ of the forward rate that resets k periods after time $T_{\exp}$ and pays one period after that. From these expressions one can easily see that the payoff is simply a function of the realizations of a set of forward rates at the time $T_{\exp}$ of the price-sensitive event, and that, conditional on a particular realization of the yield curve having been obtained, the corresponding payoff is independent of the future volatility. In particular, no expectations have to be calculated once time $T_{\exp}$ has been reached, and this grants this type of product the name of 'single-look simple'.

A second example of single-look option (type-2 payoff), but of the compound variety, is a caption. This instrument gives the right to purchase at time $T_{\exp}$ an n-period cap struck at K (the cap or rate strike) for £X (the money strike). The payoff at time $T_{\exp}$ is therefore

$$\text{Payoff}(T_{\exp}) = [\text{CAP}(T_{\overline{\exp}}) - X]^+,$$

$$\text{CAP}(T_{\exp}) = \sum_{k=1}^{n} \text{Caplet}_k(T_{\exp}),$$

$$\text{Caplet}_k(T_{\exp}) = [\tilde{f}_k(T_{\exp})N(h_{1,k}) - KN(h_{2,k})]B(T_{\exp}, T_{k+1}),$$

$$h_{1,k} = \frac{\ln(\tilde{f}_k/K) + \frac{1}{2}v_k}{\sqrt{v_k}},$$

$$h_{2,k} = \frac{\ln(\tilde{f}_k/K) - \frac{1}{2}v_k}{\sqrt{v_k}},$$

$$v_k = \int_{T_{\exp}}^{T_k} \sigma_k(u)^2 \, \mathrm{d}u \qquad T_k \geq T_{\exp},$$

where $\sigma_k(u)$ is the instantaneous volatility of the kth forward rate at time u, with $T_{\exp} \leq u \leq T_k$, $\tilde{f}_k(T_{\exp})$ is the drift-adjusted realization of the kth forward rate in the measure associated with the chosen numeraire (see Chapter 5) and $B(T_{\exp}, T_{k+1})$ is the value at time $T_{\exp}$ of a discount bond maturing at the payment time of the kth forward rate. In order to price this product, the yield curve must be evolved to the time of the price-sensitive event, that is, the caption expiry. This could be done exactly and in a single step if the forward rate were exactly jointly log-normal. This is not the case, but in Chapter 5 I shall show how this evolution can still be achieved in a single step even if the process of the forward rates is not jointly log-normal. Once the curve has been evolved to time T_{exp}, the trader will have to decide, given the particular realization of the forward rates, whether it will be more valuable to exercise the option (i.e., to pay £X to buy the underlying cap) or to let it lapse. To make this decision, the money-strike X will have to be compared with the sum of the time-T_{exp} conditional expected values of the payoffs from the caplets. These, in turn, can be evaluated, given the yield curve and the residual variances v_k, by applying the Black formula to each of the forward rates $f_k(T_{\text{exp}})$ to obtain (as shown in the formulas above) the value of the cap.

The important difference to notice in this second example is that the evaluation of the price at time T_{exp} of the various caplets will require knowledge not only of the forward rates, but also of their future root-mean-square volatility (linked to the quantity v_k above). Given the assumption of deterministic volatilities enforced in the standard LIBOR market model, however, these future quantities are not only independent of the realization of the yield curve, but also known exactly, and therefore computable, at time zero (T_0). The payoff is therefore again measurable with respect to the filtration generated by the realizations of the forward rates at the time of the single price-sensitive event, T_{exp}. If we call this forward-rate-generated filtration $\mathcal{F}_{T_{\text{exp}}}$, we can simply say that the payoff is $\mathcal{F}_{T_{\text{exp}}}$-measurable. Note carefully, however, that, unlike the European-swaption example presented above, this would no longer have been the case if we had been dealing with a stochastic-volatility model (see Chapter 12).

Non-trivial single-look products share the important feature that, by expiry time, T_{exp}, at most one of the forward rates will have come to its own expiry. When this is the case, the market-related information accessible from the caplet prices is not sufficient to specify how much of the total variance has been 'used up' by the non-resetting forward rates by time T_{exp}. Therefore different allocations of the instantaneous volatilities over the life of each forward rate will give rise to different root-mean-square volatilities from time T_0 (today) to time T_{exp}. This will be true even if these different ways of apportioning volatility are all compatible with the same market-visible caplet prices (i.e., with the Black implied volatilities).

In turn, each of the different market-compatible specifications of the volatility give rise to different future evolutions of the model term structure of volatilities. One of the central messages of this book is that monitoring the model-implied evolution of this quantity is one of the most important tools in assessing the quality of a given implementation of the LIBOR market model (see, e.g., Chapters 6, 9 and 10). It is therefore easy to see how the pricing of single-look products is intimately linked to one of the most crucial aspects of the calibration of the modern pricing framework.

4.1.4 Multi-Look Compound (Type-3) Products

The next important class of products that can be valued within the LIBOR-market-model framework are multi-look compound options (type 3), the prime example of which are Bermudan swaptions. In this case a set of price-sensitive events are pre-specified, which are made to coincide with the reset times of a set of forward or swap rates. On these dates, $\{T_i\}$, an exercise condition will have to be examined, much as in the case of the single-look compound option above. As in the case of the caption, in fact, and unlike the case of the European swaption discussed above, this exercise condition will depend not only simply on the time-T_i realization of the discrete yield curve (i.e., on the collection of forward rates $f_k(T_i)$), but also on a suitable expectation (i.e., on residual volatilities). It is also easy to see that, if there is more than one exercise opportunity, these expectations will be nested, and the resulting options will be of compound nature: in other terms, the expectations not just of payoffs, as in the case of a caption, but of functions of payoffs and of further expectations will have to be computed.

The fact that in the multi-look compound case the expectation operator has as its argument a function of the realization of the yield curve and a discounted expectation has a significant computational impact. The numerical evaluation of an expectation, in fact, typically requires the sampling of the integrand function over a significant number of points. In order to avoid an exponential explosion of the number of function evaluations, it is essential that the future yield curves should recombine at least in a suitably high-dimensional space. This recombination, however, cannot be exactly achieved within the framework of the standard LIBOR-market-model approach, because the drift terms, containing as they do the forward rates, are not just time- but also state-dependent.

One possible route to circumvent the problem is to force the recombination to take place (Hunt, Kennedy and Pelsser 2000). Another is to 'bite the bullet' and use non-recombining ('bushy') trees (Jaeckel 2000). Skillful implementations currently allow the computation of 20 steps (i.e., of a 19-fold compound option) with a five-factor implementation of the LIBOR market model.[4] An alternative way to tackle the problem is to cast it in terms of the estimation of the exercise boundary for the compound option. If the exercise boundary were known, compound-option products could still be valued using forward induction (in practice, Monte Carlo simulations), with the proviso that the evolution of the yield curve should be stopped upon breaching the boundary. Furthermore, and crucially for the measurability of the payoff, since the exercise opportunities are limited to a finite number of reset times and are not continuous, the boundary itself is simply defined, along the time axis, on a finite number of price-sensitive events (the discrete exercise oppor-

---

[4]The bushy-tree technology, when pushed to these extremes, is extremely time-consuming, and cannot be used for front-office pricing applications. It is, however, very useful for benchmarking purposes.

tunities). On the other hand, at the time of each price-sensitive event, the exercise boundary traces, in forward-rate space, a continuous hypersurface (e.g., point, curve or surface, respectively in one, two or three dimensions). This situation can be profitably contrasted with the structure of the exercise boundary in the case of, say, an American stock option, which is infinitely finer in the time dimension, but much simpler – a single point on the continuous time axis – in the dimension of the underlying. As for the estimation of this free (exercise) boundary, the underlying idea is that the value of the Bermudan swaption can be obtained via a variational approach, and will be given by the supremum (maximum value) over all the possible previsible[5] exercise strategies.

The main difficulty with this approach is that the 'boundary' is not a simple line in time-underlying space, but a hypersurface, whose dimensionality depends on the number of nested expectations. This can be seen more clearly by considering again the case of a Bermudan swaption: if there were only one exercise opportunity for each realization of the world (the Bermudan is therefore degenerate and coincides with a European swaption), the value of a single forward or swap rate (i.e., a 'point') would be sufficient to determine whether the option should be exercised or not. If there were two exercise opportunities, at the penultimate the trader would have to choose whether the intrinsic value (if positive) is worth more than the expectation of the future payoff. The early exercise boundary would therefore be a function of the realization of two forward or swap rates, and therefore traces a line in two-dimensional space. At the earlier exercise opportunity, the intrinsic value, which will have to be compared with the expectation of the previous payoff, will be a function of these forward rates. The exercise boundary is now a two-dimensional surface in the three-dimensional space spanned by the three forward or swap rates; and so on (see the exercise below).

EXERCISE 4.2 *Consider a Bermudan swaption where the exercise opportunities are located at every reset of the underlying swap. Write the exercise condition as the maximum of the intrinsic value and of (when appropriate, nested) expectations for the last, the second-to-last, the third to-last exercise opportunities. Identify clearly in each case on which variables (i.e., forward rates) the exercise opportunities depend. How can one tackle the case of a two-exercise Bermudan swaption without carrying out any numerical expectation? Making use of this result, for two model yield curves of your choice (perhaps, one upward- and one downward-sloping), construct a spreadsheet and draw the early exercise boundary as a function of two suitable variables of your choice (not necessarily two forward rates). Discuss the shape of the exercise boundary as a function*

---

[5]The previsibility condition is essential: The strategy, for instance, that follows a yield-curve path up to the final maturity in order to decide whether exercise should have taken place at an earlier time (perfect foresight) clearly violates this condition, and provides a (wide) upper bound to the true Bermudan value. This non-previsible strategy can, nonetheless, be of assistance in providing a much tighter upper bound when coupled with a contra-variate technique as suggested, in a different context, by Rogers (2000).

of the shape of the yield curve, the nature of the swaption (payer or receiver) and the level of the strike.

Since the dimensionality of the problem quickly increases with the number of exercise opportunities, the 'name of the game', when it comes to estimating the early exercise boundary in the context of the LIBOR-market-model approach, is therefore to map (collapse) the true (unknown) high-dimension boundary onto the realizations of a much smaller number (two, or, sometimes, one) representative proxy variables. Some of the popular attacks to the problem along these or related lines are to be found, for example, in Broadie and Glasserman (1997), Longstaff and Schwartz (1998), Andersen (1999), Jaeckel (2000), Broadie (2002), Haug and Kogan (2000) and Rogers (2000).

Whatever the (considerable) computational difficulties connected with the determination of the exercise boundary, the fact that, along the time axis, the latter only needs defining at the times of the price-sensitive events implies that, once again, no information about the yield curve in between the price-sensitive events affects the value of the multi-look compound option. As for the various expectations taken at the time of a generic price-sensitive event T_i, they will simply involve future residual volatilities (computable today in a deterministic-volatility setting) and future payoffs. The latter are, in turn, also fully determined by the realizations at times T_j $(j > i)$ of the discrete yield curves. Therefore, once again, the payoff of multi-look compound derivatives will still be $\mathcal{F}_T$-measurable (where $\mathcal{F}_T$ is, as in type 1, the filtration generated by the discrete forward rates observed at the times of the n price-sensitive events). Note carefully that this would no longer be the case if stochastic volatilities were used (see Chapter 12).

4.1.5 Path-Dependent Compound (Type-4) Products

Finally, it is easy to see that type-4 products share the features of path-dependent and multi-look compound options. A typical example is a multi-callable ratchet capped floater.[6] The stochastic nature of the cap strike brings about the path dependence: in order to know what the payment is today, it is not enough to know today's LIBOR reset – one also needs to know where it reset, say, six months ago. If the note is callable, the issuer has the option to redeem it at par. If it is multi-callable, this option is clearly compound.

Because of the contemporaneous presence of compound and path-dependent features, the technique of choice is forward induction (Monte Carlo) coupled with an estimate of the early exercise boundary. Once this quantity has been approximated, either the long- or the very-long-jump techniques can be applied.

---

[6]A floater is a note that pays (a function of) LIBOR. When it is capped, the coupon payment cannot exceed a certain level. If the cap is of 'ratchet' or 'cliquet' nature, this level is not deterministic, but it is a function of the LIBOR reset that occurred at the time of the previous coupon.

4.1.6 Comments on the Measurability of the Payoff

For all the products the LIBOR market model is designed to price, the filtration with respect to which their payoffs are measurable is infinitely coarser than the filtration that would be generated if the payoff were affected by the realizations of the forward rates over however small a continuous interval: the user of the model can make use of a handful of numbers (the values of the forward rates at the times of the price-sensitive events) to describe fully a path realization, or a type-3 or type-4 condition, not just as an approximation motivated by numerical convenience, but without any loss of generality. This situation should be contrasted with the traditional short-rate models (which implicitly assume the existence of a continuously compounded money-market account). In this latter case, when the same problem is mapped onto a lattice (recombining or not), the 'real' filtration describing the evolution of the *instantaneous* short rate can only be approximated by the (much larger) number of values assumed by the short rate at the various nodes along the path. In other words, no matter how many nodes one takes, in the case of short-rate models this description will always be approximate. Therefore, if the trader 'simply' wants to price a type 1–4 product, such a high-resolution description is, at the same time, approximate and unnecessarily fine. This is indeed one of the reasons why I have chosen to present a version of the LIBOR market model in which the construction of a continuously compounded money-market account has been avoided. In other words, the choice of the set-up I have presented can be regarded as providing the most apt and, as I shall show below, the easiest-to-work-with set of 'coordinates' for the types of problem at hand.

4.1.7 Common Features of the Payoffs

By means of the analysis presented above, we have reached the important conclusion that all the products that can be valued within a standard LIBOR-market-model framework share the common feature of having payoffs measurable with respect to the natural filtration generated by the discrete forward rates on a discrete set of dates (i.e., the times of the price-sensitive events). On the other hand, since we assume to know the stochastic differential equations governing the forward rates themselves (Equations (3.6) and (3.10)), we implicitly know how to construct (as a last resort, numerically, using a finely stepped Monte Carlo evolution) the individual (marginal) and joint probability densities of all the forward rates at the times of the price-sensitive events. More strongly, if the drifts of the forward rates, which we have not determined yet, depended purely on time (and not on the forward rates themselves), we would immediately know how to sample from these joint densities, since the logarithms of the forward rates would be distributed according to a joint normal law (see Sections 3.1 and 3.2). When it comes to the sampling from these joint densities, depending on the dimensionality and nature of the problem, we might still choose to effect it by using a Monte Carlo simulation, or we might prefer to carry out an explicit analytic integration. In either case, however, all these joint distributions would be fully described by the $O(N)$ expectations and the $O(N^2)$ integrated covariances at the time of each price-sensitive event.

With these considerations in mind, the classification of the payoffs presented above can be made use of together with the covariance matrices defined in the previous chapter in order to present the computationally most efficient way to tackle the various payoffs. How this task can be accomplished is presented below by introducing as a Case Study the pricing of a trigger swap and of a Bermudan swaption. The same Case Study will also bring into focus with a detailed explicit calculation the procedure based on the manipulations of the matrices $\mathbf{C}$ and $\mathbf{TOTC}$ described in Chapter 3.

4.2 Case Study: Pricing in a Three-Forward-Rate, Two-Factor World

4.2.1 Specification of the Dynamics

Let us describe the dynamics of a yield curve made up of three spanning forward rates, f_1, f_2 and f_3, in terms of a two-factor LIBOR market model. For the purpose of this discussion, I shall concentrate on the stochastic part of the evolution, and, to keep the notation as light as possible, I shall set all the drifts to zero, that is, I will assume that all three forward rates are simultaneously exponential martingales for the same choice of numeraire (which, as we know from Chapter 2, is impossible). As far as the evaluation of the covariance elements is concerned, we also know that a stochastic or time-dependent drift term would make no difference, and the results presented in this section are therefore not affected by this choice.

I shall deal with the evolution of this yield curve over three periods, each spanning two consecutive price-sensitive events. In other terms, I shall carry out three 'long jumps' to events p, $1 \leq p \leq 3$, occurring at time T_p. I will describe the three forward rates in terms of a two-factor model, and use the third formulation presented in Chapter 3, that is, I shall write

$$\frac{\mathrm{d}f_i}{f_i} = \sigma_i(t)[b_{i1}\,\mathrm{d}z_1(t) + b_{i2}\,\mathrm{d}z_2(t)] \qquad 1 \leq i \leq 3. \tag{4.2}$$

In order to keep the treatment as simple as possible, I shall assume volatilities and correlations piecewise constant over each time interval, and I will therefore omit explicit time dependence. Integrals of the type

$$\int_{T_p}^{T_{p+1}} \sigma_i(u)\sigma_j(u)\rho_{ij}(u)\,\mathrm{d}u \qquad 1 \leq i \leq 3,\ 1 \leq j \leq 3$$

therefore become simply equal to

$$\sigma_i(p)\sigma_j(p)\rho_{ij}(p)\Delta T_p \qquad 1 \le p \le 3,$$

and, to lighten the notation further, each ΔT_p is taken to be equal to one year.

4.2.2 The Inputs

I shall assume that the (piecewise constant) instantaneous volatilities of the three forward rates are given by

$$\sigma_1(1) = 20.50\%,$$
$$\sigma_2(1) = 19.50\%,$$
$$\sigma_3(1) = 18.50\%,$$
$$\sigma_2(2) = 19.25\%,$$
$$\sigma_3(2) = 18.25\%,$$
$$\sigma_3(3) = 18.00\%.$$

Notice that, as the various price-sensitive events occur, one forward rate after the other will reset, and will therefore be lost to the set of forward rates still 'alive'. Therefore at most three factors could describe the yield curve over the first step, at most two over the second, and one over the third. I then define as 'true' an exogenous correlation matrix, which has perhaps been obtained via econometric estimation, or by some 'implied' procedure (such as the one suggested by Schoenmakers and Coffey 2000, and described in Chapter 7): it is the correlation matrix we would like the model to be able to reproduce, and it will be referred to as the 'target' or 'true' correlation. The same terminology will be applied to the covariance matrices. These 'true' correlation matrices among the different forward rates are assumed to be given by

$$\begin{pmatrix} 1 & 0.904 & 0.818 \\ 0.904 & 1 & 0.904 \\ 0.818 & 0.904 & 1 \end{pmatrix}$$

$$\begin{pmatrix} 1 & 0.886 \\ 0.886 & 1 \end{pmatrix}$$

from time T_0 to time T_1 and from time T_1 to time T_2, respectively (from time T_2 to time T_3 there is only one forward rate still to reset, and therefore the correlation matrix is obviously degenerate with $\rho_{33} = 1$). This first 3×3 'true' correlation matrix will not be recoverable exactly because only two factors have been chosen to describe the dynamics of the three forward rates (see the discussion in Section 7.3).

4.2.3 Construction of the 'True' and Model Covariance Matrices

With these input data and working assumptions, one can begin to construct the 'true' covariance matrices $C(i, j, 1)$, $C(i, j, 2)$ and the degenerate

$C(i, j, 3)$. These are shown below:

$$\begin{pmatrix} 0.042 & 0.036 & 0.031 \\ 0.036 & 0.038 & 0.032 \\ 0.031 & 0.032 & 0.034 \end{pmatrix} = C(i, j, 1),$$

$$\begin{pmatrix} 0.037 & 0.031 \\ 0.031 & 0.033 \end{pmatrix} = C(i, j, 2),$$

$$0.032 = C(i, j, 3).$$

The 'true' matrix **TOTC** [obtained by adding, element by element, the matrices $C(i, j, 1)$, $C(i, j, 2)$ and $C(1, j, 3)$ as explained in Equation (3.19)] is also shown below:

$$\begin{pmatrix} 0.042 & 0.036 & 0.031 \\ 0.036 & 0.075 & 0.063 \\ 0.031 & 0.063 & 0.099 \end{pmatrix} = \textbf{TOTC}.$$

The caplet prices associated with the individual forward rates will be correctly recovered if the instantaneous volatilities are chosen to have a root-mean-square volatility equal to the desired Black implied volatility, and if the coefficients $\{b_{ij}\}$ are chosen such that the sum over factors of their squares adds up to 1, that is, $\sum_{j=1}^{2} b_{ij}^2 = 1$. Since we have chosen to use just two factors, this second condition is easily satisfied for any couplet of real numbers θ_1 and θ_2 as long as the 3×2 and 2×2 matrices $\{\textbf{b}\}$ at time T_1 and T_2 are chosen to be given by

$$\begin{pmatrix} b_{11}(T_1) = \sin\theta_1(T_1) & b_{12}(T_1) = \cos\theta_1(T_1) \\ b_{21}(T_1) = \sin\theta_2(T_1) & b_{22}(T_1) = \cos\theta_2(T_1) \\ b_{31}(T_1) = \sin\theta_3(T_1) & b_{32}(T_1) = \cos\theta_3(T_1) \end{pmatrix}$$

and

$$\begin{pmatrix} b_{21}(T_2) = \sin\theta_2(T_2) & b_{22}(T_2) = \cos\theta_2(T_2) \\ b_{31}(T_2) = \sin\theta_3(T_2) & b_{32}(T_2) = \cos\theta_3(T_2) \end{pmatrix}$$

respectively. This is certainly true because, for any θ, $\sin(\theta)^2 + \cos(\theta)^2 = 1$. (At time T_3 there is only one forward rate still alive, and therefore one factor can perfectly describe the evolution of the degenerate 'yield curve' over the next step. In other terms, one can simply choose $b_{31}(T_3) = 1$, $b_{32}(T_3) = 0$.) The angles $\{\theta\}$, arbitrarily chosen for this example, the resulting coefficients $\{\textbf{b}\}$ and the products $\tilde{b}_{ij} = \sigma_i(T_k)b_{ij}(T_k)$ are shown below:

$\theta(T_1)$	$\sin(\theta_{T_1})$	$\cos(\theta_{T_1})$	$\tilde{b}_{i1}(T_1)$	$\tilde{b}_{i2}(T_1)$
0.809	0.724	0.689	0.148	0.141
0.692	0.638	0.769	0.124	0.150
0.024	0.024	0.999	0.004	0.184

$\theta(T_2)$	$\sin(\theta_{T_2})$	$\cos(\theta_{T_2})$	$\tilde{b}_{i1}(T_2)$	$\tilde{b}_{i2}(T_2)$
0.425	0.412	0.910	0.079	0.175
0.777	0.701	0.712	0.128	0.130

Once these $\tilde{b}$ matrices have been built, one can generate the model co-variance matrix simply by carrying out the matrix multiplication $\tilde{b}\tilde{b}^T$ (where $\tilde{b}^T$ indicates the transpose of $\tilde{b}$). The result for times T_1 and T_2 are shown below:

$$\begin{pmatrix} 0.042 & 0.039 & 0.026 \\ 0.039 & 0.038 & 0.028 \\ 0.026 & 0.028 & 0.034 \end{pmatrix} = \sigma b(\sigma b)^T(T_1)$$

$$\begin{pmatrix} 0.037 & 0.032 \\ 0.032 & 0.033 \end{pmatrix} = \sigma b(\sigma b)^T(T_2).$$

These matrices should be compared with the 'true' matrices $C(i,j,1)$ and $C(i,j,2)$, displayed above. Notice, in particular, how the diagonal elements, linked to the variance of the individual forward rates, coincide, as they should, in the two cases, but the off-diagonal elements do not because of the reduced dimensionality of the model.

4.2.4 Orthogonalization of the Covariance Matrices

It is instructive to carry out an orthogonalization (principal component analysis) at time T_1 both of the 'true' matrix $C(i,j,1)$ and of the model co-variance matrix, which is given by $\tilde{b}\tilde{b}^T$. The resulting eigenvectors and eigenvalues are shown below (in both cases, the **bold** top row contains the eigenvalues and the columns below the corresponding eigenvectors) and in Figure 4.1:

- Orthogonalization of the true covariance matrix

Eig$_1$	Eig$_2$	Eig$_3$
0.1049	**0.006**	**0.002**
0.603	0.704	−0.371
0.588	−0.080	0.804
0.537	−0.704	−0.463

- Orthogonalization of the model covariance matrix

Eig$_1$	Eig$_2$	Eig$_3$
0.1012	**0.012**	**0.000**
0.621	0.459	−0.634
0.604	0.233	0.761
0.497	−0.856	−0.133

As expected, the orthogonalization of the model $\tilde{b}\tilde{b}^T$ matrix, which only has rank 2, produces only two distinct non-zero eigenvalues. No meaning should therefore be attributed to the third eigenvector. Note also, for the

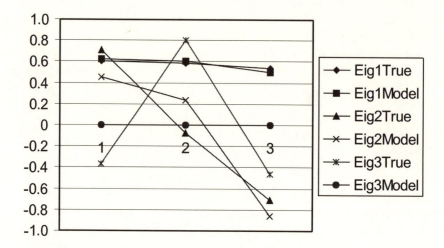

Figure 4.1   *The three eigenvectors obtained by orthogonalization of the true covariance matrix (curves labelled 'Eig1True', 'Eig2True' and 'Eig3True') and the two eigenvectors ('Eig1Model' and 'Eig2Model') from the orthogonalization of the model covariance matrix. In the 'model' case the eigenvalue associated with the third eigenvector is zero (because the rank of the model covariance matrix is 2); the third eigenvector (curve labelled 'Eig3Model') has therefore been arbitrarily set to zero. Notice the qualitative similarity between the shapes of the first two eigenvectors.*

purpose of future comparison, that the 'true' and 'model' second eigenvectors are qualitatively similar, but appreciably different.

4.2.5 First Application: a Bermudan Swaption

Having constructed these matrices, one can then proceed to the Monte Carlo evolution of the yield curve by following several distinct procedures, whose suitability depends on the type of payoff. Let us consider first the case when the nature of the security is such that, in order to evaluate the payoff, one needs to sample from the joint distribution of the three forward rates at time T_1, from the joint distribution of forward rates f_2 and f_3 at time T_2, and from the univariate distribution of the third forward rate at time T_3. One such payoff could be, for instance, that of a three-period Bermudan swaption. The 'brute-force' approach required to obtain a single realization of the world would entail evolving three forward rates over the first step using Equation (??), two forward rates (f_2 and f_3) over the second step, using the same equation with the appropriate coefficients, and one forward rate (f_3) over the last step. This would require six moves altogether, and the drawing of five $(2 + 2 + 1)$ independent normal variates.

The alternative, and conceptually totally equivalent, procedure would be to construct the three model covariance matrices at times T_1, T_2 and T_3 (the latter being degenerate), orthogonalize them, and obtain the corresponding eigenvalues and eigenvectors, as shown before. There would be two non-zero eigenvalues for the first and second steps, and one for the third. To create one realization of the world, one could then construct Monte Carlo evolutions of the yield curve by drawing, just as in the case of the 'brute-force' approach, five independent normal variates (two to shock the two orthogonal factors that move the three forward rates over the first step (T_0 to T_1), two more to move forward rates f_2 and f_3 from time T_1 to time T_2, and the last to move forward rate f_3 over the last step). As in the 'brute-force' case, six moves would be required per path (i.e., in order to carry out a single sampling from one trivariate distribution, one bivariate distribution and one univariate distribution). A very large number of these realizations of the yield curve have to be drawn following any of the equivalent procedures outlined in Section 4.1 in order to estimate the early exercise boundary, or the required expectations.

4.2.6 A Second Application: a Multi-Look Trigger Swap

In the case of a type-3 or a type-4 payoff, the building of the matrices $\mathbf{C}$ and $\mathbf{TOTC}$ therefore provides an arguably more 'elegant', but otherwise totally equivalent, approach to the 'brute-force case'. Where the building of the matrix $\mathbf{TOTC}$ acquires much greater relevance, however, is the case of path-dependent securities of type 1a, that is, such that the payoff only depends on the joint realizations of the forward rates at their own reset times. Consider, again, in fact, the case of, say, a multi-look trigger swap[7] (where the notional of the FRA resetting at time T_n depends on the resets of forward rates f_1, f_2, ..., f_{n-1}, f_n). In this case, the evaluation of the payoff can be arrived at much more efficiently by manipulating the matrix $\mathbf{TOTC}$. To see how this can be done, note first of all that, when it comes to the true and model total covariance matrices, $\mathbf{TOTC}_{\text{true}}$ and $\mathbf{TOTC}_{\text{model}}$, respectively, their orthogonalization will produce three distinct eigenvalues in both cases, as shown below and in Figure 4.2, even if the model $\mathbf{TOTC}_{\text{model}}$ matrix was built from marginal covariance matrices obtained from a two-factor description of the yield-curve dynamics, and therefore of ranks 2, 2 and 1:

$$\begin{pmatrix} 0.042 & 0.039 & 0.026 \\ 0.039 & 0.075 & 0.061 \\ 0.026 & 0.061 & 0.099 \end{pmatrix} = \mathbf{TOTC}_{\text{model}}$$

$$\begin{pmatrix} 0.042 & 0.036 & 0.031 \\ 0.036 & 0.075 & 0.063 \\ 0.031 & 0.063 & 0.099 \end{pmatrix} = \mathbf{TOTC}_{\text{true}}$$

[7]For the purpose of this discussion I shall assume that the payoff has been decomposed as explained in Section 4.1.2.

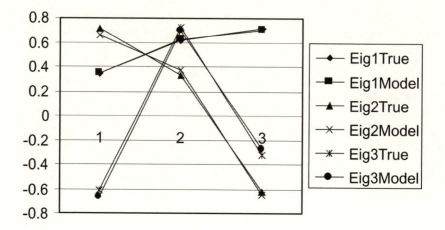

Figure 4.2   *The three eigenvectors obtained by orthogonalization of the true covariance matrix (curves labelled 'Eig1True', 'Eig1True' and 'Eig1True') and of the model ('Eig1Model', 'Eig2Model' and 'Eig3Model') covariance matrix. Notice the strong similarity, not only in the overall shapes, but also in the numerical values) between the two solutions.*

- True eigenvalues and eigenvectors

Eig_1	Eig_2	Eig_3
0.1698	**0.031**	**0.015**
0.345	0.706	−0.617
0.611	0.329	0.719
0.711	−0.626	−0.318

- Model eigenvalues and eigenvectors

Eig_1	Eig_2	Eig_3
0.1670	**0.037**	**0.012**
0.347	0.659	−0.666
0.619	0.372	0.691
0.704	−0.653	−0.278

EXERCISE 4.3 *Explain why three distinct, non-zero eigenvalues have been obtained in this case, despite the fact that only two Brownian shocks affect the yield curve. Compare the closeness of the 'True' and 'Model' second eigenvectors in Figures 4.1 and 4.2. Why is the match between the 'True' and 'Model' eigenvectors so much closer in the case to which Figure 4.2 refers? How would you choose the barriers and strikes of a multi-look trigger swap so that it 'resembles' as much as possible a given Bermudan swaption? (The discussion in Rebonato (1998, Sections 2.3 and 2.4) can be of help to answer this question.) One can empirically observe that, for most yield curves, a well-chosen set of trigger levels produces values for a multi-look trigger swap very similar to the corresponding Bermudan. Remembering that Figure 4.1 refers to a 'Bermudan-swaption-like' product,*

and Figure 4.2 to a 'multi-look-trigger-swap-like' product, what does this tell you about what is 'left behind' when approximating the more complex product (i.e., the Bermudan swaption) by the simpler one (i.e., the trigger swap)?

4.2.7 The Very-Long-Jump Procedure

Several interesting features about these results are worth noticing: First of all, as required, the elements on the main diagonal for the model and true **TOTC** matrices (linked to the values of the forward rates at their own reset times) are the same, but the off-diagonal elements are not. Furthermore, the orthogonalization procedure produces a similar partitioning of the total variability across the different modes of deformation, as can be appreciated by the relative magnitude of the eigenvalues. Finally, both the numerical values and the qualitative shape of the eigenvectors are very similar for the true and model cases (see Figure 4.2). One has therefore good reasons to believe that, for this type of product, the evolution of the forward rates obtained by using the eigenvalues and eigenvectors of the model **TOTC**$_{model}$ matrix would retain the most relevant (for a type-1a product!) features of the 'true' evolution of the yield curve, as embodied by the matrix **TOTC**$_{true}$.

Why is using the **TOTC** matrix so useful? Instead of carrying out a three-step evolution of the yield curve using the eigenvalues and eigenvectors of the marginal covariance matrices, let us carry out a single very-long-jump out to time T_3 for all the forward rates (i.e., even for those which reset before T_3) with

$$\frac{\mathrm{d}f_i}{f_i} = \sum_{j=1}^{3} \sqrt{\lambda_j}\, a_{ij} Z_j \sqrt{T_3}, \qquad (4.3)$$

with λ_j and a_{ij} equal to the eigenvectors and eigenvalues of the real symmetric matrix **TOTC**, respectively. Recall that, despite the fact that only *two* factors have been assumed to shock the yield curve, the orthogonalization of **TOTC**$_{model}$ gives rise to *three* distinct eigenvalues. Therefore, the summation in Equation (??) is correctly carried out over the number of distinct eigenvalues (three), and not over the number of factors (two) instantaneously moving the forward rates. By evolving the yield curve according to Equation (??), one can rest assured not only that the right univariate distribution of forward f_1 at time T_1, of forward f_2 at time T_2 and of forward f_3 at time T_3 can be recovered, but also that the correct joint probability of obtaining f_1 at time T_1, f_2 at time T_2 and f_3 at time T_3 is obtained. This is, by definition, all that is required to evaluate the payoffs of type-1a products. Note carefully, however, that one could not sample correctly, by carrying out a 'very long jump' for the three forward rates to time T_3 as outlined above, the correct joint distributions of, say, f_1, f_2 and f_3 at time T_1 and of f_2 and f_3 at time T_2 (required to evaluate the payoffs of type-1b products).

EXERCISE 4.4 *Explain why this is this case for type-1a and type-1b products.*

When the payoff therefore only depends on the joint realizations of the various forward rates at their own reset times, as in the case of a trigger swap, a single very long jump to time T_3 of the whole yield curve and the draw of just three univariate independent Gaussian random variates (one for each forward rate) is sufficient to price at the same time both the trigger FRA resetting at time T_2 (whose principal depends on the resets of f_1 at time T_1 and of f_2 at time T_2) and the trigger FRA resetting at time T_3 (whose principal depends on the resets of f_1 at time T_1, of f_2 at time T_2 and of f_3 at time T_3).

4.2.8 Dealing with Forward Rates That Have Already Reset

How this evaluation can be carried out in practice requires a bit more attention. In general, the trader will have chosen a particular numeraire. Let us assume that the discount bond maturing at time $T_3 + \tau$ was taken as the numeraire of choice. This choice of numeraire will affect the no-arbitrage drifts of the various forward rates, which, for simplicity, I have chosen to neglect in this section (the expressions for the drift terms will be explicitly obtained in the next chapter). Given these numeraire-induced drifts, the payoff of any security will be correctly priced, however, only if it is appropriately discounted using the chosen numeraire. The first payoff of the three-period trigger swap just described, however, will occur at time $T_1 + \tau$, and, similarly, the payoff of the second at time $T_2 + \tau$. Only the payoff of the third FRA in the trigger swap will occur at a time equal to the maturity of the numeraire. It is not obvious how these payoffs can be made to 'relate' to each other. This problem can be solved by 'rolling up' the payoffs occurring on the earlier dates to time $T_3 + \tau$ employing the same realization of the yield curve used to test the trigger condition. In other words, a triplet of independent Gaussian univariate random draws, Z_1, Z_2 and Z_3, used in conjunction with Equation (**??**) will produce three values f_1, f_2 and f_3 (at their own resets) consistent with the same chosen numeraire.[8] The realization of f_1 will determine whether the first FRA is dead or alive. If it is alive, it will produce a payoff at time T_1, which also depends on f_1. This payoff can then be rolled up to time $T_3 + \tau$ by multiplying by $(1 + f_2\tau)(1 + f_3\tau)$. It is crucial to stress again that the proposed procedure provides the values of all the forward rates, and therefore, in particular, of f_2 and f_3, at their own reset times. This is exactly what is needed to roll up the payoffs to time $T_3 + \tau$.

Similarly, the realizations of f_1 and f_2 will determine whether the second FRA is dead or alive. If alive, the realization of f_2 will produce a payoff at time $T_2 + \tau$, which can be rolled up to time $T_3 + \tau$ by multiplying by $(1 + f_3\tau)$.

---

[8]Notice that the expression 'consistent with the same chosen numeraire' is not a technical nicety. It means that the drifts for the various forward rates all have to be calculated under the same measure, and will, in general, have a different expression for any different choice of the numeraire (see Chapter 5).

And, finally, the realizations of f_1, f_2 and f_3 will determine the status (dead or alive) of the last FRA, and the outcome of f_3 will determine both the payoff, and its value at time $T_3 + \tau$.

Once the individual payoffs from the three FRAs have been accumulated (rolled up) to this point in time, they can be added together to produce the value of the total payoff at time $T_3 + \tau$. This can be consistently discounted by the chosen numeraire (i.e., the discount bond maturing at time $T_3 + \tau$) to obtain the present value of the whole trigger swap in correspondence of the triplet $\{Z_1, Z_2, Z_3\}$. The three realized forward rates have therefore been simultaneously used:

- to determine the status of the swap (dead or alive),

- to calculate the payoff (if any) of each FRA, and

- to roll up this payoff to the appropriate discounting time.

For the three-forward-rate yield curve under study, the valuation of any type-1a payoff therefore requires just three moves (the three forward rates over the single step from T_0 to T_3) and three independent random draws. Despite the fact that there are three price-sensitive events, the evolution to a single time (the final maturity of the swap) of the whole yield curve using the eigenvectors and eigenvalues obtained from the orthogonalization of the matrix **TOTC** provides the correct answer to the problem. As mentioned, this is only possible due to the particular, but by no means rare, nature of the payoff, which depends on the joint distribution of each forward rate on its own reset time (type 1a).

EXERCISE 4.5 *Obtain the term sheets for a variety of exotic interest-rate products, and determine which lend themselves to pricing through the 'very-long-jump' procedure just described. In particular, decide which of the following instruments lend themselves to evaluation by means of the 'very-long-jump' technique:*

- *ratchet caps (caps where the strike of the ith caplet is a function of the reset of the $(i-1)$th forward rate);*
- *ratchet caps with lifetime cap (as above, subject to the additional condition that no strike can be higher than X %);*
- *obligation-type flexi-caps;*
- *indexed-principal swaps;*
- *choice-type flexi-caps*
- *CMS caps (see footnote 13 in Section 3.3 for a brief description);*
- *callable capped FRNs;*
- *trigger swaps with the trigger condition dependent on forward rates;*
- *trigger swaps with the trigger condition dependent on swap rates.*

As mentioned in Chapter 3, in order to distinguish this important case from the more general situation, where the 'long jump' is carried out between one price-sensitive event and the next, I have dubbed this procedure,

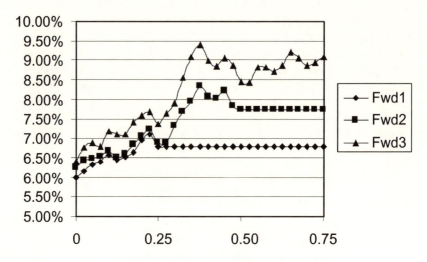

Figure 4.3   *A sample evolution of the three equivalent processes described in the text which generate the same covariance matrix as the three original forward rates.*

whereby the yield curve is evolved all the way to the last price-sensitive event, and previous payoffs rolled up to this date, the 'very-long-jump' technique.

Some readers might feel uncomfortable about the result, since it implies moving a yield curve to a point in time when some (actually, all but one) of the forward rates are no longer 'alive'. In other terms, in the example above, we were 'looking at' forward rates f_1 and f_2 after they had reset. If all the forward rates reset at the same time, the procedure would seem more obvious, since one would be simply constructing and orthogonalizing a covariance matrix for the case of three 'contemporaneous' random variables. This, however, can never be the case for spanning forward rates. Nonetheless, one can intuitively visualize the procedure described above as follows: The first and second forward rates evolve with their appropriate drifts and chosen diffusion coefficients out to their own reset, at which point both the drifts and the volatilities drop to zero. The last forward rate undergoes a 'normal' evolution out to its own expiry (see Figure 4.3). By so doing one has constructed three equivalent processes, now defined for any time between today and the last price-sensitive event, identical to the original forward rate processes up to and including their respective expiries, and such that the resultant covariance matrix coincides with the matrix **TOTC**.

4.2.9 Comparison with the 'Brute-Force' Approach

If the trader had used the 'brute-force' approach, whereby the whole yield curve is evolved, one step after the other, to each price-sensitive event, she would have had to move three forward rates from time T_0 to time T_1, for which two Gaussian draws would have been required (remember that we are using a two-factor implementation of the model). The two residual forward rates would then have had to be moved, by drawing two additional Gaussian variates. Finally, the last residual forward rate would have had to be evolved by means of an additional normal draw. In all, if the brute-force approach had been adopted, it would have been necessary to move six forward rates by means of five Gaussian draws. The 'very-long-jump' procedure, on the other hand, accomplishes the same pricing task by moving once three forward rates and drawing three independent Gaussian draws. In this particular case, the advantage over the 'brute-force' procedure might not seem substantial. This is, however, due to the very small dimensionality of the problem; the reader can perform a quick calculation in order to estimate the importance and usefulness of the approach for, say, a 10-year, quarterly trigger swap.

4.3 Overview of the Results So Far

4.3.1 Payoff Type, Numeraire and Choice of Matrix

The results obtained so far can be summarized as follows. If one goes back to the classification of payoffs provided in the previous sections, one can immediately see the following:

- Type-2 payoffs (single-look products) can always be evaluated via the (very-)long-jump procedure[9] by constructing a single matrix **TOTC** at time T_{exp}.

- Type-3 and type-4 payoffs (multiple compound options) always require the construction of as many covariance matrices (total or partial) as price-sensitive events, and therefore 'only' lend themselves to the 'long-jump' technique.

- Type-1 products (path-dependent) can be further classified into
  - type 1a, if the path-dependent conditions purely depend on the realization of quantities that have all reset at the times of the price-sensitive events (and for whose valuation a single matrix **TOTC** is sufficient, and the very-long-jump technique is appropriate); and
  - type 1b, if the path dependence entails the values of forward rates that have not reset yet at the time of the price-sensitive event (and only the long-jump procedure can be used).

As for the choice of numeraire, it will depend on the type of 'long jump' undertaken (e.g., a single jump to the final maturity, or several jumps to the

---

[9]In the case of a single-look product, there is obviously no distinction between the very-long-jump and the long-jump procedures.

intermediate price-sensitive events). More specifically, for the long-jump procedure the most 'natural' numeraire to use will be the discrete-time equivalent of the continuously compounded money-market account (which I shall therefore refer to in the following as the discretely compounded money-market account). For the very-long-jump technique, the most efficient choice of numeraire would be the discount bond maturing on the last price-sensitive event (see also the discussion in Section 5.3). Whatever the choice of numeraire, it will, in turn, uniquely determine the drift corrections to be applied to the various forward rates.

Since the drifts will in general contain the forward rates themselves, the justification of the validity of the overall procedure has not been provided yet. These topics are dealt with in the next chapter.

4.3.2 The Material So Far and the Road Ahead

Since quite a lot of material has been covered in this and previous chapters, it might be useful to retrace the conceptual path followed, and to highlight the link between the nature of the payoffs, the (total and marginal) covariance matrices, and the most efficient numerical techniques to value the various products.

The analysis has begun by observing that, in order to retain analytic tractability and positivity of interest rates, it would be desirable to model the forward rates as jointly Gaussian processes. If this were possible, the future conditional distributions would be fully described by a finite (and relatively small) number of covariance matrices and drift vectors, and closed-form solutions would be available for the evolution of the yield curve.

If the drift vector were constant or purely time-dependent, a necessary and sufficient condition for the process to be conditionally Gaussian is that its covariance matrix (and the associated quantities y_i defined in Theorem 3.1) should be deterministic. The drift condition would be (trivially) satisfied if the drifts were all zero. However, we have stated (and, for those readers who have tackled Section 2.3, we have shown) that, for a given numeraire, not all the spanning forward rates can be simultaneously log-normal martingales. Indeed, we know that one can always choose a measure (characterized by the choice of the natural payoff associated with a particular forward rate as the numeraire) under which one particular forward rate is a martingale. We also know, however, that, once the numeraire is chosen, no more than one forward rate at a time can be made drift-less. We have seen that complex products almost invariably depend on the joint dynamics of several forward rates. We have not yet explicitly evaluated the drift terms that, for a given numeraire, will affect all but one forward rate. However, let us assume for the moment that the drifts *were* purely time-dependent. If this were true, a closed-form solution would be obtainable for the evolution of the forward rate between price-sensitive events, and their joint distributions would be fully characterized by the n expectations and marginal covariance matrices $\mathbf{C}$ (see Section 3.1).

Furthermore, all the following would hold exactly:

1. The covariance matrices **C** would be useful because, once orthogonalized, they would produce eigenvalues and eigenvectors in terms of which the full evolution of all the forward rates to the very final price-sensitive event could be obtained.

2. If as many factors as spanning forward rates were retained, the orthogonalization of the matrices **C** would simply provide a description of the yield-curve dynamics equivalent to the more straightforward evolution in terms of forward-rate volatilities and correlations (Equation (3.3)). More importantly, however, it would offer a systematic approach to reducing the dimensionality of the problem whenever the trader chose to use fewer factors than forward rates. In this case the trace of the original (forward-rate) covariance matrix would still be recovered if the forward rates were evolved according to Equations (3.10) or (3.13), and the relationships

$$\sum_{i=1}^{n} \lambda_k a_{ik}^2 = \sum_{i=1}^{n} \sigma_i^2 \sum_{k=1}^{m} b_{ik}^2$$

were satisfied (see Equations (3.14) and (3.20)).

3. In addition, if the matrices **C** were constructed from instantaneous volatilities such that their root-mean-square equalled the Black implied volatility for each forward rate, then one could rest assured that the market prices of the caplets would be exactly recovered.

4. Equivalently, if the relationship

$$\sum_{k=1}^{m} b_{ik}^2 = 1$$

were satisfied, not only would the trace of the matrix be recovered, but so would be the market price of each individual caplet.

5. Any choice of possible loadings $\{b_{ik}\}$ determines a different model correlation matrix (Equation (3.9)). Only if the number of factors equals the number of spanning forward rates (i.e., only if $m = n$) can the input correlation matrix be exactly recovered, and, even in this case, this will only be true if Equation (3.14) is satisfied term by term, that is, if

$$\lambda_k a_{ik}^2 = \sigma_i^2 b_{ik}^2.$$

6. For any exotic product of type 1, 2, 3 or 4, its evaluation could always be effected using the marginal covariance matrices, **C**. Depending on the nature of its payoff, in some special but important cases, however, the total covariance matrix, **TOTC**, could be used for the purpose.

7. Since the values of the forward rates in between the price-sensitive events does not affect the payoffs, all that is required is the ability to obtain analytically, or to sample numerically, the joint distributions at the times of the price-sensitive events. I have called the procedure whereby the yield curve is evolved from one such event to the next (with the events possibly separated by several years) the 'long-jump technique'; and the technique whereby the evolution takes place all the way to the final maturity has been referred to as the 'very-long-jump' stepping.

8. If the nature of the payoff allows it (i.e., for type-1a products), I have shown that pricing by using the very-long-jump technique could provide very substantial computational savings with respect to the 'brute-force', long-jump approach. The very-long-jump procedure has been shown to be linked to the orthogonalization of the **TOTC** matrix.

9. This (very-)long-jump approach appears to have been made possible by the fact that we have imposed a log-normal distribution for the forward rates, which would seem to permit a closed-form solution for the joint (conditional) densities in terms of a deterministic covariance structure (see Section 3.1).

All these results would apply exactly if the drifts were deterministic, or, if stochastic, such that a closed-form solution for the associated stochastic differential equations was available. The last conceptual and practical step that must be undertaken in Part I is the derivation of the drifts of the forward rates. As already mentioned, it will turn out that

- the instantaneous drifts are *not* deterministic;

- *no* exact closed-form solution is available; and

- the joint distribution of the logarithms of the forward rates is *not* conditionally Gaussian.

However, I will show that it is possible to approximate the drifts as if they were (conditionally) deterministic with surprising accuracy. This result is crucial to the validity of the (very-)long-jump procedure, and, more generally, to the assumption of joint conditional normality for the forward rates which has underpinned the whole treatment. This important topic is dealt with in the next chapter.

5

Determining the No-Arbitrage Drifts of Forward Rates

I have shown in the previous chapters that the LIBOR market model is ideally suited to the evaluation of derivative products whose payoffs satisfy certain mild measurability conditions. For these products, the yield curve need only be described on a finite set of points, which correspond to the price-sensitive events (and to the payoff times). In particular, I pointed out that the evolution of a finite set of spanning forward rates, and today's value of a chosen numeraire, are all that is needed to price the payoffs above.

I have also shown (Section 3.1) that, if the set of these forward rates were exactly simultaneously log-normal, their evolution could be fully expressed in terms of a set of expectation vectors and covariance matrices. However, for this result to hold, it is necessary that the no-arbitrage drifts of the forward rates should be at most a deterministic function of time (or, if not, that a closed-form solution for the associated stochastic differential equations were available).

In this chapter I shall derive expressions for these drift terms for a variety of numeraires. I will show that, in general, the drifts unfortunately contain not only a time dependence, but also an explicit dependence on the set of the forward rates themselves, and are therefore stochastic. Since the resulting joint distribution of the logarithms of forward rates is no longer conditionally Gaussian, this might appear to invalidate most of the results obtained so far. In particular, the validity of the (very-)long-jump procedure, which has played such a central role in the set-up presented up to this point, would be jeopardized. I will show, however, that, while this is strictly correct, it is possible to introduce a very efficient numerical procedure such that the problem can still be cast (approximately, but extremely accurately) in terms of the evolution of exactly log-normal variables. All the results obtained in Chapters 3 and 4 (and, in particular, the (very-)long-jump technique, when applicable) will therefore retain their validity.

5.1 General Derivation of the Drift Terms

5.1.1 Links with the Approach in Chapter 2

For the 'fast-track' reader who decided to skip Section 2.3, I shall present in this section a self-contained derivation of the drifts of the forward rates required, for a given numeraire, to make their evolution arbitrage-free. This simplified derivation begins in the next subsection. For the more methodical reader who has gone through the mathematical treatment in Chapter 2, it is useful to link the treatment in this chapter with the development presented in the more formal setting presented earlier. To this effect, recall from Chapter 2 that the universe of assets of relevance for the problems at hand are the discrete set of bond price processes, $\{B_i(t)\}$, whose maturities coincide with the expiries and payment times of the spanning forward rates. These bond price processes were modelled in Section 2.2 in terms of strictly positive continuous semi-martingales. I have also shown that it is always possible to choose one such asset as numeraire N_i (and an associated measure Q_i) such that one particular forward rate $f_i(t)$ is a martingale under Q_i. Under this measure Q_i, however, no other forward rate will be a martingale. This is important because for non-trivial pricing problems one will in general have to work with several forward rates at the same time under a chosen numeraire-induced measure (say, Q). If $dz(t)$ is the increment of a standard Brownian motion under Q, and $dz_i(t)$ is the increment of the Q_i-standard Brownian motion in the measure under which the forward rate $f(t, T_i)$ (f_i, or $f_i(t)$, in the following for brevity) is a martingale, using Girsanov's theorem and backward induction I showed in Chapter 2 that one can write

$$df_i(t) = f_i(t)\sigma_i(t)\,dz_i(t),$$

$$z_i(t) = z(t) - \int_0^t \psi(\{\boldsymbol{\sigma}(u)\})\,du,$$

for some function $\psi(\ )$ of the deterministic forward-rate volatilities $\{\boldsymbol{\sigma}(t)\}$. It therefore follows that

$$dz_i(t) = dz(t) - \psi_i(\{\boldsymbol{\sigma}(t)\})\,dt,$$
$$\frac{df_i}{f_i} = \sigma_i(t)[dz(t) - \psi_i(\{\boldsymbol{\sigma}(t)\})\,dt].$$

The latter expression can be integrated to give

$$f_i(t) = f_i(0)\,\exp\{-\tfrac{1}{2}\int_0^t [\sigma_i(u)^2 - \psi_i(\{\boldsymbol{\sigma}(u)\})]\,du + \sigma_i(u)\,dz(u). \qquad (5.1)$$

Equation (5.1) suggests that one can interpret the Girsanov's term $\psi_i(\{\boldsymbol{\sigma}(t)\})\,dt$ as a drift adjustment that will turn the forward rate $f_i(t)$ into a Q-martingale. For this reason I will refer to this term as the drift correction to forward rate i when Q is chosen as the pricing measure (or, more briefly, as the drift correction for forward rate i, whenever the context makes the numeraire-induced measure unambiguous).

For those measures Q such that the drift correction is non-zero, the term $\psi_i(\{\sigma(t)\})$ was explicitly obtained in Section 2.2 as a function of the volatilities $\gamma(\ )$ of suitably defined forward processes. These, in turn, were shown to depend on the forward rates and on their instantaneous volatilities, and therefore the notation $\psi_i(\{\sigma(t)\})$ used above is indeed justified. See, for example, the equations below Condition 2.3' in Section 2.3. In particular, an explicit expression was obtained there for the case when the measure under which forward rate $f_i(t)$ was evolved was associated with numeraire $B(t, T_{i-1})$. The backward-induction procedure introduced in the same section (see, in particular, the treatment after Condition 2.3') then suggested how one could proceed to obtain the drift corrections for more general choices of measures or numeraires, but I stopped short of providing explicit expressions for these terms. The first task undertaken in this chapter is therefore the expression of the Girsanov's-theorem-related drift corrections in terms of directly market-accessible (or at least market-related) volatilities and correlations of forward rates, rather than the opaque volatilities of forward processes.

5.1.2 Turning Rates into Traded Assets: the Natural Payoff

The analysis to obtain the drift terms proceeds by noticing that forward rates, per se, do not belong to the universe of traded assets in the economy. In general, however, given a forward or swap rate, one can also define its natural payoff[1] as the (linear combination of) traded assets (i.e., in our universe, bonds) such that the product of the forward or swap rate and the natural payoff itself is a traded asset. Since, in general, interest rates are always defined as the ratio of two portfolios of assets,[2] it is quite simple to prove that one (portfolio of) asset(s) enjoying the properties of a natural payoff will always exist. In the case of forward and swap rates, in particular, the portfolios that define the rates are the floating and the fixed leg of a swap (of a one-period swap, i.e., an FRA, in the case of a forward rate):

$$f_i(t) = \frac{B_i(t) - B_{i+1}(t)}{B_{i+1}(t)\tau_i}, \tag{5.2}$$

$$\mathrm{SR}_i(t) = \frac{B_i(t) - B_{n_i+1}(t)}{\sum_{k=1}^{n_i} B_{k+i}(t)\tau_k}, \tag{5.3}$$

---

[1] I believe the terminology was first introduced in a narrower context by Doust (1995).

[2] Interest rates provide (annualized) returns on an investment, and the total return, that is, the quantity $(1 + \text{interest rate})$, is therefore always of the form

$$\frac{[\text{Asset price at period end}] - [\text{Asset price at period start}]}{[\text{Asset price at period start}]}.$$

where $B_i(t)$ is the value at time t of the bond price of maturity T_i, n_i is the number of periods in the ith swap, $B_i(t) - B_{i+1}(t)$ is the time-t value of the floating leg of the ith FRA, $B_i(t) - B_{n_i+1}(t)$ is the time-t value of the floating leg of the ith swap, and $B_{i+1}(t)\tau_i$ and $\sum_{k=1}^{n_i} B_{k+i}(t)\tau_k$ the time-t value of the fixed legs of the ith FRA and of the ith swap rate, respectively. (See Section 2.2 for a simple derivation of these results, or Rebonato 1998 for an extension to the cases when the equilibrium swap rates are not bullet rates – for example, amortizing swap rates.)

We know (Section 2.3) that a necessary and sufficient condition for the absence of arbitrage is that there should always exists a measure Q under which the relative prices of all (portfolios of) assets should be Q-martingales. Our strategy to find the no-arbitrage drifts for the forward rates will therefore be to convert forward rates into traded assets and to impose the martingale condition. As for the first part of this strategy, looking at Equations (5.2) and (5.3), it is clear that, if one multiplies a given forward rate by the denominator that enters its definition – which is in itself an asset – one obviously gets back another asset (or, rather, portfolio of assets), that is, the numerator. The denominator in the definition of a rate is therefore by construction the natural payoff of the rate itself. In the absence of arbitrage, it is also easy to see that the natural payoff is unique. It follows that, by its definition, the natural payoff is also the unique numeraire under whose associated measure Q the rate in question is a Q-martingale: such a measure always exists because of the assumed absence of arbitrage; it is unique because the natural payoff is unique. By the uniqueness of the natural payoff, one can also conclude that, given a measure Q under which a given forward or swap rate is a martingale, no other forward or swap rate can be simultaneously a Q-martingale.

Summarizing:

Result 1 Every forward or swap rate admits a natural payoff.

Result 2 This natural payoff is given by the denominator that defines the rate itself.

Result 3 For each (spanning) forward or swap rate the associated natural payoff is unique.

Result 4 The natural payoff is the numeraire under whose associated measure the forward or swap rate is a martingale.

Result 5 Such a numeraire is unique (to within a multiplicative constant).

Result 6 No two forward or swap rates can be simultaneously exponential martingales in the measure induced by the same numeraire.

5.1.3 A Systematic Strategy to Obtain the Drift Terms

These preliminary considerations can provide an indication of how the measure-dependent drift correction that turns an arbitrary forward rate into

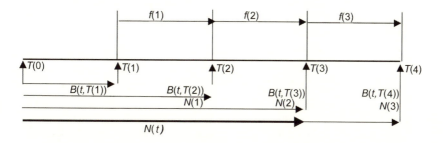

Figure 5.1 *The securities and timings of cash-flows associated with a set of three spanning forward rates. The instruments traded in the economy are the four discount bonds $B(t, T(i))$, $1 \leq i \leq 4$. $N(1)$, $N(2)$ and $N(3)$ indicate the natural payoffs of $f(1)$, $f(2)$ and $f(3)$. Note that the $(i + 1)$th bond is the ith natural payoff associated with the ith forward rate. In this example, a common numeraire, $N(t)$, was chosen for all the forward rates, namely, the natural payoff of the second forward rate. With this numeraire, forward rate $f(1)$ will have a drift given by equation (5.4), forward rate $f(2)$ will have no drift [equation (5.5)] and forward rate $f(3)$ will have a drift given by equation (5.3). Note that $f(0)$ and $N(0)$ have not been shown in this picture.*

an exponential martingale (i.e., that makes the forward rate drift-less) can be obtained. The indexing of the various forward rates, bonds and numeraires is shown in Figure 5.1 for ease of reference. After requiring that there should exist no possibility of arbitrage, the reasoning proceeds as follows:[3]

1. Consider a set of n spanning forward rates, and the associated $n + 1$ discount bonds (the available assets).

2. Choose an arbitrary numeraire, $N(t)$, from the universe of available assets.

3. Take an arbitrary forward rate, $f_i(t)$, from the set of n spanning forward rates, for which the drift correction is sought.

4. Construct the product of the chosen forward rate and its own natural payoff, $N_i(t)$, that is, $f_i(t)N_i(t)$, and remember that, by definition of natural payoff, the product thus constructed is itself a tradable asset (or, to be more precise, a portfolio of tradable assets) belonging to the universe of securities.

5. Consider the ratio $f_i(t)N_i(t)/N(t)$, and notice that, since both numerator and denominator are (portfolios of) assets, it is a relative price, $Z(t)$, as defined in Section 2.3.

---

[3]I am grateful to Noel Vailliant for first presenting to me the line of reasoning that follows in the steps below, and the formalism of the accompanying Vailliant brackets.

6. Since $Z(t)$ is a relative price, absence of arbitrage implies the existence of a measure Q_N, dependent on the choice of numeraire $N(t)$, under which Z is a martingale.

7. Write the quantity $f_i(t)N_i(t)/N(t)$ as $f_i(t)X_N(t)$, with

$$X_N(t) \equiv N_i(t)/N(t),$$

and notice that the quantity $XN(t)$ is itself a relative price (i.e., the ratio between two of the tradable assets). As such, it also is a martingale under the same measure Q_N. Furthermore, it is a forward price process as defined in Section 2.3.

8. Using the short-hand differential Ito notation, evaluate the quantity $d[f_i(t)X_N(t)]$. A straightforward calculation gives

$$d[f_i(t)X_N(t)] = d[f_i(t)]X_N(t) + f_i(t)\, d[X_N(t)] + \langle f_i, X_N \rangle,$$

where the last term is the quadratic covariation between f_i and X_N, which we know, given the working assumptions laid out in Chapter 2, to exist and to be finite and non-zero.

9. Recall from the definitions and the theorems presented in Section 2.3 that, since X is a *strictly positive* Q_N-martingale, it can be expressed as an exponential martingale with percentage volatility terms $\gamma(t, T_N, T)$, that is, it is always possible to write

$$dX(t, T_N, T)/X(t, T_N, T) = \gamma(t, T_N, T)\, dz\, Q_N(t).$$

(One should bear in mind, as usual, that, despite the notation commonly adopted in the literature and in this book, the martingale representation theorem neither requires nor ensures that the volatility $\gamma(t, T_N, T)$ should be purely a function of time.) Furthermore f_i was constructed in Chapter 2 to be strictly positive, and so is therefore the product $a \equiv f_i(t)X(t)$ (see point 10 below).

10. Since both f_i and X_N have finite quadratic variation, the quadratic covariation between f_i and X_N, that is, loosely speaking, the product $(df_i/f_i) \times (dX_N/X_N)$, is always well-defined, finite, non-zero and equal to

$$\left\langle \frac{df_i}{f_i} \frac{dX_N}{X_N} \right\rangle = f_i(t)\sigma_i(t)X_N(t)\gamma(t, T_N, T)\rho_{f_i, X_N}\, dt.$$

11. Given the observations made in points 8–10, and recalling that the product $f_i(t)X_N(t)$ has been denoted by the symbol a (i.e., $a \equiv f_i(t)X_N(t)$), one can define

   • μ_a to be the drift of a,

- μ_{X_N} to be the drift of X_N,
- μ_{f_i} to be the drift of f_i,

and one can use Ito's lemma to write the processes for $f_i(t)$, X_N and a, respectively, as

$$\frac{\mathrm{d}f_i(t)}{f_i(t)} = \mu_{f_i}\,\mathrm{d}t + \sigma_i(t)\,\mathrm{d}z_i,$$

$$\frac{\mathrm{d}a}{a} = \mu_a\,\mathrm{d}t + \sigma_a(t)\,\mathrm{d}z_a,$$

$$\frac{\mathrm{d}X_N(t)}{X_N(t)} = \mu_{X_N}\,\mathrm{d}t + \gamma(t, T_N, T)\,\mathrm{d}z_{X_N},$$

with

$$\mu_a = \mu_{f_i} + \mu_{X_N} + \sigma_i(t)\gamma(t, T_N, T)\rho_{f_i, X_N}.$$

12. From the definitions and the steps above, however, it follows that

$$\mu_a = 0 \qquad \text{(because } a \text{ is a martingale)},$$
$$\mu_{X_N} = 0 \qquad \text{(because } X_N \text{ is a martingale)}.$$

13. Finally, by equating the terms in $\mathrm{d}t$ in the equation for $\mathrm{d}a(t)$ one obtains

$$
\begin{aligned}
\mu_a a &= \mu_a f_i(t) X_N(t) \\
&= 0 \\
&= f_i(t) X_N(t) \mu_{X_N} + \mu_{f_i} f_i(t) X_N(t) \\
&\quad + f_i(t)\sigma_i(t) X_N(t)\gamma(t, T_N, T)\rho_{f_i, X_N} \\
&= 0 + \mu_{f_i} + \sigma_i(t)\gamma(t, T_N, T)\rho_{f_i, X_N} \\
&= 0 \\
\Longrightarrow \mu_{f_i} &= -\sigma_i(t)\gamma(t, T_N, T)\rho_{f_i, X_N},
\end{aligned}
$$

that is, in order to avoid arbitrage, the drift of forward rate $f_i(t)$ must be set equal to minus the quadratic (percentage) covariation between the forward rate itself and the relative price $X(t)$.

EXERCISE 5.1 *Obtain the equations in point 13 above.*

The result that follows from steps 12 and 13 has been obtained simply by imposing absence of arbitrage, and that the bond price processes should be strictly positive and monotonically decreasing in their maturities (the strict positivity of the forward rates, of X and of a, follows from this). It therefore provides a formal general answer to the problem of finding a no-arbitrage drift for the ith forward rate. In other words, given a numeraire N, if all the forward rates evolve according to

$$\frac{\mathrm{d}f_i(t)}{f_i(t)} = -\sigma_i(t)\gamma(t, T_N, T)\rho_{f_i, X_N}\,\mathrm{d}t + \sigma_i(t)\,\mathrm{d}z_i$$

or, equivalently,

$$\mathrm{d}\ln[f_i(t)] = -[\sigma_i(t)\gamma(t, T_N, T)\rho_{f_i, X_N} + \tfrac{1}{2}\sigma_i^2(t)]\,\mathrm{d}t + \sigma_i(t)\,\mathrm{d}z_i(t),$$

where $\mathrm{d}z_i(t)$ is the increment of a standard Brownian process under the measure Q_N, then one can rest assured that no arbitrage opportunities will arise among the traded assets.

The suggested procedure to obtain the no-arbitrage drifts might appear cumbersome. For the specific case where the non-zero drift of a forward rate arises from a choice of numeraire other than its natural payoff, there are simpler and more direct ways to obtain the same results. The great advantage of the procedure, however, is that it can be extended with very little effort to more complex situations. These will arise, for instance, if the discount bond is in a different currency, if the numeraire is an annuity, if the rate is a swap rate, etc. The generality of the approach makes the slightly tortuous line of reasoning well worth pursuing.

5.2 Expressing the No-Arbitrage Conditions in Terms of Market-Related Quantities

5.2.1 The Vailliant Brackets

The expression derived in the previous section provides the formal solution to the problem of assigning drifts to the forward rates such that arbitrage should be prevented. In the LIBOR world, however, there is no traded asset that can give direct market information about the volatility of a bond price. Therefore, it is still not obvious how to express the drift term in terms of market-accessible information, that is, how to estimate from more or less directly available market information the volatility of the relative price and its correlation with the forward rate itself. To this effect, let us denote the quadratic (percentage) covariation of two geometric Brownian motions x and y by the symbol $[x, y]_t$, which I have elsewhere (Rebonato 1998) called the Vailliant bracket, that is,

$$[x, y]_t \equiv \sigma_x(t)\sigma_y(t)\rho_{x, y}(t).$$

Then, Ito's lemma and the properties of quadratic covariations give the following simple properties:

$$[x, y] = [y, x],$$
$$[x, yz] = [x, y] + [x, z],$$
$$[x, y] = -[x, 1/y].$$

EXERCISE 5.2 *Prove the three properties above.*

5.2.2 Using the Vailliant Brackets to Express the Drifts as a Function of Market Observables

These properties can be profitably made use of in order to express the volatility of X_N and its correlation with f_i in terms of instantaneous volatilities of and correlations among the forward rates in the spanning set. The general strategy is to recognize again that, in the case of forward rates, the term $X(t)$ will be, in general, a forward price process, that is, a quantity of the form $B_i(t)/B_j(t)$, where i and j, which label the maturities of the bonds, can be such that $i > j$, $j > i$ or $i = j$. The last case is trivial, since the numeraire chosen is the natural payoff itself, and the forward rate is therefore drift-less (see Figure 5.1). The cases $i > j$ and $i < j$ will give rise to non-zero drifts. Let's analyze the two possibilities in turn.

If $j > i$, that is, if the chosen numeraire (the discount bond B_j) matures *after* the payoff of the ith forward rate, the forward process can be written as

$$\frac{B_i(t)}{B_j(t)} = \prod_{k=i}^{j-1} y_k,$$

with

$$y_k \equiv (1 + f_k \tau_k).$$

Similarly, if $i > j$, that is, if the chosen numeraire (the discount bond B_j) matures *before* the payoff of the ith forward rate, one can write

$$\frac{B_i(t)}{B_j(t)} = \prod_{k=j}^{i-1} y_k^{-1}.$$

From the properties of the Vailliant brackets presented above, and after defining $s \equiv i+1$, one can immediately write for the case when the numeraire has been chosen to be the discount bond maturing at time T_j, that is, $N(t) = B_j(t)$:

$$[f_i, X_N] = \left[f_i, \frac{N_i(t)}{N(t)} \right] = \left[f_i, \frac{B_s(t)}{B_j(t)} \right] = \left[f_i, \prod_{k=s}^{j-1} y_k \right] = \sum_{k=s}^{j-1} [f_i, y_k] \qquad (5.4)$$

or

$$[f_i, X_N] = \left[f_i, \frac{N_i(t)}{N(t)} \right] = \left[f_i, \frac{B_s(t)}{B_j(t)} \right] = \left[f_i, \prod_{k=j}^{s-1} y_k^{-1} \right] = - \sum_{k=j}^{s-1} [f_i, y_k] \qquad (5.5)$$

as appropriate, depending on whether $j > s$ (Equation (5.4)) or $j < s$ (Equation (5.5)). In obtaining these expressions, use has been made of the fact that the natural payoff, N_j, of forward rate j, f_j, is given by $B(t, T_{j+1})$ (see again Figure 5.1).

One can, at this point, notice that, if f_k is a strictly positive semi-martingale, so is $y_k = (1 + f_k \tau_k)$, and the representation

$$\frac{\mathrm{d}y_k}{y_k} = \mu_{y_k} \, \mathrm{d}t + \sigma_{y_k}(t) \, \mathrm{d}z_k(t) \tag{5.6}$$

is always possible (see, e.g., Nielsen 1999). (As usual, the expression $\sigma_{y_k}(t)$ does not imply that the volatility of $\mathrm{d}y_k$ is purely a function of time.) A straightforward application of Ito's lemma, and some algebraic manipulations, then lead to the following fundamental result. Let the natural payoff, N_j, of forward rate f_j be the chosen numeraire (i.e., let $B(t, T_{j+1})$ be the chosen numeraire); then the drift to be imparted to the ith forward rate, f_i, in order to prevent arbitrage is given by

$$\mu_{f_i} = \sigma_i(t) \sum_{k=j+1}^{i} \frac{\sigma_k(t) \rho_{ik}(t) f_k(t) \tau_k}{1 + f_k(t) \tau_k} \qquad \text{if } i > j, \tag{5.7}$$

$$\mu_{f_i} = -\sigma_i(t) \sum_{k=i+1}^{j} \frac{\sigma_k(t) \rho_{ik}(t) f_k(t) \tau_k}{1 + f_k(t) \tau_k} \qquad \text{if } i < j, \tag{5.8}$$

$$\mu_{f_i} = 0 \qquad \text{if } i = j. \tag{5.9}$$

EXERCISE 5.3 *Derive Equations (5.7) and (5.8) from Equations (5.4), (5.5) and (5.6).*

5.2.3 More General Applications

For the specific task tackled in this section, several equivalent and simpler, but less general, logical paths might have been followed to obtain results (5.6), (5.7) and (5.8). The small extra price that one has to pay in order to familiarize oneself with the procedure outlined above, however, brings the great added benefit that the same technique can be employed with very little change for a variety of rates and numeraires. The reader might want to follow virtually the same steps, for instance, in order to obtain the drift corrections for constant-maturity-swap (CMS) FRAs and caps, or for the forward rate underlying a serial option (see Section 2.2.6). It is also very interesting and instructive to use the technique just described to derive the analytic solution to the problem of finding the value of a multi-look trigger swap.[4] Indeed, detailed calculations showing how these expressions simplify in the cases of LIBOR-in-arrears swaps and quanto FRAs have been presented else-

---

[4]The solution will indeed be analytic, but involve, for an n-look trigger swap, the n-dimensional cumulative normal distribution.

where (see Rebonato 1998, which also deals along the same lines with the derivation of the drifts of swap rates), and will not be repeated here. The important conclusion that one can draw from all these different applications is that the equations arrived at following the procedure above always express the 'drift corrections' in terms of the market-related instantaneous volatilities and correlations that constitute the natural inputs to the LIBOR market model. The task outlined in the introductory section of this chapter of expressing the Girsanov's-theorem-related drift corrections in terms of market-related volatilities and correlations has therefore been accomplished, and the paths of the 'fast-track' and of the 'methodical' readers join at this point.

5.2.4 Implications of the Drift Functional Form

Looking at Equations (5.7)–(5.9), the first important observation is that, given the assumptions of deterministic volatilities for the forward rates, the stochastic state variables $\{\mathbf{f}\}$ have been shown to enter the drift terms, which are therefore not pure functions of time. Also, the dependence of the drifts on $\{\mathbf{f}\}$ is such that the quantities x_i are not deterministic functions of time either. This being the case, the appealing (very-)long-jump procedure presented in the previous chapter would appear to be no longer justifiable. The evolution of a forward rate can still be formally written (for the case, for instance, when the expiry, T_{j+1}, of the chosen numeraire bond is shorter than the payment time of the ith forward rate, T_{i+1}) as

$$f_i(t) = f_i(0) \exp \int_0^t [\mu_i(\{\mathbf{f}\}, u) - \tfrac{1}{2}\sigma_i^2(u)]\, du + \sigma_i(u)\, dz_i(u)$$

$$= f_i(0) \exp \int_0^t \left[\sigma_i(u) \sum_{k=j+1}^{i} \frac{\sigma_k(u)\rho_{ik}(u) f_k(u)\tau_k}{1 + f_k(u)\tau_k} - \tfrac{1}{2}\sigma_i^2(u) \right] du$$

$$+ \sigma_i(u)\, dz_i(u),$$

but, in general, now we no longer know how to integrate the quantity under the integral sign over a finite time interval, since the integrand is not a pure function of time, and we are no longer dealing with a Gaussian process. Equivalently, we can no longer say that the (joint) conditional distribution of the logarithms of the forward rates follows a (joint) Gaussian law, and we cannot therefore pursue the reasoning presented in the two previous chapters that led to the (very-)long-jump procedure. Notice that, however, that if one could write

$$\int_0^t \sum_{k=j+1}^{i} \frac{\sigma_i(u)\sigma_k(u)\rho_{ik}(u) f_k(u)\tau_k}{1 + f_k(u)\tau_k}\, du$$

$$\simeq \sum_{k=j+1}^{i} \frac{f_k(0)\tau_k}{1 + f_k(0)\tau_k} \int_0^t \sigma_i(u)\sigma_k(u)\rho_{ik}(u)\, du,$$

that is to say, if one made the approximation that the stochastic term $f_k(t)\tau_k/[1 + f_k(t)\tau_k]$ could be assumed to be deterministic – actually, a constant – and that this constant could be satisfactorily approximated by its value today, then the drift integrals would still be exactly computable. Furthermore, they would simply be proportional – via the now-constant factor $f_k(0)\tau_k/[1 + f_k(0)\tau_k]$ – to the very covariance elements that were examined in Chapter 3, and that made up the matrices **C** and **TOTC**.

As it stands, this approximation is unfortunately too crude to be of use for accurate calculations, especially if the trader wanted to carry out the very long jump to the final maturity date of a type-1a derivative product in order to exploit the advantages that can be reaped by using the matrix **TOTC** (see the Case Study in Section 4.2). Hull and White (2000) claim this approximation to be 'innocuous', but this can only be the case if the step size used in the Monte Carlo simulation is of the order of a forward-rate tenor, that is, three, six or, sometimes, twelve months. If this is the typical step size for the approximation above to be acceptably accurate, the user of the model would in practice be restricted to using the long-jump procedure. However, in the previous chapter it was argued that it is always desirable for the trader to make use whenever possible of the very-long-jump technique, and the results reported later on in Section 5.4 clearly show that, in the very-long-jump case, the crude approximation suggested above is by no means adequate for pricing purposes. Furthermore, not only does the accuracy of the naive approximation above rule out in most realistic cases the desirable very-long-jump procedure, it can often also cause hindrance in the simpler and more general long-jump case, whenever there are non-look or lock-out features. With the naive approximation, in these cases one has to introduce a large number of 'artificial' price-sensitive events when 'nothing happens', simply in order to bridge the gap present between, say, 'today' and the first true price-sensitive event, which can occur after an initial non-look period often as long as several years. The occurrence of such long non-call periods in real pricing applications is actually quite common, especially when the option is embedded in issuer-driven structured products: the typical term sheet of the once-popular long-dated zero-coupon multi-call Bermudan swaptions, for instance, often includes non-call periods as long as five years.

In an ideal world, one would like to find an efficient approximation to deal with the stochastic integrals above over step sizes of 10 or 20 years (so that the very-long-jump procedure, when appropriate, can be used); and one would also like, at the same time, to be able to treat the complex process with state-dependent drifts in such a way that the properties of conditionally Gaussian processes, and the computational procedures they afford, could still be exploited. Obviously, it is impossible to do so exactly, but some of the results available in the Gaussian setting can still be recovered. To see along what lines the 'rescue program' might be undertaken, recall, from Section 3.1, that failure to satisfy the conditions required for a process to be conditionally Gaussian has two consequences: first of all, a relatively small number of drift and covariance vectors are no longer sufficient to describe the evolution of the process; furthermore, the process itself ceases to be Markovian (see Jaeckel 2000a,b). This latter problem, despite several attempts, has not been solved so far in a satisfactory way.[5] The former difficulty, however, can be substantially reduced by the predictor–corrector (Runge–Kutta-like) approximation presented in the next section, which can accomplish to a surprisingly high degree of accuracy the task of making the drift terms conditionally deterministic.

5.3 Approximations of the Drift Terms

5.3.1 The Runge–Kutta Weak Approximation

Weak stochastic Taylor approximations of order greater than unity are well known in numerical analysis (see, e.g., Kloeden and Platen 1992), and can be profitably applied to those situations where weak[6] (rather than strong) convergence is required. Given a stochastic process $Y(t)$ with stochastic differential equation given by

$$\mathrm{d}Y(t) = \mu(Y, t)\,\mathrm{d}t + \sigma(Y, t)\,\mathrm{d}z(t),$$

the Taylor scheme of order unity gives the well-known Euler approximation

$$Y(t + \Delta t) = Y(t) + \mu(Y, t)\Delta t + \sigma(Y, t)\Delta z(t)$$

with $\Delta z(t) = z(t + \Delta t) - z(t)$.

The second- and higher-order Taylor approximations, however, require the evaluation of first and second derivatives of the drift and of the diffusion terms, and can therefore soon become cumbersome. To circumvent this problem, quite some time ago Kloeden and Platen (1992) introduced Runge–

---

[5]The solution to the problem of mapping approximately but accurately the non-Markovian evolution of the forward rates onto a recombining tree appears tantalizingly close. In the case of one factor and constant volatilities, for instance, the yield curve that results from an up shock followed by a down shock over two time-steps of, say, a quarter or half a year is indeed different from, but indeed very similar to, the yield curve produced by a down shock followed by an up shock. The similarity of these yield curves, and the apparently mild violation of the Markov property, have suggested that it might be profitable to 'combine' the resulting yield curves in some suitable way into an 'equivalent yield curve' and impose recombination of the 'bushy' tree (see Jaeckel 2000a,b for a discussion of related issues). Since, along this now-recombining tree, the bond prices are no longer exactly recovered (and the trader is therefore exposed to the possibility of arbitrage), a first set of corrections modifies the resulting mesh so as to re-obtain the market bond prices. Unfortunately, more (and more difficult) problems arise with several factors and with non-constant instantaneous volatilities. Much as in the case of nuclear fusion, a practically working solution of this problem always appears to be 'just around the next corner'.

[6]In our context, a sequence of functions $p_n(x)$ converges weakly to $p(x)$, if, for any continuous test function $f(\ )$ vanishing outside some bounded interval,

$$\lim_{n \to \infty} \int f(x)p_n(x)\,\mathrm{d}x = \int f(x)p(x)\,\mathrm{d}x.$$

Kutta-like weak approximations that do not require derivatives. These approximations were then recently applied by Hunter et al. (2001), to my knowledge for the first time, to the interest-rate derivatives arena. More precisely, Kloeden and Platen show that, given a stochastic process, Y, with state-dependent drifts and volatilities, $\mu(Y,t)$ and $\sigma(Y,t)$, respectively, and of known value, $Y(t)$, at time t, one can approximate its value at time $t + \Delta t$, that is, $Y(t + \Delta t)$, as

$$
\begin{aligned}
Y(t + \Delta t) \simeq \ & Y(t) + \tfrac{1}{2}[\mu(Y,t) + \mu(\widehat{Y},t)]\Delta t \\
& + \tfrac{1}{4}[\sigma(\widehat{Y}^+,t) + \sigma(\widehat{Y}^-,t) + 2\sigma(Y,t)]\Delta z(t) \\
& + \tfrac{1}{4}[\sigma(\widehat{Y}^+,t) - \sigma(\widehat{Y}^-,t)][\Delta z(t) - \Delta t]/\sqrt{\Delta t} \quad (5.10)
\end{aligned}
$$

where

$$
\begin{aligned}
\widehat{Y} &= Y(t) + \mu(Y,t)\Delta t + \sigma(Y,t)\Delta z(t), \\
\widehat{Y}^+ &= Y(t) + \mu(Y,t)\Delta t + \sigma(Y,t)\sqrt{\Delta t}, \\
\widehat{Y}^- &= Y(t) + \mu(Y,t)\Delta t - \sigma(Y,t)\sqrt{\Delta t}.
\end{aligned}
$$

Note that the term $\widehat{Y}$ is simply equal to the first-order Taylor approximation (Euler scheme) result, that is, in the forward-rates context of interest to us, to the value for $Y(t + \Delta t)$ that would be obtained using what Hull and White (2000) call the 'innocuous' approximation. Furthermore, the quantities $\sigma(\widehat{Y},t)$, $\sigma(\widehat{Y}^+,t)$ and $\sigma(\widehat{Y}^-,t)$ will all be equal to $\sigma(Y,t)$ if the diffusive term is purely time-dependent, that is, if it is of the form $\sigma(t)$. This being the case, Equation (5.10) simply becomes

$$
Y(t + \Delta t) \simeq Y(t) + \tfrac{1}{2}[\mu(Y,t) + \mu(\widehat{Y},t)]\Delta t + \sigma(Y,t)\Delta z(t). \quad (5.11)
$$

5.3.2 Application of the Approximation to Forward Rates

If one makes the identification of the variable Y with the logarithm of a forward rate, the simpler form (5.11) is perfectly suited to the case of the stochastic evolution of forward rates with no-arbitrage drifts, since, as we have seen, the drifts do contain the stochastic state variables, but the volatility terms are purely time-dependent.

The scheme (5.11) allows a very simple interpretation, and directly suggests why the approximation should work well. Dealing with the interpretation first, the general idea is that, before the step, one does not know what values the drift will assume during the time interval. One would naturally be tempted to try to estimate some average drift, where the averaging should be carried out along a given path, and to use it as an 'effective' deterministic drift. The simplest way to estimate this average is to give equal weights to to-day's value for the drift (which is known exactly) and to the value of the drift at the end of the step. The problem is that this terminal value of the drift is not known today, depending as it does on the particular (drift-dependent) path. This is where the predictor–corrector method provides a simple but accurate approximate solution: by (5.11) one first of all carries out a Gaussian draw,[7] and evolves the process of interest Y_t from time t to time $t + \Delta t$ using the usual Euler scheme. Since the volatilities are purely time-dependent, one can then simply recalculate the drift using as values for the state variable(s) the realization obtained performing the initial Euler step. This quantity is the predictor–corrector approximation for the unknown value of the drift at the end of the step. It is clearly not exact, because the wrong drift was used to obtain it, but, as long as the naive drift was not too off the mark, it should be reasonably accurate. This new value for the drift is then averaged with the initial one, and the process is evolved again from time t to time $t + \Delta t$ starting from the same initial value Y_t, but now using the averaged drift.

It is important to point out that three different approximations enter the overall procedure. In order to appreciate their implications as clearly as possible, let us look again at the expression for the evolution of the variable Y_t:

$$Y(T) = Y(t) + \int_t^T \mu(Y(u), u) \, du + \int_t^T \sigma(u) \, dz(u), \qquad (5.12)$$

with $T = t + \Delta t$. As mentioned above, the difficulty stems from the fact that at time t the values of the process Y (which determines the drift) are not known for times $u > t$. Let us assume for a moment, however, that the expression

$$Y(T) = Y(t) + \int_t^T \mu(Y(t), u) \, du + \int_t^T \sigma(u) \, dz(u), \qquad (5.12')$$

with $Y(t)$ now a constant, provides an 'acceptable' estimate of the value $Y(T)$. In other terms, one can hope that the process will evolve from the value $Y(t)$ to somewhere in the vicinity of the value

$$Y(t) + \int_t^T \mu(Y(t), u) \, du + \int_t^T \sigma(u) \, dz(u).$$

This constitutes the first part of the approximation.

Assuming that $Y(T)$ is now exactly known, and despite the fact that any path could, in principle, have been followed from time t to time T, it is plausible to expect that the average drift along the path, $\langle \mu \rangle$, can be reasonably approximated as

$$\langle \mu \rangle = \tfrac{1}{2}[\mu(Y(t)) + \mu(Y(T))].$$

This is the second part of the approximation.

Finally, one can hope that substituting a stochastic drift with a determinis-

---

[7]As long as one is only interested in weak convergence, it is not strictly necessary to draw a Gaussian variate, and one could replace the increment Δz with another random variable with similar moment properties (see Kloeden and Platen 1992). I do not pursue this avenue here.

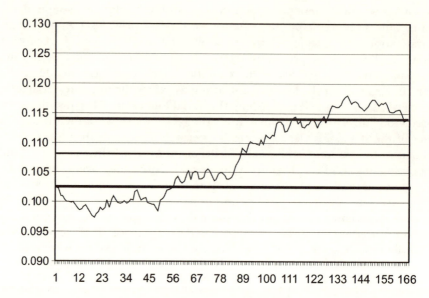

Figure 5.2   *The stochastic drift (jagged curve), the drift obtained with the initial value of the state variable, $\mu(Y(t))$ (bottom full line), the drift obtained with the final value of the state variable, $\mu(Y(T))$ (top full line), and the average drift $\frac{1}{2}[\mu(Y(t)) + \mu(Y(T))]$ (middle full line).*

tic drift (i.e., with the approximate average drift calculated with the approximate value $Y(T)$) might not entail too large a loss of accuracy. This is the third part of the approximation.

This procedure is graphically illustrated in Figure 5.2, which shows the true stochastic drift, the drift obtained with the initial value of the state variable, the drift obtained with its final value, and the average drift suggested by the predictor–corrector procedure; and in Figure 5.3, which compares the evolutions of the stochastic variable Y evolved using the true drift ('True'), the naive drift approximation ('Initial'), the constant drift obtained using the terminal value of Y ('Final'), and the average of the naive and terminal drift ('Mean'). Looking carefully at Figure 5.3, it is interesting to note that the 'true' process, estimated using a very finely stepped Monte Carlo simulation over the step size, hugs more closely the curve labelled 'Initial' over the first part of the path (as it should, since, in this portion of the evolution, the 'naive' approximation produces a drift obviously closer to the true drift). However, the processes produced by the 'true' and predictor–corrector drifts become almost exactly superimposed by the end of the step size.

Note that, if one worked with the stochastic variable Y_t given by the logarithm of the forward rates, the procedure above is equivalent (again for deterministic volatilities) to averaging the outcome $Y(t + \Delta t)$ of the usual Euler scheme with the outcome obtained using the drift term calculated with

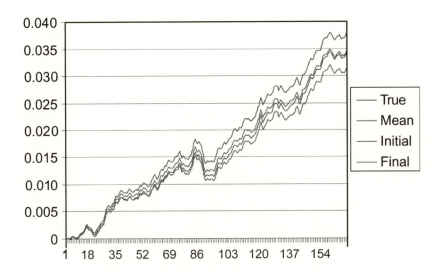

Figure 5.3 *The paths of the stochastic variable Y with state-dependent drift obtained with (i) integration of the true process (curve 'True'), (ii) a constant drift calculated using the initial value of the state variable (curve 'Initial'), (iii) a constant drift calculated using the final value of the state variable (curve 'Final'), and (iv) a constant predictor–corrector drift calculated as the average of (ii) and (iii) above (curve 'Mean'). Notice how the 'True' process, estimated using a very finely stepped Monte Carlo simulation over the step size, hugs more closely the curve labelled 'Initial' over the first part of the path (since, in this portion of the evolution, the 'naive' approximation produces a drift obviously closer to the true drift); but how the process produced by the 'True' and predictor–corrector drifts become almost exactly superimposed by the end of the step size.*

$Y(t + \Delta t)$ instead of $Y(t)$:

$$Y(t + \Delta t) \simeq \tfrac{1}{2}[Y(t) + \mu(Y, t)\Delta t + \sigma(Y, t)\Delta z(t)]$$
$$+ \tfrac{1}{2}[Y(t) + \mu(\widehat{Y}, t)\Delta t + \sigma(Y, t)\Delta z(t)].$$

Note also that the drift does depend on the Gaussian draw, but, for any given such draw, Equation (5.11) allows the user to carry out the evolution of the forward rates as if the drift were deterministic. This is exactly the type of result that we would have liked to obtain, since it allows the preservation of some of the very powerful results available in the case of vectors of conditionally Gaussian random processes (long and very long jumps included). As mentioned in Chapter 3, however, the independence of the drifts from the realization of the forward rates, which is the second requirement for a process to be conditionally Gaussian, is not achieved by this approximation, and the user is therefore still left with a non-Markovian process.

5.3.3 Numerical Results

Hunter et al. (2001) apply this technique to the case of the evolution of forward rates in a LIBOR-market-model setting (i.e., in the presence of stochastic drifts), and convincingly argue that the problem should lend itself very efficiently to this treatment. The proof of the pudding, as usual, is in the eating, and Table 5.1 provides evidence that the approximation proposed by Hunter et al. (2001) based on the insight of Kloeden and Platen is indeed extremely effective, for typical values of forward-rate volatilities, even when the time-step between price-sensitive events is as long as 10 or 20 years. Table 5.1 displays the market values and the model values of the equilibrium three-month forward rates for a real yield curve (GBP, 23 October 2000)[8]. The model values were obtained using either the 'simple' method, that is, by making use of the crude approximation

$$\int_0^t \sum_{k=j+1}^i \frac{\sigma_i(u)\sigma_k(u)\rho_{ik}(u)f_k(u)\tau_k}{1+f_k(u)\tau_k} \, du$$

$$\simeq \sum_{k=j+1}^i \frac{f_k(0)\tau_k}{1+f_k(0)\tau_k} \int_0^t \sigma_i(u)\sigma_k(u)\rho_{ik}(u) \, du,$$

or the Runge–Kutta-like approximation described above. Table 5.1 also reports the absolute errors incurred in the two approximations. For the purpose of the calculation, the rather extreme case was chosen of a mismatch between the numeraire and the forward rates as large as 20 years. More precisely, the zero-coupon bond maturing at time $T = 20$ years was chosen as numeraire.[9] The total covariance matrix **TOTC** was then built as discussed in Section 3.2 (see Equation (3.2.19)), by using one of the parametrizations of the instantaneous volatility and correlation functions for the various forward rates discussed in Chapters 6 and 7. In particular, care was taken to ensure that the root-mean-square instantaneous volatilities should reproduce exactly the corresponding implied market Black volatility. After orthogonalization of the matrix **TOTC**, as many driving factors ($79 = 20 \times 4 - 1$) were retained as forward rates. A 'smart' Monte Carlo simulation (with $2^{17} \sim 130\,000$ simulation paths) was then carried out and the value of each individual FRA calculated as the average over simulations of quantities such as

$$\text{NPV(FRA)}_{i,j} = \left\{ [f_N^{i,j}(T_i) - K]\tau \prod_{k=i}^N [1 + f_N^{k,j}(T_k)\tau] \right\} B(0,T_N), \qquad (5.13)$$

where the index j labels the simulations, $B(0, T_N)$ is today's value of the nu-

---

[8]For ease of display, only half as many forward rates have been shown in Table 5.1.
[9]Accurate numerical calculations carried out by Peter Jaeckel are gratefully acknowledged.

Table 5.1   *The exact values of the equilibrium forward rates for a market yield curve built out to 20 years (column 'Market'); the values of the strikes that give zero value to the FRAs expiring every quarter out to the final maturity, when the zero-coupon bond maturing at $T = 20$ years is chosen as numeraire, in the cases of the naive approximation ('column 'Simple') and the Hunter et al. (2001) Runge–Kutta approximation (column 'RK'); and the absolute errors for these two cases (columns 'Error Simple' and 'Error RK').*

Expiry	Market(%)	Simple(%)	RK(%)	ErrorSimple	ErrorRK
0	6.15				
0.5	6.155	6.156	6.155	0.00000	-0.00000
1.0	6.214	6.215	6.213	0.00001	-0.00000
1.5	6.265	6.268	6.264	0.00004	-0.00000
2.0	6.289	6.297	6.288	0.00008	-0.00001
2.5	6.263	6.275	6.262	0.00012	-0.00001
3.0	6.227	6.244	6.225	0.00017	-0.00002
3.5	6.215	6.238	6.213	0.00023	-0.00002
4.0	6.167	6.197	6.165	0.00029	-0.00003
4.5	6.155	6.191	6.152	0.00036	-0.00003
5.0	6.081	6.122	6.077	0.00042	-0.00004
5.5	6.056	6.104	6.052	0.00048	-0.00005
6.0	6.032	6.086	6.027	0.00054	-0.00006
6.5	6.008	6.070	6.002	0.00062	-0.00007
7.0	6.000	6.069	5.992	0.00069	-0.00008
7.5	5.975	6.050	5.966	0.00076	-0.00009
8.0	5.932	6.014	5.922	0.00082	-0.00010
8.5	5.906	5.995	5.895	0.00089	-0.00011
9.0	6.004	6.098	5.991	0.00095	-0.00012
9.5	5.991	6.092	5.977	0.00101	-0.00013
10.0	5.838	5.944	5.824	0.00106	-0.00014
10.5	5.805	5.916	5.790	0.00110	-0.00015
11.0	5.793	5.909	5.777	0.00116	-0.00017
11.5	5.765	5.884	5.748	0.00119	-0.00017
12.0	5.598	5.723	5.580	0.00124	-0.00019
12.5	5.561	5.686	5.542	0.00125	-0.00019
13.0	5.518	5.641	5.499	0.00123	-0.00019
13.5	5.480	5.600	5.461	0.00121	-0.00019
14.0	5.435	5.552	5.417	0.00116	-0.00018
14.5	5.396	5.507	5.378	0.00111	-0.00018
15.0	5.390	5.495	5.373	0.00106	-0.00017
15.5	5.339	5.438	5.323	0.00099	-0.00016
16.0	5.280	5.371	5.266	0.00091	-0.00014
16.5	5.236	5.318	5.223	0.00082	-0.00013
17.0	5.191	5.262	5.180	0.00071	-0.00011
17.5	5.150	5.209	5.141	0.00059	-0.00009
18.0	5.100	5.145	5.093	0.00045	-0.00007
18.5	5.057	5.088	5.053	0.00031	-0.00005
18.75	5.057	5.081	5.054	0.00023	-0.00003
19.0	5.024	5.039	5.021	0.00015	-0.00002
19.25	5.024	5.031	5.022	0.00007	-0.00002
19.5	4.976	4.975	4.975	-0.00001	-0.00001
19.75	4.976	4.967	4.976	-0.00009	-0.00000
20.0					

meraire (the discount bond maturing at time $T_N = 20$, $N = 80$) and $f_N^{k,j}(T_k)$ is the value of the kth forward rate in the jth simulation when $B(0, T_N)$ is taken as numeraire. Note carefully that, since all but one forward rate (the Nth) have a payment time $(T_i + \tau)$ before the maturity of the discount bond chosen as numeraire, the payoff from the reset will have to be 'rolled up' to time T_N using the later-resetting forward rates realized during the course of the same simulation, as described in Section 4.1, and in greater detail in the Case Study presented in Section 4.2. This 'rolling up' is accomplished by the term $\prod_{k=i}^{N}[1 + f_N^{k,j}(T_k)\tau]$. As for the drifts applied to all the forward rates (with the exception of the 79th and last, for which $B(t, T_{80})$ is the natural payoff), they were given by

$$\mu_{f_i} = -\sigma_i(t) \sum_{k=i+1}^{j} \frac{\sigma_k(t)\rho_{ik}(t)f_k(t)\tau_k}{1 + f_k(t)\tau_k} \qquad 1 \le i < 79,\ j = 79. \qquad (5.14)$$

Notice that, for both approximations, the error has to go to zero as the forward rate approaches the 79th, because for this forward rate the chosen numeraire is the natural payoff. Incidentally, this observation recommends a choice of numeraire closest in expiry to those price-sensitive events or forward rates that are likely to have the greatest impact on the value of a given structure.

One can see that the improvement over the 'simple' approach afforded by the scheme suggested by Kloeden and Platen is substantial, and that, for typical market values of the caplet volatilities, very long jumps spanning periods of up to 20 years become feasible. Needless to say, if the need for greater accuracy was felt for particular applications, the user can always introduce a price-sensitive event where 'nothing happens', in order to break up an excessively long jump, but, given the accuracy of the approximation, it is difficult to think of practical cases where the user might be forced to do so.

The error pattern displayed in Figure 5.4 is also worth commenting about. The existence of a maximum in the absolute error is an unavoidable feature whenever the numeraire is chosen to be the longest natural payoff: when this choice for the numeraire is made, in fact, the largest drift, and consequently the largest approximation, will be associated with the first forward rates (see Equations (5.7)–(5.9)). These forward rates, however, have relatively little time to expiry and therefore the exponential term $\exp[\int_0^{T_i} \mu(u)\, \mathrm{d}u]$ is correspondingly rather small. The opposite is true for the late-expiring forward rates: the time to expiry has now become longer and longer, and the integral covers longer and longer periods, but the number of terms in the drift correction becomes smaller and smaller. In particular, the last forward rate displays no drift correction at all, and the corresponding FRA is estimated exactly by the Monte Carlo procedure described above. The same pattern would not be found if one chose as numeraire, say, the natural payoff of the first forward rates: in this case, in fact, the first few forward rates would be extremely accurate (short time to expiry, and small correction term), but the late-expiring

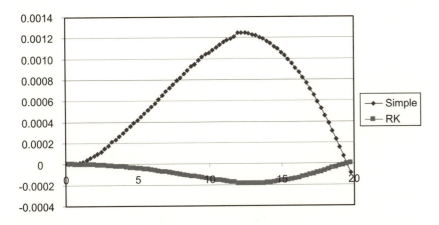

Figure 5.4   *The FRA errors in Table 5.1 corresponding to the naive approximation (curve labelled 'Simple') and to the Hunter et al. (Runge–Kutta) scheme (curve labelled 'RK').*

forward rates would suffer both from a long time to expiry and from a large drift term.

5.4 Conclusions

I have presented in this chapter the explicit expressions for the numeraire-dependent drifts of the forward rates necessary to produce an arbitrage-free evolution of the discrete yield curve. These drifts have been shown to be state-dependent (stochastic), and, therefore, for a given numeraire, every forward rate apart from, at most, one will have a distribution other than log-normal. Given these stochastic drifts, no exact closed-form solutions are available for the joint conditional densities of the forward rates. However, we have presented the results of Hunter et al. (2001) who show that a simple and computationally efficient deterministic approximation to the drifts can be obtained using a variation of the Runge–Kutta weak approximation to the solution of stochastic differential equations with stochastic drifts (and volatilities, a case not needed in this context).

The importance of these results for the practical implementation of the market model should not be underestimated:

1. If these approximations were not effective, one would have to carry out a short-stepped stochastic integration, which would negate the computational and conceptual advantages of the (very-)long-jump procedure.

2. In a way, somewhat fortuitously, once these approximations are enforced, the drifts turn out to be expressible in terms of those very same covari-

ance elements that drive the stochastic part of the evolution of the forward rates.

3. By virtue of the fact that the approximations convert a stochastic drift into an equivalent conditionally[10] deterministic one, the conditional densities of the finite set of forward rates can be accurately approximated by a set of joint Gaussian distributions.

Putting together the results presented in Chapters 3 and 4 with those obtained in this chapter, one can conclude that these sets of (approximately) jointly conditionally Gaussian distributions are fully described by the marginal covariance elements, which therefore truly constitute all that is needed in order to specify the no-arbitrage evolution of the forward rates.

The tasks for Part I that I had laid out at the beginning of the book have therefore been fully accomplished: both the conceptual architecture of the LIBOR-market-model approach (as embodied by the no-arbitrage drift conditions and by its multi-factor stochastic components), and the accompanying powerful computational engine (the (very-)long-jump procedure) have been presented purely in terms of the marginal covariance elements, and of the quantities that can be built from them. These covariance elements are in turn simply a function of instantaneous volatilities and correlations. It is therefore clear that the whole approach rests on the specification of these quantities, and that the quality of its results can be no better than the financial reasonableness and desirability of its inputs. For these reasons, the chapters of the following Part II will be completely devoted to providing theoretical and practical indications as to how these all-important marginal covariance elements can be constructed in a financially appealing manner from plausible correlations and volatilities.

---

[10]The drift is conditionally deterministic because it depends on the particular random draw.

Part II

The Inputs to the General Framework

6

Instantaneous Volatilities

6.1 Introduction and Motivation

6.1.1 Review of the Results So Far

The treatment of the no-arbitrage evolution of forward rates in the standard LIBOR-market-model framework presented in Part I has led to the following results:

1. The coefficients that multiply the Brownian increments, and that therefore affect the stochastic part of the evolution of the logarithms of the forward rates, are purely deterministic functions of time (the forward rates, in particular, do not appear). They can be expressed in terms of deterministic instantaneous volatilities and correlation functions. These two deterministic functions have been shown to appear together in the form of the total or marginal covariance elements defined in Chapter 3 – see Section 3.3.1, Equations (3.17)–(3.19).

2. The deterministic (drift) part of the evolution of a set of spanning forward rates, which reflects the conditions of no arbitrage, can be expressed as a function of deterministic instantaneous volatilities, of deterministic instantaneous correlations and of the stochastic state variables themselves (i.e., the forward rates).

3. I have shown (Chapter 5) that the no-arbitrage drifts can be expressed in terms of sums of covariance elements with stochastic weights containing the forward rates. By virtue of the fact that these weights were shown to be non-deterministic, a set of spanning forward rates turned out not to be jointly conditionally log-normally distributed.

4. An approximation was presented and justified, however, thanks to which these weights could be accurately approximated by means of quantities (conditionally)[1] known today – see Section 5.4.

---

[1] These quantities can be computed simply using information in the current yield curve only once a Gaussian draw has been performed. Hence the term 'conditionally deterministic' that I have used in Chapter 5 to describe the procedure.

5. As a result of point 4, the covariance elements (weighted now by deterministic quantities) were shown to constitute the fundamental building
   blocks both for the deterministic and for the stochastic evolution of the
   forward rates.

6. Finally, I have shown (Chapter 4) that, as long as the payoffs satisfy certain measurability conditions, and can be expressed as a function that
   is homogeneous of degree one in the bond prices,[2] the set of forward
   rates only need to be observed on a finite number of dates. As a consequence, the short rate and the instantaneous money-market account are
   not needed, and the dynamic hedging strategy required to reproduce a
   payoff as above only requires taking positions in the discount bonds (or
   forward rate aggrements) maturing (expiring) at the times of the price-
   sensitive events and of the payoffs.

By virtue of the results above, in order to price LIBOR derivatives using the
market model, the set of (the logarithms of) the spanning forward rates can
be approximately – but accurately – modelled as if they were a set of discretely
sampled, jointly conditionally Gaussian processes.

The pivotal role played by the (marginal) covariance elements justifies
the convergence of lines from the stochastic and deterministic blocks in the
graphic representation of the book plan presented in the subsection 'Plan and
structure of the book' in the 'Introduction'. I discuss the two building blocks
of the covariance elements, that is, volatilities and correlations, in Chapters 6
and 7.

6.1.2 Parametrizing the Covariance Elements

In principle, one could attempt to treat these covariance elements as the
primary (and, in a sense, the only relevant) inputs to the model and to undertake a totally non-parametric approach towards their estimation. If this line
of approach were taken, the individual marginal covariance elements could
be seen as the 'fitting parameters' to be used in order to reproduce as best
as one can the prices of a set of transparent plain-vanilla options. With a
given complex product with n price-sensitive events one can associate $O(n^2)$
prices of plain-vanilla instruments and up to $O(n^3)$ distinct covariance elements. This 'brute-force' (i.e., totally non-parametric) approach is therefore
likely to succeed, at least if by 'success' one simply means the correct recovery
of today's plain-vanilla prices. Apart from numerical considerations, however,
such a procedure makes the strong assumption that the prices of caplets and
European swaptions should be perfectly consistent with each other. Given the
practical difficulties to 'rectify' possible price discrepancies generated, for instance, by supply and demand effects via 'quasi-arbitrage trades' (see Sections
1.2, 6.1.3 and 9.1.3), the validity of this assumption should not be taken for

---

[2]Or, equivalently, as the product of a bond price and a function homogeneous of degree zero
in the forward rates.

granted. If there were indeed a noticeable lack of consistency between the two plain-vanilla markets, a non-parametric approach would be likely to give rise to a set of financially implausible instantaneous volatilities and/or correlations. These, in turn, would produce undesirable future evolutions of the term structure of volatilities and/or of the swaption matrix. The trader who made use of a model calibrated in this way would therefore be likely to carry out future re-hedging transactions in caplets and swaptions at a cost different from what the model predicts today. Almost certainly, the trader who has won the deal in a competitive tender situation will find these 'surprises' to be more negative than positive.

As I have advocated in Chapter 1, what one needs is therefore an overarching financially justifiable structure to be imposed on these over-abundant degrees of freedom. This structure can be imposed by noticing, first of all, that the covariance elements can be expressed in terms of (time integrals of) instantaneous volatility and correlation functions. As a second step one might want to specify some financially motivated criteria on the basis of which the functional forms for the volatilities and correlations can be chosen. These functional forms will then contain a much smaller number of free parameters, and the following logical chain can therefore be established:

- the prices of the plain-vanilla instruments can be expressed as a function of covariance elements;

- these can be built from integrals of instantaneous volatilities and correlations;

- the latter can be expressed via the chosen functional forms;

- and these can finally be parametrized by means of a handful of coefficients.

This four-step process is schematically illustrated in Figure 6.1.

It is clear from this account that the most delicate step in the whole procedure is the specification of the form of the instantaneous volatility and correlation functions: if they are not flexible enough, they might fail to produce a good fit to financial prices simply because the world is genuinely 'more complex' than they allow for. If, on the other hand, they achieve great flexibility by means of a large number of opaque parameters, it will be difficult to tell whether the fitting procedure has produced a sensible description of financial reality, or whether one has simply forced an over-parametrized model to yield results it is ill-suited to produce. Finally, if the chosen functional form intrinsically fails to capture important essential features, or imposes spurious behavior on the evolution of market observables, no degree of fitting will redress this situation. It is for this reason that the present and the next chapters analyze in great detail the desiderata of 'good' volatility and correlation functions. For the same reason, considerable time will be spent showing why

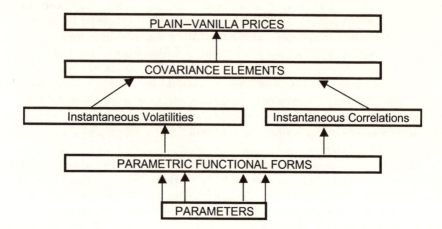

Figure 6.1   *Schematic representation of the logical chain linking the parameters of the instantaneous volatility and correlation functions to the prices of plain-vanilla instruments that can be used for calibration.*

certain formulations, perhaps superficially appealing, do not provide a good picture of financial reality.

6.1.3 Isn't Fitting to Prices Enough? Comments on Market Completeness

The trader might well ask why she should be concerned at all with the model producing a financially believable picture of financial reality, as long as the prices of the plain-vanilla instruments that will be used for hedging are perfectly reproduced by the model. The deterministic setting provided by the modern pricing approach promises, after all, perfect replication of any (suitably measurable) payoff. This line of argument is surprisingly widespread, and is often encountered in the pricing of complex instruments such as, for instance, Bermudan swaptions: 'As long as I have managed to reproduce today's prices of all the co-terminal European swaptions, and of all the caplets that I might possibly want for hedging, why should I worry about anything else?'

The dangers of this type of reasoning have been clearly highlighted, for instance, in Longstaff et al. (2000a,b), who clearly point out how exact fitting to the market prices of the European co-terminal swaptions is per se no guarantee of a reasonable model choice. From a somewhat different angle, one can begin to analyze the implications of the rhetorical question above by noticing that the deterministic-volatility framework that constitutes the backbone of the standard market model approach is, at best, a good working approximation for a more realistic state of affairs, where volatilities and correlations are neither known perfectly a priori, nor deterministic; where discontinuous jumps might occur; where the jump amplitude and frequency might, in turn, be stochastic; etc.

Furthermore, even if the process for the forward rates were indeed a diffusion, the volatilities were deterministic and their root-mean-square perfectly known by the trader via the caplet market information, exotic products depend not purely on the volatilities but on the derived covariance elements. Even for a fixed set of root-mean-square volatilities, these covariance elements strongly depend not only on the instantaneous correlation function, but also on the details of the time dependence of the volatility functions. If trading only in bonds and caplets is permitted, however, the market in instantaneous volatilities is no longer complete. If European swaptions are added to the market, some additional information about the instantaneous volatilities becomes available, but the introduction of the dependence of their prices on the instantaneous correlation still prevents the completion of the market. Only if serial options were liquidly traded (out to 30 years!) could the market in instantaneous volatilities and correlations be completed. (See footnote 9 in Chapter 1, Section 2.2.6 and Rebonato 1999c for a more detailed discussion of this point. See also Babbs and Selby 1996 on the nature of assumptions about the nature of the economic uncertainty made when invoking market completeness.)

Since the markets in instantaneous volatilities and correlations are, in reality, emphatically not complete, the available plain-vanilla market instruments do not allow the trader to 'lock in' via a self-financing trading strategy the time dependence of, say, the instantaneous volatilities, and the trader's replicating strategy will only work if her 'guess' of the instantaneous volatilities and correlations turns out to be correct.

For this reason, the trader should and does care about the financial plausibility of the assumptions she has to make about those quantities whose values cannot be 'locked in' due to the lack of completeness of the market in instantaneous volatilities and correlations. In particular she will care about the quality of the assumptions for those fundamental inputs to the model (that is, the volatilities and correlations) that are at the root of the lack of completeness. (See also Rebonato 2001a for a more careful discussion of these points, and of the different pricing measures implicitly used by a trader when making a price and when engaging in a dynamic hedging strategy.) One of the main tasks of this and the next chapter is therefore the specification of financially appealing descriptions for the input volatility and correlation functions. The chapters in Part III will then show how exact calibration to market prices can be achieved, if and when desired, while retaining these desirable qualitative features.

6.1.4 Is Imperfect Instantaneous Correlation Necessary to Produce Decorrelation?

Before embarking on the analysis proper of the instantaneous volatility functions, it is useful to say a few words about how these functions are related to the decorrelation among rates. These observations, in turn, are closely linked to the question of how many factors are needed in order to price exotic products realistically. It is widely recognized that the answer depends on the specific instruments (see Sidenius 2000 for a careful analysis of the dependence on the number of factors of the prices of a variety of exotic products), but the general point is also commonly made that many (and certainly more than one) factors are needed in order to produce a significant decorrelation among rates. There is a lot of truth in this statement, but the point that is often overlooked is that what influences the price of an exotic product (and, for that matter, of plain-vanilla products such as European swaptions) is not the instantaneous correlation or volatility functions per se, but, once again, the covariance element or, equivalently, the germane *terminal* (as opposed to *instantaneous*) correlation, $\bar{\rho}_{ij}(T)$, defined by

$$\bar{\rho}_{ij}(T) = \frac{\int_0^T \sigma_i(u)\sigma_j(u)\rho_{ij}(u)\,\mathrm{d}u}{\sqrt{v_i v_j}} \tag{6.1}$$

$$v_i = \int_0^T \sigma_i(u)^2\,\mathrm{d}u.$$

Expression (6.1) makes clear that, as long as the instantaneous volatilities are not constant, a significant terminal decorrelation can be brought about by time-dependent volatilities even in the presence of perfect instantaneous correlation (i.e., even if a single-factor description of the forward-rate dynamics were employed). This can occur, for instance, if the volatility of forward rate i, that is, σ_i, assumes large values whenever the volatility of forward rate j, that is, σ_j, is small, and vice versa.[3] Actually, one can show that when the instantaneous correlation between stochastic variables is high (as is plausibly the case for same-currency forward rates) the decorrelation mechanism stemming from the time dependence of the instantaneous volatilities becomes particularly effective (see Section 3.2 of Rebonato 1999c on this point).

Specifying a desirable time-dependent volatility is very straightforward when working with the LIBOR market model. With many of the traditional short-rate-based models, however, the functional form of the forward-rate instantaneous volatility is not a user-specified input. Given this lack of flexibility, these models have often attempted to provide a convincing description of financial reality, and, specifically, to account for decorrelation, by introducing extra factors. Since short-rate models have typically been implemented on trees or finite-difference lattices, it soon becomes computationally very burdensome to deal with more than two or three factors. Low-dimensionality (i.e., two- or three-factor) models, however, pose strong constraints on the

---

[3]This situation is not at all contrived, and, for the type of instantaneous volatility functions suggested in this chapter, it is actually very common when the forward rates in question are two forward rates belonging to the same swap rate but with significantly different expiries. See the discussion in Section 8.3.

possible shape of the instantaneous correlation between forward rates. In particular, unless 'many' factors are used, the convexity of the correlation function between contiguous forward rates tends to be negative, implying a model-induced low speed of initial decorrelation (see Sections 7.3.1 and 7.3.2). Furthermore, some (although, admittedly, not all) of the popular traditional short-rate models imply, once fitted to caplets, virtually flat instantaneous volatilities. This can have undesirable consequences in the pricing of complex products. As Equation (6.1) shows, in fact, for 'reasonable' values of the instantaneous correlation, $\rho(t)$, the attempt to produce terminal decorrelation (i.e., the type of decorrelation that 'matters' for pricing) can easily be frustrated both by low decorrelation between contiguous forward rates and by instantaneous volatilities that do not display a significant and/or plausible time dependence. Blindly 'throwing factors' at a model is therefore not necessarily the most computationally cost-effective way to obtain the desired terminal decorrelation.

The discussion that follows Equation (6.1) shows that one *can* achieve a significant terminal decorrelation even with a single-factor model. However, is it *desirable* to do so? One of the advantages of the modern pricing approach is that this choice is up to the trader, and is not an opaque implicit assumption of the model. If the trader believed, perhaps on the basis of econometric analysis, that the instantaneous correlation decreases sharply and quickly as the difference in maturity between two forward rates increases, she will choose to use a large number of factors. This approach is made possible by the fact that with the LIBOR market model a very large number of factors can easily be used for most products. On the other hand, if the trader believed that the instantaneous volatilities of forward rates are strongly non-constant throughout their lives, she would have at her control the most direct input to the LIBOR market model (i.e., the volatility functions themselves) to express this view. Personally, I prefer to 'share the burden' of achieving a realistic terminal decorrelation in an approximately even manner between instantaneous volatilities and correlations. If forced to make a choice between the two mechanisms, I would probably be more reluctant to price and hedge most exotic products with a multi-factor model that implied flat volatilities for the various forward rates (and that, as a consequence, puts all the burden of achieving terminal decorrelation among rates on the instantaneous correlation function), than with a one-factor model with a plausible behavior for the instantaneous volatility functions.

6.2 Instantaneous Volatility Functions: General Results

6.2.1 General Features and Requirements of Volatility Functions

If a modeller wanted to describe in the most general terms the no-arbitrage evolution of a set of spanning forward rates by means of a diffusive process, the instantaneous volatility, σ_{inst}, of a forward rate, f, could display a very complex functional dependence on a variety of drivers. To begin with, it could be a deterministic function of

  (i)   calendar time: $\sigma_{\text{inst}}(t)$;

 (ii)   specific features of the forward rate itself, known exactly at time t for any $\tau > t$, such as its maturity, T: $\sigma_{\text{inst}}(T)$;

(iii)   specific features of the forward rate itself, whose future values are known at time t only in a statistical sense – the instantaneous volatility at time τ, $\tau > t$, could be made to depend, for instance, on the realization of the forward rate itself at time τ: $\sigma_{\text{inst}}(T) = g(\tau, T, f_\tau)$;

(iv)   the full history of the yield curve and/or of its stochastic drivers (jumps, diffusions, etc.) up to time t, as described, for instance, by the natural filtration, $\mathcal{F}_t$, generated by the evolution of these stochastic processes: $\sigma_{\text{inst}}(\mathcal{F}_t)$.

In addition, future values of the instantaneous volatility function can display a stochastic dependence on

 (v)   the future realizations of stochastic processes, such as, for instance, Wiener processes, other than those driving the forward rates – in other terms, the instantaneous volatility could itself be a diffusion, a jump process, etc.

The distinction between (iii) and (v) is important, from both a practical and a conceptual point of view. Both types of dependence, in fact, render the instantaneous volatility a stochastic quantity. In case (iii), however, the natural filtration generated by the forward rate process up to time τ is all that is needed to know the corresponding time-τ value of the volatility. The latter will indeed be stochastic, but perfectly functionally dependent on the forward rate (I call this type of dependence has been called 'restricted' stochastic volatility and is dealt with in Chapter 11). Computationally, the same random draw necessary to evolve the forward rate from time t to time $t + \Delta t$ is sufficient to determine the value of the instantaneous volatility, $\sigma_{\text{inst}}(t + \Delta t)$, that will prevail from time $t + \Delta t$ to $t + 2\Delta t$. In case (v) on the other hand, the realization of stochastic processes other than the diffusion driving the forward rates are necessary in order to determine the future value of the volatility.

Type-(iii) and type-(v) volatility functions are examined in Chapters 11 and 12, respectively. As for the type of dependence (iv), it is, for instance, described by models of the autoregressive conditional heteroskedasticity (ARCH) family. These are not treated in this book. The literature in the field is vast, and the reader is referred, for instance, to Engle and Bollerslev (1986), Nelson (1990) and Bollerslev et al. (1992) for a review of the theory and of the empirical evidence.

In the general diffusive setting, the most important condition is perhaps the square-integrability of the volatility function. This stems from the need to compute well-defined covariance elements. In the financial context, esthetic considerations tend to require that the instantaneous volatility function should belong to L^2 (the class of Lebesgue square-integrable functions), but square-integrability in the Riemann sense is perfectly adequate for all the LIBOR-derivatives pricing applications I can think of. The next additional requirement is that the volatility should be an adapted process (i.e., loosely speaking, that its value at time t should not depend on the realization of any stochastic quantity at time $\tau > t$). Finally, in order to guarantee the existence of a unique (strong) solution to a stochastic differential equation of the form

$$\mathrm{d}X_t = \mu(X_t, t)\,\mathrm{d}t + \sigma(X_t, T)\,\mathrm{d}z_t,$$

it is safe to impose Lipschitz and growth conditions on μ and σ. Neither condition is financially restrictive for the applications dealt with in this book, and therefore they will not be considered here. The interested reader can pursue the topic in Duffie (1996, appendix E).

Looking back (Section 2.3) at the formulation I have chosen for the LIBOR market model, one can see that the crucial characterizing assumption is that the volatility functions of the forward rates should be restricted to being deterministic functions of time. In other words, it is exactly this choice that characterizes the LIBOR market model as such. When this choice is made, it is easy enough to choose deterministic functions of time with well-defined (Riemann or Lebesgue) integrals of their squares. Similar considerations apply to the requirement that the deterministic volatility function should satisfy a Lipschitz and growth condition. As for the desideratum that volatility should be an adapted process, it becomes irrelevant (or, rather, becomes trivial) in the context of the standard (deterministic-volatility) LIBOR market model. It will reappear, however, in Chapter 12 where I deal with stochastic instantaneous volatilities.

Summarizing, in the present chapter I shall deal with square-integrable instantaneous volatility functions (where the precise type of integration is, for practical purposes, largely irrelevant, and can, therefore, be chosen to the reader's liking), further restricted by requiring that they should depend at most on calendar time, t, and on the expiry of the forward rate itself, T:

$$\sigma_{\mathrm{inst}} = \sigma_{\mathrm{inst}}(t, T). \tag{6.2}$$

(Note that in the expression above I have chosen to indicate by the symbol 'T' the residual maturity of the forward rate as of 'today'. This argument therefore identifies the specific forward rate, and does not change as calendar time flows.)

6.2.2 Financial Interpretation of the Dependence on t and T

By Equation (6.2) different forward rates can respond differently to the same Brownian shock at the same point in time via their dependence on T. Similarly, the same forward rate might respond differently to Brownian shocks of the same magnitude for different values of its residual maturity (i.e., of $(T - t)$). Both these features are in principle desirable: it is plausible, for instance, to impose that a forward rate expiring in, say, nine months' time should respond more strongly to economic news than a forward rate expiring in 10 years' time. Conversely, one can reasonably expect that the same forward rate will display a greater or smaller change in its level because of the arrival of pieces of news of identical financial importance, depending on whether it has several years or a few months to expiry.

An important aspect in the construction of a market model is therefore the specification of what values the volatilities of different forward rates should assume when, as time goes by, one after the other the various forward rates have the same residual maturity. A trader, for instance, may have views about what the 'natural' level is now, and will be in the future, for the volatility of forward rates that have, say, three, six or 12 months to expiry. One possible, and plausible, set of beliefs is that forward rates that will have three, six or 12 months of residual maturity in the future will have approximately the same volatility as the forward rates that today have three, six or 12 months to go before expiry. Similarly, the trader might believe that forward rates, when of a given residual maturity, will have the same volatility that forward rates of the same residual maturity have had, on average, over a chosen representative period of time in the more or less recent past.

Alternatively, the trader might believe that, for whatever reason, the future will look neither like the present nor like the more or less recent past. This latter type of belief can have at least two distinct orientations: the trader might think that all forward rates will be more or less volatile in the future; or might believe that forward rates of certain expiries might become more or less volatile than other portions of the term structure of volatilities.

All these different types of belief find different expressions in the specification of the instantaneous volatility function, and, in a way, constitute the most crucial and delicate aspect in the specification of a LIBOR market model. Much as I believe that the modern pricing framework is powerful and practically useful, I must stress that it is only as good as the input volatilities (and, to a lesser extent, correlations) that are fed into it. A simplistic or ill-thought-out choice for the forward-rate volatility function can easily produce little more than a cumbersome and computationally expensive implementation of a poor one-factor short-rate-based model.

6.2.3 Time-Homogeneity in the Evolution of the Term Structure of Volatilities and of the Swaption Matrix

Special emphasis will be given in this chapter and in the rest of the book to the desideratum that the term structure of volatilities (and/or the swaption matrix) should evolve in a time-homogeneous manner. In the absence of more precise information, I shall therefore always assume that it is 'by default' desirable for a particular instantaneous volatility function to be able to reproduce (at least approximately) the current term structure of volatilities in the future, and in the following I will analyze various possible functional forms for the instantaneous volatility in this light. If the instantaneous correlation is not a function of calendar time, a set of instantaneous volatilities that produces a time-homogeneous evolution of the term structure of volatilities will also give rise to a similarly time-stationary swaption matrix. Imposing either of these requirements is motivated by the empirical observation that both the term structure of volatilities and the swaption matrix of the major currencies do change in level, but tend to retain their qualitative shape and some structural features over very extended periods of time (see, for instance, Figure 6.2 later in this chapter for an illustration of this feature over a relatively short but typical period of time). Occasionally, however, term structures of volatilities undergo brief but sometimes dramatic changes in shape (see Figure 6.3 later in this chapter, and the detailed analysis in Chapter 13). The ability to deal with such stochastic transitions in shape requires a fundamental extension of the LIBOR market model. For pricing purposes, however, the trader might want to assess what the price of a complex product would be if the term structure of volatilities certainly (i.e., deterministically) assumed a given future shape (possibly very different from today's). I will therefore also explore the ability of a specific instantaneous volatility function to reproduce a desired exogenously assigned (as long as admissible) future term structure of volatilities different from today's (see Section 8.4).

For the trader who thinks that the future (or, more precisely, the future term structure of volatilities) will look exactly like today (the 'time-homogeneous assumption'), the task is mathematically quite simple.[4] Let us define the term structure of volatilities precisely first. The most general definition would be the function, $\sigma_{\text{Black}}(\tau)$, $\mathcal{R}^+ \to \mathcal{R}^+$, that associates an implied volatility σ_{Black} to each caplet of maturity τ.[5] However, the version of the LIBOR market model I have introduced does not deal with a continuum of forward rates. Therefore, every pricing problem defines a set of spanning forward rates, each with a finite and (possibly different) tenor. The term structure of volatilities today is the function $(\mathcal{I} \to \mathcal{R}^+)$ that has as domain the set of the integers that label the forward rates, and as range the positive real axis (i.e., implied volatility associated to the n caplets). The term structure of volatilities

---

[4]Condition (6.2) ensures time-homogeneity of the term structure of volatilities when the instantaneous volatilities are purely time-dependent. When these latter quantities are stochastic, so becomes the term structure of volatilities, and the concept of time-homogeneity requires more careful handling. This topic is touched upon in Chapter 12.

[5]There should be a different implied volatility for each possible caplet tenor. If a continuum of possible tenors were available, the implied volatility function would be $(\mathcal{R}^+)^2 \to \mathcal{R}^+$. The extension is straightforward and, for the sake of simplicity, is not covered explicitly.

is linked to the instantaneous volatility by

$$\int_0^{T_i} \sigma_{\text{inst}}(u, T_i)^2 \, du = \sigma_{\text{Black}}^2(T_i) T_i \qquad 1 \leq i \leq n.$$

Consider now a time τ: $T_{k-1} \leq \tau \leq T_k$. A future (time-$\tau$) term structure of volatilities, denoted by $\sigma_{\text{Black}}^2(\tau, T_i)$, is then given by

$$\int_\tau^{T_i} \sigma_{\text{inst}}(u, T_i)^2 \, du = \sigma_{\text{Black}}^2(\tau, T_i)(T_i - \tau) \qquad 1 \leq i \leq n - k.$$

Notice that, given this definition, as time goes by and one forward rate after the other reaches its own reset time, the future term structure of volatilities contains fewer and fewer terms. Strictly speaking, given the infinite number of possible combinations of spanning forward rates covering a fixed time interval, there is a correspondingly infinite number of possible term structures of volatilities associated with a yield curve in its entirety. In the absence of smiles, in practice all these values will be typically obtained using a simple interpolation technique from a reference grid (in expiry–tenor space) of implied volatilities.

For a given current term structure of volatilities, if the trader wants to ensure its time-homogeneity, she will simply have to ensure that

$$\int_0^T \sigma_{\text{inst}}(u, T)^2 \, du = \int_\tau^{T+\tau} \sigma_{\text{inst}}(u, T + \tau)^2 \, du \qquad (6.3)$$

for any τ. It is straightforward to show that this condition will be satisfied for all values of τ if the functional form (6.1) reduces to

$$\sigma_{\text{inst}}(t, T) = \sigma_{\text{inst}}(T - t).$$

If that is the case, in fact,

$$\int_\tau^{T+\tau} \sigma_{\text{inst}}(u, T+\tau)^2 \, du = \int_\tau^{T+\tau} \sigma_{\text{inst}}(T + \tau - u)^2 \, du = \int_0^T \sigma_{\text{inst}}(T - u)^2 \, du.$$

6.2.4 Conditions for Recoverability of an Exogenous Term Structure of Volatilities with Time-Homogeneous Instantaneous Volatilities

Note that, however, if one wants to recover exactly an arbitrary current market term structure of volatilities, it is not always possible to find a function $\sigma_{\text{inst}}(T - t)$ such that the time-homogeneity condition will hold. This can be seen in more general terms as follows. The condition that today's market prices of caplets (i.e., today's term structure of volatilities) should be correctly recovered is tantamount to requiring that

$$\int_0^T \sigma_{\text{inst}}(T - u)^2 \, du = \sigma_{\text{Black}}^2(T)T \tag{6.4}$$

for any T, where $\sigma_{\text{Black}}(T)$ indicates the market-given implied (root-mean-square) volatility for the forward rate expiring at time T. In particular, the market pricing condition for the caplet maturing $T + \tau$ years from today is

$$\int_0^{T+\tau} \sigma_{\text{inst}}(u, T)^2 \, du = \sigma_{\text{Black}}^2(T + \tau)(T + \tau). \tag{6.5}$$

The time-homogeneity Condition (6.2) can then be rewritten as

$$\int_0^T \sigma_{\text{inst}}(T - u)^2 \, du = \sigma_{\text{Black}}^2(T)T = \int_\tau^{T+\tau} \sigma_{\text{inst}}(u, T + \tau)^2 \, du. \tag{6.6}$$

Taking the ratio of (6.5) to (6.6) one gets

$$
\begin{aligned}
\frac{\sigma_{\text{Black}}^2(T + \tau)(T + \tau)}{\sigma_{\text{Black}}^2(T)T} &= \frac{\int_0^{T+\tau} \sigma_{\text{inst}}(u, T)^2 \, du}{\int_\tau^{T+\tau} \sigma_{\text{inst}}(u, T + \tau)^2 \, du} \\
&= \frac{\int_0^\tau \sigma_{\text{inst}}(u, T)^2 \, du + \int_\tau^{T+\tau} \sigma_{\text{inst}}(u, T)^2 \, du}{\int_\tau^{T+\tau} \sigma_{\text{inst}}(u, T + \tau)^2 \, du} \\
&= 1 + \frac{\int_0^\tau \sigma_{\text{inst}}(u, T)^2 \, du}{\int_\tau^{T+\tau} \sigma_{\text{inst}}(u, T + \tau)^2 \, du}.
\end{aligned}
\tag{6.7}
$$

The second term in the last line in Equation (6.7) is a strictly positive quantity for any possible choice of the function $\sigma_{\text{inst}}(\ )$, and the whole right-hand side is therefore always greater than unity. This must be true for any arbitrary τ, and therefore the quantity $\sigma_{\text{Black}}^2(T)T$, as evaluated from today's term structure of volatilities, must be a strictly increasing function of T if one wants to be able to ensure, at the same time, that today's caplet prices are correctly recovered and that the term structure of volatilities can evolve in a time-homogeneous fashion. The exogenous quantity $\sigma_{\text{Black}}^2(T)$, however, is chosen by the market and is not always observed to be increasing. Therefore, it is not always possible to satisfy Equation (6.7) for a function $\sigma_{\text{inst}}(t, T)$ of the form $\sigma_{\text{inst}}(T - t)$. It is important to point out that the result does not depend on the details of the functional form of the (possibly unknown) instantaneous volatility function; and that the condition just obtained links in a very strong fashion the future behavior of the term structure of volatilities (namely, its time-homogeneity) with its market-given shape today. In other terms, if we live in a perfect Black world and if the market prices of the caplets are such that the quantities $\sigma_{\text{Black}}^2(T)T$ are not monotonically increasing in T,

Table 6.1   *The elements* $S(k, j) \equiv \int_{T(k-1)}^{T(k)} \sigma_{\text{inst}}(u, T_j)^2 \, du$ *of the matrix* **S** *described in the text for the case of* $1 \le k \le 5$, $1 \le j \le 5$.

$S(1,1)$				
$S(1,2)$	$S(2,2)$			
$S(1,3)$	$S(2,3)$	$S(3,3)$		
$S(1,4)$	$S(2,4)$	$S(3,4)$	$S(4,4)$	
$S(1,5)$	$S(2,5)$	$S(3,5)$	$S(4,5)$	$S(5,5)$

then the market must imply[6] that the term structure of volatilities will change in shape over time. Needless to say, the converse is not true: a term structure of volatilities today such that the quantity $\sigma_{\text{Black}}^2(T)T$ is non-decreasing can be compatible both with a time-homogeneous and with a time-varying evolution of forward-rate volatilities.

What I have just shown is that, if the instantaneous volatility function is of the form $\sigma_{\text{inst}}(T - t)$, then the quantities $\sigma_{\text{Black}}^2(T)T$ must be strictly increasing. Since, however, the implied volatilities are market-given, the implication is, so to speak, 'the wrong way around'. It is more useful to explore whether, given an arbitrary (as long as strictly increasing) function $\sigma_{\text{Black}}^2(T)T$, one can always rest assured that there will exist some function $\sigma(T - t)$ such that to-day's caplet market is correctly priced and the term structure of volatilities will evolve in a time-homogeneous fashion. That this is the case can be seen by means of a simple tabular construction, which will be used frequently in this and in the following chapters. Since, as seen in Chapters 3 and 4, for the products that the LIBOR market model is designed to price, 'nothing happens' in between the discretely spaced price-sensitive events, let us first define the quantities

$$S(k, j) \equiv \int_{T_{k-1}}^{T_k} \sigma_{\text{inst}}(u, T_j)^2 \, du,$$

where the index k labels the price-sensitive event, and the index j the forward rate. Incidentally, by the definition given, $S(k, j) = C(j, j, k)$, where the marginal covariance elements were defined in Equation (3.17). Clearly

$$\sum_{k=1}^{j} S(k, j) = \sigma_{\text{Black}}^2(T_j)T_j. \tag{6.8}$$

I will then organize these quantities in a matrix with time in the columns and maturities in the rows, as shown in Table 6.1 for the case of five forward rates.

In the case of an instantaneous volatility function of the form $\sigma_{\text{inst}}(t, T) = \sigma_{\text{inst}}(T - t)$, it is easy to see from Equation (6.6) that the matrix in Table 6.1

---

[6]I am neglecting at this stage the possible existence of smiles (see Chapters 11–13 for the inclusion of this feature).

Table 6.2 *The shape of the matrix **S** for the case of* $1 \leq k \leq 5$, $1 \leq j \leq 5$ *when the instantaneous volatility function is of the form* $\sigma_{\text{inst}}(t, T) = \sigma_{\text{inst}}(T - t)$.

$S(1,1)$				
$S(1,2)$	$S(1,1)$			
$S(1,3)$	$S(1,2)$	$S(1,1)$		
$S(1,4)$	$S(1,3)$	$S(1,2)$	$S(1,1)$	
$S(1,5)$	$S(1,4)$	$S(1,3)$	$S(1,2)$	$S(1,1)$

becomes the one shown in Table 6.2.

EXERCISE 6.1 *Prove that, if the instantaneous volatility function has the functional form* $\sigma_{\text{inst}}(t, T) = \sigma_{\text{inst}}(T - t)$, *then the matrix **S** in Table 6.1 assumes the shape of the matrix **S** in Table 6.2.*

If, as assumed, $\sigma_{\text{Black}}^2(T)T$ is a strictly increasing quantity in T, and since $S(1,1) = \sigma_{\text{Black}}^2(T_1)T_1$, one can always find[7] a $S(1,2) > 0$ such that $S(1,1) + S(1,2) = \sigma_{\text{Black}}^2(T_2)T_2$:

$$S(1,2) = \sigma_{\text{Black}}^2(T_2)T_2 - S(1,1) = \sigma_{\text{Black}}^2(T_2)T_2 - \sigma_{\text{Black}}^2(T_2)T_2. \qquad (6.9)$$

Extending the reasoning to later expiries, one can notice that, for any maturity k, there will only be one element, $S(1, k)$, left to be determined by the pricing condition for the kth caplet. The solving relationship

$$S(1,2) = \sigma_{\text{Black}}^2(T_k)T_k - \sigma_{\text{Black}}^2(T_{k-1})T_{k-1} \qquad (6.10)$$

will always be satisfied because, for any k, $S(i, k)$ is a strictly positive quantity by construction, and so is the difference $\sigma_{\text{Black}}^2(T_k)T_k - \sigma_{\text{Black}}^2(T_{k-1})T_{k-1}$, given the assumption about the increasing nature of $\sigma_{\text{Black}}^2(T)T$.

6.2.5 The Correspondence Between the Instantaneous Volatility Functions and the Future Term Structure of Volatilities

We have seen so far which forms of the instantaneous volatility functions are, or are not, compatible with a time-homogeneous evolution of the term structure of volatilities. The last link to be established is the correspondence between these two quantities in the deterministic-volatility LIBOR market model. To this effect, remember that we are only going to be interested in pricing products whose payoffs depend on a finite number of price-sensitive events. Also recall that the pricing of these products has been shown to depend on the marginal covariance elements defined in Chapter 4. Therefore,

---

[7]Given the definition, all the terms $S(j, k)$ must be strictly greater than zero.

any two instantaneous volatility functions, σ^1 and σ^2, such that

$$\int_{T_k}^{T_{k+1}} \sigma^1(T_j, u)\sigma^1(T_i, u)\rho_{ji}(T_j, T_i, u)\, \mathrm{d}u$$

$$= \int_{T_k}^{T_{k+1}} \sigma^2(T_j, u)\sigma^2(T_i, u)\rho_{ji}(T_j, T_i, u)\, \mathrm{d}u,$$

will give the same covariance elements and the same prices. For a given (sufficiently regular) correlation function, if these equalities are satisfied for any pair of forward rates (i and j) and for any price-sensitive event (k), the two functions σ^1 and σ^2 will be said to be 'equivalent over the given set of price-sensitive events' (or, more simply, 'equivalent' where no ambiguity can arise). If the same relationship has to hold for *any* (sufficiently regular) correlation function, then the two volatility functions must be, for all practical purposes, identical (apart from the usual set of measure zero). They will be called 'indistinguishable'. . In particular, for any two indistinguishable instantaneous volatility functions it is true that

$$\int_{T_k}^{T_{k+1}} \sigma^1(T_j, u)^2\, \mathrm{d}u = \int_{T_k}^{T_{k+1}} \sigma^2(T_j, u)^2\, \mathrm{d}u$$

for any j and k. Having established these definitions, it is then straightforward to prove:

PROPOSITION 6.1 *Any member of a set of indistinguishable instantaneous volatility functions gives rise to identical present and future term structures of volatilities.*

This follows immediately from the definition:

$$\sigma_{\mathrm{Black}}(\tau, T)^2 (T - t) = \int_{\tau}^{T+\tau} \sigma_{\mathrm{inst}}(T + \tau, u)^2\, \mathrm{d}u, \qquad \tau \in \{T_1, T_2, \ldots, T_n\}.$$

Going in the opposite direction requires more care. There is an infinity of (distinguishable!) instantaneous volatility functions that can be associated with (i.e., give rise to) a given term structure of volatilities. All these functions, however, will in general produce different covariance elements and, therefore, different prices for complex instruments (i.e., in this context, for instruments other than caplets).

EXERCISE 6.2 *Prove Proposition 6.1.*

EXERCISE 6.3 *'Since the yield curve is only sampled on the price-sensitive events, I can just as well use piecewise-constant instantaneous volatility functions. The algebra will be easier and I will get exactly the same results.' Discuss.*

Unless there is a possibility of ambiguity, in the following I shall loosely say, for instance, that a particular instantaneous volatility function gives rise to a

Table 6.3   *The elements $S(k, j) \equiv \int_{T(k-1)}^{T(k)} \sigma_{\text{inst}}(u, T_j)^2 \, du$ of the matrix $\mathbf{S}$ described in the text for the case of $1 \leq k \leq 5$, $1 \leq j \leq 5$. The elements of the matrix shown in bold type indicate the matrix $\mathbf{S}$ that will prevail in one period's time, and therefore completely determine the future term structure of volatilities.*

$S(1,1)$				
$S(1,2)$	**S(2,2)**			
$S(1,3)$	**S(2,3)**	**S(3,3)**		
$S(1,4)$	**S(2,4)**	**S(3,4)**	**S(4,4)**	
$S(1,5)$	**S(2,5)**	**S(3,5)**	**S(4,5)**	**S(5,5)**

given term structure of volatilities, without making reference to the equivalent indistinguishable instantaneous volatilities in the set. See Table 6.3 for an example.

6.2.6 Summaries of the Properties So Far

Summarizing and putting together the results obtained so far, one can state the following propositions (some of which are logically equivalent):

PROPOSITION 6.2 *If the instantaneous volatility function is of the form $\sigma_{\text{inst}}(t, T) = \sigma_{\text{inst}}(T - t)$, the quantity $\sigma_{\text{Black}}^2(T)T$ must be an increasing function of T (see Equation (6.7)).*

PROPOSITION 6.3 *If the quantity $\sigma_{\text{Black}}^2(T)T$ is a strictly increasing function of T, then there always exists an instantaneous volatility function of the form $\sigma_{\text{inst}}(t, T) = \sigma_{\text{inst}}(T - t)$ such that the caplet market is perfectly priced.*

PROPOSITION 6.4 *If the instantaneous volatility function is of the form $\sigma_{\text{inst}}(t, T) = \sigma_{\text{inst}}(T - t)$, then the term structure of volatilities evolves in a time-homogeneous manner.*

PROPOSITION 6.5 *If the quantity $\sigma_{\text{Black}}^2(T)T$ is an increasing function of T, then the term structure of volatilities may, but need not, evolve in a time-homogeneous manner.*

PROPOSITION 6.6 *If the quantity $\sigma_{\text{Black}}^2(T)T$ is not an increasing function of T, then (in the absence of smiles) the market implies that the term structure of volatilities will change its shape in the future.*

PROPOSITION 6.7 *If the matrix*

$$\mathbf{S} = \begin{pmatrix} S(1,1) & & & & \\ S(1,2) & S(2,2) & & & \\ S(1,3) & S(2,3) & S(3,3) & & \\ \vdots & \vdots & \vdots & \ddots & \\ S(1,n) & S(2,n) & S(3,n) & \dots & S(n,n) \end{pmatrix}$$

is of the form

$$
\begin{pmatrix}
S(1,1) & & & & \\
S(1,2) & S(1,1) & & & \\
S(1,3) & S(1,2) & S(1,1) & & \\
\vdots & \vdots & \vdots & \ddots & \\
S(1,n) & S(1,n-1) & \cdots & S(1,2) & S(1,1)
\end{pmatrix}
$$

and its elements correctly price the caplet market via Equation (6.8), then: (i) the matrix **S** *has been produced by an instantaneous volatility function of the form* $\sigma_{\mathrm{inst}}(t,T) = \sigma_{\mathrm{inst}}(T-t)$; *(ii) the quantity* $\sigma_{\mathrm{Black}}^2(T)T$ *obtained by applying Equation (6.8)* n *times is an increasing function of* T; *and (iii) the term structure of volatilities will evolve in a time-homogeneous manner.*

PROPOSITION 6.8 *If the instantaneous volatility function is of the form* $\sigma_{\mathrm{inst}}(t,T) = \sigma_{\mathrm{inst}}(T-t)$, *then the matrix* **S** *for* n *forward rates is fully described exactly by* n *independent values.*

PROPOSITION 6.9 *If the quantity* $\sigma_{\mathrm{Black}}^2(T_i)T_i$, $1 \le i \le n$, *is an increasing function of* T_i, *then it is always possible to find a matrix* **S** *described by exactly* n *independent elements such that all the caplets are perfectly priced.*

PROPOSITION 6.10 *For any market-given term structure of volatilities, there always exists an infinity of possible matrices* $\{\mathbf{S}\}$ *capable of reproducing today's caplet market.*

PROPOSITION 6.11 *There is a one-to-one correspondence between the future evolution of the term structure of volatilities and a set of indistinguishable (but not of equivalent!) instantaneous volatility functions.*

EXERCISE 6.4 *Prove Propositions 6.2–6.11, and show the implication links between them.*

6.2.7 A Strategy for Choosing Instantaneous Volatility Functions

The propositions above can provide some theoretical guidance as to how an instantaneous volatility function might be chosen. This task can be tackled as follows. First of all, one can begin by distinguishing two different market conditions, according to whether the quantity $\sigma_{\mathrm{Black}}^2(T)T$ is or is not strictly increasing. If it is, one might be tempted to dispense with the specification of an instantaneous volatility function altogether, and simply bootstrap the elements $S(i,k)$ as indicated in the discussion of Tables 6.1 and 6.2 (see Proposition 6.3 and Equation (6.10)). Tempting as this approach might be, I shall argue below that, even in the special case of increasing $\sigma_{\mathrm{Black}}^2(T)T$, it is not advisable to proceed in this way, for both numerical and conceptual reasons.

Postponing the discussion of why this should be the case until later, if the market-given quantity $\sigma_{\mathrm{Black}}^2(T)T$ is not strictly increasing, the bootstrapping procedure will certainly not work. In this case, no time-homogeneous solution can be found, but there still exists an infinity of ways to determine the elements $S(i, k)$ such that today's market is correctly priced (see Proposition 6.9). The existence of this infinity of solutions has profound pricing implications, because each specification for the matrix **S** capable of pricing today's caplet market will, at the same time, uniquely determine a different evolution of the term structure of volatilities. In order to choose among the infinitely many possible solutions, one must first of all decide what functional dependence on t and T one wants to give to the instantaneous volatility function. In order to appreciate the advantages and drawbacks of the different possible choices, from both the computational and the financial points of view, it is important to analyze in some detail a few possible candidate functional forms for the instantaneous volatility function. This task is carried out in the following section.

6.3 Functional Forms for the Instantaneous Volatility Function – Financial Implications

In this section I shall place particular emphasis on the ability of a functional specification to price an arbitrary current caplet market, and to produce, at the same time, a time-homogeneous evolution for the term structure of volatilities. The desirability of the first condition is self-evident. The financial motivation for imposing the latter condition is the 'default' requirement discussed in Section 6.2, that, unless precise information to the contrary is available to the trader, it is reasonable to impose that the future term structure of volatilities should look as similar as possible to the present (see, for instance, Figure 6.2 (but keep also in mind Figure 6.3)).

Both these requirements are directly or indirectly linked to observable caplet market prices. In addition, financial intuition and indirect information from the swaption market can suggest that certain types of qualitative behavior for the instantaneous volatility functions might be more desirable than others. The financial case for a particular qualitative shape of the forward-rate instantaneous volatility functions is made in the following section.

6.3.1 *The Financial Argument for a Humped Instantaneous Volatility Function*

One can attempt to find some qualitative financial indications as to the shape of the instantaneous volatility curve by conceptually dividing the maturity spectrum into three portions. The first would approximately correspond to the maturity period from spot to, say, the expiry of the first, or of the first two, futures contract(s). The second would span the period from the expiry of the first, or of the first two, futures contract(s) to, approximately, 12–18 months from spot. Finally, the third portion would be associated with longer maturities.

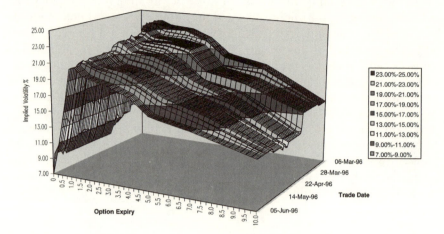

Figure 6.2   *Historical implied volatilities for different maturities collected over a period of approximately three months in 1996 for GBP. Notice the similarity over calendar time of the structural features of the surface, down to rather fine details such as the existence of a 'knuckle' around the five-year-maturity point. The implied volatilities have been shown only for a relatively short period (three months) for the sake of clarity, but these features persist over much longer periods. Occasionally, exceptional events (Russia crisis, Y2K year turn, etc.) disrupt this shape (see Figure 6.3), normally for short periods of time.*

Starting with the very short end of the maturity spectrum (the first segment), one can argue that the movements of the associated forward rates tend to fall into one of two very distinct modes: in 'normal' conditions, unexpected actions of the monetary authorities, which directly influence the short end of the yield curve, are not anticipated by the market. The instantaneous volatility of forward rates with a short time to reset can therefore be expected to be relatively low.

In periods of high uncertainty, on the other hand, the continuous analysis carried out by the market of the information relating to the future behavior of forward rates ('Will rates be left on hold, or, say, hiked by 25 or 50 basis points?') can generate very pronounced revisions of expectations[8] at the very short end of the yield curve. Similarly, if a currency is perceived to be vulnerable to speculative attacks, and the market believes that the monetary authorities will attempt a currency defense by raising short-term interest rates, the short end of the curve can experience very high volatility. By way of illustration, Figure 6.3 shows one instance of this situation, as exemplified by the period (summer 1996) when the now-legacy currency FRF came under

---

[8]The level of forward rates, of course, is not purely determined by expectations, and a risk premium enters the price-making process. At the very short end of the yield curve, however, the impact of the risk premium is very limited, and, for simplicity, I choose to concentrate in this qualitative discussion on the pure expectation component.

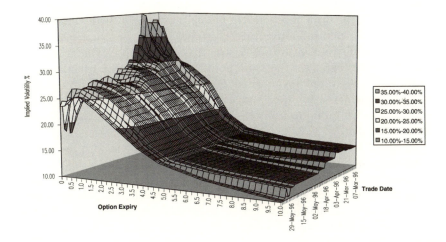

Figure 6.3 *Historical implied volatilities for different maturities collected over a period of approximately three months in 1996 for FRF, showing that the time-homogeneity constraint must not be accepted blindly. Note carefully that the figure shows the implied, rather than instantaneous, volatilities. At the short end, however, it is plausible to assume that the shape for the two functions should be closely related.*

speculative attack in the pre-euro period. The transition between a 'normal' and an 'excited' period (and the reversion back again to normality) is clearly evident. By generalizing these qualitative observations, it therefore appears plausible to assume that the volatilities of the forward rates closest to their own expiries tend to be either very low ('normal' conditions) or very high ('uncertain' conditions),[9] and that the transition between the two regimes can be rather sudden.

Moving to the opposite end of the maturity spectrum (i.e., to the third of the segments defined above), it is plausible to expect that the daily arrival of 'normal' economic news should have a rather limited impact on the revision of expectations about future rates expiring, say, 10 years in the future, which should be mainly affected by structural, rather than short-term, changes in expectation about future inflation and real rates. The volatility associated with this portion of the yield curve should therefore be relatively low.

The arrival of financial information, on the other hand, has a much more profound impact on the intermediate maturities between, say, six and 18 months (the middle segment). This is the area of the yield curve most influenced by the continuously revised market assessment of: the full extent of a rate tightening/easing cycle ('How many more rate hikes/cuts are in the pipeline?');

---

[9]The transition from one state to the other cannot be captured by any deterministic-volatility model. See however Chapter 12 (Figures 12.6 and 12.7 in particular), and the discussion at the end of Chapter 13 for a possible way to model this feature.

the positioning of the peak/trough of the futures curve ('By when will the Fed be done?'); the direction of the next rate move ('Will the Fed move from a tightening to a neutral/loosening bias?'); etc. It is therefore plausible to expect the volatility of forward rates expiring between approximately six and 18 months to be higher, at the same point in time, than the volatility of forward rates of longer and (in 'normal' conditions) shorter maturities. If this argument is correct, a humped shape is therefore appropriate for 'normal' conditions, and a monotonically decreasing one for periods of high short-term uncertainty.

The only statistical study of which I am aware that deals with the topic of the shape of the instantaneous volatility function of forward rates has been performed by Dodds (1998), and his findings confirm very nicely the qualitative picture presented above. More precisely, Dodds carried out an analysis of the volatility of constant-maturity three-month forward rates for the GBP curve in the period between 1 January 1993 and 23 June 1997. The forward rates were obtained using time series for the three-month LIBOR rate and via interpolation of euro–sterling short futures contracts. The first element in Dodds' data set is therefore the volatility of the three-month (spot) rate, the second entry is the volatility of the three-month forward rate expiring in three months' time from the current spot, and so on until the last entry, which is the volatility of the three-month forward rate expiring in 2.25 years. The results of this study are reported in Figure 6.4, and they confirm the qualitative description presented above. Notice, in particular, the location of the maximum (approximately one year), the steepness of the increase in the volatility, (the volatility almost doubles over one year), and the more gradual decline in the volatility level on the longer-maturity side of the hump.

6.3.2 Relevance of the Time Dependence of Instantaneous Volatilities for Pricing

If one accepts this qualitative account of why the instantaneous volatility of a given forward rate might display a noticeable and systematic time dependence, the relevance of the discussion above for the pricing of complex derivatives is apparent: we have concluded, in fact, in Chapters 3 and 5 that covariance integrals of the type

$$\int_{T_i}^{T_{i+1}} \sigma_j(u)\sigma_k(u)\rho_{jk}(u)\,\mathrm{d}u$$

are crucial for both the deterministic and the stochastic evolution of forward rates, and directly determine the prices of LIBOR products. In particular, the more the instantaneous volatility function is non-constant, and, in particular, the more it displays a 'hump', the more the terminal decorrelation (directly linked to the covariance integral displayed above) can be lower than unity even if the instantaneous correlation is perfect. Furthermore, the terminal decorrelation mechanism afforded by time-dependent instantaneous volatil-

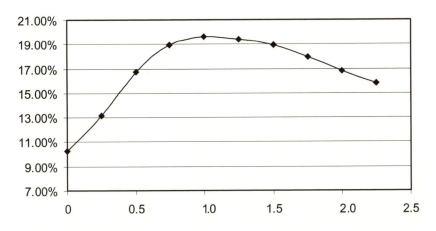

Figure 6.4 *The volatilities of forward rates of constant expiries from current spot for the GBP curve (data collected over the period 1 January 1993 to 23 June 1997). Data courtesy of Stephen Dodds.*

ities is particularly effective when the instantaneous correlation is high (see Rebonato 1999c, chapter 3), as is typically the case among same-currency forward rates. These observations should be kept in mind in the context of the discussion presented in Section 7.2.

6.3.3 Estimating Instantaneous Volatilities from Prices as an Inverse Problem

In physics and applied mathematics, two problems are often described as 'direct' and 'inverse', or inverse to each other (see, e.g., Engl 1993). Typically, if one wants to predict the future evolution of a process or physical system given its present state and a knowledge of the parameters that describe its dynamics, the problem is said to be 'direct'. The associated 'inverse' problem is that of imputing its parameters from (some properties of) its future evolution. Loosely speaking, inverse problems are often concerned with identifying causes from observed effects: for example, determining the heat distribution given initial conditions and the diffusion coefficient is a direct problem, while deducing the diffusion parameters from a future heat distribution constitutes the associated inverse problem. In a financial context, the most obvious application of these concepts is in the estimation of the instantaneous volatility given a set of prices for plain-vanilla instruments and an assumed process for the underlying.

One salient feature of inverse problems is that very often they do not satisfy the conditions for being 'well-posed'.[10] In particular, either the uniqueness or

---

[10]A problem is said to be well-posed if (i) for all admissible input data, a solution exists, (ii) for all admissible input data, the solution is unique, and (iii) there is continuous dependence of the solution on the input data (Hadamard definition).

the continuous dependence of the solution on the input data can fail to be satisfied. Traders who have tried to fit the local-volatility models of Dupire (1994), Derman and Kani (1994) and Derman et al. (1996) to market data will be familiar with these problems.

In the applications directly linked with the LIBOR market model, this implies that a totally non-parametric naive approach to estimating the volatility functions is likely to produce a solution that might change significantly for small perturbation of the noisy input prices. There are well-established ways to tackle this problem, which can be broadly described under the umbrella term of 'regularization', and of which Tikhonov's approach is probably the most common. When the 'physical' qualitative nature of the solution is not known a priori, a common feature of these techniques is to reduce or constrain its high-frequency components, and there exists a copious literature in this area (see again Engl 1993).

An alternative and, when applicable, more powerful approach to regularization is to require that the solution should belong to a class of functions identified on the basis of the modeller's understanding of the financial or physical characteristics of the problem. This is exactly the approach taken in this chapter in attacking what is an eminently inverse problem, that is, the estimation of the instantaneous volatility functions from the prices of plain-vanilla caplets and European swaptions. The financial discussion about the likely shape of an instantaneous volatility function presented in Section 3.1 provides some indications as to what a plausible solution should look like. Similarly, the requirement that an instantaneous volatility function should produce an (approximately) time-homogeneous evolution for the term structure of volatilities can provide another set of constraints on the solution.

The functional forms discussed in the remainder of Section 6.3, and their proposed parametrization, are therefore chosen so as to reflect the underlying financial requirements and to ensure that the resulting solution will indeed depend continuously on the input data. Taken together, the financial insight and the choice of a simple but flexible functional form to translate this insight into a tractable function constitute, in my opinion, an effective way of regularizing this particular inverse problem.

6.3.4 Possible Choices for the Instantaneous Volatility Functions

From the discussion above it is clear that it is important to specify functional forms for the instantaneous volatilities capable both of reproducing the caplet prices and of providing a financially satisfactory description of their observed time behavior. With these desiderata in mind, I shall analyze in detail the following functional forms:

$$\sigma_{\text{inst}}(t, T) = h(t), \tag{6.11a}$$

$$\sigma_{\text{inst}}(t, T) = g(T), \tag{6.11b}$$

$$\sigma_{\text{inst}}(t, T) = h(t)g(T), \tag{6.11c}$$

$$\sigma_{\text{inst}}(t, T) = h(T - t)g(T), \tag{6.11d}$$

$$\sigma_{\text{inst}}(t, T) = h(T - t)g(t), \tag{6.11e}$$

$$\sigma_{\text{inst}}(t, T) = h(T - t)g(t)f(T). \tag{6.11f}$$

[Needless to say, in the expressions above all the functions $h(\ )$ and $g(\ )$ that appear on the different lines are in general different; the same symbols have been used to save a few letters of the alphabet for a rainy day.] These functional forms do not exhaust all the conceivable possibilities, but variations on the theme can be easily constructed and analyzed following the discussion presented below.

6.3.5 Analysis of $\sigma_{\text{inst}}(t, T) = h(t)$

The first choice (6.11a) assumes that the volatilities of different forward rates do not depend on the specific forward rate, but are purely a function of time. According to this specification, when economic news arrives, all forward rates have the same 'responsiveness' to the shocks, irrespective of their maturity. This form for the instantaneous volatility function is designed to capture the occurrence of time-localized shocks to the yield curve as a whole – the textbook examples never fail to quote scheduled elections as an example of the type of events that could be modelled this way. Given the inability of this specification of instantaneous volatility function to assign, at a given point in time, a different responsiveness to forward rates of different maturities, the financial appeal of this assumption is, however, rather limited. Despite this shortcoming, this type of description of the volatility of forward rates used to be rather common in the early implementations of the LIBOR market model, probably for numerical reasons. With assumption (6.11a), in fact, ensuring the correct pricing of a single caplet can always be easily achieved, since it simply means choosing the function $h(t)$ to be such that

$$\sigma_{\text{Black}}^2(T)T = \int_0^T \sigma_{\text{inst}}^2(u)\, du = \int_0^T h(u)^2\, du.$$

However, when one considers today's prices for a collection of caplets, one can immediately see that, depending on the current shape of the market term structure of volatilities, an insurmountable problem can be encountered: since

$$\sigma_{\text{Black}}^2(T_1)T_1 = \int_0^{T_1} h(u)^2\, du$$

$$\sigma_{\text{Black}}^2(T_2)T_2 = \int_0^{T_2} h(u)^2\, du,$$

it follows that (for $T_1 < T_2$)

$$\sigma_{\text{Black}}^2(T_2)T_2 - \sigma_{\text{Black}}^2(T_1)T_1 = \int_{T_1}^{T_2} h(u)^2 \, du. \tag{6.12}$$

The right-hand side, being the integral of a strictly positive quantity, must be positive. The left-hand side of Equation (6.12), however, is market-given, and need not be positive for all values of T_1 and T_2. Therefore, for some shapes of the market term structure of volatilities, one might end up with an imaginary instantaneous volatility.

As for the ability of assumption (6.11a) to produce a time-homogeneous evaluation of the term structure of volatilities, one can immediately see that it entails for the matrix $\mathbf{S}$ the following shape:

$$\begin{pmatrix} S(1,1) \\ S(1,1) & \mathbf{S(2,2)} \\ S(1,1) & \mathbf{S(2,2)} & S(3,3) \\ S(1,1) & \mathbf{S(2,2)} & S(3,3) & S(4,4) \\ S(1,1) & \mathbf{S(2,2)} & S(3,3) & S(4,4) & S(5,5) \end{pmatrix}$$

In particular, the elements in bold show the term structure of volatility at time 2, which is, in general, different from the corresponding portion of the term structure of volatilities at time 1. In view of its poor financial justification, its inability to recover exactly all possible market-given term structures of volatilities, and its very strongly time-inhomogeneous nature, it is surprising how Equation (6.11a) attracted some considerable interest in the days of the first implementations of the LIBOR market model – in particular, it was often used to analyze the relative value of forward-staring swaptions. Today its interest is of mainly 'historical' character, and it will therefore not be analyzed any further.

6.3.6 Analysis of $\sigma_{\text{inst}}(t, T) = g(T)$

Option (6.11b), that is, $\sigma_{\text{inst}}(t, T) = g(T)$, is probably the simplest to implement. Not surprisingly, owing to its simplicity, historically it was also often chosen in the earliest implementations of the LIBOR market model. It is easy to show that the only way in which all the caplets can be correctly priced with the instantaneous volatility purely a function of the individual forward rate is by imposing, for any T,

$$g(T) = \sigma_{\text{Black}}(T). \tag{6.13}$$

The matrix $\mathbf{S}$ now becomes

$$\begin{pmatrix} S(1,1) \\ S(2,2) & \mathbf{S(2,2)} \\ S(3,3) & \mathbf{S(3,3)} & S(3,3) \\ S(4,4) & \mathbf{S(4,4)} & S(4,4) & S(4,4) \\ S(5,5) & \mathbf{S(5,5)} & S(5,5) & S(5,5) & S(5,5) \end{pmatrix}$$

with the elements in bold displaying again the (time-inhomogeneous) term structure of volatilities at time 2. Comparing the structure of the **S** matrices obtained for choices (6.11a) and (6.11b), one can appreciate that they correspond to two 'diametrically opposed' ways of apportioning the total variance of each forward rate across time: notice, in fact, how rows are constant for choice (6.11b), and columns for (6.11a). If one remembers that the condition for time-homogeneity can be translated into the requirement that the **S** matrix should have constant elements along diagonal lines (Proposition 6.7), one can see these three structures (i.e., the time-homogeneous, the purely time-dependent and the purely forward-rate-specific) as the fundamental building blocks of all the more complex and realistic separable functional specifications.

Going back to choice (6.11b), by displaying the term structure of volatilities in this tabular form, one can see that a feasible solution will always be found, since each (strictly positive) element $S(k, k)$ is simply obtained[11] by dividing by j the (strictly positive) quantity $\sigma^2_{\text{Black}}(T_j)T_j$. By imposing Condition (6.13) one can therefore rest assured automatically by construction that the whole term structure of volatilities will be exactly recovered for any arbitrary set of market caplet prices.

This choice, however, also suffers from very severe problems insofar as its financial justification is concerned; it in fact entails that

- a given forward rate will have the same volatility throughout its life, irrespective of whether it has three months or 10 years to expiry, and

- all forward rates will behave differently throughout their lives if looked at in terms of their residual maturities.[12]

As a consequence of this, today's term structure of volatilities will, in general, always change shape in the future: the portion of the term structure of volatilities between T_1 and T_2 years implied by the model to prevail in τ years' time will look exactly like today's term structure of volatilities between maturities $T_1 + \tau$ and $T_2 + \tau$ (see Figure 6.5).

Because of these features, choice (6.11b) is in general intrinsically incapable of reproducing a time-homogeneous evolution of the term structure of volatilities even if the collection of today's price is such that $\sigma^2_{\text{Black}}(T_1)T_1 < \sigma^2_{\text{Black}}(T_2)T_2$, for any $T_1 < T_2$. Despite its computational simplicity, Option (6.11b) is therefore both financially unappealing and unduly restrictive from the mathematical point of view. It can be of some interest, however, for model risk evaluation purposes, because simple heuristic arguments and empirical observations (Kainth et al. 2001) indicate that the evolution of the yield curve it implies is very similar (and, therefore, so are the prices of exotic products)

---

[11]I have assumed for simplicity that the time intervals $[T_k, T_{k+1}]$ are all of equal length. Generalizations of this setting are straightforward.

[12]The only exception to this statement is, of course, the unrealistic case of a perfectly flat term structure of volatilities.

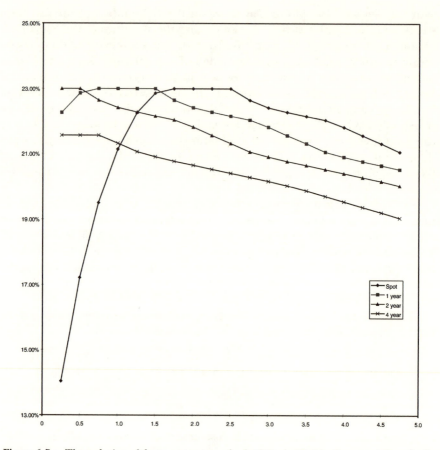

Figure 6.5   *The evolution of the term structure of volatilities implied by the assumption of a flat instantaneous volatility over four years. The spot term structure of volatilities (GBP in 1998) is labelled 'Spot'. The implied volatility curve in one year's time can be obtained by translating the spot curve by one year to the left along the maturity axis, and similarly for the two- and four-year curves.*

to what is obtained using the BDT model (Black et al. 1990). As for the latter, despite its well-known shortcomings, it allows, unlike the LIBOR market model, easy mapping onto a recombining lattice, and it is therefore still used by some banks when bidding for Bermudan swaptions. Apart from this aspect, I see little merit in the volatility specification (6.11b), and it will not be analyzed any further.

6.3.7 Analysis of $\sigma_{\text{inst}}(t, T) = g(T)h(t)$

As for Option (6.11c), that is, $\sigma_{\text{inst}}(t, T) = g(T)h(t)$, it appears to have more financial appeal than either of the choices analyzed so far: in fact, it splits the responsiveness to financial innovations of a given forward rate into a component that is purely time-dependent and one that is specific to the individual forward rate. (Note carefully again that, with the notation chosen, the argument T in $g(T)$ identifies today's maturity of a forward rate – and hence the forward rate itself – and not its residual maturity.) With choice (6.11c), pricing a single caplet correctly means imposing that, for any T,

$$g(T)^2 = \frac{\sigma_{\text{Black}}^2(T)T}{\int_0^T h(u)^2 \, du}. \tag{6.14}$$

From this expression it is easy to see that, for any arbitrarily chosen function $h(\ )$ and any exogenous market term structure of volatilities, a function $g(\ )$ can always be found so that the simultaneous pricing of all the caplets is ensured.

The next condition to be examined is the ability of choice (6.11c) to produce a time-homogeneous evolution of the term structure of volatilities and correct pricing of an arbitrary exogenous caplet market when the quantity $\sigma_{\text{Black}}^2(T)T$ is a strictly increasing function of T.[13] From Propositions 6.2 and 6.3, one can immediately conclude that this will not be the case (since Equation (6.11c) is not of the form $h(T-t)$). It can be instructive, however, to look from a different angle at the reason for the failure of specification (6.11c) in satisfying these joint conditions. This is done in Appendix I at the end of this chapter.

This inability to produce, in general, a time-homogeneous evolution of the term structure of volatilities argues against its use as a desirable instantaneous volatility function. The simple procedure (6.14) whereby the price of a caplet is automatically recovered will, however, be made use of later on for more financially appealing functional descriptions.

6.3.8 Analysis of $\sigma_{\text{inst}}(t, T) = h(T - t)g(T)$

Moving on to the choice (6.11d), it also splits the instantaneous volatility into a component that is specific to the individual forward rate, $g(T)$, but, unlike choice (6.11c), it allows for a second (multiplicative) term that depends on the residual maturity of the caplet (i.e., on $(T-t)$), rather than on calendar time:

$$\sigma_{\text{inst}}(t, T) = h(T - t)g(T). \tag{6.15}$$

The caplet market pricing condition now becomes, for any T:

$$g(T)^2 = \frac{\sigma_{\text{Black}}^2(T)T}{\int_0^T h(T - u)^2 \, du}, \tag{6.16}$$

---

[13]If this condition were not satisfied, we have already seen that no functional form for the instantaneous volatility could produce a term structure of volatilities evolving in a time-homogeneous manner.

and the time-homogeneity condition reads

$$g(T + \tau)^2 \int_{\tau}^{T+\tau} h(T + \tau - u)^2 \, \mathrm{d}u = g(T)^2 \int_{0}^{T} h(T - u)^2 \, \mathrm{d}u. \qquad (6.17)$$

The only function $g(\ )$ for which Equations (6.17) can be satisfied for any T is clearly when it is equal to a constant, k:

$$g(T) = k. \qquad (6.18)$$

This condition, of course, is nothing other than the time-homogeneity condition obtained before, but, at the same time, it suggests an easy criterion for choosing the function $h(T-t)$, if one wants to ensure correct pricing of the caplet market and approximate time-homogeneity. One can begin by choosing a functional form for $h(\ )$ parametrized by a set of parameters $\{a_i\}$. One can then choose as a requirement to determine the 'best' coefficients $\{a_i\}$ the condition that, after pricing all the caplets correctly (Equation (6.16)), the function $g(\ )$ should be as constant as possible across forward rates (i.e., should be as independent of the individual forward rates as possible). In other words, this approach finds the parametrization of the chosen function, $h(\ )$, of the residual maturity, $(T - t)$, that best preserves time-homogeneity.

Note that, as discussed above, as long as the quantity $\sigma_{\text{Black}}^2(T)T$ is a strictly increasing function of T, there always exists (see Proposition 6.3 and the discussion after Table 6.2) some function $h(T - t)$ such that all the caplets are priced, and the term structure of volatilities evolves in a time-homogeneous manner. However, if the extra requirement is imposed that the time-homogeneous component, $h(\ )$, should have a certain functional form, such as the one, for instance, suggested by the discussion before Equation (6.12), then one can no longer rest assured that it will turn out to be a solution to the pricing equations for today's caplets. Determining the parameters of $h(\ )$ in such a way that the function $g(\ )$ is as constant as possible therefore fulfills the task of finding the most time-homogeneous evolution for the term structure of volatilities *compatible with the chosen qualitative shape for $h(\ )$*. I shall show in the following a possible functional form for this function, and the results obtained using market data.

The reader who remembers Proposition 6.3 might well ask why one should use a function $g(T)$ at all when the market term structure of volatilities is strictly increasing in T. It is true that, when this condition is satisfied, a caplet-pricing, time-homogeneous solution can always be found. There is no guarantee, however, that the resulting function should display the financially desirable features described in Section 3.1. The introduction of the function $g(T)$, if it is used as suggested, can insure that the best time-homogeneous solution will be found, compatible with the observed market prices and with the financial desiderata discussed above.

There is one drawback of this approach that should be pointed out. If the best fit to the function $h(\ )$ produced a solution function $g(T)$ displaying a significant variation across forward rates (i.e., across initial maturities T), the resulting dynamics would imply that, over time, any two forward rates will respond very differently to economic information shocks of the same magnitude, even when they are of the same residual maturity: if the optimization produced a $g(T_2)$, say, twice as large as $g(T_1)$, it would mean that the forward rate maturing T_2 years from today will be twice as responsive today as the T_1-maturity forward rate was when it had the same residual maturity. This feature is clearly unsatisfactory, and would give an indication that the market data reject the joint hypotheses of time-homogeneity for the evolution of the term structure of volatilities and of correctness of the qualitative behavior postulated for the function $h(\ )$. If this were the case, an instantaneous volatility function of the form (6.11d) should not be used. I shall show below that, empirically, this is rarely the case, and that the choice of functional dependence on t and T described by Equation (6.11d) is both simple and satisfactory for most practical applications.

6.3.9 Analysis of $\sigma_{\text{inst}}(t, T) = h(T - t)g(t)$ and of $\sigma_{\text{inst}}(t, T) = h(T - t)g(t)f(T)$

The next functional form that I will briefly analyze is Equation (6.11e), which splits the instantaneous volatility into a component that is purely time-dependent, $g(t)$, and one that depends on the residual maturity of the caplet:

$$\sigma_{\text{inst}}(t, T) = h(T - t)g(t). \tag{6.19}$$

The responsiveness of all forward rates to the arrival of economic news is therefore modulated through time by the same function $g(t)$: via the function $h(\ )$ all forward rates have a responsiveness depending on their residual maturity, but, as a function of time, they might also all become more (or less) responsive. If the 'normal' responsiveness of a 10-year-maturity forward rate is, say, two-thirds of the 'normal' responsiveness of a 12-month-maturity forward rate, their relative magnitude will be maintained by the multiplication by a function of time $g(t)$. This is, arguably, a financially more appealing description of financial behavior than what is implied by function (6.11d). The caplet market pricing condition, however, now becomes, for any T,

$$\sigma_{\text{Black}}^2(T)T = \int_0^T g(u)^2 h(T - u)^2 \, du. \tag{6.20}$$

Notice that it is now no longer possible to impose a simple condition such as Equations (6.13) or (6.14) in order to price the caplets exactly, since the quantity $g(u)$ cannot now be brought outside the integral sign. The obvious computational solution is to make the function $g(t)$ piecewise constant over each interval $[T_k, T_{k+1}]$. This choice, however, must be implemented with care, because, if the integration interval is long, by making the function $g(\ )$ piecewise constant, one can end up altering significantly the terminal decorrelation that would result if a non-constant function were used (see Exercise 6.3 at the end of Section 6.2.5).

Finally, it is left to the reader to combine the analyses presented so far in order to discuss the case (6.11f), $\sigma_{\mathrm{inst}}(t, T) = h(T - t)g(t)f(T)$. It will be shown in a later chapter (Chapter 8) how choice (6.11f) lends itself to a simple three-stage procedure whereby a given (present or future) term structure of volatilities can be reproduced by placing as much explanatory burden first of all on the time-homogeneous component, $h(T - t)$, then on the purely time-dependent component, $g(t)$, and finally on the forward-rate-specific term, $f(T)$.

6.3.10 The Matrix S Revisited

In closing this section, it is useful for future calibration applications to express in a more convenient form the matrix $\mathbf{S}$ in the presence of separable time, maturity and residual-maturity (i.e., $(T - t)$) dependences. To this effect, remember first that, if the instantaneous volatility is of a purely time-homogeneous form, $\sigma_{\mathrm{inst}}(t, T) = h(T - t)$, the matrix $\mathbf{S}$ assumes the shape:

$$
\begin{pmatrix}
S_{\mathrm{th}}(1,1) & & & & \\
S_{\mathrm{th}}(1,2) & S_{\mathrm{th}}(1,1) & & & \\
S_{\mathrm{th}}(1,3) & S_{\mathrm{th}}(1,2) & S_{\mathrm{th}}(1,1) & & \\
\vdots & \vdots & \vdots & \ddots & \\
S_{\mathrm{th}}(1,n) & S_{\mathrm{th}}(1,n-1) & \cdots & S_{\mathrm{th}}(1,2) & S_{\mathrm{th}}(1,1)
\end{pmatrix}.
$$

(Notice that the subscript 'th' stands in this context for 'time-homogeneous', rather than the more usual 'theoretical'.) In the presence of a separable time-dependent component, that is, if $\sigma_{\mathrm{inst}}(t, T) = h(T - t)g(t)$, and assumes for simplicity a piece-wise constant time-dependent function, $g(t) = \epsilon_k$, $T_{k-1} \leq t < T_k$, $k = 1, 2, \ldots, n$, the matrix $\mathbf{S}$ becomes

$$
\begin{pmatrix}
S_{\mathrm{th}}(1,1)\epsilon_1^2 & & & & \\
S_{\mathrm{th}}(1,2)\epsilon_1^2 & S_{\mathrm{th}}(1,1)\epsilon_2^2 & & & \\
S_{\mathrm{th}}(1,3)\epsilon_1^2 & S_{\mathrm{th}}(1,2)\epsilon_2^2 & S_{\mathrm{th}}(1,1)\epsilon_3^2 & & \\
\vdots & \vdots & \vdots & \ddots & \\
S_{\mathrm{th}}(1,n)\epsilon_1^2 & S_{\mathrm{th}}(1,n-1)\epsilon_2^2 & \cdots & & S_{\mathrm{th}}(1,1)\epsilon_n^2
\end{pmatrix}
$$

Finally, if the instantaneous volatility function has the more general form $\sigma_{\mathrm{inst}}(t, T) = h(T - t)g(t)f(T)$, then the matrix $\mathbf{S}$ can be written as

$$
\begin{pmatrix}
S_{\mathrm{th}}(1,1)\epsilon_1^2 f(T_1)^2 & & \\
S_{\mathrm{th}}(1,2)\epsilon_1^2 f(T_2)^2 & S_{\mathrm{th}}(1,1)\epsilon_2^2 f(T_2)^2 & \\
S_{\mathrm{th}}(1,3)\epsilon_1^2 f(T_3)^2 & S_{\mathrm{th}}(1,2)\epsilon_2^2 f(T_3)^2 & S_{\mathrm{th}}(1,1)\epsilon_3^2 f(T_3)^2 \\
\cdots & \cdots & \cdots
\end{pmatrix}
$$

The usefulness of this decomposition in the calibration process will be shown in Chapter 8.

6.4 Analysis of Specific Functional Forms for the Instantaneous Volatility Functions

In the previous sections I have discussed in very general terms the financial implications of different possible types of functional dependence of the instantaneous volatility functions on calendar time (t) and residual maturity (T). In particular, I have argued that functions of the general form

$$\sigma_{\text{inst}}(t, T) = g(T)h(t)f(T - t) \tag{6.21a}$$
$$\sigma_{\text{inst}}(t, T) = g(T)f(T - t) \tag{6.21b}$$

display several positive features, from both the financial and the computational perspective. What remains to be specified is the actual functional form for the different functions, that is, $f(\ )$, $g(\ )$ and $h(\ )$, that together make up the instantaneous volatility.

6.4.1 A Possible Functional Form for $f(T - t)$

Starting from the time-homogeneous component, $f(T-t)$, the main desiderata are that

- it should have a reasonably flexible functional form, so as to be able to reproduce either a humped or a monotonically decreasing instantaneous volatility;

- its parameters should lend themselves to a reasonably transparent econometric interpretation, so as to allow a 'sanity check' almost by inspection; and

- it should afford easy analytical integration of its square, thereby greatly facilitating the evaluation of the necessary variance (and covariance) elements.

I have argued elsewhere (Rebonato 1999c) that the functional form

$$f(T - t) = [a + b(T - t)] \exp[-c(T - t)] + d \tag{6.22}$$

fulfills these criteria to an acceptable degree. Appendix II at the end of this chapter gives the closed-form expression for the indefinite integral of the instantaneous covariance obtainable with a time-independent correlation function. As for the possible shapes obtainable with function (6.22) for different choices of the parameters, a few representative examples are shown in Figure 6.6. One can readily see that these qualitative shapes display most of

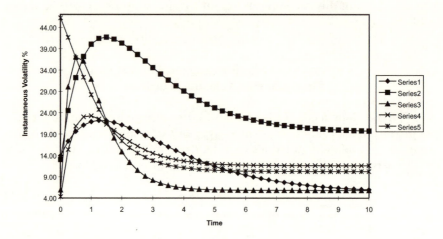

Figure 6.6   *Possible shapes of the proposed time-homogeneous component for the instantaneous volatility function.*

the salient and plausible characteristics that one might want from the time-homogeneous component of a candidate instantaneous volatility function. The proposed functional form in fact easily allows both for monotonically decreasing shapes (as could be appropriate if exceptional volatility is expected for the earliest-expiring forward rates in the immediate future, and as depicted in the curve labelled 'Series 5'), and for the more common humped shape. The hump, in turn, can be either sharp and relatively localized (see curve labelled 'Series 3), or smooth and 'diffuse' (see curves 'Series 4' and 'Series 1'). This degree of flexibility might be particularly desirable to model the instantaneous volatility functions for different currencies, since it is plausible to expect that different degrees of liquidity for the futures contracts after the first two or three might affect the resultant forward-rate instantaneous volatility.

6.4.2 Constraints on the Parameters of $f(T-t)$ and Link to Financial Observables

As for the possible financial and econometric constraints on the parameters, one can immediately notice that, for the interpretation of the function as a well-behaved instantaneous volatility to be valid, the following conditions must be satisfied:

- $a + d > 0$,

- $d > 0$,

- $c > 0$.

Furthermore, as $\tau = T - t$ tends to zero, instantaneous and average volatilities tend to coincide, and therefore the quantity $a + d$ should at least approximately assume the values given by the shortest-maturity implied volatilities. The parameter d, to which the instantaneous volatility is forced to converge asymptotically as τ goes to infinity, is instead more directly linked to the level of very-long-maturity volatilities. If the trader believes that 'normal' trading conditions are to be expected at the short end of the curve, the instantaneous volatility function should be rising for small values of τ. This implies that a should be smaller than b/c, if $b > 0$. Furthermore, the combination of parameters $(b - ca)/cb$ provides the location of the extremum of the humped curve. The condition for this extremum to be a maximum is that $b > 0$. If $b < 0$, no maximum will be present. Finally, if the financial justification for the existence of a hump in the instantaneous volatility is correct, the combination of parameters $1/c - a/b$ should give a value not too dissimilar from unity. For ease of reference, the most salient characteristics of the instantaneous volatility function and of its derivatives are listed below:

First derivative:	$(b - ca - cb\tau)\exp(-c\tau)$
Second derivative:	$c^2(a + b\tau)\exp(-c\tau) - 2cb\exp(-c\tau)$
First derivative at the origin:	$b - ca$
Location of extremum:	$(b - ca)/cb$
Second derivative at extremum:	$-bc\exp(-c\tau)$

It is also important to stress again that the simplicity of the chosen functional form allows easy analytical integration and evaluation of the covariance integrals, thereby making both the calibration and the pricing practicable and expedient. The expression for the definite integral of the square of the instantaneous volatility is given in Appendix II at the end of this chapter.

Since it is easy and natural to associate semi-observable features of the instantaneous volatility function with simple linear combinations of the parameters, the stochastic-volatility extension of the LIBOR market model presented in Chapters 12 and 13 will be formulated by positing appropriate stochastic processes for the parameters themselves.

6.4.3 Possible Functional Form for $h(t)$

Moving now to the possible functional form for the purely time-dependent function, $\epsilon(t)$, its most desirable qualitative features are less easy to identify. As usual, if the function is allowed too many degrees of freedom, it is in general more prone to mis-specification and, in particular, to picking up undesirable noise in the market term structure of volatilities. If it is too simple or too rigid, it might miss some of the important features it is supposed to capture. Another way to express the same need for balance between flexibility and over-specification is to Fourier-analyze the residuals and to retain only a pre-chosen number of frequencies. The higher the number of frequencies retained, the

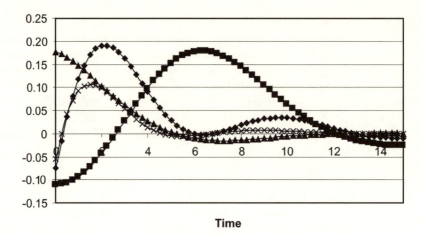

Figure 6.7   *Some possible shapes obtained with the functional choice (6.23) and n = 3 for the time-dependent component. Time in quarters along the x axis. Curve 1 (triangles) might be appropriate to capture an environment of future decreasing volatility; curves 2 (diamonds) and 3 (crosses) could account for a localized source of uncertainty (elections, scheduled Fed meetings, etc.); and curve 4 (squares) could describe a situation such as GBP joining the EUR.*

greater the ability of the function to pick up localized time dependences (say, the textbook example of a forthcoming election), but the greater the danger of chasing market noise. The functional form I propose below attempts to recover this intuition, and is made up of a linear combination of a small number of sine waves with phases and amplitudes to be optimized to the available data, and a multiplicative exponentially decaying term (with decay constant also optimized to obtain an acceptable fit). The proposed function is given by

$$\epsilon(t) = \left[\sum_{i=1}^{n} \epsilon_i \, \sin\left(\frac{t\pi i}{\mathrm{Mat}} + \epsilon_{i+1} \right) \right] \exp(-\epsilon_7 t), \qquad (6.23)$$

with n as small as 2 or 3, and the quantity 'Mat' equal to the longest caplet maturity.

As Figure 6.7 shows, three sine frequencies provide all the flexibility (and possibly even more) that a prudent model user might desire for the time-dependent function $h(t)$. The results of actual optimizations using this function are displayed in Case Study 2 in Chapter 7.

6.4.4 What the Function g(T) Should Look Like if Everything Has Worked Well

Finally, as far as the forward-rate-specific function $g(T)$ is concerned, in the case of fitting to a single market-given term structure of volatilities, the requirement that the prices of the caplets should be exactly recovered uniquely determines the quantities $g(T_i) = (1 + \delta_i)$, $1 \leq i \leq n$. If the procedure has worked properly, the variation of the term δ as a function of the forward-rate index might contain high frequencies, but should be of very small amplitude. In other terms, the forward-rate dependence might not be smooth, but should be small. Case Study 1, discussed in Chapter 7, shows for a typical example that this is indeed the case.

6.5 Appendix I – Why Specification (6.11c) Fails to Satisfy Joint Conditions

The time-homogeneity condition applied to Equation (6.11c) gives

$$g(T + \tau)^2 \int_\tau^{T+\tau} h(u)^2 \, \mathrm{d}u = g(T)^2 \int_0^T h(u)^2 \, \mathrm{d}u. \tag{6.24}$$

If one couples (6.24) with the market pricing Condition (6.14) one obtains

$$\frac{\sigma_{\text{Black}}^2(T+\tau)(T+\tau) \int_\tau^{T+\tau} h(u)^2 \, \mathrm{d}u}{\int_0^{T+\tau} h(u)^2 \, \mathrm{d}u} = \sigma_{\text{Black}}^2(T)T, \tag{6.25}$$

and therefore

$$\frac{\sigma_{\text{Black}}^2(T+\tau)(T+\tau) \int_\tau^{T+\tau} h(u)^2 \, \mathrm{d}u}{\sigma_{\text{Black}}^2(T)T} = 1 + \frac{\int_0^\tau h(u)^2 \, \mathrm{d}u}{\int_\tau^{T+\tau} h(u)^2 \, \mathrm{d}u}. \tag{6.26}$$

This expression looks deceptively similar to Equation (6.7), obtained for the general case of $\sigma_{\text{inst}} = \sigma_{\text{inst}}(t, T)$. However, if one displays the instantaneous volatilities in tabular form (as I have done in Table 6.4), one can easily see that, in general, it will not be possible to recover the caplet market prices and ensure time-homogeneity: the element, say, $g(2)$ is fixed by the pricing Condition (6.14) for the second caplet. For time-homogeneity it would be necessary that $g(1)h(1)$ be equal to $g(2)h(2)$ (Proposition 6.4), which fixes $h(2)$. The same $h(2)$, however, appears in all the entries of the second column, while $g(3)$, $g(4)$ and $g(5)$ are determined by the exogenous prices for caplets 3, 4 and 5, respectively. Therefore, unless the term structure of volatilities is exactly flat, it will not be possible to ensure (by Proposition 6.3 again) that $g(3)h(2)$, $g(4)h(2)$ and $g(5)h(2)$ should be equal to $g(2)h(1)$, $g(3)h(1)$ and $g(4)h(1)$, respectively. Choice (6.11c) is therefore intrinsically incapable of representing a time-homogeneous evolution of the term structure of volatilities.

6.6 Appendix II – Indefinite Integral of the Instantaneous Covariance

Consider the case when the correlation function between two forward rates is time-independent, and only depends on the relative separation in their ex-

Table 6.4   *The equivalent of Table 6.1 for the case of $\sigma(t,T) = g(t)h(T)$.*

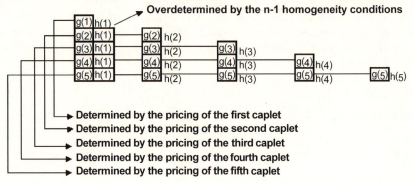

piries. This is the case, for instance, for the correlation function

$$\rho_{ij} = \exp(-\beta|T_i - T_j|),$$

discussed in Chapter 7. If ρ has this functional form $\rho(T_i, T_j)$, and the instantaneous volatility function is given by Expression (6.22), then

$$\int \sigma_{\text{inst}}(t, T_i)\sigma_{\text{inst}}(t, T_j)\rho(T_i, T_j)\, dt$$

$$= \frac{\exp(-\beta|T_i - T_j|)}{4c^3}\Bigg(4ac^2d\{\exp[c(t - T_j)] + \exp[c(t - T_j)]\} + 4c^3d^2t$$

$$- 4bcd\exp[c(t - T_i)][c(t - T_i) - 1] - 4bcd\exp[c(t - T_i)][c(t - T_j) - 1]$$

$$+ \exp[c(2t - T_i - T_j)]\{2a^2c^2 + 2abc[1 + c(T_i + T_j - 2t)]$$

$$+ b^2[1 + 2c^2(t - T_i)(t - T_j) + c(T_i + T_j - 2t)]\}\Bigg).$$

The expression for the variance is easily obtained by setting $\rho_{ij} = 1$ and $T_i = T_j$.

Specifying the Instantaneous Correlation Function

7.1 General Considerations

7.1.1 Mathematical requirements of correlation functions

A great deal of attention has been devoted in the previous chapter to forward-rate instantaneous volatilities. Nothing, however, has so far been said about the associated instantaneous correlation. In general, this correlation function can be assigned a functional dependence on calendar time and on the maturities of the two forward rates:[1]

$$\rho_{ij} = \rho(t, T_i, T_j). \tag{7.1}$$

In order for the covariance element $\int_{T_k}^{T_{k+1}} \sigma_i(u)\sigma_j(u)\rho_{ij}(u)\,\mathrm{d}u$ to be well defined, once suitably square-integrable volatility functions have been chosen, it is enough to assign that the correlation function should be (Riemann or Lebesgue) integrable over any interval $[T_k, T_{k+1}]$ (by Schwartz inequality). For the interpretation of the function ρ as a correlation to hold, for any i, j and for any time t, we also require

$$-1 \leq \rho_{ij}(t) \leq 1.$$

As in the case of instantaneous volatilities, it is in general a convenient and financially desirable feature for the instantaneous correlation function to display a time-homogeneous behavior. Therefore the functions I shall work

---

[1]As in the case of instantaneous volatilities, the correlation function could, in principle, display a more complex set of dependences, such as, for instance, on the past history, or could, for instance, be driven by an independent stochastic factor. Neither of these angles is explored in this book, or has, to my knowledge, been explored elsewhere in the literature.

with in this chapter will be of the form

$$\rho_{ij} = \rho(T_i - t, T_j - t). \tag{7.2}$$

In some cases a specification of the form

$$\rho_{ij} = \rho(T_i - T_j) \tag{7.3}$$

will be used (with $\rho(\ )$ an even function of its argument), but Equation (7.3) imposes conditions much stronger than simple time-homogeneity, and, for reasons to be discussed, it suffers from some drawbacks of financial nature.

7.1.2 Difficulties in estimating the correlation: weak dependence on swaption prices

Despite the similarity of the formal set-up described by Equations (7.1) and (7.2) with the corresponding description of instantaneous volatilities, the task of modelling the instantaneous correlation is considerably more complex for several reasons.

First of all, the price of no plain-vanilla instrument depends purely on the correlation function and no other quantity. This can be contrasted with the case of volatilities, where the information obtainable from the market price of caplets directly relates to (the root-mean-square of) one instantaneous volatility function of one forward rate at a time.

Second, the only plain-vanilla instruments that display any sensitivity at all to the instantaneous correlation function are European swaptions. Using the terminology of Chapter 4, these are single-look derivative securities, and their prices therefore depend on covariance elements of the type

$$\int_0^{T_{\exp}} \sigma_i(u)\sigma_j(u)\rho_{ij}(u) \, du, \tag{7.4}$$

where the indices i and j run over the forward rates underlying a given swap rate, and $T_{\exp}$ is the expiry time of the European swaption. The correlation function therefore always appears together with the somewhat opaque instantaneous volatility functions. Since these are in general time-dependent, this joint occurrence makes the estimation of the correlation function from swaption prices difficult. The reason why this should be the case can be seen as follows: one can express the value of the terminal (de)correlation between forward rates i and j, $\bar{\rho}_{ij}(T)$, in terms of the covariance matrix elements (7.4) (which, as we have seen in Chapter 4, fully determine the price of European swaptions) as

$$\bar{\rho}_{ij}(T) = \frac{\int_0^T \sigma_i(u)\sigma_j(u)\rho_{ij}(u) \, du}{\sqrt{v_i(T)v_j(T)}} \tag{7.5}$$

with

$$v_i(T) = \int_0^T \sigma_i(u)^2 \, du.$$

This equation shows that it is the *terminal* and not the instantaneous correlation that directly affects the prices of swaptions, and this is in turn influenced both by the instantaneous correlation and by the time dependence of the instantaneous volatilities. For the typical values of instantaneous correlation between forward rates observed in the market, however, the terminal correlation is influenced by the behavior of the instantaneous volatilities just as, if not more, strongly than by the instantaneous correlation (see Rebonato 1999c and Section 8.3). As a consequence, different combinations of instantaneous volatilities and instantaneous correlations can give rise to very similar values for the terminal correlation, and, therefore, to the same covariance matrix element and to the same swaption price. Because of the difficulty in disentangling the effects from the two contributions, the estimation of the instantaneous correlation function from the swaption prices can therefore be very arduous (see, however, the approach of Schoenmakers and Coffey 2000 discussed in Section 7.6).

There is a third reason why extracting information about the correlation function from prices of swaptions is difficult. Let us remind ourselves (see Section 2.2) that a swap rate, SR, can be written as a linear combination of forward rates:

$$\mathrm{SR}(t) = \sum_{i=1}^n w_i f_i(t),$$

where $f_i(t)$ is the ith forward rate in the swap rate, and the weights w_i are given by

$$w_i = \frac{B_{i+1}\tau_i}{\sum_{i=1}^n B_{j+1}\tau_j}.$$

(In the expression above B_i is the discount bond maturing at payment time of the ith forward rate, τ_i is its tenor and n is the number of forward rates in the swap.) If each forward rate follows a diffusion with instantaneous volatility $\sigma_i(t)$, and if the Brownian motions, $\{dw\}$, driving the forward rates are linked by $E[dw_i \, dw_j] = \rho_{ij}$, then the expression for the swap-rate instantaneous volatility, $\sigma_{\mathrm{SR}}(t)$, can be written (see Chapter 10) as

$$\sigma_{\mathrm{SR}}(t)^2 = E\left[\left(\frac{d\mathrm{SR}}{\mathrm{SR}}\right)^2\right] = E\left[\sum_j \sum_k \varsigma_j(t)\varsigma_k(t)\sigma_j(t)\sigma_k(t) \, dw_j \, dw_k\right]$$

with

$$\varsigma_j = \frac{(w_j + \sum_{r=1}^n \partial w_r/\partial f_j)f_j}{\sum_{r=1}^n w_r f_r}.$$

If we accept for the moment the result justified in Section 10.3 that, for the purpose of estimating the swap-rate volatility the stochastic quantities $\varsigma_j(t)$ can be assumed to be deterministic (actually, constant) and to be equal to their value today, $\varsigma_j(0)$, it follows that the instantaneous volatility of a swap rate can be approximated by the expression

$$\sigma_{SR}(t)^2 \cong \sum_j \sum_k \varsigma_j(0)\varsigma_k(0)\sigma_j(t)\sigma_k(t)E[dw_j\,dw_k]. \qquad (7.6)$$

From this general expression one can immediately derive some special cases:

(Case 1) Perfect correlation: $E[dw_j\,dw_k] = 1$ for any j, k

$$\sigma_{SR}(t)^2 \cong \left[\sum_j \varsigma_j(0)\sigma_j(t)\right]^2.$$

(Case 2) Zero correlation for the off-diagonal elements: $E[dw_j\,dw_k] = \delta_{jk}$

$$\sigma_{SR}(t)^2 \cong \sum_j [\varsigma_j(0)\sigma_j(t)]^2.$$

(Case 3) Identical correlation $\rho < 1$ for off-diagonal elements: $E[dw_j\,dw_k] = \delta_{jk} + (1 - \delta_{jk})\rho$

$$\sigma_{SR}(t)^2 \cong \sum_j [\varsigma_j(0)\sigma_j(t)]^2(1-\rho) + \rho\left[\sum_j \varsigma_j(0)\sigma_j(t)\right]^2.$$

EXERCISE 7.1 *Derive the three relationships in Cases 1–3.*

Therefore the square of the instantaneous swap-rate volatility in the identical-correlation case is given by the linear combination of the perfect- and zero-correlation solutions with weights ρ and $(1 - \rho)$, respectively. This relationship between the swap-rate instantaneous volatility and the constant correlation ρ is shown in Figure 7.1 for the simple case of a 10-period (5×5 semi-annual) swaption, with the same and flat instantaneous volatility function for all the forward rates, and a flat term structure of volatilities (20.00%). The first observation is that, while the overall variation is very pronounced, in the region of typical values for instantaneous correlations among same-currency forward rates (i.e., for an average correlation of, say, 80%) the change in swap-rate instantaneous volatility, while noticeable, is considerably smaller (from 20.00% to 18.11%). The really interesting observation, however, is about the impact of the shape of the correlation function on the swap-rate instantaneous volatility.

In order to explore this aspect, one can reason as follows: The constant-correlation assumption for all the non-diagonal elements of the correlation matrix represents the crudest possible shape for a non-degenerate correlation surface (i.e., for a correlation matrix that is neither diagonal nor with '1's for

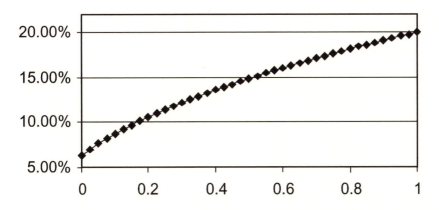

Figure 7.1 *The swap-rate instantaneous volatility as a function of the identical off-diagonal correlation ρ.*

all its elements). I deliberately choose this matrix form as the 'stress case' of a financially 'implausible', but mathematically possible,[2] correlation surface. In order to see what the shape effect might be, let us then assign a more realistic shape, that is, let us assume that the correlation between two forward rates should be given by the still very simple, but financially more appealing, function

$$\rho_{ij} = \exp(-\beta|T_i - T_j|).$$

Given this correlation matrix, and making use of the approximation (7.6), one can calculate the swap-rate instantaneous volatility as

$$\sigma_{\text{SR}}(t)^2 = [\mathbf{w}\boldsymbol{\sigma}_{\text{f}}(t)]^{\text{T}}\boldsymbol{\rho}\,[\mathbf{w}\boldsymbol{\sigma}_{\text{f}}(t)], \tag{7.7}$$

where $\mathbf{w}\boldsymbol{\sigma}_{\text{f}}(t)$ is the $n \times 1$ vector whose jth element is the product $(w_j\sigma_j)$, ρ is the correlation matrix and the superscript 'T' denotes matrix transposition (see Chapter 10 for a fuller discussion). A flat yield curve was chosen to calculate the weights $\{\mathbf{w}\}$. For a given decay constant, β, one can

- evaluate the instantaneous swap-rate volatility from Equation (7.7);
- calculate the average of the off-diagonal elements of the resulting correlation;
- set this average number equal to the identical constant correlation for all the non-diagonal elements of the 'implausible' correlation matrix;
- calculate the resulting swap-rate instantaneous volatility with the new correlation function; and

---

[2]A symmetric matrix with constant off-diagonal elements only produces positive eigenvalues (i.e., is positive definite) for certain ranges of the constant. I shall always assume that a feasible constant has been chosen.

Table 7.1   *The swap-rate instantaneous volatilities obtained with an exponential (column la-belled 'Exponential') or identical off-diagonal (column labelled 'Constant') correlation matrix, for the 5 × 5 European swaption case described in the text. The columns labelled 'Beta', 'AvgCor-rel' and 'MinCorr' display the exponential decay constant, and the corresponding average and minimum off-diagonal correlation, respectively, in the resulting exponential matrix.*

Beta	AvgCorrel	MinCorr	Exponential (%)	Constant (%)
0.05	0.913 789	0.798 516	19.2101	19.2089
0.10	0.837 483	0.637 628	18.4828	18.4805
0.15	0.769 74	0.509 156	17.8121	17.8088
0.20	0.709 42	0.406 57	17.1928	17.1887
0.25	0.655 552	0.324 652	16.6202	16.6153
0.30	0.607 305	0.259 24	16.0900	16.0845

- compare the resulting swap-rate volatilities for the constant and expo-nentially decaying correlation (i.e., for two radically different shapes that give rise to the same average off-diagonal correlation).

The result of this exercise is displayed in Table 7.1 and Figure 7.2. The most noteworthy feature is the almost total lack of dependence on the shape of the correlation function of the swap rate volatility (provided that the same average correlation is preserved).

The example chosen is admittedly rather stylized: in particular, a non-flat yield curve would introduce a more complex, although not substantially dif-ferent, behavior. Despite these caveats, this discussion has shown that the in-

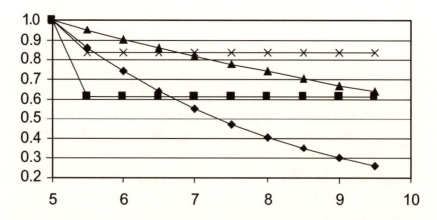

Figure 7.2   *A depiction of two pairs of correlation functions with the same average off-diagonal correlation (0.8375 and 0.6073, respectively). By reading the corresponding swap-rate volatili-ties from Table 7.1, one can appreciate to what extent radically different shapes can give rise to virtually identical instantaneous swap-rate volatilities (see Table 7.1).*

stantaneous volatility of a swap rate is significantly, although not very strongly, affected by the average correlation (see Figure 7.1). But the more important result from the discussion above is that, for a given *average* correlation, the swap-rate volatility is very weakly dependent on the shape of the correlation function. This conclusion should be coupled with the observation that the time dependence of realistic forward-rate instantaneous volatility functions produces terminal decorrelations (see Equation (7.5)) that typically lower the root-mean-square swap-rate volatility by one to two vegas with respect to the constant-volatility case (i.e., as discussed in detail in Section 8.3, unlike caplet prices, swaption prices, even for a fixed root-mean-square volatility to the expiry of the underlying forward rates, do depend on the shape of the instantaneous forward-rate volatility functions). Putting these two observations together, one can therefore conclude not only that the price of a European swaption is virtually independent of the shape of the correlation function, but also, and more importantly, that it is affected to very similar degrees by the instantaneous correlation and by the time dependence of the forward-rate instantaneous volatilities. In practice it is therefore very difficult to extract information about the instantaneous correlation matrix from the prices of European swaptions.

7.1.3 Difficulties in estimating the correlation: statistical problems

A further obstacle encountered by modellers of the forward-rate correlation surface has a completely different origin, and compounds the well-known difficulties in obtaining in a statistically robust way correlation functions in general. This is due to the fact that the required time series of changes in forward rates must be obtained from different portions of the yield curve and from different instruments: LIBOR cash deposit rates at the very short end; futures contracts for intermediate maturities; equilibrium (par) swap rates for expiries between two years and the end of the LIBOR curve. While the whole yield curve is generally referred to *tout court* as the LIBOR curve (and, indeed, the modelling approach analyzed in this book is called the 'LIBOR market model'), the joining of the various segments of the curve is not totally seamless, and different types of trader (futures traders, FRA traders, swap traders) are active along its various portions. Apart from these problems of mild but noticeable market segmentation, historical time series needed to estimate correlation tend to contain LIBOR deposit rates, futures prices and swap rates whose markets close at different times during the day. As a consequence, a naive correlation estimation from daily data suffers from problems of non-synchronicity and often displays a sharp (and spurious) fall as the maturity difference between two forward rates is such that one is extracted from, say, the cash curve, and the other from the values of swap rates.[3]

---

[3] See, for instance, the fall in correlation for the forward rate associated with the 12-month LIBOR rate reported in the empirical data in the work by Longstaff et al. (2000b) discussed below.

7.1.4 Difficulties in estimating the correlation: factor dependence

Even if an instantaneous correlation surface could be reliably estimated, the trader could still be faced with severe modelling difficulties arising for a completely different reason: as I shall show in the following (see Section 7.3) the possible shapes of the instantaneous correlation functions are strongly dependent on the number of factors used to drive the dynamics of the yield curve. Therefore, for a small number of driving factors, the ability to reproduce an exogenous (however estimated) instantaneous correlation function can be rather limited. This might not be a great problem in the case of path-dependent products, where reasonably clever implementations – such as the (very-)long-jump procedure presented in Chapter 4 – can allow simulations with a large number of factors in realistic (trading) computational times. However, it becomes a more serious constraint in the pricing of, say, Bermudan swaptions. This aspect is analyzed in detail in Section 7.3.

In the light of all these difficulties, I advocate a modelling strategy that leverages off the results of the few reliable econometric studies of forward-rate correlation and some plausible financial intuition (with which the reader might or might not agree), and keeps the translation of this scarce evidence and intuition into a model as simple and transparent as possible. In particular, I shall recommend in the following that the whole correlation function should be parametrized by exceedingly few – perhaps just one or two – parameters.

7.2 Empirical Data and Financial Plausibility

As mentioned in the introductory section, reliable statistical data about instantaneous correlation is difficult to extract, and, as a consequence, relatively few good-quality studies have appeared in the literature. Principal-component-analysis-based studies are more common (see, for instance the copious references in Martellini and Priaulet (2001)), but, not surprisingly, most studies tend to analyze zero-coupon yields, rather than forward rates. The reason for this preference is that yields, being an integral of instantaneous forward rates, are by construction smoother than the latter, and therefore give rise to 'optically' better-behaved correlation surfaces. Unfortunately this impression of stability is mainly cosmetic, since a small difference in correlation between two long-dated yields of similar maturities translates into a large difference in the implied correlation between the forward rate connecting the two (see the following exercise). When it comes to implementations of the LIBOR market model, it is the correlation among forward rates (as opposed to yields) that is needed, and the translation to the forward-rate world of yield-derived correlation data, while theoretically possible, is in practice unsatisfactory.

EXERCISE 7.2 *Consider two zero-coupon yields, y_1 and y_2, associated with maturities T_1 and T_2, $T_2 > T_1$, respectively; let B_1 and B_2 be the prices of the corresponding* *discount bonds; and denote by f_k the forward rate spanning the period $[t_{k-1}, t_k]$, with f_1 equal to the spot rate from today to time t_1. So*

$$B_i = \exp(-y_i T_i) = \exp\left(-\sum_{j=1}^{n_i} f_j \Delta t_j\right), \qquad i = 1, 2.$$

Assume the correlation structure ρ_{ij} between the forward rates to be given by

$$\rho_{ij} = \exp(-\beta|T_i - T_j|).$$

Assume a diffusive behavior for the forward rates, and, using Ito's lemma, work out the correlation ρ_{y_1, y_2} between the two yields as a function of the correlation between forward rates. Consider the behavior of this quantity as a function of T_1, T_2 and $\Delta T = T_2 - T_1$, especially when T_1 and T_2 become large but ΔT is small. In particular, comment on the sensitivity on the yield correlation of the correlation between the forward rate expiring at T_1, and spanning the period $[T_1, T_2]$ and the previous forward rates, for ΔT small. Finally, compare the eigenvalues and eigenvectors that you obtain by orthogonalizing the yield and forward-rate correlation matrices.

7.2.1 Analysis of two empirical studies

Despite these difficulties, some general and qualitative empirical information about the shape of the correlation surface can nonetheless be gleaned from some of the studies based on carefully estimated forward rates that have been published. I shall make no attempt to present a systematic survey, but shall focus instead on a very small number of selected studies that illustrate some general findings. The two works I would like to examine were carried out by Fisher et al. (1994) and by Longstaff et al. (2000b). The first was carried out just before the February 1994 bond market upheaval (and might therefore have produced a somewhat lower overall correlation estimate if it had been conducted, say, 12 months later). The second includes data that belong to the 1998 period of even greater market turmoil (and its correlation estimates are therefore likely to be significantly lower than in similar pre-1998 studies). The correlation structures they report are shown in Figures 7.3–7.9.

Despite the different numerical values presented in the two studies, and the differences in estimation procedures, some interesting common features appear: First of all, the correlation between the first (shortest-expiry) forward rate and the following shows no sign of having a negative convexity. The importance of this observation in the context of low-dimensionality implementations of the LIBOR market model is discussed in the next section.

In the data reported in Longstaff et al. (2000b) there appears to be a striking loss of correlation between the first and the second forward rates, partially reversed for the third, fourth, etc., forward rates. In order to explain this unexpected feature, and to ascertain whether it is a 'true' effect or an artifact of the estimation methodology, it might be useful to point out that, in the case

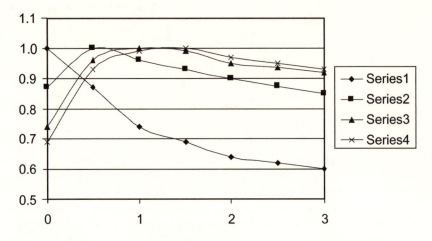

Figure 7.3   *The correlation between the first and other forward rates ('Series 1'), between the second and the others ('Series 2'), between the third and the others ('Series 3') and between the fourth and the others ('Series 4'). The forward rates were semi-annual, and only the front portion of the correlation matrix (out to three years) is shown. US$ data from the work by Fisher et al. (1994).*

of the Longstaff et al. data, the first two rates used for estimation were the six-month and the 12-month LIBOR rate. While the six-month LIBOR rate is actively traded, the 12-month LIBOR rate is one of the most illiquid of the

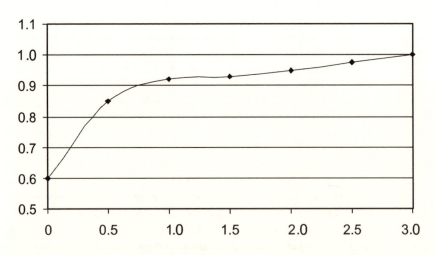

Figure 7.4   *The correlation between the sixth and the six earlier-expiring forward rates (time to expiry on the x axis). The forward rates were semi-annual, and only the front portion of the correlation matrix (out to three years) is shown. US$ data from the work by Fisher et al. (1994).*

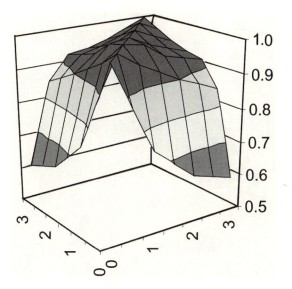

Figure 7.5   *The correlation surface for the US$ data from the work by Fisher et al. (1994).*

LIBOR cash deposit set, since traders prefer to switch to futures contracts as soon as these contracts are liquid and actively traded. If a particular deposit rate is not very actively traded, its price is updated less regularly, and it is well known that a spurious lack of co-movements between an illiquid and a more liquid rate can strongly affect their correlation estimate. I therefore suggest that this liquidity effect might account for the sharp drop in correlation between the first forward rate, expiring in six months' time, and the second, expiring in 12 months (see also Figures 7.3, 7.5, 7.6 and 7.8).

If one focusses one's attention on the later-expiring forward rates, the picture changes radically, and the convexity of the correlation surface across the main diagonal changes sign (see Figures 7.4, 7.7 and 7.9). Note also that, as this set of forward-rate data is extracted from more homogeneous market sources (swap rates), the estimates display much less variability across forward rates, and trace much smoother curves. The data, in other words, appear to be less noisy, and the conclusions about the convexity of the correlation surface can be drawn with more confidence.

As for the level of the long-term decorrelation (i.e., the correlation between, say, the first and the longest-expiring forward rate), the Longstaff et al. data do appear to suggest that the asymptotic correlation value should be non-zero, although the precise level is likely to depend on the specific estimation period.

Qualitatively similar conclusions can be drawn from the data presented by Fisher et al. (1994); in particular, the same change in convexity can be noticed

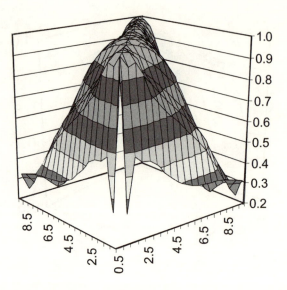

Figure 7.6   *The correlation surface for the US$ data from the work by Longstaff et al. (2000b) seen with the short-expiry forward rates towards the reader.*

as one moves perpendicularly to the main diagonal. The asymptotic value of the correlation appears to be higher, but it is more difficult to say from the data what the truly long-term correlation might be, because the matrix covers a shorter span of expiries. Furthermore, as mentioned before, the Fisher et al. data do not include the 1994 rate moves, while the Longstaff et al. estimates do include the market turmoil of 1998. Finally, the greater smoothness of correlation matrix can probably be explained by the fact that Fisher et al. estimate the correlation among *instantaneous* forward rates, which, in turn, must be obtained from a fitting of the discount curve. The smoothness of the final result is therefore likely to depend on some degree of 'pre-processing'.

7.2.2 Salient empirical features of correlation functions

Summarizing, the most salient conclusions that one can draw from the empirical correlation surfaces examined in this section are that:

- a convex shape for the correlation function between the front forward rates and later-expiring ones seems to be appropriate;

- a good case can be made for a negative convexity for the portion of the correlation surface that refers to late-expiring forward rates; and

- asymptotically the correlation appears to tend to a non-zero, positive level, $\lim_{j \to \infty} \rho_{1,j} = K$, $K > 0$.

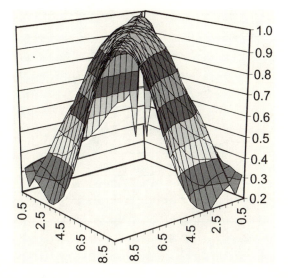

Figure 7.7 *The correlation surface for the US$ data from the work by Longstaff et al. (2000b) seen with the longest-expiry forward rates towards the reader.*

These qualitative features should be kept in mind, together with the discussion presented in Section 7.1, when analyzing the behavior of different possible functional forms for the correlation function. For future reference, it is also interesting to highlight that the correlation shape, and the change in convexity in particular, displayed by Figures 7.5–7.7, can be produced by a particular specification of the yield-curve dynamics discussed at the end of Section 9.5. The empirical observations presented in this section can therefore be profitably revisited in that context.

Having discussed the main empirical qualitative features displayed by correlation surfaces (at least, for the selected cases examined), the next logical step is the specification of suitable functional forms to capture this behavior. Before embarking on this task, however, the next section will highlight some features of the model correlation surface that are to a large extent independent of the specific functional form chosen to describe it, and depend much more strongly on the number of factors chosen to drive the yield curve.

7.3 Intrinsic Limitations of Low-Dimensionality Approaches

As mentioned in Section 7.1 and at the end of the previous section, it is important to point out certain intrinsic limitations of low-dimensionality models insofar as the recovery they allow of an arbitrary shape for the correlation function. These can be most easily appreciated by examining the two simplest

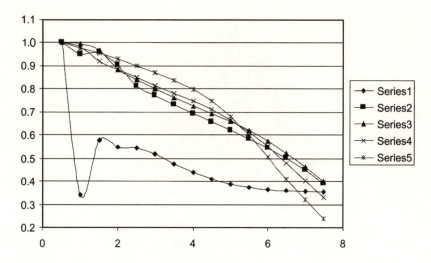

Figure 7.8   *The correlation between the first five and the subsequent forward rates: 'Series 1' shows the correlation between the first forward rate (expiring in six months' time) and all the forward rates of expiry up to seven-and-a-half years; 'Series 2' presents the correlation between the second forward rate (expiring in 12 months' time) and the forward rates expiring half a year, one year, ..., up to seven-and-a-half years thereafter; ... 'Series 5' shows the correlation between the fifth forward rate (expiring in two-and-a-half years' time) and the forward rates expiring in three, three-and-a-half, ..., ten years' time. The forward rates were semi-annual, and only the portion of the correlation matrix out to seven-and-a-half years' residual maturity is shown. US$ data from the work by Longstaff et al. (2000b). A possible reason for the sharp decorrelation between the first and the second forward rates is discussed in the text.*

non-trivial cases, that is, two- and three-factor implementations of a LIBOR market model.

7.3.1 The correlation function in a two-factor model

Using the notation introduced in Chapter 3 one can write

$$\frac{\mathrm{d}f_i}{f_i} = \mu_i(t)\,\mathrm{d}t + \sigma_{i1}\,\mathrm{d}z_1 + \sigma_{i2}\,\mathrm{d}z_2 \tag{7.8}$$

and

$$\frac{\mathrm{d}f_i}{f_i} = \mu_i(t)\,\mathrm{d}t + \sigma_{i1}\,\mathrm{d}z_1 + \sigma_{i2}\,\mathrm{d}z_2 + \sigma_{i3}\,\mathrm{d}z_3, \tag{7.9}$$

respectively, for the two- and three-factor LIBOR market models. The various Brownian increments, $\mathrm{d}z_i$, have, as usual, been taken to be orthogonal to each other: $\mathrm{d}z_i\,\mathrm{d}z_j = \delta_{ij}\,\mathrm{d}t$. If the instantaneous volatility of the ith forward rate is

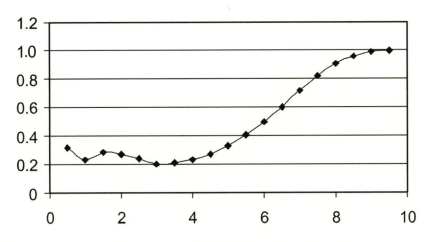

Figure 7.9 *The correlation between the forward rate expiring in nine-and-a-half years' time and all the forward rates with earlier expiries. US$ data from the work by Longstaff et al. (2000b).*

denoted by $\sigma_i(t)$, and using again the notation of Chapter 3, one can write

$$\frac{\mathrm{d}f_i}{f_i} = \mu_i(t)\,\mathrm{d}t + \sigma_i(b_{i1}\,\mathrm{d}z_1 + b_{i2}\,\mathrm{d}z_2) \qquad (7.8')$$

and

$$\frac{\mathrm{d}f_i}{f_i} = \mu_i(t)\,\mathrm{d}t + \sigma_i(b_{i1}\,\mathrm{d}z_1 + b_{i2}\,\mathrm{d}z_2 + b_{i3}\,\mathrm{d}z_3), \qquad (7.9')$$

with $\sum_{k=1}^{s} b_{ik}^2 = 1$, and $s = 2$ or 3, depending on the model dimensionality. In two dimensions the constraint $b_{i1}^2 + b_{i2}^2 = 1$ can always be satisfied for any arbitrary, forward-rate-dependent, set of real values $\{\vartheta_i\}$ as long as one takes

$$b_{i1} = \sin(\vartheta_i)$$
$$b_{i2} = \cos(\vartheta_i).$$

(This is obviously true, because $\sin^2 x + \cos^2 x = 1$, for any x.) Calculating the correlation between any two forward rates means evaluating

$$\rho_{ij} = \frac{E[\mathrm{d}f_i/f_i, \mathrm{d}f_j/f_j]}{\sqrt{v_i v_j}},$$

with $v_i = E[\mathrm{d}f_i/f_i, \mathrm{d}f_j/f_j]$. Making use of the orthogonality of the Brownian increments one immediately obtains from Equation (7.8') that

$$\rho_{ij} = \sin(\vartheta_i)\sin(\vartheta_j) + \cos(\vartheta_i)\cos(\vartheta_j).$$

By invoking use of the well-known trigonometric identity $\sin x \sin y + \cos x \cos y = \cos(x - y)$, this can then be rewritten as

$$\rho_{ij} = \cos(\vartheta_i - \vartheta_j). \tag{7.10}$$

If the dependence of the angle function ϑ on the forward rate is sufficiently smooth,[4] one can see that, for any two-factor implementation of the LIBOR market model, as the expiries of two forward rates are made to approach, their correlation must behave like a cosine function. Furthermore, the decorrelation between two couples of forward rates (i, j) and (r, s) separated by the same difference in expiries (i.e., $|T_i - T_j| = |T_r - T_s|$) can only be different if the dependence of θ on i contains terms higher than linear. (This can be seen most simply from Equation (7.10), by writing $\theta_j = a + bT_j$, and noticing that the 'phase' a cancels out when taking the difference, and one is left with $\theta_{ij} = \cos\{b(T_j - T_i)\}$.) If these higher-than-linear terms are not present, one will therefore always have $\rho_{ij} = \rho_{rs}$ for any i, j, r, s such that $|T_i - T_j| = |T_r - T_s|$. A simple calculation actually shows that, in order to obtain a positive convexity at the origin, the non-linear dependence must be rather pronounced. The relevance of this observation will become apparent in the following sections.

7.3.2 The correlation function in a three-factor model

Moving to three factors, one can express, still retaining maximum possible generality,

$$b_{i1} = \cos(\vartheta_i) \sin(\phi_i),$$
$$b_{i2} = \sin(\vartheta_i) \sin(\phi_i),$$
$$b_{i3} = \cos(\phi_i),$$

where, in analogy with the two-factor treatment, $\{\phi_i\}$ and $\{\vartheta_i\}$ are arbitrary sets of forward-rate-dependent real numbers ('angles'). Since, for any x, y, $(\cos x \sin y)^2 + (\sin x \sin y)^2 + (\cos y)^2 = 1$, all the instantaneous volatilities, and hence all the caplet prices, will still be perfectly recovered (see Equation (7.9')). It then takes only a few more trigonometric manipulations to obtain, for the three-factor case,

$$\rho_{ij} = \cos(\phi_i - \phi_j) - \sin(\phi_i) \sin(\phi_j)[1 - \cos(\vartheta_i - \vartheta_j)]. \tag{7.11}$$

EXERCISE 7.3 *Derive Equations (7.10) and (7.11).*

---

[4]At this stage, the fact that the dependence of the angle on the forward rate should be, in some sense, smooth is purely a conjecture. Also, some care should be paid to the precise definition of smoothness, since we are dealing with a discrete set of forward rates. I will show in Chapter 9 (see, in particular, the discussion in Section 9.4 after Figures 9.9 and 9.10) that actual calculations confirm this actually to be the case.

Comparing this expression with Equation (7.10), it is interesting to point out that there is now a term $(\sin(\phi_i)\sin(\phi_j))$ that no longer purely depends on the difference between two angles. Therefore, even if the dependence of the function ϑ on the forward-rate index i were exactly linear, a third factor makes it possible to obtain a more complex dependence of the correlation than on the pure angular difference. The importance of this observation will become apparent in the next section, and in Section 9.3.

7.3.3 Factor dependence of the correlation function: generalizations

These conclusions, drawn for the two- and three-factor cases, can be easily generalized: If one carries out the orthogonalization of an $n \times n$ correlation matrix (of rank n) and only retains the first $m < n$ components, one is effectively discarding the high-frequency components of the 'signal'. This being the case, it is then not surprising that the resulting model correlation, obtained by retaining a small number of principal components, should not display the ability to change rapidly around the origin. What is more surprising is that the number of frequencies necessary to reproduce globally a simple behavior – such as, say, a decaying exponential – is remarkably high (see, e.g., Rebonato and Cooper 1995, Rebonato 1999a). The qualifier 'globally' is important. If one concentrates on a small portion of the correlation matrix, it is indeed possible to recover locally a strongly varying correlation function, but, by so doing, one is giving excessive weight to the highest-frequency components available given the chosen number of factors. These, in turn, can often give rise to an undesirable oscillating behavior for the correlation function away from the tightly fitted portion of the correlation surface, at the expense of the quality of the global fit. These topics are examined in detail in Chapter 9, and have been discussed in Rebonato (1999a,c).

7.4 Proposed Functional Forms for the Instantaneous Correlation Function

In view of the comments, of the empirical data and of the theoretical results presented in Sections 7.1–7.3, respectively, I propose a few simple functional forms that can describe to an acceptable degree of accuracy the most salient desirable features of correlation surfaces.

7.4.1 Problems with a non-parametric estimation

In principle, a non-parametric approach could be employed: After choosing a particular instantaneous volatility function, one could, for instance, determine the piecewise-constant correlation needed for each of the elements of the covariance matrices associated with a full set of European swaptions. While theoretically acceptable, this 'bootstrapping' approach would be prone to severe numerical problems, and, in the presence of unavoidable market noise (bid/offer spreads, non-synchronous data, interpolated volatilities for illiquid swaptions, etc.), would be very likely to produce a wildly fluctuating correlation surface. Furthermore, the results from this approach would be strongly influenced by the assumed time dependence of the forward-rate instantaneous volatilities, which is not directly available from the market (see the discussion in Section 8.3). Finally, a non-parametric estimation of this type would also require a very strong belief in the fundamental congruence of the caplet and swaption markets, which has proven to be questionable during (and after) periods such as the summer/autumn of 1998 (see, in this respect, the discussion in Section 9.1). I will therefore restrict myself to parametric (or semi-parametric, see below) approaches.

7.4.2 Desiderata of the model function

As for the desiderata of the parametric model functions, and given the paucity of reliable empirical data, I also believe that it would be unprofitable to assign an independent time-dependent behavior to the correlation matrix. More precisely, the most general functional dependence on calendar time that I shall allow will be of the type

$$\rho(t, T_i, T_j) = \rho(T_i - t, T_j - t).$$

In view of the results presented in Section 7.2, it is also financially desirable to prescribe that the maximum asymptotic decorrelation between same-currency forward rates should not go to zero, but to a finite positive limiting value, LongCorr:

$$\lim_{p \to \infty} \rho_{1,p} = \text{LongCorr}.$$

In addition, it would be desirable for the matrix $[\rho]$ to enjoy the following properties:

1. The function $\rho_{i,i+p}$ should be, for fixed p, an increasing function of i, that is, the decorrelation between, say, forward rates expiring in one and three years should be greater than the decorrelation between forward rates expiring in, say, 17 and 20 years). This can be equivalently expressed by requiring that the correlation function should display decreasing convexity as a function of maturity of the first forward rate.[5]
2. The dynamics for the yield curve produced by the chosen volatility and correlation functions should be such that its movements should be explainable by the 'canonical' orthogonal modes of deformations of parallel shifts, slope changes and curvature modifications, in this order of importance (as obtained by standard principal component analysis).

---

[5]As discussed in Section 7.2, it might be desirable to temper this requirement by the observation that the convexity of the correlation surface could change sign for sufficiently long expiries of the first forward rate (see, e.g., Figures 7.6 and 7.7).

The above requirements find their justification in financial plausibility. The chosen model function must, however, also satisfy the mathematical requirements for them to be possible correlation functions. Therefore:

- $\rho_{ii} = 1$ for any i,

- $-1 \leq \rho_{ji} \leq 1$ for any i, j,

- $\rho_{ji} = \rho_{ij}$,

- the matrix $[\rho]$ should be positive definite.

The requirement that the prescribed correlation function should give rise to eigenvectors congruent with those observed empirically is somewhat unusual, and therefore merits a few words of comment. The shape of the eigenvectors, and the relative importance of the eigenvalues, resulting from the orthogonalization of a correlation matrix clearly depend on the magnitude of the different elements of the matrix. A large number of econometric studies (see, e.g., the references in Martinelli and Priaulet 2001) have shown that level, shape and curvature, in this order, are the most important modes of deformation of the forward-rate curve. It is therefore reasonable to require that, upon orthogonalization, the model correlation matrix should give rise to eigenvectors displaying these qualitative shapes, and to eigenvalues of the correct relative magnitude. This criterion will be used extensively in Section 7.5.

Finally, before presenting the functions, it is useful to point out that they all belong to the exponential family. The reason for this choice is that decaying exponentials naturally arise as *the* possible solution, once two assumptions (one of mathematical and one of financial nature) are imposed on the correlation function (see Section 7.5). Furthermore, I shall show in the same section that, when these two assumptions are relaxed, the more general solutions can often be regarded as relatively small perturbations of the simplest fundamental exponential solution, if financial plausibility (and the eigenvector/eigenvalue requirement in particular) is to be retained.

7.4.3 Specific functional forms and their qualitative features

- Functional form 1

$$\rho_{ij}(t) = \text{LongCorr} + (1 - \text{LongCorr}) \exp[-\beta|(T_i - t) - (T_j - t)|]$$
$$= \text{LongCorr} + (1 - \text{LongCorr}) \exp[-\beta|T_i - T_j|]. \qquad (7.12)$$

- Functional form 2

$$\rho_{ij}(t) = \text{LongCorr} + (1 - \text{LongCorr}) \exp[-\beta|(T_i - t)^\gamma - (T_j - t)^\gamma|],$$
$$\text{for } t \leq \min(T_i, T_j). \qquad (7.13)$$

• Functional form 3 (see Rebonato 1999c)

$$\rho_{ij}(t) = \text{LongCorr} + (1 - \text{LongCorr}) \exp[-\beta|T_i - T_j| + \alpha \max(T_i, T_j)],$$
$$\text{for } t \leq \min(T_i, T_j). \tag{7.14}$$

As far as the first functional form is concerned, one should notice that it is obviously a particular case of the second ($\gamma = 1$); however, for this particular value of the exponent γ, the dependence on time, t, disappears. This has desirable computational characteristics, but somewhat unpleasant financial implications. From the numerical point of view, the time independence of the instantaneous correlation allows the rewriting of the all-important covariance elements in the form:

$$\int_0^T \sigma_i(u)\sigma_j(u)\rho_{ij}(u)\,du = \rho_{ij}(T_i, T_j)\int_0^T \sigma_i(u)\sigma_j(u)\,du.$$

For many of the desirable instantaneous volatility functions presented in the previous chapter, the integral over the volatility functions can be computed analytically, and the absence of the correlation term under the integral sign therefore greatly simplifies matters. This very feature is, however, at the origin of the financial unattractiveness of specification (7.12): As time goes by, the decorrelation between two given forward rates separated by a fixed difference in expiry times remains the same, irrespective of whether the first of the two is one or 10 years from expiry. Furthermore, the convexity of the correlation surface across the main diagonal cannot change sign for the case of $\gamma = 1$. This is no longer the case for $\gamma < 1$, as shown in Figure 7.10, obtained with $\gamma = 1/3$ and $\beta = 0.24$. It is interesting to compare the qualitative shape of this surface with the empirical results presented in Figures 7.5 and 7.6 of Section 7.2. These features are also shown in Figures 7.11–7.13, where the curves with the square and diamond markers show, for the cases of $\gamma = 0.5$ and $\gamma = 1$,

• the correlation between the forward rate expiring an infinitesimal time ϵ from today and successive forward rates of increasing differences in maturity ranging from zero to 10 years (Figure 7.11);

• the correlation between the forward rate expiring five years from today and forward rates of increasing differences in maturity ranging from zero to five years, that is, expiring from year 0 to year 10 (Figure 7.12); and

• the correlation between the forward rate expiring 10 years from today and forward rates of increasing differences in maturity ranging from five to 15 years, that is, expiring from year 5 to year 15 (Figure 7.13).

Notice also from Figure 7.12 how the curve with square markers (corresponding to the $\gamma = \frac{1}{2}$ case) shows a qualitative and quantitative behavior

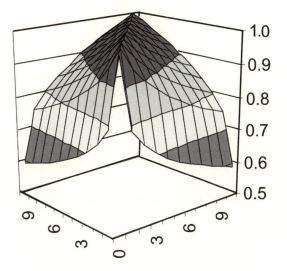

Figure 7.10 *Correlation surface obtained using functional form 2 (equation (7.13)) with $\gamma = 1/3$ and $\beta = 0.24$. Notice the change in convexity of the surface across the main diagonal. It is interesting to compare this shape with the empirical surfaces shown in Figures 7.5 and 7.6.*

markedly different as one considers correlations with the earlier- or later-expiring forward rates. The decorrelation today (i.e., at time $t = 0$) between

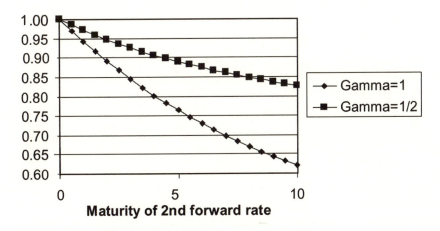

Figure 7.11 *The correlation between the first forward rate (i.e., the forward rate expiring an infinitesimal time ϵ after time 0) and the forward rates expiring at the times indicated on the x axis, for the exponential ($\gamma = 1$) and exponential square-root ($\gamma = \frac{1}{2}$) cases. The same decay constant was used in both cases.*

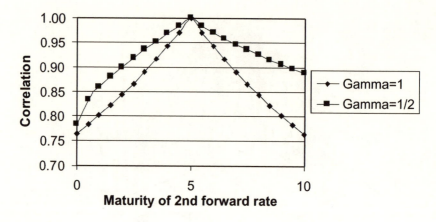

Figure 7.12   *The correlation between the forward rate expiring at time 5 and the forward rates expiring at the times indicated on the x axis, for the exponential ($\gamma = 1$) and exponential square-root ($\gamma = \frac{1}{2}$) cases. The same decay constant was used in both cases.*

the forward rate expiring on year 5 and, say, the forward rate expiring five years thereafter is more pronounced than the decorrelation today between the forward rate expiring in five years' time and the one expiring today. A similar picture is conveyed by Figure 7.13. Notice also how, for the $\gamma = \frac{1}{2}$ case, the decorrelation between, say, the five-year- and the 10-year-expiring forward rates is noticeably different from the decorrelation between the 10- and 15-year forward rates. This is not the case for $\gamma = 1$. Furthermore, Figures 7.12

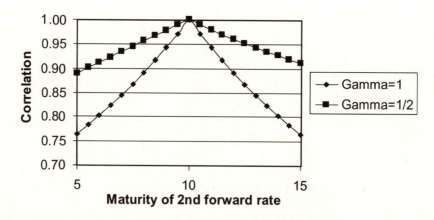

Figure 7.13   *The correlation between forward rate expiring at time 10 and the forward rates expiring at the times indicated on the x axis, for the exponential ($\gamma = 1$) and exponential square-root ($\gamma = \frac{1}{2}$) cases. The same decay constant was used in both cases.*

and 7.13 show the asymmetric, and financially desirable, shape of the correlation surface for increasing or decreasing expiries from a given reference forward rate.

It is also interesting to examine carefully in greater detail than possible from Figure 7.10 the convexity of the $\gamma = \frac{1}{2}$ curve, as shown in Figure 7.12. In particular, the change in second derivative (which cannot occur in the $\gamma = 1$ case) implies that the speed of decorrelation increases significantly as the difference in expiries from the five-year forward increases in the direction of the front end of the curve. In other words, this simple functional form can capture the financially desirable feature of the front forward rates being more decorrelated than the others with the remaining parts of the yield curve. This feature therefore appears to be in agreement both with financial intuition (Section 7.1) and with the empirical data presented in Section 7.2.

As for the third specification, i.e.

$$\rho_{ij}(t) = LongCorr$$
$$+ (1 - LongCorr)\exp[-\beta|T_i - T_j| + \alpha \max(T_i, T_j)], t \le \min(T_i, T_j)$$

the term in α, if judiciously chosen, has the ability to make the speed of the decay depend on the position along the curve of the two forward rates (more specifically, on the maturity of the longer-expiring of the two forward rates). This formulation can therefore enjoy the desirable feature that the decorrelation between two forward rates separated by the same 'distance' should decrease as the first forward rate increases in maturity. Unfortunately, both the specifications 2 and 3 (Equations (7.13) and (7.14)) are not guaranteed to produce a positive definite correlation matrix, and the user must therefore always check the positivity of the associated eigenvalues for any desired choice of the parameters. Since there is no natural way of defining the region of positivity for the eigenvalues in the parameter space, this can constitute a serious drawback if a numerical optimization is undertaken.[6]

In all the above cases, the whole correlation surface has been described by a very small number of parameters: the asymptotic correlation, LongCorr, the decay constant, β, and, possibly, either γ or α. The user might also want to fine-tune the exponent β, but the paucity of reliable statistical information, and the relatively mild dependence of European swaptions on the fine features of the shape of the correlation surface, advocate against over-zealous fitting of this parameter.

An important common feature of the three approaches proposed above is that the structure of the correlation surface is time-homogeneous. This is a feature that has been embedded in the functional form from the very start, since it is highly unlikely that a trader should have firm views about the time evolution of the instantaneous correlation surface. Needless to say, if the

---

[6]Rebonato and Jaeckel (2000) suggest a systematic methodology to produce the closest admissible correlation function to a non-positive definite real symmetric matrix.

user did have such beliefs, she could easily introduce time dependence in the correlation by assigning, for instance, a time-dependent decaying exponent $\beta(t)$ and/or LongCorr(t), or by introducing a separable function of time. In general, however, I must caution against attempting to impute a time dependence from fitting to, say, the European swaption matrix: the dependence of these instruments on the finer features of the correlation function is so mild that, in the presence of unavoidable noise, the resulting functions $\beta(t)$ and LongCorr(t) are more than likely to turn out extremely irregular, and econometrically implausible. If European swaption prices are only mildly sensitive to details in correlation, however, this is not necessarily the case for other exotic products, and the mis-pricing arising from a 'pathological' correlation function can be severe.

The simple (constant-β) exponential functional form (7.12) has so far been amply criticized on several grounds, and it would appear that not much apart from simplicity and numerical expediency can be said in its favour. In reality, closer analysis can show that it is actually less ad hoc and arbitrary than one might expect, and can be arrived at in several ways as a financially justifiable first-order building block of more realistic correlation functions. The exploration of this important feature of the correlation function is therefore presented in the next section. The argument presented is mainly of theoretical interest and totally self-contained, and the following section can therefore be skipped on a first reading without detriment to the understanding of later material.

7.5 Conditions for the Occurrence of Exponential Correlation Surfaces

In this section I intend to show that refinements of the simple, constant-β, exponential functional form are likely to be relatively small perturbations, if financial plausibility and, in particular, the eigenvalue/eigenvector condition are to be retained. One can gain financial intuition about what is captured and what is left out by a specification of the form[7] $\rho_{ij}(T) = \exp(-\beta|T_i - T_j|)$ either by following a simple argument presented by Joshi (2000) or along the lines of the semi-parametric approach presented later on (see Section 7.6).

7.5.1 A toy model: first version

To begin with Joshi's argument, let us consider three forward rates, say f_1, f_2 and f_3, with $T_1 < T_2 < T_3$, shocked by the arrival of financial information, and let us assume that:

---

[7]The discussion can obviously be extended to the case

$$\rho_{ij} = \text{LongCorr} + (1 - \text{LongCorr})\exp(-\beta|T_i - T_j|).$$

1. the correlation must be of the form $\rho = \rho(|T_i - T_j|)$, and

2. the portion of the response to the arrival of information of f_1 that is uncorrelated with the response of f_2 is also uncorrelated with the change in f_3.

In other terms, by 2 we are assuming that there is a common shock, say dZ_2, that affects, albeit to different extents, df_1, df_2 and df_3. In addition, we assume that there are also two other shocks, say dZ_1 and dZ_3, such that the first, dZ_1, only affects df_1, and the second, dZ_3, only impacts df_3. In this set-up, no shock therefore affects both df_2 and df_3 that does not affect df_1 as well. Considering only three forward rates is, of course, artificial. Even the analysis of this simple case can capture, however, the most salient features of the dynamics of the yield curve, because it constitutes the simplest non-trivial structure allowing for the existence of the three fundamental modes of deformation of a yield curve (i.e., changes in level, slope and curvature). Also, nothing constrains the three forward rates in the example below to span short periods, such as three or six months. They could be of, say, five-year tenor each, or of uneven length, and, if so interpreted, would provide a very coarse but still useful description of a given yield curve.

Neglecting the drift terms, irrelevant for the argument, we can therefore write the stochastic differential equations for their diffusive evolution as

$$\frac{df_1}{f_1} = \sigma_1\left(\sqrt{1 - \rho_{12}^2}\, dZ_1 + \rho_{12}\, dZ_2\right), \tag{7.15}$$

$$\frac{df_2}{f_2} = \sigma_2\left(dZ_2\right), \tag{7.16}$$

$$\frac{df_3}{f_3} = \sigma_3\left(\rho_{23}\, dZ_2 + \sqrt{1 - \rho_{23}^2}\, dZ_3\right), \tag{7.17}$$

with dZ_1, dZ_2 and dZ_3 independent Brownian increments. The term dZ_2 accounts for the common shock to f_1, f_2 and f_3; the terms dZ_1 and dZ_3 are idiosyncratic to f_1 and f_3. This situation is symbolically depicted in Figure 7.14.

Already at this stage it is relatively easy to appreciate the nature of the constraint on the forward-rate dynamics brought about by enforcing assumption 1: one is simply requiring that $\rho_{i,i+p}$ should always have the same value, no matter what index i one chooses (in our three-forward-rates world, this would mean that, for any T_1, T_2 and T_3 such that $T_2 - T_1 = T_3 - T_2$, $\rho_{12} = \rho_{23}$).

Assumption 2, on the other hand, has somewhat more opaque economic implications, and it is difficult at this stage to gauge whether it is financially more or less restrictive than assumption 1. The analysis of the relative financial importance of these two assumptions will therefore be undertaken later on. In the meantime, we can first of all work out the implications that can be derived from them.

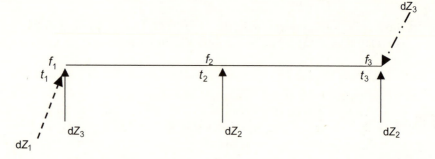

Figure 7.14   *The same shock* dZ_2 *(depicted by continuous arrows) affects forward rates* f_1, f_2 *and* f_3. *An uncorrelated shock* dZ_1 *(shown as a dashed arrow) affects* f_1 *only; similarly another uncorrelated shock* dZ_3 *(symbolized by the mixed arrow) affects* f_3 *only. No special meaning should be attached to the length or direction of the arrows.*

The construction in Figure 7.14 shows that the common shock dZ_2 is responsible for a roughly parallel (same direction) movement of the three-period yield curve. Given that the responsiveness to dZ_1 and dZ_3 of df_1 and df_3, respectively, are positive (see Equations (7.15) and (7.17)) and remembering that dZ_1 and dZ_3 are uncorrelated, these modes of deformation produce instantaneously either a change in curvature or a change in slope of the yield curve depending on the (equiprobable) signs of the shocks, but, on average, simply give rise to 'shapeless' deformation noise for the yield curve.[8] This conclusion should be compared with the discussion after Figure 7.15.

If one then calculates the correlations between the three forward rates, one immediately obtains that the correlation between the first and the second and between the second and the third forward rates are given by ρ_{12} and ρ_{23}, respectively, and that $\rho_{13} = \rho_{12}\rho_{23}$. If, however, by assumption 1, the dependence on the forward rates is purely of the form

$$\rho_{ij} = \rho(|T_i - T_j|),$$

it then follows that

$$\rho(|T_3 - T_1|) = \rho(|T_3 - T_2|)\rho(|T_2 - T_1|).$$

In other terms, the logarithm of ρ must be a linear function (i.e., $f(a + b) = f(a) + f(b)$ with $f(\ ) = \ln\{\rho(|\ \ |)\}$ and with $a = T_3 - T_2$, $b = T_2 - T_1$,

---

[8]Strictly speaking, for $\sigma_1 = \sigma_2 = \sigma_3$, the shock dZ_2 will not produce an exactly parallel shock of the yield curve; however, to the extent that ρ_{12} and ρ_{23} are not too different from unity, as is commonly the case for same-currency forward rates, the statement is approximately correct.

$a + b = (T_3 - T_2) + (T_2 - T_1) = T_3 - T_1)$ and the function ρ itself must satisfy

$$\rho(a + b) = \rho(a)\rho(b),$$
$$\rho(0) = 1,$$
$$1 \geq \rho > 0.$$

There must therefore exist some $\beta \geq 0$ such that

$$\rho_{ij} = \rho(T_i - T_j) = \exp(-\beta|T_i - T_j|).$$

The important point is that, since the same reasoning applies for every i and j, the *same decay constant β must apply to the whole set of forward rates*. This simple exponential functional form, which is a particular case of specification (7.12), is therefore the only functional form compatible with the assumptions made above about the impact of financial information on the changes of different forward rates and about the type of functional dependence of the function ρ on T_i and T_j. It therefore follows that any feature more complex than what is embodied by $\rho_{ij} = \exp(-\beta|T_i - T_j|)$ must come from either

(i) movements of f_1 uncorrelated with movements in f_2 but correlated with movements of f_3, or

(ii) a dependence of ρ other than on $|T_i - T_j|$.

Let us examine these two possible sources of deviation from the fixed-β exponentially decaying behavior in turn, with a view to ascertaining their relative importance. To this end, one can extend the argument presented above as follows.

7.5.2 A toy model: second version

One possible source of deviation from the simple exponential behavior can arise from a violation of assumption 2, that is, from the fact that the joint dynamics of the three forward rates differs from Equations (7.15)–(7.17) by the terms A and B

$$\frac{\mathrm{d}f_1}{f_1} = \sigma_1\left(\sqrt{1 - \rho_{12}^2}\,\mathrm{d}Z_1 + \rho_{12}\,\mathrm{d}Z_2\right), \tag{7.18}$$

$$\frac{\mathrm{d}f_2}{f_2} = \sigma_2\left(\mathrm{d}Z_2\right), \tag{7.19}$$

$$\frac{\mathrm{d}f_3}{f_3} = \sigma_3\left(A\,\mathrm{d}Z_1 + \rho_{23}\,\mathrm{d}Z_2 + B\,\mathrm{d}Z_3\right), \tag{7.20}$$

with

$$B^2 = 1 - \rho_{23}^2 - A^2 \quad \text{and} \quad A = \frac{\rho_{13} - \rho_{12}\rho_{23}}{\sqrt{1 - \rho_{12}^2}}. \tag{7.21}$$

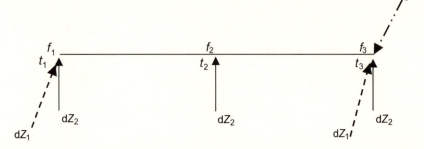

Figure 7.15   *The same shock* dZ_2 *(depicted by continuous arrows) affects forward rates* f_1, f_2 *and* f_3. *An uncorrelated shock* dZ_3 *(shown as a mixed arrow) affects* f_3 *only; another shock,* dZ_1 *(shown as a dashed arrow) affects both* f_1 *and* f_3, *but not* f_2. *Again, no special meaning should be attached to the length or direction of the arrows.*

Note that the term B is simply needed in order to preserve unchanged the total responsiveness of df_3, that is, in order to ensure that $E[df_3/f_3, df_3/f_3] = \sigma_3^2$, or, in the terminology of Chapter 3 and of Equation (3.12), that $\sum_{i=1}^{3} b_{3i}^2 = 1$. The change in the correlation structure therefore fully comes from the term A, by means of which some of the change in df_3 is due to the shock that affects df_1 but not df_2 (i.e., dZ_1). It is also important to note that the new shock structure (with one, two and three shocks, for the second, first and third forward rate, respectively) is now the most general possible for this re-duced yield curve, since by the Choleski decomposition any 3×3 correlation structure can always be rewritten in this manner. We are therefore no longer dealing with a special case, and the conclusions we will draw can therefore be extended to any three-segment yield curve. The new correlation structure can be symbolically represented as in Figure 7.15.

The construction in Figure 7.15 shows that, depending on the relative signs of the responsiveness of df_1 and df_3 to the common shock dZ_1, this Brownian increment is responsible for either a change in slope (opposite sign of respon-siveness) or curvature (same sign of responsiveness) of the three-period yield curve. More precisely, since the quantity $\sqrt{1 - \rho_{12}^2}$ is certainly non-negative (and strictly positive in non-degenerate cases), the extra mode of deforma-tion introduced in Figure 7.15 is either a curvature or a slope term depending on whether A is positive or negative, respectively. The sign of B is obviously immaterial, since dZ_3 only affects df_3. Note also that, if it is still the case that $\rho_{13} = \rho_{12}\rho_{23}$, then the term A is necessarily equal to zero. Therefore a significant curvature or slope mode of deformation for the yield curve will be present if the correlation between the first and the third forward rates is greater or smaller than the product of the correlations between the first and the second and between the second and the third. In other terms, the greater the difference between ρ_{13} and $\rho_{12}\rho_{23}$, the larger the second and third eigenvalues from the orthogonalization of the correlation matrix can be expected to be relative to the first. It is also important to stress that departures from the simple exponential solution can only occur, in this simple three-forward-rate world, because of either of two possible reasons:

(i) ρ_{23} is different from (and greater than) ρ_{12}, thereby violating assumption 1, or

(ii) A is different from zero, violating assumption 2.

Looking at Equations (7.18)–(7.20), however, one can see that the first cause of deviation has no effect on the slope and curvature changes, since the responsiveness coefficient ρ_{23} only affects the third forward rate via the common shock dZ_2. Let us therefore concentrate our attention on the implications of $A \neq 0$. The occurrence of a curvature or slope deformation can be conveniently determined in terms of the quantity Δ defined to be the amount by which ρ_{13} differs from the product $\rho_{12}\rho_{23}$, that is,

$$\rho_{13} = \rho_{12}\rho_{23} + \Delta.$$

From this definition it follows that

$$A = \frac{\rho_{13} - \rho_{12}\rho_{23}}{\sqrt{1 - \rho_{12}^2}} = \frac{\Delta}{\sqrt{1 - \rho_{12}^2}}.$$

Clearly, if $\Delta = 0$ then $A = 0$ and one is back to the case $\rho_{13} = \rho_{12}\rho_{23}$ that produces little systematic curvature or slope contribution. By studying the sign of Δ one can then conclude that if one wants

(i) positive convexity for the correlation function, that is, $\rho_{13} > (1 - 2\rho_{12})$,

(ii) decreasing monotonicity for the function ρ, and

(iii) increasing correlation for same-separation correlations as the maturity increases (i.e., $\rho_{23} > \rho_{12}$),

then $\rho_{23} > \rho_{12}$ and Δ must be either positive but smaller than $\rho_{12}(1 - \rho_{23})$ or negative but greater than $\rho_{12}(2 - \rho_{23}) - 1$. If Δ is positive then A is positive, the second most important mode of deformation is a curvature change, and the correlation function shows a pronounced convexity. If Δ is negative then A is negative, the second most important mode of deformation is a slope change, and the correlation function displays limited convexity. This state of affairs is shown in Figures 7.16 and 7.17, which display the eigenvectors obtained from the orthogonalization of the correlation matrix, with $\rho_{23} > \rho_{12}$ and for the two cases of Δ approaching its upper (positive) or lower (negative) bounds. In both cases the requirements of decreasing monotonicity and positive convexity for the correlation function were satisfied.

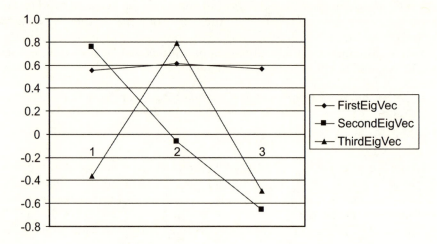

Figure 7.16   *The three eigenvectors from the orthogonalization of the correlation matrix given by* $\rho_{12} = 0.8$, $\rho_{23} = 0.85$, $\rho_{13} = 0.605$, $\Delta = -0.075$. *Notice that a recognizable slope mode of deformation is clearly visible.*

As is apparent from Figures 7.16 and 7.17, making Δ (and therefore A) positive has the effect of changing the nature of the second most important deformation mode away from a slope change and towards a curvature change. If one believes, as required by Condition 4.6 in Chapter 4, that slope changes

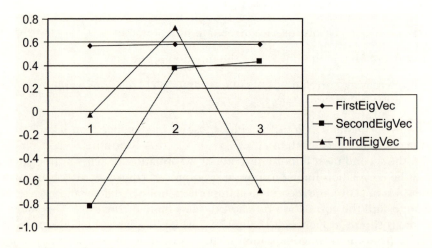

Figure 7.17   *The three eigenvectors from the orthogonalization of the correlation matrix given by* $\rho_{12} = 0.8$, $\rho_{23} = 0.85$, $\rho_{13} = 0.78$, $\Delta = 0.115$. *Notice that a recognizable slope mode of deformation has now virtually disappeared.*

should be (after parallel shifts) more important than curvature changes to explain the dynamics of yield curves, then the Δ-negative case is therefore more appealing (see Figure 7.16). When Δ is negative, however, and for plausible values of the correlation, the correlation function soon ceases to be convex. Therefore, the range of values for Δ that retain a significant *positive convexity* for the correlation function and attribute greater importance to *slope* than curvature changes is rather limited and close to zero. Given the definition of Δ, obviously the same applies to A.

In summary, the convexity and decaying monotonicity constraints can be satisfied by either a positive or a negative Δ (A). For reasonable values of the correlation function, the range of possible values for Δ is not symmetrically positioned around zero, but biassed toward positive values. Increasingly positive values of Δ, in turn, correspond to a slope eigenvector becoming increasingly more similar to a curvature mode of deformation (see Figure 7.17). Negative values of Δ retain the traditional shape for the eigenvectors, but, as mentioned above, the possible range of negative values for Δ compatible with the desired monotonicity and convexity are limited. Therefore, if we deem the financial properties highlighted above desirable, ρ_{13} cannot be too different from $\rho_{12}\rho_{23}$. On the other hand, the difference between ρ_{13} and $\rho_{12}\rho_{23}$ had been identified above as one of the two possible reasons for the financial need to model the correlation in a more complex fashion than simply as a decaying exponential. The conclusions we have just drawn, however, indicate that, if one believed that the correlation function should display a behavior substantially different from the exponential one, the cause would have to be found in reasons other than a large A term in Equations (7.18)–(7.20). Equations (7.15)–(7.17) should therefore provide a financially acceptable description of the dynamics of the three forward rates, and, by this analysis, the financial impact of the assumption $\rho = \rho(|T_i - T_j|)$, which forces $\rho_{12} = \rho_{23}$, appears decidedly more severe than assumption 2.

In addition to the considerations above, the user should remember that, having chosen and parametrized a given instantaneous correlation function, its precise shape will be recovered only if as many factors are retained in the yield-curve evolution as there are forward rates in the problem. As discussed in Section 7.3, if this is not the case, the actual shape of the correlation function will be strongly dependent on the number of factors. Indeed, Chapter 9, in the part of the book devoted to issues of calibration, will indicate how it is possible, given a fixed number of factors, to price caplets exactly, to recover an arbitrarily chosen shape for the instantaneous volatility functions, and, at the same time, to match as closely as possible (in a sense to be discussed) an arbitrary exogenously assigned correlation surface.

Before moving on to this task, however, it is worth pointing out an interesting possible semi-parametric specification for the correlation surface proposed by Schoenmakers and Coffey (2000), which displays many interesting and appealing features. This task is carried out in the concluding section of this chapter.

7.6 A Semi-Parametric Specification of the Correlation Surface

The approach presented by Schoenmakers and Coffey (2000) can be most easily formulated if the stochastic differential equations describing the evolution of n forward rates are expressed in the form $(7.8')$ presented above (see also Chapter 3):

$$\frac{\mathrm{d}f_i}{f_i} = \mu_i(t)\,\mathrm{d}t + \sigma_i \sum_{j=1}^{n} b_{ij}\,\mathrm{d}z_j \qquad \text{for } 1 \le i \le n, \qquad (7.22)$$

where the $\mathrm{d}z_i$ are, as usual, orthogonal Brownian increments, and $\sum_{j=1}^{n} b_{ij}^2 = 1$ to retain correct recovery of the desired instantaneous volatility function. (Note carefully that as many factors as forward rates have been retained in Equation (7.22).) If one defines $\mathbf{b}_1, \mathbf{b}_2, \ldots, \mathbf{b}_n$ to be the n column vectors of elements $\{b_{11}, b_{12}, \ldots, b_{1n}\}, \{b_{21}, b_{22}, \ldots, b_{2n}\}, \ldots, \{b_{n1}, b_{n2}, \ldots, b_{nn}\}$, respectively, then, as shown in Chapter 3,

$$\rho_{ij} = \mathbf{b}_i^{\mathrm{T}} \mathbf{b}_j.$$

Let us now define

$$\rho_{ij} = \mathbf{b}_i^{\mathrm{T}} \mathbf{b}_j = \frac{\min(d_i, d_j)}{\max(d_i, d_j)} \qquad (7.23)$$

for constants $\{d_i\}$, $1 \le i \le n$, such that

-
$$d_i > d_j \qquad \text{for } i > j, \qquad (7.24)$$

- the ratio d_i/d_{i+1} should be strictly increasing as a function of i, that is,

$$d_i/d_{i+1} > d_j/d_{j+1} \qquad \text{for } j > i, \qquad (7.25)$$

-
$$d_1 = 1. \qquad (7.26)$$

In their paper Schoenmakers and Coffey (2000) first of all show that Equations (7.24)–(7.26) indeed define possible candidates for correlation matrices. In particular, Conditions (7.24) and (7.25) together ensure a positive convexity to the correlation function for any i and j, and reflect the desirable feature that the loss in correlation between two couples of forward rates separated by the same difference in maturities (say, between one and two years, and 19 and 20 years) should become smaller as one moves down the maturity spectrum, that is, that $\rho_{i,i+p}$ should be an increasing function of i.

Schoenmakers and Coffey then proceed to prove that it is always possible to represent coefficients $\{d_i\}$ satisfying (7.24)–(7.26) by means of a sequence of non-negative numbers Δ_i, $2 \leq i \leq n-1$, as

$$d_i = \exp\left[\sum_{k=2}^{n-1} \min(k-1, i-1)\Delta_k\right]$$

and

$$d_i = \exp\left[\sum_{k=i+1}^{n-1} \min(k-1, j-1)\Delta_k\right] \qquad \text{for } i < j. \qquad (7.27)$$

Irrespective of whether one adopts Representation (7.23) or (7.27), the correlation surface is in general described in terms of $O(n)$ parameters (the ratios d_i/d_{i+1} or the coefficients Δ). This over-abundant number of degrees of freedom is, however, reduced by making some drastic assumptions about their dependence on the index i. (Incidentally, for a fully non-parametric approach, the correlation matrix would be described by $O(n^2)$ entries. Schoenmakers and Coffey's approach only requires the specification of $O(n)$ quantities and, for this reason, they call their strategy 'semi-parametric'.) The first assumption about the parameters Δ is to impose

$$\Delta_2 = \Delta_3 = \ldots = \Delta_{n-2} = \alpha \geq 0$$
$$\Delta_{n-1} = \beta \leq 0.$$

If this is the case, Schoenmakers and Coffey prove that the correlation function can be given a two-parameter representation as

$$\rho_{ij} = \exp\{-[\beta + \alpha(T_{n-1} - T_{(i+j+1)/2})]|T_i - T_j|\}. \qquad (7.28)$$

Schoenmakers and Coffey also propose a richer three-parameter structure given by

(i) $\Delta_2 = \alpha_1 \geq 0$,

(ii) $\Delta_{n-2} = \alpha_2 \geq 0$,

(iii) Δ_k varying linearly for $3 \leq k \leq n-3$ between α_1 and α_2, and

(iv) $\Delta_{n-1} = \beta \geq 0$.

The resulting form for the exponential is simple but rather involved, and the reader is referred to Schoenmakers and Coffey (2000) for the details. Both specifications are appealing, because they ensure a positive definite correlation matrix, a positive convexity and produce a function $\rho_{i,i+p}$ that is an increasing function of i. Furthermore, actual numerical calibration to swaption prices (EUR, 14 April 1998) carried out by the authors using the second formulation produced a good-quality fit, and econometrically plausible results, such as an asymptotic correlation of 77%, and a convexity decreasing with increasing maturity. The qualitative shape of the correlation function obtained with the optimized parameters obtained from this Case Study

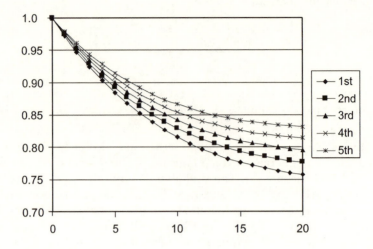

Figure 7.18   *The correlation between the first, second, third, fourth and fifth (annual) forward rates and forward rates maturing the number of years on the x axis implied by Schoenmakers and Coffey's approach. Therefore, the curve labelled '1st' denotes the correlation between the first forward rate (expiring today) and the forward rates expiring 1, 2, . . . , 20 years from today; the curve labelled '2nd' shows the correlation between the forward rate expiring one year from today and the forward rates expiring 2, 3, . . . , 21 years from today; and so on.*

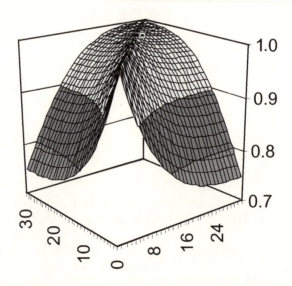

Figure 7.19   *The correlation surface implied by Schoenmakers and Coffey's approach. Notice the change in convexity of the surface across the main diagonal as the expiry of the forward rates increase. Compare this diagram with Figures 7.5 and 7.6 in Section 7.2 and with Figure 7.10 in Section 7.4.*

is shown in Figure 7.18. Furthermore, as shown in Figure 7.19, this approach allows for the change in convexity across the main diagonal that, as suggested by the works discussed in Section 7.2, appears to be an empirically observed feature. The approach proposed by Schoenmakers and Coffey (2000) therefore appears interesting and able to recover several financially plausible features. It also presents the advantage over the second and third functional forms presented in Section 7.4 (Equations (7.13) and (7.14)) that the resulting correlation surface is guaranteed to be positive definite. Despite the fact that the authors employ their approach in an 'implied' manner (i.e., they extract the parameters of the correlation function implied by the prices derived from an exogenous market swaption matrix), their specification of a correlation function could also be used for fitting a statistically obtained correlation matrix. In particular, once the fitting has been carried out, the correlation surface obtained from the three-parameter specification presented above could profitably constitute the 'target correlation' discussed and used in Chapter 9.

Part III

Calibration of the LIBOR Market Model

8

Fitting the Instantaneous Volatility Functions

8.1 General Calibration Philosophy and Plan of Part III

In Parts I and II I have gathered the tools required to undertake a robust and financially appealing calibration strategy of the LIBOR market model. More precisely, after laying out the conceptual foundations of the approach in Part I, I have highlighted in Part II the financial criteria that can guide the user in her choice of instantaneous volatility and correlation functions (see Chapters 6 and 7, respectively). Once this choice has been made, the task remains to pin down the free parameters that appear in the specification of these functions. This task is often referred to as the calibration of the LIBOR market model, and is dealt with in the chapters of Part III.

8.1.1 The wider meaning of calibration

The meaning I give to the word 'calibration' has a much wider scope than simply choosing the parameters of the model in such a way that today's prices of the plain-vanilla instruments (swaps and caplets) are correctly recovered. This goal is important but limited, and only insures that the time-0 delta and vega hedging costs predicted by the model are the same as the corresponding market prices. The trader, however, will in general have to readjust the option hedges in her portfolio throughout the life of the deal. As long as the trader manages to recalibrate the model day after day to the future market prices, these re-hedging trades will always take place at the prices implied by the model at *that* point in time and in the *then*-prevailing state of the world. Unless, however, the future conditional market prices of the hedging instruments are identical to the corresponding future conditional prices implied by the deterministic volatility and correlation functions calibrated to today's prices, the strategy engaged in by the trader will not be self-financing.

It is important to point out that the common, and in practice unavoidable, procedure of recalibrating every day the model to the current market prices by itself renders the associated hedging trading strategy non-self-financing. In other terms, every day the trader 'discovers' that the model calibrated yesterday was 'wrong'. The practical success of a hedging strategy largely depends on the ability to choose, for a given model, a calibration such that the parameters of the model have to be adjusted as little as possible throughout the life of the deal. This, in particular, will occur if the future realization of the term structure of volatilities and of the swaption matrix will be similar to the corresponding model-implied quantities.

8.1.2 *What financial quantities should be compared?*

One should note carefully that not all observable financial quantities meaningfully lend themselves to this type of comparison. Remember, in fact, that in the standard LIBOR market model the assumption is made that the instantaneous volatility and correlation function are deterministic. As such, they remain unchanged under a Girsanov's measure transformation. In the deterministic setting, the requirement that the evolution of the model term structure of volatilities should conform to the real-world one is actually meaningful and useful. However, the trader cannot naively require that the evolution of the yield curve predicted by the model should 'resemble' the future real-world behavior of the yields. This is because the drifts of the forward rates used in the standard LIBOR market model are risk-adjusted, and, whatever drift-related features the real-world dynamics of the forward rates might display (such as, for instance, mean reversion), these will be completely scrambled as one moves to the pricing measure. The same Girsanov transformation, on the other hand, leaves the (deterministic) volatilities, and hence the resulting term structure of volatilities, unchanged.

Similar problems arise as one moves from a deterministic-volatility to a stochastic-volatility setting. In the stochastic case the requirement that the evolution of the model-implied term structure of volatilities should 'resemble' the real-world one must be handled carefully. The reason is exactly the same: when volatilities are stochastic, their drifts are also scrambled in moving from one pricing measure to another, and making a naive comparison between observables affected by the drifts becomes impossible. This topic is dealt with in Part IV, Chapters 12 and 13 (see also Rebonato and Joshi 2001a). Up to that point I shall always work in a deterministic-volatility setting, and I shall therefore assume without any further qualifications that a close congruence between future model-implied and market volatilities is a desirable feature.

Even when using the deterministic-volatility version of the modern pricing approach, however, the trader should always remember that market incompleteness is the norm rather than the exception. Calibrating a complete-market model in an incomplete market therefore means, in practice, extracting from the traded prices as much information as possible about the market's expectations of future market observables; comparing this (never certain, but hopefully plausible) reverse-engineered market view with the trader's own; availing oneself of the available statistical information about the relevant real-world quantities (volatilities and correlations); combining all this information into a coherent whole; and, to some extent, hoping for the best. The last somewhat flippant remark simply highlights the fact that, despite the appealing simplicity and elegance of the deterministic-volatility models with which the trader works, the underlying markets are intrinsically incomplete, and, therefore, the ability to 'lock in' quantities erroneously implied by the market consensus is in practice very limited (see again, in this respect, the discussions in Sections 2.2.6, 2.2.7 and 11.1).

8.1.3 The general calibration philosophy

In the light of these considerations, I propose an overall fitting strategy whereby the market-related (if not fully market-determined) information is conceptually split from the statistical/econometric data. Indeed, this modelling philosophy was at the root of the decomposition of the stochastic differential equations for the forward-rate dynamics in the form presented in Section 3.2 (see, e.g., Equation (3.10)). The instantaneous volatility will be linked via its root-mean-square value to the market-implied volatility of caplets and, via the appropriate covariance elements, to swaption prices (see Section 8.3.1). Information about the (measure-invariant) correlation function will then be assumed to be derived from econometric analysis of real-world data.

This split is, to some extent, arbitrary and questionable: it would seem natural, for instance, to attempt to recover correlation information from the joint prices of caplets and European swaptions. While in principle certainly possible, I have discussed in Section 7.1 why I consider this approach in general fraught with great practical difficulties: ultimately, the validity of this very delicate joint analysis that attempts to combine swaption and caplet information stands or falls with the efficiency and congruence of the two sister markets – two features taken less and less for granted in the aftermath of the Russia crisis events of 1998. (See Section 9.1.3; see also, for a different view, the work by Schoenmakers and Coffey (2000) discussed in Section 7.6.)

The structure of the present and of the following chapters in Part III will therefore attempt to mirror, as far as possible, this overall calibration philosophy. Chapter 8 will show how the information available from the caplet and swaption markets, and the accompanying hypothesis of approximate time-homogeneity, when appropriate, can provide information about the instantaneous volatility functions. In Chapter 9 I will then assume that these instantaneous volatility functions have been determined to the trader's satisfaction, and that the model should then be calibrated to a target (econometrically determined) correlation structure. It is essential, for the overall strategy to be viable, that this second part of the calibration should be effected without spoiling the volatility part of the parametrization.

The underlying situation that I have in mind in this and in the following chapter is therefore that of a trader who believes that the complex product she has to price mainly depends on forward-rate (as opposed to swap-rate) volatilities, and who will hedge the volatility exposure by trading in caplets. In Chapter 10 I will then take the complementary view, and I will put myself in the shoes of a trader who is pricing a swaption-driven (and swaption-hedged) product, but who, at the same time, realizes that the behavior of forward rates will ultimately affect the price to a non-negligible extent (and that some caplet hedging will therefore be required as well). In this context, I intend to show how information both from the caplet and from the European swaption markets can be brought together in order to see if, and to what extent, a coherent picture can be plausibly obtained. We will also show how virtually exact pricing of a set of co-terminal European swaptions can be obtained (and in an infinity of ways), even using the much-easier-to-work-with forward-rate formulation of the LIBOR market model.

8.2 A First Approach to Fitting the Caplet Market: Imposing Time-Homogeneity

In Part II of this book I have set the groundwork required for the calibration program. More precisely

- I have highlighted the financial implications of different choices for the instantaneous volatility and correlation functions;
- I have dealt with their ability to recover a given set of market caplet prices;
- I have shown in very general terms the conditions under which these functions can produce a time-homogeneous evolution for the term structure of volatilities and for the swaption matrix; and
- I have suggested some simple functional forms for the instantaneous volatility and correlation functions that satisfy the joint requirements of analytical tractability and financial plausibility.

We are now in a position to implement the proposed strategy to choose a volatility function capable of pricing the caplet market and of producing a financially appealing evolution of the term structure of volatilities. On the basis of the discussion in Chapter 6, the two functional forms for the instantaneous volatility function will be

$$\sigma_{\text{inst}}(t, T) = g(T)h(T - t),$$
$$\sigma_{\text{inst}}(t, T) = g(T)h(T - t)f(t).$$

If the market-given quantity $\sigma_{\text{Black}}^2(T)T$ were strictly increasing, one could always find (by bootstrapping) a solution in terms of the matrix elements $S(i, j)$. This procedure, however, while theoretically perfectly acceptable, suffers from financial and practical drawbacks. I therefore intend to propose a general strategy to price the current caplet market and to produce an (approximately) time-homogeneous evolution of the term structure of volatilities that can be followed irrespective of whether $\sigma^2_{\text{Black}}(T)T$ is strictly increasing or not. I shall then show that this strategy can easily be extended to the more complex problem of pricing today's caplet market and reproducing as well as possible a user-chosen future deterministic term structure of volatilities (possibly quite different from today's).

8.2.1 Fitting the time-homogeneous part

Let us denote the time-homogeneous part of the instantaneous volatility function, expressed in terms of a (small) number, m, of parameters $\{\alpha\}$ as:[1]

$$\sigma_{\text{inst}}(T - t) = \sigma^{\text{th}}(T - t) = g(T - t; \alpha_1, \alpha_2, \ldots, \alpha_m).$$

For a given set of parameters $\{\alpha\}$, one can calculate, for an n-forward-rate problem, the n distinct elements of the matrix $\mathbf{S}^{\text{th}}$, defined by

$$S^{\text{th}}(k, j) = \int_{T_{k-1}}^{T_k} g(T_j - t; \alpha_1, \alpha_2, \ldots, \alpha_m)^2 \, du. \tag{8.1}$$

Note carefully the difference between the matrix $\mathbf{S}^{\text{th}}$ and the matrix $\mathbf{S}$: the latter contains the integrals of the square of the general (i.e., T- and t-dependent) instantaneous volatility function, $\sigma(t, T)$; the former contains the similar integrals evaluated using a time-homogeneous instantaneous volatility function, $\sigma^{\text{th}}(T - t)$. One can then define the quantities

$$\chi^2 = \sum_{j=1}^{n} \eta_j^2$$

and

$$\eta_j^2 = \left[\sigma^2_{\text{Black}}(T_j)T_j - \sum_{k=1}^{j} S^{\text{th}}(k, j) \right]^2$$

and carry out the minimization

$$\min_{\{\alpha_1, \alpha_2, \ldots, \alpha_m\}} \chi^2 \tag{8.2}$$

over the set of parameters $\{\alpha\}$ of the time-homogeneous component of the instantaneous volatility function.[2] By so doing one can find the parameters of the time-homogeneous function $g(T - t; \alpha_1, \alpha_2, \ldots, \alpha_m)$ that can best ac-

---

[1]Notice again that the index 'th' stands in this chapter for 'time-homogeneous', rather than the more common 'theoretical'.

[2]The quantities $\{\eta\}$ could be calculated directly using caplet prices rather than implied volatilities. The two procedures implicitly give different weights to out-of-the-money options.

count for the observed term structure of volatilities. With the first step of the procedure I have therefore attempted to account as much as possible for the observed market prices by means of the chosen time-homogeneous instantaneous volatility function. Notice that the fit will, in general, not be perfect even if the market-given quantity $\sigma^2_{\text{Black}}(T)T$ happens to be strictly increasing. I shall argue below that, somewhat counter-intuitively, this feature is actually desirable.

8.2.2 *Fitting the time-dependent part*

As a second step, I then propose to add a time dependence, in separable form, to the function $\sigma^{\text{th}}(T - t)$. I will do so by working directly with the elements $S(i, j)$, and by modifying the matrix $\mathbf{S}$ as shown in Chapter 6: that is, to the time-homogeneous matrix $\mathbf{S}^{\text{th}}$ a separable time-dependent component is added, transforming the matrix $\mathbf{S}$ from

$$
\begin{pmatrix}
S_{\text{th}}(1,1) \\
S_{\text{th}}(1,2) & S_{\text{th}}(1,1) \\
S_{\text{th}}(1,3) & S_{\text{th}}(1,2) & S_{\text{th}}(1,1) \\
\vdots & \vdots & \vdots & \ddots \\
S_{\text{th}}(1,n) & S_{\text{th}}(1,n-1) & \cdots & S_{\text{th}}(1,2) & S_{\text{th}}(1,1)
\end{pmatrix}
$$

into

$$
\begin{pmatrix}
S_{\text{th}}(1,1)\epsilon_1^2 \\
S_{\text{th}}(1,2)\epsilon_1^2 & S_{\text{th}}(1,1)\epsilon_2^2 \\
S_{\text{th}}(1,3)\epsilon_1^2 & S_{\text{th}}(1,2)\epsilon_2^2 & S_{\text{th}}(1,1)\epsilon_3^2 \\
\vdots & \vdots & \vdots & \ddots \\
S_{\text{th}}(1,n)\epsilon_1^2 & S_{\text{th}}(1,n-1)\epsilon_2^2 & \cdots & S_{\text{th}}(1,1)\epsilon_n^2
\end{pmatrix}
$$

The quantities χ^2 and $\{\eta\}$ now become

$$
\chi^2 = \sum_{j=1}^{n} \eta_j^2
$$

and

$$
\eta_j^2 = \left[\sigma^2_{\text{Black}}(T_j)T_j - \sum_{k=1}^{j} S^{\text{th}}(k, j)\epsilon_k^2 \right]^2 ,
$$

and the minimization is carried out over the n quantities $\{\epsilon\}$, leaving the previously determined parameters $\{\alpha\}$ unchanged:

$$
\min_{\{\epsilon_1, \epsilon_2, \dots, \epsilon_n\}} \chi^2. \tag{8.3}
$$

Once again, in order to avoid that the numerical procedure might end up amplifying the 'noise' likely to be found in the input market data, it is advisable to constrain the possible time variation of the quantities $\{\epsilon\}$ by imposing a simple parametrized functional form $\epsilon_i = \epsilon(t_i; \beta_1, \beta_2, \ldots, \beta_r)$ (such as, for instance, the one suggested in Chapter 6) with $r \ll n$. Keeping the discussion in general terms, at this stage, if this choice is made the minimization exercise now becomes

$$\min_{\{\beta_1, \beta_2, \ldots, \beta_r\}} \chi^2. \tag{8.4}$$

8.2.3 Fine-tuning using the forward-rate-specific component

With the first and second steps (i.e., with the optimization over the $\{\alpha\}$ and the $\{\epsilon\}$ or $\{\beta\}$ parameters), one attempts to account for the observed market prices by putting first as much explanatory burden as possible on the time-homogeneous part of the evolution; and to explain then as much as possible of the residual discrepancies between market and model caplet price in terms of a purely time-dependent (parametrized) separable component.

Even after carrying out this step, the caplet prices will in general not be exactly recovered. To obtain the correct prices, one can at this point define a set of n quantities, k_i^2, $1 \le i \le n$,

$$k_i^2 = \frac{\sigma_{\text{Black}}^2(T_i)T_i}{\sum_{k=1}^{i} S^{\text{th}}(k, i)\epsilon_k^2}, \tag{8.5}$$

which by construction ensure that the correct variance to expiry is perfectly recovered. After Equation (8.5) has been solved, one has finally found a particular caplet-pricing solution

$$S(k, i) = S^{\text{th}}(k, i)\epsilon_k^2 k_i^2. \tag{8.6}$$

This three-step procedure might seem unnecessarily convoluted. One could have, for instance, directly and jointly optimized over the quantities $S^{\text{th}}(k, i)\epsilon_k^2$ before proceeding to the last step (8.5), or employed a variety of other possible schemes. The problem, however, is not that finding a solution to the caplet pricing is too difficult, but that it is, if anything, too easy. The procedure I have proposed ensures that a clear financial meaning is attributed to each stage in the optimization procedure. First of all one finds the parameters of a chosen time-homogeneous function that best account for the caplet prices and that would produce a perfectly time-homogeneous evolution of the term structure of volatilities. If the market quantity $\sigma_{\text{Black}}^2(T_i)T_i$ is not strictly increasing, the market must however imply a change in the future shape of the term structure of volatilities (see Propositions 6.5 and 6.6 in Section 6.2). This change could in principle be accounted for by introducing in the instantaneous volatility function either a pure dependence on time or a pure dependence on the forward rate. I have argued in Section 6.3 that the first mechanism can often be financially more appealing, and I have therefore attempted to account for as much as possible of the residual price discrepancies by introducing the time-dependent terms $\{\epsilon\}$. If the user felt uncomfortable with introducing an explicit time dependence, the second stage of the procedure could obviously be by-passed. In either case, in order to ensure exact pricing of the caplets, whatever residual price discrepancies were still left over after the first step(s) can be taken up by means of the forward-rate-specific terms $\{k\}$. If the time-dependent component is not introduced, the more these terms are constant, the more the procedure has succeeded in producing a time-homogeneous evolution of the term structure of volatilities. By controlling, as indicated above or in similar related manners, the behavior across forward rates of the terms $\{k\}$, the trader can therefore 'induce' the model to behave in the most time-homogeneous manner (compatible with the chosen function form for the volatility function) while exactly pricing the caplet market. The ability to do so should be contrasted with the state of affairs to be found in the 'old-fashioned' short-rate-based models, and in my opinion constitutes one of the strongest points in favour of the modern pricing approach.

EXERCISE 8.1 *Calibrate to a set of bond prices and to a market-given term structure of volatilities a BDT model (Black et al. 1990). Rebonato (1998, 1999c) can provide some help with the task. Having built the tree, estimate the implied instantaneous volatilities of a series of forward rates, and the future term structure of volatilities after, say, one, two and five years. (Finding the future term structure of volatilities at a given node is a laborious but conceptually easy task; estimating the future instantaneous volatilities of the forward rates, on the other hand, will require a bit more ingenuity.) Do you find these quantities financially appealing? If not, is there anything left for you to adjust or modify in the BDT approach, if you still want to price correctly the exogenous bond and caplet markets? Comment.*

8.3 A Second Approach to Fitting the Caplet Market: Using Information from the Swaption Matrix

The previous section has dealt with the task of determining the forward-rate instantaneous volatility functions by making use of the information from the caplet market, and of the requirement that the evolution of the term structure of volatilities should be as time-homogeneous as possible. This section addresses the calibration problem from a different angle, that is, it shows how it is possible to extract useful complementary information about the instantaneous volatility functions of the forward rates by examining in a joint fashion the caplet and European swaption markets. This line of approach to the calibration is particularly useful if the trader is pricing a complex product that depends on both swaption and caplet volatilities (see the discussion in Section 10.2). The usual caveats about assuming in an uncritical way the congruence of these two markets should, of course, be kept in mind.

8.3.1 How swaption prices convey information about the shape of time-dependent volatilities

The first step in the analysis is to review the way in which the price of a European swaption contains information about the instantaneous volatilities of forward rates. Remember first (Section 2.2) that it is market practice to obtain the price of a particular (say, the ith) European swaption by using the Black formula with an implied volatility for the ith swap rate given by

$$[\sigma_{\text{Black}}^{\text{SR}_i}]^2 T_{\exp} = \int_0^{T_{\exp}} \sigma_{\text{inst}}^{\text{SR}_i}(u)^2 \, du, \tag{8.7}$$

where $T_{\exp}$ is the expiry time of the European swaption in question, $\sigma_{\text{inst}}^{\text{SR}_i}(t)$ is the instantaneous volatility of the relative swap rate at time t, and $\sigma_{\text{Black}}^{\text{SR}_i}$ is the market-implied volatility for the swaption associated with swap rate SR_i. Recall also that the swap rate whose root-mean-square volatility is given by the expression above is in turn given by a linear combination of forward rates

$$\text{SR}_i = \sum_{k=1}^{n_i} w_{ik} f_k,$$

where the weight, w_{ik}, on the kth forward rate needed to produce the ith swap rate is equal to

$$w_{ik} = \frac{B_{k+1} \tau_k}{\sum_{j=1}^{n_i} B_{j+1} \tau_j}$$

in which τ_k is the tenor – e.g. 0.5 years – of the swap, B_k the market price of a pure discount bond maturing at time t_k and n_i the number of periods in the ith swap.

If one makes a joint log-normal assumption for all the forward rates and for the swap rate, a straightforward application of Ito's lemma then links the instantaneous volatility of a given swap rate with the instantaneous volatilities, $\{\sigma_i(t)\}$, of all the underlying forward rates:

$$\sigma_{\text{inst}}^{\text{SR}_i}(t)^2 = \sum_{j,k} \zeta_j(t) \zeta_k(t) \rho_{jk}(t) \sigma_j(t) \sigma_k(t) \tag{8.8}$$

with

$$\zeta_j^i(t) = \frac{w_{ij}(t) + \sum_{k=1}^{n_i} f_k(t) \partial w_{ik} / \partial f_j}{\sum_{m=1}^{n_i} w_{im}(t) f_m(t)}.$$

As is well known, the assumption of joint log-normality cannot be correct for all the forward rates and the swap rate at the same time (see Rebonato 1999b for a discussion of the pricing implications). More importantly, and as discussed in detail in Chapter 10, the expression above clearly shows that purely deterministic (time-dependent) instantaneous volatilities for the forward rates must, strictly speaking, produce a stochastic volatility for the associated swap rate (both the forward rates and the weights $\{\mathbf{w}\}$ that appear in the expression for $\sigma_{\text{inst}}^{\text{SR}}(t)$ are in fact stochastic quantities). In the same Chapter 10, however, I show why it is a good approximation to assume that the expression above can be treated as deterministic with the forward rates and weights replaced by their values today, that is,

$$\sigma_{\text{inst}}^{\text{SR}_i}(t)^2 \simeq \sum_{j,k} \zeta_j(t_0)\zeta_k(t_0)\rho_{jk}(t)\sigma_j(t)\sigma_k(t). \tag{8.9}$$

If, for the moment, one simply accepts this result, it is easy to see that the price of a European swaption contains useful information about the instantaneous volatilities of the underlying forward rates. The price of the European swaption will in fact be obtained using in the Black formula the implied (root-mean-square) swap-rate volatility, $\sigma_{\text{Black}}^{\text{SR}}$, that is, in turn, linked via the swap-rate instantaneous volatility to the instantaneous volatilities of the forward rates by

$$
\begin{aligned}
[\sigma_{\text{Black}}^{\text{SR}_i}]^2 T &= \int_0^{T_{\text{exp}}} \sigma_{\text{inst}}^{\text{SR}_i}(t)^2 \, dt \\
&= \int_0^{T_{\text{exp}}} \sum_{j,k} \zeta_j(t)\zeta_k(t)\rho_{jk}(t)\sigma_j(t)\sigma_k(t) \, dt \\
&\simeq \int_0^{T_{\text{exp}}} \sum_{j,k} \zeta_j(t_0)\zeta_k(t_0)\rho_{jk}(t)\sigma_j(t)\sigma_k(t) \, dt \\
&= \sum_{j,k} \zeta_j(t_0)\zeta_k(t_0) \int_0^{T_{\text{exp}}} \rho_{jk}(t)\sigma_j(t)\sigma_k(t) \, dt. \tag{8.10}
\end{aligned}
$$

Since only one (the first) of the forward rates in the swap will arrive to its own expiry by expiry of the European swaption, all the others will affect the root-mean-square volatility of the latter only through an interval in the 'life' of their (time-dependent) instantaneous volatility. This interval will constitute a different fraction (albeit of the same length) of the overall 'life' of the various forward rates. This is clearly shown in Figure 8.1 for the case of a semi-annual 3×3 swaption.[3] In this example, the instantaneous volatilities of all the six forward rates have been assumed, for the sake of simplicity, to be described by the same (purely time-homogeneous) volatility function. The first forward rate in the swaption (labelled 'Fwd$_1$') will come to its own expiry by expiry of the swaption. At time 0 (today) it will therefore have the volatility of a three-year-residual-maturity forward rate. Since we have assumed that the instantaneous volatility of every forward rate should be described by the same time-homogeneous function, and given that this function displays a hump in

[3]The swaption notation '$m \times n$' indicates an n-year swaption expiring in m years' time.

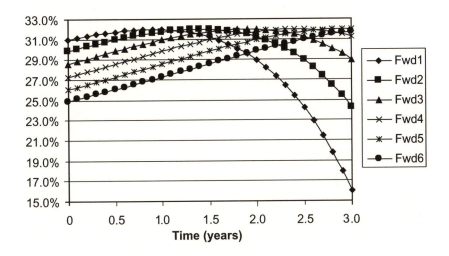

Figure 8.1 *The instantaneous volatilities of the six forward rates in a* 3×3 *semi-annual swaption. See the text for a detailed description. All the forward rates were assumed to have the same time-homogeneous instantaneous volatility function.*

approximately a year's time, as time increases from today the instantaneous volatility of the first forward rate will rise slowly to reach a maximum approximately 13 months from today, and then will begin to decline sharply as its expiry approaches.

The second forward rate (i.e., the forward rate, labelled 'Fwd$_2$', that will expire half a year after the expiry of the swaption) has at time 0 the volatility 'appropriate' to a forward rate with three-and-a-half years to expiry. As seen from 'today' (time 0) its instantaneous volatility then keeps increasing for approximately 18 months (i.e., six months more than the first forward rate). By the swaption expiry (i.e., three years from today) it will still have half a year to its own expiry, and its instantaneous volatility will therefore not have declined as much as the volatility of the first forward rate. A similar reasoning can be applied to all the other forward rates, and, by the last and sixth forward rate ('Fwd$_6$') its instantaneous volatility curve has not reached its maximum yet by the time of the expiry of the European swaption. (Remember that, given the assumption of time-homogeneity enforced in this example, all the instantaneous volatility curves displayed in Figure 8.1 are identical in shape, and, as a consequence, are represented by the same curve translated by half a year along the x axis).

Looking back at Equation (8.9), one can notice that the Black implied volatility of the swap rate can (approximately but accurately) be written as a (function of a) suitably weighted sum of covariance elements of the form

$$\int_0^{T_{\exp}} \sigma_j(t)\sigma_k(t)\rho_{jk}(t)\,\mathrm{d}t.$$

In general, this covariance integral will strongly depend not only on the average level of each component volatility, but also on whether, over the integration interval, any two volatilities have high and low values 'in phase' or 'out of step' with each other. For a given correlation,[4] the values of these integrals, which directly determine the European swaption price, will therefore display a significant dependence on the relative shape of the various instantaneous volatility functions over the integration time, and not just on their root-mean-squares. In particular, looking at Figure 8.1, one can readily appreciate that the covariance element between the first and the sixth forward rates will be much lower than the product of their root-mean-square volatilities, even if the instantaneous correlation were exactly equal to unity, since one volatility is large when the other is small, and vice versa. In general, the more the instantaneous volatility function displays a pronounced hump,[5] the more this effect will be pronounced.

EXERCISE 8.2 *Assume an instantaneous correlation function of the form $\rho_{ij} = \exp(-\beta|T_i - T_j|)$. Using Formula (8.9), calculate the implied swap-rate volatility for swaptions of different expiries and maturities, varying, in turn, the shape of the instantaneous volatility function (keeping their root-mean-square unchanged) and the correlation coefficient β. Comment on the sensitivity of the swaption price to changes in β and the shape of the instantaneous volatility function. (Make sure that you vary β in such a way that the resulting instantaneous correlations do not become unreasonably low – the correlation between the most distant forward rates should not become lower than, say, 40%.)*

EXERCISE 8.3 *A forward-starting swaption is the option to enter at time t_1 a swap starting at time t_2 and maturing at time t_3. Assume that all the caplets and the plain-vanilla (i.e., non-forward-starting) European swaptions trade at 20% implied volatility. Assume also that the instantaneous volatility function common to all the forward rates displays a pronounced hump, with a maximum located at 18 months. Discuss qualitatively what would you expect the implied volatility to be for the forward-starting swaptions with*

$t_1 = 1\ year,\quad t_2 = 2\ years,\quad t_3 = 5\ years;$
$t_1 = 1\ year,\quad t_2 = 2\ years,\quad t_3 = 10\ years;$
$t_1 = 1.5\ years,\quad t_2 = 3\ years,\quad t_3 = 5\ years;$
$t_1 = 0.5\ years,\quad t_2 = 3\ years,\quad t_3 = 5\ years.$

---

[4]Recall that I have shown in Section 7.1, that the prices of European swaptions display a very mild dependence on the shape of the instantaneous correlation function, provided that the same average correlation is obtained.

[5]That is, for the functional form proposed in Chapter 6, this will occur, for instance, when both the coefficients b and c are large.

(You might want to re-read the discussion about serial options in the final part of Section 2.2.)

8.3.2 The calibration strategy

Accepting again the assumption mentioned above about the validity of setting the quantities $\zeta_j(t)$ equal to constants given by their values today, one can state the problem as follows: The total variance, $[\sigma_{\text{Black},m}^2 SR_m T_{\exp,m}]_{\text{model}}$, of the mth swaption in the swaption matrix implied by a given set of time- and forward-rate-dependent instantaneous volatility functions (which price all the caplets perfectly) is equal to

$$[(\sigma_{\text{Black}}^{SR_m})^2 T_{\exp,m}]_{\text{model}}$$

$$= \int_0^{T_{\exp,m}} \sigma_{\text{inst}}^{SR_m}(t)^2 \, dt$$

$$= \sum_{j,k=1}^{n_m} \zeta_j(t_0)\zeta_k(t_0) \int_0^{T_{\exp,m}} \rho_{jk}(t)\sigma_j^{\text{inst}}(t)\sigma_k^{\text{inst}}(t) \, dt$$

$$= \sum_{j,k=1}^{n_m} \zeta_j(t_0)\zeta_k(t_0)k_j k_k$$

$$\times \int_0^{T_{\exp,m}} \rho_{jk}(t)\sigma_j^{\text{inst,th}}(T_j - t; \{\boldsymbol{\alpha}\})\sigma_k^{\text{inst,th}}(T_k - t; \{\boldsymbol{\alpha}\})\epsilon(t; \{\boldsymbol{\beta}\})^2 \, dt.$$

In the expression above, $[(\sigma_{\text{Black}}^{SR_m})^2 T_{\exp,m}]_{\text{model}}$ is the value of the variance of the mth swap rate implied by the chosen functional form for the forward-rate volatilities[6] and, as before, I have assumed that the instantaneous volatility function for the jth forward rate, $\sigma_j^{\text{inst}}(\ )$, can be decomposed into a time-homogeneous component, denoted by $\sigma_j^{\text{inst,th}}(T_j - t; \{\boldsymbol{\alpha}\})$, described by a set of parameters $\{\boldsymbol{\alpha}\}$, times a forward-rate-specific part, k_j, and times a purely time-dependent contribution, $\epsilon(t; \{\boldsymbol{\beta}\})$. The latter is in turn described by a set of parameters $\{\boldsymbol{\beta}\}$. If one then defines

$$\chi^2 = \sum_{m=1}^{N} \left([\sigma_{\text{Black},m}^{SR_m}]_{\text{model}} - [\sigma_{\text{Black},m}^{SR_m}]_{\text{market}}\right)^2, \tag{8.11}$$

one can look for the optimal set of parameters $\{\boldsymbol{\alpha}\}$ and $\{\boldsymbol{\beta}\}$ that minimizes the χ^2 quantity.[7] (In Equation (8.11) N is the number of European swaptions in the swaption matrix, or in the particular portion of interest thereof.) As before, one might want to carry out the optimization over the time-homogeneous

---

[6]If the associated annuity $A(T_{\exp}, T_{\text{Mat}})$ is chosen as numeraire.

[7]One could minimize the sum of the square discrepancies between the Black swaption prices, possibly after introducing some weights. Minimizing over the root-mean-square differences, as done in Equation (8.10), places all the swaptions on roughly the same footing, irrespective of whether their fixed-leg annuity, on which the price depends linearly, is large or small.

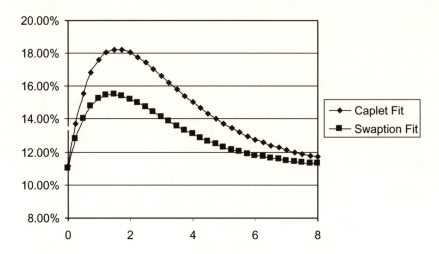

Figure 8.2   *The time-homogeneous part of the forward-rate instantaneous volatility, as obtained by fitting to the caplet or to the swaption market (curves 'Caplet Fit' and 'Swaption Fit', respectively) using EUR 1-Sept-2000 market data. Note that imposing the best possible fit to the caplet prices with a time-homogeneous forward-rate instantaneous volatility is equivalent to requiring that the evolution of the term structure of volatilities should be as self-similar as possible.*

$\{\alpha\}$ parameters first, so as to identify the most time-homogeneous solution possible, given the market prices of the European swaptions. Detailed empirical results are reported in Case Study 3 (Section 8.5.3) for a particular choice of the functional form and of the parameters of $\sigma^{\text{inst,th}}(T_j - t; \{\alpha\})$ and $\epsilon(t; \{\beta\})$, but it is important to point out already at this stage that, as shown in Figures 8.2–8.4, by following the procedure highlighted above for a variety of currencies, one 'naturally' and independently finds that the shape for the time-homogeneous instantaneous volatility function that best fits the swaption matrix is the same as the one that best preserves the time-homogeneity of the term structure of volatilities, that is, the humped one.

8.3.3 Comparison between the instantaneous volatilities obtained using the two procedures

Despite the obvious differences between the curves obtained by imposing the most time-homogeneous evolution of the term structure of caplet volatilities (curves labelled 'Caplet Fit' in Figures 8.2–8.4) and the curves that came out of the best fit to the prices from the swaption matrices, the overall similarity and congruence of the general shape (down to such details as the location

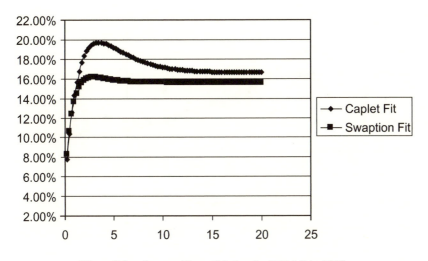

Figure 8.3   *Same as Figure 8.2, but for GBP 1-Sept-2000.*

of the maximum of the hump) is remarkable.[8] Similarly remarkable, and encouraging, is the fact that the location of the maximum and the overall shape
of the curves are consistent both with the financial 'story' presented in Section
6.3, to justify the existence of a humped volatility function in the first place,
and with the statistical data by Dodds (1998). It therefore appears that econometric evidence, financial intuition, the requirement that the term structure
of caplet volatilities should be as time-homogeneous as possible, and the best
fit to the market swaption matrices, all point to the same coherent picture of
a non-constant (and, in particular, humped) instantaneous volatility for the
forward rates.

Despite the similarities, it is also apparent that the instantaneous volatilities
obtained from the swaption data are significantly lower than the corresponding quantity estimated from caplet prices and by imposing time-homogeneity.
This observation is, in my opinion, not coincidental, and is linked to the imbalance of supply and demand between swaption and caplet volatility. Since
derivatives in general can theoretically be regarded as 'redundant' securities,
it is not a priori obvious how supply and demand can affect their prices. I
discuss this topic in detail in Section 9.1.3, where I provide an argument to explain why the instantaneous volatility curve derived from swaption data might
lie systematically below the caplet-derived curve.

---

[8]I only discuss and display here the results for a single day per yield curve. A systematic time-
series analysis shows the main qualitative features to be persistent and robust to the details of the
calculation.

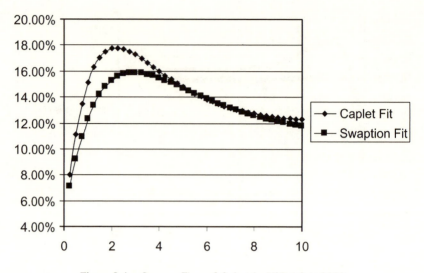

Figure 8.4   *Same as Figure 8.2, but for USD 1-Sept-2000.*

8.4 A Third Approach to Fitting the Caplet Market: Assigning a Future Term Structure of Volatilities

So far we have always assumed that the trader is driven by two possible distinct sets of joint objectives: either

- fitting today's observed caplet market and producing a future term structure of volatilities as similar as possible to the one observed today (or to some average of recently observed term structure of volatilities); or

- fitting today's caplet market while simultaneously accounting as satisfactorily as possible for the observed European swaption market.

The first strategy is well suited to the needs of the exotic trader, who simply accepts the prices of the plain-vanilla hedging instruments. The second is more suitable to the cap/swaption relative-value trader, who is required to express a trading view about the relative cheapness or dearness of different portions of the term structure of volatilities and of the swaption matrix.

The approach to caplet fitting presented in the present section attacks the problem from yet another point of view, that is, it addresses the question of how to recover today's caplet prices and, at the same time, to obtain as best as possible a user-defined deterministic future term structure of volatilities different from today's.

8.4.1 When is assigning a future term structure of volatilities possible (and useful)?

At the time of writing (and, I suspect, for quite some time to come), the possibility of the British pound joining the euro could constitute an obvious possible application for this type of exercise. More generally, I have in mind three possible applications for the procedure I am about to describe. In the first, the chosen future deterministic term structure of volatilities simply reflects a trader's view at odds with the market. This would have an obvious impact on the price of an exotic product, but an even greater relevance for its hedge parameters. This is because, in the case of market incompleteness, the approximate success of the trader's hedging program will hinge on the assigned future term structure of volatilities resembling the future realized ones. Therefore, the trader will base her hedges on *her* (not necessarily the market's) best guess of the future realization of the term structure of volatilities.

In the second application, the trader does not have firm views about the future volatility, but believes that there might be a strong variability in volatility outcomes around the market consensus.[9] The trader will therefore re-price the complex product under a variety of future volatility scenarios, in order to estimate the sensitivity of the model price to these difficult-to-hedge factors. Each of the exogenously assigned sets of future implied volatilities would constitute one of the possible future scenarios for the term structure of volatilities consistent with today's plain-vanilla market prices which are explored in making a price in an exotic product. This aspect of the price-making process is important, and deserves a few words of comment. The exotic trader who observes a set of market prices for caplets does not know for certain which set of instantaneous volatility functions the market has chosen in arriving at the prices of the caplets, but knows that these different possible choices will produce different prices for a given exotic product. In other words, the trader will know the root-mean-square of the forward-rate instantaneous volatility, but not the shape of this function. They will therefore re-price the exotic product under a variety of possible (market-consistent) volatility scenarios, estimate the sensitivity of the price of the exotic instrument, and make her price accordingly. If seen in this light, the technique proposed below to create an exogenous assigned future term structure of volatilities compatible with the current caplet market prices could constitute a first, approximate, step towards a stochastic-implied-volatility extension of the LIBOR market model (see Chapters 11 and 12, and Section 12.1.2 in particular).

In the third application, the technique I propose below can be used by a risk manager and it can be used in the context of model stress testing: the range of prices for an exotic product (or for a book thereof) compatible with

---

[9]In other words, this trader subscribes to a stochastic-volatility view of the forward-rate dynamics, and uses a deterministic-volatility model *faute de mieux*. The approach presented in Part IV would give an answer both more satisfactory and more coherent (but also considerably more complex to obtain).

Table 8.1   *The present and future term structures of volatilities, as reflected by the matrix* **S**. *See the text for a precise description.*

$S(1,1)$				
$S(1,2)$	$S(2,2)$			
$S(1,3)$	$S(2,3)$	**S(3,3)**		
$S(1,4)$	$S(2,4)$	**S(3,4)**	**S(4,4)**	
$S(1,5)$	$S(2,5)$	**S(3,5)**	**S(4,5)**	**S(5,5)**

today's term structure of volatilities and with a plausible set of future term structures of volatilities can be used to estimate the associated model reserve (see Rebonato 2001a).

The extent to which a future term structure of volatilities can be freely assigned by a trader without incurring the risk of model-independent arbitrage is a subtle question (see, for instance, Rebonato 2001a, Rebonato and Joshi 2001b and Jaeckel and Rebonato 2001b, who address the topic by introducing the concept of Kolmogorov compatibility). If the trader were to assign an arbitrary future term structure of volatilities, she could not rest assured that the derived prices would not expose her to the possibility of model-independent arbitrage. The procedure proposed in this section might not exactly recover the user's desired future term structure of volatilities, but is constructed to produce a (very) close approximation to it, and, at the same time, to guarantee that the solution so obtained will be free of arbitrage.

8.4.2 Setting of the problem

For the purpose of the present discussion I will make use again of the matrices **S** and $\mathbf{S}^{\text{th}}$ defined above (see Section 8.2), and modify the notation used so far for the implied Black caplet volatilities by introducing an argument indicating the point in time to which the corresponding market prices apply. Therefore, today's market-given implied volatilities, which have so far been denoted as $\sigma_{\text{Black}}(T_i)$, $1 \leq i \leq n$, will now be written as $\sigma_{\text{Black}}(0, T_i)$. The term structure of volatilities prevailing at time T_k will be fully described by the collection of $(n - k)$ terms $\sigma_{\text{Black}}(T_k, T_i)$ (often more simply denoted as just $\sigma_{\text{Black}}(k, T_i)$ or $\sigma_{\text{Black}}(k, i)$).

In order to present the suggested procedure in the simplest possible way, let us consider again the case of, say, a five-period term structure of volatilities. I shall then assume that the trader has views about the future (three-period) term structure of volatilities in two periods' time. The corresponding **S** matrix therefore looks as shown in Table 8.1, where the elements in bold reflect the trader's views about the future term structure of volatilities.

In Table 8.1, using all the entries one can directly obtain the term structure of volatilities today ($\sigma_{\text{Black}}(0, T_i)$, $1 \leq i \leq 5$). The entries in bold then give the term structure prevailing at time 2 ($\sigma_{\text{Black}}(2, T_i)$, $1 \leq i \leq 3$):

$$\sigma_{\text{Black}}(3, 1)^2 T_1 = S(3, 3),$$
$$\sigma_{\text{Black}}(3, 2)^2 T_2 = S(3, 4) + S(4, 4),$$
$$\sigma_{\text{Black}}(3, 3)^2 T_3 = S(3, 5) + S(4, 5) + S(5, 5).$$

(Note that, in agreement with the definitions given in Section 6.2.3, the 'length' of the term structure of volatilities at time 0 is equal to five years, but it is only equal to three years when standing at time 2).[10] The entries above corresponding to the future term structure of volatilities can be arbitrarily chosen by the trader, simply subject to the constraint that they should be compatible with today's observed market prices. In other words, the trader need not worry at this stage about the possibility of model-independent arbitrage. The fitting can then be carried out using two strategies, discussed below.

8.4.3 The fitting strategy: first approach

Given the target (present and future) term structures of volatilities, one could in principle proceed along either of two similar routes. The first procedure follows very closely the conceptual path presented in the previous section. Also in this case one can begin by choosing a parametric form for a time-homogeneous instantaneous volatility function, and calculate the elements of the matrix $\mathbf{S}^{\text{th}}$ as

$$S^{\text{th}}(k, j) = \int_{T_{k-1}}^{T_k} \sigma_{\text{inst}}(T - t; \alpha_1, \alpha_2, \dots, \alpha_m)^2 \, du.$$

After calculating these elements, a minimization similar to the one described in the previous section can then be carried out, but this time with an extended target function. More precisely one can write (note carefully the different ranges of the summations)

$$\chi^2 = \sum_{j=1}^{8} \eta_j^2,$$

$$\eta_i^2 = \left[\sigma_{\text{Black}}^2(0, T_i) T_i - \sum_{k=1}^{i} S^{\text{th}}(k, i) \right]^2 \qquad 1 \leq i \leq 5,$$

$$\eta_i^2 = \left[\sigma_{\text{Black}}^2(2, T_{i-5}) T_{i-5} - \sum_{k=3}^{i-3} S^{\text{th}}(k, i - 3) \right]^2 \qquad 6 \leq i \leq 8,$$

---

[10]The reader can profitably revisit the definition of term structure of volatilities I have given in Section 6.2.3.

and carry out the minimization

$$\min_{\{\alpha_1,\alpha_2,\ldots,\alpha_m\}} \chi^2.$$

By so doing, one attempts again to produce as accurate a simultaneous fit as possible both to today's prices ($1 \le i \le 5$), and to the future desired term structure of volatilities ($6 \le i \le 8$) by means of the time-homogeneous component of the instantaneous volatility function. As before, this first step therefore accomplishes the task of putting as much explanatory burden as possible on an instantaneous volatility function capable of producing a self-similar future term structure of volatility. Proceeding exactly as in Section 8.4, one can then continue by minimizing in turn the χ^2 quantities defined by

$$\chi^2 = \sum_{j=1,8} \eta_j^2,$$

$$\eta_i^2 = \left[\sigma_{\text{Black}}^2(0, T_i)T_i - \sum_{k=1}^{i} S^{\text{th}}(k, i)\epsilon_k^2 \right]^2 \qquad 1 \le i \le 5,$$

$$\eta_i^2 = \left[\sigma_{\text{Black}}^2(3, T_{i-5})T_{i-5} - \sum_{k=3}^{i-3} S^{\text{th}}(k, i-3)\epsilon_k^2 \right]^2 \qquad 6 \le i \le 8,$$

with the minimization over

$$\min_{\{\epsilon_1,\epsilon_2,\ldots,\epsilon_r\}} \chi^2,$$

and by

$$\chi^2 = \sum_{j=1}^{8} \eta_j^2,$$

$$\eta_i^2 = \left[\sigma_{\text{Black}}^2(0, T_i)T_i - \sum_{k=1}^{i} S^{\text{th}}(k, i)\epsilon_k^2 k_i^2 \right]^2 \qquad 1 \le i \le 5,$$

$$\eta_i^2 = \left[\sigma_{\text{Black}}^2(3, T_{i-5})T_{i-5} - \sum_{k=3}^{i-3} S^{\text{th}}(k, i-3)\epsilon_k^2 k_{i-3}^2 \right]^2 \quad 6 \le i \le 8,$$

with the minimization, this time, carried out directly over the five forward-rate-specific parameters k_i, $1 \le i \le 5$.

8.4.4 The fitting strategy: second approach

The strategy described above is perfectly possible, and its effectiveness will be explored in Case Study 3a (Section 8.5.4). Remember, however, that our ultimate goal, in this exercise, is to produce a (user-specified) future term structure of volatilities different from the current one, and time-homogeneity is therefore no longer a necessary, or perhaps even a desirable, requirement. The rationale for putting as much explanatory burden as possible on the time-homogeneous component becomes after all somewhat dubious when, as is now the case, the trader wants to impose a time-dependent change to the term structure of volatilities. It is therefore reasonable to expect that it might be better, for the specific problem tackled in this section, to follow a different route by conflating the two first steps of the procedure just described, and carrying out a simultaneous optimization over the coefficients of the time-homogeneous and the time-dependent parts. By so doing one would find the best common pattern of forward-rate responsiveness to innovations as a function of residual maturity (as embodied by the time-homogeneous component, which, after time translation, is the same for all forward rates) compatible with a modulation of the volatilities by a time-dependent term (which also affects all the forward rates exactly to the same extent). The forward-rate-specific components can then be calculated so as to pick up whatever price discrepancies have been left over, exactly as described above.

8.5 Results

Up to this point I have presented simple and plausible procedures in order to achieve the fitting to (market- and/or trader-assigned) term structures of volatilities. What remains to be explored is how well these techniques actually fare with real market data. These empirical issues are dealt with in the following Case Studies: Case Studies 1 and 2, presented in the next subsections, deal with the simpler case of fitting a current market term structure of volatilities. The relative merits of the two procedures suggested above to fit simultaneously a current market and a future exogenously assigned term structure of volatilities are then explored in Case Studies 3a and 3b (Sections 8.5.4 and 8.5.5).

8.5.1 Case Study 1: fitting a term structure of volatilities by imposing time-homogeneity – 'synthetic' data

In the first Case Study, I deal with the problem of fitting an exogenous, market-given term structure of volatilities following the procedure recommended in Sections 8.3 and 8.4. The first 'market' term structure of volatilities analyzed in this Case Study was created by combining several actual market term structures of volatilities, chosen and 'spliced together' in order to display simultaneously as many as possible of the most typical observed features, such as

- an initial very steep portion;

- a plateau area, followed by a rapid decline in implied volatilities;

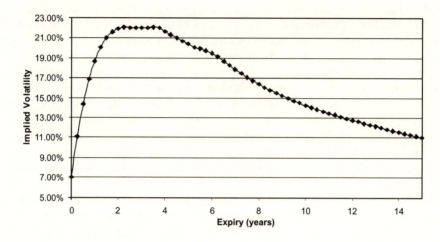

Figure 8.5 *A 'synthetic' term structure of volatilities created from actual market data for fitting purposes.*

- portions where the derivative of the implied volatility with respect to expiry changes very rapidly (approximately around the four- and six-year-maturity areas in Figure 8.5);

- areas where the quantity $\sigma^2_{\text{Black}}(T)T$ is not increasing (approximately around the six-year-maturity area).

The resulting 'synthetic' target term structure of volatilities is shown in Figure 8.5.

Given the synthetic 'market' term structure of volatilities shown in Figure 8.5, the first part of the fitting procedure was undertaken by minimizing the χ^2 quantity given by

$$\chi^2 = \sum_{j=1}^{n} \eta_j^2,$$

$$\eta_j^2 = \left[\sigma^2_{\text{Black}}(T_j)T_j - \sum_{k=1}^{j} S^{\text{th}}(k,j)\right]^2$$

over the parameters $\{\alpha\}$ of the time-homogeneous component of the instantaneous volatility function

$$\min_{\{\alpha_1,\alpha_2,\ldots,\alpha_m\}} \chi^2.$$

The quantities $S^{\text{th}}(k,j)$ indicate the time-homogeneous integrals defined by Equation (8.1). The parameters $\{\alpha\}$ in the minimization were chosen to be

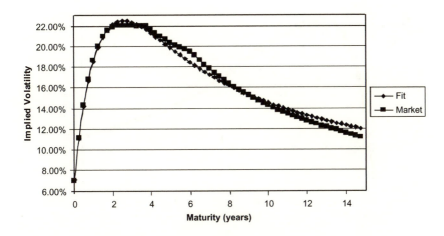

Figure 8.6 *The market and model term structures of volatilities (curves 'Market' and 'Fit', respectively); the latter was obtained using the time-homogeneous fit.*

the parameters $\{a, b, c, d\}$ in

$$\sigma_{\text{inst}}(T - t) = [a + b(T - t)] \exp[-c(T - t)] + d.$$

The results of this first stage in the optimization are shown in Figure 8.6. As it will be recalled from Chapter 6, the necessary condition for a time-homogeneous instantaneous volatility function to be able to account for the observed caplet market prices is that the associated quantity $\sigma_{\text{Black}}^2(T)T$ should be non-decreasing. It is therefore not surprising that this first stage of the fitting procedure should fail to produce a very good fit in the portion of the term structure of volatilities around the six-year area, that is, exactly where the quantity $\sigma_{\text{Black}}^2(T)T$ is non-increasing.

In order to improve the quality of the fit in a financially desirable way, the next step was then the introduction of a purely time-dependent part:

$$S^{\text{th}}(k, j) \rightarrow \epsilon_k^2 S^{\text{th}}(k, j).$$

As discussed in Section 6.6, the functional form expressing the dependence of the quantity ϵ on time was chosen as a linear combination of a few sine waves of increasing frequency, multiplied by a 'dampening' decaying exponential factor:

$$\epsilon(t) = \left[\sum_{i=1}^{3} \epsilon_i \sin\left(\frac{t\pi i}{\text{Mat}} + \epsilon_{i+1} \right) \right] \exp(-\epsilon_7 t).$$

(Recall that the quantity 'Mat' is equal to the longest caplet maturity.) The resulting fit obtained using a time-dependent component is shown in Figure 8.7, and, as one can readily see, the match between model and market prices is

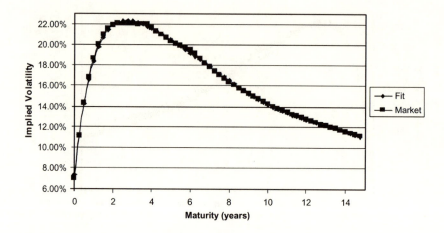

Figure 8.7   *The fit to the market term structure of volatilities obtained after introducing a time-dependent component into the instantaneous volatility function. Notice the improvement over the fit obtained using just a time-homogeneous component (Figure 8.6).*

now almost perfect. Notice that no forward-rate-specific component has been used yet in the specification of the instantaneous volatility function.

In order to obtain an exact fitting to the 'market' caplet prices, idiosyncratic (forward-rate-specific) factors k_j are then introduced, as discussed in Section 8.2 (Equation (8.5)). The factors required to bring about a perfect

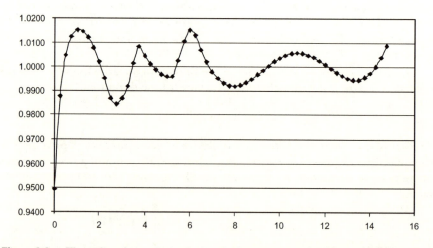

Figure 8.8   *The scaling factor obtained after the first two steps of the fitting procedure for the 'market synthetic' case. Despite the apparently 'wild' fluctuations, notice the scale: all the scaling factors but one are greater than 0.98 and smaller than 1.02.*

price match are shown in Figure 8.8. Notice that, by proceeding in this manner, the normalization factors k_j have turned out to be very close to unity, thereby ensuring that perfect pricing of the caplets has been obtained while putting as little burden as possible on the shoulders of the financially unappealing forward-rate-specific component. As a result, the overall evolution of the term structure of volatilities has been constructed to be made up, as much as possible, of a time-homogeneous component plus a time-dependent component that affects all the forward rates to the same extent.

8.5.2 Case Study 2: fitting a term structure of volatilities by imposing time-homogeneity – market data

Since the excellent fitting shown in Figures 8.5–8.8 was, after all, obtained with a 'made-up' term structure of volatilities, as a second example I present below the results obtained for two 'true' (as opposed to 'synthetic') market curves, GBP and USD 20-Sept-2000 (Figures 8.9–8.12). The fits in these cases were carried out without making use of the time-dependent component, to show (see Figures 8.10 and 8.12) that, even with this simpler fitting scheme, the forward-rate-specific component needed to price the caplets exactly can remain reasonably small.[11] I also directly show, in Figures 8.9 and 8.11, how time-homogeneous the resulting evolution of the term structures of volatilities actually remains after the market-matching forward-rate-specific terms have been introduced.

In concluding this Case Study, it is interesting to point out the link between the maturities of the forward-rate volatilities that require a non-negligible rescaling in order to price the caplet correctly (between 0.25 and 1.5 years in Figure 8.12), and the time after which the term structure of volatilities becomes almost exactly time-homogeneous (after one year) – see Figure 8.11.

8.5.3 Case Study 3: simultaneous fitting to a current and to a future exogenously assigned term structure of volatilities

The problem is tackled in this third Case Study of fitting not only today's market caplet prices, but also a future user-assigned term structure of volatilities. The task can be undertaken in two different ways. If one follows the first procedure, the first two steps are carried out in exactly the same fashion as in Case Studies 1 and 2. Note that, however, for the problem at hand, even after the last stage (i.e., even after the introduction of a set of forward-rate-specific terms), a perfect simultaneous fit cannot be guaranteed both to the presented and to the future desired term structure of volatilities. Instead of solving for the factors $(1 + \delta_j)$ that *exactly* price today's caplet market, a fit over the n parameters $\{\delta\}$ that can produce the best overall fit must therefore be carried

---

[11]The help provided by Dr. Peter Jaeckel with some calculations and with the production of the accompanying graphs is gratefully acknowledged.

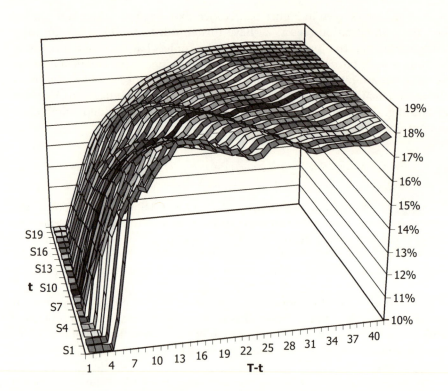

Figure 8.9 *The evolution of the future term structure of volatilities from time-homogeneous instantaneous volatility for the case of GBP 20-Sept-2000.*

out. Needless to say, if one so wanted, greater weights could be given to the current prices than to the future prices. The necessary modification of the equations reported in Section 8.5 are obvious, and are not displayed in detail in this Case Study.

A second line of attack is however possible. As mentioned in Section 8.4, the rationale behind splitting the time-homogeneous fitting from the remaining part of the procedure has been justified on the basis of an attempt to describe as much as possible of the evolution of a given term structure of volatilities in terms of a time-homogeneous component. The justification for this line of attack is no longer as compelling if one is actually trying to capture an explicit time-dependent evolution of the term structure of volatilities. It might therefore make more sense to optimize simultaneously the time-homogeneous and the time-dependent parameters. Since, as usual, the proof of the pudding is in the eating, the results from both these two possible fitting procedures are presented, and examined separately, in Case Studies 3a and 3b. In both cases the current observed and future assigned term structure of volatilities are shown in Figure 8.13 (labelled 'Present' and 'Desired',

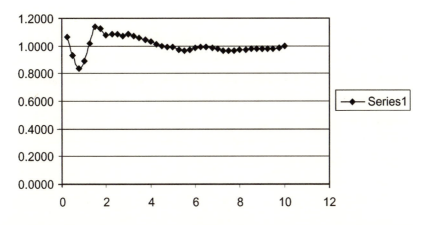

Figure 8.10 *The scaling factor necessary to bring about the perfect pricing of the caplets for the same GBP market data (no purely time-dependent component of the instantaneous volatility was used).*

respectively). The 'future' time was assumed to be three years from today. As one can see from Figure 8.13, in this example the trader first of all believed that future volatilities would be lower. But she also believed that this fall in volatilities would not be uniform across maturities (more than two vegas in the two-year area, and less than one vega at the long end). Clearly, the quality of the fit will in general depend on the degree of 'deformation' the trader wants to impose on today's term structure of volatilities: it is always possible to choose such a 'twisted' future term structure of volatilities that the procedure

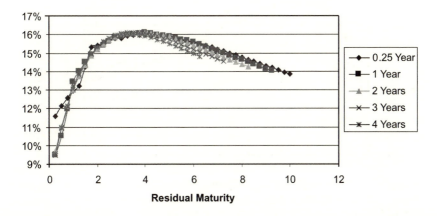

Figure 8.11 *The evolution of the future term structure of volatilities from time-homogeneous instantaneous volatility for the case of USD 20-Sept-2000.*

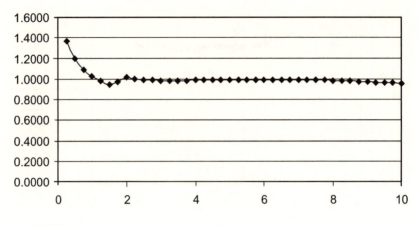

Figure 8.12   *The corresponding scaling factor for the USD market data.*

will fail to produce an accurate fit. The more relevant question, however, is to what extent the trader can prescribe a sufficiently rich, yet financially reasonable, pattern of deformation, and still obtain acceptably accurate results. The 'trader's views' presented above should therefore be seen in this context, and are meant to represent significantly different, but still financially realistic, future volatility scenarios. With this proviso in mind, the two possible fitting procedures mentioned above are examined separately in Case Studies 3a and 3b.

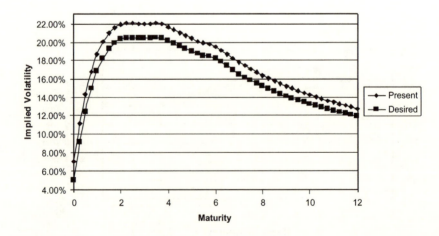

Figure 8.13   *The current ('Present') market given and the future desired ('Desired') term structure of volatilities. The future point in time about which the trader is assumed to express a view is in three years' time from today.*

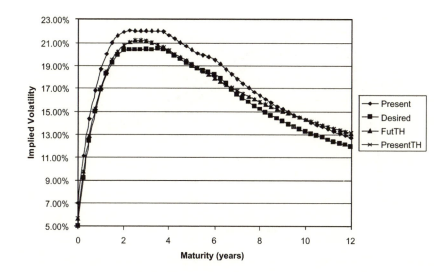

Figure 8.14   *The fits to the current and future assigned term structure of volatilities obtained with a time-homogeneous fit. The two model curves that attempt to fit today's and the future term structure of volatilities are obviously superimposed (curves labelled 'FutTH' and 'PresentTH'), since a time-homogeneous form for the instantaneous volatility function must produce a self-similar term structure of volatilities.*

8.5.4 Case Study 3a: three-step fitting

Case Study 3a presents the results obtained by fitting separately to the parameters of the time-homogeneous function, of the time-dependent component and to the forward-rate-specific terms. The quality of the fit resulting from the first step (i.e., the fit to parameters $\{\alpha\}$ of the time-homogeneous function) is shown in Figure 8.14. Note that, given the time-homogeneous assumption enforced in this first step, the resulting model term structure of volatilities will be the same today and after three years, and the same optimized curve must therefore attempt to fit both the present and the future term structure of volatilities. It is therefore not surprising that the fitting procedure should produce a curve that is approximately equal to the average between the two input curves.

The next step is then to introduce a time-dependent component to the instantaneous volatility function. The same functional form used for the first Case Study (Section 8.5) was employed, and the results are shown in Figure 8.15. Note that, since a time-dependent component is now present in the instantaneous volatility function, the model present (curve labelled 'PresentTD') and the model future term structure of volatilities (curve labelled 'FutTD') are no longer superimposed.

As Figure 8.15 shows, the fit obtained by optimizing separately over the

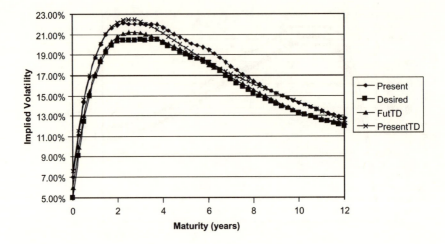

Figure 8.15 *The fits to the current and future assigned term structure of volatilities obtained from an instantaneous volatility function made up of a time-homogeneous and a time-dependent part with a three-stage procedure. The two model curves that attempt to fit today's and the future term structure of volatilities are no longer superimposed (curves labelled 'FutTD' and 'PresentTD'), since a time-dependent component has been added to the instantaneous volatility function.*

time-homogeneous and time-dependent coefficients is far from perfect, and there remain several poorly fitted portions of the current term structure of volatilities, especially around the six-year area. This poor fitting will have to be taken up by a substantial idiosyncratic component, which, as we have discussed at length in Chapter 6, is a priori financially unappealing. The procedure has therefore produced not very satisfactory results. For this reason, the quality of the fit that could be obtained for the same present and future term structures of volatilities by optimizing simultaneously over both sets of parameters is examined in Case Study 3b.

8.5.5 Case Study 3b: two-step fitting

The fitting in Case Study 3b is now carried out over the sets of parameters $\{\alpha\}$ and $\{\epsilon\}$ simultaneously. The results obtained by carrying out this first joint step is shown in Figure 8.16.

Comparing Figure 8.16 with Figure 8.15, the much better quality of the fit obtainable employing the simultaneous optimization is clearly visible. The residual discrepancies to be accounted for by means of the second and last step (i.e., the optimization over the n factors k_j) should therefore be very small. It is important to stress that this feature is appealing not only, and not so much, from the computational point of view, but even more so from a financial perspective. Figure 8.17, for instance, shows the time-dependent function

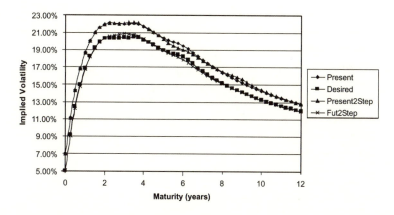

Figure 8.16 *The results of the simultaneous fitting to the target term structure of volatilities over the time-homogeneous coefficients* $\{a, b, c, d\}$ *and over the time-dependent coefficients* ϵ_i. *The curves labelled 'Present2Step' and 'Fut2Step' indicate the fits to the current and future term structure of volatilities obtained via the joint optimization to the time-homogeneous and the time-dependent coefficients.*

that has produced the best fit. Reassuringly, and, a posteriori, not surprisingly given the assumption about the future user-assigned term structure of volatilities, the overall shape turned out to be smooth and monotonically decreasing.

The last step is now to carry out a fit over the quantities k_j, which should turn out to be reasonably close to unity. This indeed turned out to be the case, as shown in Figure 8.18.

On the basis of the results shown in the last two Case Studies, one can

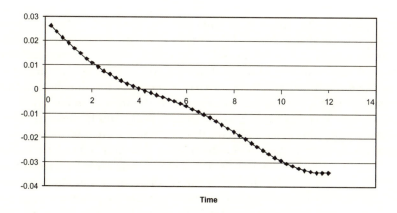

Figure 8.17 *The time-dependent function* $\epsilon(t_k) = \{\sum_{i=1}^{3} \epsilon_i \sin[(t_k \pi i / \mathrm{Mat}) + \epsilon_{i+1}]\} \exp(-\epsilon_7 t_k)$ *that produced the fit displayed in Figure 8.16.*

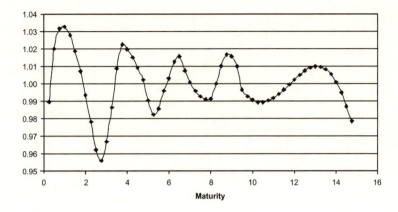

Figure 8.18   *The forward-rate-specific factor k_j obtained from the two-step fitting procedure.*

therefore conclude that the second procedure proposed in Section 8.4.4 can provide a computationally effective and financially appealing strategy to carry out the fitting of the instantaneous volatility function both to a present observed and to a future exogenously assigned term structure of volatilities.

8.5.6 Case Study 4: simultaneous fitting to a current caplet term structure of volatilities and to a swaption matrix

The last Case Study I examine in this chapter deals with the simultaneous fitting to a market term structure of caplet volatilities and to a market swaption matrix. Such an application would be of great importance whenever the trader is faced with the task of pricing a complex product that depends on both forward-rate and swap-rate volatilities (and that will be hedged using both caplets and European swaptions) (see Section 10.2). This Case Study is also of relevance to the choice of the best overall parametrization to be used in the consistent risk management and hedging of a complex interest-rate derivatives book that contains a variety of instruments. I shall assume in this Case Study the same functional forms discussed above for the time-homogeneous component of the instantaneous volatility of the forward rates, and for the time-dependent component. It is essential to point out, however, that in this case the results will depend also on the functional form and on the specific parameters for the instantaneous correlation function, $\rho(t)$. I have argued (see Section 7.1.2) that, as long as the same average correlation is retained, different, but reasonable, choices of the shape of the instantaneous correlation have a relatively small effect on the European swaption prices (see also the discussion in De Jong et al. 1999). I have therefore chosen the simplest of the functional forms discussed in Chapter 7:

$$\rho_{ij}(t) = \exp[-\beta|(T_i - t) - (T_j - t)|],$$

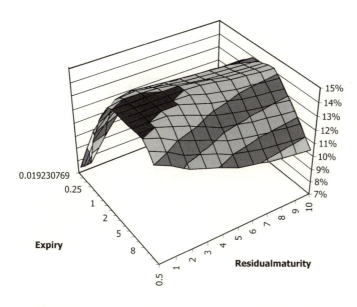

Figure 8.19 *The market swaption matrix (USD 18-Oct-2000).*

with $\beta = 0.1$. The merits (and the drawbacks) of this simple choice have been discussed at length in that chapter, but the gist of the results presented in this Case Study would still hold if a different functional form had been chosen.

Given this choice of instantaneous correlation,[12] and the market swaption volatility matrix shown in Figure 8.19 (USD 18-Oct-2000), the first step in the procedure was to obtain the 'optimal' parameters $\{a, b, c, d\}$ of the time-homogeneous part of the forward-rate instantaneous volatility function. This was achieved by initially carrying out the χ^2 optimization over the coefficients $\{\alpha\}$ as shown in Equation (8.10). Figures 8.19 and 8.20 show the qualitative similarities between the market and model swaption matrices, even when the latter was obtained using a purely time-homogeneous forward-rate instantaneous volatility function.

It is also important to point out again that the same feature noticed in Section 8.3 was observed again, that is, without imposing any constraint on the shape of the instantaneous volatility function, the optimized shape turned out to be qualitatively very similar to the shape resulting from imposing the time-homogeneous requirement on the term structure of caplet volatilities (see Figure 8.21). This important feature therefore points to the ability of the general fitting 'philosophy' proposed in this chapter to provide a coherent, although, naturally, somewhat different, description of the yield curve dynamics in its entirety (caplets and swaptions).

---

[12]The help provided by Dr. Peter Jaeckel with the coding and with the computations used in producing the results in Case Study 3 is gratefully acknowledged.

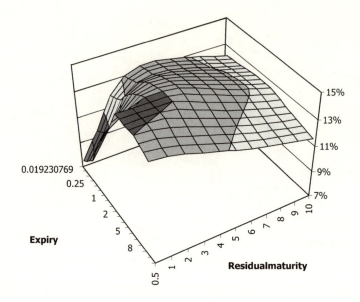

Figure 8.20   *The best-fit model swaption matrix to the market data presented in Figure 8.19 obtained by allowing only a purely time-homogeneous component for the instantaneous volatility of the forward rates.*

The next step in the procedure was then the introduction of a time-dependent component in the instantaneous volatility function. On this occasion, rather than choosing from the start a specific functional form, each time segment was allowed to assume the component ϵ_t that produced the best overall fit. The

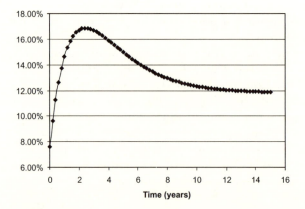

Figure 8.21   *The time-homogeneous instantaneous volatility that best fits the swaption market in Figure 8.19.*

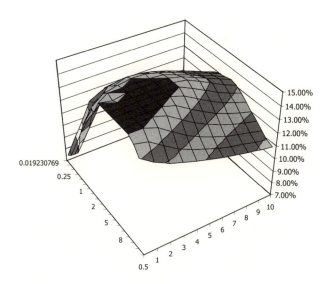

Figure 8.22 *The best fit obtained by allowing a time-dependent component in the forward-rate instantaneous volatility function. This surface should be compared with the surfaces in Figures 8.19 and 8.20.*

resulting model swaption matrix is shown in Figure 8.22. Needless to say, this procedure can, in general, be dangerous because it can easily amplify unavoidable market noise. If, however, it ends up producing a reasonably well-behaved shape, it might provide further comfort that the overall procedure is indeed well grounded. Since three-dimensional graphs can be pictorially dazzling,

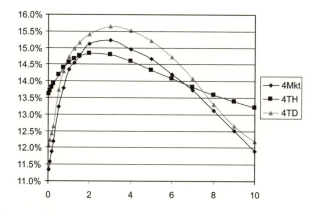

Figure 8.23 *Cross-sections of previous figures across the four-year residual maturities. The curves labelled '4Mkt', '4TH' and '4TD' indicate the market (Figure 8.19), time-homogeneous (Figure 8.20) and time-dependent (Figure 8.22) fits, respectively.*

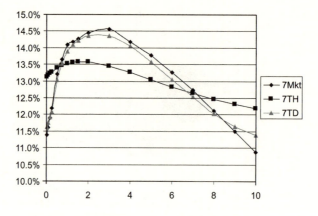

Figure 8.24   *Cross-sections of previous figures across the seven-year residual maturities. The curves labelled '7Mkt', '7TH' and '7TD' indicate the market (Figure 8.19), time-homogeneous (Figure 8.20) and time-dependent (Figure 8.22) fits, respectively.*

but make the reading of actual values rather difficult, Figures 8.23–8.25 show cross-sections of the market, time-homogeneous and time-dependent swaption matrices for different residual maturities of the swap entered into.

It is clear that the improvement brought about by the time-dependent component is substantial (see, in particular, Figures 8.23 and 8.24, and, to a lesser but still significant extent, Figure 8.25). Furthermore, one can notice a clearly recognizable structure in the piecewise-constant quantities ϵ_t, which appear to follow a systematic pattern: as Figure 8.26 illustrates, the time de-

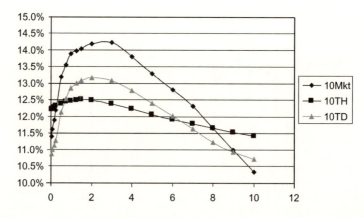

Figure 8.25   *Cross-sections of previous figures across the 10-year residual maturities. The curves labelled '10Mkt', '10TH' and '10TD' indicate the market (Figure 8.19), time-homogeneous (Figure 8.20) and time-dependent (Figure 8.22) fits, respectively.*

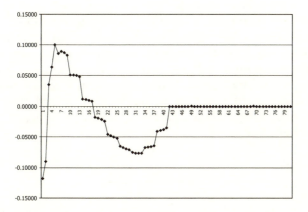

Figure 8.26 *The time-dependent function required to bring about the best fit between the model and market swaption matrices.*

pendence shows a clear maximum after approximately six months, followed by another clear minimum after approximately two-and-a-half years.

Finally (see Figure 8.27) the scaling factors needed to bring about, if desired, perfect pricing of the caplets turn out to be very close to unity, thereby ensuring that the a priori undesirable idiosyncratic (forward-rate-specific component) is relatively small. Therefore, for the market case analyzed in Case Study 3, a simple, plausible and well-behaved time-dependent component has been shown to allow for a substantially richer and more rapidly varying structure of the swaption matrix than a purely time-homogeneous instantaneous volatility function could.

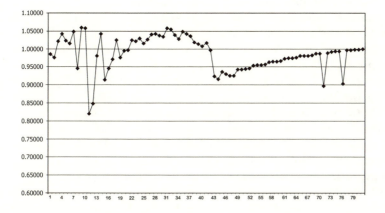

Figure 8.27 *The scaling factors needed to bring about exact fitting to the caplets for the same example, after the time-dependent component has been introduced.*

Clearly, the crucial question for the trader is whether the swaption market is indeed 'trying' to convey information about future levels of volatility, or whether the procedure is simply picking up market noise (or, possibly, mis-priced options or liquidity effects). In the absence of liquid serial options, the market in instantaneous volatilities is intrinsically incomplete, and therefore the ability to 'lock-in' via a dynamic trading strategy inconsistencies between different portions of the swaption matrix is rather limited, and all relative-value model 'arbitrages' include substantial basis risk (see also the discussion in Sections 1.2 and 9.1.3).

8.6 Conclusions

The Case Studies presented in this chapter have shown how information about the shape of the instantaneous volatility functions can be obtained from a variety of sources: from swaption prices, when taken together with caplet prices; from the requirement that the term structure of volatilities should be-have in an (approximately) time-homogeneous manner; from a financial un-derstanding of the responsiveness of different portions of the yield curve to the arrival of economic news; etc. I have stressed that time-homogeneity of a directly observable quantity, such as the term structure of volatilities, can be a useful guiding principle for modelling the evolution of forward rates. I have pointed out that sometimes the market can provide some information about the time behavior of the volatilities through the prices of caplets and swaptions. I have stressed, however, that such information should always be analyzed very carefully and critically, and should only be accepted if a coher-ent and plausible financial explanation can be provided.

By the end of this chapter the reader should have at her disposal the tools for distilling from the available market data as much direct or indirect infor-mation as possible about the parameters of the instantaneous volatility func-tions. These functions and their parametrization are then taken as a given for the analysis presented in the next chapter, which shows how caplets can be exactly priced with the 'favorite' chosen instantaneous volatility function, while recovering, at the same time, an exogenous target correlation matrix as well as possible.

Information about this correlation matrix could in principle also be ex-tracted from the traded prices of caplets and swaptions. For reasons men-tioned in Chapter 7, however (namely, the relatively low dependence of swap-tion prices on 'reasonable' correlation structures), I prefer to assume that the relevant correlation information has been arrived at via econometric estima-tion. This splitting of market-related and 'historical' (statistical) information is readily dealt with from the analytic point of view by the description of the forward-rate dynamics introduced in Section 3.2.

Simultaneous Calibration to Market Caplet Prices and to an Exogenous Correlation Matrix

9.1 Introduction and Motivation

9.1.1 Working with fewer factors than forward rates

One of the most important messages conveyed in Part I has been that the marginal covariance matrices, **C**, of elements

$$C(i, j, k + 1) = \int_{T_k}^{T_{k+1}} \sigma_i(u)\sigma_j(u)\rho_{ij}(u) \, du$$

(and sometimes just the total covariance matrix, **TOTC**), are all that matters for option pricing using the standard LIBOR market model. These quantities are in turn fully determined once the time-dependent (but deterministic) instantaneous volatilities and correlations are specified. A great deal of attention has therefore been devoted to the specification of desirable general functional forms for these two sets of functions (see Chapters 6 and 7). Given the parametric approach that I have chosen to embrace, I have also pointed out that, once the functional type of dependence on the relevant variables (calendar time and forward-rate expiry) has been selected, there remains a set of coefficients at the user's disposal in order to fit a specified subset of market observables.

Let us assume that the desired parametrization of the volatility and correlation functions has been carried out. These two sets of quantities fully specify the (marginal) covariance matrices. Therefore, if the trader can afford to retain as many factors as forward rates, the problem is exactly solved by orthogonalizing either the matrix **TOTC** or a series of matrices **C**, as appropriate, and evolving the forward rates using the resulting eigenvectors and eigenvalues (see Chapter 4, and, in particular, Equation (3.11) in Chapter 3). In many applications, however, the sheer size of the problem makes this brute-force approach impracticable, and the trader will have to work with fewer factors than forward rates. When this is the case, the desired (target) covariance matrix cannot be exactly recovered, and the trader will have to sacrifice 'something' in the calibration procedure.

When fewer factors than the number of forward rates are retained, any possible choice for the apportioning of the variance of the forward rates (i.e., any possible choice for the real numbers σ_{ik} or b_{ik} in Equations (3.10) or (3.13) in Chapter 3), and for the time dependence of the instantaneous volatilities will give rise to different terminal correlations, covariance elements and, ultimately, exotic option prices (see, e.g., Sidenius 1998, 2000). The user is therefore left with the task of optimizing a very-high-dimensional problem to a target (time-dependent) marginal covariance matrix. This task appears very daunting and one finds in the literature statements like (Sidenius 1998):

> With such a large number of variables a straightforward optimization is impractical at best. The problem is that finding the global best fit [...] is very difficult in high dimensions. [...] The question of calibrating the correlation matrix is very interesting, but it seems impractical to undertake this calibration in parallel with the volatility calibration.

I propose in this chapter a simple and computationally efficient methodology that, contrary to the statement above, does recover exactly the instantaneous volatilities of all the forward rates in the problem, and, at the same time, fits in the 'best' possible way, given the dimensionality of the approach, the correlation matrix. More precisely, I intend to show that one can

1. recover exactly the prices of caplets,

2. retain the chosen forward-rate instantaneous volatility function and, at the same time,

3. approximate optimally an arbitrary exogenous forward-rate correlation matrix.

The next chapter will show how the complementary task can be accomplished, that is, how one can obtain the (almost) exact recovery of co-terminal European swaption prices while simultaneously reproducing, as best as one can, an exogenous forward-rate covariance matrix. When dealing with either of these calibration tasks, I shall advocate that a judicious fitting to global quantities (such as the whole correlation or covariance matrix) can produce more robust and financially appealing results than an attempt to over-fit more specific variables (such as, for instance, caplet prices in isolation).

9.1.2 Different types of best-fit calibration

It is important to distinguish conceptually between the need to calibrate a model because the dimensionality of the approach does not allow the recovery of an exogenous correlation matrix (the case dealt with in this chapter) and the calibration that must be carried out because one is dealing with two complementary sets of variables (the case analyzed in Chapter 10). The first case applies when the user wants to recover correctly the prices of the plain-vanilla options which have as underlying one set of state variables and, at the same time, to recover an exogenous correlation matrix between the same state variables as accurately as possible (i.e., the two possible cases are: caplets and the forward-rate correlation matrix, or European swaptions and the swap-rate correlation matrix). This source of imperfect recovery of the correlation matrix can be made smaller and smaller simply by using more and more factors.

The other, and, arguably, more fundamental, reason for using a calibration procedure arises when one tries to recover the correct prices of the plain-vanilla options of one set of state variables together with an exogenous correlation matrix among the complementary set of state variables. This can occur if the user attempts to recover[1]

1. caplet prices and an exogenous swap-rate correlation matrix,

2. caplet prices and an exogenous swap-rate/forward-rate correlation matrix,

3. European swaptions prices and an exogenous forward-rate correlation matrix,

4. European swaptions prices and an exogenous forward-rate/swap-rate correlation matrix.

In these four cases the fit to an exogenous correlation matrix will in general be impossible even if as many factors are used as state variables (forward or swap rates). The inability to recover these matrices exactly is therefore of fundamental nature, stemming as it does from the possible lack of coherence between the caplet and swaption markets, and could prompt questions about the possible existence of trading opportunities, as discussed in the next subsection.

9.1.3 Congruence between the caplet and swaption markets

The reader might find it surprising that a noticeable and systematic lack of price 'congruence' should arise and persist between the caplets and the European swaptions. After all, the same state variables, that is, forward rates, can

---

[1]Some of the combinations listed might seem rather 'unnatural' or artificial. This is not necessarily the case, since, as discussed in detail in Case Study 1 of Chapter 10, the value of important instruments such as trigger swaps can display, for certain combinations of the trigger and strike levels, a marked dependence on the forward-rate/swap-rate correlation.

describe both sets of market quantities, and either caplets or swaptions could theoretically be regarded as 'redundant' securities. A partial explanation for the possible existence and persistence of this price discrepancy clearly stems from the fact that swaptions can be deemed to be cheap or dear with respect to the underlying forward rates only in a model-dependent sense – the 'trading opportunity' might disappear, or perhaps even change sign, if the trader used, say, a different correlation between forward rates, or a different shape for the forward-rate instantaneous volatility functions.[2] This is simply a reflection of the lack of completeness in the market in instantaneous volatilities and correlations. Looking at Figures 8.2–8.4, however, one gets the impression that the cheapness of swaptions relative to caplets is a rather clear and systematic feature, which should persist under a wide range of reasonable assumptions about the shape of the instantaneous volatility functions or the level of the correlation. I believe that a possible explanation for this can be found in the natural supply and demand dynamics in the interest-rate-option markets. The argument goes as follows: Investment houses are the natural buyers of swaption optionality (as embedded in issuer- or investor-driven products) and natural sellers of caplet optionality (in the form of interest-rate protection for borrowers). A rather detailed description of some of the most common structures is given in chapter 2 of Rebonato (1998). For the purpose of the present discussion, it is sufficient to recall that issuers will attempt to lower their funding costs by issuing puttable bonds and investors to increase their yield by purchasing callable paper. The investors who have bought the 'low-coupon' puttable bonds and the issuers who have issued the 'high-coupon' callable paper (and who are therefore long a payers' and a receivers' swaption, respectively) are theoretically compensated for their 'low' investment yield or 'expensive' funding cost by the fact that they are long a valuable option. Neither the investors nor the issuers will, in general, attempt to capture via dynamic hedging the value of this long option, but they will swap the cash-flows and the option with a trading firm in exchange for an attractive investment yield or funding cost. This type of trade makes investment houses naturally long swaption volatility.

At the same time, there exists regular demand for interest-rate protection from floating-rate corporate borrowers, and this protection is typically provided by financial institutions in the form of products of the 'cap family' (plain-vanilla caps, flexi-caps, pay-as-you-go caps, etc.). As a consequence, the trading books of the investment houses which engage in these types of activity end up being naturally *long* swaption and *short* caplet volatility, and their bids and offers are adjusted accordingly. In general, when supply-and-demand effects skew a market in a given direction, arbitrageurs, who do not have a pre-

----

[2]Another way to look at the problem is to notice that swaptions would be redundant securities only if the forward-rate volatility and correlation functions were perfectly known and deterministic. When this is not the case, liquid and long-dated serial options (see the discussion at the end of Section 2.2) would be required to complete the market and to make one of the three sets of securities (caplets, swaptions or serial options) exactly replicable in a model-independent fashion, and therefore truly redundant.

ferred habitat, are immediately enticed to move in, and to bring the markets in line with each other. As in the case of equity out-of-the-money puts, discussed in Rebonato (1999c), however, the swaption/caplet 'arbitrage' trade is not at all trivial. Some of the difficulties in this 'arbitrage' trade can be understood as follows. Because of the perceived 'cheapness' of swaption volatility, a vega-hedged 'arbitrage' portfolio would typically be long swaption straddles and short caplet volatility (say, straddles). By swaption expiry, however, only one of the underlying caplets will also come to expiry. This can create a severe gamma mismatch between the swaption position and the portfolio of caplets. The problem can, to some extent, be remedied by adjusting (i.e., widening) the strikes of the receiver and payer swaptions so as to reduce their gamma (i.e., by trading in swaption strangles rather than straddles). This partial solution, however, requires dealing in significantly out-of-the-money options and brings therefore to the fore rather complex smile-related considerations. Furthermore, for the 'arbitrage' trade to be profitable, the expiry of the 'cheap' swaption must be quite long. When this is the case, mark-to-market swings might push even a fundamentally correct strategy violently into the red before it can be proven 'right'. This is indeed what happened to some investment houses in the autumn of 1998, and the trading community has retained a vivid memory of the losses incurred by some players who were engaging in this type of model-driven 'arbitrage' in the aftermath of the Russia events. For all these reasons, a systematic lack of congruence between the caplet and the swaption markets can (and, in my opinion, does) exist, and its pricing and hedging consequences should always be carefully factored into the evaluation of a complex product.[3] (See also the discussion in Section 1.2.)

The most important conclusion that one can draw from these observations is therefore that swaption information should be 'taken into account' when describing the forward-rate dynamics, and vice versa, but that enforcing too strong a congruence between the two markets might be counterproductive.[4]

---

[3]In the USA, the situation is complicated by the existence of a very large market in fixed-rate-mortgage-backed securities, which implicitly contain a short pseudo-Bermudan option (the prepayment right). This, to some extent, balances the swaption vega position of investment houses. However, the long swaption volatility position from issuer- and investor-related trades, and the short swaption volatility position from the mortgage-backed securities market, have significantly different expiries and maturities. The overall exposure tends therefore to be more to changes in *shape* rather than in *level* of the swaption matrix (see Chapter 13). The considerations above therefore mainly apply in the form just presented to the European and British interest-rate option markets, and would have to be qualified and altered significantly to be extended to the much more complex US situation.

[4]It might seem that the project carried out in the next chapter, that is, the exact recovery of European swaption prices by means of a forward-rate-based LIBOR market model, runs against this piece of advice. This is, however, not the case, because the FRA-based framework adopted in Chapter 10 is only chosen as a computational tool to facilitate the evaluation of the drift terms and the specification of the correlation and volatility structure. Indeed, I will recommend to focus on the recovery of the root-mean-square volatilities of one set of variables (the swap rates) exactly, and obtain the forward-rate dynamics in an approximate and 'global' fashion, rather than attempt to recover perfectly, as one could do, the caplet prices. See, in particular, the discussion in Section 4.6 (Case Study 4).

This important point is taken up again in a quantitatively more precise way in Section 10.2 and Case Study 2 of Chapter 10.

9.1.4 Historical versus market information: a hedging philosophy

The treatment presented in this chapter carries out an important part of the programme sketched in Chapter 3. I have argued, in fact, that if the dynamics of the forward rates is expressed in the form

$$\frac{\mathrm{d}f_i}{f_i} = \mu_i\,\mathrm{d}t + \sigma_i \sum_{k=1}^{m} b_{ik}\,\mathrm{d}z_k,$$

one can naturally distinguish a 'market component' (the instantaneous volatility, σ_i), related via its root-mean-square to caplet prices, and a 'historical component', linked via the coefficients $\{b_{jk}\}$ to the statistical correlation matrix. I think that this decomposition is not only conceptually but also practically useful. This is because hedging the volatility exposure of a forward-rate-based complex product can be carried out to a satisfactory degree by trading in caplets. Hedging the correlation exposure is, on the other hand, much more complex, and this difficulty is one of the causes of the market incompleteness discussed in the previous section. When perfect hedging is not possible (see Section 6.1.3) one cannot expect to 'lock-in' the price-implied values of volatilities or correlations by means of a self-financing dynamic trading strategy. Therefore the statistical and financial 'reasonableness' of the corresponding model-implied quantities becomes all-important. In other terms, the philosophy behind my proposed approach can be summarized as: 'Hedge what you can, and guess as accurately as possible what you cannot.'

The topic covered in this chapter fits in perfectly with this approach. Guessing correlations or instantaneous volatilities is difficult enough. In addition, the trader will in general find constraints dictated by the dimensionality of the chosen model, which will further reduce her ability to recover either the market-implied or the statistically determined quantities of interest. The decomposition above and the accompanying calibration procedure are constructed so as to allow the trader to recover exactly the market-related hedgeable volatilities and, as best as possible, via the choice of the coefficients $\{b_{jk}\}$, the target statistical correlation matrix.

9.2 An Optimal Procedure to Recover an Exogenous Target Correlation Matrix

9.2.1 Description of the setting

The most convenient m-factor setting for the evolution of forward rates is provided by the equations for the evolution of the forward rates expressed in terms of orthogonal Brownian increments, as presented in Chapter 3. These are repeated below (and renumbered) for ease of reference:

$$\frac{\mathrm{d}f_i}{f_i} = \mu_i \,\mathrm{d}t + \sigma_i \sum_{k=1}^{m} b_{ik} \,\mathrm{d}z_k, \tag{9.1}$$

$$\sum_{k=1}^{m} b_{ik}^2 = 1, \tag{9.2}$$

$$f_i(t) = f_i(0) \exp \int_0^t [\mu(\{\boldsymbol{\sigma}(u)\}, u) - \tfrac{1}{2}\sigma_i^2(u)] \,\mathrm{d}u$$

$$\times \exp \int_0^t \sigma_i(u) \sum_{k=1}^{m} b_{ik}(u) \,\mathrm{d}z_k(u). \tag{9.3}$$

It is important to recall that

- the Brownian increments $\{\mathrm{d}z_k\}$ have been assumed to be orthogonal;

- fewer factors (m) than forward rates (n) are assumed to shock the discrete yield curve; and

- Condition (9.2) ensures that all the caplets are correctly priced – as one can immediately verify by direct calculation of the terms $E[(\mathrm{d}f_i/f_i)\,(\mathrm{d}f_i/f_i)]$, and by making use of the orthogonality of the increments $\{\mathrm{d}z_k\}$.

Equation (9.1) can then be rewritten (see also Chapter 7) in vector form as

$$\underbrace{\frac{\mathrm{d}\mathbf{f}}{\mathbf{f}}}_{[n\times 1]} = \underbrace{\boldsymbol{\mu}\,\mathrm{d}t}_{[n\times 1]} + \underbrace{\mathbf{S}}_{[n\times n]}\underbrace{\boldsymbol{\beta}}_{[n\times m]}\underbrace{\mathrm{d}\mathbf{z}}_{[m\times 1]}$$

where[5] $\mathrm{d}\mathbf{f}/\mathbf{f}$ and $\boldsymbol{\mu}$ are the $n \times 1$ vectors containing the percentage increments in the forward rates and their drifts, respectively, $\mathbf{S}$ is the $n \times n$ diagonal matrix containing the instantaneous volatilities, σ_i, along the main diagonal

$$\mathbf{S} = \begin{pmatrix} \sigma_1 & 0 & 0 & \cdots & 0 \\ 0 & \sigma_2 & 0 & \cdots & 0 \\ 0 & 0 & \sigma_3 & \cdots & 0 \\ \vdots & \vdots & \vdots & \ddots & \vdots \\ 0 & 0 & 0 & \cdots & \sigma_n \end{pmatrix},$$

[5]As elsewhere in this book, and in order to keep notation simple, the division operator must be understood to act term by term on the elements of a vector: so, $[\mathrm{d}f/f] = [\mathrm{d}f_1/f_1, \mathrm{d}f_2/f_2, \ldots, \mathrm{d}f_n/f_n]$.

dz is the $m \times 1$ vector containing the Brownian increments, and the $n \times m$ matrix β is obtained by stacking the n row vectors $\mathbf{b}_i$, $1 \leq i \leq n$, each containing m elements, given by the loadings b_{ik}, $1 \leq k \leq m$, in Equation (9.1)

$$\beta = \begin{pmatrix} \mathbf{b}_1 \\ \mathbf{b}_2 \\ \dots \\ \dots \\ \mathbf{b}_n \end{pmatrix} = \begin{pmatrix} b_{11} & b_{12} & \dots & b_{1m} \\ b_{21} & b_{22} & \dots & b_{2m} \\ \dots & \dots & \dots & \dots \\ \dots & \dots & \dots & \dots \\ b_{n1} & b_{n2} & \dots & b_{nm} \end{pmatrix}. \tag{9.4}$$

As long as the coefficients $\{b_{jk}\}$ satisfy Equation (9.2), the norm of all the row vectors $\{\mathbf{b}_i\}$ is equal to unity. This being the case, the Representation (9.4) is very useful, because the correlation ρ_{jk} between two forward rates, say, the jth and the kth, can immediately be written as

$$\rho_{jk} = \mathbf{b}_j \mathbf{b}_k^{\mathrm{T}} = \mathbf{b}_k \mathbf{b}_j^{\mathrm{T}}, \tag{9.5}$$

as can be directly verified by multiplying the right-hand sides of the appropriate Equations (9.1), and remembering that $dz_j\, dz_k = \rho_{jk}$. In other terms, by Equation (9.5) one obtains the correlation between two forward rates as the cosine of the angle between the two associated vectors $\mathbf{b}_j$ and $\mathbf{b}_k$. More generally, the whole correlation matrix ρ can be written as

$$\rho = \beta \beta^{\mathrm{T}}. \tag{9.6}$$

From Equation (9.6) one can see that the matrix β is the pseudo-square-root of the correlation matrix, ρ. It is also instructive to construct the matrix β by juxtaposing m column vectors, say, γ_i, $1 \leq i \leq m$, instead of stacking n rows:

$$\beta = \begin{pmatrix} \gamma_1 & \gamma_2 & \dots & \gamma_m \end{pmatrix} = \begin{pmatrix} b_{11} & b_{12} & \dots & b_{1m} \\ b_{21} & b_{22} & \dots & b_{2m} \\ \dots & \dots & \dots & \dots \\ \dots & \dots & \dots & \dots \\ b_{n1} & b_{n2} & \dots & b_{nm} \end{pmatrix} \tag{9.7}$$

with

$$(\gamma_j)^{\mathrm{T}} = \{b_{1j}, b_{2j}, \dots, b_{nj}\}, \qquad j = 1, 2, \dots, m.$$

Note that the constraints (9.2), which reflect the caplet-pricing condition, have no bearing on the norm of the vectors $\{\gamma\}$: the caplet-pricing condition requires $\sum_{k=1}^{m} b_{ik}^2 = 1$, but the norm of the kth vector γ_k is related to $\sum_{i=1}^{n} b_{ik}^2$ (notice the different index of summation). Furthermore, no special meaning can be attributed to the angle between any two vectors γ_j and γ_k. However, if one had retained as many driving Brownian processes as forward rates ($m = n$), there would always be at least one solution such that all the $\{\gamma\}$ vectors were orthogonal to each other, and of norm 1. One such solution would be given by the eigenvectors resulting from the orthogonalization of the correlation matrix, and, for this solution, the sum of the squares of the elements of each row and each column would indeed add up to unity.

It is important to stress that, when fewer factors are retained than driving Brownian motions, only the norm of the $\{b\}$ row vectors matters if one simply wants to ensure that the caplet prices are correctly reproduced. Despite the fact that the orthogonality requirement between any pair of column vectors $\{\gamma\}$, as mentioned above, has no impact on the prices of caplets, I shall show below that it can be made of use in order to 'mimic' the results of a full principal component analysis with fewer than n factors.

From the discussion above it follows that an arbitrary exogenous correlation matrix will in general not be recovered via Equations (9.5) and (9.6). We would nonetheless like to find a solution such that

1. the caplets are still correctly priced,

2. the exogenous correlation matrix is approximated as closely as possible (in a precise sense to be defined), and

3. the solution should 'resemble' (also in a sense to be precisely defined later) as much as possible the principal-component-analysis solution.

Conditions 1 and 2 have obvious pricing implications. Condition 3 does not have a direct pricing impact, as long as conditions 1 and 2 are met, but it is desirable for an intuitive interpretation of the resulting solution vectors in terms of the familiar level, slope, curvature, etc., modes of deformation. I will show how the third desideratum can be obtained without 'paying any extra price', that is, without spoiling in any way the pricing of the caplets or worsening the fit to the exogenous correlation matrix.

9.2.2 An efficient computational technique

In principle, conditions 1 and 2 could be satisfied by following a 'brute-force' approach, that is, by defining a 'penalty function', which reflects the quality of the fit between the model correlation matrix (9.6) and the exogenously assigned target correlation matrix, and by optimizing over the coefficients $\{b_{jk}\}$. This procedure, however, would be computationally fraught with difficulties, because the search would be subject to the caplet-pricing constraints (9.2). This is indeed the source of the difficulties mentioned by Sidenius (1998) in Section 9.1. In order to circumvent this problem, it is useful to extend and generalize the approach presented in Section 7.3, and to express the coefficients $\{b_{jk}\}$ in terms of angular coordinates as follows:

$$b_{ik}(t) = \cos\theta_{ik}(t) \prod_{j=1}^{k-1} \sin\theta_{ij}(t), \qquad k = 1,\ldots,s-1, \qquad (9.8)$$

$$b_{ik}(t) = \prod_{j=1}^{k-1} \sin \theta_{ij}(t), \qquad k = s. \tag{9.8'}$$

For an arbitrary set of real numbers ('angles') $\{\theta_{ij}\}$, Equations (9.8) and (9.8') define the position of a point on the surface of an m-dimensional unit-radius hypersphere in terms of its angular coordinates. The requirement that the hypersphere should have unit radius translates requirement (9.2) linked to the correct pricing of the caplets. From Equations (9.8) and (9.8'), in fact, for any $\{\theta_{ij}\}$, $\sum_{k=1}^{m} b_{ik}^2 = 1$, which is exactly the caplet-pricing Condition (9.2). Clearly, for two factors the Expressions (9.8) and (9.8') reduce to

$$b_{i1} = \sin(\theta_i), \qquad b_{i2} = \cos(\theta_i), \qquad 1 \le i \le n,$$

which always ensures correct caplet pricing for a two-factor implementation of the LIBOR market model, since $\sin^2(x) + \cos^2(x) = 1$ for any x (see Section 7.3). The advantage in effecting the transformation (9.8), (9.8') is that, once it has been carried out, the optimization to obtain the best fit to the correlation matrix can be effected over the abstract 'angles' $\{\boldsymbol{\theta}\}$ in an unconstrained manner for any chosen number of factors. More precisely, one can

- start from $(m-1)$ random n-dimensional vectors of real numbers ('angles');

- produce the coefficients $\{b_{jk}\}$ using Equations (9.8), (9.8');

- create the matrix $\boldsymbol{\beta}$ by stacking the vectors $\mathbf{b}_i$;

- calculate the model correlation matrix by Equation (9.6);

- evaluate the penalty function (see below) that expresses in some suitable way the 'distance' between the model and target correlation matrices;

- vary the angles using any of the fast unconstrained non-linear minimization algorithms (e.g., conjugate gradients) so as to make the distance between the matrices as small as possible.

Note carefully that, if one directly optimized over the coefficients $\{b_{jk}\}$, one would have $n \times m$ 'free fitting parameters', subject to n constraints (Equations (9.2)). The optimization procedure I have suggested, on the other hand, is not only unconstrained, but also carried out over a smaller number of variables (the $n \times (m-1)$ angles).

I shall discuss in the following a few different possible choices for the penalty function. Before discussing this important topic, however, let us assume that we have found an optimal solution, made up of $n \times (m-1)$ angles $\{\tilde{\theta}_{jk}\}$, or, equivalently, of $n \times m$ coefficients $\{\tilde{b}_{jk}\}$ linked by Equations (9.2). By the procedure carried out so far, conditions 1 and 2 have been met, but no consideration has been given to ensuring that the 'not strictly necessary', but desirable condition 3 should be satisfied. From the optimal vectors $\hat{\mathbf{b}}_i$, we can, however, always construct the matrix $\hat{\beta}$ and the optimal model-implied correlation matrix, $\hat{\rho}$:

$$\hat{\rho} = \hat{\beta}\hat{\beta}^{\mathrm{T}}. \tag{9.9}$$

This will be a real symmetric matrix of rank m. Its orthogonalization will therefore produce m non-zero eigenvalues, λ_i, $1 \leq i \leq m$, with the associated eigenvectors, $\mathbf{a}_i$, of elements a_{ik}, $1 \leq i \leq n$, $1 \leq k \leq m$. Note that these eigenvectors will now be both orthogonal to each other and normalized to unity. Furthermore, by construction, they will reproduce the same correlation matrix, and, after rescaling by the eigenvalues, they will preserve the caplet-pricing condition 1. In other terms, the solution $\{\tilde{b}_{jk}\}$ has been 'rotated' by the orthogonalization procedure in such a way that the fulfillment of conditions 1 and 2, already satisfied by the solution $\{\tilde{b}_{jk}\}$, has not been 'spoiled'. In addition, the new rotated vectors 'resemble' the principal-component-analysis solution (that would be obtained if n factors were retained) in the sense of being orthogonal to each other and of unit norm.

9.2.3 Choice of the penalty function

As for the choice of the penalty function, the most natural choice is to define a 'distance', χ^2, between the model and target matrices as

$$\chi^2 = \sum_{j,k=1}^{N} \omega_{jk}(\rho_{jk}^{\mathrm{target}} - \rho_{jk}^{\mathrm{mod}})^2 = \sum_{j,k=1}^{N} \omega_{jk}(\rho_{jk}^{\mathrm{target}} - \mathbf{b}_j\mathbf{b}_k^{\mathrm{T}})^2, \tag{9.10}$$

where $N = n + n(n-1)/2$, n is the number of forward rates in the problem, $\rho_{jk}^{\mathrm{target}}$ is the (j,k)th element of the exogenously assigned (target) correlation matrix, ρ_{jk}^{mod} is the (j,k)th element of the model-implied correlation matrix, given by $\mathbf{b}_j\mathbf{b}_k^{\mathrm{T}}$ (see Equation (9.5)), and ω_{jk} are suitably defined non-negative weights. The empirical results reported below (see Section 9.5) will address the topic of how desirable it might be to have instrument-specific optimal weights $\{\omega\}$, but, for the moment, the simplest choice can be taken to require $\omega_{jk} = 1$ for any j, k.

This concludes the description of the procedure required in order to carry out the optimization to the correlation matrix. The following sections will then

- explore how well an exogenous correlation matrix can be recovered in practice by following this procedure (in particular, as a function of the number of factors);
- examine the qualitative shape of the vectors $\mathbf{b}_j$;
- discuss the nature of the transformation brought about by the last orthogonalization step; and
- comment on the desirability of choosing instrument-specific non-constant weights $\{\omega\}$.

Table 9.1   *The 'target' or 'market' correlation matrix.*

	1	2	3	4	5	6	7	8	9	10
1	1	0.961935	0.927492	0.896327	0.868128	0.842612264	0.819525	0.798634	0.779732	0.762628
2	0.961935	1	0.961935	0.927492	0.8963273	0.868128018	0.842612	0.819525	0.798634	0.779732
3	0.927492	0.961935	1	0.961935	0.9274923	0.896327288	0.868128	0.842612	0.819525	0.798634
4	0.896327	0.927492	0.961935	1	0.961935	0.927492301	0.896327	0.868128	0.842612	0.819525
5	0.868128	0.896327	0.927492	0.961935	1	0.961934967	0.927492	0.896327	0.868128	0.842612
6	0.842612	0.868128	0.896327	0.927492	0.961935	1	0.961935	0.927492	0.896327	0.868128
7	0.819525	0.842612	0.868128	0.896327	0.9274923	0.961934967	1	0.961935	0.927492	0.896327
8	0.798634	0.819525	0.842612	0.868128	0.8963273	0.927492301	0.961935	1	0.961935	0.927492
9	0.779732	0.798634	0.819525	0.842612	0.868128	0.896327288	0.927492	0.961935	1	0.961935
10	0.762628	0.779732	0.798634	0.819525	0.8426123	0.868128018	0.896327	0.927492	0.961935	1

9.3 Results and Discussion

9.3.1 Best overall fit

In order to study how well the procedure suggested above can reproduce an exogenous correlation matrix when fewer factors are used than the number of underlying forward rates, I shall start from the simplest possible correlation function, that is,

$$\rho_{jk} = \text{LongCorr} + (1 - \text{LongCorr}) \exp[-\beta(|T_j - T_k|)],$$

which has been discussed extensively in Chapter 7. For the purpose of this investigation, I have assumed that the discount curve could be described by 10 forward rates, the decay constant, β, was taken to be 0.1, and the asymptotic correlation, LongCorr, to be 0.6. This choice of parameters produces the correlation between the ten 12-month forward rates shown in Table 9.1. This correlation matrix is assumed to have been obtained independently – probably from econometric estimation – and is exogenously assigned. It will be referred to as the 'market' or 'target' correlation matrix.

Following the approach described in Equations (9.1)–(9.8), three distinct cases are analyzed in this section, that is, the forward-rate dynamics is in turn assumed to be driven by two, three or four factors. As shown above, the model correlation matrix is then fully determined once the 10×2, 10×3 and 10×4, respectively, **B** matrix is given – see Equations (9.5) and (9.6). We also know that, if the elements b_{ik}, $1 \leq i \leq 10$, $1 \leq j \leq 2, 3, 4$, of the **B** matrix are given by Equations (9.8) and (9.8'), the instantaneous volatilities will be exactly recovered (and if the latter have been chosen to have the correct root-mean-square value, so will the caplet prices). Finally, Equations (9.8) and (9.8') express the elements $\{b_{ik}\}$ in terms of matrices of angles, θ, of dimensions 10×1, 10×2 and 10×3, respectively. In other terms, these matrices of angles fully specify the correlation structure among the 10 forward rates for the two-, three- and four-factor cases. The correlation produced by any possible combination of angles is referred to in the following as the 'model' correlation matrix.

Table 9.2 *The best overall fit (i.e., the fit with identical weights) to the target matrix in Table 9.1 obtained using two factors.*

	1	2	3	4	5	6	7	8	9	10
1	1	0.9989	0.994797	0.985012	0.958227	0.884172	0.82389	0.780794	0.74456	0.713004
2	0.998900389	1	0.99848	0.992015	0.970582	0.905101	0.849555	0.809227	0.775038	0.745093
3	0.99479736	0.99848	1	0.997459	0.982378	0.927163	0.87734	0.840381	0.808692	0.780725
4	0.98501179	0.992015	0.997459	1	0.993198	0.951499	0.909298	0.876859	0.848545	0.823259
5	0.958226955	0.970582	0.982378	0.993198	1	0.98085	0.951569	0.926873	0.904384	0.883758
6	0.88417159	0.905101	0.927163	0.951499	0.98085	1	0.993224	0.982233	0.970175	0.957974
7	0.823889708	0.849555	0.87734	0.909298	0.951569	0.993224	1	0.997387	0.991772	0.984819
8	0.780793734	0.809227	0.840381	0.876859	0.926873	0.982233	0.997387	1	0.998429	0.994786
9	0.744559662	0.775038	0.808692	0.848545	0.904384	0.970175	0.991772	0.998429	1	0.998938
10	0.713004448	0.745093	0.780725	0.823259	0.883758	0.957974	0.984819	0.994786	0.998938	1

In the numerical experiment presented below the procedure was started by

- choosing random values for the elements of the angle matrices (10, 20 or 30 numbers, respectively, for the two-, three- and four-factor cases);

- assigning identical weights, ω, to all the elements in the correlation matrix,

- varying the angles using a reasonably efficient, but otherwise absolutely standard, minimization technique (Powell–Fletcher conjugate gradient, as described, for example, in Press et al. 1996) until the distance between the model and target correlation matrices was rendered as small as possible, given the dimensionality of the problem – see Equation (9.10).

Since the matrix, ω, contained identical weights, an attempt was made to obtain the best global fit to the correlation matrix. The resulting optimal solutions are shown in Tables 9.2–9.4, for the two-, three- and four-factor cases, respectively.

Table 9.3 *The best overall fit (i.e., the fit with identical weights) to the target matrix in Table 9.3 obtained using three factors.*

	1	2	3	4	5	6	7	8	9	10
1	1	0.996692	0.97811	0.918304	0.863906	0.822078	0.79415	0.792001	0.790052	0.7835
2	0.996692441	1	0.991783	0.947196	0.900169	0.860311	0.82872	0.814255	0.802976	0.790156
3	0.978109589	0.991783	1	0.980096	0.945598	0.909726	0.873195	0.839929	0.814279	0.79185
4	0.918303773	0.947196	0.980096	1	0.989641	0.965756	0.928481	0.87316	0.828858	0.793807
5	0.863906058	0.900169	0.945598	0.989641	1	0.992036	0.965617	0.909797	0.860836	0.822126
6	0.822077683	0.860311	0.909726	0.965756	0.992036	1	0.989462	0.945334	0.900203	0.863344
7	0.794150216	0.82872	0.873195	0.928481	0.965617	0.989462	1	0.980251	0.947791	0.918522
8	0.792000716	0.814255	0.839929	0.87316	0.909797	0.945334	0.980251	1	0.991929	0.978061
9	0.790051858	0.802976	0.814279	0.828858	0.860836	0.900203	0.947791	0.991929	1	0.996579
10	0.783499931	0.790156	0.79185	0.793807	0.822126	0.863344	0.918522	0.978061	0.996579	1

Table 9.4   *The best overall fit (i.e., the fit with identical weights) to the target matrix in Table 9.1 obtained using four factors.*

	1	2	3	4	5	6	7	8	9	10
1	1	0.994768	0.945321	0.892026	0.853796	0.837259	0.827084	0.809508	0.778207	0.755324
2	0.994768199	1	0.973649	0.931847	0.894046	0.865579	0.844	0.822485	0.798148	0.778555
3	0.945321044	0.973649	1	0.986101	0.95173	0.899378	0.855305	0.828153	0.821814	0.81076
4	0.892026382	0.931847	0.986101	1	0.986247	0.939906	0.89041	0.855417	0.842971	0.827194
5	0.853795738	0.894046	0.95173	0.986247	1	0.979661	0.939345	0.898652	0.866167	0.83807
6	0.83725884	0.865579	0.899378	0.939906	0.979661	1	0.985982	0.950059	0.894912	0.85283
7	0.827084329	0.844	0.855305	0.89041	0.939345	0.985982	1	0.984718	0.932244	0.889403
8	0.80950777	0.822485	0.828153	0.855417	0.898652	0.950059	0.984718	1	0.976338	0.94646
9	0.778207106	0.798148	0.821814	0.842971	0.866167	0.894912	0.932244	0.976338	1	0.993817
10	0.755323804	0.778555	0.81076	0.827194	0.83807	0.85283	0.889403	0.94646	0.993817	1

In order better to visualize the results, Figure 9.1 shows the correlation between the first forward rate and the following nine forward rates for the target case, as obtained using two, three and four factors.

One can easily notice the inability to reproduce the rapid decorrelation implied by the target correlation between the first and the second and third forward rates. This feature is due to the low dimensionality of the underlying model. It has been discussed at length in Chapter 7, and will therefore not be analyzed here again. Figure 9.2 then shows the differences between the elements in the first column of the target and model correlation matrices for the same three cases. One can notice that the discrepancies become smaller in magnitude and assume higher-frequency components as the number of factors increases. In particular, if one employed one less factor than the number

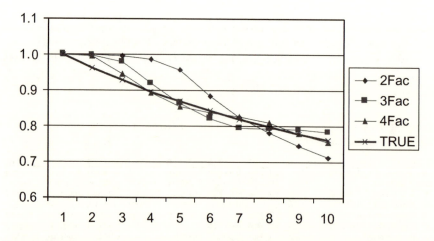

Figure 9.1   *The correlation between the first and the following forward rates for the target correlation matrix (curve labelled 'TRUE') and as obtained after the best overall fit for two, three and four factors (curves labelled '2Fac', '3Fac' and '4Fac', respectively).*

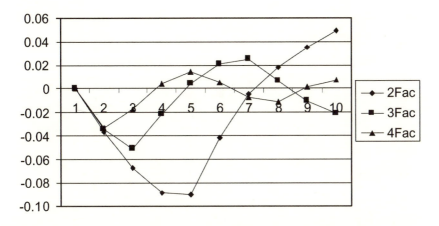

Figure 9.2 *The differences between the elements of the first column of the target and model correlation matrices for the two-, three- and four-factor cases (same labelling of the curves as in Figure 9.1).*

of forward rates, one would notice that, given the chosen functional form for the target correlation matrix, the (now very small) discrepancies would have opposite signs for any two consecutive forward rates. Figure 9.3 then shows the market and model correlation between the fifth forward rate and all the others. The differences between the two associated correlation functions are shown in Figure 9.4.

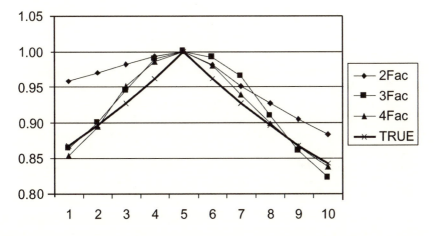

Figure 9.3 *The correlation between the fifth and the other forward rates for the target correlation matrix (curve labelled 'TRUE') and as obtained after the best overall fit for two, three and four factors (curves labelled '2Fac', '3Fac' and '4Fac', respectively).*

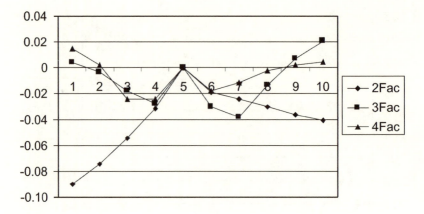

Figure 9.4   *The differences between the elements of the fifth column of the target and model correlation matrices for the two-, three- and four-factor cases (same labelling of the curves as in Figure 9.1).*

The first observation from Figures 9.1–9.4 is that increasing the number of factors brings about rather slow, and at the margin diminishing, improvements. Looking at the magnitude of the errors in Figures 9.2 and 9.4 in more detail, it is also apparent that, as the index of the 'reference' forward rate increases from the first to the fifth, the overall discrepancies between the model and target correlations do not decrease significantly for the same number of factors. In other terms, the decorrelation between the first and the remaining forward rates is as poorly captured, for a fixed number of factors, as the decorrelation between, say, the fifth and the other forward rates. Ultimately, this feature stems from the inability of the small number of 'basis functions' used (ultimately, sines and cosines, as discussed in Chapter 7) to reproduce globally a rapidly varying function such as a decaying exponential. It should be noted, however, that, given the particular choice of target correlation function described by an exponential with a constant decay constant β, the target decorrelation between, say, the fifth and sixth forward rates has been assumed to be just as pronounced as the decorrelation between the first and second. If a target correlation matrix had been chosen such that this feature were not present, for a given model dimensionality the model correlation function might have been able to capture the decorrelation between the ith and other forward rates somewhat better as the index i increases. See again, in this respect, the discussion in Sections 7.2 and 7.4.

9.3.2 Comparison between the optimal and the principal-component-analysis solution

It is interesting to examine the vectors **b** obtained from the optimization procedure, and to compare them with the eigenvectors **a** obtained by orthogo-

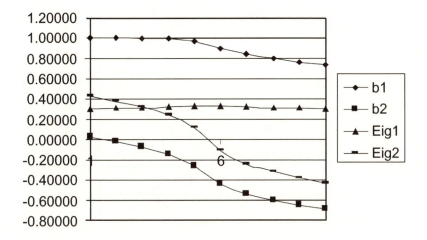

Figure 9.5 *The first and second eigenvectors (curves labelled 'Eig1' and 'Eig2', respectively), and the vectors* $\mathbf{b}_1$ *and* $\mathbf{b}_2$ *(curves labelled 'b1' and 'b2', respectively) for the two-factor case.*

nalizing the model correlation matrix for the two-, three- and four-factor cases (see Figures 9.5–9.8).

It is evident, and somewhat surprising, that the optimization procedure, which is required neither to produce orthogonal vectors **b**, nor to ensure any resemblance between these vectors **b** and the eigenvectors **a**, ends up obtaining a very principal-component-analysis-like solution.

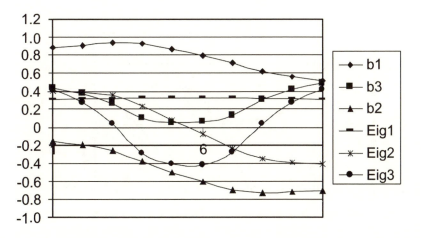

Figure 9.6 *The first, second and third eigenvectors (curves labelled 'Eig1', 'Eig2' and 'Eig3', respectively), and the vectors* $\mathbf{b}_1$, $\mathbf{b}_2$ *and* $\mathbf{b}_3$ *(curves labelled 'b1', 'b2' and 'b3', respectively) for the three-factor case.*

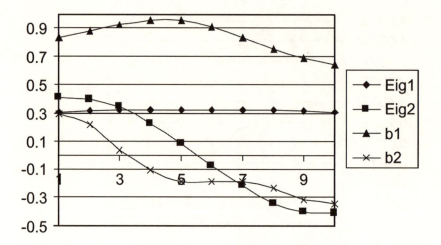

Figure 9.7 *The first and second eigenvectors (curves labelled 'Eig1' and 'Eig2', respectively), and the vectors b_1 and b_2 (curves labelled 'b1' and 'b2', respectively) for the four-factor case.*

Indeed, there was no a priori reason to expect that the curves traced by the various vectors **b**, obtained by means of a 'blind' unconstrained optimization procedure, should be at all smooth as a function of the forward rates; nor, for that matter, that the vectors, say, b_1 or b_2 obtained in the two- or three-factor cases should have had any resemblance to the corresponding vectors obtained with four factors.

Figures 9.9 and 9.10 show that, despite the fact that these features were

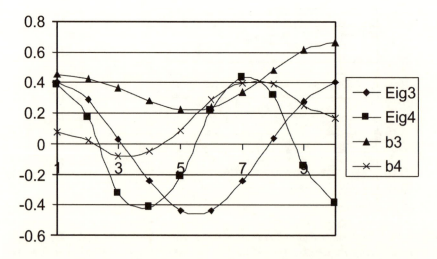

Figure 9.8 *The third and fourth eigenvectors (curves labelled 'Eig3' and 'Eig4', respectively), and the vectors b_3 and b_4 (curves labelled 'b3' and 'b4', respectively) for the four-factor case.*

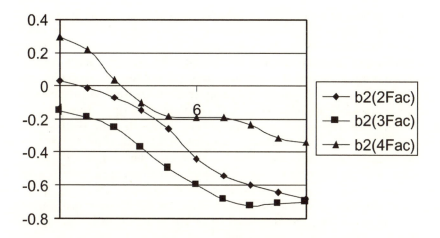

Figure 9.9 *The vectors* **b**₂ *obtained from the optimization for the two-, three- and four-factor cases (curves labelled, 'b2(2Fac)', 'b2(3Fac)' and 'b2(4Fac)', respectively).*

in no way embedded in the search routine, the vectors **b** always turned out to be smooth, and retained the same approximate shape when the independent optimizations were carried out for the two-, three- and four-factor cases. The smoothness property, in particular, is important because the arguments presented in Section 7.3, regarding the qualitative shape of the correlation as a function of the forward rate index for low-dimensionality implementations of the LIBOR market model, relied on the smoothness of the dependence of the angle function on the index – see, for example, Equations (7.10) and

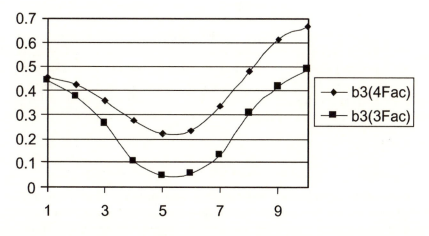

Figure 9.10 *The vectors* **b**₃ *obtained from the optimization for the three- and four-factor cases (curves labelled 'b3(3Fac)' and 'b3(4Fac)', respectively).*

(7.11). There is little doubt that these features are partly due to the fact that the 'target' ('market') correlation matrix was assumed to be smooth and well-behaved, and that they would most likely have been lost (or, rather, masked) if a noisy input target matrix had been used. This observation, however, suggests that it might be useful to pre-fit a statistically observed correlation matrix to a simple and smooth functional form, thereby creating a 'synthetic' input market matrix, before embarking on the optimization procedure.

Finally, it is interesting to comment on the fact that the vectors $\{\mathbf{b}\}$ display similar oscillatory behavior as the eigenvectors obtained from the final orthogonalization. This observation is interesting because, for the latter, in fact, introducing higher and higher frequency oscillation of the eigenvectors is a 'natural' way to enforce mutual orthogonalization. There is no a priori reason, however, why this should be the case for the $\{\mathbf{b}\}$ vectors, which, unlike the eigenvectors, are not required by construction to be orthogonal to each other. I find very interesting this should turn out to be the case.

The results presented in this section have therefore shown that, if one attempts a best fit to the overall correlation matrix, that is, if one gives identical weights, ω_{jk}, to all the elements, $(\rho_{jk}^{\text{target}} - \rho_{jk}^{\text{mod}})^2$, of the distance matrix, one obtains as a solution vectors $\{\mathbf{b}\}$ that are smooth, well-behaved and remarkably similar to eigenvectors obtained via the principal-component-analysis route. I have also shown that the vector rotation induced by the last (facultative) orthogonalization step brings about a relative minor change in the vectors. One can therefore truly say that the equal-weights technique proposed above provides a systematic procedure to obtain the perfect pricing of caplets and a principal-component-analysis-like dynamics with fewer factors than forward rates.

It is important to stress, however, that these results have been obtained after imposing a *global* best fit to the whole correlation matrix. On the other hand, it might be tempting to assign in a product-specific manner non-constant importance weights to the elements $(\rho_{jk}^{\text{target}} - \rho_{jk}^{\text{mod}})^2$ that make up the total distance between the target and model correlation matrices (see Equation (9.10)). More precisely, the trader might want to assign weights specifically chosen to reflect the (perceived) importance of different particular portions of the correlation matrix for a given derivative product. What remains to be analyzed is whether this procedure can succeed at all, and whether it is desirable to proceed in this direction. This task is undertaken in the next section.

9.3.3 Best fit to portions of the correlation matrix

I discuss in detail in this section the quality of the calibration to a model correlation matrix obtainable from a low-dimensionality implementation of the LIBOR market model when, in order to capture the specific features of a given exotic product, non-constant weights $\{\omega\}$ are assigned to the elements of the χ^2 distance function. In particular, I shall analyze in detail the cases of a ratchet cap and of a trigger swap.

As far as the first instrument is concerned, it can be decomposed into a series of caplets and/or floorlets with stochastic strikes. More precisely, the strike for the jth caplet is a function of the reset of the $(j-1)$th forward rate. Typically, the strike will be given by the reset of the previous forward rate shifted by a known number of basis points. It is therefore plausible to surmise that the crucial features of the forward-rate dynamics that must be correctly captured by a given modelling approach should be (i) the portion of the instantaneous volatility corresponding to the last few months of the life of each forward rate and (ii) the correlation between contiguous forward rates.

EXERCISE 9.1 *The payoff at time $t_j + \tau$ of the jth caplet in a ratchet cap is given by $[f(t_j, t_j, t_j + \tau) - K]^+ \tau$ and the strike K is given by $f(t_{j-1}, t_{j-1}, t_j) + h$, with h a constant $(t_j = t_{j-1} + \tau)$. Provide a qualitative argument to justify the statements (i) and (ii) in the text above.*

Criteria that can guide the trader in the choice of the instantaneous volatility function have been examined elsewhere (see Chapters 6 and 8), and we already know that, for any chosen number of factors, this quantity can always be recovered so as to display the desired shape. The fulfillment of the desideratum in point (i) above can therefore always be achieved irrespective of the number of factors. As far as the correlation matrix is concerned, on the other hand, we know that retaining fewer Brownian drivers than forward rates can significantly affect the shape of the resulting model correlation matrix. If the trader believes that it is desirable to recover as accurately as possible the correlation between contiguous forward rates, it is tempting to try to use the available 'degrees of freedom' in an efficient way, and to prescribe that the diagonal lines above and below the main diagonal of the target matrix should be recovered as accurately as possible.

In order to achieve this, the optimization procedure described in the previous section was modified by assigning identical weights to the elements on these diagonal lines, and zero weight to the remaining elements, $(\rho_{jk}^{\text{target}} - \rho_{jk}^{\text{mod}})^2$:

$$\omega_{ij} = \delta_{j,i} + \delta_{j,i+1} + \delta_{j,i-1},$$

where, for any two indices a and b, the Kronecker delta symbol, δ_{ab}, is defined as $\delta_{ab} = 1$ if $a = b$ and $\delta_{ab} = 0$ otherwise. The overall target correlation was left unaltered.

As for the case of the multi-look trigger swap, the situation was considered of a swap with strike K that would come to life if any of a series of forward (index) rates reset above a pre-known barrier level, H (up-and-in trigger swap). So, for the ten-forward-rate case covered by the correlation matrix, if the first forward rate reset above H, a nine-forward-rate swap would come to life; if the second, but not the first, forward rate reset above H, an eight-forward-rate swap would appear; and so on. It was also assumed that, given the shape of the yield curve, the most likely forward rates to reset above the barrier would be,

Table 9.5   *The target correlation matrix.*

	1	2	3	4	5	6	7	8	9	10
1	1	0.961935	0.927492	0.896327	0.868128	0.84261226	0.819525	0.798634	0.779732	0.762628
2	0.961934967	1	0.961935	0.927492	0.896327	0.86812802	0.842612	0.819525	0.798634	0.779732
3	0.927492301	0.961935	1	0.961935	0.927492	0.89632729	0.868128	0.842612	0.819525	0.798634
4	0.896327288	0.927492	0.961935	1	0.961935	0.9274923	0.896327	0.868128	0.842612	0.819525
5	0.868128018	0.896327	0.927492	0.961935	1	0.96193497	0.927492	0.896327	0.868128	0.842612
6	0.842612264	0.868128	0.896327	0.927492	0.961935	1	0.961935	0.927492	0.896327	0.868128
7	0.819524654	0.842612	0.868128	0.896327	0.927492	0.96193497	1	0.961935	0.927492	0.896327
8	0.798634122	0.819525	0.842612	0.868128	0.896327	0.9274923	0.961935	1	0.961935	0.927492
9	0.779731586	0.798634	0.819525	0.842612	0.868128	0.89632729	0.927492	0.961935	1	0.961935
10	0.762627864	0.779732	0.798634	0.819525	0.842612	0.86812802	0.896327	0.927492	0.961935	1

say, the first, second and third. This being the case, it is plausible to impose that a low-dimensionality LIBOR market model should be implemented so as to recover the first three columns of the correlation matrix as accurately as possible: the first column would be associated with the correlation between the first forward (index) rate and the nine-period swap rate; the second column with the second forward (index) rate and the eight-period swap rate; and so on (see Section 10.2). This could be achieved by specifying that the weights $\{\omega\}$ should be as follows:

$$\omega_{jk} = 1 \qquad \text{for } k = 1, 2, 3,$$
$$\omega_{jk} = 0 \qquad \text{otherwise.}$$

EXERCISE 9.2 *Analyze carefully how the correlation affects the value of a trigger swap, and justify the statement above. Compare a trigger swap with a Bermudan swaption with the same strike, and with exercise dates coinciding with the look-times of the trigger swap, and comment on the relative value of the two. Ceteris paribus, how do you think that imperfect correlation will affect the value of a Bermudan swaption?*

Apart from the fact that different weights were assigned, the procedure followed was then exactly the same as described in the previous section. The resulting model correlation matrices obtained for the ratchet cap and the trigger swap matrices for a three-factor implementation of the yield-curve dynamics are shown in Tables 9.6 and 9.7, respectively (Table 9.5 shows again, for ease of reference, the target correlation matrix).

The first observation is that, *prima facie*, the procedure appears to have been successful in both cases: the first three columns of the target correlation matrix for the trigger-swap case (see Table 9.7), and the three main diagonals for the ratchet-cap case (see Table 9.6) have been recovered exactly or almost perfectly, respectively. It·is interesting to notice, however, that, as one moves away from the areas of the correlation matrix which had been specifically targeted, the overall agreement becomes much worse than in the case of the identical-weights fit, as shown in Figures 9.12 and 9.13 (Figure 9.11 shows the target correlation surface for ease of comparison).

Table 9.6 *The model correlation matrix for the case of the ratchet cap.*

	1	2	3	4	5	6	7	8	9	10
1	1	0.961928	0.853107	0.720585	0.580054	0.41474826	0.295101	0.467902	0.561058	0.616134
2	0.96192802	1	0.96188	0.866074	0.778117	0.64681137	0.529687	0.654071	0.686776	0.671671
3	0.853106901	0.96188	1	0.961977	0.919811	0.81721963	0.693623	0.751155	0.711911	0.622745
4	0.720585433	0.866074	0.961977	1	0.962015	0.85153134	0.690318	0.675172	0.566411	0.419062
5	0.580053824	0.778117	0.919811	0.962015	1	0.96204366	0.856604	0.815231	0.682678	0.501385
6	0.414748264	0.646811	0.81722	0.851531	0.962044	1	0.962098	0.906185	0.767596	0.572244
7	0.295100518	0.529687	0.693623	0.690318	0.856604	0.96209776	1	0.961961	0.85236	0.67798
8	0.467901531	0.654071	0.751155	0.675172	0.815231	0.9061845	0.961961	1	0.961867	0.850795
9	0.561057886	0.686776	0.711911	0.566411	0.682678	0.76759561	0.85236	0.961867	1	0.962074
10	0.616133927	0.671671	0.622745	0.419062	0.501385	0.57224428	0.67798	0.850795	0.962074	1

It is apparent from these figures that the price paid in order to force perfect agreement with specific portions of the target correlation matrix can become very high in the 'neglected' areas of the surface. It therefore takes a very strong confidence in one's financial intuition to focus the attention almost exclusively on a product-dependent subset of the correlation matrix. If, for instance, the price of a ratchet cap were to depend (as in reality it does) on the correlation between forward rates other than the contiguous ones, the pricing errors introduced by this procedure could become very serious.

Another indication of the dangers of this procedure can be gleaned by examining the resulting **b** vectors and the associated eigenvectors for the ratchet-cap case (see Figure 9.14). Despite the fact that, once again, there is a noticeable resemblance between the vectors $\mathbf{b}_i$ ($i = 1, 2, 3$) and the three eigenvectors resulting from the orthogonalization of the rank-three model correlation matrix, it is now difficult to interpret the modes of deformation in terms of a shift, slope and curvature change of the yield curve. In other terms, the yield curve will now evolve, under the shocks produced by the three resulting eigenvectors, in a manner very different from what is statistically observed.

On the basis of the results from these 'case studies', one can conclude that imposing the perfect fit of a specific portion of the correlation matrix with a view to capturing the relevant features of a specific product can be a dan-

Table 9.7 *The model correlation matrix for the case of the trigger swap.*

	1	2	3	4	5	6	7	8	9	10
1	1	0.961944	0.927513	0.896355	0.868097	0.842637	0.819532	0.798549	0.77973	0.762638
2	0.961943971	1	0.962004	0.927565	0.896285	0.868147	0.84265	0.819534	0.798669	0.779705
3	0.927513249	0.962004	1	0.994337	0.98329	0.97062	0.957574	0.944747	0.932487	0.920863
4	0.896354528	0.927565	0.994337	1	0.997067	0.990691	0.982771	0.974223	0.965577	0.957061
5	0.868096544	0.896285	0.98329	0.997067	1	0.998204	0.994034	0.988629	0.98265	0.976435
6	0.842637188	0.868147	0.97062	0.990691	0.998204	1	0.998783	0.995862	0.991995	0.987608
7	0.819532162	0.84265	0.957574	0.982771	0.994034	0.998783	1	0.999132	0.997016	0.994147
8	0.798548987	0.819534	0.944747	0.974223	0.988629	0.995862	0.999132	1	0.999366	0.997783
9	0.779730075	0.798669	0.932487	0.965577	0.98265	0.991995	0.997016	0.999366	1	0.99952
10	0.762638274	0.779705	0.920863	0.957061	0.976435	0.987608	0.994147	0.997783	0.99952	1

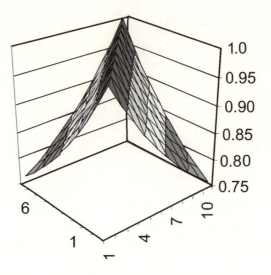

Figure 9.11   *The exponentially decaying target correlation matrix.*

gerous exercise. If the trader were fully confident that only the correlation between specific forward rates mattered for a given instrument, the strategy might prove very effective. If the financial intuition of the trader, however, were to be imperfect, the serious mis-specification of the non-fitted areas of

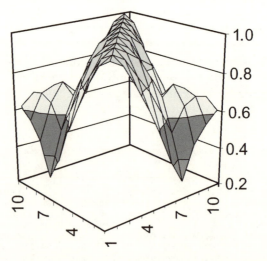

Figure 9.12   *The correlation surface obtained by imposing the best possible fit to the three main diagonals (ratchet-cap case).*

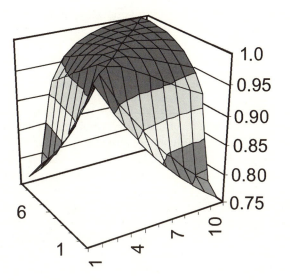

Figure 9.13 *The correlation surface obtained by imposing the best possible fit to the first three columns (trigger-swap case).*

the correlation matrix could have a profound and undesirable pricing impact. It seems therefore reasonable to close this section with the recommendation that a global fit to the correlation matrix, while intrinsically imperfect because

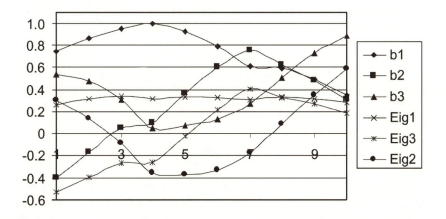

Figure 9.14 *The first three eigenvectors (curves labelled 'Eig1', 'Eig2' and 'Eig3', respectively), and the vectors $\mathbf{b}_1$ to $\mathbf{b}_3$ (curves labelled 'b1', 'b2' and 'b3', respectively) in the ratchet-cap case. Notice that, contrary to the identical-weight fit, little resemblance is now left between the canonical principal-component-analysis solution (yield-curve deformations explainable in terms of level, slope and curvature changes) and the vectors $\{\mathbf{b}\}$.*

of the dimensionality constraints, will in general be more robust, easier to understand in its financial implications and better suited to the portfolio management of a book of complex products.

9.3.4 An 'accidental' observation

The conclusion reached at the end of the previous section can be tempered by an almost 'accidental' observation. Looking back at the model correlation surface obtained in the trigger-swap case (see Figure 9.13), one can observe that its shape closely matches (by construction) the corresponding target matrix for the first three columns, but then changes convexity. Given the assumed (decaying-exponential) shape of the target matrix, this constitutes a 'failure' of the procedure. The resulting model correlation surface, however, turns out to bear a strong resemblance with some of the econometric correlation surfaces discussed in Section 7.2 (see, e.g., Figures 7.5 and 7.6). In particular, these figures display a change in convexity as one moves away from the first few forward rates: the correlation between the first and the remaining forward rates does display positive convexity, but the second derivative becomes negative when one looks at the correlation between a late-expiring forward rate and all the others. In the trigger-swap case the particular choice for the weights attempted to combine the relatively slowly varying basis functions in such a way as to produce as rapid a change in correlation as possible for the first few columns of the matrix. Since truly high-frequency components are actually not in the basis set when one works with a small number of factors, the price that the procedure has to pay is that there is little variation 'left' to describe the remaining portions of the correlation surface. This, however, can be a blessing in disguise if one wanted to reproduce correlation surfaces such as the ones depicted in Figures 7.5 and 7.6: one could start from a target decaying-exponential correlation function fitted to the first few columns of the econometric matrix; retain a small number of factors; impose weights in the distance function that quickly decrease with the index of the first forward rate; and proceed as in the case of the trigger swap. Exploration of this avenue is left as a small research project (rather than just an exercise) for the reader.

9.4 Conclusions

In this chapter I have suggested a methodology by means of which the simultaneous calibration of the LIBOR market model to the market caplet prices and to an exogenous correlation matrix can be achieved. As explained in the opening section, the need to carry out a calibration for this type of problem is purely 'technical', that is, it stems from the decision (or, more likely, the need) to use fewer driving factors than forward rates in the problem. For a problem dimensionality up to, say, 30 or 40, this computational constraint can often be overcome for path-dependent options (which can be priced by propagating forward the yield curve using a Monte Carlo simulation) by employing a 'brute-force' approach (i.e., by retaining as many factors as forward rates). This is particularly true for those products (of type 1a, as described in Chapter 4), for which the very-long-jump procedure can be employed. Also for products for which 'only' the long-jump procedure is applicable, however, answers in 'trading times' can be obtained with 30 or 40 factors. This line of attack, however, becomes impracticable for very large numbers of forward rates, as could be found, for instance, in a 30-year product with quarterly or monthly resets; and it becomes virtually impossible for Bermudan swaptions, and for compound options in general. For these products the methodology presented in this chapter provides the 'best' possible solution (in the sense described above). It also shows how the resulting forward-rate dynamics can be made to resemble in a systematic manner, for a given small number of factors, the evolution obtainable using the eigenvectors and eigenvalues from the orthogonalization of the full-rank correlation matrix.

The next chapter will tackle a different problem, that is, how to ensure that the joint dynamics of forward and swap rates should be as self-consistent and, at the same time, as econometrically desirable as possible, while pricing exactly a set of co-terminal European swaptions. The setting is therefore fundamentally different, and, even if the trader used as many factors as forward rates, there would be no guarantee that a perfect fit could be found. Despite superficial formal similarities with some of the techniques used in this chapter – such as the angular decomposition – the reader should therefore keep in mind this underlying conceptual difference.

10

Calibrating a Forward-Rate-Based LIBOR Market Model to Swaption Prices

10.1 The General Context

10.1.1 How a trader would like to use a model

The no-arbitrage restrictions on the drifts of the forward rates do not fully characterize, by themselves, the LIBOR market model, but only do so when specific functional forms for the volatility and correlation functions are chosen. I have shown that these functions are under-determined by the market prices of the plain-vanilla instruments (caplets and European swaptions). This is of great practical relevance, because a remarkable richness of behaviors (and exotic option prices) can be generated by relatively simple choices of market-consistent instantaneous volatility or correlation functions (see, e.g., Sidenius 1998, 2000). The trader is therefore left with a variety of possible choices for these unobservable quantities, which all give rise to, say, the same caplet and/or European swaption prices, but produce substantially different prices for exotic products.

These over-abundant 'degrees of freedom' can be reduced in a variety of ways. I have discussed in Chapters 6 and 8 (see also Chapter 12) that imposing time-homogeneity for the term structure of volatilities is an appealing strategy in order to reduce substantially the number of degrees of freedom in the problem. Another effective way to do so is by taking into account the congruence of the two related plain-vanilla liquid option markets for caplets and European swaptions.[1] Either strategy forces the trader to express views about something that is not fully 'contained' in the observed prices. One of the main differences between the LIBOR market model and the traditional

---

[1] See Sections 1.2 and 9.1 for a discussion of the congruence (or lack thereof) between the caplet and the swaption markets.

short-rate-based approaches is to be found in the set of quantities about which these trading views can be expressed. I would argue that traders find it more 'natural' to express views about the time dependence of forward-rate volatilities, than, say, about the risk-adjusted speed of reversion of the instantaneous short rate. In other words, given the degrees of freedom that any model affords, something or someone *has* to express trading views that go beyond the information embedded in the market prices. I believe that it is more desirable that these trading views should be consciously and explicitly expressed by the trader in terms of quasi-observable, quasi-tradable quantities, rather than equivalently but opaquely introduced via the back door by a black-box model.

I propose below a method to bring explicit trading views directly to bear on the choice of instantaneous volatilities. In particular, I shall show how this can be achieved when dealing with complex products (such as CMS derivatives and Bermudan swaptions) that have as natural hedges not forward rates and caplets, but swap rates and European swaptions.

10.1.2 An overview of some of the results so far, and plan of the chapter

I intend to carry out this program by building on some of the results that have been established in the previous chapters. These can be summarized as follows:

1. The time dependence of the instantaneous volatilities of forward rates plays a crucial role in the pricing of European swaptions and exotic LIBOR products (see Chapter 8 and Sidenius 2000).

2. If one works in a forward-rate-based LIBOR-market-model framework, it is possible to choose an infinity of functional forms for the instantaneous volatilities, such that the prices of all the caplets linked with the underlying forward rates are perfectly recovered (see Chapters 3 and 6).

3. In the same forward-rate-based framework, it is possible to recover the caplet prices and at the same time to obtain an optimal fit to a user-specified correlation matrix in an infinite number of ways (see the results in Chapter 9). Once a choice has been made for the instantaneous volatility function, the resulting covariance matrix is therefore also optimal (Rebonato 1999a).

4. The joint information from the caplet/European swaption markets is not sufficient to determine the time-dependent volatilities and correlation functions uniquely. Different choices for these functions can give rise to the same prices for either set of plain-vanilla options (caplets or European swaptions) that constitute the market reference points. Therefore the user has to invoke some exogenous source of financial information in order to choose among the many combinations of instantaneous volatility and correlation functions that can produce a desired covariance matrix.

Building on these results, I have two main goals in mind for this chapter. First I intend to expand on point 4 above, by showing that there is a surprisingly simple and effective way to examine the congruence of the swaption and caplet markets, given a choice of instantaneous volatilities and correlations. More precisely, I show how to 'deduce' in an accurate way what the model prices of European swaptions are given a certain specification for the dynamics for the *forward* rates without having to carry out a series of computationally demanding computer simulations.[2] These results allow the trader to carry out a rapid examination of the model-implied swaption prices, but do not provide any indication as to how to ensure that the chosen forward-rate dynamics should indeed produce swaption prices close to the market, or a desirable overall evolution of the yield curve.

This brings me to the second task. I will in fact show that the same approximations that allow an efficient and accurate calculation of the swaption prices allow one to specify the stochastic evolution of forward rates in such a way as to recover virtually exactly the prices of a full set of co-terminal European swaptions. More importantly, I will indicate how it is possible and practicable to do so while obtaining, at the same time, the best possible fit to market prices of caplets (if so desired) or to a forward-rate/forward-rate covariance matrix.

10.1.3 Comparison with the optimal fit to the correlation matrix

This task is deceptively similar to that presented in Section 9.3, where we saw how to price exactly the caplets underlying, for instance, a European swaption, while obtaining at the same time the optimal fit to an exogenously assigned forward-rate correlation matrix. The task I undertake in this chapter is different for at least two reasons. First, what I deal with in the following sections is the recovery of European swaption prices, which depend on, but are not uniquely determined by, the correlation matrix, even when all the underlying caplets are exactly priced (see Chapter 7 about the dependence of European swaption prices on the correlation function). Second, the need to calibrate the forward-rate dynamics to the forward-rate correlation matrix simply arises when fewer factors than forward rates are retained in the chosen implementation of the LIBOR market model. When it comes to the description of European swaptions in a forward-rate-based implementation of the LIBOR market model, the situation is intrinsically different, and the need to carry out a calibration is of more fundamental nature. There is no guarantee, in fact, that a market-given set of co-terminal swaption prices can be recovered together with an exogenous forward-rate correlation matrix, even if as many factors as forward rates are used in the modelling (see the discussion in Section 9.1.3). It is therefore unavoidable for the user of the model to obtain an optimal, but not perfect, solution.

---

[2]The formulas in Case Study 3 (Section 10.3.5) that contain some of the results of this chapter have already been independently obtained and have appeared in the literature, albeit in a different form (see Jamshidian 1997, Andersen and Andreasen 1997, Hull and White 2000).

10.1.4 Should one prefer a swap-rate-based model to price swaption-based products?

I shall provide in the second part of this chapter the tools to evolve forward (rather than swap) rates in such a way that the market prices of a set of co-terminal European swaptions are correctly obtained (and other desirable features are simultaneously recovered). It might appear that working in a swap-rate-based LIBOR-market-model setting would provide a more natural set of 'coordinates' to deal with swaption problems. This used, indeed, to be my view, but I have recently come to the conclusion that the ability to recover 'intelligently' European swaption prices in a forward-rate-based framework has a two-fold appeal: The first is computational, since an effective numerical implementation of a forward-rate-based stochastic simulation is technically and computationally considerably less demanding than its swap-rate-based counterpart.[3] The second is conceptual, since the approach I propose affords a natural way to analyze and take trading views about the congruence of the two sister plain-vanilla markets. The inability of a model to fit perfectly a set of market quantities might be frustrating for the trader, but, after all, a model that can fit everything perfectly by construction loses all explanatory power (see Section 1.1).

Finally, it is often argued that a forward-rate based on the LIBOR market model is unsuitable for a product (such as a Bermudan swaption) that the trader will want to hedge using mainly European swaptions. Such an implementation, the objection goes, might well produce after calibration the same prices as the swap-rate-based version. However, when calculating the model hedges, it will 'naturally' express the risk statistics in terms of FRAs and caplets, rather than the swap rates and European swaptions that the trader would like to use. This, however, need not be the case, and the same approximations that can be used to calibrate the model to the prices of co-terminal European swaptions can also be employed to produce the required swaption hedges. I therefore prefer to work in a forward-rate-based setting even when pricing swaption-related instruments.

These results are applied in detail in Section 10.6 to the special case of fitting the European swaptions associated with a given Bermudan swaption, and the pricing implications are discussed. The numerical quality of the approach is discussed in Section 10.7 by presenting the results of detailed calculations. Before embarking on this project, however, I will attempt to highlight why bringing together the information from the caplet and swaption markets is so important for relative-value trading, and for the pricing of exotic products. I undertake this task in the next section.

---

[3] See also the discussion at the end of Chapter 3.

10.2 The Need for a Joint Description of the Forward- and Swap-Rate Dynamics

In this section I intend to show that, when pricing a complex product, a trader should almost always care about the *joint* dynamics of forward and swap rates. I shall do so by analyzing in detail two case studies. In particular, the swaption prices implied by a set of forward-rate volatilities and correlations will be shown to be very important. This will provide a motivation for the results presented in Section 10.3.

10.2.1 The special importance of co-terminal swap rates

Forward rates have been the traditional building blocks of the LIBOR-market-model approach. The reason is more likely to be 'historical' rather than fundamental since the modern pricing approach evolved out of the HJM model, and the latter is naturally expressed in term of instantaneous forward rates. If one wants to be able to describe the (continuous) discount function in its entirety, instantaneous forward rates are by far the most natural choice of instruments for the task, because the discount function at time t for maturity T, $P(t, T)$, is directly linked to the time-t instantaneous forward rate expiring at time T, $f(t, T)$, by the relationship

$$f(t, T) = -\frac{\partial \ln P(t, T)}{\partial T}.$$

When moving from instantaneous to discrete-tenor forward rates, however, as one does with the HJM to LIBOR-market-model transition, the discount function is defined and used only at a discrete set of points, that is, at the times at which the price-sensitive events occur. If the values of the discount function at a discrete number of points are all that is needed, forward rates lose their privileged status and the prices of other sets of financial quantities can provide the same information about the discount curve: Both co-starting and co-terminal swap rates, for instance, provide an equivalent set of state variables in terms of which the discrete discount function can be expressed. Figure 10.1, displays the co-terminal swap rates that allow the determination of the discount function at the required discrete times.

EXERCISE 10.1 *With reference to Figure 10.1, express the values of the discount factors at times $t_1, t_2, \ldots, t_7$, given the values of the swap rates SR_0, SR_1, $\ldots$, SR_6. The brute-force solution entails the inversion of an upper-diagonal matrix. Try to find a shrewder, and much simpler, solution.*

Co-starting and co-terminal swap rates are not the only sets of market-traded quantities in terms of which the discount curve can be recovered: several other, albeit less elegant, combinations of forward rates and swap rates can, in theory, equivalently be used for the purpose. Co-terminal swap rates,

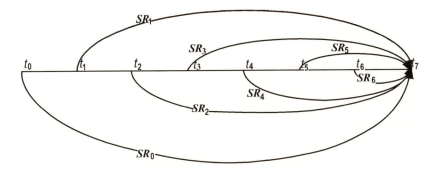

Figure 10.1 *The set of (seven) co-terminal swap rates* $(SR_i, \ i = 0, 1, 2, \ldots, 6)$ *underlying swaps that all mature at time* t_7, *and begin at times* t_0 *(spot)*, t_1, t_2, $\ldots$, t_6. *From the value of these seven swap rates, it is possible to express the value of the discount factors at times* t_i, $i = 1, 2, \ldots, 7$, *in terms of the value of the discount factor at time* t_0. *Since* SR_0, *however, is a spot swap rate, the value of the discount function at time* t_0 *is known to be equal to unity, and the absolute, rather than relative, values for the other discount factors can be determined. Note also that the last swap rate* (SR_6) *coincides with the one-period forward rate resetting at time* t_6 *and paying at time* t_7. *For the case at hand, co-starting swap rates can be similarly defined with reference to this figure, as the swap rates all beginning at the same time* t_0 *and maturing at times* $t_1, t_2, \ldots, t_7$.

however, enjoy a somewhat special status because they are linked to the instruments underlying one of the most important 'exotic' products, that is, Bermudan swaptions. The European swaptions expiring at the various reset dates and all maturing on the same terminal date are in fact the natural hedging instruments for the associated Bermudan. The exact recovery of their prices is therefore the first (although by no means the only) requirement for a satisfactory pricing and hedging of the Bermudan product.

10.2.2 Interrelation between volatilities and correlations associated with different state variables

The price of virtually no exotic product depends exclusively on the volatilities of, and correlations among, one single set of state variables. Trigger swaps, for instance, depend strongly on the volatility of forward rates, on the volatility of swap rates and on the correlation between swap rates and forward rates. Similarly, Bermudan swaptions depend to first order on the volatility of the underlying co-terminal swap rates (as one can easily surmise), but also on the correlation amongst swap rates and on the volatility of forward rates. When implementing the LIBOR market model, it is very easy to fit exactly the volatility of the chosen set of state variables (forward or swap rates). As shown in Chapter 9, in the case of forward rates it is also relatively simple to obtain, at the same time, the best possible fit to the forward-rate/forward-rate correlation matrix. Once these 'degrees of freedom' have been used up, however, the volatility of, and the correlation among, the complementary set of state variables (say, the co-terminal swap rates) are uniquely determined. Given that the price of complex products depends on the interrelation between several sets of state variables, it is essential to ensure that the output of the implemented LIBOR market model should be consistent with these cross-relationships. Suppose, for instance, that we have chosen a forward-rate-based description to model a particular product and fitted in the best possible way the discrete covariance elements among these variables. Hopefully, given our choice, the exotic product will depend on the volatilities of the forward rates more strongly than on the volatilities of the associated swap rates. Financial intuition, however, can be seriously stretched by this kind of judgement: I show in the Case Study 1 (Section 10.2.3) that instruments such as trigger swaps can depend to a different extent on forward-rate or swap-rate volatilities, depending on the specific terms of each individual deal (i.e., depending on the relative levels of the strike, of the barrier and of the forward rate itself). Therefore, whether it is more important to capture in a satisfactory way the correlation among forward rates, or among forward and swap rates, can depend on the individual deal's specific terms. Trigger swaps are therefore treated in some detail in Case Study 1, not only because of their intrinsic interest, but also as a representative example of a product where it can be very difficult to tell a priori which set of state variables is more important for correct pricing.

10.2.3 Case Study 1: forward- and swap-rate volatility in the pricing of trigger swaps

I present in Case Study 1 an analysis of the simplest possible case of trigger swap, that is, the case of an up-and-in trigger swap whose barrier is monitored at a single point in time. The purpose of this Case Study is to show how, depending on the details of each trade, its present value can be affected to a different extent by several different sets of variables: sometimes swaption volatilities will have the largest impact, sometimes caplet volatilities. I will show that also the correlation between swap and forward rates can have a very different impact on the value of trigger swap, depending on the shape and level of the yield curve. Since, for the same trade, this dependence can vary over time as the yield curve evolves, the calculations below show the importance of modelling realistically the dynamics of both sets of variables.

The product description is as follows: The forward swap starting at time T, maturing at time T_{Mat} and with strike K will come to life if a particular forward rate (also referred to in the following as the 'index rate') at the same time T resets above a barrier level H. Neglecting the barrier condition, the value of the swap at time T would be

$$\mathrm{PV(Swap)} = [\mathrm{SR}(T, T_{\mathrm{Mat}}) - K]A(T, T_{\mathrm{Mat}}), \qquad (\mathrm{CS}10.1.1)$$

where $A(T, T_{\text{Mat}})$ is the time-T value of the fixed leg annuity of the swap covering the accrual periods from the swap beginning (time T) to its maturity (time T_{Mat}), and $\text{SR}(T, T_{\text{Mat}})$, also referred to in the following as the 'asset rate', is the time-T equilibrium swap rate for maturity T_{Mat}. This payoff will be received only if the index rate resets above the barrier level H.

Given this product description, let me begin by analyzing in a qualitative way the possible factors that might plausibly affect the present value of an up-and-in trigger swap. First of all, the value of the structure will clearly depend on the correlation between the asset rate and the index rate: if the index rate is positively correlated with the asset rate, the swap will come to life when it is likely to be in the money. If there is no correlation between the asset and index rates, the swap will come to life when it is just as likely to be in as out of the money. In the case of no correlation, one can therefore expect that increasing the asset volatility will create more dispersion in the possible outcomes at trigger time, but will not affect the expectation. Conversely, if the correlation is negative, when the asset (swap) rate would be out of the money, the swap itself is likely to come to life, and this should have a negative effect on the present value of the trigger swap.

Correlation and volatilities are, therefore, not important by themselves. If the correlation between the index forward rate and the asset swap rate were, say, positive, a high volatility of the asset can be expected to be beneficial. Looking at the swap in isolation, a higher asset volatility produces both higher positive and negative outcomes, and therefore has no net impact on its value. With positive correlation, however, in those states of the world where the swap would be out of the money, the index is unlikely to bring the swap to life. Because of this asymmetry between large losses and larger gains, the payoff has option-like features, and a positive correlation therefore favors conditions of high asset volatility.

Furthermore, if the barrier level is sufficiently high, what determines whether the swap comes to life at all should mainly be the volatility of the index. When this is the case, for a given correlation the asset volatility can be expected to play a much more limited role.

Finally, if the barrier is located close to the money level for the index, the volatility of the latter should have a very limited impact: a greater index volatility will increase the dispersion of the index around (approximately) the at-the-money level, but the probability of knocking the swap into life is largely unaffected.

These qualitative features can be seen more precisely in Tables 10.1–10.3, which have the index and asset volatilities horizontally and vertically respectively, and which have been produced for different correlation and barrier levels. The calculations have been carried out for a look time, T, of one year, with the index and asset rates at the initial values of 5% and with a strike of 4.5%. The (semi-annual) swap rate was assumed to have a maturity of one year, and the fixed-rate annuity, A, turned out to have the value of 0.950 01.

The pricing formula for the one-look trigger is then given by

$$\text{PV(Trigger)} = [FN(h_1) - KN(h_2)]A, \qquad (\text{CS10.1.2})$$

where F = asset (swap) rate, A = fixed leg annuity,

$$h_1 = \frac{\ln(I/H) - \frac{1}{2}\sigma_I^2 T + 2\sigma_I \sigma_A \rho_{I,A} T}{\sigma_I \sqrt{T}},$$

$$h_2 = \frac{\ln(I/H) - \frac{1}{2}\sigma_I^2 T}{\sigma_I \sqrt{T}},$$

I = drift-adjusted index rate, H = barrier level, $\rho_{I,A}$ = correlation between the asset rate and the index rate, σ_I = index volatility, σ_A = asset volatility and T = look time. (Note that, in this formula, the index rate must be drift-adjusted because of the choice of a non-'natural' numeraire.)

Using this formula the values of the trigger swap for different combinations of asset volatility, index volatility and index/asset correlation were calculated, and are presented in Tables 10.1–10.3 for three distinct cases of positive (+0.75), zero and negative (−0.75) correlation (the value of the swap has been reported in basis points). The values in bold give the barrier level, and, as mentioned above, both the index and the asset rates were assumed to be 5.00% today. For all cases the strike was assumed to be 4.5%. The volatilities of the index and of the asset are reported horizontally and vertically. Finally, Tables 10.1–10.3 contain the value of the trigger swap in basis points per unit notional.

Looking at the positive-correlation case first, it is apparent from the 8.00% barrier case that, when the barrier level is far away from the level of the index rate today, the index volatility, as surmised above, is indeed much more important than the asset volatility in determining the value of the trigger swap. The situation is reversed when the correlation is still positive, but the barrier level is at 5.00%, that is, approximately at-the-money. In this case the changes in value are almost exclusively driven by the asset volatility. In either case, as long as the correlation is positive, the present value of the trigger swap always shows a positive dependence on the asset volatility.

Moving to the zero-correlation case, one can first of all notice that the dependence on the asset volatility has now virtually disappeared. This also is in agreement with the qualitative arguments outlined above. For the zero-correlation case also the index volatility plays virtually no role when the barrier is exactly at-the-money. One can therefore have a situation – which will change dynamically over time – where the quantity of greatest importance in the modelling of the trigger swap is neither the volatility of the index nor the volatility of the asset rate, but, by far, the index/asset correlation. The zero-correlation case might not be realistic if the index and the asset belong to the same-currency yield curve, but might be of relevance for cross-currency trigger swaps.

Case 1   Asset/index correlation = 0.75. See text for a detailed description.

Barrier level	Asset vol.	Index vol.				
		14%	15%	16%	17%	18%
8.00%	14%	0.18	0.36	0.64	1.04	1.55
	15%	0.19	0.39	0.70	1.12	1.68
	16%	0.21	0.43	0.76	1.22	1.81
	17%	0.23	0.46	0.82	1.31	1.95
	18%	0.25	0.50	0.88	1.41	2.10
7.00%	14%	2.75	3.95	5.31	6.79	8.35
	15%	2.97	4.26	5.72	7.31	8.98
	16%	3.20	4.58	6.15	7.84	9.62
	17%	3.44	4.92	6.58	8.39	10.27
	18%	3.69	5.26	7.03	8.95	10.95
6.00%	14%	21.88	24.40	26.68	28.74	30.60
	15%	23.34	26.00	28.40	30.57	32.52
	16%	24.83	27.62	30.15	32.42	34.47
	17%	26.34	29.27	31.92	34.30	36.44
	18%	27.87	30.95	33.72	36.21	38.44
5.00%	14%	62.12	62.03	61.94	61.85	61.76
	15%	64.93	64.85	64.76	64.67	64.58
	16%	67.74	67.65	67.57	67.48	67.40
	17%	70.54	70.46	70.37	70.29	70.20
	18%	73.33	73.25	73.17	73.09	73.00
4.00%	14%	55.06	56.36	57.57	58.68	59.69
	15%	55.69	57.12	58.45	59.68	60.80
	16%	56.30	57.85	59.31	60.66	61.90
	17%	56.89	58.57	60.15	61.62	62.97
	18%	57.46	59.27	60.97	62.56	64.02

Finally, looking at the case of negative correlation between index and asset, one can note again that the index volatility is proportionally more important as the barrier level increases. Furthermore, increasing the asset volatility now has a negative effect on the present value of the trigger swap. In addition, a new feature appears, that is, the change in sign for the value of the structure when the barrier level goes from above to below the strike.

In the context of a LIBOR-market-model implementation, the most important conclusion that can be drawn from this Case Study is therefore that the relative importance of fitting exactly to forward-rate (index) volatilities, to swap-rate (asset) volatilities or to the correlation between the two can change substantially according to the precise terms of a deal (the level of in- or out-of-the-moneyness of the barrier, for instance). Furthermore, for a given deal,

Case 2   *Asset/index correlation = 0. See text for a detailed description.*

Barrier level	Asset vol.	Index vol.				
		14%	15%	16%	17%	18%
8.00%	14%	0.01	0.03	0.06	0.10	0.16
	15%	0.01	0.03	0.06	0.10	0.16
	16%	0.01	0.03	0.06	0.10	0.16
	17%	0.01	0.03	0.06	0.10	0.16
	18%	0.01	0.03	0.06	0.10	0.16
7.00%	14%	0.32	0.49	0.69	0.93	1.19
	15%	0.32	0.49	0.69	0.93	1.19
	16%	0.32	0.49	0.69	0.93	1.19
	17%	0.32	0.49	0.69	0.93	1.19
	18%	0.32	0.49	0.69	0.93	1.19
6.00%	14%	4.04	4.68	5.29	5.87	6.41
	15%	4.04	4.68	5.29	5.87	6.41
	16%	4.04	4.68	5.29	5.87	6.41
	17%	4.04	4.68	5.29	5.87	6.41
	18%	4.04	4.68	5.29	5.87	6.41
5.00%	14%	22.42	22.33	22.24	22.14	22.05
	15%	22.42	22.33	22.24	22.14	22.05
	16%	22.42	22.33	22.24	22.14	22.05
	17%	22.42	22.33	22.24	22.14	22.05
	18%	22.42	22.33	22.24	22.14	22.05
4.00%	14%	44.47	43.75	43.02	42.28	41.56
	15%	44.47	43.75	43.02	42.28	41.56
	16%	44.47	43.75	43.02	42.28	41.56
	17%	44.47	43.75	43.02	42.28	41.56
	18%	44.47	43.75	43.02	42.28	41.56

this relative importance can also change as time goes by and a barrier level becomes closer or more distant from the current level of the (index) forward rates. In addition, the Case Study has also made clear that reproducing a plausible correlation between forward and swap rates (index/asset correlation) can be extremely important. If one extended the study to multi-look trigger swaps, it would become apparent (see Rebonato 1998) that the forward-rate/forward-rate (index/index) correlation can also become very important. For a reliable and robust model implementation it is therefore essential to check the simultaneous plausibility of the values of all these quantities, as they are produced by the chosen model parametrization.

Case 3   *Asset/index correlation = −0.75. See text for a detailed description.*

Barrier level	Asset vol.	Index vol.				
		14%	15%	16%	17%	18%
8.00%	14%	−0.06	−0.14	−0.25	−0.41	−0.62
	15%	−0.07	−0.14	−0.26	−0.43	−0.66
	16%	−0.07	−0.15	−0.28	−0.46	−0.70
	17%	−0.08	−0.16	−0.29	−0.48	−0.74
	18%	−0.08	−0.17	−0.30	−0.51	−0.77
7.00%	14%	−1.13	−1.65	−2.24	−2.88	−3.56
	15%	−1.21	−1.76	−2.40	−3.09	−3.83
	16%	−1.28	−1.87	−2.55	−3.30	−4.09
	17%	−1.35	−1.98	−2.70	−3.49	−4.34
	18%	−1.42	−2.08	−2.84	−3.68	−4.58
6.00%	14%	−9.36	−10.38	−11.29	−12.09	−12.79
	15%	−10.16	−11.29	−12.30	−13.19	−13.98
	16%	−10.94	−12.18	−13.29	−14.27	−15.14
	17%	−11.71	−13.05	−14.26	−15.33	−16.28
	18%	−12.46	−13.91	−15.21	−16.37	−17.40
5.00%	14%	−16.70	−16.76	−16.81	−16.87	−16.93
	15%	−19.42	−19.48	−19.53	−19.59	−19.64
	16%	−22.14	−22.19	−22.24	−22.29	−22.34
	17%	−24.84	−24.89	−24.93	−24.98	−25.02
	18%	−27.53	−27.57	−27.62	−27.66	−27.70
4.00%	14%	29.90	26.81	23.86	21.08	18.49
	15%	28.69	25.41	22.30	19.38	16.65
	16%	27.46	24.00	20.72	17.64	14.79
	17%	26.20	22.56	19.11	15.89	12.89
	18%	24.91	21.09	17.48	14.10	10.98

10.2.4 Case Study 2: a two-period Bermudan swaption

In this Case Study I shall look in detail at the case of a two-period Bermudan swaption. One of the goals of this analysis is to show with the simplest non-trivial example that, even when all the market prices of the co-terminal European swaptions *and* of the underlying caplets are correctly recovered by a model, the price of the Bermudan swaption can still assume a wide range of possible values. Recovery of the prices of the 'most relevant' benchmark options, or even of European swaptions and caplets at the same time (desirable as it might appear), therefore provides no guarantee that the price for the exotic product will necessarily be 'correct'. The other goal is to provide a concrete and simple example of the pricing importance of the swap-rate and forward-rate instantaneous volatilities.

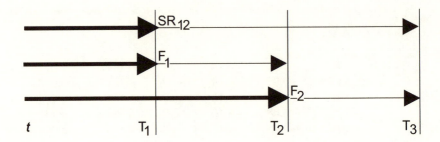

Figure CS10.2.1   *The timing of the expiries and maturities for the two forward rates. The first forward rate, expiring at time T_1, and spanning the period from time T_1 to time T_2, is labelled F_1; similarly the second forward rate, expiring at time T_2 and spanning the period from time T_2 to time T_3, is called F_2; the two-period swap rate resetting at time T_1 and maturing at time T_3 is called SR_{12}. The end of the thick arrows denote expiry times and the end of the thin arrows denote maturity times.*

Let us focus the attention on a two-period Bermudan swaption, on the two associated underlying European swaptions and on the one-period caplet expiring at the same time as the first (i.e., the two-period) European swaption. Given the simplicity of the case analyzed in this example, the second European swaption (i.e., the swaption expiring at time T_2) will simply be a caplet. These four instruments – that is, the two European swaptions, the caplet and the Bermudan swaption – therefore constitute the universe of traded security of relevance for this example.

The market provides direct information about the prices of the caplet expiring at time T_1, of the two-period European swaption also expiring at time T_1, and of the caplet (one-period swaption) expiring at time T_2; the final maturity is time T_3 (see Figure CS10.2.1). The actual times used in the calculation are shown in Table CS10.2.1, which also displays the implied Black volatilities for the two caplets and for the two-period European swaption (denoted Vol_1, Vol_2 and $\text{Vol}_{\text{Swapt}}$, respectively).

Table CS10.2.1   *The expiry times of the two caplets and of the European swaption (Exp_1, Exp_2), the tenor of each caplet and of the swap in years (Tenor), the Black and piecewise-constant volatilities for the caplets, as explained in the text (Vol_1, Vol_2, Vol_{1-01}, Vol_{2-01}, Vol_{2-12}), and the volatility of the European swaption (Vol_{Swapt}).*

Exp_1	1	Vol_1	20.00%
Exp_2	2	Vol_2	20.00%
		$\text{Vol}_{1\text{-}01}$	20.00%
Tenor	1	$\text{Vol}_{2\text{-}01}$	21.89%
FinMat	3	$\text{Vol}_{2\text{-}12}$	17.91%
		$\text{Vol}_{\text{Swapt}}$	19.00%

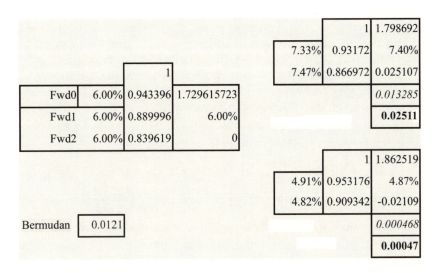

Figure CS10.2.2 *The evolution of a yield curve over two steps. See the text for details.*

Furthermore, Table CS10.2.1 displays the volatilities (assumed piecewise constant) of the first and second forward rates (F_1 and F_2) from time 0 to time T_1, and of the second forward rate from time T_1 to time T_2. These quantities are labelled $\text{Vol}_{1\text{-}01}$, $\text{Vol}_{2\text{-}01}$ and $\text{Vol}_{2\text{-}12}$. With this notation I have denoted with the first subscript the forward rate, and with the next two subscripted indices the beginning and end time of the period to which the volatility refers. So, for instance, $\text{Vol}_{2\text{-}01}$ is the volatility of the second forward rate from time T_0 to time T_1. Clearly $\text{Vol}_{1\text{-}01}$ is the same as Vol_1, since there is only one period for the first caplet. Note also that, despite the fact that the volatilities have been assumed to be constant over each period, they are not so over the life of the second forward rate, and their root-mean-square therefore does not contain all the relevant information.

As for $\text{Vol}_{2\text{-}01}$ and $\text{Vol}_{2\text{-}12}$, the relationship

$$\text{Vol}_2^2 T_2 = \text{Vol}_{2\text{-}01}^2 T_1 + \text{Vol}_{2\text{-}12}^2 (T_2 - T_1) \qquad \text{(CS10.2.1)}$$

must hold true. A particular set of values such that this relationship is satisfied is shown in Table CS10.2.1.

Figure CS10.2.2 then depicts three distinct 'blocks': the left-hand one provides information about the state of the world (i.e., about the values of the chosen state variables, in this case the forward rates) prevailing at time 0. The two blocks on the right provide the same type of information after an up and a down move of the yield curve. More precisely, starting from the left-hand side, the first block describes the initial (time-0) yield curve (flat at 6.00%), made up of a spot rate (Fwd$_0$), spanning the period from time 0 to time T_1, and two forward rates (Fwd$_1$ and Fwd$_2$), covering the periods from time T_1 to time T_2, and from time T_2 to time T_3, respectively. The column next to the forward rates displays the discount function at times 0, T_1, T_2 and T_3. With these discount factors one can calculate both the equilibrium swap rate (obviously also at 6.00%) and the fixed-leg annuity. Both these quantities are shown in the next column, together with the present value of a 6.00%-strike payer's swap (clearly zero, given the chosen strike, at time 0).

The yield curve is then assumed to evolve to an 'up' and a 'down' state, by moving the forward rates Fwd$_1$ and Fwd$_2$ according to

$$\text{Fwd}_1(T_1) = \text{Fwd}_1(0)\exp[-\tfrac{1}{2}\text{Vol}_{1\text{-}01}^2 T_1 + \mu_1 T_1 \pm \text{Vol}_{1\text{-}01}\sqrt{T_1}],$$

$$\text{Fwd}_2(T_1) = \text{Fwd}_2(0)\exp[-\tfrac{1}{2}\text{Vol}_{2\text{-}01}^2 T_1 + \mu_2 T_1 \pm \text{Vol}_{2\text{-}01}\sqrt{T_1}].$$

In this expression, μ_i ($i = 1, 2$) is the forward-rate-specific drift necessary to ensure no-arbitrage pricing given the chosen numeraire (the discretely compounded money-market account). In both states of the world, the discrete discount factors thus obtained are shown next to the forward rates, together with the fixed rate annuity, the new equilibrium swap rate and the present value in one period's time of the 6.00%-strike swap. For the sake of simplicity, the assumption has been made of a perfect correlation between the two forward rates. Therefore the up (down) move for the first is associated with probability = 1 to the up (down) move for the second. The number in italics below shows the expectation at time T_1 of the payoff of the one-period caplet expiring at time T_2 (also struck at 6.00%). This quantity is calculated using the balance of volatility, Vol$_{2\text{-}12}$ (see Equation (CS10.2.1)) as input to the Black caplet formula, with residual time to expiry equal to $(T_2 - T_1)$. Finally the cells in bold underneath represent the greater of the intrinsic value (i.e., the value of the two-period swap) and the expectation (the value of the caplet expiring at time T_2). These two quantities are finally averaged and discounted to produce the value for the Bermudan swaption in the bottom left-hand cells of the picture.

Needless to say, the particular value of 121 basis points obtained in this example depends on the particular choice for Vol$_{2\text{-}01}$ and Vol$_{2\text{-}12}$. A different 'split' of the total variance of the second forward rate between the two subperiods consistent with Equation (CS10.2.1) would, in general, have given rise to a different residual volatility for the time-T_1 caplet, a different intrinsic value, and a different Bermudan price.

If, in addition to requiring that the two caplets should be correctly priced, the constraint had also been imposed that the European swaption price should be correctly recovered, one would have had to alter the correlation between the stochastic movements of the first and second forward rates. The 'geometry' illustrated in the picture just described would therefore no longer have been appropriate. In order to recover an exogenously assigned European swaption volatility, in fact, the correlation between the forward rates could

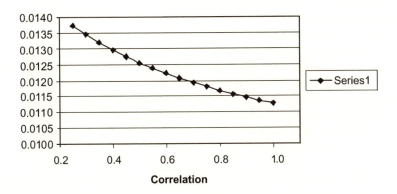

Figure CS10.2.3 *Values of the two-period Bermudan swaption as a function of the implicit correlation described in the text.*

not, in general, have been chosen to be unity, as implicitly assumed by the construction described above. This can be seen more precisely as follows (see Figure CS10.2.3).

After recalling (see, e.g., Chapter 2) that the swap rate, $SR_{1,2}$, resetting at time T_1 can be written as

$$SR_{1,2} = w_1 f_1 + w_2 f_2, \qquad (CS10.2.1)$$

let us define

$$\text{Var}(\text{Fwd}_1) = \int_0^{T_1} \text{Vol}_1^2(u)\, du = \int_0^{T_1} \text{Vol}_{1\text{-}01}^2(u)\, du$$

and

$$\text{Var}(SR_{1,2}) = \int_0^{T_1} \text{Vol}_{\text{Swapt}}^2(u)\, du,$$

and let us assume for the moment that the expression

$$\text{Vol}_{\text{Swapt}}^2 = \qquad\qquad\qquad (CS10.2.2)$$

$$\frac{w_1^2 \text{Fwd}_1^2 \text{Vol}_{1\text{-}01}^2 + w_2^2 \text{Fwd}_2^2 \text{Vol}_{2\text{-}01}^2 + 2\text{Fwd}_1 \text{Fwd}_2 w_1 w_2 \text{Vol}_{1\text{-}01} \text{Vol}_{2\text{-}01} \rho}{SR_{1,2}^2}$$

provides a good approximation for the European swaption volatility (in Equation (CS10.2.2) ρ is the correlation between the two forward rates). Why this should be the case is explained later in this chapter. The important point to notice at this stage is simply that this expression contains the quantity $\text{Vol}_{2\text{-}01}$. This quantity is not directly linked to any market observable, since it is the volatility of the second forward rate from time T_0 to time T_1, and the market provides information only about the integral of the square of this volatility from time T_0 to time T_2. We know, however, as long as one keeps the root-mean-squares associated with the quantities $\text{Var}(\text{Fwd}_1)$, $\text{Var}(\text{Fwd}_2)$ and $\text{Var}(\text{SR}_{1,2})$ equal to the respective Black implied volatilities, all the market prices (for the two caplets and for the European swaption) will be correctly recovered. In order to do so, for any chosen (piecewise-constant) correlation from time T_0 to time T_1, one can solve the quadratic Equation (CS10.2.2) for $\text{Vol}_{2\text{-}01}$. Having computed this quantity, and, by using Equation (CS10.2.1) (the balance-of-variance condition), one can then obtain the volatility of the second forward rate from time T_1 to time T_2, $\text{Vol}_{2\text{-}12}$. By so doing, all the market prices for the plain-vanilla instruments are by construction perfectly recovered. Furthermore, one can proceed to evaluate the values of the caplets in one period's time using the Black formula with the appropriate volatility as input, as described in the first part of this Case Study. This expectation can be compared with the intrinsic value, and the Bermudan value can be calculated as described above.

We have reached the conclusion that, if one imposes that the three market prices for the plain-vanilla options should be correctly recovered, there is a one-to-one relationship between the volatility of the second forward rate from time T_0 to time T_1, and the correlation ρ, and between either of these two quantities and the present value of the Bermudan swaption. This latter quantity can therefore be plotted as a function, for instance, of the correlation, which can be regarded as the only quantity it depends on if the prices for all the plain-vanilla options are to be exactly recovered. (Needless to say, the alternative viewpoint is possible: the Bermudan price could be regarded as depending exclusively on the shape of the instantaneous volatility of the second forward rate, that is, on $\text{Vol}_{2\text{-}01}$ and $\text{Vol}_{2\text{-}12}$.)

As noted at the beginning of this Case Study, one can clearly see that, even for a case as simple as this, the theoretical range of prices is quite wide (approximately 30%), and that the exact recovery of the plain-vanilla market prices is not sufficient to pin down the value of the complex product. If one knew the correlation function, clearly the ambiguity would cease to exist. Conversely, if one insisted that all the plain-vanilla instruments should be exactly priced, any choice for the volatility of the second forward rate from time T_0 to time T_1 would uniquely determine both a price for the Bermudan swaption and an 'implied' correlation. One tempting criterion in order to choose among the infinity of possible prices would be to impose that this correlation should assume a desired 'plausible' value and to let the instantaneous volatility function 'take up the slack'. Another possible route could be to require that the instantaneous volatility function should give rise to a financially justifiable future term structure of volatilities, and determine the implied correlation that prices the market correctly. Both these avenues are explored later in this chapter, but it is important to stress at this stage that, if the exact recovery of all the plain-vanilla market prices is imposed in a 'blind' fashion, either procedure can often give rise to financially unsatisfactory results.

10.2.5 The congruence between the caplet and the swaption markets revisited: relevance for relative-value trading

In Case Study 2 the 'congruence' of the caplet and swaption markets has been accepted without question. As discussed in Sections 9.3 and 10.1, in reality this assumption should not be taken for granted. More subtly, the user might, for instance, reach the conclusion that, depending on the currency, the European swaption market is, say, less liquid and/or developed than the caplet market, and its prices correspondingly less trustworthy. If this view were correct, the information from the caplet market could be deemed to contain more direct and reliable information about the dynamics of the yield curve, and a forward-rate-based approach could allow a (riskier) hedging strategy that might unlock more value from the original Bermudan swaption trade than an 'unquestioning' swap-rate-based approach. The approach just described could also be of use in a relative-value trading context. In this case neither market is assumed to be 'right'. Rather, the trader concludes that the lack of coherence between the prices of caplets and European swaptions cannot be eliminated by any plausible (as opposed to possible) choice for the input instantaneous volatilities and correlations. As a consequence, coupled long and short positions are taken in the cheap and expensive instruments, respectively, with the hedge ratio dictated by the model. The technical difficulties of such trades have already been discussed in Chapter 9. It is important to stress, however, that the trader who might want to engage in these relative-value strategies relies not only on the validity of the model used, but also on the future availability of market liquidity (see Scholes 2000). As a consequence, the trader implicitly enters an even-more-difficult-to-analyze long position in liquidity.

Whether the trader engages in a relative-value type of activity or not, she should always check the sensitivity of the model price to the 'secondary' variables, keeping the prices of the 'primary' instruments constant. If the trader had chosen a swap-rate-based implementation of the LIBOR market model, this could be achieved, for instance, by calculating the price of the exotic product (in this case the Bermudan swaption) using different parametrizations for the function describing the instantaneous volatilities of the co-terminal swap rates, whilst still recovering the correct prices of the European swaptions. Alternatively, the user could change the correlation amongst the different co-terminal swap rates, since this operation has no effect on the prices of the associated European swaptions. Furthermore, it is always advisable to check whether the 'best-compromise solution' finally arrived at provides a reasonable answer for the whole caplet/European swaption markets: one should look, that is, beyond the volatilities of the co-terminal swap rates and examine the whole swaption matrix. If the latter looked locally good, but globally implausible, the user should question very carefully whether the different underlying cap and swaption markets are trading in a congruous and coherent way, and whether the chosen model implementation is indeed plausible and believable.

The conclusion that can be drawn from the discussion in this section is that it is extremely important to ascertain the implications for the dynamics of the swap rates of a particular choice of dynamics for the forward rates, and vice versa. More precisely, once the time-dependent instantaneous volatilities and correlations of the forward rates have been specified, what can one say about the instantaneous volatilities of the corresponding co-terminal swap rates? How do the model and market prices of European swaptions compare? How are time-homogeneity constraints linked to the resulting functional form for the swap-rate instantaneous volatilities? And, from a trading perspective, the following question has great practical relevance: Once the dynamics of the forward rates in a given problem have been chosen to the trader's satisfaction (e.g., so as to recover all the prices of the corresponding caplets or so as to produce a time-homogeneous evolution for the forward-rate term structure of volatilities), is there a quick and effective way to calculate the corresponding 'implied' swaption matrix? These topics are addressed in the following sections.

10.3 Approximating the Swap-Rate Instantaneous Volatility

10.3.1 Deterministic forward-rate volatilities imply stochastic swap-rate volatilities

I analyze in this section the implication of different choices of functional forms of the forward-rate instantaneous volatility for the dynamics of the corresponding co-terminal swap rates. To this end, one can begin by conceptually placing oneself in a forward-rate-based framework. As shown in Chapter 5, the no-arbitrage evolution of the forward rates is specified by the choice of a particular functional form for the forward-rate instantaneous volatilities and for the forward-rate/forward-rate correlation function. The task at this point is to obtain the corresponding swap-rate instantaneous volatilities. If one denotes by $\sigma_{n \times m}(t)$ the percentage instantaneous volatility at time t of a swap rate expiring n years from today and maturing m years thereafter, and one recalls that a swap rate, SR, can be expressed as a function of the underlying forward rates as[4]

$$SR = \sum_i w_i f_i(t),\qquad(10.1)$$

a straightforward application of Ito's lemma gives

$$\sigma_{n \times m}^2(t) = \frac{\sum_j \sum_k [\partial SR/\partial f_j][\partial SR/\partial f_k] f_j(t) f_k(t) \rho_{jk}(t) \sigma_j(t) \sigma_k(t)}{[\sum_i w_i f_i(t)]^2},\qquad(10.2)$$

---

[4]It will be recalled from Section 2.2 that the weights w_i are given by $B_{i+1}\tau_i / \sum_{j=1}^n B_{j+1}\tau_j$, where B_{i+1} is the discount bond maturing at payment time of the ith forward rate, τ_i is the tenor of the ith forward rate and n is the number of forward rates in the swap.

where, as usual, $\sigma_j(t)$ is the time-t instantaneous volatility of log-normal forward rate j, and $\rho_{jk}(t)$ is the instantaneous correlation at time t between forward rate j and forward rate k. Looking at Equation (10.1), it is tempting to write

$$\frac{\partial \text{SR}}{\partial f_j} = w_j. \tag{10.3}$$

This is not quite correct, since the weight w_j depends on f_j. The correct expression for the derivative is presented below in Case Study 3. Since it is conceptually simple, but algebraically somewhat convoluted, for clarity of exposition I shall assume in the first part of the chapter that Equation (10.3) holds exactly. The modification of the results is totally straightforward and will be shown in Case Study 3.

Expression (10.2) shows that the instantaneous volatility at time $t > t_0$ of a swap rate is a stochastic quantity, depending as it does on the coefficients, $\{\mathbf{w}\}$, and on the future realization of the forward rates underlying the swap rate, $\{\mathbf{f}\}$. Insofar as the weights $\{\mathbf{w}\}$ are concerned, if one looks at their definition one might be tempted to claim that their volatility should be very low compared to that of the swap or forward rates, and, as such, negligible. The same argument, however, certainly cannot be made about the forward rates themselves that enter equation (10.2).

It therefore appears that, starting from a purely deterministic function of time for the instantaneous volatilities of the forward rates, one arrives at a rather complex, and stochastic, expression for the instantaneous volatility of the corresponding swap rate. In order to obtain the price of a European swaption corresponding to a given choice of forward-rate instantaneous volatilities, the trader seems to be faced with a rather difficult task. To begin with, in order to obtain the total Black volatility of a given (say, the $n \times m$) European swaption to expiry, one first has to integrate its swap-rate instantaneous volatility to the expiry of the swaption, T_n:

$$[\sigma_{n \times m}^{\text{Black}}]^2 T_n = \int_0^{T_n} \sigma_{n \times m}^2(u)\, du. \tag{10.4}$$

As Equation (10.2) shows, however, at any time u there is one such (different) swap-rate instantaneous volatility for any future realization of the forward rates from today to time u. But since every path gives rise to a particular swap-rate instantaneous volatility via the dependence on the path of the quantities $\{\mathbf{w}\}$ and $\{\mathbf{f}\}$, there seems to be no such thing as a single unique root-mean-square (Black) volatility for the swap rate. Rather, if one starts from a description of the dynamics of forward rates in terms of a deterministic volatility structure, there appears to be one Black volatility for a given swap rate associated with each and every realization of the forward rates along the path of the integral. Notice that the implications of Equation (10.2) are farther-reaching than the usual (and correct) claim that log-normal forward rates are incompatible with log-normal swap rates. By Equation (10.2) one can conclude that, starting from a purely deterministic volatility for the (logarithm of) the forward rates, the instantaneous volatility of the corresponding swap rate is a stochastic quantity, and that the quantity $\int_0^{T_n} \sigma_{n\times m}^2(u)\,du$ is a path-dependent integral that cannot be directly equated to the (path-independent) real number $[\sigma_{n\times m}^{\text{Black}}]^2 T_n$. Calculating the value of several European swaptions, or, perhaps, of the whole swaption matrix, therefore appears to be a very burdensome task, the more so if the coefficients of the forward-rate instantaneous volatilities are not given a priori but are to be optimized via a numerical search procedure so as to produce, say, the best possible fit to the swaption market.

10.3.2 The link between forward-rate and swap-rate volatilities: a first approximation

While all of the above is, strictly speaking, correct, some simple but powerful approximations are possible. In order to gain some insight into the structure of Equation (10.2), one can begin by regarding it as a weighted average of the covariance terms $\rho_{jk}(t)\sigma_j(t)\sigma_k(t)$, with (new) double weights, $\zeta_{jk}(t)$, given by[5]

$$\zeta_{jk}(t) = \frac{w_k(t)f_k(t)w_j(t)f_j(t)}{[\sum_i w_i f_i(t)]^2}. \qquad (10.5)$$

For a given point in time, and for a given realization of the forward rates, these weights are, in general, far from constant or deterministic, and their stochastic evolution is fully determined by the evolution of the forward rates. One can distinguish, however, two important cases: the first (case 1) refers to (proportionally) parallel moves in the yield curve; the second (case 2) occurs when the yield curve experiences more complex changes. One can intuitively regard the results presented in the following as pertaining to movements of the yield curve under shocks of the first principal component for case 1, or to higher principal components[6] for case 2. For the purpose of the discussion to follow, it is also important to keep in mind the typical relative magnitude of the first principal component shocks relative to the higher modes of deformation (the first eigenvalue often accounts for more than 80% of the yield-curve variability). In the first case (log-parallel moves), each individual weight is only mildly dependent on the stochastic realization of the forward rate at time t. Intuitively this can be understood by observing that each forward rate occurs both in the numerator and in the denominator of Equation (10.5). As a consequence, the effects on the weights $\{\zeta\}$ of a (reasonably small) identical change in the forward rates tend to a large extent to cancel out. This is shown in Figures 10.2–10.4 for the particular case study illustrated in Table

---

[5]If the correct expression for the derivative of the swap rate with respect to the jth forward rate were used instead of (10.3), in Equation (10.5) one would have to replace the quantity w_j in the numerator with $\partial SR/\partial f_j$. The terms w_j in the denominator remain unchanged.

[6]Since, as discussed below, the weights are approximately constant for identical proportional changes in the forward rates, the principal components should be thought of as referring to log changes.

Table 10.1 *The initial yield curve and the column of weights corresponding to the longest co-terminal swap for the European swaptions whose weights* $\{\zeta\}$ *are analyzed in Figures 10.2–10.10.*

Time	Disc	Forward (%)	Weights
0	1	5.278	
0.25	0.986976	5.747	
0.50	0.972996	6.178	
0.75	0.958196	6.572	
1.00	0.942707	6.928	
1.25	0.926657	7.246	
1.50	0.910169	7.526	
1.75	0.89336	7.768	
2.00	0.87634	7.972	0.072409
2.25	0.85922	8.138	0.070965
2.50	0.84208	8.265	0.069529
2.75	0.82504	8.355	0.068106
3.00	0.80816	8.406	0.066704
3.25	0.79152	8.419	0.065329
3.50	0.77521	8.393	0.063987
3.75	0.75928	8.329	0.062681
4.00	0.74379	8.227	0.061418
4.25	0.7288	8.087	0.060201
4.50	0.71436	7.908	0.059034
4.75	0.70051	7.692	0.05792
5.00	0.68729	7.437	0.056863
5.25	0.67474	7.144	0.055865
5.50	0.6629	6.814	0.054929
5.75	0.6518	6.445	0.054058
6.00	0.64147		

10.1. More precisely, Figure 10.2 shows the changes to which the yield curve was subjected (rigid up and down shifts by 25 basis points); Figure 10.3 displays the percentage changes in the weights $\{\zeta\}$ for the longest co-terminal swap in moving from the initial yield curve to the yield curve shocked upwards by 25 basis points. Figure 10.4 then shows the average of the percentage changes in the weights $\{\zeta\}$ corresponding to the equiprobable up and down 25 basis point shifts.[7]

For more complex changes in the shape of the yield curve, the individual weights $\{\zeta\}$ become less and less constant with increasing order of the associated principal component. In the less benign cases of tilts and bends in the

---

[7]Strictly speaking, the relative (not the absolute) up and down changes in forward rates should be identical. If their magnitude is small, there will be little difference between absolute and proportional up and down changes, and, for the sake of simplicity, the absolute case is discussed in the following.

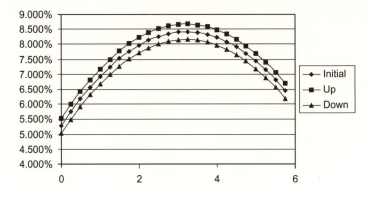

Figure 10.2   *The rigid changes in the yield curve (rigid up and down shifts by 25 basis points) used to calculate the weights in Equation (10.5).*

forward curve, the difference between the weights calculated with the initial values of the forward rates and after the yield curve move will in general be significant (see Figures 10.5, 10.6, 10.8 and 10.9). However, in these cases one

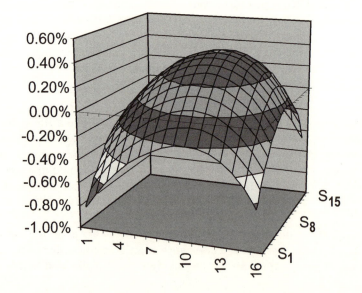

Figure 10.3   *The percentage changes in the weights $\{\zeta\}$ – see Equation (10.5) – in moving from the initial yield curve to the yield curve shocked upwards by 25 basis points.*

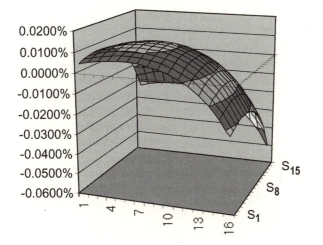

Figure 10.4 *The average of the percentage changes in the weights $\{\zeta\}$ corresponding to the equiprobable up and down shifts by 25 basis points.*

observes that the average of each individual weight corresponding to a positive and negative move of the same magnitude (clockwise and counterclockwise tilt, increased and decreased curvature) is still remarkably constant (see Figures 10.7 and 10.10). This feature, needless to say, is even more marked for the parallel movement, as shown in Figure 10.4.

These 'symmetric' deformations are important, because they are equiprobable, and one can expect that, over a very large number of realizations, each

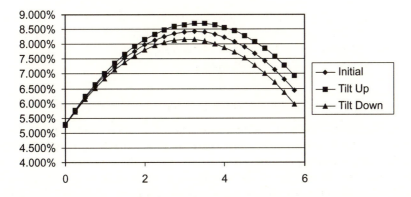

Figure 10.5 *The tilt changes in the yield curve used to calculate the weights in Equation (10.5).*

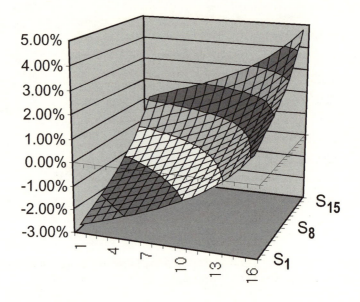

Figure 10.6 *Same as Figure 10.3 for the tilts in Figure 10.5.*

principal-component shock to the yield curve will occur, on average, with the same frequency as its own antithetic counterpart.

On the basis of these observations, we are therefore in a position to reach two simple but important conclusions:

1. To the extent that the movements in the forward curve are dominated by a first (log-parallel) principal component, the weights $\{\zeta\}$ are only very mildly dependent on the path realizations.

2. Even if higher principal components are allowed to shock the forward curve, the expectation of the future swap-rate instantaneous volatility is very close to the value obtainable by using today's values for the coefficients $\{w\}$ and the forward rates $\{f\}$.

10.3.3 Reasons for the accuracy of the approximation

The second of the statements above has wider applicability (it does not require that the forward curve should only move in parallel), but yields weaker results, only referring as it does to the average of the instantaneous volatility. Note also that the average of the weights over symmetric shocks becomes less and less equal to the original weights as the complexity of the deformation increases. On the other hand, we know that relatively few principal components

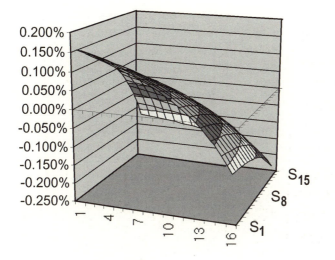

Figure 10.7   *Same as Figure 10.4 for the tilts in Figure 10.5.*

can describe the yield-curve dynamics to a high degree of accuracy. Therefore, the negative impact of a progressively poorer approximation becomes
correspondingly smaller and smaller. Given the linearity of the integration operator, which allows the user to move from instantaneous volatilities to Black
volatilities via Equation (10.4), the second conclusion can be transferred to
these latter quantities. The second conclusion above can therefore be restated

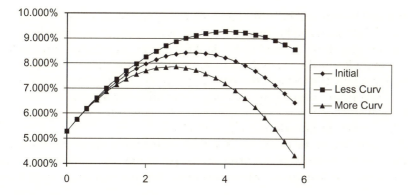

Figure 10.8   *The changes in curvature of the yield curve used to calculate the weights in Equa-*
tion (10.5).

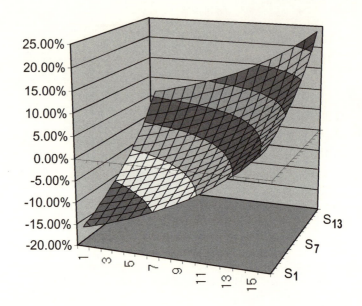

Figure 10.9   *Same as Figure 10.6 for changes in curvature of the yield curve shown in Figure 10.8.*

as:

2′. Even if higher principal components are allowed to shock the forward curve, the expectation of the average Black volatility is very close to the value obtainable by integrating the swap-rate instantaneous volatilities calculated using today's values for the coefficients $\{\mathbf{w}\}$ and the forward rates $\{\mathbf{f}\}$.

It is well known, on the other hand, that the price of an at-the-money plain-vanilla option, such as a European swaption, is to a very good approximation a linear function of its implied Black volatility.[8] Therefore it follows that, as long as one includes in the average all possible changes in shape of the forward curve in a symmetric fashion, the resulting average of the prices for the at-the-money European swaption under study obtained using the different weights, $\zeta_{jk}(t)$, will be very close to the single price obtained using the current values for $\{\mathbf{f}\}$ and $\{\mathbf{w}\}$ in Equations (10.2) and (10.4).

This conclusion, by itself, would not be sufficient to authorize the trader to quote as *the* price for the European swaption the (approximate) average over the price distribution. More precisely, the situation faced by a trader

---

[8]See, for example, Levin and Singh (1995) and Chapter 12, where this result is repeatedly made use of.

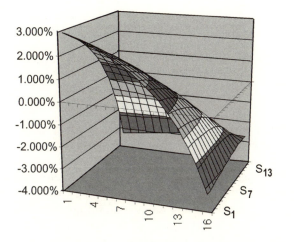

Figure 10.10 *Same as Figure 10.7 for changes in curvature of the yield curve shown in Figure 10.8.*

who uses a forward-rate-based implementation for pricing and hedging is as follows: Starting from a dynamics for the forward rates described by a deterministic volatility, a different root-mean-square volatility is obtained for each different path, and the trader obtains a distribution of swaption prices. Therefore, by engaging in a self-financing trading strategy in forward rates to hedge a swaption assuming that

1. both sets of quantities are log-normally distributed, and

2. their volatilities are simultaneously deterministic,

she will not, in general, manage to produce an exact replication of the swaption payoff by its expiry, even if the deterministic forward-rate volatilities and correlations were known perfectly. Therefore, the combined portfolio (swaption plus dynamically re-hedged holdings of forward rates) will have a finite variance (and higher moments) at expiry. Strictly speaking, the risk-averse trader will therefore not make a price simply by averaging over the final portfolio outcomes. I have shown, however, that the dispersion of the swaption prices around their average is very small. If one therefore assumes that swaptions and forward rates can have simultaneously deterministic volatilities, and makes use of the results in Rebonato (1998) about the likely impact of the joint log-normal assumption, it is possible to engage in a trading strategy that will produce, by expiry, an imperfect but 'very good' replication. In other terms, a trader who were to associate to the swaption a price significantly different from the average would have to have a utility function exceedingly sensitive to small variations in her final wealth. Therefore, taken together, statements 1 and 2 together lead one to surmise that the expression

$$\sigma_{n\times m}^2(t) = \frac{\sum_j \sum_k [(\partial SR/\partial f_j)|_0][(\partial SR/\partial f_k)|_0] f_j(0) f_k(0) \rho_{jk}(t)\sigma_j(t)\sigma_k(t)}{[\sum_i w_i f_i(0)]^2}$$

$$= \sum_j \sum_k \zeta_{jk}(t_0)\rho_{jk}(t)\sigma_j(t)\sigma_k(t) \qquad (10.6)$$

should yield a useful approximation to the instantaneous volatility of the swap rate, and, ultimately, to the European swaption price. (The notation $(\partial SR/\partial f_j)|_0$ indicates that the derivative should be taken using the time-0 yield curve.) It is essential to note that the above equation differs fundamentally from Equation (10.2) in that the weights $\zeta_{jk}(t_0)$ are no longer stochastic quantities, but are evaluated using today's known values for the forward rates and the discount factors. The empirical results presented in the following section indicate that the quality and simplicity of this approximation is such as to make it a powerful and practicable tool.

10.3.4 The link between forward-rate and swap-rate volatilities: refining the formulas

The approximation just discussed can be easily improved upon by using the correct derivative $(\partial SR/\partial f_j)|_0$ rather than its approximate value $w_j(0)$. In order not to break the logical flow too much, this useful but conceptually straightforward set of approximations (see Jaeckel and Rebonato 2001a for the algebraic details) is reported in the next Case Study, which could be skipped on a first reading.

10.3.5 Case Study 3: refining the Approximation (10.5)

The expression

$$\frac{\partial SR}{\partial f_j} = w_j \qquad (CS10.3.1)$$

was proposed in Equation (CS.10.3.1) as the derivative with respect to f_i of the swap rate given by

$$SR = g(\{f_i\}) = \sum_i w_i f_i(t). \qquad (CS10.3.2)$$

Equation (CS10.3.1) is actually correct only if one assumes that the weights $\{w\}$ are independent of the forward rates $\{f\}$. In reality (neglecting deterministic terms in dt, irrelevant for this discussion) Ito's lemma gives

$$\frac{\mathrm{dSR}}{\mathrm{SR}} = \sum_i \frac{\partial \mathrm{SR}}{\partial f_i} \frac{f_i}{\mathrm{SR}} \sigma_i \, \mathrm{d}z_i.$$

From (CS10.3.2) the partial derivatives above become

$$\frac{\partial \mathrm{SR}}{\partial f_i} = w_i + \sum_k f_k \frac{\partial w_k}{\partial f_i}. \qquad (\mathrm{CS10.3.3})$$

Given the definition

$$w_i = \frac{B_{i+1}\tau_i}{\sum_j B_{j+1}\tau_j},$$

after some algebra (see Jaeckel and Rebonato 2001a) the partial derivative can be written as

$$\frac{\partial \mathrm{SR}_i}{\partial f_k} = w'_k = \left\{ w_k + \frac{\tau_k}{A_i(1 + f_k\tau_k)} \left[X_i \frac{A_k}{A_i} - X_k \right] \right\} \mathbf{1}_{k \geq i} \qquad (\mathrm{CS10.3.4})$$

with

$$A_i = \sum_{j=1}^{n_i} B_{j+1}\tau_j,$$

$$X_i = \sum_{j=1}^{n_i} B_{j+1}f_j\tau_j.$$

(Notice that in the two definitions above the dependence on the index i comes from the summation range.)

One can therefore conclude that all the expressions obtained above can be modified in such a way as to take into account the correction term above by substituting the new weights $\{\mathbf{w}'\}$ for $\{\mathbf{w}\}$ in the numerator of Equation (10.6), and then proceeding exactly as before. In particular, the double weights $\{\zeta_{jk}\}$ now become

$$\zeta'_{jk}(t) = \frac{w'_k(t) f_k(t) w'_j(t) f_j(t)}{[\sum_i w_i f_i(t)]^2}.$$

(Notice that the $\{\mathbf{w}'\}$ only appear in the numerator.)

When the quantities $\zeta'_{jk}(t)$ are calculated, Jaeckel and Rebonato (2001a) show that the extra terms disappear if all the forward rates have the same value, and that they will make a significant contribution if the yield curve is steep (upward or downward), or, more generally, appreciably non-flat. For this reason they call the whole term the 'shape correction'. For a flat yield curve the weights $\{\mathbf{w}'\}$ will have exactly the same form as Equation (10.5). The improvements brought about by the inclusion of the more precise derivative can become significant for realistically steep yield curves (see, e.g., Table

10.4 and Figure 10.11). This is not only practically useful, but also intrinsically interesting because it shows that the limitations of the approach are due only in very small measure to the inconsistent joint assumptions of simultaneous log-normality and deterministic volatility.

10.4 Computational Results on European Swaptions

10.4.1 The model inputs to carry out the tests

The results and the arguments presented so far indicate that it is indeed plausible that the instantaneous volatility of a swap rate might be evaluated with sufficient precision by calculating the stochastic weights $\{\zeta\}$ using the initial yield curve. As usual, the proof of the pudding is in the eating, but, in order to carry out the necessary empirical comparisons between the approximate and the correct swaption prices, one needs to specify both the forward-rate instantaneous volatilities and a forward-rate correlation function, ρ_{jk}. In general, this latter function will depend both on calendar time and on the expiry time of the two forward rates. If one makes the assumptions that (i) the correlation function is time-homogeneous and (ii) it only depends on the relative 'distance' in years between the expiries of the two forward rates in question, that is, on $|T_j - T_k|$ (see Chapter 7 for a discussion of the mathematical and financial implications of these assumptions), further simplifications are possible, because the expression for the average Black volatility then becomes

$$[\sigma_{\text{Black}}^{(n\times m)}]^2 T_n = \int_0^{T_n} \sigma_{n\times m}^2(u)\,\mathrm{d}u$$

$$= \int_0^{T_n} \sum_j \sum_k \zeta_{jk}(t_0)\rho(|T_j - T_k|)\sigma_j(u)\sigma_k(u)\,\mathrm{d}u$$

$$= \sum_j \sum_k \zeta_{jk}(t_0)\rho(|T_j - T_k|) \int_0^{T_n} \sigma_j(u)\sigma_k(u)\,\mathrm{d}u. \quad (10.7)$$

(In Equation (10.7), T_n denotes the expiry of the European swaption.) This choice is particularly expedient, since, by making the correlation function depend only on the difference $|T_j - T_k|$ and not on calendar time, one can take the correlation out of the integral sign.

As for the instantaneous volatility function, if the simple yet flexible functional form discussed in Chapters 6 and 8 is chosen, that is, if $\sigma_j(t)$ is taken to be equal to

$$\sigma_j(t) = k_j\{[a + b(T_j - t)]\exp[-c(T_j - t)] + d\}, \quad (10.8)$$

then the integrals in Equation (10.7) can be easily carried out analytically,[9] and a whole swaption matrix can be calculated in under a second. The values

---

[9]See Appendix II in Chapter 6.

of a, b, c and d for the instantaneous volatility function used in the calculation were given by $a = -5.97\%$, $b = 0.1677$, $c = 0.5403$ and $d = 17.10\%$.

Given the difficulties in estimating correlation functions in a reliable and robust fashion (let alone in trying to estimate their possible time dependence), the assumption of time-homogeneity for the correlation function is rather appealing. The further assumption that $\rho_{jk} = \rho(|T_j - T_k|)$ is more difficult to defend on purely econometric grounds: it implies, for instance, that the decorrelation between, say, the front and the second forward rate should be the same as the decorrelation between the ninth and the tenth. (But see again the discussion in Section 7.5, which indicates that this choice is not, after all, as arbitrary as it might seem.) Luckily, as discussed in Section 7.1, European swaption prices turn out to be relatively insensitive to the detailed shape of the correlation function, and this assumption has been shown to produce in most cases prices for European swaptions very little different from those obtained using more complex and realistic correlation functions.

10.4.2 Description of the test

The following test was carried out:

1. First the instantaneous volatility function described above (Equation (10.7)) was used, with its parameters chosen so as to ensure a realistic and approximately time-homogeneous behavior for the evolution of the term structure of volatilities. This feature was not strictly necessary for the test, but the attempt was made to create as 'realistic' a case study as possible. In particular, the values of the vector $\{\mathbf{k}\}$ implicitly defined by Equation (10.7) were very close to unity, thereby ensuring an approximately time-homogeneous evolution of the term structure of volatilities (see the discussion in Chapters 6 and 8).

2. Given this parametrized form for the forward-rate instantaneous volatility, the instantaneous volatility of a given swap rate was obtained by using Equation (10.6). This equation was then integrated out to the expiry of the chosen European swaption. The correlation amongst the forward rates was assumed to be given by $\rho_{jk} = \exp(-\beta|T_j - T_k|)$, with $\beta = 0.1$. The value of this integral could therefore be evaluated analytically and gave the required approximate implied volatility for the chosen European swaption.

3. With this implied volatility, the corresponding approximate Black price was obtained.

4. Given the initial yield curve and the chosen instantaneous volatility function for the forward rates, an 'exact' FRA-based LIBOR-market-model Monte Carlo evaluation of the chosen European swaption price was then carried out. In the simulation the same correlation function used in the

Table 10.2   *Errors in swaption prices (quarterly, 10-year maturity) using the simple approximation [Equation (10.6)]. The table shows the 'true' (i.e., full 20-factor Monte Carlo) and approximate swaption prices obtained by inputting in the Black formula the volatility obtained by integrating Equation (10.6) for a variety of quarterly swaptions with final maturity of 10 years. The 'True price' was obtained using the Black formula. The approximation error has been expressed both in absolute terms and as a fraction of one vega, which is a good proxy for a typical bid–offer spread. Even the worst-case approximation is therefore well within bid–offer spread.*

Expiry	Swap length	True price	Approx. price	Error /vega	Absolute error
0.5	9.5	0.0284	0.0289	0.3652	0.000524
1	9	0.0345	0.0351	0.3487	0.000594
2	8	0.0389	0.0394	0.2646	0.000503
3	7	0.0384	0.0387	0.1643	0.000305
4	6	0.0356	0.0358	0.0953	0.000162
5	5	0.0314	0.0315	0.0605	0.000090
6	4	0.0265	0.0266	0.0298	0.000036
7	3	0.0208	0.0208	0.0174	0.000016
8	2	0.0144	0.0145	0.0146	0.000009
9	1	0.0074	0.0074	0.0032	−0.000001
9.5	0.5	0.0038	0.0038	0.0062	−0.000001

estimation of the approximate price was employed, and as many stochastic driving factors as forward rates in the problem were retained. This meant retaining 20 and 40 factors for the Case Studies presented below.

5. The values of the swaps that can be obtained as a by-product of the procedure were calculated separately to check against the possible presence of drift biases. The results (not shown in the following tables) indicated discrepancies from the theoretical swap prices always less than one basis point, and most of the time less than a quarter of a basis point.

6. The prices for the European swaptions obtained from the simulation and the corresponding price obtained using the approximate Equation (10.6) were then compared.

10.4.3 The results with and without the shape correction

The results obtained using this simple approximation are shown in Tables 10.2 and 10.3.

As one can see, the agreement is already very good even without using the shape correction mentioned in Case Study 3. It should also be kept in mind that, given the final maturity of the underlying swap, the tests shown in Tables 10.2 and 10.3 can be considered stress cases. Shorter underlying swaps produce even better results. However, even in the most unfavorable case, that of a

Table 10.3 *Same as Table 10.2 for semi-annual swaptions, final maturity 20 years.*

Expiry	Swap length	True price	Approx. price	Error /vega	Absolute error
1	19	0.0488	0.0510	0.7667	0.002126
2	18	0.0581	0.0561	0.6207	0.001971
4	16	0.0608	0.0595	0.3833	0.001284
6	14	0.0582	0.0575	0.2437	0.000773
8	12	0.0533	0.0528	0.1649	0.000467
10	10	0.0467	0.0464	0.1240	0.000298
12	8	0.0381	0.0380	0.0555	0.000106
14	6	0.0291	0.0291	0.0106	0.000015
16	4	0.0195	0.0195	0.0039	−0.000004
18	2	0.0099	0.0099	0.0164	0.000007

1×19 years semi-annual swaption with 38 forward rates in the underlying swap, the error from the 'simple' method is less than the typical bid–offer spread of approximately one vega. For swaptions with longer expiries, and consequently fewer forward rates in the underlying swap, the agreement quickly becomes excellent, becoming as small as 5% of one vega (or one basis point in absolute terms) for a 12×8 semi-annual swaption. The quality of the approximation is better for quarterly than for semi-annual swaptions, and is largely insensitive to the choice of the decay factor β.

An analysis of the improvement brought about by the shape correction is then displayed in Table 10.4, which reports both the case of a hypothetical flat yield curve (where the shape correction produces no improvement) and the case of a market yield curve (GBP, 10-Aug-2000), where the improvement brought about by the shape correction is noticeable. The errors from the simple and 'refined' (shape-corrected) approximations are also shown in Figure 10.11.

10.4.4 Summary of the results so far

Up to this point in the present chapter, I have provided a tool to compare the model prices of European swaptions implied by a forward-rate-based implementation of the LIBOR market model with the corresponding market prices. By using the Approximation (10.5), possibly refined as explained in Case Study 3, the trader can tell in a quick and accurate way how well the swaption matrix is reproduced by the chosen functional form for the forward-rate instantaneous volatilities and correlations. This has been accomplished as follows. The model prices of the European swaptions in the swaption matrix have been obtained by inputting the appropriate volatility in the Black formula. This volatility is given by the time integral of the swap-rate instantaneous volatility. The latter has been shown to be a stochastic (path-dependent) quan-

Table 10.4   *Comparison between the errors incurred when estimating the prices of co-terminal semi-annual European swaption prices (final maturity 20 years) when using the simple approximation in Equation (10.6) (columns labelled 'Constant'), and the approximation described in Case Study 3 (columns labelled 'ShapeCorr'), for the case of a flat (7.00%) yield curve, and for a market yield curve (GBP, 10-Aug-2000). The 'true' prices for the European swaptions were calculated using a series full-factor Monte Carlo simulation (columns labelled 'MC Price'). The value of one vega for each swaption is also provided in order to give an idea of the quality of the approximation (columns labelled 'Vega'). Note how, in the case of a flat yield curve, the simple and the shape-corrected approximations give exactly the same value.*

| Time [years] | Flat at 7% annually | | | | GBP for 10 / August / 2000 | | | |
	Constant	ShapeCorr	MC Price	Vega	Constant	ShapeCorr	MC Price	Vega
0.5	0.0257	0.0257	0.0257	0.0020	0.0242	0.0247	0.0247	0.0019
1.0	0.0347	0.0347	0.0347	0.0027	0.0327	0.0334	0.0334	0.0025
1.5	0.0404	0.0404	0.0403	0.0032	0.0380	0.0389	0.0388	0.0030
2.0	0.0443	0.0443	0.0442	0.0035	0.0415	0.0425	0.0424	0.0033
2.5	0.0470	0.0470	0.0468	0.0037	0.0440	0.0450	0.0449	0.0035
3.0	0.0489	0.0489	0.0487	0.0039	0.0456	0.0466	0.0465	0.0036
3.5	0.0502	0.0502	0.0500	0.0040	0.0467	0.0477	0.0476	0.0037
4.0	0.0511	0.0511	0.0509	0.0041	0.0473	0.0483	0.0482	0.0037
4.5	0.0515	0.0515	0.0513	0.0041	0.0476	0.0486	0.0485	0.0038
5.0	0.0517	0.0517	0.0515	0.0041	0.0476	0.0486	0.0484	0.0037
5.5	0.0516	0.0516	0.0513	0.0041	0.0474	0.0483	0.0481	0.0037
6.0	0.0512	0.0512	0.0510	0.0040	0.0469	0.0477	0.0476	0.0037
6.5	0.0507	0.0507	0.0504	0.0040	0.0463	0.0471	0.0469	0.0036
7.0	0.0499	0.0499	0.0497	0.0039	0.0455	0.0462	0.0461	0.0035
7.5	0.0490	0.0490	0.0488	0.0038	0.0445	0.0452	0.0451	0.0034
8.0	0.0480	0.0480	0.0477	0.0037	0.0435	0.0441	0.0440	0.0033
8.5	0.0468	0.0468	0.0466	0.0036	0.0423	0.0429	0.0427	0.0032
9.0	0.0455	0.0455	0.0453	0.0034	0.0410	0.0415	0.0414	0.0031
9.5	0.0441	0.0441	0.0439	0.0033	0.0396	0.0401	0.0400	0.0030
10.0	0.0426	0.0426	0.0424	0.0032	0.0382	0.0386	0.0385	0.0028
10.5	0.0411	0.0411	0.0409	0.0030	0.0366	0.0370	0.0369	0.0027
11.0	0.0394	0.0394	0.0392	0.0029	0.0351	0.0354	0.0353	0.0026
11.5	0.0377	0.0377	0.0376	0.0028	0.0334	0.0337	0.0336	0.0024
12.0	0.0360	0.0360	0.0358	0.0026	0.0317	0.0319	0.0318	0.0023
12.5	0.0341	0.0341	0.0340	0.0025	0.0300	0.0302	0.0301	0.0022
13.0	0.0323	0.0323	0.0321	0.0023	0.0283	0.0284	0.0284	0.0020
13.5	0.0304	0.0304	0.0302	0.0021	0.0265	0.0266	0.0266	0.0019
14.0	0.0284	0.0284	0.0283	0.0020	0.0248	0.0248	0.0248	0.0017
14.5	0.0264	0.0264	0.0263	0.0018	0.0229	0.0230	0.0230	0.0016
15.0	0.0244	0.0244	0.0243	0.0017	0.0211	0.0212	0.0211	0.0014
15.5	0.0223	0.0223	0.0223	0.0015	0.0193	0.0193	0.0193	0.0013
16.0	0.0202	0.0202	0.0202	0.0014	0.0175	0.0175	0.0175	0.0012
16.5	0.0181	0.0181	0.0181	0.0012	0.0157	0.0157	0.0157	0.0010
17.0	0.0160	0.0160	0.0159	0.0010	0.0138	0.0138	0.0138	0.0009
17.5	0.0138	0.0138	0.0138	0.0009	0.0119	0.0120	0.0119	0.0008
18.0	0.0116	0.0116	0.0116	0.0007	0.0101	0.0101	0.0101	0.0006
18.5	0.0094	0.0094	0.0094	0.0006	0.0081	0.0081	0.0081	0.0005
19.0	0.0071	0.0071	0.0071	0.0004	0.0061	0.0061	0.0061	0.0004
19.5	0.0048	0.0048	0.0048	0.0003	0.0042	0.0042	0.0041	0.0002
20.0	0.0024	0.0024	0.0024	0.0001	0.0021	0.0021	0.0021	0.0001

tity. This would appear to make the evaluation of the prices of several swaptions (or of the whole swaption matrix) a very demanding task. A set of simple but accurate approximations, and a justification for their use, have therefore been provided. Together, they allow the quick computation of the instanta-

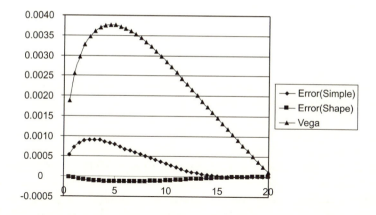

Figure 10.11   *The absolute errors incurred when calculating the prices of a set of semi-annual co-terminal European swaptions using Equation (10.6) [curve labelled 'Error(Simple)'] or equations (CS10.3.3) and (CS10.3.4) [curve labelled 'Error(Shape)']. The yield curve was taken to be the market curve observed for GBP, 10-Aug-2000. In order to give a feel for the quality of the approximation, the vega of the underlying European swaptions is also shown (curve labelled 'Vega'), and can be taken as a proxy for the typical bid–offer spread. (The help with computations carried out by Peter Jaeckel is gratefully acknowledged.)*

neous volatilities, the average volatilities and the desired European swaption prices analytically from quantities known today. A full swaption matrix can therefore be obtained in under a second.

10.4.5 From the estimation to the choice of the swap-rate volatilities

The results presented so far simply indicate how to 'deduce' the prices of European swaptions given the volatilities of, and the correlation among, the forward rates. The issue of how the parameters of the forward-rate instantaneous volatility function should be chosen is assumed to have been separately resolved to the trader's liking. The approach described in Section 8.3, in particular, might have been followed in arriving at the best choice. More precisely, the trader could be interested in obtaining the best fit to the overall swaption matrix while pricing the caplets exactly. This would be appropriate if she were pricing a complex product mainly dependent on, and hedged with, caplet volatility, such as, for instance, a high-barrier up-and-in trigger swap. In order to obtain the best fit, one can first optimize iteratively over the parameters so as to find the set $\{\hat{a}, \hat{b}, \hat{c}, \hat{d}\}$ (or $\{\hat{a}, \hat{b}, \hat{c}, \hat{d}; \hat{\beta}\}$) that best accounts for the swaption matrix. After this solution is found, perfect pricing of the caplets can be obtained via the normalization vector $\{\hat{k}\}$, as described in Chapter 8. If the vector $\{\hat{k}\}$ needed to price the caplets exactly with the parameters found by best-fitting to the swaption matrix were significantly non-constant, one would be led to choose between the following logical alternatives:

(i) either the chosen functional form for the instantaneous volatilities of the forward rates and/or their correlation is inadequate;

(ii) or the caplet and swaption market display a low degree of congruence (see the discussion in Section 9.1).

An alternative way of using the results presented so far would be the recovery of the prices of European swaptions exactly (while still working in a forward-rate-based version of the LIBOR market model), and the simultaneous recovery of the caplet prices as best as possible. The pricing and hedging of a Bermudan swaption would be a product for which this approach is particularly appropriate. This second case is treated in detail in Sections 10.8–10.10.

With this task in mind, in the next section I intend to show how one can achieve a virtually exact calibration of a forward-rate-based implementation of the LIBOR market model to a set of co-terminal swaption prices, in such a way that the European swaption prices are (almost) exactly recovered, and a desired forward-rate/forward-rate covariance matrix is approximated as well as possible. Unlike the case of the best fit to a whole swaption matrix, I will show how the calibration to a set of co-terminal European swaptions can be achieved by simple matrix algebra and without using any numerical search procedure. These results are then applied in the following section to the detailed analysis of Bermudan swaptions.

10.5 Calibration to Co-Terminal European Swaption Prices

The main result obtained so far in this chapter is that one is justified in assuming that, as long as one is interested in the price of plain-vanilla European swaptions, the weights, $\zeta_{jk}(t)$, introduced in Equation (10.5), can be effectively approximated by neglecting their stochastic nature, and they can be calculated using today's yield curve. This result is used in this section in order to achieve the calibration of a forward-rate-based implementation to the co-terminal European swaption prices underlying a given Bermudan swaption in such a way that the forward-rate dynamics is as close as possible to a desired ('target') one.

10.5.1 Restating the problem in vector form

In order to move from the estimation to the choice of the swap-rate volatilities, one can begin by rewriting Equation (10.5) in matrix form, that is,

$$\underbrace{\mathbf{SR}}_{[m\times 1]} = \underbrace{\mathbf{w}}_{[m\times m]}\ \underbrace{\mathbf{f}}_{[m\times 1]}$$

where the vector **SR** contains the m co-terminal swap rates, the vector **f** represents the underlying forward rates (i.e., the forward rates in the longest co-terminal swap) and the $m \times m$ matrix **w** contains the weights

$$
\mathbf{w} = \begin{pmatrix}
w_{11} & w_{12} & w_{13} & \cdots & w_{1m} \\
0 & w_{22} & w_{23} & \cdots & w_{2m} \\
0 & 0 & w_{33} & \cdots & w_{3m} \\
\vdots & \vdots & \vdots & \ddots & \vdots \\
0 & 0 & 0 & \cdots & 1
\end{pmatrix}
$$

More precisely, the element w_{ij} represents the weight of the jth forward rate in the average (Equation (CS10.3.2)) that produces the ith co-terminal swap rate. Notice that the mth co-terminal swap rate coincides with the mth forward rate: therefore $w_{mm} = 1$. See Figure 10.1 for the case $m = 6$.

If a joint log-normal assumption is made for the forward rates and the swap rates, one can write

$$
\frac{\mathrm{d}f_r}{f_r} = \mu_{f_r}\,\mathrm{d}t + \sigma_{f_r}\,\mathrm{d}z_r^f, \tag{10.9}
$$

$$
\frac{\mathrm{d}\mathrm{SR}_i}{\mathrm{SR}_i} = \mu_{\mathrm{SR}_i}\,\mathrm{d}t + \sigma_{\mathrm{SR}_i}\,\mathrm{d}z_i^{SR}. \tag{10.10}
$$

In this expression σ_{f_r} and σ_{SR_i} denote the instantaneous volatility for forward rate r and swap rate i, respectively. Since the assumption of joint log-normality for a given swap rate and the underlying forward rates is incorrect, and so is the assumption that the forward-rate and swap-rate volatilities can be assumed to be simultaneously deterministic, the validity of the results presented in this section hinges on the accuracy of the approximations discussed in Sections 10.3 and 10.4. Note also that, at this stage, we have not chosen the Brownian increments to be independent, that is, with hopefully obvious notation,

$$
E[\mathrm{d}z_i^f\,\mathrm{d}z_j^f] = \rho_{ij}^f\,\mathrm{d}t
$$

and, similarly,

$$
E[\mathrm{d}z_i^{\mathrm{SR}}\,\mathrm{d}z_j^{\mathrm{SR}}] = \rho_{ij}^{\mathrm{SR}}\,\mathrm{d}t.
$$

10.5.2 Calibration of the swap-rate covariance matrix

Let us evaluate the instantaneous covariance between two generic swap rates, say, the ith and the jth, belonging to the same co-terminal set. Using the approximations and the definitions introduced in this chapter (and neglecting drifts as usual) we can write

$$E\left[\frac{\mathrm{dSR}_i}{\mathrm{SR}_i}\frac{\mathrm{dSR}_j}{\mathrm{SR}_j}\right] = E\left[\frac{\sum_{r=1}^{n_i} w_{ir}\,\mathrm{d}f_r}{\sum_{r=1}^{n_i} w_{ir}f_r}\frac{\sum_{r=1}^{n_j} w_{jr}\,\mathrm{d}f_r}{\sum_{r=1}^{n_j} w_{jr}f_r}\right]$$

$$= E\left[\frac{\sum_{r=1}^{n_i} w_{ir}f_r\sigma_r^f\,\mathrm{d}z_r^f}{\sum_{r=1}^{n_i} w_{ir}f_r}\frac{\sum_{s=1}^{n_j} w_{js}f_s\sigma_s^f\,\mathrm{d}z_s^f}{\sum_{s=1}^{n_j} w_{js}f_s}\right]$$

$$= \frac{\sum_{r=1}^{n_i} w_{ir}f_r\sigma_r^f\sum_{s=1}^{n_j} w_{js}f_s\sigma_s^f\rho_{rs}^f}{\sum_{r=1}^{n_i} w_{ir}f_r\sum_{s=1}^{n_j} w_{js}f_s},$$

where n_i is the number of forward rates in the ith swap and, to obtain the last line, use has been made of the usual Ito's differentiation rules symbolically expressed as $E[\mathrm{d}z_r^f\,\mathrm{d}t] = 0$ and $E[\mathrm{d}z_r\,\mathrm{d}z_s] = \rho_{rs}^f$.

It is easy to recognize that the quantities

$$\frac{w_{ir}f_r}{\sum_{r=1}^{n_i} w_{ir}f_r}$$

are linked to the quantities ζ_{rs}^i introduced before (Equation (10.5)); namely

$$\zeta_{rs}^i = \zeta_r^i\zeta_s^i$$

with

$$\zeta_r^i = \frac{w_{ir}f_r}{\sum_{r=1}^{n_i} w_{ir}f_r}.$$

(In order to avoid the proliferation of symbols, a slight abuse of notation has been employed, by using the same symbol, ζ, for different but related quantities, and by distinguishing them by the number of subscripts. Note also that the superscript i, present in the equation above but absent in Equation (5), simply identifies the swap rate.)

With this definition one can write more concisely

$$\mathrm{cov}\left[\frac{\mathrm{d\mathbf{SR}}}{\mathbf{SR}}\right] = E\left[\frac{\mathrm{dSR}_i}{\mathrm{SR}_i}\frac{\mathrm{dSR}_j}{\mathrm{SR}_j}\right] = \sum_{r=1}^{n_i}\sum_{s=1}^{n_j}\zeta_r^i\zeta_s^j\sigma_r^f\sigma_s^f\rho_{rs}^f \qquad (10.11)$$

or, in matrix form,

$$\mathrm{cov}\left[\frac{\mathrm{d\mathbf{SR}}}{\mathbf{SR}}\right] = \mathbf{Z}\,\mathbf{S}^f\boldsymbol{\beta}^f(\boldsymbol{\beta}^f)^{\mathrm{T}}(\mathbf{S}^f)^{\mathrm{T}}\mathbf{Z}^{\mathrm{T}}, \qquad (10.12)$$

where the superscript 'T' indicates the transpose of a matrix, $\mathbf{Z}$ is the $n \times n$ matrix containing the weights $\{\zeta\}$, n is the number of co-terminal swaps, $\mathbf{S}^f$ is the $n \times n$ diagonal matrix containing on the main diagonal the instantaneous volatility of the different forward rates, σ_r^f $(1 \leq r \leq n)$, that is,

$$
\mathbf{S}^f \equiv \begin{pmatrix}
\sigma_1^f & 0 & 0 & \cdots & 0 \\
0 & \sigma_2^f & 0 & \cdots & 0 \\
0 & 0 & \sigma_3^f & \cdots & 0 \\
\vdots & \vdots & \vdots & \ddots & \vdots \\
0 & 0 & 0 & \cdots & \sigma_n^f
\end{pmatrix}
$$

and

$$
\boldsymbol{\beta}^f (\boldsymbol{\beta}^f)^{\mathrm{T}} = \boldsymbol{\rho}^f. \tag{10.13}
$$

Notice that the matrix $\boldsymbol{\beta}^f$ is not uniquely defined by Equation (10.13). We will obtain explicitly the components of $\boldsymbol{\beta}^f$ in the following.

10.5.3 Calculation of the forward-rate covariance matrix

In order to establish the correspondence between the swap-rate/swap-rate covariance matrix and the forward-rate/forward-rate covariance matrix, it is useful to rewrite the equations that translate the log-normal character of the forward and swap rates in terms of orthogonal Brownian increments (denoted by $\mathrm{d}\widehat{\mathbf{Z}}$ in the rest of this section[10]). For maximum generality, I shall retain as many factors, m, as forward rates, n_i. Also, I neglect in the following the drift terms stemming from the no-arbitrage conditions, since the terms in $\mathrm{d}t$ will prove irrelevant for the computation of the covariances. Once these choices have been made one can write

$$
\frac{\mathrm{d}f_r}{f_r} = \sum_{m=1}^{n_i} \sigma_{rm}^f \, \mathrm{d}\widehat{Z}_m \qquad 1 \leq r \leq n_i. \tag{10.14}
$$

In matrix form this can be written[11]

$$
\frac{\mathrm{d}\mathbf{f}}{\mathbf{f}} = \boldsymbol{\sigma}^f \, \mathrm{d}\widehat{\mathbf{Z}},
$$

with

$$
\boldsymbol{\sigma}^f = \begin{pmatrix}
\sigma_{11}^f & \sigma_{12}^f & \sigma_{13}^f & \cdots & \sigma_{1n}^f \\
\sigma_{21}^f & \sigma_{22}^f & \sigma_{23}^f & \cdots & \sigma_{2n}^f \\
\sigma_{31}^f & \sigma_{32}^f & \sigma_{33}^f & \cdots & \sigma_{3n}^f \\
\vdots & \vdots & \vdots & \ddots & \vdots \\
\sigma_{n1}^f & \sigma_{n2}^f & \sigma_{n3}^f & \cdots & \sigma_{nn}^f
\end{pmatrix}.
$$

---

[10]A remark on notation: because of the proliferation of symbols, and to avoid confusion with the matrix of weights $\mathbf{Z}$, in this section a vector of orthogonal Brownian motions is denoted by $\widehat{\mathbf{Z}}$.

[11]As elsewhere in this book, in order to keep notation simple, the division operator must be understood to act term by term on the elements of a vector: so, $[\mathrm{d}f/f] = [\mathrm{d}f_1/f_1, \mathrm{d}f_2/f_2, \ldots, \mathrm{d}f_n/f_n]$.

Let us now divide and multiply each term in Equation (10.14) by the quantity

$$\sqrt{\sum_{m=1}^{n_i} [\sigma_{rm}^f]^2}.$$

By so doing one can write

$$\frac{\mathrm{d}f_r}{f_r} = \sqrt{\sum_{m=1}^{n_i} [\sigma_{rm}^f]^2} \sum_{m=1}^{n_i} \frac{\sigma_{rm}^f}{\sqrt{\sum_{m=1}^{n_i} [\sigma_{rm}^f]^2}} \, \mathrm{d}\widehat{Z}_m.$$

However, given the orthogonality of the increments $\mathrm{d}\widehat{Z}_m$,

$$\sqrt{\sum_{m=1}^{n_i} [\sigma_{rm}^f]^2} = \sigma_r^f. \qquad (10.15)$$

Therefore, if one defines

$$\frac{\sigma_{rm}^f}{\sqrt{\sum_{m=1}^{n_i} [\sigma_{rm}^f]^2}} \equiv b_{rm}^f, \qquad (10.16)$$

one can rewrite Equation (10.14) as

$$\frac{\mathrm{d}f_r}{f_r} = \sigma_r^f \sum_{m=1}^{n_i} b_{rm}^f \, \mathrm{d}\widehat{Z}_m.$$

If one now defines by $\mathbf{B}^f$ the $n \times n$ matrix containing the elements $\{b_{rm}^f\}$ from Equation (10.16) and makes use of the definition of the $\mathbf{S}^f$ matrix presented above, one can write

$$\underbrace{\frac{\mathrm{d}\mathbf{f}}{\mathbf{f}}}_{[n\times 1]} = \underbrace{\mathbf{S}^f}_{[n\times n]} \underbrace{\mathbf{B}^f}_{[n\times n]} \underbrace{\mathrm{d}\widehat{\mathbf{Z}}}_{[n\times 1]} \qquad (10.17)$$

Equation (10.17) expresses in a convenient matrix form the stochastic part of the dynamics of the forward rates.

10.5.4 The link between the swap-rate and the forward-rate covariance matrix

Exactly the same reasoning could have been applied to swap rates rather than forward rates. In the notation above, the superscript 'f' would simply have to be replaced by 'SR'. Notice that, since one set of variables (say, the swap rates) can be exactly expressed as a function of the other set (say, the forward rates), exactly the same orthogonal Brownian increments shock both sets of quantities. The only quantities that change in moving from forward to swap rates are the loadings $\{b^f_{rm}\}$ and $\{b^{SR}_{jm}\}$. Therefore Expression (10.17) can be rewritten by inspection as

$$\frac{d\mathbf{SR}}{\mathbf{SR}} = \mathbf{S}^{SR}\,\mathbf{B}^{SR}\,d\widehat{\mathbf{Z}},$$

where $d\widehat{\mathbf{Z}}$ is the vector of increments of the same orthogonal Brownian motions that affect the forward rates. From this, the swap-rate/swap-rate covariance matrix can be written as

$$\mathrm{cov}\left[\frac{d\mathbf{SR}}{\mathbf{SR}}\right] = \mathbf{S}^{SR}\,\mathbf{B}^{SR}(\mathbf{B}^{SR})^{T}(\mathbf{S}^{SR})^{T},$$

where use has been made of the fact that $d\widehat{\mathbf{Z}}\,d\widehat{\mathbf{Z}}^{T} = \mathbf{I}$.

Equating this expression with the equation previously obtained for the swap-rate/swap-rate covariance matrix in terms of forward-rate volatilities and correlation (Equation (10.12)), one can write

$$\mathbf{S}^{SR}\,\mathbf{B}^{SR}(\mathbf{B}^{SR})^{T}(\mathbf{S}^{SR})^{T} = \mathbf{Z}\,\mathbf{S}^{f}\boldsymbol{\beta}^{f}(\boldsymbol{\beta}^{f})^{T}(\mathbf{S}^{f})^{T}\mathbf{Z}^{T}$$

(Recall that $\mathbf{Z}$ is the matrix containing the weights $\zeta^i_{jk}(t)$). However, from the definitions above, and by direct calculation, one can easily see that $\mathbf{B}^f(\mathbf{B}^f)^T = \rho^f$, and therefore $\mathbf{B}^f = \boldsymbol{\beta}^f$. Putting all the pieces together, it therefore follows that

$$\mathrm{cov}\left[\frac{d\mathbf{SR}}{\mathbf{SR}}\right] = \sigma^{SR}(\sigma^{SR})^{T}, \tag{10.18}$$

$$\mathrm{cov}\left[\frac{d\mathbf{f}}{\mathbf{f}}\right] = \sigma^{f}(\sigma^{f})^{T}, \tag{10.19}$$

$$\sigma^{SR}(\sigma^{SR})^{T} = \mathbf{Z}\sigma^{f}(\sigma^{f})^{T}\mathbf{Z}^{T}, \tag{10.20}$$

$$\sigma^{f}(\sigma^{f})^{T} = \mathbf{Z}^{-1}\sigma^{SR}(\sigma^{SR})^{T}(\mathbf{Z}^{T})^{-1}. \tag{10.21}$$

In the equations above σ^{SR} is the exact equivalent for the co-terminal swap rates of the matrix σ^f for forward rates. These results give the elements of the (instantaneous) covariance matrix between co-terminal swap rates in terms of the weights, $\{\zeta\}$ and of the elements of the (instantaneous) covariance matrix between forward rates. These relationships allow the direct translation from the stochastic dynamics of one set of variables (say, forward rates) to the complementary set (swap rates). The crucial assumption underpinning these results is that the quantities $\mathbf{Z}$ can be treated as constants while performing the expectations. Sections 10.3 and 10.4 have shown why and to what extent this can be justified. Given the very good quality of these approximations, Equations (10.18)–(10.21) then provide tools for evolving forward rates in such a way that an arbitrary set of market values for the corresponding co-terminal swaptions is (almost) exactly recovered. The details of the procedure are given in the following section, which deals with the problem of the valuation of Bermudan swaptions and of the calibration to the associated European swaptions. The important point to stress, however, is that it will become apparent that the almost exact recovery of the European swaptions prices by evolving forward rather than swap rates can be achieved in an infinity of ways. To each of these possible solutions there will correspond a different dynamic for the forward and swap rates. I will supply criteria to choose between these possible solutions on the basis of financial judgement. Producing the forward-rate dynamics capable of reflecting as accurately as possible a set of user-defined financial desiderata will be shown to be closely linked to specifying the forward-rate instantaneous volatility functions. If these are parametrized, perhaps as described in Chapter 6, the ability to perform a numerical search in this parameter space under the constraint of the correct recovery of the European swaption prices will hinge crucially on the availability of quick and efficient 'translation rules' such as the ones in Equations (10.18)–(10.21). How this can be accomplished is presented in detail in the next section.

10.6 An Application: Using an FRA-Based LIBOR Market Model for Bermudan Swaptions

10.6.1 Making use of the link between the covariance matrices for calibration

In order to see how the results presented above can be profitably used in practice, one can turn to the task of producing a calibration of the LIBOR market model suitable for the evaluation of Bermudan swaptions. As discussed above, the first and most important desideratum is, of course, the exact recovery of the prices of the co-terminal European swaptions. However, many specifications of the swap-rate instantaneous volatility functions can produce this result, and yet give rise to significantly different prices for the underlying Bermudan swaption. This is exactly what has been shown in detail with Case Study 2. It is therefore essential to ensure that, given the correct pricing of the European swaptions, the resulting forward-rate dynamics should be as realistic and convincing as possible: the prices of the caplets are of course important, but the implied forward-rate/forward-rate, forward-rate/swap-rate and swap-rate/swap-rate correlations also play a significant role. This is exactly where the links established above become useful. The task of ensuring an acceptable overall description of the forward-rate dynamics while pricing the European swaptions correctly can in fact be accomplished as follows. To begin with, from the market values of European swaptions one can choose a set of instantaneous volatilities for the swap rates, $\sigma_i^{\mathrm{SR}}(t)$, such that their root-mean-squares fit the market (see Equation (10.4)). After choosing the number s of orthogonal factors, one can write[12]

$$\frac{\mathrm{dSR}_i}{\mathrm{SR}_i} = \mu_i^{\mathrm{SR}}\,\mathrm{d}t + \sigma_i^{\mathrm{SR}}\,\mathrm{d}w_i = \mu_i^{\mathrm{SR}}\,\mathrm{d}t + \sum_{r=1}^{s}\sigma_{ir}^{\mathrm{SR}}\,\mathrm{d}z_r.$$

Making use for the dynamics of the swap rates of the third formulation discussed in Chapter 3, this can be rewritten as

$$\frac{\mathrm{dSR}_i}{\mathrm{SR}_i} = \mu_i^{\mathrm{SR}}\,\mathrm{d}t + \sigma_i^{\mathrm{SR}}\sum_{r=1}^{s} b_{ir}^{\mathrm{SR}}\,\mathrm{d}z_r$$

with

$$\sum_{r=1}^{s}[b_{ir}^{\mathrm{SR}}]^2 = 1. \tag{10.22}$$

As shown in Chapter 9, constraint (10.22) can always be satisfied if one chooses the coefficients $\{\mathbf{b}\}$ to be such that

$$b_{ik}^{\mathrm{SR}}(t) = \begin{cases} \cos[\theta_{ik}(t)]\prod_{j=1}^{k-1}\sin[\theta_{ij}(t)], & k = 1,\ldots,s-1, \\ \prod_{j=1}^{k-1}\sin[\theta_{ij}(t)], & k = s. \end{cases} \tag{10.23}$$

For any choice of these angles $\{\boldsymbol{\theta}\}$, all the swap-rate instantaneous volatilities are exactly recovered and, therefore, the co-terminal European swaptions are always perfectly priced. Each choice of angles will uniquely determine not only the covariance matrix of the swap rates, but also of the forward rates (and therefore the caplet prices and the forward-rate/forward-rate correlation matrix). The latter dependence, however, is rather implicit and opaque. How can it be made more transparent?

For s factors, $(s-1)$ vectors, each made up of n angles, will 'contain' the quantities $\{b_{ik}\}$. As in Chapter 9, one can begin by choosing the angle vectors at random. This will produce a correlation matrix $\mathbf{B}\,\mathbf{B}^{\mathrm{T}}$, and, in conjunction with the chosen instantaneous volatility function, a matrix $\boldsymbol{\sigma}^{\mathrm{SR}}$. By making use of Equation (10.18), from this one can calculate the covariance matrix between swap rates as

$$\mathrm{cov}\left[\frac{\mathrm{d}\mathbf{SR}}{\mathbf{SR}}\right] = \boldsymbol{\sigma}^{\mathrm{SR}}(\boldsymbol{\sigma}^{\mathrm{SR}})^{\mathrm{T}}.$$

The covariance matrix between the forward rates as a function of these initial random angles can be written using Equations (10.16) and (10.18) as

$$\mathrm{cov}\left[\frac{\mathrm{d}\mathbf{f}}{\mathbf{f}}\right] = \boldsymbol{\sigma}^f(\boldsymbol{\sigma}^f)^{\mathrm{T}} = \mathbf{Z}^{-1}\boldsymbol{\sigma}^{\mathrm{SR}}(\boldsymbol{\sigma}^{\mathrm{SR}})^{\mathrm{T}}(\mathbf{Z}^{\mathrm{T}})^{-1}. \tag{10.24}$$

---

[12]I have reverted in this section to the standard notation used elsewhere in this book: increments of orthogonal Brownian motions are denoted again by $\mathrm{d}z_i(t)$.

By making use of this relationship, and by carrying out just a few matrix operations, one can therefore immediately obtain the forward-rate/forward-rate covariance matrix as a function of the initial (possibly random) choice for the angles $\{\theta\}$. In particular, the elements on the main diagonal are directly linked to the caplet volatilities, and allow, after integration over time, direct comparison with market observables. More generally, one can extract both the instantaneous volatilities of, and the correlation among, the forward rates, and appraise their financial desirability. If this were found wanting, one could iteratively vary the angles (which had originally been chosen at random) by requiring that the discrepancies between a desired forward/forward (instantaneous) covariance matrix and $\mathbf{Z}^{-1}\sigma^{\mathrm{SR}}(\sigma^{\mathrm{SR}})^{\mathrm{T}}(\mathbf{Z}^{\mathrm{T}})^{-1}$ should be as small as possible. Clearly the optimization can be carried out either over the whole covariance matrix or over specific portions thereof. For instance, minimizing the errors in the trace of $\sigma^{f}(\sigma^{f})^{\mathrm{T}}$ ensures the correct instantaneous volatility of the various forward rates and, ultimately, the best possible pricing of the various caplets consistent with the (almost) exact recovery of the European swaption prices. Therefore, all the underlying caplets or the forward-rate/forward-rate covariance matrix are obtained as best as possible under the constraint that all the co-terminal European swaptions should at the same time be priced correctly. Furthermore, once the volatilities of the forward rates have been obtained, the volatilities of swaptions other than the co-terminal ones can be easily obtained, as long as their expiries and maturities are bracketed by the expiry and maturity of the longest co-terminal ones. See, in this respect, the interesting analysis in Dodds (2002).

In order to illustrate the procedure more precisely I analyze in Case Study 4 the stylized case of a forward-rate implementation with constant (time-independent) instantaneous volatilities. More realistic numerical experiments that illustrate the quality of the approximations and the practical applicability of the approach are presented in the following and last section of this chapter.

10.6.2 Case Study 4: recovering swap-rate volatilities while fitting to the FRA covariance matrix

In order to illustrate in detail the procedure outlined in the previous section, the case is considered of a semi-annual Bermudan swaption, with which five forward rates and five co-terminal European swaptions are associated. The swap- and forward-rate Black volatilities are assumed to be exogenously available from the market. They are displayed in the columns 'VolFRA' and 'Vol-Swap' in Table CS10.4.1. The five semi-annual forward rates and the spot rate are shown in the column labelled 'FwdRates'. The column 'SwapRates' contains the various co-terminal swap rates; the first entry is the (spot) swap rate from today to the final maturity. The contents of the other columns should be obvious from the labelling. For simplicity, the instantaneous volatilities of the forward rates have been assumed in this case study to be constant (i.e., maturity-dependent but time-independent).

Table CS10.4.1 *The inputs to Case Study 4. The columns labelled 'VolFRA' and 'VolSwap' give the market implied Black volatilities for the caplets and the co-terminal swaptions, respectively. See the text for a description of the labelling of the other columns.*

Time	FwdRates (%)	Discount	SwapRates (%)	VolFRA (%)	VolSwap (%)
0	6.00	1	6.456		
0.5	6.25	0.970 873 786	6.557	20.00	18.31
1	6.50	0.941 453 369	6.640	22.00	18.68
1.5	6.65	0.911 819 243	6.689	20.00	18.21
2	6.70	0.882 476 887	6.710	19.00	18.19
2.5	6.72	0.853 872 169	6.720	18.50	18.50
3		0.826 114 715			

The purpose of the exercise is to produce an (almost) exact recovery of the swap-rate volatilities while, at the same time, producing the 'best' possible fit to selected portions of the forward-rate/forward-rate covariance matrix. I intend to highlight how different choices for the optimization target (e.g., caplets versus the whole matrix) can give rise to significantly different solutions.

Following the procedure described in Section 6.1, the angles $\{\theta\}$ were first varied in such a way as to produce the best possible fit to the trace of $\sigma^f(\sigma^f)^{\mathrm{T}}$ by making use of the trigonometric relationships (10.23) and of Equations (10.18)–(10.21). The usual functional form for the correlation function, that is, $\rho_{ij} = \exp(-\beta|T_i - T_j|)$, with $\beta = 0.1$, was chosen for the exercise. Given the assumption of constant instantaneous volatility, imposing the best fit to the trace of the matrix $\sigma^f(\sigma^f)^{\mathrm{T}}$ is automatically equivalent to ensuring the best possible fit to the caplet prices. Indeed, after varying over the angles, the resulting fit to the caplet prices turned out to be virtually perfect, as shown in Table CS10.4.2.

With the angles so obtained, one can then examine the resulting forward-rate and swap-rate matrices. A cross-section of these matrices is shown in Figures CS10.4.1 and CS10.4.2. It is apparent that, by 'forcing' the fit to a specific portion of the covariance matrix (i.e., to its main diagonal), both the

Table CS10.4.2 *Target and model caplet prices when the optimization over the angular coefficients $\{\theta\}$ was carried out so as to obtain the best possible fit to the trace of $\sigma^f(\sigma^f)^{\mathrm{T}}$.*

Target (%)	Model (%)
20.00	20.00
22.00	22.00
20.00	20.00
19.00	19.00
18.50	18.50

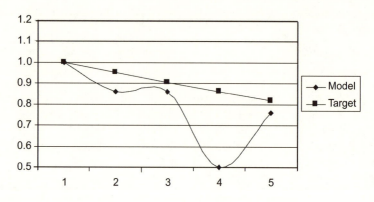

Figure CS10.4.1 *The forward-rate/forward-rate correlation produced by the best fit to the main diagonal of the forward-rate/forward-rate covariance matrix. The line labelled 'Target' corresponds to the correlation function $\rho = \exp(-\beta|t_i - t_j|)$, with $\beta = 0.1$.*

resulting forward-rate/forward-rate and swap-rate/swap-rate correlation matrices turned out to be highly implausible.

Despite, or, rather, because of, the perfect fit to caplet prices, the resulting correlation functions are financially very unappealing, and are the by-product of attempting to achieve 'too good' a fit of some subset of the target surface. This should come as no surprise given the related results reported in Chapter 9 and in Rebonato (1998, 1999a).

These findings can be contrasted with the results that can be obtained if, instead, one optimizes the angles $\{\boldsymbol{\theta}\}$ so as to obtain the overall best possible

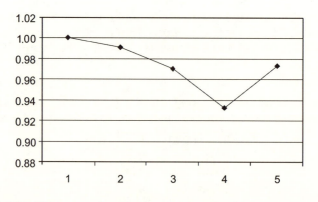

Figure CS10.4.2 *The swap-rate/swap-rate correlation produced by the best fit to the main diagonal of the forward-rate/forward-rate covariance matrix.*

Table CS10.4.3   *Model and target caplet volatilities when the optimization over the angular co-efficients {θ} was carried out so as to obtain the best possible fit to the whole forward-rate/forward-rate covariance matrix.*

Target (%)	Model (%)
20.00	19.64
22.00	22.05
20.00	19.78
19.00	18.86
18.50	18.50

fit to the whole covariance matrix. Once the optimization has been carried out, the prices of the individual caplets are now no longer exactly recovered (see Table CS10.4.3). The discrepancies, however, between model and target prices turn out in this case to be very small. More importantly, the resulting forward-rate/forward-rate and swap-rate/swap-rate correlation matrices now display a much more plausible and desirable behavior. This is shown in Table CS10.4.4 and Figures CS10.4.3–CS10.4.5.

The main message of this Case Study is therefore that it is indeed possible to obtain an efficient fit to selected portions of an exogenous forward-rate/forward-rate covariance matrix while recovering the prices of the European co-terminal swaptions. I also tried to show, however, that focussing on specific areas of the target covariance matrix can be dangerous, the more so if the caplet and swaption markets are not highly congruous. A modest price in terms of caplet mis-pricing can be more than offset by a much more plausible correlation structure between the various variables. The importance of a globally plausible description of the yield-curve dynamics, and the dangers of focussing too closely on the recovery of certain quantities to the detriment of others, have been highlighted in Section 10.1 and in Case Study 1.

What this Case Study has not shown is the quality of the recovery of the European swaption prices in realistic market cases. This task is therefore undertaken in the next and final section of this chapter. Before that, it is useful to show how the framework presented so far can be used to obtain accurate

Table CS10.4.4   *The swap-rate/swap-rate correlation matrix when the optimization over the angular coefficients {θ} was carried out so as to obtain the best possible fit to the whole forward-rate/forward-rate covariance matrix.*

1	0.99434	0.97846	0.95044	0.90855
0.99434	1	0.99222	0.9698	0.93075
0.97846	0.99222	1	0.98882	0.95596
0.95044	0.9698	0.98882	1	0.98008
0.90855	0.93075	0.95596	0.98008	1

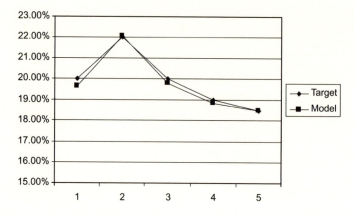

Figure CS10.4.3 *Target and model caplet prices in the case of a fit to the whole matrix* $\sigma^f(\sigma^f)^{\mathrm{T}}$.

hedge statistics in terms of swap rates and swaption volatilities (deltas and vegas) despite the fact that one is working in a forward-rate-based framework.

10.6.3 Making use of the link between covariance matrices to recover swap-based hedge parameters

One of the reasons why swap-rate-based versions of the LIBOR market model are sometimes preferred to forward-rate-based implementations is because it is thought that, when using swap rates as the state variables, the risk

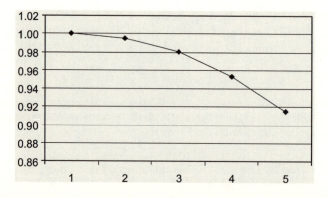

Figure CS10.4.4 *The swap-rate/swap-rate correlation produced by the best fit to the whole forward-rate/forward-rate covariance matrix.*

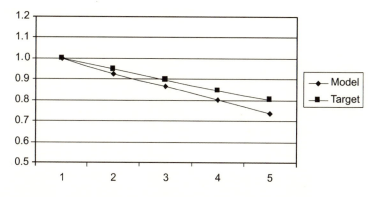

Figure CS10.4.5 *The forward-rate/forward-rate correlation produced by the best fit to the whole forward-rate/forward-rate covariance matrix.*

statistics are naturally obtained in terms of the instruments the trader will need for hedging (i.e., swaps and European swaptions). This, however, need not be the case, and the approximations presented in this chapter can provide an almost exact translation from one set of coordinates to the other. This can be accomplished as follows. (The case of a vega calculation is shown, as the calculations for the delta are similar and simpler.)

Recall that $\mathbf{S}^{\text{SR}}$ ($\mathbf{S}^f$) denotes the $n \times n$ matrix containing on the main diagonal the volatilities of the n co-terminal swap rates (or the n underlying forward rates), and zeros elsewhere. Let

- NPV( ) denote the function that gives the price today of a complex swap-rate-based product;

- $\partial \text{NPV}/\partial \mathbf{S}^{\text{SR}}_{ii}$ be the $n \times 1$ vector containing the vega derivatives of the NPV function with respect to the volatilities of the ith co-terminal swaption;

- $\mathbf{C}^f$ be the matrix with the instantaneous covariance between the forward rates; and

- $\mathbf{C}^{\text{SR}}$ be the matrix with the instantaneous covariance between the co-terminal rates.

Thanks to the approximate relationships established in this chapter, one can write

$$\mathbf{Z}\,\mathbf{C}^f\mathbf{Z}^{\text{T}} = \mathbf{C}^{\text{SR}}, \tag{10.25}$$

$$\mathbf{Z}\,\sigma^f(\sigma^f)^{\text{T}}\mathbf{Z}^{\text{T}} = \mathbf{C}^{\text{SR}} = \sigma^{\text{SR}}(\sigma^{\text{SR}})^{\text{T}}, \tag{10.26}$$

$$\mathbf{Z}\,\mathbf{S}^f\beta^f(\beta^f)^{\text{T}}(\mathbf{S}^f)^{\text{T}}\mathbf{Z}^{\text{T}} = \mathbf{S}^{\text{SR}}\beta^{\text{SR}}(\beta^{\text{SR}})^{\text{T}}(\mathbf{S}^{\text{SR}})^{\text{T}}. \tag{10.27}$$

Table 10.5   *The market inputs for the test problem analyzed in the text. The labelling of the columns is (hopefully) self-explanatory, and the prices correspond to a notional principal of $100 000 000.*

Underlying forward rates				Co-terminal swaps			
Reset time (yrs)	Pay time (yrs)	Accrual factor	Forward rate	Market swpn vols (%)	Swap rate (%)	Swaption price	Swaptio vega
10.0	10.50	0.50	6.21	15.5	5.94	3,551,759	139,983
10.5	11.00	0.50	6.21	16.0	5.91	3,202,308	127,467
11.0	11.50	0.50	6.15	16.4	5.86	2,842,528	114,333
11.5	12.00	0.50	6.15	17.1	5.82	2,507,729	100,666
12.0	12.50	0.50	5.80	17.8	5.76	2,151,316	86,566
12.5	13.00	0.50	5.80	18.7	5.75	1,856,393	72,211
13.0	13.50	0.50	5.79	19.7	5.73	1,533,658	57,683
13.5	14.00	0.50	5.79	20.8	5.71	1,187,145	43,086
14.0	14.50	0.50	5.67	21.6	5.67	805,100	28,554
14.5	15.00	0.50	5.67	22.1	5.67	408,532	14,244

Since the matrix $\mathbf{S}^{SR}$ contains on its main diagonal the volatilities of the co-terminal swap rates, these can be shocked in turn one at a time, the corresponding forward-rate matrix re-calculated using Equation (10.27), and the price today of the complex product evaluated accordingly. The result of this calculation will give the quantity $\partial \mathrm{NPV}/\partial \mathbf{S}_{ii}^{SR}$, as required.

10.7 Quality of the Numerical Approximation in Realistic Market Cases

10.7.1 Price recovery

This section illustrates how well the prices of European swaptions can indeed be recovered while fitting to the forward-rate/forward-rate covariance matrix in a realistic market case. To carry out this test, the case of a semi-annual 15-year non-call 10 Bermudan swaption was considered, and a market yield curve, swaption matrix and term structure of volatilities were chosen. The relevant market information is displayed in Tables 10.5 and 10.6.

Table 10.7 then shows the values of the optimal parameters $\{a, b, c, d\}$ for the forward-rate instantaneous volatility function described in Chapter 6 (see also Equation (10.8) for ease of reference). This set of parameters was obtained by imposing the best possible fit to the overall forward-rate/forward-rate covariance matrix. In the exercise the value of the decay constant β in the correlation function was kept fixed at 0.15.

By so doing, the caplet prices are not exactly recovered. Also displayed in Table 10.8 are therefore the scaling factors $\{k\}$ that would be necessary if one wanted to ensure exact pricing of the caplets. It is important to notice

Table 10.6 *The portion of the swaption matrix (values in per cent) relevant for the problem at hand: the values in the first column indicate the expiry times of the European swaptions, and the numbers in the first row the maturity of the swap entered into. Entries in bold indicate the volatilities of the co-terminal swaptions.*

	0.5	1.0	2.0	3.0	4.0	5.0
10.0	20.1830	20.8121	19.6060	18.8559	18.2280	**18.0275**
11.0	20.7028	21.3204	19.8983	19.0612	**18.4186**	18.2188
12.0	20.5271	21.1702	20.1548	**19.2541**	18.7024	18.3425
13.0	20.9900	21.6330	**20.7289**	19.7999	19.0515	18.6879
14.0	21.5220	**22.1505**	21.6154	20.2533	19.5773	18.9879
15.0	22.6495	23.3050	22.3177	20.9617	20.0347	19.4349

that all the scaling factors (column 'Vol Scale') are smaller than unity, and remarkably constant, despite the fact that this criterion did not enter the optimization. This indicates that the caplet prices implied by the model will be systematically biased downwards, but that the resulting evolution of the term structure of volatilities is approximately time-homogeneous. This latter feature is both important and reassuring, since it had not been imposed at all in the fitting procedure. The fact that the caplet model prices implied by the co-terminal swaption prices turned out to be 'cheap' is in agreement with the discussion in Section 9.1.3.

With the parameters for the forward-rate instantaneous volatility, a Monte Carlo evaluation of the European swaption prices was carried out retaining as many factors as forward rates in the problem (i.e., 10). The price thus obtained was then compared with the corresponding Black price. It is important to highlight the joint approximations and assumptions that enter this calculation:

- first of all it is assumed that the instantaneous volatilities of forward and swap rates can be simultaneously deterministic;

- it is also assumed that both sets of state variables can all be log-normal at the same time;

- the approximation is then made that the weights that link a given swap

Table 10.7 *The values of the parameters $\{a, b, c, d\}$ for the forward-rate instantaneous volatility function [equation (10.7)] obtained by imposing the best possible fit to the overall forward-rate/forward-rate covariance matrix. In the exercise the value of the decay constant β in the correlation function was kept fixed at 0.15.*

a	b	c	d	β
−0.0228	0.0466	0.3404	0.1818	0.15

Table 10.8   *The caplet implied volatilities obtained by the optimization procedure and the scaling factors {k} (column labelled 'Vol scale') that would be needed to bring the model prices in line with the corresponding market values. Notice the small variation across the rescaling factors, which implies an approximately time-homogeneous evolution of the term structure of volatility (and of the swaption matrix).*

Reset date	Pay date	Accrual factor	Forward rate (%)	Market caplet vol (%)	Model caplet vol (%)	Vol scale
10.00	10.25	0.25	6.16	22.7	21.0	0.926
10.25	10.50	0.25	6.16	22.7	21.0	0.924
10.50	10.75	0.25	6.16	22.7	20.9	0.923
10.75	11.00	0.25	6.16	22.7	20.9	0.922
11.00	11.25	0.25	6.10	22.7	20.9	0.921
11.25	11.50	0.25	6.10	22.6	20.8	0.920
11.50	11.75	0.25	6.10	22.6	20.8	0.919
11.75	12.00	0.25	6.10	22.6	20.8	0.917
12.00	12.25	0.25	5.76	22.5	20.7	0.923
12.25	12.50	0.25	5.76	22.4	20.7	0.922
12.50	12.75	0.25	5.76	22.4	20.7	0.922
12.75	13.00	0.25	5.76	22.4	20.6	0.921
13.00	13.25	0.25	5.74	22.4	20.6	0.921
13.25	13.50	0.25	5.74	22.3	20.6	0.921
13.50	13.75	0.25	5.74	22.3	20.5	0.921
13.75	14.00	0.25	5.74	22.3	20.5	0.920
14.00	14.25	0.25	5.63	22.2	20.5	0.923

rate to its underlying forward rates can be regarded as constant when using Equations (10.18)–(10.21);

- finally it is assumed that the 'true' forward-rate instantaneous volatility and correlation functions can be adequately described by the chosen functional forms.

Table 10.9 presents the main results, that is, the quality of the recovery of the European swaption prices obtained by evolving the forward rates.

10.7.2 The resulting caplet prices

The agreement between the market and the model prices of the co-terminal swaptions can be clearly seen to be excellent, both in percentage terms and as a fraction of the typical bid–offer spread (taken to be one vega). From Table 10.8 one can see that the resulting caplet prices are indeed not perfectly recovered, and that there is a systematic downward bias. If one so desired, this bias could be substantially reduced by changing the value for the decay

Table 10.9 *Comparison between the model prices of the European co-terminal swaptions obtained by evolving the forward rates as described in the text [column labelled 'European (model)'] and the corresponding market prices [column labelled 'European (Black)']. The last two columns display the error both in percentage terms and as a percent of one vega (taken as a proxy of a typical bid–offer spread).*

European (Black)	European (model)	Swaption vega	Error (%)	Error (vega)
3551,759	3553,400	139,983	−0.046	−1.17
3202,308	3204,566	127,467	−0.071	−1.77
2842,528	2841,692	114,333	0.029	0.73
2507,729	2505,399	100,666	0.093	2.31
2151,316	2149,243	86,566	0.096	2.39
1856,393	1855,077	72,211	0.071	1.82
1533,658	1533,030	57,683	0.041	1.09
1187,145	1187,068	43,086	0.006	0.18
805,100	804,925	28,554	0.022	0.61
408,532	408,373	14,244	0.039	1.12

constant β, but the resulting correlation function would assume implausibly low values.

Strictly speaking, this inability to recover the caplet market with a higher degree of accuracy might theoretically be due to several factors, such as, for instance, an inadequate parametric form for the correlation or volatility functions. Despite the fact that these explanations are logically possible, I believe that it is more likely that supply and demand conditions, coupled with relatively poor market liquidity, might act as a deterrent to the activity of arbitrageurs. In other terms, in the particular currency (GBP) and for the date chosen for this example, the caplet and swaption markets would appear to be trading with a palpable lack of internal coherence. The discussion in Section 9.1 can be profitably revisited at this point.

Part IV

Beyond the Standard Approach: Accounting for Smiles

11

Extending the Standard Approach – I: CEV and Displaced Diffusion

11.1 Practical and Conceptual Implications of Non-Flat Volatility Smiles

11.1.1 Flat smiles and the log-normality of forward rates

In Parts I–III of this book I have presented a modelling approach for a set of spanning forward rates that is underpinned by the assumption of log-normality. More precisely, the crucial assumption was made in Chapter 2 that it was possible to find a measure (the 'terminal' measure) under which one forward rate at a time could be described in terms of a (strictly positive) exponential martingale with deterministic volatility (see Condition 2.3 and Equations (2.28) and (2.28′) in Section 2.3). Despite the fact that other forward rates were shown not to be log-normal under the same terminal measure (see Section 5.2.2, Equations (7)–(9), in particular), the caplet prices for different strikes to which they give rise are perfectly consistent with a log-normal distribution (under their own associated terminal pricing measure) and therefore with the market-standard Black formula. If, by inversion of the Black formula, these prices were translated into implied volatilities for a fixed expiry, the latter would give rise to a perfectly flat curve as a function of the caplet strike.

The exact recovery of the Black caplet prices under a measure other than the terminal one is a point worth looking at a bit more closely. To see why, recall three results from Chapter 2:

1. There exists some (equivalent) measure under which any one forward rate can be exactly log-normally distributed (i.e., under which it is an exponential martingale with deterministic volatility).

2. If a measure other than the terminal one is used, the drift of a given forward rate will contain the stochastic state variables and, therefore, the resulting distribution will not be log-normal.

3. The transformation from one measure to another brought about by Girsanov's theorem (see Section 2.3) changes the drifts but not the volatility components in the diffusion equation for the forward rates. In particular, therefore, if a forward rate displays a deterministic volatility under one measure, it will display a deterministic volatility under any of the Girsanov-related equivalent measures.

When it comes to the pricing of caplets, this seems to give rise to a paradox: Since, when moving between measures, the drifts change but the volatilities do not – and, in particular, they remain deterministic – how can the same (log-normal) caplet price be recovered? What is left to 'take up the slack', and ensure the invariance of the price across measures?

To see how this is possible, one can begin by noticing that, under the terminal measure, a discount bond that matures at payoff time is used to present-value the payoff itself. Given the particular choice for its maturity, the value of this discounting factor is independent of the state of the caplet payoff at maturity. In particular, there will be no systematic bias in the price arising from a non-zero covariance between the discounting and the payoff. For any other numeraire, however, the discounting asset will assume different values in the states of the world associated with different payoffs. Therefore, in general, there will be a non-zero covariance between the discounting and the payoffs themselves, which alters the value of the expectation, and hence the caplet price. This covariance term is exactly compensated for by the numeraire-dependent drift imparted to the forward rate. (Incidentally, by the reasoning just presented, it is clear that these compensating drifts, obtained in Chapter 5, must contain the state variables.) A detailed derivation of the drifts that follows this line of reasoning can be found in chapter 5 of Rebonato (1998).

We can summarize these points as follows:

- If, under its own terminal measure, a given forward rate produces caplet prices across strikes consistent with the log-normal Black formula, under a different measure it will still have to produce the same prices, even if it is no longer log-normally distributed.

- A log-normal distribution for a given forward rate is a necessary condition for achieving Black-consistent prices of its associated caplets across strikes only under the terminal measure associated with the forward rate itself.

- The Girsanov drift transformation brings about the 'correction' that exactly compensates for the fact that, under a 'non-natural' payoff (see Section 3.2, and chapter 5 in Rebonato 1998), there will be a non-zero covariance term between the payoff and the discounting.

These considerations will have to be kept in mind when, in the remainder of this chapter and the next, I shall discuss, briefly, deviations from log-normality for the distribution of the forward rates: the qualifier 'under their own terminal measure' should always be understood.

11.1.2 *The changing market environment: appearance of non-monotonic smiles*

One of the main virtues of the standard LIBOR market model presented in the previous chapters is that it allows the exact recovery of the prices of the plain-vanilla options associated with at least one set of state variables (i.e., with caplets or European swaptions). It was indeed this important feature that earned the approach the label of 'the market model'. Unfortunately, in the past few years the market prices of the plain-vanilla benchmark securities have ceased agreeing with the predictions from the market model increasingly. As early as, approximately, 1996 the implied volatility for caplets of a given maturity began to assume a marked monotonically decreasing behavior as a function of strikes. (The case of JPY, where very low levels of rates were prevalent before 1996, is rather *sui generis* and has never been satisfactorily dealt with within the standard market-model framework.) This source of discrepancy from the log-normal behavior can be accounted for in a relatively straightforward way, and is amenable to a simple and convincing financial explanation. From the perspective of the LIBOR market model, not only is accounting for this feature relatively simple, but the powerful calibration procedures described in the log-normal setting can be recovered and adapted in a very straightforward way. In the presence of a monotonically decaying implied volatility curve, the degree of 'surgery' needed in order to bring about a satisfactory agreement between market and model prices for the plain-vanilla instruments, and to price exotic instruments consistently, is therefore rather limited. This is the general line of approach towards accounting for smiles that has been taken, for instance, by Andersen and Andreasen (1997) (see also Zuehlsdorff 2001 for a generalization).

During the second half of 1998, however, the implied volatility 'smile'[1] began to assume more complex shapes ('hockey stick'[2]) (see Figures 11.1–11.3), which cannot be reproduced by simple 'tinkering at the edges' of the market-model approach. In my opinion I believe that this further change in shape in the implied volatility smile can be convincingly explained in terms of a new source of deviation from the log-normal behavior *added to*, but not substituting, whatever cause was responsible for the monotonically decreasing smiles which had been visible since the second half of the 1990s.

---

[1] In this book a 'smile' is any non-constant function expressing the implied volatility (discussed and defined precisely in the following) as a function of strike, for a fixed maturity, irrespective of the shape of the function itself. The term 'smile surface' will be used in order to describe the collection of implied volatilities as a function of both strike and maturity.

[2] In this book I desribe as 'hockey stick' any smile that is not monotonically declining with strike (and, of course, displays only one minimum). Some traders prefer to use the terms 'U-shaped' or 'V-shaped' to highlight different features of the smile curve.

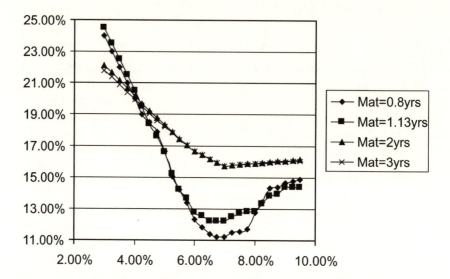

Figure 11.1 *The implied volatility as a function of strike for selected caplet expiries (USD, 28-Jul-2000), displaying a very pronounced hockey-stick shape at short maturities, and a less strong, but still visible, minimum for maturities out to five years.*

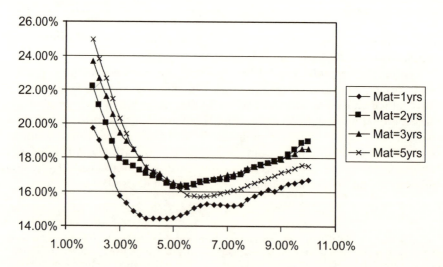

Figure 11.2 *The implied volatility as a function of strike for selected caplet expiries (EUR, 4-Aug-2000), displaying a clearly noticeable hockey-stick shape for all maturities.*

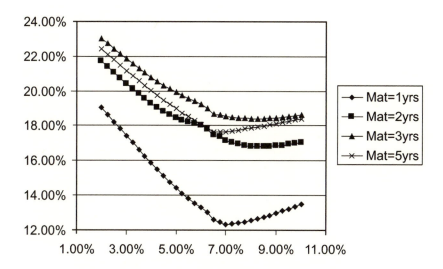

Figure 11.3 *The implied volatility as a function of strike for selected caplet expiries (GBP, 1-Aug-2000), displaying a pronounced hockey-stick shape at short maturities, and a shallow minimum for maturities of two and three years.*

11.1.3 Comparison with FX and equity smiles – the importance of time-homogeneity

This focus on the financial origin of smiles is important. Non-monotonic smiles have been around in the equities and FX world for a much longer period of time (in the case of equity indices, at the very least since the crash of 1987), and it has therefore been very tempting for modellers in the interest-rate world to turn to the work that had been carried out for over a decade by their colleagues in the sister option markets. I believe that such an approach is not desirable, since, in my opinion, the financial mechanisms at the basis of the appearance of smiley implied volatilities are fundamentally different in the equity and FX case on the one hand, and in the interest-rate area on the other. Therefore, I shall argue that a simultaneous description of the decreasing behavior of the implied volatility as a function of strike and of the more recent hockey-stick behavior by means of a single mechanism could be a tempting but misguided effort. Departing from the approach that has been followed in the literature so far, I shall therefore present in the following the results of fits to market data using simultaneously two distinct and independently financially justifiable sources for interest-rate smiles.

In this respect the recently acquired proficiency that has been developed in the equity and FX areas to fit almost exactly a bewildering variety of volatility smile surfaces is less desirable and more dangerous than one might initially think. The ability to reproduce today's prices exactly by means of a given modelling approach, in fact, often fails to address the issue of the desirability of the implications of the underlying financial mechanism. In the case of implied volatility curves derived from the prices of JPY caplets, for instance, a very good fit can be obtained (see, e.g. Glasserman and Kou 2000) by requiring that the process for the forward rate should be a jump diffusion with a time-dependent jump frequency and jump distribution parameters. The quality of the fit is certainly high (see again, for instance, Figure 2 in Glasserman and Kou 2000), but, as is often the case with jump diffusions, the jump frequency required in order to obtain a good fit across maturities turns out to be markedly time-dependent and, in particular, decaying. This would give rise to strongly non-time-homogeneous – in particular, flattening – term structures of volatilities. In other words, tomorrow's smile is predicted by the model to be very different from today's. I believe that the trader should question very carefully whether she finds this feature convincing.

11.1.4 Is price-matching all one should care about? Market completeness revisited

At a more fundamental level, the reason why I believe that a good fit to current market prices might be less reassuring than one might think is the following. One might be tempted to argue that, as long as today's prices are fully recovered, the exotic trader need not worry about the realism of the model producing the prices themselves, and can trade her way out of a possibly unrealistic process specification simply by hedging according to the chosen (price-reproducing) model. Unfortunately, this line of argument suffers from two shortcomings. To begin with, its validity is predicated on the chosen model, and its parametrization, to be correct. Even if, for instance, a jump-diffusion model with time-dependent parameters could account perfectly for all of today's caplet prices, it would fail to recommend the correct hedges if the world were instead driven by, say, a stochastic-volatility dynamics (see also, in this respect, the discussion in Section 11.2). Furthermore, as soon as one moves away from a deterministic-volatility, log-normal forward-rate universe, derivatives markets in which one can only trade in the 'underlying' (the discount bonds or the FRAs and swaps) soon cease to be complete, and investors' preferences and attitudes towards risk enter the price-making process. To some extent the markets can be completed by adding plain-vanilla options to the universe of the traded instruments at the trader's disposal. After doing so one can sometimes attempt to impute the risk-adjusted parameters of the chosen model – which embed the market's aversion to the corresponding sources of risk – from the cross-sectional analysis of today's market prices. When markets lack completeness, however, these risk-adjusted parameters will be associated with one of the infinite number of possible pricing measures compatible with the observed prices,[3] namely with the particular measure currently chosen

---

[3]It might be useful to recall that, given a set of market prices and the requirement that no arbitrage should be allowed, three possible situations can arise: either (i) there is a single pricing measure (the market is complete, the true model and its parameters are known exactly, and, with continuous trading, perfect dynamic replication is possible); or (ii) no pricing measure exists; or (iii) there exists an infinity of pricing measures (the market is incomplete) (see, e.g., Pliska 1997).

by the market. There is no guarantee, however, that the market (which, in the incomplete-market case, is, as Bjork 1998 puts it, the ultimate chooser of the pricing measure) might not 'change its mind' as to which pricing measure it will favor in the future. In more financially transparent terms, there is no guarantee as to what market price of risk the market will exact in the future for the different unhedgeable risk factors. See also Rebonato (2001a) on this point. In this respect, one should note carefully that, even when using complete-market models, the trader has always been engaged in two different types of hedging activities. The former, and the theoretically easily justifiable one, is the ('delta') hedging carried out by engaging in a trading strategy in the underlying (ultimately, the discount bonds, or the FRAs and the swaps) constructed so as to compensate for the changes in value of the complex product due to the changes in the fundamental stochastic variables stemming from the innovation part (see Sections 2.2 and 2.3). In this hedging mode, these latter changes are, on the one hand, totally unpredictable, but, on the other, assumed to be statistically perfectly known (the forward rates, for instance, are supposed to follow a continuous path, with infinite first and finite second variation, deterministic volatilities, and known first and second moments). In real life, the exotic trader has always carried out in parallel a second hedging program, whereby she undergos the transition from being a 'model-believer' to being a mild 'model-agnostic'. Typically the trader will assume, in this mode of operation, that the model is still correct in its general specification (for instance, the forward rates will still possess a diffusive behavior with deterministic volatility), but the possibility is now entertained that, in the phenomenological description of the forward-rate dynamics, the parameters might have been wrongly chosen. In particular, the trader will consider the possibility that the volatilities, while still deterministic, might have different values than those obtainable from today's plain-vanilla prices. In simple terms, she will vega-hedge. As is well known, the robustness of this approach, which is universally used in the option world, relies on the fact that, in a Black world, the 'cross-terms' (i.e., the mis-specification in the delta due to the incorrect knowledge of the volatility) produce relatively small hedging mistakes.

This second modus operandi, which I have called elsewhere 'outside-model hedging', becomes dramatically more important in the case of non-flat implied volatility curves, and is discussed in more detail in Section 11.2. There exist, in fact, only two (closely related) classes of diffusive models (both dealt with in this chapter) which can account for smiley implied volatility surfaces and retain market completeness if trading is to be allowed only in the underlying discount bonds. This is the case for no other smile-producing mechanism: irrespective of whether these other mechanisms give rise to future *deterministic* smiles (as in the case of jump diffusions with deterministic parameters) or to future *stochastic* smiles (as in the case of jump diffusions with stochastic coefficients), they all introduce sources of market incompleteness.

As mentioned above, in some cases it might be possible to recover, from a cross-sectional analysis of today's prices, the risk-adjusted parameters that describe the forward-rate dynamics (say, the risk-adjusted jump frequency). However, even if the real-world jump frequency were truly constant over time, the risk-adjusted one would only remain constant if the market's risk aversion to jumps were also not to change in the future. See again the discussion in Rebonato (2001a). In practice, this cannot be counted upon, and the market events that have followed, for instance, the Russia crisis have shown that risk aversion to certain risk factors (such as swap spread risk) can in reality change dramatically over a very short period of time.

The existence of non-flat smile surfaces therefore confronts the trader with a much greater degree of complexity in her hedging program: she now has to hedge not only against moves in the underlying (the 'delta' hedging) or against the possibility that the parameters of an otherwise 'true' complete-market model might be mis-specified (the 'vega' hedging); but also the trader must try to hedge against the possibility that the 'fickle market' might change its mind in its choice of the pricing measure (see Joshi 2001f). This type of hedging is both qualitatively different, and substantially more subtle and complex, than the traditional 'delta' and 'vega' hedging. As for the promise, often encountered in the literature, that the market can be completed, and dynamic replication re-introduced, simply by introducing one or more plain-vanilla options in the set of hedging instruments, this is true if one assumes to know not only the prices today, *but also the full processes* (i.e., the prices in all possible future states of the world) of these additional options (see, e.g., Rebonato 2001a).

11.1.5 Root-mean-square volatility in the presence of smiles

Another casualty of the more complex world brought about by the existence of smiles is the ability to identify the implied volatility with the root-mean-square of the instantaneous volatility. As soon as implied volatility surfaces are non-flat (as a function of strike), it is no longer true that

$$\sigma_{\text{Black}}^2 T = \int_0^T \sigma_{\text{inst}}(u)^2 \, du,$$

and the implied volatility simply becomes the 'wrong number to put in the wrong (Black) formula to obtain the right price' (see Rebonato 1999c). The conceptual changes brought about by this state of affairs are not insurmountable, especially if one still regards the identification of the root-mean-square instantaneous volatility with the implied volatility as a useful, albeit imprecise, first-order approximation. What becomes much more delicate, however, is the calibration procedure to caplet prices. I will show in this and the next chapter that an efficient and accurate calibration is still possible, but now one will have to tread very carefully where it was possible, for instance, to achieve perfect agreement between model and market prices by taking a simple ratio. Compare, for instance, Equation (6.16) in Section 6.3, on the one hand, and Equations (12.17)–(12.21) in Section 12.4, on the other.

11.1.6 Requirements of a practical extension of the LIBOR market model

The LIBOR-market-model pricing framework, as it has evolved from its inception to the present day, is much more than a set of equations for the no-arbitrage evolution of a set of spanning forward rates. It includes a very rich body of calibration procedures and approximate, but very accurate, numerical techniques for the evolution of the forward rates. It is this body of techniques that has turned the approach into today's most popular pricing tool for complex interest-rate derivatives. Much of the success of the standard market-model approach has also been due to the fact that these numerical approximations have turned out to be not only accurate but also surprisingly simple. Extending the LIBOR market model in such a way that the observed smiles can be accounted for in a financially convincing way is therefore a very tall order: not only must the resulting modelling choices make 'financial sense', but the calibration and evolution results presented in Parts I–III for the deterministic-volatility case must also be recovered.

The treatment to be found in the remainder of this book has therefore been influenced by these joint requirements of financial plausibility and ease of practical implementation of the calibration and evolution techniques that have been presented in the chapters so far. In particular, this chapter will introduce the financial underpinning and the theoretical structure of the constant-elasticity-of-variance (CEV)/displaced-diffusion approach; the next chapter will tackle the stochastic-volatility case. The empirical analysis of the extension of the above-mentioned calibration procedures to the joint displaced-diffusion/stochastic-volatility case is presented in the next chapter for the combined case: if, as we will show, all the various approximations remain as good as in the deterministic case even when both modifications are applied to the standard model, they will a fortiori work at least as well if the reader wanted to implement only one of the two suggested extensions. Therefore virtually all the numerical experiments needed to substantiate the claims made about the effectiveness of the numerical procedures are presented in Chapter 12. The only exceptions are some results specific to caplet fitting in the displaced-diffusion case, which can be made use of instead of the suggested joint calibration procedure suggested in the next chapter if the reader only wanted to make use of the displaced-diffusion extension of the modelling approach. These results are reported in Section 11.3.

Before undertaking these tasks, however, I think it is important to discuss some often-misunderstood conceptual issues regarding the meaning of non-flat implied volatility curves (as a function of strike). These considerations have a direct bearing on the calculation of deltas and other derivatives in the presence of smiles, but, more generally, can provide a guideline towards choosing the most appropriate modelling approach to account for the observed market smiles. This topic is dealt with in the next section.

11.2 Calculating Deltas and Other Risk Derivatives in the Presence of Smiles

11.2.1 The relationship between the true call price functional and the Black formula

When dealing with a non-flat implied volatility surface, it is essential to draw a clear distinction between the true price functional that gives the value of a call (caplet) as a function of the state variables, and the market-reference Black pricing formula. In the presence of smiles, as is well known, the latter is simply a convenient agreed-upon way of quoting a price. I shall analyze in the following the problem of a trader who observes with infinite accuracy[4] a smiley implied volatility surface, but has not formed any opinion yet as to what deviations from the set of Black model assumptions are giving rise to the observed market prices from which the implied volatility surface itself has been derived. At this stage the trader is therefore agnostic as to what the true process for the forward rates might be, and only knows that the true caplet pricing functional might depend on

- today's value of the stock price,

- the residual time to maturity,

- the strike of the option,

- a discount factor (numeraire),

- an unknown set of parameters describing the 'true' dynamics (such as diffusion coefficients, jump amplitudes, etc.), and,

- possibly, the past history.

The parameters describing the process of the underlying (volatility, jump frequency, jump amplitude, etc.) can, in turn, be themselves stochastic. However, they are all, obviously, strike-independent. The unknown 'true' parameters and the full history up to time t will be symbolically denoted by $\{\alpha_t\}$ and $\{\mathcal{F}_t\}$, respectively.

The Black formula, on the other hand, used to translate contemporaneous observed market prices for different strikes and maturities into a set of implied volatility numbers, depends in the presence of smiles on

---

[4]When we say that the trader knows the smile surface with 'infinite' accuracy, we mean that they have carried out an interpolation/extrapolation of the caplet smile surface and/or of the swaption matrix in such a way that they can associate a unique and certain implied volatility with a continuum of strikes, and with all the maturities of interest.

- today's value of the stock price,

- the residual time to maturity,

- a discount factor (numeraire),

- the strike of the option, and

- a single *strike-dependent* parameter (the implied volatility).

Since, in this section, I shall deal with only one forward rate, and to lighten the notation, I shall depart slightly from the conventions I have used elsewhere in this book. Therefore, I shall denote the single forward rate I shall be focussing on simply as F, its maturity as T and the volatility of the diffusion part of its unknown true process as σ. The symbol K, as elsewhere, has been reserved for the strike of the caplet, and I shall denote the true functional by $C(F_t, t, T, K, \{\alpha_t\}, \{\mathcal{F}_t\}, \sigma)$ and the Black formula by $\text{Black}(F_t, T - t, K, \sigma_{\text{impl}}(t, T, F, K))$.

11.2.2 Calculating the delta using the Black formula and the implied volatility

The trader is aware that, given the existence of a non-flat implied volatility curve, she does not inhabit a Black world, and that, in particular, the Black implied volatility, σ_{impl}, is not linked in any simple way to the volatility, σ, of the true process – more specifically, she knows that it is not equal to its root-mean-square. The implied volatility is just 'the wrong number to put in the wrong (Black) formula to get the right price'. Therefore, as of 'today' (time 0), by the very definition of implied volatility, the trader can only write

$$C(F_0, 0, T, K, \{\alpha_0\}, \{\mathcal{F}_0\}, \sigma) = \text{Black}(F, T - 0, K, \sigma_{\text{impl}}(0, T, F, K)). \quad (11.1)$$

(Since, for simplicity, I shall always deal in the following example with a single expiry time, T, as seen from today, I shall lighten the notation by writing $\sigma_{\text{impl}}(0, T, F, K) = \sigma_{\text{impl}}(F, K)$.)

The trader would then like to be able to calculate the delta, that is, to compute

$$\Delta_{\text{Black}} = \frac{\partial C(F, 0, T, K, \{\alpha_0\}, \{\mathcal{F}_0\}, \sigma)}{\partial F}. \quad (11.2)$$

The task appears difficult because the trader does not know the true functional. Today, however, thanks to (11.1), she can always write

$$\Delta_{\text{Black}} = \frac{\partial \text{Black}(F, T, K, \sigma_{\text{impl}}(F, K))}{\partial F}, \quad (11.3)$$

which, because of the dependence of the implied volatility on F, she knows to be given by

$$\Delta_{\text{Black}} = N(h_1) + \frac{\partial \text{Black}(F, T, K, \sigma_{\text{impl}}(F, K))}{\partial \sigma_{\text{impl}}(F, K)} \frac{\partial \sigma_{\text{impl}}(F, K)}{\partial F}$$

$$= N(h_1) + \text{BlackVega}(F, T, K, \sigma_{\text{impl}}(F, K)) \frac{\partial \sigma_{\text{impl}}(F, K)}{\partial F}. \quad (11.4)$$

In Equation (11.4) the quantity BlackVega is the derivative of the Black function with respect to the implied volatility, $N(\ )$ denotes the cumulative normal distribution and h_1 is the usual argument of $N(\ )$ in the Black formula (see, e.g., Section 2.2). From Equation (11.4) it is clear that the only difficulty in calculating the delta is associated with the term $\partial \sigma_{\text{impl}}(F, K)/\partial F$. How can the trader estimate this quantity?

11.2.3 The different dependences of implied volatilities on strike and forward rate

From today's caplet market, she can, at least in principle, observe a continuous series of implied volatilities as a function of the caplet strikes, or, more precisely, observe a series of contemporaneous caplet prices for different strikes given today's forward rate, F_0. The trader, by inversion of the Black formula, then knows how to convert these prices into implied volatilities. In other terms, for a given F_0, she observes the variation of the function $\sigma_{\text{impl}}(F, K)$ along the K dimension, $\sigma_{\text{impl}}(F_0, K)$, but cannot say anything about how it varies, if at all, when F changes. For the sake of concreteness, let us assume that the trader observes from the market that, as a function of K, the quantity $\sigma_{\text{impl}}(F_0, K)$ increases as K decreases (for a fixed F_0). Let us also assume that the trader knows a lot more about the 'true' process, for instance, that it is a diffusion, that the true process volatility – which bears no direct relationship with the implied volatility – is of the form $\sigma(F)$, and that this true volatility function, say, decreases when F (not K!) increases, that is,

$$\frac{\mathrm{d}F}{F} = \sigma(F)\,\mathrm{d}z, \quad (11.5)$$

$$\frac{\partial \sigma(F)}{\partial F} < 0. \quad (11.5')$$

(The drift has been neglected for simplicity.) How would she obtain the delta $\partial C(F, 0, T, K, \{\alpha_0\}, \{\mathcal{F}_0\}, \sigma)/\partial F$? Naturally enough, she would like to use the expression

$$\Delta_{\text{Black}} = N(h_1) + \text{BlackVega}(F, T, K, \sigma_{\text{impl}}(F, K)) \frac{\partial \sigma_{\text{impl}}(F, K)}{\partial F},$$

because, even if the true process (11.5) were known, it might be difficult to calculate its derivative with respect to F analytically. The market-given plot of $\sigma_{\text{impl}}(F_0, K)$, however, only gives the trader information about how the implied volatility changes as a function of K, not of F. If the trader assumed, for instance, that the implied volatility were of the form $\sigma_{\text{impl}}(F - K)$, then she could easily switch from $\partial/\partial F$ to $\partial/\partial K$, and could read the information she needed directly off today's market function $\sigma_{\text{impl}}(F_0, K)$. Alternatively, if the trader knew that the implied volatility function is of the form $\sigma_{\text{impl}} = \sigma_{\text{impl}}(\ln(F/K))$, the change in implied volatility as a function of F could be read off today's chart for the change of σ_{impl} as a function of K. For a process of the general form (11.5), however, she cannot know a priori whether the implied volatility function will indeed turn out to be of the form, say, $\sigma_{\text{impl}}(F - K)$, that is, whether the prices implied by the true process (11.5) will actually give rise to an implied volatility that only depends on the difference $(F - K)$. In general, therefore, the trader will have to extend her information about the implied volatility function along the F dimension. How can she find out the dependence of $\sigma_{\text{impl}}(F, K)$ on F?

If we continue to assume that she believes the true process volatility to be of the form $\sigma = \sigma(F)$, with $\partial \sigma(F)/\partial F < 0$, she could conceptually attempt to answer this question by proceeding as follows: she could begin by running a Monte Carlo simulation of process (11.5) starting with $F_0 + \delta F$ and using for the initial process volatility $\sigma(F_0 + \delta F)$. She could calculate the prices of several calls for different strikes, and convert these prices into an implied volatility function $\sigma_{\text{impl}}(F_0 + \delta F, K)$. She could then repeat the exercise with today's forward rate shifted down by the same amount; that is, she could re-run the Monte Carlo simulation with starting point equal to $F_0 - \delta F$ (and volatility $\sigma(F_0 + \delta F)$), calculate the prices for the same set of strikes and convert them into a new function $\sigma_{\text{impl}}(F_0 - \delta F, K)$. Now, for each strike K, she would finally be in a position to compute the term $\partial \sigma_{\text{impl}}(F, K)/\partial F$ by approximating it as

$$\frac{\partial \sigma_{\text{impl}}(F, K)}{\partial F} \simeq \frac{\sigma_{\text{impl}}(F_0 + \delta F, K) - \sigma_{\text{impl}}(F_0 - \delta F, K)}{2\delta F}. \tag{11.6}$$

It will turn out that, if the true process volatility did have a declining behavior in F (see Equation (11.5) and the assumption above), the implied volatility curve will indeed display a monotonically decreasing shape in K. The important point, however, is that the true process volatility was *assumed* to be a decreasing function of F, and that the implied volatility was *found* to be a decreasing function of K. A priori, that is, before doing the price calculations outlined above, one could not have immediately concluded that a decreasing true volatility with F would give rise to a decreasing implied volatility with K (although some good financial intuition could have suggested that this might have been the case).

From this thought experiment, one can draw a first conclusion. In general, even if the trader knew perfectly today's implied volatility curve as a function of the strike K for the current forward rate, F_0, she could not in general and in a model-neutral way determine the delta. The only exception would be if she made a very strong set of assumptions, such as, for instance, $\sigma_{\text{impl}}(F, K) = \sigma_{\text{impl}}(F - K)$ or $\sigma_{\text{impl}}(F, K) = \sigma_{\text{impl}}(\ln(F) - \ln(K))$, or, more generally, $\sigma_{\text{impl}}(F, K) = \sigma_{\text{impl}}(g(F) - g(K))$, where $g(\ )$ is some function. (This, incidentally, is one of the crucial necessary conditions for a smile to be called 'floating'. See, for a detailed discussion, Rebonato and Joshi 2001b.)

Are these assumptions reasonable? The question can be rephrased as: 'How do caplet prices across strikes (i.e., the implied volatility curve) change in the real world when F changes?' Clearly, the question is difficult, because, when the trader observes a market change in F (say, via the change in price of FRA), and simultaneously observes a change in the call price, she cannot be sure that the true (and possibly stochastic) volatility function might not have changed as well at the same time – model (11.5) does not allow it, but the validity of that model is only the trader's, not the market's, speculation. However, it is reasonable to invoke a sort of 'adiabatic approximation', that is, to say that the volatility should change more slowly than the price,[5] and therefore, with some care, the trader can attempt to answer the question empirically.

11.2.4 Floating and sticky smiles and what they imply about changes in caplet prices

It is important to stress that the evaluation of the delta is therefore purely a statement as to how the implied volatility changes as a function of caplet prices. If, for instance, the assumption $\sigma_{\text{impl}}(F, K) = \sigma_{\text{impl}}(F - K)$ were to be true, then, as F moves to $F + \delta F$, the trader would observe that the price of the call with strike $K + \delta F$ would now be recoverable by inputting the same implied volatility in the Black formula. If the assumption

$$\sigma_{\text{impl}}(F, K) = \sigma_{\text{impl}}(\ln(F) - \ln(K)) = \sigma_{\text{impl}}(\ln(F/K))$$

were true, then the trader would observe that, as F moves to $(1 + \delta)F$, the call price with strike $K(1 + \delta)$ would be recoverable by inputting in the Black formula the same implied volatility and strike $K(1 + \delta)$, and so on. I have called elsewhere this behavior the (absolute or relative, respectively) floating smile. Recall, however, that the Black formula is homogeneous of degree one in F and K, that is, if both F and K are multiplied by the same constant $(1 + \delta)$, the whole caplet price is simply multiplied by $(1 + \delta)$. Therefore, if the smile were, for instance, relatively floating, when both the forward rate and the strike move from F and K to $F(1 + \delta)$ and $K(1 + \delta)$, respectively, the ratio of the forward rate to the strike would not change, the (relatively floating) implied volatility would be the same, and the price of a caplet would simply be

---

[5]The observation that implied volatilities change more slowly than the underlying is, after all, the reason for quoting prices of options in terms of the implied volatilities themselves, rather than directly in pounds or dollars: over short time periods, this quoting convention allows the trader not to change their prices every time the underlying moves by one tick.

multiplied by $(1 + \delta)$. More generally, it is only by observing how real caplet prices change when F changes that one can deduce the dependence on F of the implied volatility and, therefore, calculate the correct delta.

The fundamental question is therefore not theoretical but empirical: Which way do caplet prices behave when F changes? I am not aware of any empirical published work in the interest-rate option area.[6] In my experience, the changes in caplet prices in the interest-rate world can, by and large, be poorly explained by assumptions such as $\sigma_{\text{impl}}(F - K)$ or $\sigma_{\text{impl}}(\ln(F) - \ln(K))$, or, more generally, $\sigma_{\text{impl}}(g(F) - g(K))$, which, I believe, apply much better to the FX/equity world, but, at the time of writing, I cannot provide solid evidence to this effect. Work is under way in this direction.

Finally, the trader could ask another, related, question: 'What process would give rise to prices such that, if the price of a K-strike caplet with $F = F_0$ is given by $\text{Black}(F_0, T - 0, K, \sigma_{\text{impl}}(F_0, K))$, then, when the forward goes to $F_0 + \delta F$, the price of the K-strike call is given by $\text{Black}(F_0 + \delta F, T - 0, K, \sigma_{\text{impl}}(F_0, K))$?' Prices that behave this way give rise to what I call a sticky smile. Note carefully that the implied volatility $\sigma_{\text{impl}}(F_0, K)$ used to calculate the price when F moved from F_0 to $F_0 + \delta F$ has not changed to $\sigma_{\text{impl}}(F_0 + \delta F, K)$ (although the caplet price obviously has changed). If this is the case, then the implied volatility is independent of F, one can write $\sigma_{\text{impl}}(F, K) = \sigma_{\text{impl}}(K)$,

$$\frac{\partial \sigma_{\text{impl}}(F, K)}{\partial F} = 0,$$

and, in evaluating the delta,

$$\Delta_{\text{Black}} = N(h_1) + \text{BlackVega}(F, T, K, \sigma_{\text{impl}}(F, K)) \frac{\partial \sigma_{\text{impl}}(F, K)}{\partial F},$$

the last term disappears and the trader recovers the old simple Black expression:

$$\Delta_{\text{Black}} = N(h_1). \tag{11.7}$$

Possibly the most important conclusion that one can draw from this discussion is that it is impossible to deduce just by inspection of the smile curve as a function of K for a given F_0 what process gives rise to this pattern: today's smile just gives us a snapshot and we would actually need a (short) movie. Indeed, one can prove that an infinity of processes are compatible with any (admissible) set of market call prices today (no matter how finely spaced in expiry and/or strike) (see, e.g., Britten-Jones and Neuberger 1998). When it comes to forward-rate modelling, the standard LIBOR-market-model approach, underpinned as it is by the Black formula, clearly produces not only

---

[6]Very interesting studies along these lines have been carried out in the equity and FX worlds (see, e.g., Derman 1999, Derman and Kamal 1997, Alexander 2000, Johnson 2001). Given the fundamentally different nature of the interest-rate market, on the one hand, and of the equity and FX markets, on the other, these results unfortunately have limited relevance to the topic of this chapter.

a flat, but also a floating, smile (i.e., a smile that will remain flat as the yield curve moves). In a very imprecise way one can say that the displaced-diffusion process presented in this chapter progressively introduces more and more 'stickiness' to a floating smile as the displacement coefficient increases. This, however, is just an approximate statement, and by no means exact (see the exercise below).

EXERCISE 11.1 *Assume that the true process is given by a normal diffusion, that is, in Equation (11.5), assume $\sigma(F) = \sigma_0/F$. Calculate, using the appropriate closed-form expression for normal diffusions, a set of prices for different strikes starting from a given F_0. Repeat the exercise for $F_0 + \delta F$ and $F_0 - \delta F$. Obtain $\sigma_{\mathrm{impl}}(F_0, K)$, $\sigma_{\mathrm{impl}}(F_0 + \delta F, K)$, $\sigma_{\mathrm{impl}}(F_0 - \delta F, K)$. Calculate the derivatives $\partial \sigma_{\mathrm{impl}}(F_0, K)/\partial F$ and $\partial \sigma_{\mathrm{impl}}(F_0, K)/\partial K$. Comment on their relative magnitude, and compare with the relative magnitude of the same derivatives in the truly log-normal (Black) case. What can you conclude about the degree of 'stickiness' of the normal-diffusion smile?*

Note that, if the trader managed to fit the observed smile satisfactorily with a displaced diffusion, and believed this to be indeed the appropriate model for the forward rate, she would not have to run the 'conceptual' Monte Carlo simulation I described before in order to discover the behavior of $\partial \sigma_{\mathrm{impl}}(F_0, K)/\partial F$, since all the prices would be given by a simple, closed-form, Black-like formula. This will indeed be the approach taken in Section 11.3.

11.2.5 *Criteria to choose an appropriate model in the presence of smiles*

The approach to choosing an appropriate process and to evaluating the delta of a caplet (and, by extension of the reasoning, the other derivatives) can therefore be profitably split into two components:

1. An empirical part, which addresses the question: 'What is the functional dependence of the implied volatility on F and K, $\sigma_{\mathrm{impl}}(F, K)$?' The answer to this question can only be obtained by observing price changes (not just prices). The observation of these price changes should, in theory, be separated by small time intervals (to avoid that the true process volatility might change at the same time, polluting the price picture). There is no hiding, however, the practical difficulties of such an investigation, especially because most of the 'trading action' is around the at-the-money strikes.

2. A modelling part: Once the function $\sigma_{\mathrm{impl}}(F, K)$ has been determined, one can either determine the delta directly using Formula (11.4) or one can fit a model that simultaneously produces today's prices with F_0 (a relatively easy task) and the prices that give rise to the function $\sigma_{\mathrm{impl}}(F, K)$ (a much more difficult task).

The second route in point 2 is more appealing because, if one can think in terms of a model, one's intuition is significantly enhanced. If the model allows for closed-form solutions, then the deltas, gammas, vegas, etc., can be obtained easily and quickly, without having to contend with numerical problems, which, especially for gammas, can often be burdensome. More generally, once a model is specified, one can do a lot more than just calculating the risk statistics, and the evaluation of complex derivatives becomes possible.

Given the paucity of reliable, simultaneous quotes, especially away from the at-the-money level, the practical difficulties of the empirical investigation mentioned in point 1 should not be under-estimated. Despite the near-impossibility of obtaining a set of statistically watertight results, however, the need for the trader to express an opinion on the 'origin' of the smile (rather than just its shape at one point in time) is unavoidable. I shall therefore begin in the next section to present the rationale for one possible and appealing smile mechanism.

11.3 Accounting for Monotonically Decreasing Smiles

11.3.1 CEV processes

If one accepts the log-normal assumption, the implication about the absolute basis point move of a particular forward rate due to the arrival of a given information shock is that the move should be exactly proportional to the level of the forward rate itself. Therefore, in an upward-sloping yield curve where the front end is, say, at 3% and the long-end forward rates at 6%, the response to the arrival of a given innovation shock should be twice as large (in basis points) for the later-expiring forward rates.[7]

While there appears to be common agreement among traders (but, to my knowledge, a surprising lack of hard econometric evidence[8]) that the absolute rate movement does depend on the level of the forward rate, the market consensus seems to point in the direction that an exactly proportional scaling would make this dependence too strong: in other terms, according to 'market lore', the forward rate at 6% should move, in basis points, more than, but not twice as much as, the forward rate at 3%.

If the problem is looked at in this light, it is natural to see the log-normal and normal models for the evolution of forward rates (which imply that their basis point moves should be proportional to or independent of, respectively, the level of the forward rates themselves) as limiting members of the same family of diffusions, often referred to as the constant-elasticity-of-variance (CEV)

---

[7]Identical and constant instantaneous volatility functions for all the forward rates have been implicitly assumed in presenting this argument. The modifications needed to deal with more realistic cases are straightforward.

[8]Marsh and Rosenfeld (1983) find no evidence to reject the log-normal model, while Chan et al. (1992) find evidence for $\beta > 1$. Campbell et al. (1996) also support these findings, and report results that show that the heteroskedasticity of the short rate is significantly reduced as the exponent β is increased from 0 to 1.5. See also the discussion in Ahn and Gao (1999).

family (see, e.g., Beckers 1980):

$$\mathrm{d}f_i(t) = \mu_i(\{\mathbf{f}\}, t)\,\mathrm{d}t + \sigma_i^{(\beta)}(t)f_i^\beta\,\mathrm{d}z_i(t) \qquad 0 \le \beta \le 1. \tag{11.8}$$

(Note that, in Equation (11.8), the superscript β indicates exponentiation when it appears next to the forward rate, but simply labels the time-dependent component of the volatility function when it is used in the expression $\sigma_i^{(\beta)}(t)$. For simplicity, the volatility in the log-normal case will in the following often be simply denoted by $\sigma_i(t)$, that is, $\sigma_i^{(1)}(t) = \sigma_i(t)$.)

Clearly, the value of $\beta = 1$ corresponds to the log-normal case that has been examined so far; $\beta = 0$ gives rise to the normal case; $\beta = \frac{1}{2}$ produces the square-root process; etc. Extensions of the LIBOR market model along these lines have recently been introduced by Andersen and Andreasen (1997). See also the related approach by Zuehlsdorff (2001).

A specification such as (11.8) implies that, for $0 < \beta < 1$, the assumption made in Chapter 2 about the deterministic nature of the volatility of the exponential martingale describing the forward-rate process is no longer valid. Indeed, for $\beta \neq 1$, the process for the forward rate need not be a strictly positive martingale (for $\beta = \frac{1}{2}$, for instance, zero becomes an absorbing barrier), and its representation in terms of an exponential martingale is no longer possible. Note, however, that the volatility, $\sigma_i(t) = \sigma_i^{(\beta)}(t)f_i^\beta$, in Equation (11.8) is assumed to depend purely on the realization of the forward rate itself. As a consequence, the knowledge of the future value of f_i, and of no other stochastic variable, fully determines the state, and, in a statistical sense, its future evolution (more precisely, the natural filtration $\mathcal{F}_t$) is still generated by the evolution up to time t of the forward-rate process. This should be contrasted with the stochastic-volatility case, dealt with in the next chapter, where the realizations of the Wiener processes describing the forward rates and their volatilities from the time origin to time τ are necessary to specify fully the state at time τ.

As for the analytic tractability of the specification (11.8), explicit closed-form solutions exist for $\beta = 0$, $\frac{1}{2}$, $\frac{2}{3}$ and 1. The general solution for arbitrary values of β, however, requires an infinite sum of Gamma functions, and can be both awkward and numerically delicate to evaluate[9]

---

[9]It is often claimed that the CEV model 'allows for closed-form solutions'; indeed, caplet and European swaption prices can be expressed in terms of the non-central chi-squared distribution, as Hull and White (2000) correctly point out. This statement can however be somewhat misleading, since it might suggest that one can write a closed-form expression for the realization of a forward rate at a time $T + \tau$, given its value at time T, as one can do in the normal and log-normal cases. In reality, for an arbitrary value of the exponent β, no simple closed-form solution for the stochastic differential equation describing the evolution of a forward rate exists, one has to resort to a short-stepped Monte Carlo evolution, and the (very-)long-jump procedure described in Chapter 4 is therefore jeopardized.

11.3.2 Displaced diffusion: the process

An alternative description of the state of affairs described at the beginning of this section can be achieved by means of the following model (often referred to as the 'displaced-diffusion' model (see Rubinstein 1983)):

$$\frac{d(f_t + a)}{f_t + a} = \frac{df_t}{f_t + a} = \mu_a \, dt + \sigma_a(t) \, dz(t) \qquad a > 0, \qquad (11.9)$$

whereby the quantity $(f_t + a)$ is modelled as a log-normally distributed stochastic variable. Alternatively and equivalently one can write (Marris 1999):

$$df_t = \mu \, dt + [\gamma f_t + f_0(1 - \gamma)]\sigma_\gamma \, dz(t). \qquad (11.10)$$

Note that, in Expression (11.10) f_0 is today's known value of the forward rate and the whole expression $f_0(1 - \gamma)$ is therefore just a constant, say, ξ. For $\gamma \neq 0$, rewriting (11.10) as

$$df_t = \mu \, dt + [f_t + (\xi/\gamma)]\gamma\sigma_\gamma \, dz(t), \qquad (11.10')$$

one can readily see that (11.10) is equivalent to (11.9), with

$$f_t + a = f_t + \frac{\xi}{\gamma} \implies \frac{\xi}{\gamma} = \frac{f_0(1 - \gamma)}{\gamma} = a$$

$$\sigma_a(t) = \gamma\sigma_\gamma(t).$$

The relationship between γ and the displacement coefficient a for different initial values of today's forward rate, f_0, is shown in Figure 11.4. One can notice that, as the coefficient a approaches a value of approximately unity, the corresponding γ is almost zero, irrespective of the initial value f_0, leading towards a normal (Gaussian) behavior for the forward rate.

Equation (11.10') lends itself to the interpretation of the forward rate being driven by a mixture of a normal and a log-normal responsiveness to the same shock, and therefore constitutes a plausible way of translating into a tractable model the financial desiderata mentioned at the beginning of this section. (The reason for expressing a displaced diffusion in the somewhat convoluted manner as in (11.10) will become apparent in the following.) Clearly, $\gamma = 0$ corresponds to the normal case, and $\xi = a = 0$ to the log-normal one.

11.3.3 Displaced diffusion: closed-form solution for the forward-rate evolution and caplet prices

The closed-form solution for the value of the forward rate at time t is easily found to be given by

$$f(t) = (f(0) + a)[exp \int_0^t \mu_a(u) - \frac{1}{2}\sigma_a^2(u)du + \int_0^t \sigma_a(u)dz(u)] - a \qquad (11.11)$$

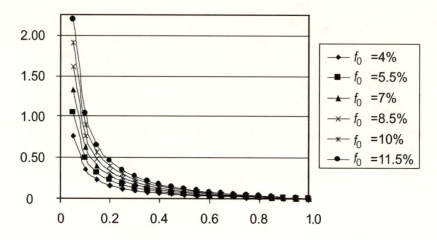

Figure 11.4   *The link between γ (on the y axis) and the displacement coefficient a (on the x axis) for different initial values of f_0. Since, as shown later, a correspondence can be established between the exponent β and γ, the same values on the y axis also express the approximate link between the displacement coefficient a and the CEV exponent β. Notice that for values of a $\approx$ 1, the coefficient γ and the exponent β are already virtually identical to zero irrespective of f_0, and an almost exactly normal behavior has been recovered.*

or

$$f(t) = \frac{f(0)}{\gamma} [exp \int_0^t \mu(u) - \frac{1}{2}\gamma^2\sigma_\gamma^2(u)du + \gamma \int_0^t \sigma_\gamma(u)dz(u) - 1] \qquad \gamma \neq 0$$

$$(11.11')$$

in terms of Specifications (11.10) or (11.10′) respectively. When $\gamma = 0$ the Solution (11.11′) is clearly non-valid, but the $\gamma = 0$ solution is easily recognized to correspond to the normal diffusion for the forward rate, and in this case (neglecting the drift to keep notation light, and denoting the absolute volatility in the normal case by σ_{abs}) one can write

$$f(t) = f_0 + \int_0^t \sigma_{abs}(u)\,dz(u) \qquad \gamma = 0. \qquad (11.12)$$

Therefore, given today's values of the forward rates, the displaced-diffusion setting allows a closed-form expression for the realizations of the same forward rates after an arbitrarily large time t,[10] and therefore readily lends itself to the (very-)long-jump procedure described in Chapter 4.

[10]For the result to be true exactly, the usual caveat should apply that the drift μ_a must be at most a deterministic function of time. When the no-arbitrage conditions are introduced, this will turn out not to be the case. The same approximations presented in Chapter 5 are however possible (see, in particular, Sections 12.3 and 12.8.2). The statement above about the availability of a closed-form solution therefore remains true, albeit in an approximate sense.

Another desirable feature of the displaced-diffusion approach is that the integration of a caplet payoff over the terminal probability distribution yields an extremely simple result. This can be obtained either by direct integration of Equations (11.4) or (11.4′) – the route followed by Marris (1999) – or, much more simply, as follows. For a given caplet, let us

- choose as numeraire the natural payoff of the underlying forward rate,

- call Q the associated terminal measure, and

- denote the present value at time $t = t_0 = 0$ of a K-strike caplet of maturity T when the forward rate follows a displaced diffusion with displacement coefficient a as $\mathrm{Caplet}_a(f_0, K, t_0, T)$.

Then

$$
\begin{aligned}
\mathrm{Caplet}_a(f_0, K, t_0, T) &= E_Q[(f_T - K)^+]B(t_0, T + \tau) \\
&= E_Q[(f_T + a - (K + a))^+]B(t_0, T + \tau) \\
&= \left[\int_{K'}^{+\infty} (f_T + a)\Phi(f_T + a)\,\mathrm{d}(f_T + a) \right. \\
&\quad \left. - K' \int_{K'}^{+\infty} \Phi(f_T + a)\,\mathrm{d}(f_T + a) \right] B(t_0, T + \tau) \\
&= [(f_0 + a)N(h_1^a) - K'N(h_2^a)]B(t_0, T + \tau) \quad (11.13)
\end{aligned}
$$

with $N(\ )$ the cumulative normal distribution, $K' = K + a$, $B(t_0, T + \tau)$ the value at time t_0 of the natural payoff of forward rate f_T (i.e., the discount bond maturing at time $T + \tau$), $\Phi(\ )$ the probability density function in the terminal measure Q for the variable $(f_T + a)$, and

$$
h_1^a = \frac{\ln[(f_0 + a)/K'] + \frac{1}{2}v_a^2}{v_a},
$$

$$
h_2^a = \frac{\ln[(f_0 + a)/K'] - \frac{1}{2}v_a^2}{v_a},
$$

$$
v_a^2 \equiv \int_0^T \sigma_a^2(u, T)\,\mathrm{d}u.
$$

Equation (11.13) lends itself to a very simple interpretation: the last line in Equation (11.13) is simply the familiar (log-normal) Black caplet formula with the variable $f_T(0) + a$ replacing $f_T(0)$, a displaced strike $K' = K + a$ and a root-mean-square volatility given by $v_a/\sqrt{T}$.

EXERCISE 11.2 *Using the result presented in Equation (11.13), repeat Exercise 11.1 in Section 11.2 for the case of displaced diffusions. Comment on the relative magnitude of the derivatives $\partial\sigma_{\mathrm{impl}}(F_0, K)/\partial F$ and $\partial\sigma_{\mathrm{impl}}(F_0, K)/\partial K$ as a function of the displacement coefficient a, and draw a comparison with the normal case.*

11.3.4 Displaced diffusion: derivation of the approximate equivalent volatility

Equation (11.13) therefore gives a very simple formula for the value of a caplet, but gives no indication as to how a given at-the-money market price for a caplet, quoted in terms of an implied log-normal volatility, can be easily recovered in a displaced-diffusion setting. In other words, given a log-normal implied volatility σ_{impl}, and for a chosen a, it is not a priori obvious which displaced-diffusion volatility σ_a will produce the same at-the-money price. One can, of course, obtain the correct answer by making use of the fact that closed-form expressions exist for the value of a call (caplet) for any value of strike. By equating the at-the-money prices one can attempt to solve (Marris 1999) for the volatility, σ_a, given the log-normal volatility, σ, by inverting the Black formula.[11] While conceptually straightforward, the procedure is not without some computational problems, because one cannot neatly solve for the volatility σ_a. Fortunately, a much simpler, but remarkably accurate, approximate result can be used: one can in fact empirically observe that the at-the-money caplet prices obtained with different values, say, a' and a'', of the displacement coefficient, a, are almost identical as long as one chooses the volatility $\sigma_{a'}$ and $\sigma_{a''}$ using the formula

$$\sigma_{a''}(t)(f_0 + a'') = \sigma_{a'}(t)(f_0 + a'). \tag{11.14}$$

In particular, this result holds true for $a = 0$, that is, in the log-normal case, and one can write, for a generic a,

$$\sigma_a(t) = \sigma(t)\frac{f_0}{f_0 + a}, \tag{11.14'}$$

where $\sigma(t) = \sigma_{a=0}(t)$. (Note that in Equation (11.14') the term $f_0/(f_0 + a)$ is just a constant, which can be evaluated given the knowledge of today's value of the forward rate.) The values of at-the-money caplet prices obtained using different values of the displacement coefficient a when the volatility is scaled according to (11.14) are shown in Table 11.1 for a variety of maturities up to 10 years, for the case of a percentage volatility ($a = 0$) of 20% and an at-the-money forward rate of 6.00%. As I shall show in the next chapter, this property can be of assistance in the calibration of the model to at-the-money caplet prices, and gives the first indication that even the extended LIBOR-market-model approach continues to enjoy the benefit of very simple but very accurate approximations.

---

[11]The 'correct' approach suggested by Marris (1999) is superior to the approximate solution suggested in this section not so much for the greater accuracy (which is rather limited) but because it allows one to find the volatility σ_a that matches the caplet prices for *any* strike, not necessarily for the at-the-money one. In practice this conceptual advantage is rather limited.

Table 11.1 *At-the-money forward (i.e., undiscounted) caplet prices for different values of the displacement coefficient and different maturities (in years, in the first column). The prices in the table were obtained by setting the volatility σ_a equal to $\sigma_a = \sigma f_0 / (f_0 + a)$. The prices are expressed in units of principal, and for a tenor of one year. No discounting was applied to the prices, in order to avoid dampening possible discrepancies by a large discounting factor.*

			a		
Expiry	0.4	0.3	0.2	0.1	0.0
1	0.0048	0.0048	0.0048	0.0048	0.0048
2	0.0068	0.0068	0.0068	0.0067	0.0067
5	0.0107	0.0107	0.0106	0.0106	0.0106
10	0.0150	0.0150	0.0150	0.0149	0.0149

11.3.5 Displaced diffusion: comparative analysis of prices and implied volatilities

Figure 11.5 shows, for the different values of the strikes marked on the x axis, the ratio of displaced-diffusion caplet prices to the prices obtained with a geometric Brownian motion (for a maturity of one year, and an initial forward-rate value of 6.00%). Figure 11.6 then shows the implied volatilities associated with caplet prices of different strikes (also for a maturity of one year and an initial value for the forward rate of 6.00%), and indicates that the displaced-diffusion approach does indeed have the ability to reproduce the monotonically decreasing smile referred to above. Similarly, Figure 11.7

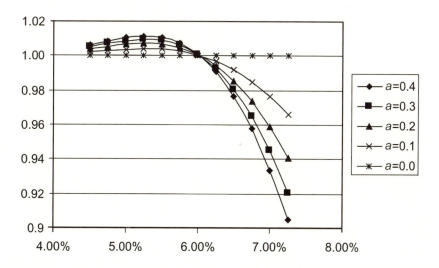

Figure 11.5 *The ratios for different strikes of the displaced-diffusion caplet price to the price for the log-normal caplet (displacement coefficient a =0.4, 0.3, 0.2, 0.1 and 0, corresponding to the log-normal price), for a maturity of one year and an at-the-money forward rate of 6%.*

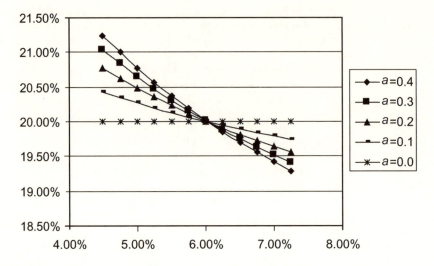

Figure 11.6   *Implied volatilities obtained from caplet prices corresponding to different values of the displacement coefficient a, for expiry time of one year and $f_0 = 6.00\%$.*

displays, again for different strikes, the dependence on the displacement coefficient a of the percentage difference in caplet price in moving from the log-normal case ($a = 0$) to the case of $a = 0.20$; a maturity of five years was used for this example. It is apparent that the changes in the relative discrepancy become progressively smaller as the value of the displacement coefficient increases. Finally, Figure 11.8 shows the changes in implied volatility for the same option as a function of the displacement coefficient a (the same strikes were used as in Figure 11.7). Also in this case it is apparent that the effect (i.e., the change in discrepancy from the log-normal case) becomes progressively smaller as the displacement coefficient a increases.

11.3.6 The link between CEV and displaced diffusion

Given the treatment up to this point, the CEV and the displaced-diffusion approaches to modelling the deviation of the behavior of forward rates from log-normality appear to be two plausible, but otherwise unrelated, approaches. Marris (1999), however, shows, and gives a justification for, an unexpected and very useful property: if β in Equation (11.8) is taken to be equal to γ in Equation (11.10), then the caplet prices, and hence the implied volatilities, produced by the two approaches are almost identical over a very wide range of strikes, as shown in Figure 11.9 (see also Figure 11.4 for the link between a and γ (or, equivalently, β)).

Needless to say, the approximate agreement between the displaced-diffusion and the CEV prices must break down for very low strikes, since the displaced-

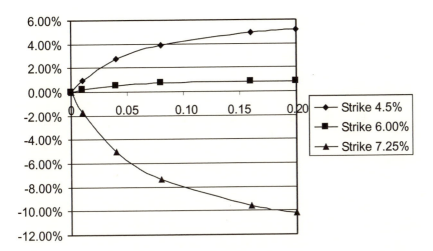

Figure 11.7 *The dependence of the percentage difference in caplet price from the log-normal case (for expiry of five years and at-the-money forward rate of 6.00%) on the displacement diffusion coefficient a (on the x axis). Note that the range of values for a typically found when fitting the displacement coefficient to market smiles data is centred around 0.02/0.05.*

diffusion model implies that each forward rate must be greater than $-a$, but that it can be negative; the CEV model, on the other hand, implies non-negative forward rates for any $\beta > 0$. Plausible values of a, however, are found to be no larger in magnitude than a few percentage points, and the likelihood of the forward rate becoming negative is therefore very small (for $f_0 = 6.00\%$, for $\beta = \gamma = \frac{3}{4}$, one obtains $a = 0.02$; see Figures 11.4 and 11.10). As one can see from Figure 11.9, however, even values of the displacement coefficient considerably larger than a few percent produce implied volatilities for very low and high strikes barely distinguishable from the corresponding CEV values.

Marris (1999) provides an interesting explanation of why the agreement is so good over such a large range of strikes (the argument is based on the expansion of the cumulative normal and of the non-central chi-squared distributions). From a different but related angle, Figures 11.10 and 11.11 show the log-normal probability density in three and 10 years' time, respectively, for a forward rate with initial value (today) of 6.00%, obtained with a root-mean-square volatility of 15%. The same figures also show the corresponding densities for the case of a displacement coefficient of 0.05 (typical values obtained in fitting real market data tend to produce smaller values, of the order of 0.02 or 0.03) and of 1000 (i.e., for a virtually normal distribution). The volatilities of the normal and displaced-diffusion processes were chosen so as to give the same price for the at-the-money caplet in all the three cases. This was achieved by making use of approximation (11.14). It is interesting to notice that the three probability densities have a visibly different skewness, and

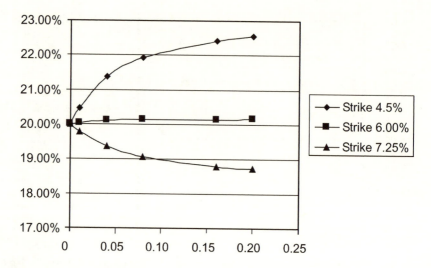

Figure 11.8   *The dependence of the implied volatility (for expiry of five years and at-the-money strike of 6.00%) on the displacement diffusion coefficient a (on the x axis). The same considerations about 'typical' values for a in the caption to Figure 11.6 apply.*

that the integrated probability density over negative values corresponding to the displaced-diffusion coefficient of 0.05 remains very small even after a 10-years' period (4.25% for a displaced-diffusion coefficient a of 0.05, and 1.72% for $a = 0.03$).

11.3.7 Reasons for choosing the displaced-diffusion formalism

This equivalence property between the CEV and the displaced-diffusion approaches is very useful and important, since it allows an immediate translation back and forth between the CEV world (which has been more extensively treated in the literature and has more attractive theoretical properties, since it preserves non-negative rates) and the displaced-diffusion setting (which always allows closed-form analytical solutions, and therefore more readily lends itself to natural extensions of the numerical manipulations presented in Parts I–III). So, for instance, the treatment presented in Section 2.3 (where the formal set-up to describe the dynamics of the forward rates is presented) proceeds unaltered up to Equation (2.28) of that chapter. At this point, in the displaced-diffusion framework, we simply impose the two conditions that

1. the quantity $f_i + a$ should be strictly positive, and therefore representable by means of an exponential martingale, and

2. the volatility that appears in this exponential representation (i.e., the volatility of $f_i + a$) should be a deterministic function of time (cf. Conditions 2.3 and 2.3′ in Section 2.3).

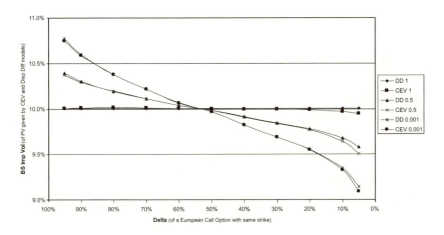

Figure 11.9 *The implied volatility obtained for call option prices with strikes corresponding to different (Black) delta values from 95% to 5%, for the log-normal case (curves 'DD 1', 'CEV 1'), the (almost or exactly) square-root process (curves 'DD 0.5', 'CEV 0.5') and the (almost) normal case (curves 'DD 0.001', 'CEV 0.001'). From work by Marris (1999), whose help is gratefully acknowledged.*

Similarly, when it comes to obtaining the explicit expressions for the drift corrections presented in Chapter 5, the reasoning proceeds substantially unaltered up to point 7 in Section 5.1.3, where the Conditions (i) and (ii) above are then invoked. (Note that, if $N_i(t)$ is the natural payoff of the forward rate f_i, then the quantity $(f_i + a)N_i(t)$ is still a traded asset, and division by the chosen numeraire still produces a relative price.) The no-arbitrage drift of the quantity $f_i + a$, μ_a, is then given by

$$\mu_a = -\sigma_a \sigma_X \rho_{(f+a),X},\tag{11.15}$$

with X exactly defined as in point 6 in Section 5.1.3. In deriving this equation, use has been made of the fact that $f_i + a$ can be represented in terms of an exponential martingale. The explicit expression for the drift in the displaced-diffusion case in terms of volatilities of and correlations among forward rates is given in Section 12.2.

EXERCISE 11.3 *Derive Equation (11.15).*

More importantly, for an arbitrary exponent β, the CEV approach does not allow computationally efficient closed-form solutions of the stochastic differential equations of the forward rates. Even for the standard case of $\beta = \frac{1}{2}$, the closed-form expression for the value of the forward rate after a finite time is computationally rather burdensome. Therefore the long-jump and very-long-jump procedures cannot, in general, be used efficiently, and the trader must

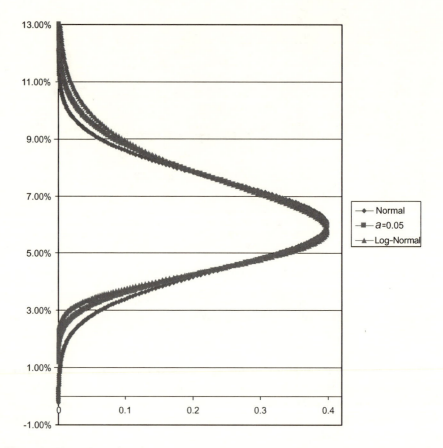

Figure 11.10   *The probability densities obtained for a forward rate with constant volatility of 15% over a three-year horizon in the case of a normal, log-normal and displaced-diffusion process (a = 0.05). The volatilities of the normal and displaced-diffusion processes were chosen so as to give the same price for the at-the-money caplet. This was achieved by making use of equation (11.14).*

evolve the process by means of a relatively short-stepped Monte Carlo simulation. In this respect, statements often found in the literature that the CEV model 'allows for analytic solutions in terms of the non-central chi-squared density' should be strongly qualified. It is indeed possible to express in this form the expectations that produce the prices of caplets and European swaptions (Hull and White 2000). This feature, however, only simplifies one (admittedly important) aspect of the calibration procedure, but does not easily give back the more important and powerful evolution techniques described in Chapters 3 and 4. As shown below, these are, however, naturally recovered in the displaced-diffusion setting.

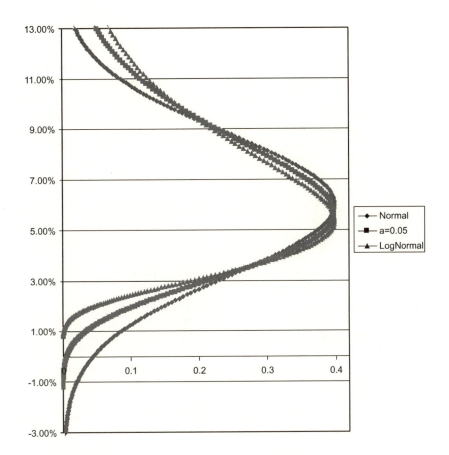

Figure 11.11 *The probability densities obtained for a forward rate with constant volatility of 15% over a 10-year horizon in the case of a normal, log-normal and displaced-diffusion process (displacement coefficient a = 0.05). The volatilities of the normal and displaced-diffusion processes were chosen so as to give the same price for the at-the-money caplet [i.e., by making use of Equation (11.14)]. The integrated probability for the forward rate to become negative is 4.25% for a displaced-diffusion coefficient a = 0.05, 1.72% for a = 0.03 and 0.87% for a = 0.02. Fits to actual market data tend to give a value for a of the order of 0.02.*

11.3.8 Should the displacement coefficients be made time-dependent?

Another important issue in this preliminary analysis of the general properties of the displaced-diffusion approach is the desirability of introducing a dependence of the displacement parameter a (or, equivalently, of the exponent β) on the forward rate:

$$\mathrm{d}f_i(t) = \mu(\{\mathbf{f}\}, t)\,\mathrm{d}t + \sigma_i^{(\beta_i)}(t)f_i^{\beta_i}\,\mathrm{d}z_i(t) \qquad 0 \leq \beta \leq 1, \qquad (11.16)$$

$$\frac{d(f_i + a_i)}{f_i + a_i} = \mu(\{\mathbf{f}\}, t)\, dt + \sigma_{a_i}(t)\, dz_i(t). \tag{11.17}$$

Needless to say, the fitting flexibility of this version is greatly (and perhaps excessively) increased. On purely financial grounds, it might superficially appear plausible and desirable to allow for a dependence on the level of the forward rate in the deviation from log-normality. So, for instance, a given forward rate that stands today at 6% might display a more log-normal behavior than a 3% forward rate in the same yield curve. This approach, however, which has recently been proposed in the literature and by some practitioners, not only creates some unpleasant computational problems, but largely fails to capture the very effect it is supposed to describe. To begin with the latter problem, if one believed that forward rates behaved in a more normal (as in 'Gaussian') way when they reach low values, and more log-normally when they are higher, one should make the exponent, or the displacement coefficient, dependent on the level of the forward rate *as it evolves over time*, not on the level of the forward rate in today's yield curve. So, the displacement coefficient should be of the form $a_i(f_i(t))$, and it would become stochastic. The computational complexities would be substantial, and the underlying financial justification somewhat dubious. Furthermore, for a model to be of practical use, it must lend itself to effective numerical implementation. In particular, the speedy recovery of European swaption prices and the ready calibration to co-terminal swaptions, treated in Chapter 10, and extended to the stochastic-volatility displaced-diffusion setting in the next chapter, are essential ingredients of a successful pricing engine. If the same displacement coefficient a is retained for all the forward rates, I shall show that simple modifications of the procedures presented so far allow one to retain the general structure and validity of the approximations. This would no longer be the case if the displacement coefficient were made forward-rate-dependent. Therefore, in the following the same exponent and displacement coefficient for all the forward rates will always be used.

11.3.9 Plan of the work ahead

These preliminary considerations have laid out the fundamental properties of the displaced-diffusion extensions of the LIBOR market model. My next task is to recast the driving equations and the approximations presented in the previous chapters in terms of the displaced-diffusion model and to explore to what extent they retain their effectiveness. More precisely, I have shown in Parts I–III that, insofar as the standard LIBOR market model is concerned,

1. the predictor–corrector method allows one to express (approximately, but very accurately) the drift terms in terms of quantities computable today (and therefore makes the (very-)long-jump procedure practicable);

2. the prices of (at-the-money) European swaptions can be calculated very efficiently and analytically simply from the knowledge of the deterministic instantaneous volatility and correlation function, and of today's yield curve;

3. the prices of caplets can be exactly recovered while producing as time-homogeneous an evolution of the term structure of volatilities as possible;

4. a forward-rate-based model can be efficiently, rapidly and almost perfectly calibrated to co-terminal European swaptions, while simultaneously providing the best possible fit to an exogenous forward-rate co-variance matrix.

I will examine to what extent these approximations can still be relied upon when moving to the displaced-diffusion case will be examined. As mentioned above, I shall make use of the displaced-diffusion approach for ease of computation, despite the greater theoretical appeal of the CEV model. In the back of her mind, the trader can always effect a translation to the closely equivalent CEV world by means of Marris's (1999) insight. For the sake of economy of presentation, these extensions are undertaken in the following chapter, together with the treatment of the stochastic-volatility case.

Before leaving this chapter, however, it is useful to revisit the concept of time-homogeneity for the term structure of volatilities, which was, after all, one of the main desiderata that informed the choice of the instantaneous volatility functions in the deterministic case. This important topic is dealt with in the next section.

11.4 Time-Homogeneity in the Context of Displaced Diffusions

11.4.1 Time-homogeneity, caplet prices and log-normality

I have already shown in Section 11.2 how the at-the-money caplet prices corresponding to different values of the displacement coefficient a can be made almost identical without any numerical fitting procedure simply by imposing relationship (11.14′):

$$\sigma_a(t) = \sigma(t)\frac{f_0}{f_0 + a}.$$

Therefore, if a satisfactory set of coefficients for the log-normal instantaneous volatility function capable of reproducing the at-the-money caplet prices has already been found, the scaling provided by Equation (11.14′) is guaranteed to produce a percentage volatility for the quantity $f(t) + a$ capable of reproducing almost exactly the same at-the-money prices.

One of the criteria proposed so far to determine the coefficients of the log-normal instantaneous volatility functions has been the time-homogeneity of the resulting term structure of volatilities. As mentioned in Section 11.1, however, in the presence of smiles the link between implied volatilities (that make up the term structure of volatilities) and the root-mean-square instantaneous volatility is lost, and one must examine much more carefully what one means by time-homogeneity. To this effect, let us revisit the implications of time-homogeneity in the context of a log-normal model. In Chapter 6, the time-homogeneity condition of the term structure of volatilities was written as

$$\int_0^T \sigma(T,u)^2 \, du = v(0,T)^2 = \int_\tau^{T+\tau} \sigma(T+\tau,u)^2 \, du = v(\tau,T+\tau)^2. \quad (11.18)$$

At time τ the forward rate that has value f_0 today will have assumed the stochastic value $f(\tau)$. Given the fact that the Black formula, Black( ), is homogeneous of degree one in the forward rate and strike,[12] one can write, if Condition (11.18) (i.e., the time-homogeneity condition) holds and under the assumption of log-normality,

$$\text{Caplet}(t_0, T, f_T(0), K, v(0,T)) = \text{Black}(f_T(0), K, T, v(0,T)) \quad (11.19)$$

and

$$\begin{aligned}
&\text{Caplet}(\tau, T+\tau, f_{T+\tau}(\tau), Kh, v(\tau, T+\tau)) \\
&= \text{Black}(f_{T+\tau}(\tau), Kh, T+\tau, v(\tau, T+\tau)) \\
&= \text{Black}(f_{T+\tau}(\tau), Kh, T+\tau, v(0,T)), \quad (11.20)
\end{aligned}$$

with h a multiplicative constant necessary to ensure that the degree of at-the-moneyness at time τ for the caplet, given the realization of $f_T(\tau)$, is the same as the at-the-moneyness at time t_0 for a caplet with the same residual maturity. Given the log-normal assumption, this means that h must be equal to $f_T(\tau)/f_T(0)$. Therefore

$$\begin{aligned}
&\text{Caplet}(\tau, T+\tau, f_{T+\tau}(\tau), Kh, v(\tau, T+\tau)) \\
&= \text{Black}\left(f_{T+\tau}(\tau), K\frac{f_{T+\tau}(\tau)}{f_T(0)}, T+\tau, v(0,T)\right) \\
&= \text{Black}\left(f_T(0)\frac{f_{T+\tau}(\tau)}{f_T(0)}, K\frac{f_{T+\tau}(\tau)}{f_T(0)}, T+\tau, v(0,T)\right) \\
&= \frac{f_{T+\tau}(\tau)}{f_T(0)} \text{Black}(f_T(0), K, T+\tau, v(0,T)) \\
&= \frac{f_{T+\tau}(\tau)}{f_T(0)} \text{Caplet}(0, T, f_T(0), K, v(0,T)), \quad (11.21)
\end{aligned}$$

---

[12] Recall that a function, $f( )$, is said to be homogeneous of degree one if $f(kx) = kf(x)$. In the case of the Black function, if both the forward rate and the strike are multiplied by the same constant, the arguments of the cumulative normal distributions do not change, and the call (caplet) price is simply multiplied by the constant itself.

where in the last two lines use has been made of the homogeneity-of-degree-one property of the Black formula. Therefore, by imposing the time-homogeneity condition in a log-normal world, we are imposing that the future prices of same-residual-maturity and same-at-the-moneyness caplets should scale exactly as the ratio $f_{T+\tau}(\tau)/f_T(0)$. In particular, if the forward rate at time τ, $f_{T+\tau}(\tau)$, were, say, twice as large as the forward rate $f_T(0)$, the caplet price for the same residual maturity and the same degree of at-the-moneyness would be twice as large in basis points.

11.4.2 Time-homogeneity, caplet prices and displaced diffusion

If one instead still enforced the time-homogeneity condition for the instantaneous volatility, but now made, say, a normal assumption for the underlying forward rates, one could write

$$\text{Caplet}(\tau, T + \tau, f_{T+\tau}(\tau), K + h, v(\tau, T + \tau))$$
$$= \text{Caplet}(\tau, T + \tau, f_{T+\tau}(\tau), K + h, v(0, T)), \qquad (11.22)$$

where the quantity v has been redefined for an absolute instantaneous volatility, and the factor h, needed to ensure the same degree of at-the-moneyness, is now additive rather than multiplicative, and given by $f_{T+\tau}(\tau) - f_T(0)$. One can therefore write

$$\text{Caplet}(\tau, T + \tau, f_{T+\tau}(\tau), K + h, v(\tau, T + \tau))$$
$$= \text{Caplet}(\tau, T + \tau, f_T(0) + f_{T+\tau}(\tau) - f_T(0) + K$$
$$+ f_{T+\tau}(\tau) - f_T(0), v(0, T))$$
$$= \text{Caplet}(0, T, f_T(0), K, v(0, T)), \qquad (11.23)$$

that is, enforcing the time-homogeneity condition and making the normal-distribution assumption is equivalent to imposing that future caplet prices for the same residual maturity and the same degree of at-the-moneyness should be totally independent of the future level of the forward rate, $f_{T+\tau}(\tau)$.

With the CEV or displaced-diffusion models the trader is therefore implicitly saying that, if the term structure of volatilities is time-homogeneous, future prices of caplets will neither be independent of the level of forward rates nor scale exactly as the ratio $f_{T+\tau}(\tau)/f_T(0)$; rather, they will display an intermediate behavior. This observation is very important, because it is quite plausible that the original introduction of monotonically decreasing smiles might have been motivated by this very observation of the caplet *price* behavior as a function of the yield-curve level.

The conclusions that one can draw from this discussion are that the concept of time-homogeneity must be analyzed much more carefully in the displaced-diffusion (or CEV) setting, and that time-homogeneity now becomes a property that affects prices rather than simply volatilities. Furthermore, this price behavior is intimately linked with the dependence of the implied volatility, $\sigma_{\text{impl}}(f, K)$, on f and K, as discussed in Section 11.2.

With this last proviso clearly in mind, one can move to the extension of the evolution and calibration procedures alluded to above in the displaced-diffusion/stochastic-volatility setting. This is the task presented in the next chapter.

12

Extending the Standard Approach – II: Stochastic Instantaneous Volatilities

12.1 Introduction and Motivation[1]

12.1.1 Criteria to extend the displaced-diffusion approach

In the previous chapter, I have presented the possible financial reasons for describing the forward-rate dynamics in terms of a displaced-diffusion or CEV model. I would like to stress that I find the CEV approach theoretically more appealing, since it is guaranteed to preserve non-negative forward rates (for $\beta \neq 0$). Unfortunately, for arbitrary values of the exponent β (see Equation (11.8)), it does not readily lend itself to simple closed-form solutions. As pointed out in Section 11.3, however, there exists a simple relationship (see Marris 1999) between the CEV exponent and the displacement factor of the displaced diffusion model that allows the establishment of a very close correspondence between the two approaches (see, in particular, Figure 11.9). In the treatment presented in Part IV of this book, I have therefore chosen displaced diffusions over CEV simply for computational simplicity, and I keep in the back of my mind the theoretically more appealing, and closely equivalent, CEV setting.

In Chapter 11 I have also indicated that, by means of either of these approaches, it is possible to account in a realistic way for the perceived deviations from the log-normal behavior of the absolute basis point moves of the forward rates. I have also pointed out that more complex features have recently appeared in the smile surface (see Figures 11.1–11.3), which cannot

---

[1](Extended parts of this chapter have been adapted from an article by Joshi and Rebonato 2001, which is still in the submitted-for-publication stage. I would like to thank Dr. Mark Joshi for allowing the material to appear in this book while still publicly available only in working-paper form.

be reconciled with the simple explanation of the smile as being due to a lack of proportionality between the move sizes and the forward-rate level. It is not at all obvious which avenue should be explored in order to account for these features. Even a cursory examination of the three figures mentioned above presents a somewhat contradictory picture. Looking at Figure 11.1 (USD), for instance, one can notice that the steepness of the smile appears to decrease as the expiry of the forward rate increases. In both the EUR and GBP cases (Figures 11.2 and 11.3), on the other hand, the slope remains approximately constant across maturities, or, if anything, becomes more pronounced as the expiry increases. The former behavior is more commonly associated with jump-diffusion processes, the latter with stochastic volatility. Needless to say, both modelling approaches can be 'forced' to produce either pattern, but, in general, only at the expense of making the process parameters strongly time-dependent. The lack of time-homogeneity in the smile surface that this choice would entail strongly reduces the desirability of going down this route.

Another pertinent consideration in trying to choose the correct smile-producing mechanism is that, historically, the origin of the hockey-stick shape[2] has been associated with the market turmoil of the post-Russia events. In this period, forward rates did experience significant moves, but the most pronounced dislocations occurred in the implied volatility surfaces[3] (and in the relative value of caplets and swaptions in particular). It is plausible, and confirmed by anecdotal evidence, that traders who were hedging their positions on the basis of models which implied a deterministic term structure of volatilities were severely hurt by the moves in the volatility surfaces. The same traders, according to this reconstruction of events, began to feel an acute need for models that could account for stochastic implied volatility surfaces. Several mechanisms can give rise to such stochastic smiles, and requiring that the volatility of the forward-rate process should be stochastic is by no means the only way to produce the desired effect. The knee-jerk reaction whereby stochastic implied volatilities are automatically associated with a stochastic-volatility process is indeed as common as it is unfortunate. It is a fact, however, that a jump-diffusion process with deterministic coefficients does give rise to a smile, but not to a stochastic one. Therefore, if the feature the traders were trying to incorporate was the propensity of smile surfaces to change shape over time, a jump-diffusion model with deterministic coefficients would simply not have done the job.

One could, of course, introduce jump processes with stochastic jump amplitude ratios or jump frequencies. One obvious drawback is that the model becomes increasingly less parsimonious as its complexity is increased, and the estimation task more and more daunting. More fundamentally, I have shown

---

[2]As mentioned in Chapter 11, any smile that is not monotonically decreasing with the strike is called a 'hockey stick'.

[3]Historical events had already had a profound impact on implied volatility surfaces in the equity world, which has seen the appearance of pronounced asymmetric volatility smiles in the aftermath of the 1987 equity market crash.

elsewhere (Rebonato and Joshi 2001b) that, even if the process for the underlying were a jump-diffusion process with stochastic jump intensity, it is very often possible to define an associated deterministic-coefficient equivalent process that produces almost indistinguishable prices for plain-vanilla calls and puts, and for path-dependent securities. This, however, is not the case for stochastic-volatility models, for which this reduction to an effective deterministic setting can only be carried out at the expense of considerable loss of information.

On the basis of these considerations, I have attempted to account for the observed smiles in a financially convincing way by embracing the stochastic-volatility approach. I would like to point out that, in doing so, I do not regard fitting the caplet/swaption volatility surface as closely as possible the main purpose of this project. I have attempted, instead, to retain a simple and transparent financial justification for the smile-inducing mechanisms proposed, and to regard the production of a good fit as an important and desirable by-product. In other terms, I am ready to pay a price in terms of closeness of fit in order to retain financial plausibility and explanatory power for the model. As it happens, the quality of fit has turned out to be very good, but this should be regarded, if anything, as an indirect corroboration of the reasonableness of the approach, rather than a justification for it, or an in-built feature.

12.1.2 'What does a stochastic-volatility model really buy me?'

Let us put ourselves in the shoes of a trader who is pricing a complex product using a deterministic-volatility version of the LIBOR market model. Let us assume that the trader has chosen a satisfactory form for the deterministic instantaneous-volatility function and that she is reasonably happy with its parametrization. With this parametrized function, the prices of the main hedging instruments (caplets or swaptions) have been exactly recovered, and the resulting evolution of the term structure of volatilities displays a satisfactory time-homogeneous evolution (assuming that this is indeed the view of the trader). Finally, the trader has carried out a series of vega-hedging transactions that, thanks to the successful calibration, have been executed in the market at the prices implied by the model.

The trader, however, believes that the future implied volatility surface will, in reality, not be deterministic, but stochastic. She accepts that, as the future term structure of volatilities changes over time, she will have to re-balance her vega-hedging positions. But above all, she is concerned about the future term structure of volatilities evolving in ways not allowed by the deterministic-volatility model used to arrive at the price. The model simply does not 'know' about these future states of the world, and has therefore associated zero weight to the corresponding conditional prices. In order to get a 'feel' for the situation, the trader will typically shift simultaneously all the implied volatilities first up and then down by a small amount and will re-calculate the required vega hedges in both states of the world. Depending on the product and on the shape of the yield curve and of volatility structure, four possible situations can in general arise. In order to be vega-neutral after the move, the trader might have to re-hedge by

- buying volatility when the implied volatilities have gone up and selling volatility when the volatilities have gone down;

- buying volatility when the implied volatilities have gone down and selling volatility when the volatilities have gone up;

- buying volatility both when the implied volatilities have gone up and when they have gone down, and approximately by the same amount;

- selling volatility both when the implied volatilities have gone up and when they have gone down, and approximately by the same amount.[4]

The situation is clearly reminiscent of being long or short gamma in the first two cases, or of being gamma-neutral but long or short delta in the third and fourth cases. This analogy has given rise to a variety of colorful names for the associated statistics (i.e., for the second derivative of the price with respect to a rigid shift in the volatilities), such as gamma-vega or vol-gamma.

These names have been chosen in an apt way. Even neglecting transaction costs, if the trader has sold the complex product, what she is really afraid of is clearly the first situation. Not only will she have to buy volatility when it is expensive and sell it when it is cheap (the more so, the more volatile the volatility is). More worryingly, the deterministic model used in valuing the complex product cannot know about these combinations of future yield curves and volatility surfaces. Therefore it cannot know about this *systematic* bias, which is in no way reflected in the deterministic-volatility price. In short, the trader has sold the option too cheaply.

Traders who use deterministic-volatility models perform this kind of sensitivity check on a regular basis, and tend to avoid, or to charge for, products where the gamma-vega is the 'wrong way around'. However, a rigid shift up and down of the volatilities is obviously very crude, and associating a dollar value to the systematic price bias arising from the future re-hedging costs is imprecise at best.

This is one of the areas where a stochastic-volatility model provides the greatest assistance to the trader. Loosely speaking, to the extent that a variety of combinations of future yield curves and of future volatility surfaces are explored by their chosen joint dynamics in a meaningful and realistic way, the model will know about the associated conditional prices and will produce the (risk-adjusted!) average price accordingly. In which measure will this average be carried out? If the trader has calibrated the model to the current option prices, the measure will be the one chosen by the market (see Bjork 1998). This measure will reflect the market's aversion to volatility risk today and its

---

[4]Typically the last two situations will only arise if the trader was not originally vega-neutral.

current overall systematic sensitivity to random volatility changes (i.e., its own gamma-vega). There is no guarantee that this volatility risk aversion will not change in the future, and for this reason the trader's exposure to this factor will only be imperfectly hedgeable.

Because of market incompleteness, the trader might not be able to replicate perfectly the payoff of an individual complex product. However her prices will be shifted in the right direction with respect to the deterministic case, and these price 'adjustments' will be consistent across different instruments. We know that, when markets are not complete, the uniqueness of the pricing measure is lost and attitudes towards risk do matter. However, by using a consistent arbitrage-free stochastic-volatility model, at least for *some* utility function (the market's if not the trader's), the set of prices for different products will reflect (a particular but important) aversion to volatility risk in a coherent manner.

12.1.3 *Computational desiderata of a stochastic-volatility LIBOR market model*

In concluding this introductory section, I would like to emphasize again that, on the practical side, I consider one of the main contributions of the approach proposed below is not so much the formulation of the stochastic-volatility, displaced-diffusion version of the LIBOR market model – which is, after all, rather straightforward. Instead, following Joshi and Rebonato (2001) and Rebonato (2001b), my aim is to present a new set of precise and numerically efficient calibration and implementation procedures, which translate to the new setting those results that have played such an important role in the acceptance of the LIBOR market model as a market standard. More precisely, I intend to show that it is still possible to achieve:

- the efficient recovery of at-the-money caplet prices;

- the accurate semi-analytic evaluation of European swaption prices, given the parameters of the instantaneous volatility and correlation functions;

- the accurate recovery of the prices of the co-terminal European swaptions underlying a given Bermudan swaption; and

- the rapid pricing of path-dependent exotic options.

As for the (very-)long-jump evolution, which was shown to be one of the linchpins of the practical implementation of the LIBOR market model, I will show that it can still be recovered, albeit only conditionally on a particular volatility path being realized.

12.2 The Modelling Framework

12.2.1 Specification of the stochastic instantaneous volatility process

One of the central building blocks of the standard LIBOR market model is the specification of the instantaneous volatility function. Indeed, in the classic treatment (see, e.g., Musiela and Rutkowski 1997a or Jamshidian 1997 and the discussion in Chapter 2), the LIBOR market model is characterized by imposing that the volatility of forward rates, $\sigma_{\text{inst}} = \sigma_{\text{inst}}(T, t)$, should be deterministic. In the following I shall take as a natural starting point for a discussion of the volatility function the particular specification I have presented in Chapters 6 and 8 in the deterministic setting:

$$\sigma_{\text{inst}}(t, T) = k(T)g(T - t). \tag{12.1}$$

By Equation (12.1) the total instantaneous volatility is expressed in separable form as the product of a time-homogeneous component, $g(T - t)$, times an idiosyncratic (forward-rate-specific) part, $k(T)$.[5] As explained in detail in Chapter 8, in the standard (deterministic-volatility) LIBOR-market-model setting and in the absence of smiles, by means of this separation one can ensure correct pricing of caplets for any choice for $g(\ )$ simply by imposing that

$$k(T)^2 = \frac{\sigma_{\text{Black}}^2 T}{\int_0^T g(t - u)^2 \, du}. \tag{12.2}$$

Furthermore, if one chooses the time-homogeneous function $g(\ )$ in such a way that the function $k(\ )$, as implied by (12.2), varies as little as possible as a function of the forward rates, one can rest assured that, for a given $g(\ )$, the evolution will be as time-homogeneous as possible. I have also argued in Part II of this book also argued that the functional form

$$g(T - t) = [a + b(T - t)] \exp[-c(T - t)] + d \tag{12.3}$$

provides a sufficiently flexible, easy-to-interpret and analytically tractable choice.

I shall use Equation (12.3) will be used as the reference deterministic instantaneous volatility, and report my results based on a stochastic extension of this function as indicated below. The treatment proposed, however, can easily be generalized, and can be adapted to different parametric functional choices for the instantaneous volatility. With this proviso in mind, the

---

[5]A separable time-dependent function $h(t)$ could easily be added, as discussed in Chapters 4 and 6. The extension is straightforward, and it is not treated explicitly in this chapter.

proposed stochastic extension of the LIBOR market model is therefore the following:[6]

$$\frac{d(f_i + \alpha)}{f_i + \alpha} = \mu_i^\alpha(\{\mathbf{f}\}, \mathbf{t})\, dt + \sigma_\mathbf{i}^\alpha(\mathbf{t}, \mathbf{T_i})\, dz_\mathbf{i}, \tag{12.4}$$

$$\sigma_i^\alpha(t, T_i) = [a_t + b_t(T - t)]\, \exp[-c_t(T - t)] + d_t, \tag{12.5}$$

$$da_t = RS_a(RL_a - a_t)\, dt + \sigma_a\, dz_a, \tag{12.6}$$

$$db_t = RS_b(RL_b - b_t)\, dt + \sigma_b\, dz_b, \tag{12.7}$$

$$d\ln(c_t) = RS_c[RL_c - \ln(c_t)]\, dt + \sigma_c\, dz_c, \tag{12.8}$$

$$d\ln(d_t) = RS_d[RL_d - \ln(d_t)]\, dt + \sigma_d\, dz_d, \tag{12.9}$$

$$E[dz_i\, dz_a] = E[dz_i\, dz_b] = E[dz_i\, dz_c] = E[dz_i\, dz_d] = 0, \tag{12.10}$$

$$E[dz_a\, dz_b] = E[dz_a\, dz_c] = E[dz_a\, dz_d] = 0$$

$$E[dz_b\, dz_c] = E[dz_b\, dz_d] = 0$$

$$E[dz_c\, dz_d] = 0, \tag{12.10'}$$

with RS_a, RS_b, RS_c, RS_d, RL_a, RL_b, RL_c and RL_d the reversion speeds and reversion levels of a, b, $\ln(c)$ and $\ln(d)$, respectively, and σ_a, σ_b, σ_c and σ_d their volatilities.

12.2.2 Is the model over-parametrized?

Before proceeding any further, it is worth while commenting briefly on the number of parameters that the approach requires. If the reversion speeds, reversion levels and volatilities σ_a, σ_b, σ_c and σ_d were all to be used as fitting parameters, the approach could be criticized on the grounds of its non-parsimonious nature. The dangers of working with over-parametrized models are particularly acute when the financial interpretation of the parameters is opaque, and their main justification is the achievement of a tighter fit to a set of market data. As discussed in the previous section, however, obtaining a very close match to the smile surface is not the sole, or even the main, purpose of the approach, and the stochastic features introduced by Equations (12.5)–(12.10) are meant to provide sufficient flexibility to describe in a financially realistic way not just today's smile surface, but also the observed changes in the market term structure of volatilities (see Figures 12.6–12.9 below and the accompanying discussion, and Chapter 13). Despite the fact that no attempt was made to carry out an explicit fit to these time-dependent behaviors, this qualitative but important inter-temporal check can nonetheless afford a useful independent 'corroboration' of the parametrization obtainable from a single-time cross-sectional fit. Furthermore, one can empirically observe that the prices of caplets are mainly affected by the stochastic behavior of the

---

[6]In order to avoid confusion with the coefficients of the instantaneous volatility process, in this chapter the displaced-diffusion coefficient, denoted by a in the previous chapter and often in the literature, is written as α.

d coefficient, and that their at-the-money values are almost independent of the stochasticity of a and b (needless to say, this is not the case for more complex products). Therefore, the quality of the fit to at-the-money caplet prices, displayed and discussed in Section 8.6, would not be much worse if only the d parameter were allowed to be stochastic. If the trader felt more comfortable with a small number of parameters, and a more transparent modelling approach, she could therefore work with a, b and c deterministic, thereby gaining greater 'control' over the model and some computational efficiency, while losing relatively little in terms of quality of fit to the caplet prices. Finally, despite the fact that I present the general framework allowing, for maximum generality, for the ability to optimize over 16 parameters (the four initial values $a(0)$, $b(0)$, $c(0)$ and $d(0)$; the four volatilities σ_a, σ_b, σ_c and σ_d; the four reversion levels RL_a, RL_b, RL_c and RL_d; and the four reversion speeds RS_a, RS_b, RS_c and RS_d), when it comes to fitting market data I have chosen to restrict this flexibility by requiring that the reversion levels should be equal to today's value of a, b, $\ln(c)$ or $\ln(d)$, as appropriate. Since, as shown in detail in Section 12.4.6, even if only the d parameter is allowed to display a stochastic behavior, the quality of the resulting fit to the whole caplet smile surface is not substantially impaired, the reader who felt uncomfortable with the possibility of working with a possibly over-parametrized model could therefore follow this simpler version (a, b and c deterministic and $\mathrm{RL}_d = \ln(d(0))$) with relatively little loss of fitting accuracy.

Finally, it will be shown later on that, in complete analogy with the deterministic case (see Chapters 6 and 8), in order to obtain a perfect fit to the caplet prices, as many rescaling constants will be introduced as forward rates. This would appear to increase substantially the number of fitting parameters. Just as in the deterministic case, however, these extra multiplicative parameters are constructed to be as close to unity as possible, and only provide a very modest last-step fine-tuning, without altering in any material way the dynamics described by Equations (12.4)–(12.10).

12.2.3 The no-arbitrage drifts for the forward rates

The precise expression for the no-arbitrage drifts of the forward rates, symbolically shown as $\mu_i^\alpha(\{f\}, t)$ in Equation (12.4), depends on the specific choice of numeraire (in the following this will always be chosen to be one of the $n + 1$ pure discount bonds that define the n spanning forward rates). In particular, as shown in Chapter 4, there is always a particular discount bond, $B(t, T_{j+1})$, that can be chosen as the 'natural' numeraire, N_j, for forward rate j, f_j, such that the forward rate itself is a martingale. This 'natural' numeraire coincides with the discount bond maturing at the payoff time of the jth forward rate. For any other numeraire, the forward-rate drift will be non-zero.

The derivation of the no-arbitrage drifts for the forward rates in the standard formulation of the LIBOR market model presented in Chapter 2 by adapting the conceptual layout by Musiela and Rutkowski (1997a) and Jamshidian (1997) hinges on

1. the definition of bond processes as strictly positive continuous semi-martingales with finite second (co)variation;

2. the construction of forward-price and forward-rate processes, also described by similar strictly positive semi-martingales;

3. the requirement that the volatilities of the forward rates (and of no other quantities) should be deterministic functions of time; and

4. the application of Ito's lemma and Girsanov's theorem coupled with a backward-induction procedure to obtain the no-arbitrage drifts of the forward rates in a particular measure.

Furthermore, Jamshidian (1997) shows that, as long as the payoff of the derivatives to be priced satisfy the conditions of

(a) being a function homogeneous of degree one in the bond prices, and

(b) being measurable with respect to the filtration generated by the forward rates on their reset times,

the instantaneously compounded money-market account, and the short rate, need not be introduced. As previously pointed out (see Chapter 4), Condition (a) is equivalent to requiring that the payoff function should be expressible as the product of an arbitrary function of the forward rates (which are a function of degree zero in the bond prices) times a discount bond, and therefore affords all the flexibility we need for the common LIBOR products encountered in market practice.

In dealing with the case of stochastic instantaneous volatilities, as much of this framework as possible is retained, and the treatment carries through virtually unaltered, with two important exceptions: At point 3 above, the requirement is made that the volatility of the forward rates should be stochastic, as per Equations (12.4)–(12.10). Furthermore, the underlying probability space must be endowed with a finer filtration, generated not only by the forward rates at their reset times, but also by their stochastic variances on the same reset dates. In practice, since the Ornstein–Uhlenbeck behavior postulated for the coefficients of the instantaneous volatility (or their logarithms) does not yield a closed-form solution for the variance, the trader will have to sample their processes numerically with a frequency that might be finer than the spacings between price-sensitive events in order to estimate the required covariances.[7] However, it should be kept in mind that, for the LIBOR

---

[7]When the long-jump, as opposed to the very-long-jump, procedure is adopted, and there are no long-dated lock-out or no-look features, the time interval between price-sensitive events tends to coincide with the spacing between one forward-rate reset and the other (typically, three or six months). Such a time-step is more than adequate to produce an accurate sampling of the instantaneous volatility process, and the long-jump procedure can therefore be applied again with very few modifications. See also the discussion and the results in Section 8.1.

payoffs that the LIBOR market model is designed to tackle, the same above-mentioned measurability and homogeneity conditions imposed by Jamshidian (1997) are retained in the stochastic-volatility setting. The need for finer sampling therefore reflects a technical (numerical) rather than a conceptual (financial) constraint.

Since point 4 in the account given above of Musiela and Rutkowski's (1997a) derivation (and, in particular, the application of Ito's lemma and of Girsanov's theorem) holds true irrespective of whether the volatilities are deterministic or stochastic, the no-arbitrage drifts retain the same formal appearance, with the volatilities now a stochastic quantity. If, in addition, the process for the forward rates is assumed to be a displaced diffusion, as discussed in Chapter 11, and using the notation introduced in Chapters 3 and 5, the drifts μ_i become

$$\mu_i^\alpha = \sigma_i^\alpha(t) \sum_{k=j+1}^{i} \frac{\sigma_k^\alpha(t)\rho_{ik}(t)[f_k(t) + \alpha]\tau}{1 + f_k(t)\tau} \qquad \text{if } i > j, \qquad (12.11)$$

$$\mu_i^\alpha = -\sigma_i^\alpha(t) \sum_{k=i+1}^{j} \frac{\sigma_k^\alpha(t)\rho_{ik}(t)[f_k(t) + \alpha]\tau}{1 + f_k(t)\tau} \qquad \text{if } i < j, \qquad (12.12)$$

$$\mu_i^\alpha = 0 \qquad \text{if } i = j. \qquad (12.13)$$

In Equations (12.11)–(12.13), the symbols μ_i^α and σ_i^α indicate the percentage drift and the (now stochastic) percentage volatility of the quantity $(f_i + \alpha)$. These equations, together with Equations (12.5)–(12.10), therefore fully describe the no-arbitrage evolution of the spanning forward rates in the problem.

EXERCISE 12.1 *Using as a guideline the treatment in Chapter 5, derive Equations (12.11)–(12.13).*

12.2.4 Financial and mathematical motivation for the choice of process

The financial and mathematical motivations for the choice of the functional form above for the processes describing the dynamics of the volatility coefficients are as follows. As for the conditions of linear independence (12.10), the stochastic behavior of the instantaneous volatility function has been separated into a component that is perfectly correlated with the level of the forward rate in a CEV-like fashion, and into further components that are totally uncorrelated with the forward rates (and, for simplicity, among themselves). In other terms, the use of the CEV, or displaced-diffusion, dynamics produces an effective correlation between the percentage volatility and the level of the forward rates, and, via Equations (12.10), the assumption is made that there are no other sources of correlation. One implicitly endorses, by this modelling choice, the explanation for the monotonically decreasing part of the smile purely in terms of the trader's beliefs that the absolute (basis point) moves of forward rates are less than proportional to the level of the forward rates themselves. Then, and purely for computational reasons, a displaced diffusion is used as a proxy for the CEV dynamics, following the equivalence and transformation rules presented by Marris (1999) and discussed in the previous chapter.

Having accounted for this component of the smile, one can then attempt to capture the remaining, and more recently appeared, non-monotonic component of the smile surface by means of a diffusive stochastic instantaneous volatility driven by shocks that have no residual correlation with the level of the forward rate. This is achieved by imposing an Ornstein–Uhlenbeck mean-reverting behavior to the volatility parameters, thereby ensuring that they do not stray too much from 'reasonable' values.[8] This choice has the added advantage that closed-form solutions for their realizations after a finite time interval are available. Furthermore, as mentioned in Chapter 6, the various coefficients in the functional form (12.3) can be given a reasonably transparent financial interpretation, by noticing, for instance, that (in the risk-adjusted world!) d is equal to the asymptotic level of the long-maturity volatility, that the quantity $1/c - a/b$ gives the location of the maximum (if present), that b controls whether the initial slope of the instantaneous volatility will be negative or positive, etc., as discussed in Chapter 6. Introducing a diffusive behavior for these quantities can therefore be interpreted as allowing the overall level of the volatility to vary (via d), the location of the maximum of the hump (when present) to change, the hump to become more or less pronounced (via b and c), etc.

Despite the intuitive appeal of these interpretations, it must be kept in mind that, in the standard (deterministic-volatility) LIBOR market model, the instantaneous volatility is left unchanged by the Girsanov transformation from the real to the risk-adjusted world, and that the direct comparison between what is observed in the real world and what is predicted by the model is therefore fully justified. In the stochastic-volatility setting proposed in this chapter, on the other hand, the reversion level and the reversion speed of the instantaneous volatility (i.e., those quantities which are related to the drift of the volatility process) strictly apply to the risk-adjusted world, and a direct comparison with their counterpart in the real world is not theoretically justifiable. Despite these reservations, I concur with Britten-Jones and Neuberger (1998) that there is, nonetheless, merit in carrying out these comparisons, since a careful analysis of any systematic differences between realized and risk-adjusted volatilities is central to understanding the pricing of volatility risk. Chapter 13 suggests a methodology whereby a meaningful comparison between some carefully chosen real-world and the model-produced quantities can be carried out.

[8]A more precise, and convincing, justification for assigning a, b, $\ln(c)$ and $\ln(d)$ a mean-reverting behavior can be given by carrying out a principal component analysis of the model-produced and real-world changes in the swaption implied volatility, as shown in the next chapter and in Rebonato and Joshi (2001a). This type of analysis circumvents the problems associated with carrying out comparisons between real-world and risk-adjusted quantities.

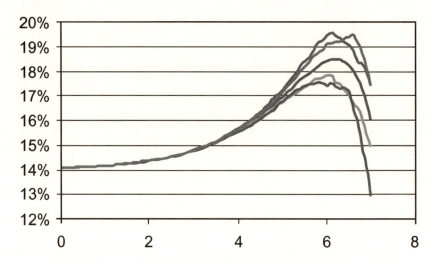

Figure 12.1   *A few sample instantaneous volatility curves for a seven-year expiry forward rate when only the a coefficient is stochastic according to Equations (12.5)–(12.10). The deterministic curve is also given as a reference. The parameters used are shown in Table 12.1. See the text for more details.*

12.2.5 Qualitative behavior of the instantaneous stochastic-volatility processes

I display in Figures 12.1–12.4 the qualitative features of the stochastic volatility functions when one coefficient after the other is allowed to assume a stochastic mean-reverting behavior. Figure 12.5 then shows the combined effect of four stochastic coefficients. The sampled paths displayed in these figures together with the deterministic volatility curve were obtained assuming the initial values $a(0)$, $b(0)$, $c(0)$ and $d(0)$ of the processes for the coefficients to be known exactly (as they could be, for instance, after a fitting procedure has been carried out). Given the perfect knowledge of the parameters $a(0)$, $b(0)$, $c(0)$ and $d(0)$ today, the current instantaneous volatility of every forward rate is known exactly. In particular, for the particular seven-year residual-maturity forward rate whose volatility is examined in Figures 12.1–12.5, its instantaneous volatility is known from $a(0)$, $b(0)$, $c(0)$ and $d(0)$ to have the value 14.00%. This level corresponds to the left-most point on the curves. The volatility of this forward rate is then evolved through the seven years of the life of the forward rate itself up to its expiry (the right-most points in each graph) using the coefficients in Table 12.1.

As mentioned above, since, in the calibration procedure proposed in the following, the values for the reversion speeds and levels will be obtained from quoted option prices, they will be risk-adjusted, rather than real-world, quantities.   Under the modelling assumptions made, on the other hand, the

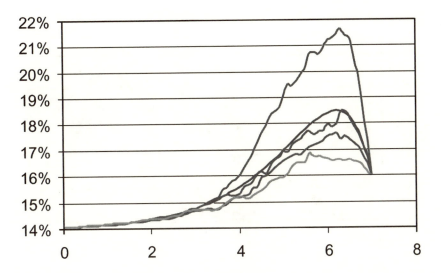

Figure 12.2 *Same as Figure 12.1 when only the b coefficient is stochastic according to Equations (12.5)–(12.10). The deterministic curve is also given as a reference. The parameters used are shown in Table 12.1. See the text for more details.*

volatilities of the coefficients (or of their logarithms) remain the same in the real and risk-adjusted worlds. Comparisons between model and real-world volatilities are therefore to some extent still possible, but must be made with great care and will be dealt with in Chapter 13. Even with this caveat, however, the qualitative behavior appears reassuringly plausible (see below). In particular, for reasonable values of c, the stochastic behavior of a and b appears to affect mainly the portion of the instantaneous volatility curve immediately prior to the reset of the forward rate, and, in particular, to influence the magnitude of the volatility hump. This feature, in turn, has been shown in the previous chapters to have a noticeable influence on the terminal decorrelation between forward rates, and can therefore be expected to have a significant influence on the covariance elements that enter the pricing of the com-

Table 12.1 *The numerical values for the a, b, c and d coefficients and their Ornstein–Uhlenbeck processes used in the calculations that produced Figures 12.1 to 12.5.*

a	0.02	RS_a	0.1	RL_a	0.02	σ_a	0.008
b	0.1	RS_b	0.1	RL_b	0.1	σ_b	0.016
c	1	RS_c	0.1	RL_c	0	σ_c	0.12
d	0.14	RS_d	0.1	RL_d	-1.96611	σ_d	0.1

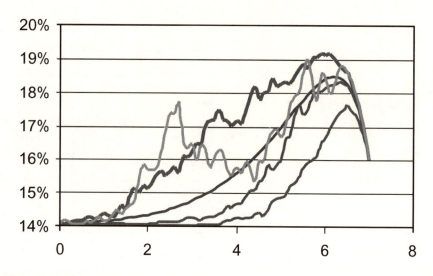

Figure 12.3 *Same as Figure 12.1 when only the c coefficient is stochastic according to Equations (12.5)–(12.10). The deterministic curve is also given as a reference. The parameters used are shown in Table 12.1. See the text for more details.*

plex products. Given the dampening effect of the decaying exponential, one can reasonably expect the stochastic behavior of a and b to have a relatively small impact on the prices of caplets, but a greater influence on the pricing of those securities that strongly depend on the decorrelation among forward rates brought about by non-flat volatility functions. The volatility of the coefficients c and d, on the other hand, has a more pronounced effect throughout the life of the forward rate, and are expected to produce an effect on caplet prices similar to the 'classic' (Hull and White 1987) stochastic-volatility model (with zero correlation between the processes for the volatility and for the underlying). In particular, they are expected to produce shallow smiles for short maturities, and more pronounced ones as the expiries increase. Finally, given assumptions (12.10), the smiles produced by the stochastic behavior of c and d will display little skew (this latter feature, of course, is introduced by the CEV/displaced-diffusion behavior).

12.2.6 *Qualitative comparison between the model and real-world evolution of the term structure of volatilities*

Since it might be difficult to appreciate the degree of plausibility of a non-directly observable quantity such as the instantaneous volatility, the latter was integrated in order to obtain the corresponding stochastic term structures of (at-the-money) volatilities implied by the model proposed in this chapter.

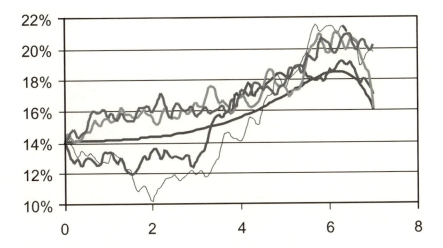

Figure 12.4 *Same as Figure 12.1 when only the d coefficient is stochastic according to Equations (12.5)–(12.10). The deterministic curve is also given as a reference. The parameters used are shown in Table 12.1. See the text for more details.*

Figures 12.6 and 12.7 display two typical results. These qualitative patterns can then be more transparently compared with observed time series of market term structures of volatilities (see Figures 12.8 and 12.9). Also in this case, however, one must bear in mind that, by so doing, one is comparing real-world and risk-adjusted quantities. A more accurate comparison should be carried out along the lines presented in Chapter 13 (see also Rebonato and Joshi 2001a).

Clearly, these figures do not allow one to make any statistically testable statement, but the similarity between the observed and model changes in the term structure of volatilities (which is one of the market variables to which the trader using a deterministic-volatility LIBOR market model is most exposed) is encouraging. (Note that, in producing Figures 12.6 and 12.7, the same parameters in Table 12.1 were used, and these were not obtained by fitting the model parameters to the historical term structure of volatilities shown in Figures 12.8 and 12.9.) The proposed approach therefore appears to produce a reasonable and financially desirable description of the dynamics of the term structure of volatilities.

In order to fulfill the program highlighted in Section 12.1, the next task is to proceed to examine whether, and to what extent, the powerful approximation procedures that have been presented in Parts I–III of this book, and which constitute the backbone of the LIBOR market model, retain their validity in the stochastic-volatility setting presented above. Section 12.3 presents the first results of this multi-task project.

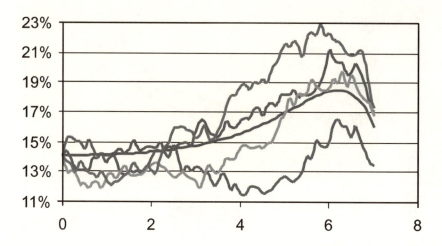

Figure 12.5   *Same as Figure 12.1 when all the coefficients (a, b, c and d) are allowed to be stochastic according to Equations (12.5)–(12.10). The deterministic curve is also given as a reference. The parameters used are shown in Table 12.1. See the text for more details.*

12.3 Numerical Techniques

12.3.1 Approximations for the drifts

Joshi and Rebonato (2001) propose an efficient general computational procedure in order to sample the joint distribution of the forward rates given the displaced-diffusion, stochastic-volatility structure postulated in Section 12.2. More precisely, they recommend performing a simple short-stepped, first-order Euler-scheme Monte Carlo evolution for the volatility process. (Given the particular functional form chosen for the processes for the coefficients, one can use the Ornstein–Uhlenbeck solutions. This might not be the case if the reader wanted to alter the proposed approach by making use of a more general choice of processes for the volatility parameters.) Once the appropriate root-mean-square volatility for the relevant portion of the path has been obtained, one can then apply the usual (very-)long-jump evolution (see Chapter 4) of the forward rates from one price-sensitive event to the next – typically, from one forward-rate reset to the next – or to the final maturity, as appropriate. In other terms, once the sampling of the volatility process by a short-stepped Monte Carlo evolution has been carried out, the problem is conditionally (i.e., for a given realized root-mean-square volatility) reduced to the deterministic case. The procedure is rendered particularly simple by the assumed independence between the forward rates and the volatility process.

As discussed in Chapter 4, there exist an important class of securities (multi-look trigger swaps are an example) characterized by the fact that their payoffs

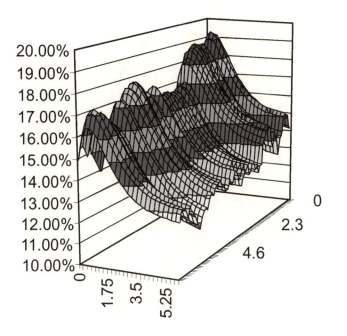

Figure 12.6 *A model stochastic evolution term structure of volatilities (at-the-money) obtained with the parameters in Table 12.1.*

can be expressed as a function of the resets of the various forward rates on their own reset dates. For these products the very-long-jump procedure can profitably be employed, and I have discussed at length in Chapter 5 that, in these cases, it is not only desirable, but indeed essential, to employ the drift approximation introduced by Hunter et al. (2001). Section 12.3.1 reports the result of numerical experiments and shows that the approximation retains its validity also for displaced diffusions and in the presence of stochastic volatilities.

Once the (conditionally deterministic) drift has been obtained, one is in a position to carry out the evolution of the forward rates in the yield curve. In order to do so, it is important to recall that the evolution of the volatility parameters is independent of the dynamics of the forward rates (see Equations (12.10)). The probability of occurrence of a particular volatility path is therefore independent of the realization of the forward rates. This being the case, one can divide (see Joshi 2001a) the time intervals between price-sensitive events (or from today to the final maturity when the very-long-jump procedure is employed) into small steps, Δs_l, $l = 1, \ldots, m$, and evolve a, b, c and d over these small steps. For each small step one can create a forward-rate

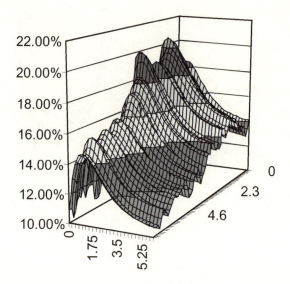

Figure 12.7   *Another model stochastic evolution term structure of volatilities (at-the-money) obtained with the parameters in Table 12.1.*

marginal covariance matrix for that step C_l^f. The (j, k)th entry of C_l^f will be

$$C_l^f(j, k) = [a_{s_l} + b_{s_l}(T_j - s_l)] \exp[-c_{s_l}(T_j - s_l) + d_{s_l}]$$
$$\times [a_{s_l} + b_{s_l}(T_k - s_l)] \exp[-c_{s_l}(T_k - s_l) + d_{s_l}]\rho_{jk}^f \Delta s_l.$$

With these quantities one can then form a covariance matrix $\mathbf{C}^f$ by summing C_l^f for $l = 1, \ldots, m$. One could now proceed as in the deterministic case and carry out a principal-component-analysis (spectral-analysis) orthogonalization of the (now conditional) covariance matrix. Since, however, the procedure will now have to be repeated for each volatility path, Joshi (2001a) shows that it is computationally more efficient to proceed by calculating a pseudo-square-root, $\mathbf{A}^f$, of $\mathbf{C}^f$ by Cholesky decomposition. In other words, one can determine the lower triangular matrix $\mathbf{A}^f$ such that

$$\mathbf{C}^f = \mathbf{A}^f(\mathbf{A}^f)^{\mathrm{T}}.$$

When this step has been carried out, one is in a position to evolve the forward rates across, say, the rth interval, $[T_r, T_{r+1}]$, according to

$$\log f_j(T_{r+1}) = \log f_j(T_r) + \mu_j(T_r)(T_{r+1} - T_r) + \sum A_{jk} Z_k$$

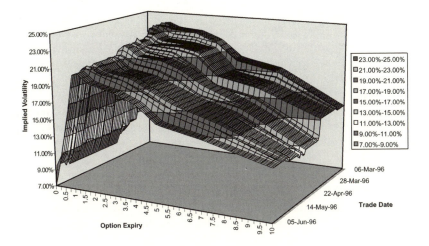

Figure 12.8 *Historical implied volatilities for different maturities collected over a period of approximately three months in 1996 for GBP.*

(with $\{\mathbf{Z}\}$ i.i.d. standard normal variates), applying on a path-by-path basis the same predictor–corrector approximation presented by Hunter et al. (2001) and discussed in Chapter 5.

It is important to stress that, by means of this technique, only the volatility process has to be short-stepped, and the ability to carry out the long- and

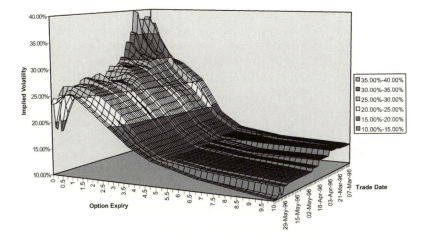

Figure 12.9 *Historical implied volatilities for different maturities collected over a period of approximately three months in 1996 for FRF.*

very-long jump evolution for the forward-rate processes is preserved. The only loss of accuracy in evolving the forward rates is in the approximation to the forward-rate drifts. This source of inaccuracy, however, already exists in the non-stochastic-volatility case, and its magnitude has been shown in Chapter 5 to be totally acceptable. Furthermore, since the instantaneous volatility process is only four-dimensional, while the forward-rate process can easily be 20- or 40-dimensional (for, say, a semi-annual or quarterly 10-year product), the procedure affords significant computational saving over the more obvious 'brute-force' procedure of evolving the forward rates and the volatility processes in 'lock-step'.

12.3.2 Exact calibration to caplet prices

The overall strategy followed in order to calibrate the stochastic-volatility version of the LIBOR market model to caplet prices is underpinned by two observations:

- Given the independence between the forward rates and volatility processes, on a path-by-path basis each problem can be reduced to its deterministic counterpart. In particular, on a path-by-path basis, the concept of root-mean-square volatility can still be recovered.

- The Black formula is almost exactly linear, at the money, in the input root-mean-square volatility.

These two simple observations can produce a surprising wealth of useful results, the first of which is the fast and numerically efficient calibration of the model to the caplet prices. Let me recall briefly the strategy suggested in Chapters 6 and 8 in order to determine the coefficients of the time-homogeneous component, $g(\ )$, of the instantaneous volatility function in Equation (12.3) in the deterministic case. For an arbitrary set of coefficients a, b, c and d, one can first of all calculate analytically for all the caplets in the term structure of volatilities the integral

$$\int_0^{T_i} \sigma_{\text{inst}}(T_i - u)^2 \, \mathrm{d}u = \int_0^{T_i} \{[a + b(T_i - u)] \exp[-c(T_i - u)] + d\}^2 \, \mathrm{d}u$$
$$\equiv [\sigma_i^{\text{BlackModel}}]^2 T_i. \tag{12.14}$$

One can then vary the coefficients in such a way as to minimize

$$\chi^2 = \sum_{i=1}^n [\sigma_i^{\text{BlackModel}} - \sigma_i^{\text{Black}}]^2. \tag{12.15}$$

By so doing, one can rest assured that, given the choice for the function $g(\ )$, as much of today's term structure of volatilities as possible will be explained by a time-invariant component. This, in turn, will imply that today's term structure of volatilities will also be as time-homogeneous (i.e., evolve in a self-similar way) as possible, given today's market prices and the chosen function $g(\ )$. The desirability of this feature has been discussed at great length in Part II of this book. Furthermore the arguments presented, for example, in Longstaff et al. (2000a) and (2000a,b) suggest that, for a deterministic-volatility model, this should be both a desirable and an important feature.

As discussed in Chapter 8, however, in the deterministic case the minimization (12.15) will not in general yield exactly the caplet market prices. Therefore, in Chapter 8, the instantaneous volatility function was separated into a time-homogeneous component, $g(T_i - t)$, and an idiosyncratic (i.e., forward-rate-specific) multiplicative correction factor, $k(T_i)$. In the deterministic setting, the latter was determined by requiring that each caplet should be correctly priced:

$$k(T_i)^2 = \frac{[\sigma_i^{\text{Black}}]^2 T_i}{\int_0^{T_i} g(T_i - u)^2 \, du}. \tag{12.16}$$

As discussed in Chapter 8, the smaller the variation of the function $k(\ )$ (i.e., without loss of generality, the closer the various terms $k(T_i)$ are to unity), the more closely will the term structure of volatilities (deterministically) evolve in a time-homogeneous fashion.

This conceptual approach can be retained substantially unaltered, and the caplet calibration approach can be modified to deal with stochastic instantaneous volatilities in the following way (see Joshi 2001b). First of all, one assumes to know the parameters of the volatility process and the initial values $a(0)$, $b(0)$, $c(0)$ and $d(0)$. One can then subdivide the time interval from today to the expiry of the ith caplet, $[0, T_i]$, $i = 0, 1, \ldots, m$, into steps, Δs_r, $r = 1, \ldots, m$, and evolve a, b, c and d over these relatively small steps[9] using these initial 'guesses' for the process parameters. Each step should be sufficiently small to allow accurate sampling of the volatility path. For each small step one can then create one element of a marginal variance matrix, V_{r_i}:

$$V_{r_i} = \{[(a_{s_r} + b_{s_r})(T_i - s_r)] \exp[-c_{s_r}(T_i - s_r)] + d_{s_r}\}^2 \Delta s_r. \tag{12.17}$$

A forward-rate-specific variance vector, V_i, for a given volatility path is then formed by summing the elements V_{r_i}, $r = 1, 2, \ldots, m$:

$$V_i = \sum_{r=1}^{m} V_{r_i}. \tag{12.18}$$

---

[9]The steps are 'small' compared to the size of the long or very long jumps over which the forward rates are evolved. The results presented later in this chapter show, however, that adequate sampling of the instantaneous volatility process can be achieved even with a rather coarse volatility step size.

To calculate the model price of the ith caplet along this volatility path, one simply has to compute the root-mean-square volatility out to its expiry and use it in the displaced-diffusion Black formula, $\text{Black}(T, V_i)$. This provides a caplet value associated with path i. Given the assumption of independence between the Brownian increments of the process for the volatility coefficients, on the one hand, and of the process for the forward rates, on the other, the model price, P_i^{model}, of the ith caplet will then be given by

$$P_i^{\text{model}} = \int \text{Black}(T_i, V_i)\phi(V_i)\,\mathrm{d}V_i. \qquad (12.19)$$

This is an adaptation of a result of Hull and White (1987). The density function $\phi(\;)$, however, is not known analytically, and therefore it must be sampled using a Monte Carlo simulation. This can be done very efficiently using low-discrepancy numbers – Joshi and Rebonato (2001), for instance, found that, in practice, as few as 64 volatility paths were sufficient to ensure convergence. See also the results presented in Section 12.4.3.

By means of the first stage of the procedure, the trader has determined a set of model caplet prices associated with the initial guess for the parameters of the volatility processes. These prices, in general, will not coincide with the corresponding market values. As a second stage in the fitting process, one can then mirror the procedure used in the deterministic-volatility case, and minimize over all the parameters the sum of the squared discrepancies, χ^2, between the model prices, obtained as shown above, and the corresponding market values, P_i^{market}, for all available maturities and strikes:

$$\min \chi^2 = \min \sum_{i=1}^{N} [P_i^{\text{model}} - P_i^{\text{market}}]^2. \qquad (12.20)$$

The only difference in this part of the algorithm is that in the stochastic-volatility case the parameter space is considerably wider, encompassing as it does the initial values, the reversion speeds, the parameter volatilities, and the displaced-diffusion coefficient. Once the best set of coefficients has been determined, the second stage of the fitting procedure is completed.

As in the deterministic case, after this optimization has been carried out, the agreement between model and market prices will not be perfect. In order to match exactly these two quantities at the money, one can now move to the third stage of the procedure and, as mentioned above, invoke the well-known result that the Black function is almost exactly linear in volatility for the at-the-money strike. (Note that, since the price of a caplet in the displaced-diffusion case has been shown in Chapter 11 to be given by the Black formula with modified inputs, this linearity property also holds in the displaced-diffusion case.) More precisely, let $k(T_i)$ be the ratio between the market and the model price. Given the linearity property, one can then set up an alternative volatility process for the ith forward rate given by

$$\sigma'_{\text{inst}}(t; a_t, b_t, c_t, d_t) = k(T_i)\sigma_{\text{inst}}(t; a_t, b_t, c_t, d_t). \tag{12.21}$$

By so doing, along any given path the root-mean-square volatility for $\sigma'(t)$ will simply be equal to $k(T_i)$ times the root-mean-square volatility for the original process, $\sigma(t)$. Given the approximate, but very accurate, linearity of the at-the-money Black prices as a function of the root-mean-square volatility (see Wilmott 1998, Brenner and Subrahmanyam 1994), the price implied by the Monte Carlo simulation will also be multiplied by (almost exactly) the same scaling factor, thereby ensuring correct pricing of each at-the-money caplet.

The effectiveness of the procedure is discussed in the numerical experiments reported in the results (Section 12.4), but it is important to stress already at this stage that one can run one simulation to price all the caplets at once. For a given volatility path, one can in fact calculate all the strikes, and one can use different stopping points along the same path for different maturities. An entire caplet surface can therefore be evaluated in a fraction of a second on a standard PC (e.g., using a 200 MHz Pentium II processor). Calibrating to a caplet surface is therefore a feasible task in real-life trading times.

12.3.3 Fast pricing of European swaptions

Another important feature of the deterministic-volatility LIBOR market model is the ability to approximate accurately and simply the at-the-money price of a European swaption, given the instantaneous volatility of, and the correlation among, the associated forward rates. An efficient procedure to accomplish this task in a deterministic setting was discussed in Chapter 10 (see also Hull and White 2000, Jamshidian 1997, Andersen and Andreasen 2000, Jaeckel and Rebonato 2001). As discussed in Part III, this is of great importance in order to explore the congruence and consistency of the caplet and swaption markets, or to ensure, if the trader so desires, that a given choice of forward-rate volatilities should reproduce as well as possible a given swaption matrix.

In order to show in detail how the procedure can be naturally extended to the more complex setting presented in this chapter, one can start also in this case from a set-up similar to the one used in the deterministic case. Following Joshi (2001c) and Joshi and Rebonato (2001), if one denotes by $\sigma^\alpha_{\text{SR}_k}(t)$ the instantaneous volatility of the kth swaption when the displacement of the diffusion has value α, the log-normal deterministic-volatility approximations presented in Chapter 10 clearly generalize in the displaced-diffusion (CEV) setting to

$$\sigma^\alpha_{\text{SR}_k}(t) \simeq \frac{\sum_{i,j=1}^{n_k}[f_j(0) + \alpha][f_i(0) + \alpha](\partial \text{SR}_k/\partial f_i)(\partial \text{SR}_k/\partial f_j)\sigma^\alpha_i(t)\sigma^\alpha_j(t)\rho_{ij}(t)}{[\text{SR}_k + \alpha]^2}$$

$$\equiv \sum_{i,j=1}^{n_k} \zeta_{ik}\zeta_{jk}\sigma_i^\alpha(t)\sigma_j^\alpha(t)\rho_{ij}(t) \tag{12.21'}$$

where n_k is the number of forward rates in the kth swap, and ζ_{ik} is given by

$$\zeta_{ik} = \frac{\partial \mathrm{SR}_k}{\partial f_i}\frac{f_i(0)+\alpha}{\mathrm{SR}_k+\alpha}, \tag{12.22}$$

which will be zero when $k < i$. (Note in passing that the matrix $\mathbf{Z} = \{\zeta_{ik}\}$ is upper triangular and non-zero on the diagonal; it will therefore have non-zero determinant and an upper triangular inverse. Use will be made of this fact in the next section.)

If the simpler, but less accurate, of the approximations in Chapter 10 is used, the derivative $\partial \mathrm{SR}_k/\partial f_i$ will simply be set equal to the weight w_{ik} (see Equations (10.2) and (10.3)). Alternatively, for a non-flat yield curve, the more accurate, but slightly more cumbersome, expression discussed in Case Study 3 in Section 10.3.5 or in Jaeckel and Rebonato (2001b) can be used. In either case, the structure of the matrix equations that follow remains unchanged. The approach is then very similar to the one presented for the calibration to caplets (see Joshi 2001c, Joshi and Rebonato 2001). Let T be the expiry of the swaption. As in the caplet case, one can again divide the interval $[0,T]$ into m small steps, Δs_r, $r = 1, 2, \ldots, m$, and evolve the coefficients a, b, c and d over these small steps. As explained in Section 12.3, and for a given choice of the forward-rate correlation function ρ_{ij}^f, along each sample path one can then form the forward-rate covariance matrix of elements

$$C_l^f(j,k) = [a_{s_l} + b_{s_l}(T_j - s_l)]\exp[-c_{s_l}(T_j - s_l) + d_{s_l}]$$
$$\times [a_{s_l} + b_{s_l}(T_k - s_l)]\exp[-c_{s_l}(T_k - s_l) + d_{s_l}]\rho_{jk}^f \Delta s_l.$$

This sample covariance matrix provides the input to Formula (12.21'), which can then be integrated to give the swap-rate root-mean-square volatility:

$$\sigma_{\mathrm{impl}}^{\alpha,\mathrm{SR}}(T) \equiv \sqrt{\frac{1}{T}\int_0^T \sigma_{\mathrm{SR}}^\alpha(\mathrm{d}u)^2\,\mathrm{d}u}.$$

Finally, this latter quantity can be used as an input to the Black formula to price the European swaption of interest corresponding to that particular volatility path. Thanks again to the independence between the processes for the forward rates and the instantaneous volatility, the desired swaption price in the presence of stochastic volatility is simply obtained by Monte Carlo averaging, exactly as shown in the previous section in the caplet case.

The numerical quality of the results is commented upon in Section 12.4.3. Recall, however, that the approximations that underpin Equations (12.21') and (12.22) are highly accurate in the deterministic case, and that, once a stochastic-volatility path has been drawn, one is effectively in a deterministic setting. There are therefore good a priori reasons to believe that the proposed procedure should work well also in the stochastic-volatility case. Numerical results to substantiate this claim are presented in Section 12.4.3.

12.3.4 Calibration to co-terminal swaptions: displaced diffusion

In this section, the problem is tackled of calibrating in a financially desirable way a forward-rate-based displaced-diffusion stochastic-volatility LIBOR market model to the prices of a set of co-terminal swaptions. As discussed in Chapter 10, this problem is of particular relevance in the pricing of those complex derivative instruments which are 'naturally' hedged using plain-vanilla European swaptions. CMS-based products and Bermudan swaptions are the most obvious examples. The deterministic case has been extensively treated in Chapter 10 and in Rebonato (2000). One significant advantage of the procedure there proposed is that virtually exact recovery of the prices of the desired set of co-terminal swaptions can be obtained even when working with a forward-rate-based LIBOR market model. This is desirable because, when these state variables are used, the no-arbitrage drifts are considerably easier to implement than the corresponding quantities in the swap-rate-based version of the market model (Jamshidian 1997). More fundamentally, we showed in Chapter 10 (see also Rebonato 2001b) that, in the deterministic-volatility case, this recovery of the co-terminal swaption prices can be obtained in an infinity of ways. Making use of this feature, we then saw how, by means of this method, one can simultaneously obtain the best possible fit to a forward-rate covariance matrix, thereby ensuring a financially appealing evolution of the yield curve.

As shown below, the exact same approach cannot be followed in the stochastic-volatility case. Just as in the deterministic-volatility case, in fact, it will become clear that an infinity of solutions still exist, such that the co-terminal swaptions are exactly priced. Unlike the deterministic-volatility case, however, it is no longer possible to pick one out of these infinity of solutions so as to simultaneously guarantee that the resulting approximation to the forward-rate covariance matrix will be optimal in the same sense as the solution obtained in Chapter 10 was shown to be optimal. I will argue that the procedure suggested below nonetheless still produces a solution that displays some very appealing financial features.

The conceptual path followed in the deterministic-volatility setting can be first briefly revisited by extending it to the still-deterministic, but displaced-diffusion, setting. This can be done in the following way (see also Joshi 2001d, Joshi and Rebonato 2001). Let $0 = t_0 < t_1 < \ldots < t_n$ be the starting times of a set of co-terminal swaptions, let $SR_j(t)$ denote the equilibrium swap rate at time t of the swap associated to the times $t_j < t_{j+1} < \ldots < t_n$ and let f_j denote the forward rate from t_j to t_{j+1} (as seen from time t). As shown in the previous section, applying Ito's lemma and ignoring drifts (irrelevant for the calculation of the volatilities), one can compute the instantaneous volatility of the kth swap rate when the diffusion displacement coefficient is α, $\sigma^\alpha_{\text{SR}_k}$, as follows:

$$\frac{\mathrm{d}(\text{SR}_k + \alpha)}{\text{SR}_k + \alpha} = \sum_{i=1}^{n_k} \frac{\partial \text{SR}_k}{\partial f_i} \frac{f_i + \alpha}{\text{SR}_k + \alpha} \sigma^\alpha_i \, \mathrm{d}w_i,$$

$$\frac{\mathrm{d}(f_i + \alpha)}{f_i + \alpha} = \sigma^\alpha_i \, \mathrm{d}w_i = \sigma^\alpha_i \sum_m b^f_{im} \, \mathrm{d}z_m,$$

$$\frac{\mathrm{d}(\text{SR}_k + \alpha)}{\text{SR}_k + \alpha} = \sum_{i=1}^{n_k} \zeta_{ik} \sigma^\alpha_i \, \mathrm{d}w_i = \sum_{i=1}^{n_k} \zeta_{ik} \sigma^\alpha_i \sum_m b^f_{im} \, \mathrm{d}z_m,$$

$$[\sigma^\alpha_{\text{SR}_k}]^2 = \sum_{i,j=1}^{n_k} \sigma^\alpha_i \sigma^\alpha_j \rho^f_{ij} \zeta_{ik} \zeta_{jk} \equiv \sum_{i,j=1}^{n_k} C^f_{ij} \zeta_{ik} \zeta_{jk}.$$

In the expressions above $E[\mathrm{d}w_i \, \mathrm{d}w_j] = \rho^f_{ij}$, $\{\mathrm{d}z_i\}$ are the increments of orthogonal Brownian motions, n_k is the number of forward rates in the kth swap rate, C^f_{ij} is the (i,j)th element of the forward-rate covariance matrix, the weights $\{\zeta_{ik}\}$ are given by Equation (12.22), and the constraint $\sum_m b^2_{im} = 1$ on the loadings $\{\mathbf{b}^f\}$ is introduced to preserve the correct recovery of the desired forward-rate instantaneous volatility, as discussed in Chapter 3. The covariance element between the swap rates r and s, C^{SR}_{rs}, is then given by

$$C^{\text{SR}}_{rs} = E\left[\frac{\mathrm{d}(\text{SR}_r + \alpha)}{\text{SR}_r + \alpha} \frac{\mathrm{d}(\text{SR}_s + \alpha)}{\text{SR}_s + \alpha}\right]$$

$$= E\left[\sum_{i=1}^{n_r} \zeta_{ir} \sigma^\alpha_i \sum_m b^f_{im} \, \mathrm{d}z_m \sum_{j=1}^{n_s} \zeta_{js} \sigma^\alpha_j \sum_q b^f_{jq} \, \mathrm{d}z_q\right]. \qquad (12.23)$$

In matrix form (12.23) can be written as

$$\mathbf{C}^{\text{SR}} = \mathbf{Z}\,\mathbf{S}^f\boldsymbol{\beta}\,E[\mathrm{d}\mathbf{z}\,\mathrm{d}\mathbf{z}^{\text{T}}]\,\boldsymbol{\beta}^{\text{T}}(\mathbf{S}^f)^{\text{T}}\mathbf{Z}^{\text{T}} = \mathbf{Z}\,\mathbf{S}^f\boldsymbol{\beta}^f(\boldsymbol{\beta}^f)^{\text{T}}(\mathbf{S}^f)^{\text{T}}\mathbf{Z}^{\text{T}}$$

$$= \mathbf{Z}\,\mathbf{S}^f\boldsymbol{\rho}^f(\mathbf{S}^f)^{\text{T}}\mathbf{Z}^{\text{T}} = \mathbf{Z}\,\mathbf{C}^f\mathbf{Z}^{\text{T}} \qquad (12.24)$$

where $\mathbf{C}^{\text{SR}}$ ($\mathbf{C}^f$) is the covariance matrix among the swap (forward) rates, $\boldsymbol{\beta}$ is the matrix containing the elements $\{b^f_{ij}\}$, $\boldsymbol{\rho}^f$ is the correlation matrix among forward rates, the matrix $\mathbf{Z}$ contains the weights ζ_{ij} and the matrix $\mathbf{S}^f$ (introduced in Section 10.5.2) is the square matrix containing on its diagonal the instantaneous volatilities of the forward rates, and zeros elsewhere. The notation in Equation (12.24) can be lightened by defining the matrix $\boldsymbol{\sigma}^f$, given by

$$\boldsymbol{\sigma}^f = \mathbf{S}^f\boldsymbol{\beta}.$$

With this definition, and neglecting drifts again, one can more succinctly write in matrix form:

$$\frac{d(\mathbf{f}_t + \boldsymbol{\alpha})}{\mathbf{f}_t + \alpha} = \boldsymbol{\sigma}_t^f \, d\mathbf{W}_t \tag{12.25}$$

$$\frac{d(\mathbf{SR}_t + \boldsymbol{\alpha})}{\mathbf{SR}_t + \alpha} = \mathbf{Z} \, \boldsymbol{\sigma}_t^f \, d\mathbf{W}_t. \tag{12.26}$$

Expressions (12.25) and (12.26) are instantaneously correct. The value of the swap-rate vector after a finite time will be given by

$$\int \frac{d(\mathbf{SR}_t + \boldsymbol{\alpha})}{\mathbf{SR}_t + \alpha} = \int \mathbf{Z}_t \, \boldsymbol{\sigma}_t^f \, d\mathbf{W}_t.$$

The matrix $\mathbf{Z}_t$ is stochastic, and in general no closed-form solution for the above equation exists. In the deterministic displaced-diffusion case, the following approximation can be made with little loss of accuracy (its validity has been justified and analyzed at length in Chapter 10 and in Rebonato (2000) for the case when $\alpha = 0$):

$$\frac{d(\mathbf{SR}_t + \boldsymbol{\alpha})}{\mathbf{SR}_t + \alpha} = \mathbf{Z}(0) \, \boldsymbol{\sigma}_t^f \, d\mathbf{W}_t,$$

where $\mathbf{Z}(0)$ is the value of the (constant) matrix $\mathbf{Z}$ evaluated given the knowledge of today's yield curve. With this approximation one can write

$$\int \frac{d(\mathbf{SR}_t + \boldsymbol{\alpha})}{\mathbf{SR}_t + \alpha} = \int \mathbf{Z}_t \, \boldsymbol{\sigma}_t^f \, d\mathbf{W}_t \simeq \mathbf{Z}(0) \int \boldsymbol{\sigma}_t^f \, d\mathbf{W}_t.$$

All the quantities under the integral sign are now deterministic, and the integral can therefore be easily evaluated analytically. Almost exact pricing of the co-terminal European swaptions in a displaced-diffusion setting can therefore be achieved by requiring that

$$\mathbf{C}^f = \mathbf{Z}^{-1} \mathbf{C}^{\mathrm{SR}} (\mathbf{Z}^{\mathrm{T}})^{-1}, \tag{12.27}$$

where $\mathbf{C}^{\mathrm{SR}}$ is a swap-rate covariance matrix such that its diagonal elements integrate correctly to produce the desired root-mean-square volatility for each swap.

12.3.5 Calibration to co-terminal swaptions: stochastic volatility

Given the existence of an infinity of such matrices $\mathbf{C}^{\mathrm{SR}}$, I have shown in Chapter 10 and in Rebonato (2000) that, in the deterministic-volatility setting and when $\alpha = 0$, a procedure based on a trigonometric decomposition is available to choose the swap-rate covariance matrix that prices the co-terminal swaptions correctly and simultaneously produces the closest match to an exogenous forward-rate covariance matrix. As mentioned above, this last part of the deterministic-volatility procedure cannot be easily adapted to the stochastic-volatility setting. The treatment presented above can therefore be mirrored in the stochastic case up to the very last step, at which point a different route must be taken in order to ensure a reasonable (although no longer optimal in the sense discussed in Chapter 10) simultaneous fit to an exogenous forward-rate covariance matrix. The conceptual path outlined in Joshi and Rebonato (2001) and Joshi (2001e) is the following.

> **STEP 1** First of all one can begin by choosing a set of parameters for the forward-rate stochastic-volatility process, such that the caplet prices, or, more generally, the elements of the forward-rate covariance matrix are satisfactorily recovered. As in Section 12.4, one can then divide the time intervals into small steps, $\Delta s_l, l = 1, 2, \ldots, m$, and evolve the coefficients a, b, c and d over these small steps. For each small step, one can create a marginal covariance matrix for that step, $\mathbf{C}_l^f$. In particular, the (j, j)th entry of $\mathbf{C}_l^f$ will be
>
> $$C_l^f(j, j) = \{[a_{s_l} + b_{s_l}(T_j - s_l)] \exp[-c_{s_l}(T_j - s_l) + d_{s_l}]\}^2 \Delta s_l$$
>
> and the off-diagonal element in position (j, k) is
>
> $$C_l^f(j, k) = [a_{s_l} + b_{s_l}(T_j - s_l)] \exp[-c_{s_l}(T_j - s_l) + d_{s_l}]$$
> $$\times [a_{s_l} + b_{s_l}(T_k - s_l)] \exp[-c_{s_l}(T_k - s_l) + d_{s_l}] \rho_{jk}^f \Delta s_l.$$
>
> One can then form a forward-rate covariance matrix $\mathbf{C}^f$ by summing $\mathbf{C}_l^f$ for $l = 0, \ldots, m - 1$. From this one can obtain an implied swap-rate covariance matrix for this particular volatility path via $\mathbf{C}^{\mathrm{SR}} = \mathbf{Z}\,\mathbf{C}^f\mathbf{Z}^{\mathrm{T}}$. Much as shown in the previous section, this covariance matrix can now be used to price the co-terminal European swaptions using the Black formula with volatilities equal to the root-mean-square volatilities implied by the diagonal elements. These are the prices of the co-terminal European swaptions implied by this particular volatility path.
>
> The prices thus obtained must then be averaged across different path realizations. This can be achieved by using a Monte Carlo sampling of the root-mean-square volatilities implied by the chosen coefficient dynamics, as outlined in Section 8.5. The averages obtained in this way provide the 'first-pass' model swaption prices implied by the chosen dynamics for the forward-rate instantaneous volatility.
>
> **STEP 2** For the chosen set of parameters a, b, c and d, which had been chosen with the forward-rate covariance matrix in mind, the co-terminal swaptions will, in general, not be correctly priced. As shown below, this is easy to remedy, but, as in the deterministic-volatility case, the challenging task is not just, and not so much, the correct recovery of the market

prices. What is more important is that, at the same time, a believable and desirable evolution for such observables as the term structure of volatilities or the swaption matrix should be obtained (see also Rebonato 2000, Longstaff 2001, Longstaff et al. 2000a,b). In order to achieve this task, Joshi (2001e) proposes the following procedure: With the forward-rate market-calibrated volatility parameters, one can expect to obtain reasonable, but not exact, prices for the co-terminal swaptions in which one is interested. Unfortunately, as mentioned above, one can no longer specify the forward-rate covariance matrix simply to be given by

$$\mathbf{C}^f = \mathbf{Z}^{-1}\mathbf{C}^{\mathrm{SR}}(\mathbf{Z}^{\mathrm{T}})^{-1}$$

because the covariance matrix is only specified on a path-by-path basis by the volatility process. There is, however, a simple solution: One can begin by noticing that, if one multiplies the prices of all the swaption instantaneous volatilities along each instantaneous volatility path by a particular set of constants, which are specific to the swaption itself but independent of the path, then, by the linearity of the expectation operator, the final prices of the swaptions will be multiplied by the same set of constants. Furthermore, as mentioned above, the at-the-money (displaced) Black formula is almost exactly linear in the volatility, or, equivalently, linear in the square-root of the variance (see, again, Wilmott 1998, Brenner and Subrahmanyam 1994). This means that, if one adjusts the variance of the ith swaption by a constant K_i^2 on every path, then the final at-the-money price will be multiplied by K_i.

STEP 3 With this observation in mind, let $\boldsymbol{\lambda}$ be the $n \times n$ matrix with the required scaling constants K_i on the diagonal and zeros elsewhere (n is here the number of co-terminal swap rates). By carrying out a particular short-stepped evolution of the instantaneous volatilities of the different forward rates, one is effectively randomly sampling a particular forward-rate covariance matrix $\mathbf{C}^f$. If $\mathbf{C}^f$ is the drawn forward-rate covariance matrix for a given path, then the corresponding swap-rate covariance matrix for that path is $\mathbf{C}^{\mathrm{SR}} = \mathbf{Z}\,\mathbf{C}^f\mathbf{Z}^{\mathrm{T}}$. In order to price the co-terminal swaptions correctly (at the money) one would however like it to be

$$\mathbf{C}^{\mathrm{SR}} = \boldsymbol{\lambda}\,\mathbf{Z}\,\mathbf{C}^f\mathbf{Z}^{\mathrm{T}}\boldsymbol{\lambda}.$$

(Note that $\boldsymbol{\lambda} = \boldsymbol{\lambda}^T$.) Let $\mathbf{X}$ be a pseudo-square-root of $\mathbf{C}$, then (i.e., let $\mathbf{X}$ be a matrix such that $\mathbf{X}\mathbf{X}^{\mathrm{T}} = \mathbf{C}^f$). Therefore, if one replaces $\mathbf{X}$ by

$$\mathbf{B} = \mathbf{Z}^{-1}\boldsymbol{\lambda}\mathbf{Z}\mathbf{X},$$

one obtains the effective swap-rate covariance matrix

$$\mathbf{Z}\mathbf{B}\mathbf{B}^{\mathrm{T}}\mathbf{Z}^{\mathrm{T}} = \boldsymbol{\lambda}\mathbf{Z}\mathbf{C}^f\mathbf{Z}^{\mathrm{T}}\boldsymbol{\lambda},$$

and the diagonal elements have been multiplied by K_i^2, as required. This means that the average price, and therefore the implied volatility of the ith swap rate, is also multiplied by K_i, and the desired at-the-money price is therefore exactly recovered.

The proposed procedure is not only very simple, but similar in spirit to the technique suggested in the deterministic-volatility setting in order to choose the forward-rate-specific terms, $k(T_i)$, when calibrating to caplet prices. More precisely, the procedure presented above has the desirable feature that it can give an idea of the extent by which the forward-rate volatilities have to be altered in order to obtain an exact fit to the relevant swaption prices: the closer, in fact, the matrix λ is to (a multiple of) the identity matrix, the more congruent will be the observed market prices of the co-terminal swaptions and of the underlying forward rates. Therefore, the initial values $a(0)$, $b(0)$, $c(0)$ and $d(0)$ and their associated stochastic parameters can be varied in such a way as to ensure that the trace of the matrix λ is as constant as possible.

Any errors in this calibration procedure will come either from the inaccuracy of the equivalent swaption formula (see Section 12.5) or from deviation from linearity of the at-the-money Black price as a function of volatility. Any errors stemming from the first possible source of inaccuracy would be equally important in the deterministic-volatility case. As discussed in Chapter 10 (see also Hull and White 2000, Jaeckel and Rebonato 2001b), however, these pricing errors are hardly noticeable on the scale of a typical bid–offer spread. As for the second possible source of inaccuracy, the approximate linearity is (at-the-money) extremely accurate. More detailed results of relevant numerical experiments are presented in Section 12.4.5.

12.3.6 Rapid pricing of complex derivatives

Once the calibration of the model has been carried out using the techniques presented in the chapter so far, the scene is set for the actual pricing of a complex derivative product. The various necessary 'ingredients' can be reviewed in turn: To begin with, and as mentioned in Section 12.2, I shall always assume that the payoff enjoys the measurability and homogeneity conditions highlighted in Jamshidian (1997) and discussed in Chapter 4. As for the evolution of the forward rates, Monte Carlo is again the obvious numerical technique of choice, at least for path-dependent derivatives. I would like to stress, however, that, given the results recently presented by Andersen (1999) and Broadie and Glasserman (1997) amongst others, more complex free-boundary problems can be reduced to the path-dependent case after estimation of the exercise boundary (see the discussion in Chapter 4). Needless to say, the Monte Carlo evolution of the forward rates should be carried out using the methodology presented in Section 5.3 devoted to the drift approximation, which can obviously be naturally applied to the case of path-dependent securities.

The main obstacle would appear to be the sheer computational burden that would be encountered if one carried out the evolution of the forward rates using a short-stepped Monte Carlo simulation. This route would prima facie seem necessary in order to accommodate the stochastic nature of the volatility process. This would be unfortunate, because, as discussed in Section 12.3, in the deterministic-volatility case the ability to carry out moves of the yield curve over periods much longer than the typical three- or six-month tenors is of great importance. This is true not only in the presence of non-call features, but also for all those instruments where the evolution of all the forward rates can be carried out in a single very long jump all the way to the final expiry. Fortunately, by virtue of Equations (12.10) and (12.10′), the four-dimensional stochastic integration of the volatility process can be decoupled from the evolution of the forward rates. As a consequence, conditionally on a given volatility path having been achieved, the evolution of the forward rates over very long steps remains possible also in the stochastic-volatility setting. Therefore, by combining the fast calibration procedures presented in Sections 12.4–12.6 with the efficient evolution of the yield curve using the predictor–corrector approximation discussed in Section 12.3, the stochastic-volatility pricing of complex derivatives in a trading environment becomes a demanding but computationally feasible numerical task.

12.4 Numerical Results

The sections up to this point have presented the extensions to the displaced-diffusion, stochastic-volatility setting of the calibration and evolution techniques that have been discussed in Parts I–III in the deterministic-volatility case (i.e., for the standard LIBOR market model). In the present section I now proceed to present the results of the numerical experiments required to substantiate the claims about the accuracy and effectiveness of the approximations presented in the sections so far.

12.4.1 Convergence of the sampling of the volatility distribution

The general procedure recommend above can be summarized as follows:

1. Sample the unknown distribution of the instantaneous volatility via a relatively short-stepped Monte Carlo simulation.

2. Compute the root-mean-square volatility along each of the volatility paths.

3. Carry out a (very) long jump for the forward rates once the appropriate root-mean-square volatility has been computed.

It is therefore necessary to explore two separate issues of convergence. To begin with, one must corroborate the statements made so far that, by using

Table 12.2   *The values of the stochastic parameters used for the convergence test.*[a]

	Normal log-normal	Initial value	Vol.	Reversion speed	Reversion level
a	0	−0.020	0.05	0.5	−0.020
b	0	0.108	0.1	0.3	0.108
c	1	0.800	0.1	0.5	0.800
d	1	0.114	0.2	0.4261	0.114

[a] In the column 'Normal/log-normal' a 0 or a 1 denote an Ornstein-Uhlenbeck process for the coefficient or for its logarithm, respectively.

low-discrepancy sequences, sufficient convergence to the desired price can be obtained with a relatively small number of volatility paths (very often, as few as 32 or 64). The second convergence issue that must also be explored is the price convergence as a function of the step size over which the volatility process is evolved. These two issues are addressed in turn in this section.

One can begin with a fixed step size (chosen, in the first instance, to be equal to $1/12$ years – see the discussion below) and explore the convergence of the model price of European swaptions evaluated using the approximations described in Section 12.5 as a function of the number of sampled volatility paths. More precisely, 15 European swaptions of varying expiries and lengths were valued using the procedure presented in Section 12.5 using a displaced-diffusion, stochastic-volatility version of the LIBOR market model. The parameters for the stochastic processes of the coefficients are shown in Table 12.2. The swaption prices were evaluated for the number of paths increasing as a power of 2, and are shown for the cases of the 1×1 and 10×10 swaptions in Figures 12.10 and 12.11. One can observe from these figures that, after as few as 64 paths, the 1×1 swaption is converged to within a small fraction of a basis point, and the 10×10 swaption is converged to within approximately

Table 12.3   *The vega in basis points for some of the swaptions used in the tests. Following market practice, one vega has been taken as a proxy for the typical bid–offer spread for an at-the-money European swaption in market size.*

	Length			
1	5	10	Expiry
0.0002	0.0010	0.0015	0.5
0.0003	0.0013	0.0021	1
0.0004	0.0018	0.0028	2
0.0005	0.0022	0.0035	5
0.0005	0.0021	0.0034	10

Table 12.4   *The convergence of the swaption prices as a function of number of paths. See the text for details.*

Length	1	5	10	Expiry
16	0.002808	0.013501	0.019882	0.5
	0.004207	0.018759	0.027485	1
	0.006743	0.025219	0.03667	2
	0.00774	0.028798	0.043695	5
	0.006901	0.026803	0.041187	10
				Expiry
32	0.002791	0.013365	0.01969	0.5
	0.00416	0.018484	0.027091	1
	0.006594	0.024692	0.035929	2
	0.007624	0.028305	0.042944	5
	0.006833	0.026712	0.041092	10
				Expiry
64	0.00279	0.013388	0.019723	0.5
	0.004155	0.018498	0.027127	1
	0.006603	0.024757	0.036062	2
	0.00767	0.028492	0.043212	5
	0.00691	0.026935	0.0414	10
				Expiry
128	0.002792	0.013386	0.019717	0.5
	0.004158	0.018492	0.027107	1
	0.006603	0.024731	0.036006	2
	0.007698	0.028563	0.0433	5
	0.006923	0.026944	0.041377	10
				Expiry
256	0.002796	0.013403	0.01974	0.5
	0.004169	0.018531	0.027158	1
	0.00662	0.024781	0.036077	2
	0.007702	0.028574	0.043329	5
	0.006927	0.026968	0.041418	10
				Expiry
512	0.002794	0.013399	0.019738	0.5
	0.004166	0.018524	0.027156	1
	0.006628	0.024817	0.036128	2
	0.00771	0.028599	0.043369	5
	0.006924	0.026965	0.041425	10
				Expiry
1024	0.002794	0.013395	0.019732	0.5
	0.004167	0.018518	0.027147	1
	0.006629	0.024809	0.036114	2
	0.007714	0.028609	0.043376	5
	0.006927	0.02697	0.041432	10
				Expiry
2048	0.002794	0.0134	0.019739	0.5
	0.004169	0.01853	0.027161	1
	0.006632	0.024809	0.036113	2
	0.007704	0.028586	0.043354	5
	0.006928	0.026973	0.041437	10

0.4 basis points. In both cases these price inaccuracies correspond to approximately a hundredth of a vega. Over a variety of tests (see Table 12.4), 64 paths always produced pricing inaccuracies substantially smaller than a tenth of a vega (as usual, one vega was taken in this context as a reasonable proxy of a

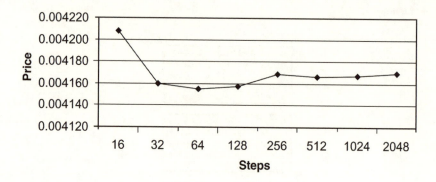

Figure 12.10   *Convergence as a function of number of paths for price of a* 1 × 1 *at-the-money European swaption.*

typical bid–offer spread for a European swaption). Table 12.3 reports, for the purpose of providing a comparison yardstick, the approximate vega for the swaptions analyzed in the tests.

As one can appreciate from these tables and figures, the convergence as a function of number of paths is indeed very rapid, and the claim made in the previous sections that as few as 64 (well-chosen) paths can produce a convergence well within market bid–offer spreads even for 'stress' cases such a 10 × 10 swaption has therefore been substantiated.

The second convergence issue to explore is the behavior of the estimated price as a function of step size. This aspect of the convergence is addressed in Figure 12.12, again for the 'stress' case of 10 × 10 swaption, for step sizes rang-

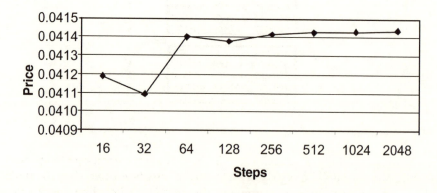

Figure 12.11   *Same as Figure 12.10 for a* 10 × 10 *swaption.*

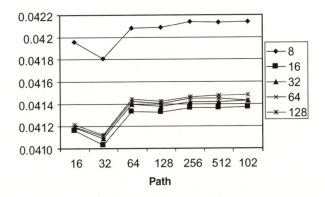

Figure 12.12   *Convergence in the price of a* 10×10 *European swaption as a function of number of paths and step size.*

ing from 1.25 years (eight steps over 10 years) to 1/12 years (120 steps over 10 years). One can see from this figure that, despite the fact that eight steps over 10 years are clearly not sufficient to produce a fully converged solution, even in this case the price error corresponds to only eight basis points, that is, a quarter of the typical bid–offer spread for the 10×10 year swaption under study. On the basis of these results, one can therefore conclude that 64 paths with a step size of 1.25 or 0.625 years should produce results well within the accuracy required for practical applications.

12.4.2 Accuracy of the drift approximation

The next issue to explore is the accuracy of the drift approximation in the stochastic-volatility case. In order to carry out this test, a 10-year semi-annual caplet was chosen, whose natural numeraire, using the terminology and notation introduced in Figure 2.1, would be called $N(20)$. Under the measure associated with the natural numeraire, the underlying forward rate would be drift-less. For any other numeraire the drift would be non-zero, and is given by Expressions (12.11) or (12.12), as appropriate, depending on the expiry of the chosen numeraire. The greater the mismatch between the expiry of the natural numeraire and any other numeraire (chosen among the universe of traded assets, i.e., pure discount bonds), the larger the drift term, and the more demanding the task for the approximation. Similarly, the longer the expiry, T, of the forward rate, the larger the exponent (because of its linear dependence on T), and the more severe the 'stress case' for the drift approximation. (See, in this respect, the discussion at the end of Chapter 5.) The test was therefore carried out as follows:

1. An approximately at-the-money (5%), 10-year-expiry caplet was selected.

Table 12.5   *The simulation parameters used in the test, together with the coefficients for the evolution of the instantaneous volatility. A displaced-diffusion coefficient α of 0.02 was used in conjunction with these parameters.*

	Normal log-normal	Initial value	Vol.	Reversion speed	Reversion level	
a	0	-0.020	0.05	0.500	-0.020	$\beta = 0.1$
b	0	0.108	0.1	0.300	0.108	Strike = 5.00%
c	1	0.800	0.1	0.500	0.800	Paths = 16 384
d	1	0.114	0.2	0.426	0.114	Steps/year = 32

2. The corresponding 10-year-expiry forward rate was evolved with a single-step 10-year evolution under a variety of numeraires ranging from $N(1)$ (largest drift) to $N(10)$ (no drift).

3. The values of both the 5%-strike caplet and floorlet were evaluated by the Monte Carlo averaging procedure described in Section 12.3.

4. The value of a 5%-strike forward-rate agreement was obtained via call–put parity, and compared with its exact theoretical value.

The results obtained for this case study and the parameters used in the simulations are displayed in Tables 12.5 and 12.6.

Since what is being investigated in this section is the quality of the drift approximation, for the simulations 32 steps per year and 16 384 (2^{14}) paths were used to ensure that numerical convergence to within one part in 10^6 in the Monte Carlo sampling had been achieved. It is clear from the results

Table 12.6   *The values of the caplet (price call) and floorlet (price put) used to obtain via call–put parity the value of the FRA.*

Numeraire	Price call	Price put	Forward rate
0	0.001 1550	0.000 9687	0.000 1863
1	0.001 1550	0.000 9687	0.000 1863
2	0.001 1538	0.000 9687	0.000 1851
3	0.001 1549	0.000 9687	0.000 1862
4	0.001 1550	0.000 9687	0.000 1862
5	0.001 1549	0.000 9687	0.000 1861
6	0.001 1549	0.000 9687	0.000 1862
7	0.001 1549	0.000 9691	0.000 1858
8	0.001 1549	0.000 9688	0.000 1861
9	0.001 1550	0.000 9688	0.000 1862
10	0.001 1549	0.000 9689	0.000 1860
Exact price of a 5% FRA			0.000 1864

Table 12.7 *The values obtained by best-fitting the displacement coefficient and the parameters of the stochastic volatility processes (12.5)–(12.9) to the GBP caplet market (February 2001). These values were then used in the fitting to the caplet prices.*

	Normal log-normal	Initial value	Vol.	Reversion speed	Reversion level	
a	0.000	−0.020	0.050	0.500	−0.020	$\beta = 0.1$
b	0.000	0.108	0.100	0.300	0.108	Displacement
c	1.000	0.800	0.100	0.500	0.800	= 0.0205
d	1.000	0.114	0.200	0.426	0.114	

in Table 12.6 that, even for this severe test, the drift approximation produces results of excellent numerical quality. It can therefore be reliably used in order to carry out very-long-stepped evolutions of the forward rates either across non-call features, or, when appropriate (i.e., for type-1a products), to the final expiry of a complex product.

12.4.3 Accuracy of the fitting to caplet prices

The next topic to investigate is the accuracy of the procedure suggested in Section 12.4 in order to produce fast and accurate fitting to the at-the money caplet prices. As it will be recalled, the fitting scheme proposed in Section 12.4 constitutes a natural extension of the fitting procedure suggested in the deterministic-volatility case in Chapters 6 and 8, and attempts to preserve its link with time-homogeneity.[10] It is important to remember, in fact, that all the coefficients of the stochastic instantaneous volatility process have been assumed to be time-independent, and, therefore, the only two additional necessary and sufficient conditions for the (now stochastic) evolution of the term structure to be time-homogeneous is that

- the scaling factors $k(T_i)$ should all be identical and

- the reversion levels should be identical to the current initial values.

With these considerations in mind, several global (i.e., all-strikes, all-maturities) fits to caplet market data were carried out and the best set of coefficients and initial values was determined by minimizing the discrepancies between model and market prices, as per Equation (12.20). In the (typical)

---

[10]When the instantaneous volatility is deterministic, so obviously is the term structure of volatilities. Therefore, in the deterministic-volatility setting, the necessary and sufficient condition for time-homogeneity is simply that $\int_0^T \sigma(T, u)^2 \, du = \int_\tau^{T+\tau} \sigma(T + \tau, u)^2 \, du$ (cf. Equation (6.2)). When the instantaneous volatility is stochastic, one can obviously no longer require that this relationship should hold in a pathwise sense; rather, one can at most require that, for any τ, the statistical properties of the quantity of interest should look exactly the same when evaluated at time t or at time τ.

case of the GBP caplet market (February 2001) the volatility coefficients, initial values and displacement coefficient displayed in Table 12.7 were used. The issue of the quality of the market fit is explored separately (see Section 8.6), but these values could not reproduce exactly the market prices exactly (as, in general, will always be the case).

The rescaling factors $k(T_i)$ were therefore determined as shown in Equation (12.21) and the results are displayed in Table 12.8. This table shows that the agreement between the model and the target prices (whose accuracy basically hinges on the linearity of the Black formula in the at-the-money volatility) is virtually perfect. It is important to stress that the goal of this numerical test was to show the effectiveness of the procedure even when the required rescaling is substantial (see column 'Rescaled Ks' in Table 12.8). Therefore, no attempt was made, in this particular test, to ensure that the factors $k(T_i)$ should be as close to unity as possible, which would have ensured as time-homogeneous an evolution of the term structure of volatilities as possible.

12.4.4 Accuracy of the European swaption approximation

The next result that requires numerical investigation is the accuracy of the extension of the European swaption approximation formula to the displaced-diffusion, stochastic-volatility setting, as discussed in Section 12.5. The same coefficients shown in Table 12.7 were used for the purpose. More precisely, a series of swaptions was valued using a full stochastic-volatility Monte Carlo simulation approach (results labelled 'Full Monte Carlo' in Table 12.9) in which the forward rates were evolved to the swaption maturity using as many factors as the number of forward rates themselves, and the volatility paths were sampled using for accuracy as many as 512 paths with sufficiently short steps to ensure convergence in price to within less than a basis point. The only approximation used in this calculation was the use of the extension Hunter et al. (2001) drift correction to the stochastic setting, discussed in Section 12.3. Given the empirical results presented in Section 8.2, and given the chosen step size, the errors introduced by using this approximation can be safely regarded as totally immaterial.

The approximate formulae given in Section 12.5 were then used to obtain the 'quick' prices for the same swaptions, and the results compared. The results are displayed in Table 12.9 for a handful of typical cases, including, as usual, the 'stress case' of a 10×10 year semi-annual swaption.

The vegas for the swaptions (i.e., a reasonable proxy for the bid–offer spread) can be read from Table 12.3. For the most severe 'stress case', that is, the 10×10 year swaption, the vega is approximately 34 basis points, while the approximation error is just two basis points. Also this extension of the procedure, which is known to work well in the deterministic-volatility case, can therefore be relied upon in the new setting.

Table 12.8 *The at-the-money market implied volatilities for a series of caplets (GBP curve, February 2001) (column 'Market ATM vols'), the model caplet prices obtained with a global coefficient fit to the market (column 'Global calib ATM vols'), the rescaling factors (column 'Rescaled Ks') and the fitted caplet prices (column 'ATM calib vols').*

Expiry times	Global Ks	Market ATM vols (%)	Global calib ATM vols (%)	Rescaled Ks	ATM calib vols (%)
0.25	1.25	9.76	17.95	0.682	9.77
0.50	1.11	9.68	17.51	0.612	9.69
0.75	0.93	9.64	15.85	0.569	9.64
1.00	0.93	11.10	16.59	0.623	11.10
1.25	1.04	13.52	19.15	0.733	13.51
1.50	1.15	15.95	21.81	0.843	15.95
1.75	1.14	16.52	21.94	0.858	16.51
2.00	1.09	16.43	21.25	0.845	16.42
2.25	1.09	16.97	21.39	0.866	16.96
2.50	1.09	17.44	21.48	0.887	17.43
2.75	1.08	17.63	21.36	0.895	17.62
3.00	1.09	18.16	21.55	0.921	18.15
3.25	1.08	18.19	21.33	0.924	18.18
3.50	1.08	18.11	21.16	0.922	18.10
3.75	1.07	18.16	21.00	0.928	18.15
4.00	1.06	18.07	20.71	0.925	18.06
4.25	1.05	17.81	20.36	0.916	17.80
4.50	1.04	17.68	20.11	0.914	17.67
4.75	1.03	17.60	19.92	0.914	17.59
5.00	1.03	17.66	19.85	0.917	17.65
5.25	1.02	17.38	19.52	0.906	17.37
5.50	1.01	17.30	19.33	0.906	17.29
5.75	1.01	17.42	19.29	0.916	17.41
6.00	1.02	17.74	19.38	0.934	17.73
6.25	1.02	17.85	19.33	0.944	17.84
6.50	1.02	17.89	19.24	0.949	17.88
6.75	1.01	17.73	19.04	0.945	17.72
7.00	1.01	17.65	18.90	0.944	17.64
7.25	1.00	17.45	18.69	0.937	17.45
7.50	1.00	17.39	18.55	0.936	17.38
7.75	1.00	17.43	18.50	0.942	17.42
8.00	1.00	17.53	18.48	0.949	17.52
8.25	1.00	17.54	18.40	0.953	17.53
8.50	1.00	17.55	18.34	0.956	17.55
8.75	1.00	17.56	18.27	0.960	17.55

Table 12.8   *continued*

Expiry times	Global Ks	Market ATM vols (%)	Global calib ATM vols (%)	Rescaled Ks	ATM calib vols (%)
9.00	1.00	17.55	18.21	0.962	17.54
9.25	1.00	17.53	18.14	0.964	17.53
9.50	1.00	17.58	18.10	0.969	17.57
9.75	1.00	17.67	18.10	0.977	17.67
10.00	1.00	17.82	18.18	0.983	17.81
10.25	1.01	17.93	18.20	0.991	17.93
10.50	1.01	17.99	18.21	0.995	17.99
10.75	1.01	17.98	18.16	0.996	17.98
11.00	1.01	17.97	18.13	0.996	17.96
11.25	1.01	17.98	18.11	0.998	17.98
11.50	1.01	18.00	18.11	1.000	18.00
11.75	1.01	18.01	18.08	1.002	18.00
12.00	1.00	17.98	18.14	0.995	17.97
12.25	1.00	17.98	18.11	0.996	17.98
12.50	1.00	17.97	18.11	0.997	17.97
12.75	1.00	17.97	18.08	0.999	17.97
13.00	1.00	17.95	18.08	0.996	17.95
13.25	1.00	17.95	18.06	0.998	17.95
13.50	1.00	17.92	18.07	0.995	17.92
13.75	1.00	17.92	18.04	0.997	17.92
14.00	1.00	17.89	18.06	0.994	17.89
14.25	1.00	17.88	18.04	0.995	17.88
14.50	1.00	17.84	18.05	0.992	17.84

Table 12.9   *The 'true' (row 'Full Monte Carlo') and approximate (row 'Approximate') prices for several European swaptions, as described in the text.*

	5×10	10×1	10×5	10×10
Full Monte Carlo	0.0286	0.0069	0.0270	0.0440
Approximate	0.0286	0.0069	0.0269	0.0438

Table 12.10 *The portion of the market swaption matrix corresponding to a set of co-terminal swaptions (GBP swaption matrix, February 2001). The at-the-money 'exact' (Monte Carlo) and approximate swaption implied volatilities are given in columns 'Input vols' and 'Output vols', respectively.*

Residual Expiry × Length	Input vols (%)	Output vols (%)
1 × 8	13.920	13.919
1.5 × 7.5	14.000	13.999
2 × 7	14.080	14.079
2.5 × 6.5	14.132	14.130
3 × 6	14.183	14.182
3.5 × 5.5	14.340	14.338
4 × 5	14.497	14.495
4.5 × 4.5	14.708	14.706
5 × 4	14.919	14.916
5.5 × 3.5	15.273	15.270
6 × 3	15.628	15.624
6.5 × 2.5	16.018	16.013
7 × 2	16.407	16.401
7.5 × 1.5	16.407	16.401

12.4.5 Accuracy of the simultaneous calibration to a set of co-terminal swaptions

In order to investigate the accuracy of the procedure suggested in Section 12.6 to produce a virtually exact fit to a set of co-terminal European swaptions (as would typically be found in a Bermudan-swaption problem), a similar procedure to the one described in the previous section was followed. More precisely, the at-the-money prices for a set of co-terminal European swaptions were first evaluated 'exactly' using a full-factor Monte Carlo simulation as described in Section 8.4. The prices for the same swaptions using the approximate formulae discussed in Section 12.6 were then estimated. Finally, the prices were converted into at-the-money implied volatilities. The results are shown in Table 12.10, and show again the excellent quality of the proposed approximation.

For the sake of brevity, information about tests run for other currencies and/or trading dates is not displayed. The results were however always of the same numerical quality as the ones displayed for this Case Study. One can therefore conclude that, also in this case, the quality of the numerical approximation is excellent.

12.4.6 Global fitting to the caplet market smile surface

Despite the fact that, as discussed in the introductory section, the main goal of the approach presented in this chapter has not been the production

Table 12.11   *The initial values a(0), b(0), c(0) and d(0) and the optimal parameters for their processes obtained by fitting globally to the whole caplet surface, and by allowing either just d (upper half of table) or all the coefficients (lower half of table) to be stochastic. The column labelled 'Vol' contains the volatilities of the coefficients or of their logarithms, as appropriate. When the volatility is set to zero (first three rows) the coefficient is deterministic, and the reversion speed becomes immaterial because the reversion level is set equal to the initial value.*

	Initial value	Vol.	Reversion speed	Reversion level
a	−0.0897	0.0000	0.2000	−0.0897
b	0.1083	0.0000	0.2000	0.1083
c	0.9677	0.0000	0.2000	0.9677
d	0.1137	0.3976	0.4261	0.1137
a	−0.1216	0.0183	0.1701	−0.1216
b	0.1683	0.0098	0.1979	0.1683
c	0.9512	0.0005	0.1995	0.9512
d	0.1212	0.1870	0.4916	0.1212

of as close a fit to the caplet smile surface as possible, it is obviously important to check the quality of the match between the model and the market smile surfaces. To this effect, I present in this section the results obtained for the global fit over the volatility coefficients, the initial values, $a(0)$, $b(0)$, $c(0)$ and $d(0)$, and the single displacement coefficient, α, to a market smile caplet surface (GBP, 1-Sept-2000). It is important to emphasize that

- the same set of parameters was used for the whole surface (i.e., all strikes and all maturities) and
- the reversion levels were not allowed to be fitting parameters, but were constrained to be equal to today's values of the appropriate quantities (thereby enhancing time-homogeneity).

Similar results were obtained in the case of the EUR caplet surface but, again for the sake of brevity, they are not shown in this section.

In order to ascertain 'how much' stochasticity is actually needed in order to achieve a sufficiently close match of the caplet surface, two distinct optimizations were run, the first allowing for a stochastic behavior for a, b, c and d (curves labelled 'all stochastic' in Figures 12.13–12.17), and the second by keeping a, b and c deterministic actually, constant and assigning a stochastic behavior only to the d coefficient (curves labelled 'Fit'). In either case, a perfect fit to the at-the-money prices was then obtained by using the rescaling factors, $k(T_i)$, as described in Section 12.4. Parameter values are shown in Table 12.11. Cross-sections of the resulting fitted smile surfaces are shown in Figures 12.13–12.17.

The following features in the graphs are worth mentioning. First of all, with the exception of the shortest-maturity smile, the agreement between

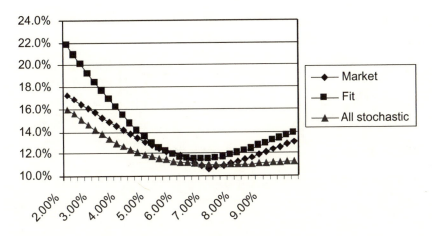

Figure 12.13 *The fit across strikes to the market implied volatilities (curve labelled 'Market') obtained with a, b, c and d stochastic (curve labelled 'All stochastic'), or just d stochastic (curve labelled 'Fit'), for a maturity of one year for the GBP surface discussed in the text.*

the market and the model smile surface remains very good in a wide region around the at-the-money strike (where model and market prices are matched by construction). Allowing for a stochastic behavior for all the coefficients obviously provides a better overall fit. The quality of the fit in which only d is stochastic, however, is not much poorer, and only appears to fail noticeably for extremely out-of-the-money strikes, where the reliability of market quotes is very questionable in any case.

It is also important to point out that (see Table 12.11) the optimal solutions obtained for the parameters of the d process and for the initial values $a(0)$, $b(0)$, $c(0)$ and $d(0)$ turned out to be very similar irrespective of whether an optimization over all the reversion speeds and volatilities (and α) was carried out, or simply over the corresponding quantities for d (and α). The similarity of the solutions (as found in this example and in other cases not reported for the sake of brevity) lends considerable reassurance as to the robustness of the procedure. It is also encouraging that the parameters obtained in the course of the optimization to the caplet surface turned out to be econometrically plausible, without any constraints to this effect having being imposed.[11] More precisely:

- The long-term level of the volatility, d, was naturally found by the optimization procedure to have a plausible magnitude of 11.4%.

---

[11]The usual caveats about comparing real-world and risk-adjusted quantities must be kept in mind when making these comparisons. See Chapter 13 and Rebonato and Joshi (2001a) on this point.

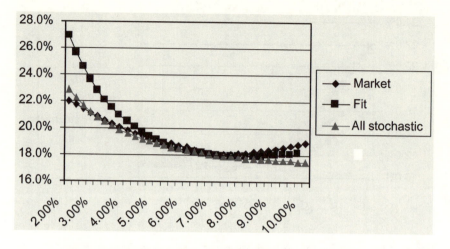

Figure 12.14   *Same as Figure 12.13, but for a maturity of three years.*

- The single displacement coefficient α, which turned out to be approximately equal to 2%, would correspond, after carrying out Marris's (1999) transformation to a CEV model, to an exponent β approximately equal to 0.60 for an initial forward of 6.00%. This compares well with 'market lore', which favours a value around 0.5.

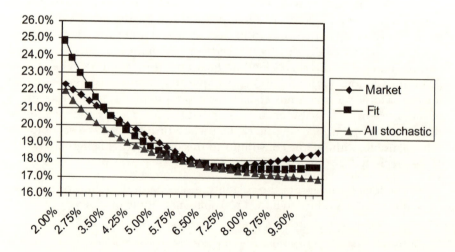

Figure 12.15   *Same as Figure 12.13, but for a maturity of five years.*

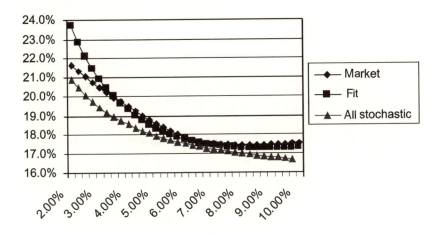

Figure 12.16 *Same as Figure 12.13, but for a maturity of seven years.*

- The initial values $a(0)$, $b(0)$, $c(0)$ and $d(0)$ turned out to be very similar to the corresponding values obtained in the deterministic case, and gave rise to a maximum in the hump for the instantaneous volatility around the one-year region, which agrees well with the maturity of the most volatile futures contracts, as discussed in Chapter 6 and in Rebonato (1998).

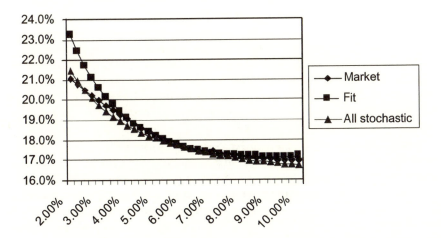

Figure 12.17 *Same as Figure 12.13, but for a maturity of eight years.*

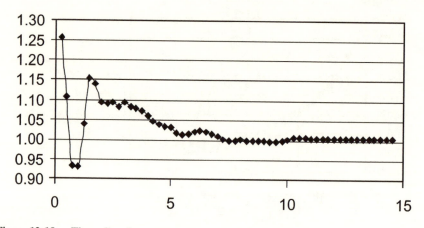

Figure 12.18   *The scaling factors necessary to ensure perfect pricing of the at-the-money caplets obtained in the case of only d stochastic.*

- Finally, the values for the mean-reversion coefficient turned out to be sufficiently high to ensure that, as desired, the dispersion around the initial values should not be too high, but not so large as to 'kill' the stochastic behavior of any of the coefficients.

It is perhaps even more important and encouraging to draw attention to the fact that the rescaling coefficients, $k(T_i)$, necessary to ensure a perfect fit to the at-the-money prices, turned out to be extremely close to unity, at least after a brief initial period of less than one year (see Figure 12.18). For the (typical) example reported in this figure, for all but four out of 60 caplets a perfect fit could be obtained with rescaling coefficients between 1.05 and 0.95. This is important, because, given the choice for the reversion levels, a set of perfectly constant coefficients $k(T_i)$ would imply an exactly time-homogeneous behavior for the stochastic evolution of the term structure of volatilities. I have argued at length in the previous parts of this book that this is, in general, a highly desirable feature, and the author fully concurs in this respect with the analysis in Longstaff et al. (2000a,b).

I would like to stress again the importance of the result just mentioned. By virtue of the fact that the optimized coefficients allow for an approximate forward-rate-independence of the scaling factors, in fact, what has been achieved is not only a perfect fit to today's at-the-money prices and a very good fit to today's smile surface, but also and simultaneously a time-homogeneous future evolution of the latter. I consider this ability to account simultaneously and convincingly not only for today's caplet surface but also for its evolution is possibly the most important feature of the approach proposed in this chapter.

It is important to stress again that it would indeed be possible to obtain a closer fit by allowing, for instance, the displacement-diffusion coefficient α to become forward-rate-specific;[12] or by allowing for the reversion levels of the coefficients a, b, c and d to be different from today's values. By so doing, however, I feel that these modifications of the proposed approach would be very ad hoc, and little would be added in terms of financial modelling. In other terms, I believe that the trader will be better served by using an imperfectly fitting, but transparent and intuitively understandable, model, than by employing an over-parametrized approach.

12.5 Conclusions and Suggestions for Future Work

I have presented in this chapter a displaced-diffusion extension of the LIBOR market model which allows for stochastic instantaneous volatilities of the forward rates. Virtually all the powerful approximations that have been devised in the past few years in the deterministic-volatility setting, and presented in Parts I–III of this book, can be successfully and naturally extended to the stochastic-volatility case. In particular, this chapter has shown that

1. the caplet market can be efficiently and accurately fitted;

2. the drift approximations that allow the evolution of the forward rates over very long time-steps can be recovered;

3. the European swaption matrix implied by a given choice of volatility parameters can be efficiently approximated with a closed-form expression without having to carry out any Monte Carlo simulation;

4. it is still possible, just as in the deterministic-volatility case, to calibrate the model virtually perfectly via simple matrix manipulations so that the prices of the co-terminal swaptions underlying a given Bermudan swaption should be exactly recovered using a forward-rate-based implementation of the approach, while retaining at the same time a desirable behavior for the evolution of the caplet term structure of volatilities.

As for the fitting to the caplet surface obtainable with this procedure, the important point has been made that the proposed approach is capable not only of pricing perfectly today's at-the-money caplets, and of obtaining a very good overall fit to today's smile surface, but also of producing a financially desirable time-homogeneous evolution for the term structure of volatilities. In other terms, a cross-sectional, single-time estimation has naturally and automatically produced in a very satisfactory way a dynamic, inter-temporal feature, without any constraint that this should be the case.

---

[12]See, in this respect, the discussion in Section 11.3, as to why this would not be desirable.

There are several natural extensions to this work: first of all one can explore the pricing impact of the approach for different types of complex derivatives products. I have already mentioned, for instance, that, for the simplest instrument of all, that is, for at-the-money caplets, allowing a stochastic behavior for the d coefficient has a strong pricing impact, but the effect of the stochasticity of a and c is very limited. In general, it is natural to expect that those complex instruments whose price strongly depends on the terminal decorrelation brought about by non-constant volatility, and, in particular, by the presence of a hump in the instantaneous volatility curve, should be noticeably affected by the stochastic behavior of the volatility. Trigger swaps, flexi-caps and Bermudan swaptions would clearly warrant close scrutiny.

The second obvious avenue would be the analysis of the hedging performance of the model using real-world data for the analysis. Also very interesting would be the exploration of the ability to obtain, at the same time, a good cross-sectional fit to a single-time smile surface and a convincing recovery of the most salient features of the inter-temporal evolution of the at-the-money implied term structure of volatilities. When one moves to a stochastic-volatility setting, this task is more complex than one might initially think, because of the need to distinguish carefully between the real-world and the risk-adjusted quantities that relate to the evolution of the term structure of volatilities. While, for instance, if the model specification were correct, the volatilities of the coefficients a, b, c and d would remain unchanged in moving from the real-world to the pricing measure, the same would not be true for the reversion speed and the reversion level. The comparison between model-produced and market-observed term structures of volatilities must therefore be undertaken with great care. A detailed analysis of this topic using swaption data is presented in the next chapter (see also Rebonato and Joshi 2001a).

All these topics can be investigated either in the stochastic-volatility framework presented above, or using the jump-diffusion approach, which has recently been presented (Glasserman and Kou 2000, Glasserman and Merener 2001, Jamshidian 1999). In order to assess which of these possible lines of enquiry might be the most profitable one, it is necessary to look in detail at some empirical data. This task is undertaken in the next chapter.

A Joint Empirical and Theoretical Analysis of the Stochastic-Volatility LIBOR Market Model

13.1 Motivation and Plan of the Chapter

13.1.1 Reasons for choosing European swaptions to test the stochastic-volatility LIBOR market model

(The results presented in this chapter are based on work done with Dr Mark Joshi (Rebonato and Joshi 2001a). It is a pleasure to acknowledge his help with computations and many useful discussions.)

One of the underlying themes of this book has been that caplets and European swaptions enjoy a privileged status in the interest-rate derivatives world, in that they are the liquid plain-vanilla reference instruments used by the complex derivatives traders to hedge the 'convexity' of their positions (i.e., for hedging beyond the delta level). In this respect, the exotic interest-rate option trader tends to regard cap(let)s and European swaptions almost as their most natural set of 'underlying' instruments, and one of the reasons for the appeal of the LIBOR market model is its ability to recover almost by construction the Black prices of these benchmark derivatives. Furthermore, a significant amount of direct screen-visible information is available for these instruments in almost real time, making their prices to a large extent model-independent.

When examined in detail, the situation is actually somewhat more complex, since brokers' quotes of *cap*, rather than *caplet*, implied volatilities are posted on the screen.[1] In the presence of smiles, it is not a simple and model-

---

[1]The market adopts the following convention in quoting a cap implied volatility: Given the strike and the expiry of the cap, the associated implied volatility is the single number that must be input into the Black formulas for all the underlying caplets in order to obtain the desired market price for the whole cap. This procedure is much more opaque than an implied volatility quote for

independent task to extract from these quotes the at-the-money volatilities of the underlying caplets. The swaption information is, on the other hand, much 'cleaner', since each screen quote refers to one single at-the-money option. The construction of the swaption implied volatility matrix, defined precisely below, is therefore a simpler and less ambiguous task, requiring as it does at most a two-dimensional interpolation/extrapolation exercise. It is for this reason that I focus the analysis presented in this chapter on swaption, rather than caplet, implied volatilities.

13.1.2 Difficulties with the naive assessments of the quality of a model

The quality of the fitting to the smile surface that a given model allows is, of course, an important criterion in order to decide whether it provides a reasonable description of the market they attempt to describe. However, a variety of financially very different modelling approaches can produce fits of essentially the same quality. Indeed, Britten-Jones and Neuberger (1998) show how an arbitrary stochastic-volatility model can be made to fit exactly by construction any (sufficiently regular) exogenous smile surface. I have therefore argued in the previous chapter that placing too much emphasis on the quality of a static fit in assessing the quality of a modelling approach can be a misguided effort.

The time-homogeneity of the evolution of the term structure of volatilities can provide a useful indication in this respect, but its appropriateness is clear only if the fit to the current market data is of good quality. If this is not the case, the ability to reproduce in the future an ill-fitting smile surface is, per se, hardly a positive feature. The question, therefore, remains open as to how the quality of a yield-curve model can be profitably assessed. Because of the difficulties in making direct use of the cap data, it is tempting to concentrate on swaption-related information, and to try to ascertain the realism of a proposed model by comparing the market-observed and the model-produced stochastic changes in the swaption matrix.

This line of enquiry appears appealing and relatively simple. The exercise is however made difficult by the fact that one set of quantities is related to the risk-adjusted and the other to the real world. If, as is the case for the approach discussed in Chapter 12, the source of randomness in the volatility dynamics is introduced by positing an additional (set of) Brownian shock(s), there intervene a set of volatility drift transformations in moving between one world and the other. Therefore, the drift term of the stochastic-volatility process, as obtained by a best fit to market prices, not only will incorporate a real-world (econometric) component, but also will reflect the risk aversion of the traders. In particular, if a mean-reverting model is chosen for the volatility, both the reversion speed and the reversion level obtained by matching market prices

---

a single option, since, even in the absence of smiles, a cap implied volatility is not directly linked in any simple way to the root-mean-square volatility of any of the underlying caplets.

will contain an inextricable combination of real-world and risk-adjusted parameters. This occurs because (see, e.g., Lewis 2000) in a stochastic-volatility setting the Girsanov's translation from the real-world to the risk-adjusted measure brings about a change in the drift of the instantaneous volatility. This change of measure, in turn, makes a naive comparison between the empirically observed and the model-predicted changes in the swaption matrix impossible.

It is worthwhile commenting further on this point. When moving between equivalent measures, Girsanov's theorem allows us to change the drifts of all Brownian motions. When one deals with forward rates, the requirement of no arbitrage, coupled with the fact that a forward rate times an appropriate bond becomes a tradable asset (see Chapter 5) forces its drift in the martingale measure to take a unique value. However, volatility is not tradable, nor is it possible to find a simple transformation (such as the multiplication by a 'natural payoff') that can turn it into a traded asset. It is therefore not possible to impose constraints that are strong enough to single out a unique drift of the volatility parameters in the martingale measure. As a consequence, an infinity of volatility drifts (each associated with a different equivalent pricing measure) are compatible with the absence of arbitrage.

In summary, the volatility of the instantaneous volatility, as usual, remains unchanged in moving between measures – because of Girsanov's theorem again, this time applied to the volatility rather than the forward-rate processes. However, the model-implied evolution of the term structure of volatilities or of the swaption matrix will be influenced also by the mean-reverting behavior of the volatility, and will not lend itself to direct comparison with the same quantities observed in the real world.

At this stage it is therefore not a priori obvious to what extent the resulting evolution of the real and model swaption matrices can be compared. Despite these difficulties, it would be highly desirable to bring statistical information to bear on the financial justification of the extensions to the LIBOR market model that are being introduced.

13.1.3 Brief description of the test methodology and plan of the chapter

I address this problem from a joint empirical/theoretical perspective. First of all I analyze in Section 13.2 market data pertaining to the USD and EUR/DEM swaption matrices. In the same section I then perform a principal component analysis of the changes in at-the-money implied swaption volatilities by calculating and orthogonalizing the correlation and covariance matrices among changes in the implied volatilities that make up the swaption matrix. An intuitive qualitative interpretation of the results is presented, and, given the complex structure of a swaption matrix, the results are more interesting than the usual level/slope/curvature decomposition.[2] I then move to the principal component analysis of the changes in the swaption matrix as predicted by the stochastic instantaneous volatility model proposed in Chapter 12 and estimate the eigenvectors and eigenvalues of the swaption matrix correlation implied by the theoretical evolution of the instantaneous volatility.

The analysis of the real-world and model eigenvectors and eigenvalues has a clear intrinsic interest. It has the added appeal of constituting a possible bridge between the pricing and real-world measures. This important advantage of the principal-component-based methodology stems from the fact that, as I discussed in Section 13.3.1, the statistical (real-world) and the risk-adjusted principal components are in the limit unchanged in moving between measures, since they only depend on the (deterministic) volatility and correlation of the volatility process, and can therefore be directly compared. This allows us to circumvent the problems alluded to above of comparing real-world and model-produced changes in the overall shape of the swaption matrix.

Section 13.4 concludes the chapter by commenting on the results and providing suggestions for future studies.

13.1.4 What does it mean to test a model? Strong and weak validation

It must be stressed that there are several levels at which the 'validity' or 'reasonableness' of a modelling approach, such as the stochastic instantaneous volatility model presented in the previous chapter, can be assessed. The most demanding test would require a substantial congruence between the relevant moments of the distributions produced by the model and observed in the real world. If this test were rigorously applied, probably all the modelling approaches (in the interest-rate, FX and equity worlds) based on a geometric-Brownian-motion assumption for the underlying would be strongly rejected. One need not look for a deeper reason for this than the well-documented leptokurtosis of most time series of financial returns (Campbell, Lo and McKinley 1993). Certainly, the standard LIBOR market model is rejected on the basis of the congruence (χ^2 test) between the empirical and the model-produced distributions. A weaker criterion of a model's adequacy and reasonableness is to explore the eigenvectors and eigenvalues obtained by orthogonalizing time series of changes in the real-world and the model-produced data. Historically, this type of principal component analysis has been one of the most common calibration strategies of yield-curve models in general, and of the LIBOR mar-

---

[2]To the best of the author's knowledge, no study either of the qualitative patterns of change of the swaption matrix or of its principal component analysis have been presented in the literature so far. The only somewhat related work of which the author is aware is Alexander's (2000) principal component study of implied equity index volatilities.

ket model in particular. The general philosophy has been

- to recognize that the true process for the underlying is not a diffusion;

- to obtain nonetheless the associated principal components; and

- to impose that the loading on the Brownian motions that describe the model dynamics should match as much as possible the econometrically-obtained eigenvalues and eigenvectors (see, e.g., Rebonato 1999a, Hull and White 2000).

It is often claimed that the strategy based on a rescaling and matching of the Brownian drivers to the real-world eigenvalues and eigenvectors will produce an exactly equivalent description of the original dynamics if as many factors are retained as forward rates. This is however only correct if the real-world processes are indeed diffusions. If they are not, the common principal component analysis approach simply provides an efficient and systematic mapping from one type of process to another, constructed in such a way that some important features of the two sets of distributions should be retained.

It is therefore important to explore not only whether the proposed stochastic instantaneous volatility model passes the more stringent test of an overall distributional match, but also whether, and under what circumstances, it can be made to satisfy the weaker criterion of a principal-component-analysis test.

More generally, the findings presented below can shed some light on the necessary ingredients for a realistic description of the stochastic evolution of the implied volatility swaption matrix. The principal component analysis of real-world swaption implied volatilities presented in the following yields, in fact, a first eigenvector which decays as time to expiry increases. In comparing this quantity with the first eigenvector obtainable from the 'artificial' time series generated by a stochastic-volatility model, one notices that this decaying behavior can be naturally obtained through the use of a mean-reverting stochastic volatility. The intuitive explanation for this is clear: a change in volatility will have less effect on the value of a long-dated swaption as the volatility will have plenty of time to mean-revert back to its reversion level. This can be taken as indirect but convincing evidence that mean reversion of volatility is an important feature when modelling changes in stochastic instantaneous volatilities.

The empirical results reported and discussed in Sections 13.2 and 13.3 have a bearing that goes beyond their intrinsic interest. More generally, the methodology suggested in this work could constitute a useful blueprint for analyzing the financial desirability of different yield-curve models which produce stochastic future swaption matrices. As mentioned in the previous chapter, there currently exist some extensions of the LIBOR market model that attempt to account for the current smile surface (see, e.g., Glasserman and Kou 2000, 2001, Glasserman and Merener 2001, Jamshidian 1999, Andersen and Andreasen 1997, Zuehlsdorff 2001). However, either they do not produce a stochastic term structure of volatilities or swaption matrices, or, if they do, they only allow for a very restrictive type of stochasticity (in these CEV-related models the stochastic percentage volatility must be perfectly functionally dependent on the underlying forward rates). Conceptually straightforward extensions of some of these approaches are however possible, which would give rise to non-deterministic implied volatility structures. (This feature could be achieved, for instance, by allowing the jump intensity in Glasserman and Kou 2000 to be a stochastic variable.) If and when these extensions are undertaken, the testing approach employed in the present chapter could provide some guidance in judging their performance and desirability.

13.2 The Empirical Analysis

13.2.1 Description of the data

The data set used for the analysis consisted of 83,136 data points (57.156 for USD and 25 980 for DEM), corresponding to all the trading dates between 1-Jan-1998 and 1-May-2001 (866 trading days, three years and four months). In the case of USD, for each trading day the following at-the-money implied swaption volatilities were available: 3m, 6m, 9m, 1y, 2y, 3y, 4y, 5y, 7y and 10y into 1y, 2y, 3y, 5y, 7y and 10y.[3] In the case of DEM/EUR, the following expiries were available: 3m, 6m, 1y, 2y and 3y for exercise into 2y, 3y, 4y, 5y, 7y and 10y swaps. Less than 0.12% of the data were missing, unreliable or corrupted. For these cases, in order to preserve equal time spacings between observations, rather than eliminating the trading day, a bilinear interpolation between the neighbouring cells was carried out. Care was taken to ensure that the interpolation procedure did not alter in any significant way the final results.

The data set is particularly significant because it encompasses both the Russia crisis and the series of rate cuts carried out by the US Fed in the first months of 2001. Indeed, non-monotonic implied volatility smiles have appeared in the swaption market after the events associated with the Russia crisis. Despite the fact that in the present study I restrict my attention to at-the-money volatilities, anecdotal market evidence indicates that it was the occurrence of dramatic changes in the swaption implied volatility matrix during this period that prompted the trading community to revise the shape of quoted volatility surfaces.

With these data the absolute[4] daily changes in implied volatilities were then calculated. The data were organized with the first column containing the

---

[3]A remark on notation and terminology: The $a \times b$ European swaption is the swaption expiring in a years', or months', time, as appropriate, to exercise into a b-year swap. So, the 6m × 5y, read '6 month into 5 years', swaption is the option to pay or receive fixed for five years in six months' time.

[4]Qualitatively very similar results were obtained by conducting the analysis using percentage, rather than absolute, daily changes.

changes for the first expiry into the first swap length, the second column containing the changes for the first expiry into the second swap length, ..., the sixty-sixth (thirtieth) column containing the changes of the eleventh (fifth) expiry into the sixth swap length for USD (DEM/EUR). In moving across columns, the data therefore naturally present a relatively smooth behavior until one expiry gives place to the next.

Since the data presented are considerably more complex than the more-familiar equity or FX implied volatility data, it is important to familiarize oneself with the data set-up in order better to appreciate the graphs and results presented in the following. More precisely, since three-dimensional graphs can be dazzling, but are rather difficult to read in detail, I present most of the graphical information in the following sections by providing on the same graph the implied volatility corresponding to the various expiries on the x axis, with differently marked curves referring to different swap lengths. The series corresponding to different expiries for a fixed swap length are called the 'into' series. So, the curve corresponding to the implied volatilities of the 3m × 4y, 6m × 4y, 1y × 4y, 2y × 4y and 3y × 4y will be referred to as the 'into 4y' series.

13.2.2 Qualitative patterns of the swaption matrix

The analysis of the data presented above can be profitably split into the USD and the EUR/DEM cases. The time series of selected at-the-money implied volatility curves are shown in Figures 13.1 and 13.2 for USD and EUR/DEM, respectively.

For the purpose of future discussions, it is interesting to notice the more complex structure of the USD data, where time series of different 'into' series appear 'optically' less correlated. Notice, in particular, the strong upward change of the 1 × 3 swaption series, associated with a large downward move for the 10 × 10 swaption volatility during October 1998. While large sudden moves can also be observed in the case of the DEM swaption matrix, these are directionally more correlated, and, therefore, are more likely to produce a level translation of the swaption matrix, rather than a change in overall shape. These qualitative observations are analyzed in more detail later in this section.

Continuing with the analysis of the USD data, the following salient features can be noticed. First of all, over the period of observation at least two main distinct patterns can be recognized: the first, that I shall call 'normal' for reasons that will become clear in the following, displays an overall humped shape for all or most of the curves (see Figures 13.3–13.5); the second, that I shall call 'excited', shows instead a monotonically decaying behavior (see Figures 13.6 and 13.7).

Within the normal pattern, further systematic shape configurations can be distinguished: in the 'ordered' case, for all expiries greater than, approximately, one year, the cross-sectional curves of the swaption matrix corresponding to the different swap lengths (i.e., the into 1y, into 2y, into 3y, into 5y, into

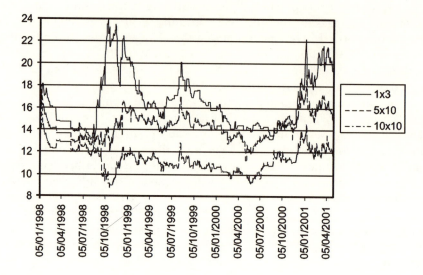

Figure 13.1   *Selected swaption implied volatility time series for USD:* 1×3 *(top curve)*, 5×10 *(middle curve) and* 10×10 *(bottom curve).*

7y and into 10y curves) are monotonically decreasing as a function of residual swap length (see Figures 13.1 and 13.2). For expiries shorter than approximately one year, the order is exactly reversed. There exists, for these 'normal' and 'ordered' shapes, a very tight range of expiries (indeed, almost a single point) where the different 'into' curves intersect. In other cases, that I shall call 'normal and scrambled', the overall shape of the surface is still humped, but the shape of some of the 'into' series is more complex – perhaps displaying several maxima (see, e.g., Figure 13.5).

As for the 'excited' (monotonically decreasing) pattern, displayed in Figure 13.6, the overall surface is monotonically decreasing as a function of the expiry for each 'into' series. These series, in turn, are monotonically decreasing in level from the shortest swap length (into 1y) to the longest (into 10y). Furthermore, all the different 'into' series occur in decreasing level from the shortest to the longest swap length (i.e., for all expiries, options to exercise into one-year swaps have a higher implied volatility than options to exercise into two-year swaps; these, in turn, have a higher implied volatility than options to exercise into three-year swaps; and so on). Finally, Figure 13.7 displays a 'mixed' case where both humped and monotonically decreasing cross-sectional curves coexist in the same surface.

Moving to the DEM/EUR data, a much simpler set of patterns can be observed during the same period of observation, that is, either a monotonically decreasing pattern (see Figure 13.8) or a steep or shallow hump (Figures 13.9 and 13.10). Notice that, for this currency, little, if any, cross-over of the different 'into' series can be observed for either the 'normal' or the 'excited' state.

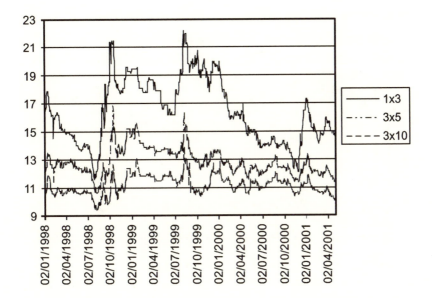

Figure 13.2 *Selected swaption implied volatility time series for DEM/EUR:* 1×3 *(top curve),* 3×5 *(middle curve) and* 3×10 *(bottom curve).*

Some features of the overall structure of the swaption matrix can be understood by noticing that the series corresponding to the shortest swap length should be approximately related to the term structure of caplet volatilities (a

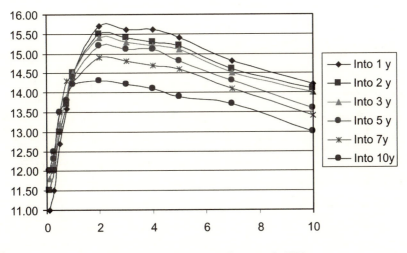

Figure 13.3 *The 'normal' pattern for USD.*

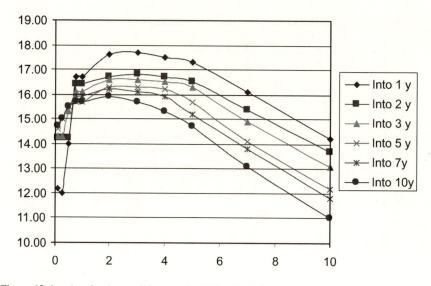

Figure 13.4   *Another 'normal' pattern for USD with a more pronounced occurrence of the cross-over of the different 'into' series.*

one-period swaption is clearly a caplet). It is therefore not surprising that the 'into 1y' and 'into 2y' series for USD and DEM/EUR, respectively, should bear a close resemblance to the typical humped shapes of the market-observed term structures of volatilities.

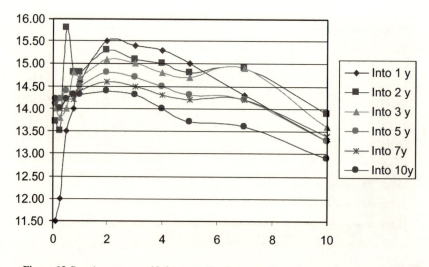

Figure 13.5   *A more scrambled pattern for the normal matrix swaption shape (USD).*

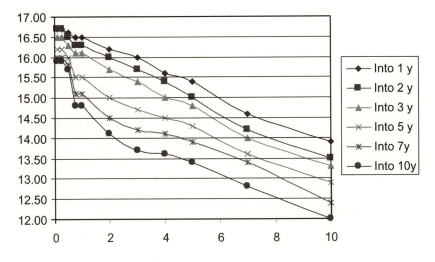

Figure 13.6 *An 'excited' pattern for the USD swaption matrix.*

The reason for labelling the matrices 'normal' or 'excited' is that the monotonically decreasing shape is associated with periods immediately following large movements in the underlying yield curve and in the swaption matrix itself. The post-Russia environment is a prime example of this pattern. The humped, 'normal' shape, on the other hand, prevails during periods of greater stability.

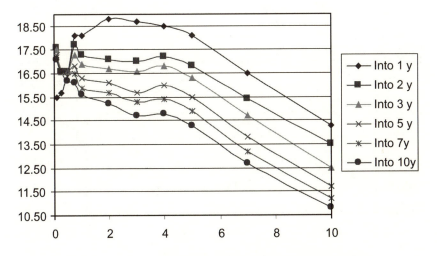

Figure 13.7 *A mixed case for the USD swaption matrix.*

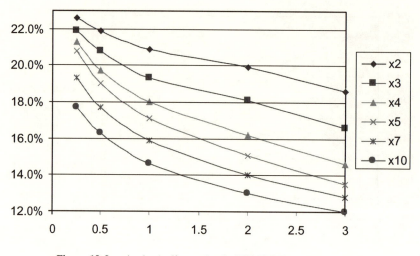

Figure 13.8   *An 'excited' state for the DEM/EUR swaption matrix.*

It is important to point out that similar patterns (i.e., normal, excited, scrambled or mixed patterns) repeat themselves at different points in the history of the swaption matrix analyzed in this study. Generalizing considerably, one can say that, especially in the USD case, the swaption matrix appears to switch rapidly and with random frequency between a few possible fundamental shapes. The existence of these well-defined patterns is important for mod-

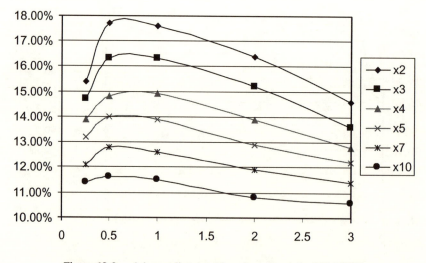

Figure 13.9   *A 'normal' state with a sharp hump for DEM/EUR.*

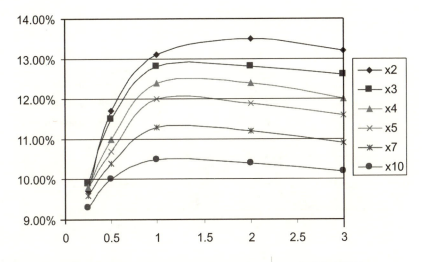

Figure 13.10   *A 'normal' state with shallow hump for DEM/EUR.*

elling purposes because, if the swaption matrix were to 'diffuse' freely over time, it would explore a variety of possible shapes, would quickly lose memory of where it started, and would be very unlikely to revisit time and time again very similar patterns. Similarly, if the diffusion of the swaption matrix were driven by a mean-reverting diffusion with a constant reversion level, one would observe a temporary departure from a particular 'basis' shape, but a long-term reversion to the same pattern. The recurrence of these well-defined patterns therefore suggests that a simple mean-reverting diffusive behavior cannot adequately capture these fine details of the swaption matrix dynamics.

13.2.3 Statistical analysis of the data

The USD swaption data turned out to be different from the DEM/EUR data not only in the sense that they showed more complex shape patterns. Even more significant is, in fact, the observation that the USD implied volatilities displayed much more rapid transitions between different shapes than observed in the case of DEM/EUR. For USD, the transition from the normal to the excited pattern sometimes occurred over a space of two or three trading days. In the DEM/EUR case, instead, a much smoother 'diffusion' from one shape to the other was observed. This observation is somewhat difficult to quantify without displaying an enormous amount of data. Some information about this feature can however be gleaned by the following analysis. If it were indeed the case that the transition between implied volatility states took place much more rapidly for USD than for DEM/EUR, one would expect to observe a different tail behavior for the changes in im-

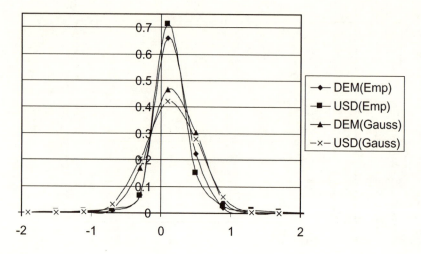

Figure 13.11 *The empirical and fitted (Gaussian) densities of changes in the implied volatility swaption matrix for DEM/EUR and USD.*

plied volatilities in the two currencies. In particular, sudden transitions between one regime and the other would be associated with very large changes in the implied volatilities, which would, in turn, give rise to fat tails. If the transitions from one regime to the other were more sudden in the case of USD, one would expect to observe fatter tails for the density of changes for this currency than for DEM/EUR. This conjecture was tested by constructing a frequency histogram for the changes in implied volatilities across all expiries and swap lengths, and by comparing its overall shape, its first four moments and its right and left tails (see Figures 13.11 and 13.12).

Prima facie, the overall shapes appear quite similar for the two currencies, and both display marked leptokurtosis (see Figure 13.11, which also shows the two Gaussian densities with the same expectation and standard deviation). In particular, the average change was quite similar in the two currencies (15.7 and 18.2 basis points for USD and DEM/EUR, respectively), with a (non-annualized) standard deviation of 37.5 (USD) and 33.2 (DEM/EUR) basis points. The skewness is also very similar for the two currencies (0.044 for USD and 0.042 for DEM/EUR), but the kurtosis differs significantly, and in the direction consistent with the speed of transition between patterns highlighted above: 0.24 for DEM/EUR and 0.41 for USD. Figure 13.12 illustrates this feature by displaying the left tails of the empirical frequency densities (the corresponding Gaussian tails are not shown in the graph because they do not show on the scale of the y axis).

Besides being of intrinsic interest, these results are of relevance for the modelling of the stochastic volatility of the forward or swap rates that drive the swaption matrix. Since this latter quantity is given by suitable integrals of

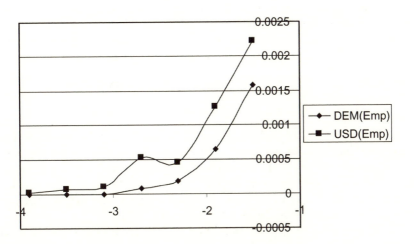

Figure 13.12   *The left tails of the empirical frequency density of implied volatility changes for DEM/EUR and USD. The corresponding Gaussian tails do not appear on the scale of the graph.*

the instantaneous volatility, these results indicate that

- the hypothesis of a purely diffusive behavior for the instantaneous volatility is strongly rejected;[5]

- very 'large'[6] changes in implied volatilities are present for both USD and DEM/EUR;

- these changes are more frequent and pronounced for USD than for DEM/EUR.

The rejection of the diffusive behavior for the implied volatility components is not surprising, and is consistent with similar findings for virtually all the financial-market quantities that have been investigated. A geometric-diffusion approach has nonetheless provided a useful first approximation both in the equity and FX worlds and in interest-rate modelling. In the latter field, in particular, it has become customary to calibrate a diffusive model to the principal components contained from the statistical data. As mentioned above, in this restricted modus operandi, modellers have accepted the fact that the real-world distributional features of the relevant underlying quantity might be poorly described by a diffusive behavior. They have however retained a Brownian-shock modelling description as long as the shape of the eigen-vectors, and the relative magnitude of the eigenvalues, could be matched in

[5]A series of χ^2 tests to check the hypothesis that the sample distribution of any of the empirical implied volatility (changes) series could have been drawn from a normal distribution with matching first two moments always gave a probability of less than 10^{-13}.

[6]The term 'large' means in this context probabilistically incompatible with the assumption of (log-)normality.

the real and risk-adjusted worlds. The results presented in the following section therefore present Principal-Component-Analysis data not only for their intrinsic interest, but also in order to explore whether a diffusive stochastic volatility LIBOR market model can be justified and calibrated along these lines.

13.2.4 The implied volatility correlation matrix

Using the data described in Sections 13.2.1 and 13.2.2, the correlation matrix between the (absolute) changes in the implied volatilities was constructed. The columns and rows in the matrix were organized as described in Section 13.2.1. Table 13.1 displays a small portion of the USD correlation matrix in order to highlight some of the main features of the whole matrix (the same considerations apply to the DEM/EUR matrix).

The 36 elements in the bordered box in the top left-hand corner of the portion of the matrix displayed in Table 13.1 contain the correlation between changes in implied volatilities of the $1y \times 1y$, $1y \times 2y$, ..., $1y \times 10y$ swaptions. Similarly, the 36 elements in the bordered box in the top right-hand corner of the matrix contain the correlation between changes in implied volatilities for the $2y \times 1y$, $2y \times 2y$, ..., $2y \times 10y$ swaptions; etc. There are several interesting features worth noting:

- For a given expiry (i.e., for a given 'into' series), the correlation tends to be a convex function of the swap lengths. This feature remains true for all expiries, and in both currencies.

- For a given swap length, the correlation displays less convexity as a function of swaption expiry.

- Given the way the matrix has been organized, there are discontinuities with a periodicity of 6 both as one moves across columns (from one 'into' series to the next) and as one moves down rows (from one swap length to the next).

- The correlation between changes in implied volatilities of very 'distant' swaptions (i.e., swaptions with greatly different expiries and swap lengths) is very low (approximately 20% for USD and 15% for DEM/EUR).

With these preliminary considerations in mind, one can better understand the shape of the overall correlation matrices for the two currencies, reported below for the case of the DEM/EUR currency (the qualitative shape of the USD matrix is the same).

One can easily recognize the jagged structural feature of the matrix due to the transition from one expiry series to the next, or from one swap length series to the next. It is important to point out that this jagged behavior, clearly displayed in Figure 13.13, is not due to noise, but to the way the two-dimensional data must be organized along a one-dimensional axis. The individual correlation curves inside each 6×6 box are indeed remarkably smooth,

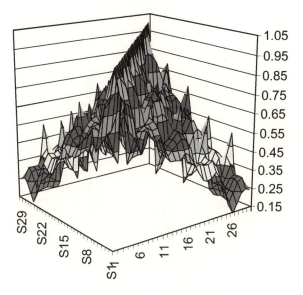

Figure 13.13   *The correlation matrix for the changes in implied volatility for DEM/EUR.*

as shown in Table 13.1 for the small sample of the DEM/EUR correlation matrix displayed, indicating that prima facie statistical noise should not be a concern as far as the interpretation of the data is concerned.

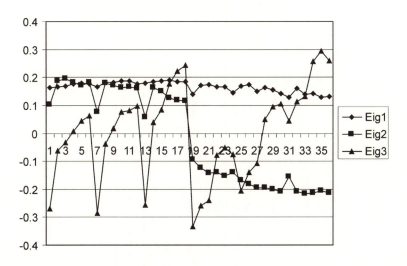

Figure 13.14   *The first three eigenvectors from the orthogonalization of the USD correlation matrix.*

Table 13.1   *A portion (top-left hand corner) of the DEM/EUR correlation matrix.*

	1 year into						2 year into					
	1	2	3	5	7	10	1	2	3	5	7	10
1	1	0.7573313	0.70383312	0.70272808	0.6829902	0.66714772	0.84221759	0.68091232	0.67311099	0.65330642	0.63271429	0.62925843
2	0.7573313	1	0.92506863	0.87005919	0.83106392	0.84816343	0.72208199	0.88853052	0.88370878	0.87442905	0.84005688	0.83917766
3	0.70383312	0.92506863	1	0.90081514	0.86441631	0.87633016	0.67399784	0.81245114	0.86123263	0.85059915	0.83775257	0.85590297
5	0.70272808	0.87005919	0.90081514	1	0.90266159	0.89152726	0.66102105	0.83970274	0.87059137	0.85980915	0.85980908	0.84799235
7	0.6829902	0.83106392	0.86441631	0.90266159	1	0.89152726	0.6565227	0.7961068	0.83785346	0.86171228	0.87911228	0.88349286
10	0.66714772	0.84816343	0.87633016	0.89152726	0.89152726	1	0.61186077	0.71600212	0.77343124	0.83632581	0.84958077	0.88349286
1	0.84221759	0.72208199	0.67399784	0.66102105	0.6565227	0.61186077	1	0.72983905	0.67236483	0.66607135	0.64950144	0.58603538
2	0.68091232	0.88853052	0.81245114	0.83970274	0.7961068	0.71600212	0.72983905	1	0.9065737	0.89238609	0.86824658	0.80100429
3	0.67311099	0.88370878	0.86123263	0.87059137	0.83785346	0.77343124	0.67236483	0.9065737	1	0.89298015	0.90110557	0.85150274
5	0.65330642	0.87442905	0.85059915	0.85980915	0.86171228	0.83632581	0.66607135	0.89238609	0.89298015	1	0.92530429	0.84412453
7	0.63271429	0.84005688	0.83775257	0.85980908	0.87911228	0.84958077	0.64950144	0.86824658	0.90110557	0.92530429	1	0.92073865
10	0.62925843	0.83917766	0.85590297	0.84799235	0.88349286	0.88349286	0.58603538	0.80100429	0.85150274	0.84412453	0.92073865	1

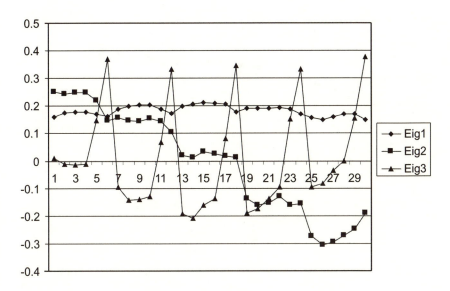

Figure 13.15 *The first three eigenvectors from the orthogonalization of the DEM/EUR correlation matrix.*

13.2.5 Orthogonalization of the correlation matrix

With these correlation matrices one is in a position to obtain, by orthogonalization, the associated eigenvectors and eigenvalues. The results for USD and DEM/EUR are shown in Figures 13.14 and 13.15.

The first noteworthy feature is the strong qualitative similarity of the results for the two currencies. The shape of the eigenvectors also lends itself to an interesting interpretation: The first principal component, as usual, displays a virtually identical loading across the various swaption implied volatilities, and therefore describes the typical up and down rigid shift of the swaption matrix.[7] This first mode of deformation, however, only accounts for less than 60% in both USD and DEM/EUR. The second mode of deformation can be interpreted as corresponding to the first three series moving up (down) and the last three series moving down (up). Finally, the third eigenvector mainly picks up movements within each series, with, say, the implied volatility of swaptions with short swap length moving up and the volatility of swaptions with long swap length moving down.

Finally, it is also worthwhile pointing out the remarkable similarity of the explanatory power of an increasing number of eigenvectors, as shown in Figure 13.16: for both currencies, it takes approximately 10 eigenvectors to ex-

---

[7]The first eigenvector is virtually flat when the correlation, as opposed to covariance, matrix is orthogonalized. Therefore the most important mode of deformation is a parallel shift only after scaling by the volatilities. See the discussion later in this section.

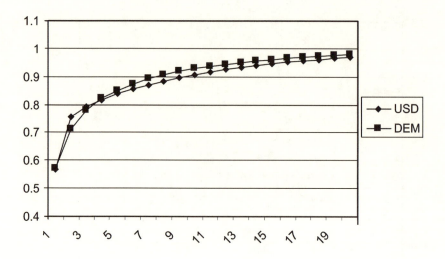

Figure 13.16 *The proportion of the variability explained by an increasing number of eigen-vectors (on the x axis).*

plain 90% of the variability across series of expiries and swap lengths. This result should be contrasted with the findings of principal component analysis on yields or forward rates, where, typically, 90% of the variability is explained by four or fewer eigenvectors (see, e.g., Priaulet et al. 2001 for a recent survey of results). It must be stressed that the data sample included two particularly 'excited' periods, that is, both the Russia crisis and its aftermath, and the aggressive easing by the FED in early 2001. It would be interesting to see whether data in more 'normal' periods would display the same features.

13.2.6 Orthogonalization of the covariance matrix

Similar, but, at the same time, noticeably different, results were obtained by orthogonalizing the covariance rather than the correlation matrix. The most noteworthy difference is that the loadings onto the various implied volatilities now display a noticeable decaying behavior as one moves across columns, indicating that the top left-hand corner of the swaption matrix is more volatile than the bottom right-hand corner. This observation, per se not surprising, will become very relevant in the discussion of the role of mean-reversion in the stochastic-volatility model analyzed in Section 13.3. Without pre-empting future results, it is worth pointing out that these findings will be shown to be compatible with a mean-reverting process for the instantaneous volatility. Figures 13.17 and 13.18 show the first three eigenvectors obtainable from orthogonalizing the covariance (as opposed to the correlation) matrix. Finally, the explanatory power of an increasing number of eigenvectors was found to be quite similar to that found by orthogonalizing the correlation matrix.

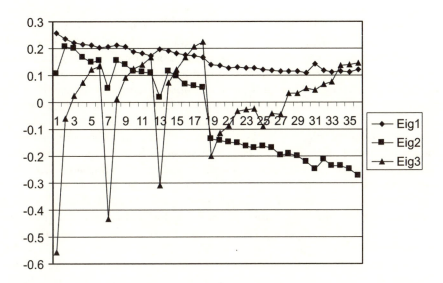

Figure 13.17   *The first three eigenvectors from the orthogonalization of the USD covariance matrix.*

13.2.7 Why choose principal component analysis to assess the quality of a stochastic-volatility model?

In closing this section it is important to recall the rationale behind the choice of the principal component analysis as the primary tool in assessing

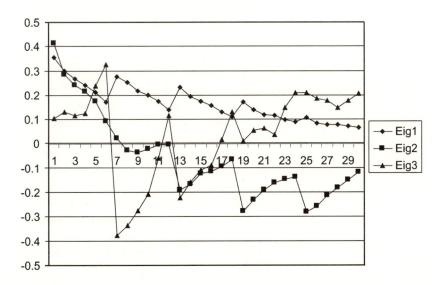

Figure 13.18   *The first three eigenvectors from the orthogonalization of the DEM/EUR covariance matrix.*

the quality of the model. Two observations are relevant: first, the stochastic evolution (under the pricing measure Q) of the swaption matrix is fully specified once the dynamics for the instantaneous volatility is given; second, as mentioned in the introductory section, the model-implied evolution of the swaption matrix takes place in the pricing measure, and, to the extent that investors display aversion to volatility risk, cannot be immediately related to the observable evolution of the same quantity in the real world. Principal component analysis, on the other hand, in general relies on the orthogonalization of covariance or correlation matrices that remain unchanged in moving between measures. In the particular application presented, the Principal-Component-Analysis results are obtained from the orthogonalization of implied volatilities, which are the inverse of the (Black) functions.[8] These inverses of the Black function are, in turn, linked to the instantaneous volatilities through a complex chain of Ito's lemmas. However complex this chain might be, given the assumption about the dynamics of the model instantaneous volatilities, the implied volatilities are themselves a diffusion. The volatility terms of these diffusions only depend on the volatilities of, and the correlation among, the coefficients of $\sigma(t, T)$. Since the volatilities of the coefficients, $\sigma_a(t)$, $\sigma_b(t)$, $\sigma_c(t)$ and $\sigma_d(t)$, have been assumed to be deterministic (and their associated Brownian motions uncorrelated), they will remain unchanged under the Girsanov transformation between measures (see, e.g., Duffie 1996). It immediately follows that the volatilities of and correlations amongst the implied volatilities will also be invariant, and so will their eigenvectors and eigenvalues.

The last statement regarding the invariance of the eigenvectors and eigenvalues deserves some further comment. It is certainly correct if one deals with the orthogonalization of *instantaneous* correlation or covariance matrices. In this case the drift-associated changes (in dt) are guaranteed to be infinitely smaller than the changes from the volatility terms (in $\sqrt{dt}$). With a real time series, however, the sampling frequency (daily in the case of the study presented in this chapter) might be small, but is always finite. Since it is very difficult to obtain information about the real-world drift, which could in theory be orders of magnitude larger than the volatility terms, one cannot rest assured, for a single sampling frequency, that the observed changes are not 'polluted' by a not-so-negligible drift correction. If this were the case, however, halving the sampling frequency would produce an even greater contamination of the observed data with the drift component, and the resulting eigenvectors and eigenvalues would depend even less on the measure-invariant volatilities. As a consequence they would turn out to be significantly sampling-frequency-dependent.

To check for this possibility, the analysis was repeated using two-day (as opposed to daily) changes in implied swaption volatility. Apart from noise,

---

[8]Note carefully that the price functions that transform the instantaneous volatilities into the prices of the European swaptions, and, ultimately, into their implied volatilities, do depend on the mean-reversion and, therefore, on the measure-dependent drift terms. This, however, does not make the results measure-dependent.

the same qualitative and quantitative features were found, confirming that, for the chosen sampling interval, the drift term is indeed negligible.

13.3 The Computer Experiments

13.3.1 The methodology to extract the model-implied principal components

This section investigates the dynamics of the swaption volatility matrix when swaptions are priced using the stochastic volatility model of Chapter 12. In particular, answers are provided to the following questions:

1. How many principal components are required in order to account for the stochastic evolution of the swaption matrix to a given percentage of explanatory power (fraction of variance explained)?

2. How does the first principal component (eigenvector) obtained from the orthogonalization of the model covariance matrix compare with the corresponding empirically observed quantity?

3. Does this first principal component change its qualitative behavior when the volatilities are mean-reverting?

4. Has the displacement coefficient a significant effect on the overall qualitative behavior of the first principal component?

The methodology employed to carry out this investigation was the following:

- The coefficients a, b, c and d were evolved over a time-step of a week using the dynamics described in Section 12.3.1. Since an Ornstein–Uhlenbeck process has been chosen for the coefficients (or their logarithms) the evolution of the instantaneous volatilities can be accomplished exactly and analytically.

- Given this joint realization of the instantaneous volatilities, the forward rates were then evolved over the same time-step.

- After performing this step, the curve was 'reset' so that the expiries of the various forward rates remained a constant time distance away from the new spot time.

- Given this state of the world, all the swaptions in the different series and for the different expiries were then priced, and their prices translated into implied volatilities.

By repeating this exercise many times, one can generate an artificial time series for the swaption implied volatilities. The changes in this time series over 1000 weeks were finally used to produce a covariance matrix, which was then diagonalized.

Table 13.2   *The parameters of the instantaneous volatility process used in the simulation.*

	Initial value	Vol. (%)	Reversion speed	Reversion level
a	−0.02	10.00	0.5	−0.02
b	0.108	10.00	0.3	0.108
$\ln(c)$	0.800	10.00	0.5	0.800
$\ln(d)$	0.114	10.00	0.4	0.114

Despite the fact that, for numerical reasons, the time-step was taken to be one week (as opposed to the daily spacing between the real-world data), the changes are fully dominated by the stochastic term: for typical values of the volatility and of the forward rates, and for the chosen time-step, the volatility terms are typically 200–500 times larger than the drift term,[9] and therefore the numerical procedure presented above accurately estimates the instantaneous covariance matrix.

The parameters used for this exercise are given in Table 13.2. In addition to the instantaneous volatility function, a functional shape for the correlation had to be chosen in order to describe the covariance matrix between the forward rates. This was taken to be given by

$$\rho_{ij} = \exp(-\beta|T_i - T_j|), \tag{13.1}$$

where ρ_{ij} is the correlation between the forward rate expiring at time T_i and the forward rate expiring at time T_j. As discussed at length in Chapter 7, this correlation function is not particularly sophisticated, but I concur with De Jong et al. (1999) who state that, although swaption prices do depend on the correlation between interest rates of different maturities, this turns out to be a second-order effect, and that swaption prices are primarily determined by the volatilities of interest rates. Mercurio and Brigo (2001) provide additional evidence that, and an explanation as to why, the detailed shape of the correlation function has a small impact on the price of European swaptions.

The parameters shown in Table 13.2, to which the results in this study refer, were typical of the ones obtained by optimizing to the caplet smile surface of EUR and USD using the market data prevailing as of 8 September 2000. They were not chosen to produce a best fit to either swaption matrix, but provide a qualitatively acceptable overall description of the swaption matrix. The qualitative features reported below, and the trends in the eigenvectors, were found to be strongly insensitive to the details of the parametrization, and mainly depend on whether the reversion speed was assumed to be zero, or equal to a finite 'reasonable' value (where 'reasonable' means similar to

---

[9]For this order-of-magnitude calculation, the forward rate was taken to be at 6.00% and the instantaneous volatility at 15.00%. A constant correlation of 90% among all the forward rates was also assumed.

the values found in the fitting to actual market data for different currencies).

Finally, the displacement coefficient α was chosen to be equal to 0.02, in close agreement with the best-fit values obtained for both currencies.

13.3.2 The results of the computer experiments

I begin the discussion of the results begins by presenting the graphs of the first principal component obtained using the methodology described above. The x axis displays the following swaptions, in the order

1×1, 2, 3, 5, 7, 10,
2×1, 2, 3, 5, 7, 10,
3×1, 2, 3, 5, 7, 10,
5×1, 2, 3, 5, 7, 10,
7×1, 2, 3, 5, 7, 10,
10×1, 2, 3, 5.

The first observation from these results, which answers the first of the questions posed in the section above, is that, in all cases (i.e., with and without mean-reversion and with and without a displacement coefficient), a very large fraction (approximately 90% for both currencies) of the variability across expiries and swap lengths is explained by the first principal component. This was observed despite the fact that four independent Brownian processes affect the instantaneous volatility process. The finding is not surprising, because it was noticed in the previous chapter that the prices of European swaptions are mainly affected by the stochastic behavior of the d coefficient.[10] On the other hand, the fraction of the total variability (percentage of variance) explained by the first principal component in the two currencies examined was empirically found to be slightly less than 60% (see Figure 13.16). Therefore the first conclusions are that a significant degree of the real-world complexity is not accounted for by the model proposed, and that the model changes in swaption volatility are too strongly correlated. This is a priori not surprising: stochastic-volatility extensions of the LIBOR market model are after all just being introduced (see, e.g., Gatarek 2001 for recent work inspired by the present approach), and one can draw a parallel with the early simple one-factor models (such as Vasicek 1977, Cox et al. 1985) that attempted to describe the evolution of the yield curve. The more relevant question is perhaps whether this initial step, albeit incomplete, is in the right direction.

In order to answer this question, one can refer again to Figures 13.17 and 13.18, which display the first principal component as estimated from the statistical data, and recall two salient empirical features:

---

[10]This observation should not be taken to imply that the stochastic behavior of the a, b and c parameters has 'no use': b and c control the location of the 'hump' in the instantaneous volatility curve, which in turn controls the degree of terminal decorrelation between forward rates. Several complex products are sensitive to different extents to this terminal decorrelation, and it would therefore be unwarranted to extrapolate conclusions from plain-vanilla to complex instruments.

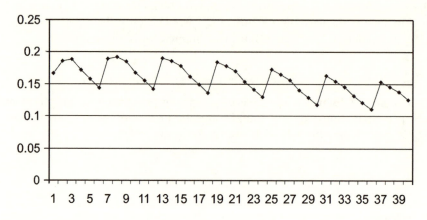

Figure 13.19   *The first model eigenvector obtained using zero reversion speed in the volatility drift and a zero displacement coefficient.*

- There is clear periodicity of all the eigenvectors as one moves from one 'into' series to the next.

- There is a difference in the qualitative shape of the first eigenvector obtained from orthogonalizing the correlation or covariance matrix: When one uses real-world correlation data, the average magnitude of the first eigenvector is roughly constant as one moves from one series to the next, giving rise to a first mode of deformation roughly parallel across the swaption matrix. When the real-world covariance matrix is orthogonalized, however, the first eigenvector displays a noticeable decay as one moves down the series.

These features can be compared with the model-obtained ones. First of all, the model-obtained eigenvector (obtained from the orthogonalization of the covariance matrix) clearly displays the same periodicity as the empirical eigenvectors (see Figures 13.19–13.21). As for the shape of the first eigenvector obtained from the model data, one can distinguish three cases (see Figures 13.19–13.21):

1. When no reversion speed and zero displacement coefficient are used in the simulation, the first eigenvector from the model covariance matrix remains roughly constant as one moves down the x axis.

2. To a limited extent, a non-zero, positive displacement coefficient, which indicates a deviation from log-normality towards normality, produces some degree of decay in the first covariance eigenvector.

3. It is only when the reversion speed has a value similar to that obtained in the fit to the smile surface that the model data display a decay similar to what can be observed from real data.

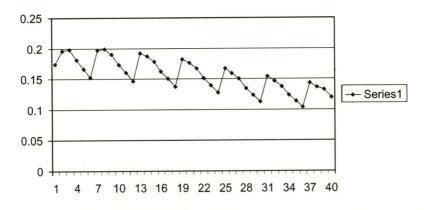

Figure 13.20   *The first model eigenvector obtained using zero reversion speed in the volatility drift and a non-zero displacement coefficient.*

This result is particularly noteworthy, because the reversion speed used in the present study was independently determined by fitting to smile data, and without any prior knowledge of the shape of the empirical eigenvalues. Therefore, it appears that the empirical data are consistent with a mean-reverting behavior for the instantaneous volatility (in the risk-adjusted world!) as posited in the approach presented in the previous chapter, and as independently calibrated to static cross-sectional data (a single-day volatility surface)

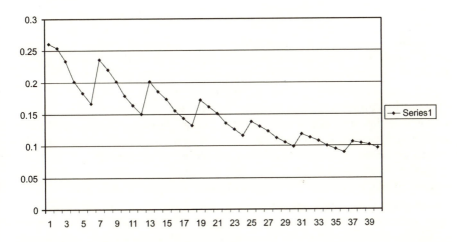

Figure 13.21   *The first model eigenvector obtained using non-zero reversion speed in the volatility drift and a non-zero displacement coefficient.*

13.4 Conclusions and Suggestions for Future Work

13.4.1 Discussion of the results so far

I have presented in this chapter some empirical work about the changes in market-implied volatility swaption matrices. This investigation has been coupled with a theoretical analysis of the particular stochastic-volatility extension of the LIBOR market model discussed in Chapter 12. The findings convey a mixed but overall encouraging picture of the adequacy of this modelling approach.

To begin with the negative results, certain important features of the real data are not captured by the proposed model: the empirical data indicate, for instance, that the swaption matrix tends to oscillate between well-defined shape patterns, with different, and sometimes quite short, transition periods. Such a behavior is compatible neither with a stochastic volatility model with constant reversion speed, nor with a jump-diffusion process (which does not produce, in its standard formulation, stochastic smile surfaces), nor with any of the CEV extensions that have been proposed. Linking the volatility in a deterministic manner to the stochastic forward rates could produce sharp moves in the level of the swaption matrix, if the forward rates displayed a discontinuous behavior (as in Glasserman and Kou 2000, Glasserman and Merener 2001). It is difficult, however, to see how a deterministic functional dependence on the forward rates could give rise to a sudden change in shape of the swaption matrix. Possibly, a reversion level for the instantaneous volatility that underwent almost instantaneous transitions between a number of pre-defined values could provide a better description of the observed dynamics. The reversion speed, however, would have to change significantly (i.e., would have to display a short-lived burst) when these transitions occur if one wants to recover at the same time the diffusive behavior of the implied volatility in 'normal times', and the quickness of the transition during 'crises', as observed, in particular, for USD. The computational and calibration problems of such a model are likely to be quite a challenge, but this modelling approach could constitute an interesting avenue for future research.

Continuing with the 'bad news', the descriptive statistics of the empirical changes in implied volatility strongly reject the hypothesis that the instantaneous volatility should follow a diffusive (mean-reverting) behavior. In particular, the empirical tails are far too fat when compared with the model-produced ones. Furthermore, the proportion of the variability across the swaption matrix explained by the first principal component is significantly smaller in reality (about 60%) than with the model-produced data.

Despite these shortcomings, the mean-reverting stochastic-volatility approach has been shown to display two important encouraging features: first of all, the qualitative shape of the first eigenvector turned out to bear a close resemblance with the corresponding empirical quantity. In particular, the same periodicity was observed in the real and model data. Second, the decaying behavior of the first principal component as a function of increasing expiry, observed in the real data when the covariance matrix is orthogonalized, was found to be naturally recoverable and explainable by the mean-reverting behavior for the instantaneous volatility. This feature in turn constitutes the most salient characteristic of the stochastic-volatility extension of the LIBOR market model presented in the previous chapter. Furthermore, the values for the mean-reversion that had been previously and independently obtained using static information (i.e., by fitting to the smile surface) turned out to be adequate to explain in a satisfactory way the qualitative features of such dynamic features as the shape of the eigenvectors (obtained from time series analysis). It is therefore fair to say that, despite the obvious shortcomings, the modelling approach analyzed in the theoretical part of the present study appears to be a useful first step in the right direction.

13.4.2 Where do we go from here?

How could one improve upon the approach presented in Chapter 12 in such a way as to take into account the empirical evidence presented in this chapter? The most salient missing features are probably the ability

(i) to reproduce rapid transitions of the swaption matrix from one 'mode' to another; and

(ii) to return, after one such transition has taken place, to a similar shape.

A simple and natural way to model these features, while retaining the simplicity and intuition behind the approach proposed above is the following.

1. One can begin by choosing a simple criterion to determine whether the swaption matrix is currently in the normal or excited state. Looking at the graphs in Chapter 12, one such criterion could be whether the n-year into one-year series displays a hump or not.

2. The instantaneous volatility function for each forward rate can be described by either of these two equations:

$$\sigma_i^n(t, T) = [a_t^n + b_t^n(T - t)] \exp[-c_t^n(T - t)] + d_t^n, \qquad (13.2)$$
$$\sigma_i^x(t, T_i) = [a_t^x + b_t^x(T - t)] \exp[-c_t^x(T - t)] + d_t^x, \qquad (13.3)$$

with different coefficients $\{a^n, b^n, c^n, d^n\}$ and $\{a^x, b^x, c^x, d^x\}$ associated with the normal (superscript 'n') and excited state (superscript 'x').

3. All the coefficients $\{a^n, b^n, c^n, d^n\}$ and $\{a^x, b^x, c^x, d^x\}$ are stochastic, and follow the same Ornstein–Uhlenbeck process described in Chapter 12. Their processes are all uncorrelated with the forward rates.[11]

---

[11] If desired, a non-zero correlation between the 'normal' and 'excited' stochastic volatility processes can easily be introduced. Provided that independence from the forward-rate processes is retained, this does not alter the computational procedure.

4. The transition of the instantaneous volatility from the normal to the excited state occurs with frequency $\lambda_{n \to x}$, and the transition from the excited state to the normal state with frequency $\lambda_{x \to n}$. Notice that both frequencies are risk-adjusted and not real-world frequencies; and that $\lambda_{n \to x} + \lambda_{x \to n} \neq 1$.

5. Since the same assumption of independence between the volatility processes and the forward-rate processes is enforced, once again along each volatility path the problem is exactly equivalent to the deterministic case, apart from the fact that, at random times, the coefficients would switch from one state to the other.

6. Because of point 5, the evaluation of the variances or covariances along each path proceeds exactly as described in Chapter 12, with possibly different coefficients 'half-way through' some of the paths if a transition has occurred. The evaluation of caplets and European swaptions would be practically unaltered.

This procedure has been explicitly designed to capture the most significant qualitative features highlighted by the empirical study. In particular,

- the transition between states and the reversion to the two basic (normal and excited modes) is built in to the model;

- the implied volatility distribution displays fatter tails than in the pure-diffusion case; and

- the explanatory power of the first eigenvector is lower than in the simple-diffusion case.

The only complication could be of computational nature, and stems from the fact that, if either $\lambda_{n \to x}$ or $\lambda_{x \to n}$ are very small, it might be necessary to use significantly more paths than discussed in Chapter 12 to carry out an accurate sampling.

Work is under way to explore this model extension in greater detail.

Bibliography

Ahn D-H, Gao B (1999) 'A parametric non-linear model of term structure dynamics', *Review of Financial Studies*, **12** (4), 721–62

Alexander C (2000) 'Principal component analysis of volatility smiles and skews', Working Paper, ISMA Centre, University of Reading

Andersen L (1999) 'A simple approach to the pricing of Bermudan swaptions in the multi-factor LIBOR market model', *Journal of Computational Finance*, **3** (2), 5–32.

Andersen L, Andreasen J (1997) 'Volatility skews and extension of the LIBOR market model', *Applied Mathematical Finance*, to appear; also Working Paper, Gen Re Financial Products

Andersen L, Andreasen J (2000) 'Volatility Skews and Extension of the LIBOR Market Model; Applied Mathematical Finance **7**, 1, March 2000

Babbs S H, Selby M J P (1996) 'Pricing by arbitrage in incomplete markets', Working Paper, Financial Options Research Centre, University of Warwick, FORC Preprint 96/69, January

Ballard P, Hughston L (1999) 'Pricing of Contingent Claims in Incomplete Markets', working paper, Merrill Lynch and King's College London

Baxter M, Rennie A (1996) *Financial Calculus*, Cambridge University Press, Cambridge

Beckers S (1980) 'The constant elasticity of variance model and its implications for option pricing', *Journal of Finance*, **35**(3),(June) 661–673

Bjork T (1998) *Arbitrage Theory in Continuous Time*, Oxford University Press, Oxford

Black F (1976) 'The pricing of commodity contracts', *Journal of Financial Economics*, **3**, 167–79

Black F, Karasinski P (1991) 'Bond and option pricing when short rates are lognormal', *Financial Analyst Journal*, **47**, (July-August) 52–59

Black F, Scholes M (1973) 'The pricing of options on corporate liabilities', *Journal of Political Economy*, **81**, 637–59

445

Black F, Derman E, Toy W (1990) 'A one-factor model of interest rates and its application to Treasury bond options', *Financial Analyst Journal*, **46**, 33–39

Bollerslev T, Chou R, Kroner K (1992) 'ARCH Modelling in Finance: a Review of the Theory and Empirical Evidence' Journal of Econometrics, 52, 5–59

Bollerslev T, Engle R, Nelson D (1994) 'ARCH Models' in R. Engle and D Macfadden (editors) 'Handbook of Econometrics', IV, Elsevier, Amsterdam.

Boyle P P (1977) 'Options: a Monte Carlo approach', *Journal of Financial Economics*, **4**, 323–38

Brace A, Gatarek D, Musiela M (1996) 'The market model of interest rate dynamics', *Mathematical Finance*, **7**, 127–54

Brenner M, Subrahmanyam M G (1994) 'A simple approach to option valuation in the Black–Scholes model', *Financial Analyst Journal*, 25–8

Brigo D, Mercurio F, (2001) 'Interest Rate Models: Theory and Practice', Springer Verlag, Heidelberg

Britten-Jones M, Neuberger A (1998) 'Option prices, implied price processes and stochastic volatility', Working Paper, London Business School, available at www.london.edu/ifa

Broadie (2002), New Methods for Pricing American and Bermudan Options: the Fast Gauss Transform Lattice Methods and the Prima-Dual Simulation Method' presented at the Global Derivatives Conference - Barcelona, May 2002

Broadie M, Glasserman P (1997) 'A stochastic mesh method for pricing high-dimension American options', Working Paper, Columbia University, New York

Campbell J Y, Lo A W, MacKinlay A C (1996) *The Econometrics of Financial Markets*, Princeton University Press, Princeton, NJ

Carverhill A (1993) 'A simplified exposition of the Heath, Jarrow and Morton model', Working Paper, Hong Kong University of Science and Technology, January

Chan K C, Karolyi G A, Longstaff F A, Sanders A B (1992) 'An empirical comparison of alternative models of the short-term interest rate', *Journal of Finance*, **68** (May), 1209–1227

Chatfiled C, Collins A J (1989) *Introduction to Multivariate Analysis*, Chapman and Hall, London

Cochrane J H (2001) *Asset Pricing*, Princeton University Press, Princeton, NJ

Cox J, Ross S A, Rubinstein M (1979) 'Option pricing: a simplified approach', *Journal of Financial Economics*, **7**, 229–63

Cox J, Ingersoll J E, Ross S A (1985) 'A theory of the term structure of interest rates', *Econometrica*, **53**, 385–407

De Jong F, Driessen L, Pelsser A (1999) 'LIBOR and swap market models for the pricing of interest-rate derivatives: an empirical comparison', Working Paper

Derman E, Kamal M (1997) 'The patterns of change in implied index volatilities', Quantitative Strategies Research Notes, Goldman Sachs

Derman E, Kani I (1994) 'Riding on a smile', *Risk Magazine*, **7** (2), 98–101

Derman E, Kani I, Chriss N (1996) 'Implied binomial trees of the volatility smile', *Journal of Derivatives*, **3** (4), 7–22

Dodds S (1998) personal communication

Dodds S (2002) 'Pricing and Hedging Bermudon Swaptions with the BGM Model', Barclays Capital working paper, presented at the Global Derivitives Conference in Barcelona, May 2002

Dothan M N (1990) *Prices in Financial Markets*, Oxford University Press, Oxford

Doust P (1995) 'Relative pricing techniques in the swaps and options markets', *Journal of Financial Engineering*, (March), 45–71

Duffie D (1996) *Dynamic Asset Pricing Theory*, 2nd edn, Princeton University Press, Princeton, NJ

Duffie D, Kan R (1996) 'A yield-factor model of interest rates', *Mathematical Finance*, **6**, 379–406

Dupire B (1994) 'Pricing with a smile', *Risk Magazine*, **7**, 18–20

Engl H E (1993) 'Regularization methods for the stable solution of inverse problems', *Surveys on Mathematics for Industry*, **3**, 71–143

Fisher M, Nyehka D, Zevros D (1994) 'Fitting the term structure of interest rates with smooth splines', Working Paper, US Federal Reserve Board, January

Gatarek D (2001) 'LIBOR market model with stochastic volatility', presented at the Maths Week Risk Conference, London, 28 November; also Working Paper, BRE Bank and Systems Research Institute

Glasserman P, Kou S G (2001) 'The Term Structure of Simple Forward Rates with Jump Risk', working paper, Colombia University

Glasserman P, Kou S G (2000) 'The term structure of simple forward rates with jump risk', Working Paper, Columbia University

Glasserman P, Merener N (2001) 'Numerical solutions of jump-diffusion LIBOR market models', Working Paper, Columbia University

Gustavsson T (1997) 'On the pricing of European swaptions', Working Paper, Department of Economics, University of Uppsala, Sweden, March

Harrison J M, Kreps D (1979) 'Martingales and arbitrage in multi-period securities markets', *Journal of Economic Theory*, **20**, 381–408

Harrison J M, Pliska S (1981) 'Martingales and stochastic integrals in the theory of continuous trading', *Stochastic Processes and their Applications*, **11**, 215–60

Haug M B, Kogan L (2000) 'Pricing American options: a duality approach', Working Paper, MIT and the Wharton School

Heath D, Jarrow R A, Morton A (1987) 'Bond pricing and the term structure of interest rates: a new methodology', Working Paper, Cornell University

Heath D, Jarrow R A, Morton A (1989) 'Bond pricing and the term structure of interest rates: a new methodology', Working Paper (revised edition), Cornell University

Hull J (1993) *Options, Futures and Other Derivative Securities*, 2nd edn, Prentice-Hall, Englewood Cliffs, NJ

Hull J, White A (1987) 'The pricing of options on assets with stochastic volatilities', *Journal of Finance*, **XLII** (2), 281–300

Hull J, White A (1990) 'Pricing Interest Rate Derivative Securites' The Review of Financial Studies, 3, 573–592

Hull J, White A (1993) 'Bond option pricing based on a model for the evolution of bond prices', *Advances in Futures and Option Research*, **6**, 1–13

Hull J, White A (2000) 'The essentials of LMM', *Risk Magazine*, (December)

Hunt P, Kennedy J, Pelsser A (2000) 'Markov-Functional Interest Rate Models', Finance and Stochastics, **4**(4), 391–408

Hunter C, Jaeckel P and Joshi M (2001) 'Getting the Drift', *Risk Magazine*, (July) 81–84 also QUARC (Quantitative Research Centre) Working Paper, 'Drift approximations in a LIBOR market model', available at www.rebonato.com

Jaeckel P (2000) 'A simple method to evaluate Bermudan swaptions in the LIBOR market model framework', Working Paper, Royal Bank of Scotland Quantitative Research Centre (QUARC), available at www.rebonato.com

Jaeckel P, Rebonato R (2001a) 'Valuing American options in the presence of user-defined smiles', *Journal of Risk*, **4** (1), 35–62

Jaeckel P, Rebonato R (2001b) 'Linking caplet and swaption volatilities in a LIBOR market model setting', *Journal of Computational Finance*, accepted for publication; also Working Paper, Royal Bank of Scotland Quantitative Research Centre (QUARC), available at www.rebonato.com

Jamshidian F (1991) 'Forward induction and construction of yield curve diffusion models', Working Paper, Financial Strategies Group, Merryll Lynch Capital Markets, New York

Jamshidian F (1997) 'LIBOR and swap market models and measures', *Finance and Stochastic,* **1** (4), 293–330

Jamshidian F (1999) 'LIBOR market model with semimartingales', Working Paper, NetAnalytic Ltd, London

Johnson T C (2001) 'Volatility, momentum and time-varying skewness in foreign exchange returns', Working Paper, London Business School, available at www.london.edu/ifa

Joshi M (2000) 'A short note on exponential correlation functions', Working Paper, Royal Bank of Scotland Quantitative Research Centre (QUARC), June

Joshi M (2001a) 'The calibration of a stochastic volatility model to caplet prices', Working Paper, Royal Bank of Scotland Quantitative Research Centre (QUARC), available at www.rebonato.com

Joshi M (2001b) 'Fast pricing of swaptions in a stochastic volatility market model', Working Paper, Royal Bank of Scotland Quantitative Research Centre (QUARC), available at www.rebonato.com

Joshi M (2001c) 'Calibration to co-terminal swaptions in a stochastic volatility market model', Working Paper, Royal Bank of Scotland Quantitative Research Centre (QUARC), available at www.rebonato.com

Joshi M (2001f) 'The concepts of mathematical finance', in preparation

Joshi M, Rebonato R (2001) 'A stochastic-volatility, displaced-diffusion extension of the LIBOR market model', *Journal of Computational Finance,* submitted; also Working Paper, Royal Bank of Scotland Quantitative Research Centre (QUARC), available at www.rebonato.com

Kainth D, Rebonato R, Joshi M (2001) 'Similarities between the prices of Bermudan swaptions obtained with the BDT and a particular implementation of the LIBOR Market Model', Working Paper, Royal Bank of Scotland Quantitative Research Centre (QUARC)

Karatzas I, Shreve S (1988) *Brownian Motion and Stochastic Calculus,* Springer-Verlag, Berlin

Kloeden P E, Platen E (1992) *Numerical Solutions of Stochastic Differential Equations,* Springer-Verlag, Berlin

Levin R, Singh K (1995) 'What hides behind the smile?', Working Paper, J P Morgan Derivatives Research, March

Lewis A L, (2000), 'Option Valuation under Stochastic Volatility', Finance Press, Newport Beach, California

Longstaff F A, Schwartz E S (1992) 'Interest rate volatility and the term structure: a two-factor general equilibrium model', *Journal of Finance,* **47,** 1259–82

Longstaff F A, Schwartz E S (1998) 'Valuing American options by simulations: a least square approach', Working Paper 25-98, Andersen School at the UCLA

Longstaff F A, Santa-Clara P, Schwartz E S (2000a) 'Throwing away a billion dollars: the cost of sub-optimal exercise strategies in the swaptions markets', presented at the ICBI Risk Conference, Geneva; also Working Paper, UCLA

Longstaff F A, Santa-Clara P, Schwartz E S (2000b) 'The relative valuation of caps and swaptions: theory and empirical evidence', presented at the ICBI Risk Conference, Geneva; also Working Paper, UCLA

Madan D B, Carr P, Chang E C (1998) 'The variance gamma process and option pricing', Working Paper, University of Maryland

Marris D (1999) 'Financial option pricing and skewed volatility', M.Phil. Thesis, Statistical Laboratory, University of Cambridge

Marsh T A, Rosenfeld E R (1983) 'Stochastic processes for interest rates and equilibrium bond prices', *Journal of Finance*, **38**, 635–46

Martellini L, Priaulet P (2001) 'Fixed-Income Securities' John Wiley's, Chichester

Merton R (1973) 'The theory of rational option pricing', *Bell Journal of Economic and Management Science*, **4**, 177–86

Mikosh T (1998) *Stochastic Calculus with Finance in View*, Advanced Series on Statistical Science and Applied Probability, Vol. 6, World Scientific, Singapore

Miltersen K, Sandmann K, Sondermann D (1997) 'Closed-form solutions for term structure derivatives with log-normal interest rates', *Journal of Finance*, **52**, 409–30

Musiela M, Rutkowski M (1997a) 'Continuous-time term structure models: forward-measure approach', *Finance and Stochastic*, **1** (4), 261–92

Musiela M, Rutkowski M (1997b) *Martingale Methods in Financial Modelling*, Springer-Verlag, Berlin

Neftci S A (1996) *An Introduction to the Mathematics of Financial Derivatives*, Academic Press, San Diego

Nelson D (1990) 'Conditional Heteroskedsticity in Asset Returns: a New Approach', Econometrica, 59, 347–370

Neuberger A (1990) 'Pricing swap options using the forward swap market', IFA Working Paper, London Business School

Nielsen L T (1999) *Pricing and Hedging of Derivatives Securities*, Oxford University Press, Oxford

Oksendal B (1995) *Stochastic Differential Equations*, 5th edn, Springer-Verlag, Berlin

Pliska S R (1997) *Introduction to Mathematical Finance*, Blackwell, Oxford

Press W H, Teukolsky S A, Vetterling W T, Flannery B P (1996) *Numerical Recipes in C*, 2nd edn (reprinted with corrections 1998), Cambridge University Press, Cambridge

Rebonato R (1998) *Interest-Rate Option Models*, 2nd edn, John Wiley, Chichester

Rebonato R (1999a) 'On the simultaneous calibration of multi-factor lognormal interest-rate models to Black volatilities and to the correlation matrix', *Journal of Computational Finance*, **2** (4), 5–27; also Working Paper, Royal Bank of Scotland Quantitative Research Centre (QUARC), available at www.rebonato.com

Rebonato R (1999b) 'On the pricing implications of the joint log-normality assumption for the cap and swaption markets', *Journal of Computational Finance*, **2** (3), 30–52; also Working Paper, Royal Bank of Scotland Quantitative Research Centre (QUARC), available at www.rebonato.com

Rebonato R (1999c) *Volatility and Correlation*, John Wiley, Chichester

Rebonato R (2000) 'Calibration to co-terminal European swaptions in a BGM setting', *Journal of Computational Finance*, submitted; also Working Paper, Royal Bank of Scotland Quantitative Research Centre (QUARC), available at www.rebonato.com

Rebonato R (2001a) 'Managing model risk', in *Mastering Risk*, Vol. II, FT–Prentice Hall Educational Carol Alexander editor, London

Rebonato R (2001b) 'The stochastic volatility LIBOR market model', *Risk*, (October), 105–10

Rebonato R, Cooper I (1995) 'Limitations of simple two-factor interest rate models', *Journal of Financial Engineering*, **5**, 1–16

Rebonato R, Jaeckel P)(2000) 'The most general methodology to create a valid correlation matrix', *Journal of Risk*,**2** (2), (Winter), 1–16

Rebonato R, Joshi M (2001a) 'A joint empirical/theoretical investigation of the modes of deformation of swaption matrices: implications for the stochastic-volatility LIBOR market model', *International Journal of Theoretical and Applied Finance*, accepted for publication also Working Paper, Royal Bank of Scotland Quantitative Research Centre (QUARC), available at www.rebonato.com

Rebonato R, Joshi M (2001b) 'The Kolmogorov Project: no-arbitrage evolution of implied volatility surfaces and applications to weak static replication', Working Paper, Royal Bank of Scotland Quantitative Research Centre (QUARC), available at www.rebonato.com

Rogers L C G (2000) 'Monte Carlo valuation of American options', Working Paper, Department of Mathematical Sciences, University of Bath

Rubinstein M (1983) 'Displaced diffusion option pricing', *Journal of Finance*, **38** (March), 213–17

Rutkowski M (1997) 'Models of forward LIBOR and swap rates', Working Paper, University of New South Wales

Rutkowski M (1998) 'Dynamics of spot, forward and futures LIBOR rates', *International Journal of Theoretical and Applied Finance*, **1** (3), 425–45

Schaefer S M (1977) 'The problem with redemption yields', *Financial Analyst Journal*, (July–August), 59–67

Schoenmakers J, Coffey B (2000) 'Stable implied calibration of a multi-factor LIBOR model via a semi-parametric correlation structure', Working Paper No. 611, Weierstrass-Institut für Angewandte Analysis und Stochastik, Berlin

Sharpe W, Alexander G (1990) 'Investments', 4th Edition, Englewood, New Jersey, Prentice Hall

Scholes M (2000) 'Crisis and risk', *Risk*, (May), 50

Shleifer A (2000) *Inefficient Markets – An Introduction to Behavioural Finance*, Clarendon Lectures in Economics, Oxford University Press, Oxford

Shleifer A, Vishny R (1997) 'The limits of arbitrage', *Journal of Finance*, **52**, 35–55

Sidenius J (2000) 'LIBOR market models in practice', *Journal of Computational Finance*,**3**, (3),(Spring), 75–99

Sidenius J (2000) 'Evaluating new research exploring practical aspects of multi-factor LIBOR market models', presented at the ICBI 7th Annual Forum – Global Derivatives 2000, Paris

Vasicek O (1977) 'An equilibrium characterization of the term structure', *Journal of Financial Economics*, **5**, 177–88

Wilmott P (1998) *Derivatives: the Theory and Practice of Financial Engineering*, John Wiley, Chichester

Zuehlsdorff C (2001) 'Extended LIBOR market models with affine and quadratic volatility', Working Paper, Department of Statistics, Rheinische Friederich-Wilhelms-Universität, Bonn, Germany

Index